THE PAPERS OF
WOODROW WILSON

VOLUME 24
1912

SPONSORED BY THE WOODROW WILSON
FOUNDATION
AND PRINCETON UNIVERSITY

THE PAPERS OF

WOODROW WILSON

ARTHUR S. LINK, *EDITOR*

DAVID W. HIRST AND JOHN E. LITTLE

ASSOCIATE EDITORS

EDITH JAMES, *ASSISTANT EDITOR*

SYLVIA ELVIN, *CONTRIBUTING EDITOR*

M. HALSEY THOMAS, *CONSULTING EDITOR*

Volume 24 · 1912

PRINCETON, NEW JERSEY

PRINCETON UNIVERSITY PRESS

1977

Note to scholars: Princeton University Press
subscribes to the Resolution on Permissions of
the Association of American University Presses,
defining what we regard as "fair use" of copyrighted works. This Resolution, intended to encourage scholarly use of university press publications and to avoid unnecessary applications
for permission, is obtainable from the Press or
from the A.A.U.P. central office. Note, however,
that the scholarly apparatus, transcripts of
shorthand, and the texts of Wilson documents
as they appear in this volume are copyrighted,
and the usual rules about the use of copyrighted materials apply.

Publication of this book has been aided by a
grant from the National Historical Publications
and Records Commission.

Printed in the United States of America
by Princeton University Press
Princeton, New Jersey

INTRODUCTION

THIS volume opens upon the eve of the Jackson Day Dinner in Washington on January 8, 1912, and the official beginning of the Democratic preconvention presidential campaign. The New York *Sun*, Wall Street's spokesman, tries to kill Wilson's candidacy by publishing a letter highly derogatory of William J. Bryan which Wilson had written in 1907. Countering, at the Jackson Day Dinner, in a warm tribute to the Nebraskan and a moving appeal for party unity, Wilson maintains his position as the frontrunner.

However, a host of troubles lie ahead. Most old-line Democrats and city bosses, fearful of the anti-machine newcomer, rally behind Champ Clark of Missouri, Speaker of the House of Representatives. The candidacy of Representative Oscar W. Underwood of Alabama draws away much support in Wilson's native region. Colonel George Harvey, Wilson's original sponsor, turns against his one-time protégé because he has become too independent and radical. The Georgia anti-Negro demagogue, Thomas E. Watson, rallies the "wool hat boys" and rednecks in a vicious campaign against Wilson. Then William Randolph Hearst moves in for the kill, orchestrating his magazines and nation-wide chain of newspapers in a violent attack portraying Wilson as anti-labor and contemptuous of immigrants from southern and eastern Europe.

Wilson goes on his lonely way, avoiding personalities; as the campaign reaches its climax, he focuses on the great issues of tariff, trusts, and Wall Street control of credit and, incidentally, foreshadows his great New Freedom addresses later in 1912. Taking personal charge of his campaign, he rallies his friends with a barrage of letters and telegrams. But there seems to be no way to stem the anti-Wilson tide. Every state controlled by old-line organizations goes for Clark, Underwood, or Governor Judson Harmon of Ohio. More discouraging still, Wilson loses the presidential primaries in every state in which Hearst and Watson have influence or ethnic or immigrant voters are numerous. Only late victories in Minnesota, Wisconsin, New Jersey, Texas, Pennsylvania, and the Carolinas keep Wilson's candidacy alive.

Clark seems the likely winner when the Democratic national convention opens in Baltimore on June 25. He appears irresistible when the Tammany-controlled delegation switches its ninety votes from Harmon to Clark on the tenth ballot, giving the Speaker a majority. But the Wilson delegates hang on with fanatical loyalty and execute an agreement with the Underwood leaders to stand together to prevent Clark from winning the necessary two thirds. Bryan switches his vote from Clark to Wilson on the fourteenth ballot. All delegates are deluged by telegrams; the two leading Democratic newspapers, the New York *World* and the Baltimore *Sun*, demand Wilson's nomination in order to avoid disaster and defeat with Clark. Through many long ballots, the Wilson managers slowly wear down Clark's strength. Victory comes on the forty-sixth ballot when the Underwood managers switch to Wilson.

The conclusion of this volume finds Wilson preparing for the great campaign that lies immediately ahead.

We refer our readers to the Introduction to Volume 23 for a discussion of the problems that we have encountered in putting together all the volumes (21–25) for the period 1910–1912. We refer our readers also to that Introduction for an explanation of our editorial methods and practices.

❖

THE CORRECTION OF CORRUPT TRANSCRIPTS OF
EXTEMPORANEOUS SPEECHES

Dealing with corrupt transcripts of Wilson's extemporaneous speeches has been our most difficult problem since we set about to edit Volume 21. Textual corruption has come from the following sources:

1. Ordinary—and inevitable—typographical errors made by a typist or typesetter.

2. Errors in punctuation and the division of sentences made by reporters, which often changed the meaning of what Wilson said.

3. Errors made by stenographers because their vocabulary did not match Wilson's.

4. Paraphrasing and compacting a speech, often because of spatial constraints, while giving the impression that the text is complete.

5. Most important, errors made by reporters because of their inability to read correctly their own shorthand. Courtroom and speech reporters during this period used the reporting style of the Gregg system. It is highly abbreviated and requires great precision; novitiates often rely heavily upon memory. Reporters rarely had an opportunity carefully to correct and edit transcripts of Wilson's speeches. Wilson often spoke at night, sometimes very late. At the end of the meeting, the reporter would have to rush to his newsroom or hotel room and pound furiously on his typewriter to produce a report in time for the morning edition.

As we explained in the Introduction to Volume 21, which

covers the gubernatorial campaign of 1910, corrupt transcripts
had become a major problem now that Wilson had gone into
politics and had begun to speak frequently and almost always ex-
temporaneously, and they are our only texts of his speeches. It
continues to be a problem even though we are, at Volume 31, well
into the presidential period.

We have had to work out our own solutions because to our
knowledge no one had yet wrestled with the problem of how to
correct corrupt transcripts or offered any guidelines, much less
solutions.

We have found that the surest and safest method is to compare
parallel reports of the same speech because, while all reporters
make errors, they rarely make the same errors. Most of Wilson's
speeches from 1910 to 1912 were reported by more than one
newspaper. In addition, we have the manuscript transcripts of
many of them. It has usually been possible to correct typographical and punctuation errors and anomalies (that is, words
that Wilson could not possibly have spoken) by comparing two or
more texts against each other.

For example, our basic texts[1] of many of Wilson's speeches
during the gubernatorial campaign of 1910 were manuscript
transcripts made by the free-lance journalist, Frank Parker
Stockbridge. He was remarkably incompetent, and his transcripts
are filled with anomalies, typographical errors, and garbled sentences. Fortunately, reporters from New York to Philadelphia
followed Wilson during this campaign. One of them, Charles
Reade Bacon, reported extensive portions of most of Wilson's
speeches for the *Philadelphia Record*. He was a suberb reporter.
The *Trenton Evening Times*, the Trenton *True American*, the
Jersey City *Jersey Journal*, the *Newark Evening News*, and even
county weeklies printed the complete texts of many of Wilson's
speeches. By putting all texts of each speech alongside each other,
we were able in all but a few cases to correct Stockbridge's texts.
The same has been true of most of Wilson's speeches printed in
subsequent volumes.

Real difficulty arises when one has only a single text of a
speech. Since our methods in dealing with such cases have
changed during the editing of Volumes 21–30, we think that
we owe to our readers an explanation of our earlier and present
methods.

We have moved gradually toward silent correction of obvious
typographical errors. So bound were we by the *verbatim et*

---

[1] The basic text of a speech is the most complete version. It is not necessarily
the best text.

literatim tradition that in the beginning we reproduced the garbled word and then repaired it within square brackets. Then we began silently to retranspose transposed letters. We now think that it would have been better silently to correct typographical errors in transcripts of speeches, and we shall do so in the future.

As for punctuation and the division of sentences, we have all along deleted and added punctuation and made our own divisions of sentences when plain meaning and common sense dictated that we do so.

Compacted and paraphrased versions of speeches have never been much of a problem because we have been able to find complete texts of most of Wilson's important speeches. However, researchers should be warned that what purports to be a complete text in, say, the *New York Times*, will probably be a paraphrase or incomplete.

The greatest problems in single texts are the anomalies that occur when the shorthand reporter misreads his notes and has Wilson saying what he could not possibly have said.

One example occurs in the following sentence from a text printed in the Flemington, N. J., *Hunterdon County Democrat*, October 10, 1911:

> Most of them know that they are guilty of a cruel and unjustifiable misrepresentation in that. And some of them do not. They do not know what the support of the progressives is. Why, by the very description of the things I have been telling you, the support of the progressives is the support of common council for the common welfare.

Other examples occur in the transcript by an anonymous reporter of a speech in Jersey City on May 25, 1912:

> Life is a short thing at best . . . but the live of a community is endless and the issues are the issues of life and death, of moral political life and death, and men are counters, mere pawns in the game. . . . Year by year in the United States this spirit more and more dispels itself.

Another anomaly appears in the official and still standard text of Wilson's first inaugural of March 4, 1913:

> We remembered well enough that we had set up a policy which was meant to serve the humblest as well as the most powerful.

The most important anomaly that we have found to date was perpetrated many times by Wilson's personal stenographer,

Charles Lee Swem, particularly in texts of Wilson's speeches during the campaign of 1912. Swem often, almost consistently, rendered Wilson's "serve" as "save." One example occurs on page 428 of this volume, when Swem reports Wilson as saying, in a speech to the Economic Club of New York: "It is by constructive purpose that you are going to govern and save the United States." Later, during the presidential campaign, Swem had Wilson saying things like "Our purpose is to save America" or "America exists not for herself but to save civilization and mankind."

Our first method was to rely upon context and our knowledge of Wilsonian vocabulary to find the right word and to correct the anomaly in square brackets. We probably chose the right word in most cases. But this method carries obvious risks. For example, our first choice as a substitute for the "supports" in the first example, which made no sense in the larger context, was "purpose." It turned out that we were wrong, as we will explain later.

A possible new method occurred to us some two months ago when we heard a lecture on problems of editing medieval manuscripts by Professor William C. Jordan of the History Department of Princeton University. One problem that medievalists encounter is the recovery of poems and chronicles in medieval Latin which have been lost and of which only vernacular translations exist. Using techniques which it is not necessary to explain here, medievalists translate the vernacular texts back into medieval Latin; and, Jordan said, they can be reasonably confident that they have recovered the original texts.

It occurred to us that we might use the same method to correct corrupt transcripts of Wilson's speeches. Their original language was Gregg shorthand, reporting style. Write out the anomalous words in the same shorthand. Then see what the alternatives in transcription are, and also possibly how the reporter could have made the error in the first instance.

We have recently used this method frequently and find that it works in most cases. The outline that the reporter read as "support" sounds in Gregg reporting style "s-p-r-t." Wilson obviously said "the spirit of the progressives" and "the spirit of common counsel." (Note "counsel," not "council." The two are indistinguishable in Gregg; one of Wilson's favorite phrases was "common counsel.") The "live" in the second example might have been a typographical error; however, the shorthand outlines for "life" and "live" are very similar, and the chances are that the reporter simply misread his notes. Wilson could not possibly have said "men are counters." We knew that he was fond of the word "ciphers" in such a context, and we were sure that was the word he used. More important, a study of the shorthand outlines for "counter" and "cipher" makes it clear how the reporter could easily have made the mistake. Writing very fast, he probably wrote an outline with the sounds "c-r." The "dispel" is an obvious anomaly; Wilson could not possibly have said it. The sounds of the shorthand for "dispels" in the Gregg reporting style are "d-s-p-l-s." Wilson obviously said "displays."

The "policy" in the sentence from Wilson's first inaugural was also an obvious error. Woodrow Wilson was a master of English prose style; it is inconceivable that he could have been guilty of so ungrammatical and gauche a phrase as "we had set up a policy." Wilson probably dictated this address to Swem from his, Wilson's, own typewritten draft now in the Wilson Collection in the Princeton University Library. Swem then made the copy that was printed as Wilson's reading copy. Swem's shorthand (about which we will have more to say in the Introduction to Volume 25) is extraordinarily abbreviated, even for the reporting style. We do not have his notes, but he undoubtedly wrote (as it would sound) "p-l-y." In this case, context and knowledge of Wilson's vocabulary would have enabled us to solve the problem. Wilson used the word "polity" hundreds of times. Knowing Swem's shorthand style, we could have assumed that he had made a mistake, and done so probably because the word "polity" was not in his vocabulary. As it turned out, "polity" is what Wilson wrote in his own typed draft, and we were able to correct this anomaly with absolute confidence that "polity" is the word that Wilson used.[2]

In the case of "save" or "serve," it is monumentally important to be sure which word Wilson used, for some writers, relying upon the Swem text, might rightly conclude that Wilson's notion that he, the Democratic party, or the United States should try to save or could save civilization and mankind was early evidence of a messianic complex.

The "save" in the sentence quoted above from the speech to the Economic Club struck us at once as a possible anomaly. Never before had Wilson talked about "saving" the United States or mankind. However, he had spoken many times about "serving." We do not have Swem's notes for the Economic Club speech.

---

[2] It might well be asked why Wilson did not take steps to see that this and another error in his reading copy ("equality or opportunity" for "equality of opportunity") were not corrected. Actually, a correspondent called his attention to the latter error, and he replied that he had of course said "equality of opportunity." But he did nothing to see that the mistakes were corrected in subsequent printings of this address. Indeed, he rarely corrected transcripts of any of his speeches or, for that matter, typographical errors in his letters written either by himself or by stenographers. Perhaps he was too busy to take the trouble; or perhaps he did not care.

However, we do have his notes for Wilson's speeches during the presidential campaign of 1912. The outlines for the two words in the reporting style are called "similar outlines." "Serve" is written $\jmath$; "save," $\jmath$. In many cases, Swem wrote the outlines for both words so that they could not be distinguished.

The presumption was now strong in our minds that Wilson said "serve." But we could not be absolutely sure, and the best that we could have done if this was all that we had known would have been to suggest that Swem probably had misread his notes and that Wilson had probably said "serve." However, in this case the problem was solved conclusively by using the method of comparing parallel texts. We do not have a parallel text for the Economic Club speech. However, we have many parallel texts of the speeches during the presidential campaign. In every instance when Swem had Wilson saying "save," the other reporters wrote "serve." Presumption now turned into certainty: Swem often misread his notes in transcribing his outlines for "serve."

We have been able to make a few corrections following the method described above in the page proofs of Volume 23 and a great many in the galley proofs of Volume 24. We have made them silently and will continue to do so unless we are not absolutely sure that we have found the correct word or words.

We trust that by using this combination of methods we will be able to recover Wilson's spoken prose in all its pristine beauty.

❖

Wilson's letter to W. G. McAdoo, November 10, 1911, Volume 23, p. 547, was incorrectly said to be in WP, DLC. It is in the W. G. McAdoo Papers, DLC.

Phyllis L. Marchand prepared the index for this volume. We are grateful for her excellent and timely work under great pressure.

We extend a warm if belated welcome to Professor William H. Harbaugh of the University of Virginia to the Editorial Advisory Committee.

THE EDITORS

Princeton, New Jersey
December 10, 1976.

CONTENTS

The Papers, January 7, 1912–August 4, 1912

ILLUSTRATIONS

Following page 324

Wilson in Governor's office, Trenton
Princeton University Library

Wilson and William Frank McCombs
Princeton University Library

William Randolph Hearst
Library of Congress

William Gibbs McAdoo
Princeton University Library

Francis Griffith Newlands
Library of Congress

Willard Saulsbury
Library of Congress

Judson Harmon
History of Ohio, by Charles B. Galbreath

Oscar Wilder Underwood
Library of Congress

Champ Clark
Library of Congress

William Jennings Bryan
Library of Congress

Convention Hall, Baltimore
Brown Brothers

Wilson greeting visitors at Sea Girt, New Jersey
Library of Congress

ABBREVIATIONS

ALS	autograph letter signed
CC	carbon copy
CC MSS	carbon copy of manuscripts
CC T MS	carbon copy of typed manuscript
CCL	carbon copy of letter
EAW	Ellen Axson Wilson
hw	handwriting, handwritten
Hw MS	handwritten manuscript
HwLS	handwritten letter signed
LPC	letterpress copy
MS	manuscript
MSS	manuscripts
T	typed
T MS	typed manuscript
T MSS	typed manuscripts
TC	typed copy
TCL	typed copy of letter
TCLS	typed copy of letter signed
TL	typed letter
TLS	typed letter signed
WW	Woodrow Wilson
WWhw	Woodrow Wilson handwriting, handwritten
WWhw MSS	Woodrow Wilson handwritten manuscripts
WWsh	Woodrow Wilson shorthand

ABBREVIATIONS FOR COLLECTIONS
AND LIBRARIES

Following the National Union Catalog
of the Library of Congress

A-Ar	Alabama Department of Archives and History, Montgomery
CU	University of California
CtY	Yale University
DLC	Library of Congress
DeU	University of Delaware
MH	Harvard University
MdBJ-Ar	Johns Hopkins University Archives
NHpR	Franklin D. Roosevelt Library, Hyde Park
NcD	Duke University
NcDaD	Davidson College
Nj	New Jersey State Library, Trenton
NjP	Princeton University
RSB Coll., DLC	Ray Stannard Baker Collection of Wilsoniana, Library of Congress
ViU	University of Virginia
ViW	College of William and Mary
WC, NjP	Woodrow Wilson Collection, Princeton University
WP, DLC	Woodrow Wilson Papers, Library of Congress

SYMBOLS

[Jan. 7, 1912]   publication date of a published writing; also date of document when date is not part of text

[[Jan. 8, 1912]]   delivery date of a speech if publication date differs

[*July* 22, *1912*]   composition date when publication date differs

THE PAPERS OF

WOODROW WILSON

VOLUME 24

1912

THE PAPERS OF
WOODROW WILSON

An Unpublished Statement About the Cleveland Letter[1]

[c. Jan. 7, 1912]

If this is in fact an authentic utterance of Mr. Cleveland's, it is, no doubt, an echo of certain controversies at Princeton which I had hoped, for the sake of the University, I should not be obliged to revert to. It has nothing to do with politics.

I can perhaps indicate in a few sentences the things that were in debate,—though the debate itself would be a very complicated thread to trace. Professor Andrew F. West, Dean of the Graduate School at Princeton, many years ago worked out a plan for a beautifully appointed house of residence for the fellows and some of the graduate students of the University of which, as he then conceived it, we all thought well. It was to be placed at the geographical heart of the University, in close neighbourhood to the libraries and laboratories, where the work of the men in residence might tell in all its seriousness upon the general life of the University, only too apt to be ignorant and negligent of the claims and interest of real scholarship and the scholarly life. But, as the years went by, and the time approached when it was thought his plan might be put into operation, it greatly changed in his own mind, and lost all promise of its general use and effect upon the University. He wished his "Graduate College," which was (in fact) only to be an elaborate hall of residence, to be surrounded by gardens,—set off at a distance from the rest of the University, in order that its residents might be secluded to a life of their own, separated from the rest of the graduate students of the University as well as from the undergraduates, whose ideals their example had originally been intended to affect,— away from the libraries and laboratories, where it would be nothing but a beautiful place of retreat. I, for one, could not support such a plan.

Mr. Cleveland was a member of the Board of Trustees of the University, and had been made chairman of its standing committee on the Graduate School. Dean West was his neighbour and was in constant attendance upon him. In the last years of his life,—the years in which Dean West's plan underwent its most undesirable changes,—Mr Cleveland's health and vigor were failing. He was much shut in, was very little in contact with the outer world, hardly at all in contact with the general life of the University. During those same years the movement of college life at Princeton (naturally one of the most democratic of the colleges) away from democracy to club life developed very rapidly indeed. As President of the University I met it and felt it at every turn. I found myself obliged to fight for a return to democracy all along the line, or else know that the young men in the University were not being properly prepared for American life or imbibing American ideals.

Mr. Cleveland did not perceive these things. He would not accept the very earnest representations I made to him of a change of conditions to which I knew he would be very sensitive if he once got sight of them. He remained under the influence of the small group of men who were always about him. He did not see how radically Dean West's plan had swung away from its first form and purpose, and continued to champion it with all his force. When I opposed it in the essential particular of its site and consequent spirit and character, and sought by every possible suggestion to bring it back to what it had originally been intended to be, he accused me of bad faith.

I can only deplore the fact that this great man should not have seen that the same forces were at work in the University which it had become our duty to fight throughout the nation,— forces which were making against democracy and for special privilege in the University which I know he conscientiously sought to serve. Since his death Professor West's ideas have been carried out. The graduate hall of residence is being erected upon a site far removed from the rest of the University buildings. It is to cost about a million dollars and is to house somewhat less than a hundred students; is to have a dining hall which will itself cost two hundred thousand dollars, a special gift by Mr. William Cooper Proctor, of Cincinnati; and the beautiful tower which is to be erected in memory of Mr. Cleveland, by the subscription of many hundreds of citizens of the republic, is to be part of the great structure. The pouring in of money has overwhelmed all opposition and Professor West's ideals of university life have for the time prevailed at Princeton.[2]

T MS (WP, DLC).

[1] About this letter, allegedly written by Grover Cleveland to Henry van Dyke, see WW to R. Garrett, Sept. 5, 1911, n. 2, Vol. 23.

[2] There is a WWsh draft of this statement dated Dec. 9, 1911, and a later and undated WWhw draft in WP, DLC.

A News Report

[Jan. 7, 1912]

WILSON LETTER ATTACKING BRYAN

WASHINGTON, Jan. 6.—The letter written by Woodrow Wilson in 1905, when he was president of Princeton University, to Adrian H. Joline of New York city was telegraphed from New York to-night and handed about among the Democratic national committeemen. The letter said:

"Cannot we devise some dignified way of getting Mr. Bryan out of the Democratic party and getting rid of him for all time?"[1]

This letter was written shortly after the defeat of Alton B. Parker for the Presidency. This excerpt of Mr. Wilson's letter was variously discussed to-night by the committeemen, nearly all of whom to the number of fifty-two are in town. They did not wish to speak of it in specific terms. When the excerpt was read to Chairman Norman E. Mack of the national committee his only comment was:

"The national committee is not here to select candidates for the Presidency." . . .

When a SUN reporter asked Mr. Joline yesterday for the letter Mr. Joline said:

"I have a letter, but apparently I have already talked about it too much. I have nothing to say at this time." He would not elucidate further.[2]

Printed in the New York *Sun*, Jan. 7, 1912; three editorial headings omitted.

[1] Wilson's letter to Joline was actually dated April 29, 1907, and is printed at that date in Vol. 17.

[2] The New York *Sun* printed the correct text of the letter on January 8, just before Bryan, Wilson, and other Democrats were to speak at the Jackson Day Dinner in Washington. About this affair, see Arthur S. Link, *Wilson: The Road to the White House* (Princeton, N. J., 1947), pp. 352-55.

To Mary Allen Hulbert Peck

The Bellevue-Stratford
Dearest Friend,   Philadelphia 7 Jan'y, 1912

I am on my way down to Washington, where I am to speak to-morrow evening. The Democratic National Committee is to meet there to-morrow (which is Jackson's birth-day) and the banquet in the evening is to be a grand dress parade of candidates for the presidential nomination on the Democratic ticket. I hate the whole thing, but it is something "expected" of me by my friends and backers, and, after all, an honest and sincere man need not be embarrassed by being put on exhibition. I can say what I really *care* to say, and really believe[,] almost as well in one set of circumstances as in another. I am getting a bit self-possessed at last!

There is a merry war on against me. I am evidently regarded as the strongest candidate at present, for all the attacks are directed against me, and the other fellows are not bothered. Kind one-time friends are giving to the newspapers letters I wrote them before I became of public consequence in which I expressed uncomplimentary opinions of Mr. Bryan. Rumours are sedulously set afoot that there is a letter which various persons have seen or been told the contents of in which Mr. Cleveland said that he thought I "lacked intellectual integrity," or words to that effect,—&c. &c. No doubt these things will have their effect and will turn various people against me, and this rain of small missles makes me feel like a common target for the malicious (by the way, practically all the darts are supplied by the Princetonians who hate me), and somewhat affect my spirits for a day at a time (the strongest nerves wince under persistent spite); but for the most part I go serenely on my way. I believe very profoundly in an over-ruling Providence, and do not fear that any real plans can be thrown off the track. It may not be intended that I shall be President,—but that would not break my heart—and I am content to await the event,—doing what I honourably can, in the meantime, to discomfit mine enemies! I keep perfectly well. Nothing from you recently except the hasty little note[1] that Allen brought by the *Tagus*, but that made me happy by reporting you well—and seemed to be written in fine spirits. All join me in affectionate messages. My warm regards to Mrs. Allen.

Your devoted friend   Woodrow Wilson

ALS (WP, DLC).
[1] It is missing.

To the Democratic Club of Philadelphia[1]

[Philadelphia, Jan. 7, 1912]

May I not have the privilege of sending to the Democratic Club on the occasion of its Jackson day banquet an expression of my warm hope that it will have a distinguished part in bringing about Democratic success in the year upon which it has just entered.   [Woodrow Wilson]

Printed in the Philadelphia *North American*, Jan. 9, 1912.
[1] On the occasion of its Jackson Day banquet at the Lu Lu Temple on January 8. Francis Fisher Kane was president of the club.

A News Item

[*Jan. 8, 1912*]

WILSON LEADS IN CLASH OF BOOMS.

WASHINGTON, Jan. 8.—While Col. Bryan was being subjected to the steam roller treatment by the old guard of the National Committeemen[1] and the faithful were getting dressed for the Jackson Day dinner there was a lot of talk about the various Presidential booms on exhibition.

That for Gov. Wilson of New Jersey attracted the most attention. The Governor himself contributed very largely to the interest in it. He reached Washington at 11 o'clock, talked with the leaders of several States, held a general reception at the Willard Hotel, made a newspaper talk at the Press Club[2] and then got ready to add his speech to the fourteen scheduled for the dinner.

The attendance at the general reception to the Governor, arranged by Lawyer McCoomb,[3] indicated the interest in his personality and reflected the wide range of curiosity in his political welfare. Next to Mr. Bryan and Mr. Murphy[4] the New Jersey Governor came in for the lion's share of attention from the Democratic hosts. He was in fine form, alert, clear-eyed, and quick in making agreeable responses to the greetings he received from the persons who called on him.

At the Press Club the Governor faced more than a hundred members of the newspaper profession. In his speech he touched lightly upon current matters, though he carefully avoided any reference to the Presidential proposition. He gave the "boys" some good advice, paid their profession a gracious compliment and then shook hands with his auditors.

While dodging Presidential talk Gov. Wilson made an indirect allusion to the Joline letter, which his hearers easily understood. . . .[5]

The Governor was emphasising the value of absolute frankness among newspaper men and the necessity of an unprejudiced statement of facts when he observed:

"Even if a man has written letters it ought not to embarrass him if they are published. Even if a man changes his mind it ought not to embarrass him."

Printed in the New York *World*, Jan. 9, 1912.

[1] A news report accompanying this item told about Bryan's defeat when he led the attempt to unseat James M. Guffey, national committeeman from Pennsylvania, and give his place to A. Mitchell Palmer, recently elected to the National Committee by the "reorganizer" state committee.

[2] Another report of this talk is printed at Jan. 9, 1912.

[3] That is, William F. McCombs.

[4] Charles Francis Murphy, leader of Tammany Hall.

[5] Here follows the text of the letter to Joline.

Two Unpublished Statements About the Joline Letter[1]

[Washington, Jan. 8, 1912]

⟨This is the Mr. Joline who was overwhelmingly defeated by the alumni of Princeton when he sought election at their hands to the Board of Trustees of the University in opposition to my democratic policy as president.

⟨I suppose that Mr. Joline's object was in some way to discredit me in the eyes of the many thousands who have for so many years loyally supported Mr. Bryan. Everybody who cared to know already knew that I was opposed to the nomination of Mr. Bryan by the party a second and a third time. My opinion was of no public interest at the time, because I was not in politics, and never expected to be. I was merely expressing my judgment as a private citizen deeply concerned for the practical success of the party to which I have all my life belonged.⟩

All the country now knows what a profound ⟨an admirable and pervasive⟩ influence Mr. Bryan has had upon the thought and upon the public policy of the country. ⟨What he conceived Mr. Roosevelt in part accomplished.⟩ Under his ⟨fearless and eloquent⟩ courageous teaching, the whole country has waked up to the realization of the meaning of things in its life which were threatening, and are still threatening, to embarrass every process of genuine democracy. The present progressive vigour of the Democratic party is in no small part ⟨in chief measure⟩ due to his ⟨fearless⟩ declaration of ⟨the truth as he saw it, and as he has now made the country see it⟩ facts now becoming abundantly clear. What he conceived the Republican leaders have already been compelled in part to translate into law.

⟨This did not make it wise, nevertheless, to renominate him in 1900 and in 1908, from the practical point of view of party success at the polls.⟩ I am not singular in having been one of the many ⟨thousands of⟩ Democrats who voted for him at the polls while wishing that his leadership might have been that of the teacher and tribune of the people, and not that of the candidate. Office could not add to the great name and place he has made for himself in the history of the country,—and the loss of it cannot ⟨take from him his natural ascendancy⟩ deprive him of his undisputed hold upon the affection and confidence of the people

❖

⟨These letters⟩ The Joline letter merely illustrates my habit,— I hope not a bad habit, however impolitic,—of speaking bluntly the opinions I entertain. ⟨With equal frankness, I hope, I am willing to learn.⟩ Since ⟨that letter was written⟩ I have come into personal contact with the actual conditions of politics, the active forces that are forming,—or attempting to form,—the policy of the government. ⟨My active participation in politics has enabled me to realize all this as I never realized it before.⟩ Of late years the conviction has grown upon me that Mr. Bryan has done the country an inestimable service,—and has done it with admirable fearlessness and constancy. The present progressive vigour of the Democratic party is in no small part due to his effective declaration of the truth as he saw it. Under his stimulation the whole country has waked up to a realization of influences which it did not fully perceive, but which were undoubtedly threatening, and still threaten, the genuine processes of Democracy. What he conceived ⟨Mr. Roosevelt in part accomplished.⟩ the Republican leaders have been compelled in part to translate into law. I hope I shall always be able to see things as they are when I come into actual contact with them, and that, whatever my views as to particular proposals, I shall be able to do justice to the gifts and characters of the men concerned. Above all, I hope I shall always continue to learn.

WWhw MSS (photostats in RSB Coll., DLC).
1 About the drafting of these statements and Wilson's decision not to issue them, see Link, *Road to the White House*, p. 354.

An Address in Washington at a Jackson Day Dinner[1]

[[Jan. 8, 1912]]

Mr. Toastmaster[2] and fellow Democrats, we are met to celebrate an achievement. It is an interesting circumstance that principles have no anniversaries. Only the men who embody principles are celebrated upon occasions like this and only the events to which their concerted action gave rise excite our enthusiasm. You know that the principles of the Democratic Party are professed by practically the whole population of the United States. The test of a Democrat is whether he lives up to those principles or not. I have no doubt there are some people in the United States who covertly question the doctrines of Democracy, but nobody challenges them openly. It goes without saying, therefore, that we have not come together merely to state the abstract principles of our party. We have come together to take

1 Delivered in the ballroom of the Raleigh Hotel.
2 Senator James A. O'Gorman of New York.

counsel as to how it is possible, by courageous and concerted action, to translate them into policy and law. The Democratic Party has had a long period of disappointment and defeat and I think that we can point out the reason. We do not live in simple times. We live in very conflicting times indeed. No man can be certain that he can say how to weave the threads of Democratic principle throughout all the complicated garment of our civilization, and the reason that the Democratic Party has had this period of successive disturbance is that it has been divided into groups just as it was as to the method of fulfilling the principles.

We have differed as to measures; it has taken us 16 years and more to come to any comprehension of our community of thought in regard to what we ought to do. What I want to say is that one of the most striking things in recent years is that with all the rise and fall of particular ideas, with all the ebb and flow of particular proposals, there has been one interesting fixed point in the history of the Democratic Party, and that fixed point has been the character and the devotion and the preachings of William Jennings Bryan.

I, for my part, never want to forget this: That while we have differed with Mr. Bryan upon this occasion and upon that in regard to the specific things to be done, he has gone serenely on pointing out to a more and more convinced people what it was that was the matter. He has had the steadfast vision all along of what it was that was the matter and he has, not any more than Andrew Jackson did, not based his career upon calculation, but has based it upon principle.

Now, what has been the matter? The matter has been that the Government of this country was privately controlled and that the business of this country was privately controlled; that we did not have genuine representative government and that the people of this country did not have the control of their own affairs.

What do we stand for here to-night and what shall we stand for as long as we live? We stand for setting the Government of this country free and the business of this country free. The facts have been disputed by a good many sections of the Democratic Party for the last half generation, but they were not clearly recognized.

I make the assertion that the Government was privately controlled. I mean to put it specifically that the Government of this country was managed by politicians who gained the contributions which they used by solicitation from particular groups of business interests, on the understanding, explicit or implied, that the first care of the Government was to be for those particular interests. I am not questioning either the integrity or patriotism of the men concerned. I have no right to. In most instances they were of that old belief, cropping up again and again in America, that the people of this country are not capable of perceiving their own interest and of managing their own affairs; that they have not the contact with large affairs; that they have not the variety of experience which qualifies them to take charge of their own affairs. It is the old Hamiltonian doctrine that those who have the biggest asset in the Government should be the trustees for the rest of us; that the men who conduct the biggest business transactions are the only men who should stand upon an elevation sufficient to see the whole range of our affairs, and that if we will but follow their leadership we may share in their prosperity. That is the Republican doctrine, and I am perfectly willing, as a tribute to their honesty though not to their intelligence, to admit that they really believe it; that they really believe it is unsafe to trust such delicate matters as the complicated business of this country to the general judgment of the country. They believe only a very small coterie of gentlemen are to be trusted with the conduct of large affairs. There was a long period in New Jersey, for example, in which no commissioner of insurance was ever chosen without first consulting or getting the consent of the head of the largest insurance company in the State, and I am willing to admit, at any rate for the sake of argument, that it was supposed he, better than anyone else, knew who was qualified for the job. He did know who was qualified for the job and he had the proper point of view in demonstrating that it was mainly for the benefit of the big interests.

Now, the other thing that has been privately controlled in this country is the business of the country. I do not mean that each man's particular business ought not to be privately controlled, but I mean that the great business transactions of this country are privately controlled by gentlemen whom I can name and whom I will name, if it is desired; men of great dignity of character; men, as I believe, of great purity of purpose, but men who have concentrated, in their own hands, transactions which they are not willing to have the rest of the country interfere with.

Now, the real difficulty in the United States, gentlemen, it seems to me, is not the existence of great individual combinations—that is dangerous enough in all countries—but the real danger is the combination of the combinations, the real danger is that the same groups of men control chains of banks, systems of railways, whole manufacturing enterprises, great mining projects, great enterprises for the developing of the natural water power of this country, and that threaded together in the personnel of a series of boards of directors is a community of interest more formidable than any conceivable combination in the United States.

It has been said that you can not "unscramble eggs," and I am perfectly willing to admit it, but I can see in all cases before they are scrambled that they are not put in the same basket and intrusted to the same groups of persons.

What we have got to do—and it is a colossal task—a task not to be undertaken with a light head or without judgment—but what we have got to do is to disentangle this colossal community of interest. No matter how we may purpose dealing with a single combination in restraint of trade, you will agree with me in this that I think no combination is big enough for the United States to be afraid of; and when all the combinations are combined and this combination is not disclosed by any process of incorporation or law, but is merely the identity of personnel, then there is something for the law to pull apart, and gently, but firmly and persistently dissect.

You know that the chemist distinguishes between a chemical combination and an amalgam. A chemical combination has done something which I can not scientifically describe, but its molecules have become intimate with one another and practically united, whereas an amalgam has a mere physical union created by pressure from without. Now, you can destroy that mere physical contact without hurting the individual elements, and you can break up this community of interest without hurting any one of the single interests combined; not that I am particularly delicate of some of the interests combined—I am not under bonds to be unusually polite, but I am interested in the business of this country, and believe its integrity depends upon this dissection. I do not believe any one group of men has vision enough or genius enough to determine what the development of opportunity and the accomplishments by achievement shall be in this country. You can not establish competition by law, but you can take away the obstacles by law that stand in the way of competition, and while we may despair of setting up competition among individual persons there is good ground for setting up competition between these great combinations, and after we have got them competing with one another they will come to their senses in so many respects that we can afterwards hold conference with them without losing our self-respect.

Now, that is the job. That is the thing that exists, and the thing that has to be changed, not in any spirit of revolution and not with the thought—for it would be a deeply unjust thought—that the business men of this country have put up any job on the Government of this country. Take even that colossal job known as the Payne-Aldrich tariff. The business men of this country did not put up that job. Some of the business men of this country did, but by no means all of them. Think what that means. Do you mean to say that the commercial men of this country are interested in maintaining the integrity of that bill? Some, and only some, of the manufacturers of this country have put up that job on us, and many of them have been unwilling beneficiaries of a system which they knew did not minister to the prosperity of their undertakings.

I am not going to make a tariff speech. It is so easy to knock holes in the present tariff there is no sport in it. I am a humane man. I would not jump on a thing like that, but I do want to point out to you that the ownership of Government—it is a harsh word to use, but I am not using it harshly, I am using it for shorthand—the ownership of the Government of the United States, by special groups of interests, centers in the tariff, and that is where the difference comes in. I have heard men say that politicians interfered too much with business. I want to say that business men interfere too much with politics. Do the statesmen of this country go to the Ways and Means Committee and the Finance Committee and beg for these favors? You know that they do not. Some Congressmen go to these committees and plead that some gentlemen back in their constituencies are pressing them hard on bills, and as public men, plead for individual interests, and their entrance into politics has been so by those who intended to control the schedules of the tariff.

I once heard a very distinguished Member of Congress give this illustration: He was talking about a great campaign fund that had been collected.[3] It was the paltry sum of $400,000. It was a great sum for that somewhat primitive day, and it was pointed out at the time—at any rate specified—that most of this money had been contributed by manufacturers who were the chief beneficiaries of the tariff, and those gentlemen pointed out that they certainly would want to get their money back. I may not be saying the thing properly, but it is simply this:

Down where I live we get most of our water from pumps, and a pump, as you know, may go dry over night, and a prudent

[3] That is, the fund collected by the department store magnate, John Wanamaker, for the first presidential campaign of Benjamin Harrison.

housekeeper will pump up a bucket of water at night before she goes to bed and leave it standing. Then, in the morning if the plunger will not suck she pours in that water, and that expands the plunger and it begins sending the pump water out; and the first water that comes out is the same water she poured in. By that I mean, gentlemen, that this $400,000 was ordered poured in to make the old pump suck, and you know that that homely illustration is fair. That is what is done and that is the way the control of Government comes in.

Well, what are we going to do? I have a practical mind, and am not interested particularly in the too-long-winded discussion of the principles upon which we are going to act. Neither am I wise enough to propose a comprehensive program. I think the rule of Donnybrook Fair is good enough for me: "Hit the heads you see." Make sure before that your shillalahs are made of good Irish hickory. By that I mean this: Lop off the special favors whenever you are certain you have identified them; lop them off. That is a pretty good rule. You do not need to be all-wise to do that. Paint some of those favors so conspicuously that all can see them. If you do not know which they are, ask the first man you meet on the street and he will tell you. He will give you a list that will keep you busy all winter. And I might add this, if you please, not to go at them haphazard, but to go steadily through the things that have become obvious excrescences and cut them off. That is a very definite program, and, then, I might add, go into an absolutely thorough investigation of the way it may best be conducted, find out just where, in dissecting, the scalpel can be introduced, and divorce these artificial unions, because I know that you will not be cutting living tissue.

I hear a great deal of talk about conservatism and radicalism. Now, what makes a man shiver when he hears a statement of the facts concerning it? He feels it is cold-blooded and indiscreet to state the facts, and yet he really is inclined, I must say, to think there is something in it. He says to himself, this man must be a radical, because if he sees the thing that way, what in God's name is he going to do, because, if he is going to go to work to thoroughly change those facts there is no telling where he will stop. Now, it is just there that he ought to stop being radical. If the prudent surgeon wants to save the patient he has got absolutely to know the naked anatomy of the man. He has got to know what is under his skin and his intestines; he has got to be absolutely indecent in his scrutiny. And then he has got to say to himself: "I know where the seat of life is; I know where my knife should penetrate; I dare not go too far for fear

it should touch the fountain of vitality. In order to save this
beautiful thing I must cut deep, but I must cut carefully; I
must cut out the things that are decayed and rotten, the things
that manifest disease, and I must leave every honest, wholesome
tissue absolutely untouched." A capital operation may be radical,
but it is also conservative. There can not be life without the
cutting out of the dead and decayed tissue.

And, as to business, after a few committees like the Stanley
committee[4] have gone on a little longer we will know a good
many particulars, and we will be versed in this high-finance
business ourselves. These things are coming out with astonishing candor. We now know how to regulate prices. We know
how to run combinations by circulars that convey intimations
and instructions. We see the little artificial threads that bind
these things together, threads which do not themselves contain
the life, but which themselves do control the vessels in which
the life blood runs. And so stage by stage we shall learn what
the practical business of a Democrat is. It is to go to the root
of the matter, seek out the processes of cure and restoration
and rehabilitation. What a travesty it is upon the name of Democracy to see any Democrat who wishes to destroy the very
thing that his principles should make him in love with, namely,
the life of the people themselves. A very thoughtful preacher
pointed out the other day that one of the first quotations in our
Lord's Prayer is, "Give us this day our daily bread," which would
seem, perhaps, to indicate that our Lord knew what every statesman must know—that the spiritual life of the Nation can not
exist unless it has physical life; that you can not be an altruist
and patriot on an empty stomach. Nothing shows the utter incapacity of a man to be a Democrat so much as his incapacity
to understand what we are after. He does not know that the
very seeds of life are in the principles and confidence and lives
and virtues of the people of this country, and so when we strike
at the trusts, or, rather, I will not say strike at the trusts, because we are not slashing about us—when we move against the
trusts, when we undertake the strategy which is going to be
necessary to overcome and destroy monopoly, we are rescuing
the business of this country, we are not injuring it, and when
we separate the interests from each other and disconnect these
communities of connection we have in mind a greater community
of interest, a vaster community of interest, the community of
interest that binds the virtues of all men together, that mankind
which is broad and catholic enough to take under the sweep of

4 Described in n. 1 to the second news report printed at June 16, 1911, Vol. 23.

its comprehension all sorts and conditions of men, and that vision which sees that no society is renewed from the top and every society is renewed from the bottom. Limit opportunity, restrict the field of originative achievement, and you have cut out the heart and root of the prosperity of the country itself.

The only thing that can ever make a free country is to keep a free and hopeful heart under every jacket in it, and then there will be an irrepressible vitality, then there will be an irrepressible ideal which will enable us to be Democrats of the sort that when we die we shall look back and say: "Yes; from time to time we differed with each other as to what ought to be done, but, after all, we followed the same vision, after all we worked slowly, stumbling through dark and doubtful passages onward to a common purpose and a common ideal." Let us apologize to each other that we ever suspected or antagonized one another; let us join hands once more all around the great circle of community of counsel and of interest which will show us at the last to have been indeed the friends of our country and the friends of mankind.[5]

Printed in the *Congressional Record*, 62nd Cong., 2nd sess., Vol. 48, pp. 4745-47.
[5] There is a WWhw outline of this address dated Jan. 6, 1912, in WP, DLC.

A News Report of Remarks to the National Press Club of Washington

[Jan. 9, 1912]

WILSON IN WASHINGTON MEETS MANY FRIENDS

WASHINGTON, Jan. 9.—Occupying the Presidential suite in the New Willard, Governor Wilson received more than 300 Jerseymen yesterday afternoon, not to say anything of a large number of members of Congress and Democrats of prominence from all sections of the country. Among them were many old Southern friends of the Governor.

The Governor remained in the New Willard rooms until 5 P. M. and then went to the National Press Club, where he was a guest of honor of the Washington newspaper men. At the Press Club he was greeted by 200 of the members and guests.

Introduced by President Frederick J. Haskins,[1] Governor Wilson made a short address. He commented on the work of the news writers, and spoke especially of their fidelity to the truth. He was less kindly in his estimate of editorial writers.

Speaking for publicity in public affairs, he said: "I do not mind getting licked in an open fight when the other man appealed to the same tribunal I appealed to. If they will lay their whole case before the people and the people decide against me, why, that's sport. What I object to is private council frame-ups, the things that are arranged and the interests that are privately safeguarded. I am against the whole business with respect to privacy with regard to the business of the United States. I cannot imagine anything connected with the public business that is not as much the business of the humblest citizen as of the most distinguished Cabinet Minister."

During the reception at the Press Club, W. K. Devereux got in line to shake hands with Governor Wilson. One of Mr. Devereux's possessions is a humorous streak. The Governor and he shook hands and Mr. Deveraux solemnly declared:

"Governor Wilson, I inform you that I have in my possession a letter written by you to General George Washington in 1776 just before the battle of Trenton, in which you criticise the Ocean Grove Campmeeting Association[2] because it objects to that resort being made a borough."

Instantly the Governor replied:

"I am aware of the existence of that letter. Be a perfect gentleman and give it to the press."

"That shall be done," answered Devereux, "and I shall have it published in full on the sporting page of The Ladies' Home Journal." . . .

Printed in the *Newark Evening News*, Jan. 9, 1912.

[1] Frederic Jennings Haskins, one of the nation's leading columnists and a regular contributor of special articles to nearly fifty newspapers.

[2] The Methodist organization that owns Ocean Grove, N. J.

A News Report

[Jan. 9, 1912]

WILSON ALSO ATTENDS NEW JERSEY DINNER

WASHINGTON, Jan. 9.—The Jersey overflow dinner at the Shoreham last night was as pronounced a success as its projectors had hoped. The table was set in the room in which the Democratic national committee held its meeting in the afternoon. . . .

Colonel Holly,[1] of Bergen County, acted as toastmaster and introduced Dudley Field Malone, of New York, as the first speaker. Just as Mr. Malone concluded Governor Wilson came in, having left the big dinner at the Raleigh to say a few words to his New Jersey friends. He was greeted with tumultuous cheering and it was a long time before the Governor could be heard. He told the diners that he felt at home, because he knew how they all felt toward him, while he was not so certain about the Democrats of the big dinner.

"I can only observe with my eyes what's going on in their minds," he said. "There are all sorts and conditions of Democrats," he continued, "and all of us are interested in bringing the Democratic party to the service of a common cause. There are all sorts of policies, and we must not assume that our policy is the only good one."

He denounced machines and boss rule. "There is a great deal of misconception about political organization," he said. "Some people have the idea that organization is bad, but the binding together of the various forces, which do not come together in haphazard fashion, is the only conceivable way in which to achieve the common purpose. A movement must be managed, but it must be managed to do things, not bossed. The only thing I shall fight is the machine. There is a difference between party and machine. Shall a man be said to be opposed to a party because he is opposed to the base uses of a party? Would you rather concoct a little private program at the head of a small number of men or march at the head of a great State?"

Governor Wilson also attacked the Payne-Aldrich bill and made a plea for conservatism of the people. "So long as they understand that their voice is going to be heard," he said, "they are going to conserve the public interest."

After the Governor had retired there were speeches by William G. McAdoo, former Judge [Robert S.] Hudspeth and others.

Printed in the *Newark Evening News*, Jan. 9, 1912.

1 Alfred T. Holley, Democratic leader of Hackensack, member of the State Board of Equalization of Taxes.

An Annual Message to the Legislature
of New Jersey

[Trenton, N. J.] Ninth of January, 1912.

To the Legislature:

With the opening of another legislative session, it is my privilege to call your attention to several matters with regard to which we have the opportunity to serve the State by well-considered changes in its law. It has interested me very deeply to note that in recent years in this State the platforms of the two great parties, which come every year into competition at the annual election for the control of the legislative body, have usually been in substantial agreement; so that one is encouraged to believe that our elections are not so much contests for party advantage, or aggrandizement, as for the opportunity to serve the people of the State—contests for the honor and satisfaction of accomplishing the reforms which the conditions obtaining in the State naturally suggest. If this is true, the winning party may count upon the co-operation of the minority in carrying out its platform program. When the legislative session opens we become colleagues in a common service, and our standard is not party advantage, but the welfare of New Jersey. We are, first of all, citizens and public servants; our party differences are secondary to our duty as representatives and trustees.

I venture upon this preface to my recommendations in order to afford myself the opportunity to say with how much pleasure I shall co-operate with the present Legislature in carrying out every program that is judged to be for the common benefit. It is my duty, as Governor of the State and representative of all its people, to be the leader of my party in the State, indeed, but not a partisan or a strategist for mere party benefit. I am glad to think, therefore, that the matters to which I shall call your attention do not lie within the field of party debate. They are matters which we can approach without party bias or prejudice. Whatever differences of judgment may arise with regard to them, they need have no flavor of party feeling about them.

At the last session we united in effecting reforms obviously necessary and long desired, upon which opinion in the State had for many years been centered, but did not address ourselves at all to certain other large questions no less necessary to deal with, which public opinion has not definitely fixed upon, simply because of their complexity and of the fact that only those who can view them from the inside can fully appreciate how vital they are to the integrity and serviceability of the State's government. I mean questions of efficiency and economy. We can get at the heart of these if we choose, and we could not render the State a greater service than by doing so. Without the very best administrative organization the government of the State cannot be administered with entire integrity or with full and candid responsibility to the people, for unless it is efficient and responsible it is in constant danger of becoming corrupt. Wastefulness and inefficiency are themselves virtually forms of graft. They afford fruitful opportunities for every kind of abuse.

It is to questions of efficiency and economy, therefore, that I first invite your serious attention.

The government of New Jersey, like the governments of most of the older States, has developed on its administrative side, not systematically, but by patchwork, and mere accretion: by the multiplication of boards and commissions, by the addition of first this piece and then that piece to existing departments. There has been constant addition, no subtraction, no elimination, no co-ordination. It has grown very much as the State House itself has grown, but without the necessity of at least some semblance of architectural unity, without the connecting corridors and the common roof which the State House must of mere physical necessity be given.

The number and variety of State boards and commissions is utterly confusing. One wonders why there might not be, for example, a department of public works, in which would be assembled all the functions affecting roads, parks, bridges and waterways, now divided up amongst a half dozen boards and commissions, permanent and temporary; why a department of public welfare might not serve as a means of co-ordinating and simplifying the supervision of the public health, the examination of practitioners of medicine, the inspection of tenement houses, of mills and factories, and the enforcement of the laws against child labor; why a department of conservation might not combine the work now scattered amongst numerous bodies concerning the preservation of fish and game, the supervision and regulation of the oyster industry, the safeguarding of the water supply and the disposition of the riparian rights of the State? Why should every oyster bed have a commission of its own? It is necessary to bring order out of this chaotic miscellany, not merely to have the satisfaction of conducting the business of the State in a businesslike and efficient way, but to prevent waste and forestall abuses of many kinds. I suggest, therefore, the constitution by law of a commission, not too large, to act promptly and harmoniously, to take into consideration the whole question of simplifying and co-ordinating the administrative agencies of the State in order that they may be put upon the best possible basis of economy and efficiency. In my judgment, the majority of the commission should be experienced and trusted business men, and they should have the benefit of the advice of men who have made a special study of scientific efficiency in practical administration. It should report to the Legislature at as early a date as possible. Its report would serve to concentrate public opinion upon one of the most vital matters of government, whether looked at from the point of view of purity or of serviceability, and with public criticism centered upon a particular scheme of reorganization, satisfactory legislation could readily be obtained.

The scope of this commission's inquiry ought to be so wide as to include our whole method of assessing and equalizing taxes. You have only to examine the reports of our State tax boards to realize how unsatisfactory our present methods are. It is not enough that there should be boards to which individuals can resort to remedy inequalities in taxation and assessment. Powers of correction fall short of accomplishing what ought to be accomplished. Uniform standards ought to be established upon the initiative and authority of some central board of supervision. That body ought to have independent and exclusive powers of reclassification within certain general limits defined in the law. In several States of the Union—in Wisconsin, for example, and in Massachusetts—commissions of this kind have been set up with exceedingly satisfactory results, whose powers are powers of active supervision, and through whose instrumentality inequalities and inequities are being corrected upon a definite plan, not in individual cases only, not merely for the persons who can afford to appeal and protest, but by systematic means and upon the initiative of the commission itself.

You have only to ask the average taxpayer whom you meet on the street what he thinks of the assessments to which he is subjected to find how many varieties of assessment there are in the State. You have only to examine the average tax assessor's books to discover how little system there is and how little he actually knows of the property he assesses. How many of the tax districts in the State are mapped and plotted? How many assessors can produce definite evidence and data to support their assessments? Undertake to debate with men from half a dozen counties the question whether we should continue to maintain our present system of county tax boards, and you will at once discover that in some counties they are valued and deemed efficient; in others smiled at and regarded as entirely unnecessary and unwarrantably expensive. Have the State Board of Assessors and our State Board for the Equalization of Taxes powers that can bring a satisfactory system out of these varieties and confusions? If they have not, somebody should have, for the whole matter needs reconsideration.

Along with this systematic reconsideration of our methods of assessments and taxation should go a very thorough examination of our tax system itself; its basis and principle. Perhaps we shall be in a better position after making our machinery suitable and adequate to discover the weak places in the bases of taxation. Sooner or later we shall be obliged to examine them to the bottom.

Are we systematic, have we properly combined our instrumentalities and adequately equipped them with authority in the great matter of the conservation of our naturally splendid and abundant resources? Conservation is not a matter which can now be satisfactorily handled by an occasional act of legislation. We must hit upon a system, and somebody in particular must be charged with the responsibility of administering it— not a half dozen different bodies, or even two or three, but some one body served and assisted by the constant and intelligent advice of experts. This great matter, too, should be brought within the scope of inquiry, which I earnestly urge you to authorize and provide for. I do not mean that immediate individual steps toward conservation cannot be taken by statute, but that we must hereafter depend upon system, not upon the casual vigilance of individual legislators.

One important matter of administration can be and should be taken up at once and promptly provided for by legislation. I mean the administration of the charitable and correctional institution of the State. These institutions have been established and developed in entire separateness. There nowhere exists any authority which can co-ordinate them or bring them into practical and serviceable co-operation. Their inmates cannot be reclassified or redistributed if once, by any mistake, they have been wrongly placed, or if they develop in a way not looked for when they were sent for treatment or segregation to a particular institution. The result is that individual institutions are authorized to do several kinds of work at once, for some of which they were not intended, and are, therefore, not equipped. They very properly have their separate establishments under separate boards of managers, but these boards and the superintendents of the several institutions should be brought into co-operation, and a comprehensive system of charity and correction made possible, which will increase efficiency and prevent waste and ineffectual effort. This can be done by a reform very similar to that so fortunately effected last winter in the administration of our State system of schools: by granting proper supervisory authority to the Commissioner of Charities and Correction and associating with him a small, responsible board, which may in turn, together with the Commissioner, advise with the superintendents and directors of the various institutions. Other States have already shown us the way in this important reform of organization, and we should feel impelled to take it by reasons of humanity as well as of efficiency and economy.

In this connection I would urge very strongly upon the Legis-

lature the need of a reformatory for women. A suitable site has
already been chosen in Hunterdon county, near Clinton, and
purchased by the authority of the State, and men and women
whom the whole State knows and trusts have prepared plans
for an institution for which all recognize the immediate need.

There is another matter which should no longer be left at
loose ends without thorough reorganization. I mean the supervision of the health of the State. I intend no criticism of our excellent Board of Health, but only repeat the testimony of its
own members when I say that our present means for safeguarding the health of the State are entirely inadequate. It is not generally realized how vast, complicated and difficult a matter it
has become since we began to perceive what it is really the duty
of the State to do for the health of its people. Every sort of infection must be guarded against. A costly war must be waged
on the mosquito and the housefly, those active breeders of disease. The dissemination of poisonous gases from factories, from
locomotive engines and from the vast bodies of smoke which
pervade our cities must be prevented. The dairy business must
be sharply supervised along with cold storage and the handling
of foodstuffs in the markets. Oyster beds must be inspected and
guarded against pollution. The adulteration of foods must be
prevented. There must be some thorough and efficient system of
keeping our lakes and streams from pollution. Sewage must be
supervised and properly regulated. Systematic war must be made
with such diseases as tuberculosis, and the State must be guarded
against the introduction of fatal epidemics from every quarter.
Garbage collection and disposal must be systematized and regulated. Thorough inspection must be carried into a score of places
where disease is most likely to originate. Have we the machinery
for these great tasks? Have we made sure of the service of experts, doctors, engineers, biologists, whose advice will enable us
to feel that we have done our duty by the people of the State
in the all important matter of the conservation of their lives and
health? Is it not our duty to consider very carefully and at once
the creation of a thoroughly effective department of health?

The duty of the State to make every service it renders the
people efficient, responsible and economical, seems to be one of
the first and most manifest duties of government. Next to that
is the duty in a self-governed country of making the representative body from which legislation proceeds in fact representative,
as nearly as possible a mirror of the character and opinion of
the communities of which the State is composed. It seems to
me of the first consequence, therefore, that the promise we have

made the people of the State, that we would at once take the initial steps necessary to effect a return to a system of Assembly districts in place of county delegations to the Legislature should be redeemed, and that a constitutional amendment for that purpose should be submitted to the vote of the people at the earliest possible time.

It is equally imperative, as it seems to me, that the use of the courts of justice by the people should be simplified and facilitated. Our legal procedure is too technical, too complicated, too expensive, too little adapted to the use of the poor and unschooled. With splendid courts of undoubted integrity we nevertheless feel that the rich litigant can tire the poor litigant out, and that the common run of men have good reason to dread litigation and doubt its outcome. We are proud of our bench; why should we not put ourselves in a position to be equally proud of our administration of justice as based upon the best reformed models? A little expert advice will put us in a way to discover the right legislation for this purpose, without waiting for amendments of the Constitution. It is not the courts we wish to change so much as the methods of procedure.

Both parties are pledged also to take up the matter of jury reform; to consider in particular the methods by which grand juries are chosen in order to devise, if possible, a process of choice by which abuses of a serious kind which have arisen to the scandal of public opinion may hereafter be prevented. I commend this deeply important subject to your very earnest consideration.

We have done much toward securing justice and safety for the workingmen of the State in our factory laws, our tenement-house legislation and our Employers' Liability Act, but we have not done enough. Our workmen very justly demand further legislation with regard to the inspection and regulation of factories and workshops, and I recommend legislation of this kind to your very careful and earnest consideration. I recommend, moreover, the passage at an early date of an act requiring the railways operating within this State to provide their trains with adequate crews. Our sister State of Pennsylvania has adopted legislation of this kind, and the railways whose lines cross from Pennsylvania into New Jersey actually carry full crews to the border of this State and then send their trains on through New Jersey with diminished crews, to the jeopardy, as I believe, of life and property, requiring more of the small crew than it can safely and thoroughly do.

The abolition of grade crossings, too, as rapidly as possible, under the direction of the Board of Public Utilities Commissioners, is an imperative necessity, if the lives of our citizens are to be properly safeguarded. However difficult it may be to effect the changes needed in this matter, I feel it to be a question of the very greatest moment. The loss of life at grade crossings in this State has been very great, quite inexcusably great, and there is no reform which public opinion more clearly or more justly demands than this.

Possibly it is not necessary to draw your attention to this important matter to which the public opinion of the State has been now for so long a time turned. It is not to be wondered at that opinion has grown very critical and very impatient of the delay in dealing with it.

The report of the Commissioner of Public Roads urges some changes in the Road Law, for which I bespeak your very careful consideration. They are intended to render the present system of administration more efficient, to remove the care of improved roads entirely from politics and to establish a definite system of highways. The changes in the conditions of road traffic in recent years certainly render many alterations in the existing law very desirable, if not imperative.

These are all matters of serious business, and it will be a great pleasure to me to be associated with you in trying to fulfill our obligations in regard to them in a manner that will satisfy the just expectation of those who have intrusted to our care the interests and the welfare of this great State.

Respectfully submitted,   Woodrow Wilson, *Governor*.

Printed in *Minutes of Votes and Proceedings of the One Hundred and Thirty-Sixth General Assembly of the State of New Jersey* (Trenton, N. J., 1912), pp. 11-19.

From Henry C. Bell[1]

My Dear Mr. Wilson: Washington, D. C. Jan. 9, 1911 [1912].

Veni, Vidi, Vici—You came, you saw, and they saw and heard you, and you conquered; and this morning Washington, and the politicians here, know, if they have not before known, that you are the choice of an overwhelming majority of Democrats of the Capital and of the nation for the Democratic nomination for President.

As it was at the great banquet last night, so it is in the nation, and I hope it will be in the national convention. It is now clearly Wilson against the field, and I do not believe that the field can

beat you. Last night I sat among the Harmon men, what few
there were, and your speech first whipped them into silence,
and then into unstinted praise, while your grand reception seemed
to absolutely daze and bewilder them. I have been hearing Bryan
speak for years, and am his devoted friend, and last night was
the first time in my life that I have ever seen a man even *divide*
the honors with him; but you did it, not by the matter of your
speech alone, but even more so in the enthusiasm and universal
favor with which it was received.

I felt sure that the heart beat of the progressive, militant
Democracy was for you in the west, and I know now that it is
even more so at the nerve center of American political life. Despite the efforts to make the banquet a distinctive Clark meeting,
it turned out, as I felt sure it would, to be a Wilson boom, and a
Clark, Harmon, Folk boomerang,—the most conspicuous one
that has ever been seen in this country. Now, if they have any
more stale and mouldy literature to spring on you let it come,
and it will share the fate that your letter touching Bryan, upon
which the opposition banked so much did, and prove their un-
doing rather than yours. If they have anything from Cleveland
that will go to show that he did not approve of your course in his
latter days, let it come, for his disapproval will only strengthen
you in the hearts of all progressive and patriotic Democrats of
the country. I am feeling good, to use a common expression,
to day, and I feel sure that you do. I know that all of your friends
here do, and that your enemies feel correspondingly cast down.
With expressions of the profoundest praise for your splendid
speech, and with hopes expanded for the future in your behalf,
I am,   Faithfully yours,   H. C. Bell.

TLS (WP, DLC).
¹ Political writer for the Baltimore *Sun*.

From Francis Fisher Kane

Personal

Dear Governor Wilson: Philadelphia Jan. 9, 1912.

Thank you very much for the telegram. To say that it was
gratefully received does not at all describe what took place. At
the first mention of your name the assembled company—we
had about three hundred present—went wild. The applause was
so loud & long as to settle the question then and there, and it
needed no resolution or anything of that kind to show who was

our choice for President. I think you really would have been pleased.

My one regret is that I did not hear your speech in Washington. From the meagre extracts in the papers it must have been of a very high order.

We "reorganizers" in Pennsylvania feel very grateful to Bryan. It was just like him to champion the popular—I mean of course the people's—side, and those of us who were not formerly his followers are something very like it now. He certainly has always made his appeal to the people—to the voters of his party, and that of course is why he is so strong today. His attitude in that Palmer-Guffey fight is just what we might have expected, although Palmer has not been a Bryan man.

I am writing too long a letter. All I intended to do was to thank you and assure you that you never had so strong a hold as you have today on the hearts of the Democrats of Pennsylvania.   Yours sincerely,   Francis Fisher Kane.

Please let me write to you without feeling that I am putting the Governor of New Jersey to the trouble of an acknowledgment.

ALS (Governors' Files, Nj).

Ellen Axson Wilson to Mary Allen Hulbert Peck

My dear Mrs. Peck,   Princeton, New Jersey. Jan. 10, 1912.

Many many thanks for your tempting invitation,—and also many apologies for my delay in answering it,—a delay due to the innummerable engagements, distractions and interruptions of the season. I need not tell you how delighted I and any one of my daughters would be to visit you and your charming island; but indeed it is quite impossible for me to leave home even for a *short* stay, and a voyage to Bermuda is necessarily rather long. The reasons, which are many, it would be—as Mrs. [Thomas] Carlyle used to say—more interesting *not* to mention. I can only regret that they force me to remain amid these icy blasts: it has been desperately cold for the last week.

Jessie and Margaret are as busy as their Mamma with their "careers" and Nell is in Mexico for a six weeks visit,—and having, she says, quite a wonderful time. The older ones beg me to give you their most sincere thanks and regrets.

Again thanking you, with all my heart, for your kind thought of me I am,   Yours most cordially,   Ellen A. Wilson.

TCL (WC, NjP).

From William Gibbs McAdoo

PERSONAL AND CONFIDENTIAL.

Dear Governor: New York January 10, 1912.

I must tell you how delighted I am with all that you did and accomplished in Washington. Your speeches were admirable, and you must have left there happily impressed with the evidences of a profound sentiment and friendly regard existing throughout the country for you. The Joline letter fell flat. Your treatment of that matter was excellent. I talked with many people from different sections of the country, and am more than ever encouraged about the future. I think one of our weakest spots, strange to say, is the South. We will have to give more attention to that section, and I hope to be able to devote more time to it in the future.

I want to congratulate you also on your message to the Legislature. You did exactly the right thing. I wish you would consider carefully Dr. Allen's suggestions, which I sent to you a few days ago.[1] The proper auditing of accounts and investigation of municipal and state bureaus, with a view to stopping waste and promoting efficiency, is a matter of prime importance, as I know from my own experience as head of a large company, and I believe that you can send a special message to the Legislature on this subject which will be productive of highly beneficial results to the people of the state, to say nothing of the incidental advantage to your own reputation.

I would also like to say how much I enjoyed the article in the January "World's Work" about the Princeton incident.[2] It was well written. The whole incident is highly creditable to you, and it is a good thing that the public is at last being informed about it. It will be of immense advantage in dispelling the effects of a lot of inuendos which your enemies have indulged in about this matter. I hope soon to have for you some information about the alleged Cleveland letter.

By the way, can you find time at an early date to see Mr. Miller,[3] editor of the "Warheit"? He wants to write an article about you, and I think it would be well for you to give him an early audience.

Very soon also I should like to have a talk with you about the Southern situation. I think Baltimore is a happy selection for the Convention,[4] and it augers well for you.

Always, with warm regards,

                    Sincerely yours,   W G McAdoo

TLS (WP, DLC).

1 Frederick Hobbes Allen of the New York law firm of Allen and Camman; chairman of the Democratic committee of Westchester County. McAdoo's letter and Allen's memorandum are missing.

2 William Bayard Hale, "What Happened at Princeton," *World's Work*, xxiii (Jan. 1912), 297-310, the fourth in Hale's biographical series. Hale described the controversies over the quadrangle plan and the Graduate College as "a conflict between a progressive and democratic president and the forces of privilege and aristocracy in an ancient university."

3 Louis E. Miller, editor of *Die Warheit*, a Yiddish-language newspaper of New York.

4 The Democratic National Committee had just voted that the Democratic national convention should meet in Baltimore on June 25, 1912.

To Richard Heath Dabney

My dear Heath: [Trenton, N. J.] January 11, 1912.

Thank you for your letter of the sixth.¹ May I drop a hint to you. There are thousands of warm friends of Mr. Bryan's in Virginia and all over the country. La Follette is regarded as a very high minded champion of progressive ideas, and I think that it is bad policy not only, but essentially unjust to indulge in flings at either of those men.

I know that you will understand, my dear fellow, my taking the liberty of dropping this hint for our hearts work together in all things.

The progress of the "campaign" is certainly most interesting, and, on the whole, promising, and you are doing yeoman service.

In haste,

Faithfully and affectionately yours,   Woodrow Wilson

TLS (Wilson-Dabney Corr., ViU).
1 It is missing.

To Alexander Mitchell Palmer

My dear Mr. Palmer: [Trenton, N. J.] January 11, 1912.

I would not fail to tell you how I felt about the contest in the National Committee. I hope that you feel as I do that in the long run the result of the vote will do not harm, but good. This is merely a line of sincere friendship, and I regret that I did not have a chance to see you during the few hours I was able to stay in the City.

Cordially and faithfully yours,   Woodrow Wilson

TLS (WP, DLC).

A Draft of a Letter
to George Brinton McClellan Harvey

My dear Colonel Harvey: [New York, Jan. 11, 1912]

Your letter written in reply to my little note from the University Club was characteristically frank and kind and manly and generous but it has left me with a very uneasy feeling. I had been so obtuse as not to realize that you were really hurt by what I said of the effect of the support of the Weekly upon the opinion of the country. Your letter shows that you were.

I was very sorry indeed not to see you when I was in Washington. I was occupied every minute with callers at my rooms while I was there, except when I was fulfilling engagements, and so found it impossible to get at you. I saw you at a distance at the dinner but lost sight of you when it was over.

I must do myself and my real feeling justice to write you again. I never doubted for a moment the genuineness or the independence of your generous support of me. I knew, on the contrary, that the support you were giving me must be causing you a great deal of embarrassment among the men whom you had been in the habit of consulting in politics. What you wrote, moreover, was far and away the best interpretation of my purpose and character that anybody had written,—secretly just the man I should like to believe myself to be. Towards yourself I felt nothing but deep regard and genuine gratitude.

When you asked me what the influence of the Weekly's support was, whether I found it embarrassing or not, I felt obliged to tell you the truth; never doubtful for a moment that you wished me to tell it; and took it for granted that you by this time knew me too well to question my feeling in the matter or misunderstand me in the least.

I cannot blame myself too severely for my apparent brusqueness, the "peremptoriness of my tone." It was an error of the manner, not of the heart. I must beg you to overlook it, as I am sure you have, now that you understand it. I should indeed be ungrateful if I did not honor you for the constant and generous support you have given me.

With sincere regard,

Faithfully yours,   Woodrow Wilson

Transcript (WWsh, WP, DLC).

To George Brinton McClellan Harvey

Hotel Astor New York

My dear Colonel Harvey,   11 Jan'y, 1910 [1912].

Generous and cordial as was your letter written in reply to my note from the University Club, it has left me uneasy,— because, in its perfect frankness, it shows that I *did* hurt you by what I so tactlessly said at the Knickerbocker Club.[1] I am very much ashamed of myself,—for there is nothing I am more ashamed of than hurting a true friend, however unintentional the hurt may have been. I wanted very much to see you in Washington, but was absolutely captured by callers every minute I was in my rooms, and when I was not there was fulfilling public engagements. I saw you at the dinner, but could not get at you, and after the dinner was surrounded and prevented from getting at you. I am in town to-day, to speak this evening, and came in early in the hope of catching you at your office.

For I owe it to you and to my own thought and feeling to tell you how grateful I am for all your generous praise and support of me (no one has described me more nearly as I would like to believe myself to be than you have!), how I have admired you for the independence and unhesitating courage and individuality of your course, and how far I was from desiring that you should cease your support of me in the *Weekly*. You will think me very stupid,—but I did not think of that as the result of my blunt answer to your question. I thought only of the means of convincing people of the real independence of the *Weekly's* position. You will remember that that was what we *discussed*. And now that I have unintentionally put you in a false and embarrassing position you heap coals of fire on my head by continuing to give out interviews favourable to my candidacy! All that I can say is, that you have proved yourself very big and that I wish I might have an early opportunity to *tell* you face to face how I really feel about it all.

With warm regard

Cordially & faithfully Yours   Woodrow Wilson

ALS (WP, DLC).
[1] He meant the Manhattan Club.

An Address in New York to the National League
of Commission Merchants[1]

[[Jan. 11, 1912]]

MR. TOASTMASTER,[2] LADIES AND GENTLEMEN: I find myself
embarrassed in view of the fact that your toastmaster did not
announce the subject upon which I am to address you, but fortunately it is printed upon your program, namely, "Business and
Politics."

There are two reasons why I am embarrassed: One is that
there is so much to attract the eye in this audience and the
other is that it distracts the thought. I am reminded by contrast
of a limerick which one of my daughters introduced to me the
other day. It runs:

> For beauty I am not a star.
> There are others more handsome by far,
> But my face, I don't mind it,
> For I am behind it,
> It's the people in front that I jar.

I hope, in the circumstances, that you will survive the shock.
Moreover, the theme is so great that I would not venture to speak
of business in the presence of business experts, and the less
said about politics the better. To address myself to so great a
theme at this time of the evening would show I had audacity
which I assure you I do not possess. I am very much in the position of the old negro who fell asleep in a railway train, and
as he slept his head fell back and his mouth was wide open. A
fellow traveler happening to have some quinine put it on the
darkey's tongue. It was some time before it soaked in, and when
he did wake up with the consciousness that something had happened, he became very much excited, and said to the passenger,
"Boss, is there a doctor on this train?" The gentleman answered,
"I don't know; what do you want a doctor for?" And the negro
said, "Boss, I done believe ma gall's busted." I have not the gall
to address you on this subject, and then I have thought as I
sat here and looked upon this company of business men how
few of us realize what business life in America means. It means
the constant readjustment to new conditions. America is one of
the countries in which business seems almost to have no laws
that run from generation to generation, because the organization

---

[1] Delivered at the Hotel Astor.
[2] William H. Bahrenburg, president of the New York branch of the National
League of Commission Merchants.

of business, the form of business, and the objects of business seem to be transformed so rapidly.

You realize, of course, that in something less than two years the routes of trade will probably have altered once for all on this continent. That ditch that is so nearly completed between the Atlantic and Pacific will switch the route of trade around almost as thoroughly as it was switched when the Turks captured Constantinople and blocked the course of the Mediterranean, and sent the venturesome seamen down the coast of Africa to discover a route around the capes. You know at that moment England, which had been at the back of the nations trading with the East, suddenly swung around and found herself occupying a place at the front of the nations, for hardly had those mariners gone down the coast of Africa when other sailors, more venturesome still, looked seaward across the unexplored waters of the open Atlantic, then set out and discovered a new continent, made new territory for the trader, new trade for the politician, and so England, that had been upon the edge of the water, darkened by ignorance, presently found all her skirts flooded with the light of the new continent arising out of the waters of the sea. Something not so great as that, but nevertheless as revolutionary in our trade, is going to happen as soon as the canal is opened. And when you reflect upon the great projects afoot on this continent, the great inland waterways that we have made up our minds to build, you will see that we have intended nothing less than the transformation of our economic life, and with the transformation of our economic life there will necessarily be a vast readjustment.

Your thoughts will have to be very nimble and your plans quickly changed after the year 1913. Are you ready to do it? Do you realize what the future of America is going to be from the point of view of trade? As I sat here to-night I was thinking of you as commission merchants and reflected that most of our science in regard to trade in this country had been a science of omission rather than commission. Most of the things we ought to have done we have not done. You know that the singular thing about America is that with a genius for new things, with inventive genius, with a capacity for organization hardly matched before in the history of the world, we, nevertheless, have drawn our own borders close about us, have made ourselves shut-in patients, have confined our energies to a continent when we might have extended them into a world. We went almost deliberately about the destruction of our own merchant marine. We swept our own flag from the seas, and while we thought that

we were a little Nation a hundred years ago, just before the
War of 1812, we competed with the greatest nations in the world
in the carrying trade as between nations. Now we, practically
the greatest Nation in the world, compete with nobody in carrying trade. We retired from the stage upon which we had already
made conquest and, turning our eyes upon ourselves, stood willing to compete with no one until we had developed our own resources.

What is the consequence? It is one unparalleled in the history
of the world. We wasted our own resources. We have believed
that you do not have to husband your resources, that you can
just scratch the surface of your mines and then go on to another mine; that you can cut your forests down for bark on the
trees in order to make tan bark and then leave the whole noble
trees to rot with the wood never used. We have confined ourselves to a sort of prodigal waste, which sooner or later will
find us unprepared in the competition with the rest of the world.
No man can compete in the great contests of the world in trade
and manufacture who has not learned how to husband his resources and use every scrap of his raw material. We have been
a prodigal people and yet have prided ourselves that we have a
genius for industry, a genius for spending, if you will, a genius
for getting, if you will, but not a genius for the niceties of industry.

Why is it we have never had, even according to our own
account, great native literature in America? We have had great
writers, great prose writers and great poets, but it is our own
complaint that we have never produced a great native literature
characteristic of America but have merely carried on and explained the traditions of England. In order to answer that question you have only to look at the progress of American civilization as a whole. You can't have a great work of art if you try
to make it in a hurry. No great work of art is made with the
flat hand. It is made with the nicety of touch that comes only
with pains and with infinite care. Nothing is artistic that is not
patiently completed, professionally completed down to its mi-
nutest detail. You can not make a great sentence unless you
love the cadences of the language, unless you look for those
words which will heighten the color, release the light, and mark
everything you say with such vividness that men shall keep it
forever in their memory. You can not do great things unless you
master the natural processes by which they are dominated. The
world determines what you are to do; you don't determine what
the world is to do. All the conditions are changing. It was just

now said very truly in your presence[3] that a man who can not change his mind gives the most capital evidence that the modern world can offer of his profound ignorance, because if your mind don't change while the world is changing, then your mind won't match the world's. If the whole economic civilization is in flux about you and you alone are crystallized and steadfast, then you will either be washed away by the flood or your position will become one in which you are serviceable only to have some worn-out craft moored to to go to rot. A friend of mine was traveling in Florida and was very curious to identify Florida crocodile. He asked a Florida gentleman how he should know one. "Well," said the friend, "if you are going through the swamp and see a brown object in the distance you will know it's either a stump or a crocodile. If it moves it's a stump."

Now, American trade has a good many crocodiles—men to whom a new thing is an incredible thing, an undesirable thing, a thing to be afraid of. If you don't learn by experience, experience will see that you don't have much time to learn anything. Some people think conservatism is to let things alone, but suppose they change overnight so that you can not recognize them? An English writer[4] used this illustration: If you want a white post to remain white, do you let it alone? If you do it won't be a white post long; it will be a black post. You have got to renew that post once every so often if you want to keep it what it was —a white post.

Now, in order to keep our civilization in repair, in order to keep our trade good and to keep our industries vigorous we have got to change them every month of our lives. I am willing to let things alone if you will guarantee that I can go to sleep and be able to recognize the same thing in the morning; but unless you guarantee me that things will not stand still I am not content and want to be part of the proposition to protect the industries of America. Everything depends upon some nice process for which you have to employ experts, and you must look to the scientific schools of the country to enable you to advance a single inch. You can sit in your office and determine what is to be done, but you can not do it. You have got to hire training; you have got to employ knowledge; you have got to give salaries to science in order to accomplish anything in America; and now you are finding, those of you who are manufacturers, that you did not even know how to keep your cost sheets; that you can not tell

---

[3] By the preceding speaker, the Rev. Dr. Robert W. McLoughlin, pastor of the Park Slope Congregational Church of Brooklyn.

[4] Walter Bagehot.

what a particular division of your business costs you, and whether it pays its own expenses or not; that you have not yet studied those niceties of readjustment, those niceties of management, which mean the difference between big or little profits or no profits at all, and that from this time out you have got to employ those brains which devote themselves to the niceties of detail. That's the future of America, not only so as to these niceties of detail, but the man who produces is going to expect the same things of machinery as of exchange that he finds and establishes in his own factory. In other words, the model man has got to be something more than an expert. I say he has got to be something more than an expert even in American training.

Have you watched the foreign balance sheets? Do you know by what leaps and bounds foreign exports have increased? Do you know that since the Spanish War pushed us out into the political field of the world circumstances have pushed us out into the trade of the world? This trade which we have seemed to despise we are now bound to undertake. Have you noticed the different figures between what has happened in the exports of the natural products of the soil and the exports of our manufactured products? Don't you know that while we used to export a vast amount of grain and feed, the rest of the world is fast approaching the point where we will consume almost all of our own grain and that our exports of foodstuffs are falling off? Now, at the same time our exports of manufactured stuffs are increasing because while we are reaching the limit of productivity of supplying the world in our field, we have exceeded the amount of production in our factories which is necessary for the domestic consumption, and now unless we use the stuff and draw our borders in we must sell our manufactured products to the world. The middleman has to be an expert in the conditions of the world. I wonder how many Americans know what patterns of carpet can be sold in China. The average American salesman, I dare say, will try to ram American patterns down, I was going to say, Chinese's throats. They will try to get rid of all the surplus things suitable for America in countries for which they are not suitable, and it won't go. You must know something more than the geography of the world, you must know something more than establishing foreign lines with commission merchants; you must know the tastes of the civilized world, economic necessities must be learned, or else you will not be serviceable to America. We have ceased to be a provincial Nation. We have got men whose mastery extends to the borders of the civilized world. That's the reason I rejoice in associations like this. Working, each in his little field, staying within his home markets, men do not realize as to the economic readjustments but wonder whether New York is going to take toll of the whole world after the canal is opened; wonder whether New York is going to take toll of all the world after we have threaded this continent with great open waterways, when everything will be reasonably rapid and cheaply transported like the veins in a great vital body.

Now, whatever changes happen, you gentlemen must see them, must act upon them, must be the agents in them. I look upon the young men in this country as the prophets of what is going to happen. Elderly men get in a rut, elderly men refuse to conceive anything new. I once had the painful duty of telling a company of well-dressed people that I understood the object of the university to be to make the young gentlemen of the country as unlike their fathers as possible, by which I meant no disrespect to the fathers but that by the time a man is old enough to have a son he got so set in his ways that it is not possible to make any change for the rest of his life.[5] We must have elastic, adaptable, malleable, young stuff to meet the exigencies of the changing age. Just as soon as America loses her elasticity, as soon as she loses her audacity and the adaptability of youth, the course of trade will be neglected, the process of our industry will be embarrassed. So we are at, I will not say the parting of the ways; we are at the opening of the ways. Our life is to have new channels, our economic processes are to take on new forms, for I call you to witness, gentlemen, that America up to this point has devoted herself chiefly only to one side of the great commercial and industrial process, America has been the scene of promotion and exploitation. Every kind of industry has been promoted in the technical sense of that word, and every resource of this rich country has been exploited in the literal meaning of that word. We have been promoters and exploiters. Isn't this coming to an end? Haven't most of the big enterprises been suggested and promoted, including some not worth promoting? Haven't we gone just about to the limit of the rough and ready exploitation of the resources of this country?

Now, what are we going to do? We are going to consider, as we are beginning to consider, scientific forms of government, skill, efficiency, economy; these things that do not come with native genius but come by training. It is all very well what you did. We haven't finished anything in America. I hope we haven't finished the governments of our cities; I hope we haven't fin-

[5] A news report of this address is printed at Feb. 6, 1909, Vol. 19.

ished our streets; I hope we haven't finished our work upon our great water courses in which we have dumped all the débris of our civilization and congested them until they run with difficulty, murmuring against us. We have not been careful of anything except to make haste, except to grow fruitless, and now we are paying the penalty. It has become vulgar in the United States to be rich. Some years ago I went to the commencement of a school which was attended, I understood, practically only by the sons of very rich men, because the courses at the school were so conducted that no others could attend. I felt bound to say to these youngsters that I looked upon them with a great deal of pity and sympathy, because in all probability they were foredoomed to obscurity; that the mere possession of wealth did not any longer lead to distinction in the United States; that in order to be distinguished you have to do something and if you were born with wealth the probability was that you would not do anything, and therefore a man born rich in the United States was likely to be born unserviceable and, being unserviceable, was foredoomed to obscurity.[6] Is it not so? Suppose you have a lot of wealth, suppose you have lavished the resources of the country upon your own bank account? Then what are you going to do with your bank account? What are you going to make of this America that you have adorned and petted and upon which you have spent the genius of organization and the energy and eagerness of development? You, gentlemen, are, so to say, the agents of all the distribution and of the readjustment which takes place, at any rate, in a large number of the products of this country. I remember when I was a youngster I was obliged to study the elements of political economy. I was taught that there were several kinds of value—that there was time value, which makes ice very valuable in the summer and coal very valuable in the winter, and that there was place value, and that a thing that was not serviceable in one place because there might be a surplus of it there was very serviceable in another where it was scarce or could not be produced. You are the servants of place value. It is your business to see that things are at the place where they are wanted at the time they are wanted. In that sense I must accuse you of being place hunters.

You are always looking for a market in which to place the product you deal in, and by the same token you must have a wide and general forecast upon the commerce of nations. You must forecast the changes that are going to take place; you must realize just how long a place is going to be the center and

6 A news report of this address is printed at June 3, 1909, *ibid.*

just when it is going to stop being the center. I remember a good many years ago I dined with a society in this city to which no one could belong whose ancestors had not lived in New York for, I think, 200 years, and I could not refrain from saying to the gentlemen assembled that I looked upon them with a good deal of curiosity, for while all the rest of America had been moving they had been sitting still for 200 years.[7] Now, I am no prophet, but I am sorry for the man who can not see the visions of our time. If you think you knew American trade by heart last year, within a decade you will be out of business. You have got to know how American trade will be next year and the year after, a whole decade, of which these years are a part. You have got to have vision; you have got to look into the future; you have got to feel the full pulses which are beating in the great round world before you will comprehend the civilization of which you dream, of which you form a part. So this is what I call the statesmanship of business. Statesmanship is merely the organization of the common life in order to conserve the common interest. That is all statesmanship is, and statesmanship of business is organization of business to conserve the economic interest of your generation.

The same Englishman from whom I was just now quoting gives this very interesting definition of a statesman in a self-governing country. He says he is a man of ordinary opinion and extraordinary ability; a man who reflects the opinion of his generation, but has extraordinary ability in giving expression to that opinion. And so I challenge you, if you know what uses to make of your organization, not to suppose that business is going to dwell in your several commission houses. You have got to get limits outside of those houses; you have got to learn not only of your fellow commission merchants, but of men who have been to the ends of the earth, of travelers, scientists, politicians, of men who have dreamed the dreams that constitute the vision that men follow.

Do you know who are the leaders of mankind? The leaders of mankind are those who lift their vision from the dusty road under their feet and look forward, and though they are determined to keep a firm footing upon the road they nevertheless gladden their eyes with the illuminated distance, to those regions which seem to rise and rise, level by level, promising happier days for mankind, easier lives, more sympathy, more cooperation, more perfect mutual understanding, more common trust, more enthusiasm, more partisanship of what is good, more

[7] Notes for this speech are printed at April 9, 1901, Vol. 12.

hatred of what is not good, more contempt for shams, more confidence in realities. They will redeem us from our errors and our mistakes, will show us that to open our eyes is to enlarge our trust, and will convince us that to lead men upon a great process of change is to keep open the love in their hearts in order to travel the road of perfection which comes only with applying ourselves to the things that are better; or, better, giving over to forgetfulness the things that are wrong. Why, gentlemen, do you know that the ancients shut themselves in and refused to trade with the rest of the world, for fear that in trading in goods they should also trade in ideas? Men did not admit foreign merchants to their markets because they said, "these men will contaminate us with foreign ideas," and so they strangled their own development for fear of invasion of ideas not their own.

I congratulate you, gentlemen, upon being traders in the thought of the world, traders in the hope of the world, full of confidence that as you receive men into your thinking you will establish the supremacy of America as we wish it to be established—not by force of arms, not by the conquest of hope, not by the conquest of aggrandizement, not by conquest, but by the free injection of our enthusiasm, our love of mankind, our confidence in human liberty.

Are not the horizons large? Is not the prospect fair? Is not the trend beautiful when it leads us to these models of human achievement?[8]

Printed in *Congressional Record*, 62nd Cong., 2nd sess., Vol. 48, pp. 3917-19.

[8] There is a WWhw and WWsh outline of this address with the composition date of Jan. 11, 1912, in WP, DLC.

Ellen Axson Wilson to Robert Ewing[1]

My dear Cousin Robert,   Princeton, N. J., January 12, 1912.

At Woodrow's suggestion, I am writing you with regard to certain extraordinary rumors concerning Col. Watterson and Col. Harvey, of Harper's Weekly, echoes of which may have reached you. We are told that Col. Watterson has "turned violently" against Woodrow, because of his alleged ill treatment of Col. Harvey. A Mr. Hemphill reports that Col. Watterson described to him "a stormy interview, in which Wilson hysterically denounced Harvey and Watterson, in turn denounced Wilson, in language unfit for publication."[2] Now, of course, Hemphill (whoever he may be) is grossly slandering Col. Watterson, giving a highly imaginative version of his conversation, for there is not *one word of truth* in this account of Woodrow's interview with the two Colonels. He met them at their request for a general conference on the political situation. From first to last, no one of the three showed a trace of excitement or irritation, and they parted, as Woodrow supposed, in perfect harmony. Yet some misunderstanding has since developed, which they date from that occasion, and Woodrow will be extremely obliged to you for anything you can do to set it right.

This is the simple story of the interview in question. For two hours they talked over the whole "situation," in the most intimately friendly and harmonious fashion, Woodrow in his usual absolutely open, frank manner. Then, as they rose to go, Col. Harvey said he wanted from Woodrow "a perfectly frank answer" to one question, viz: Whether The Weekly's constant booming of him seemed to him unwise or embarrassing (in view, of course, of Harper's alleged connection with Wall Street). Now, as it happened Col. Watterson himself had brought up that very subject with Woodrow a few weeks before; had declared that it *was* having an unfavorable effect, and that he meant to suggest to Harvey a more politic course for the time being. There had also been the same comment at the "Wilson Headquarters" in New York. So when Col. Harvey begged him to be frank, Woodrow unwillingly, for it was at best, an ungracious thing to do, told him what the general impression was. Col. Harvey took it in perfect good humour and said he would have to "put on the soft pedal." There was not for one moment the slightest sign of excitement or irritation on the part of any one of the three. They stood discussing for some time longer how best to make the public understand the *real* independence of Col. Harvey and The Weekly, and then parted in the most cordial manner. Woodrow never for a moment dreamed that they had misunderstood him, or been "hurt."

Now, this is absolutely all that happened. Imagine then how dazed we are to hear of Col. Watterson's "rage."

It is part of the general irony of things that Woodrow personally was far from convinced that Col. Watterson and the men at headquarters were right in thinking it would be wise to apply the "soft pedal." Col. Harvey was *by far* his ablest advocate, and we felt that whatever harm such championship of his cause might do in certain quarters (owing to the inflamed state of the public mind towards Wall Street) was more than counterbalanced in other quarters. Moreover, the harm, if any, in the first quarter was already done, since everybody knew that Harper's Weekly was for Wilson, and he instinctively dislikes that sort of hedging. So that Woodrow was really doing violence both to his feelings of friendship and gratitude to Col. Harvey, and, in a sense, to his own judgment, in saying what little he did. Doubtless, that was why he said it so badly. Whatever stiffness there may have been in his manner was due solely to those feelings. Perhaps he erred in saying so little, but Col. Harvey (not Woodrow) had brought up the question, and no one in the world needs less than Col. Harvey to have things elaborately explained to him, for you know what an extraordinary mind he has.

I cannot believe that you will have any difficulty in making all this clear to Col. Watterson. Woodrow wrote to Col. Harvey and received a very friendly letter, yet one that showed that he had been wounded, and I do not know when we have been more deeply distressed than at that discovery. He was Woodrow's first political friend, the one who started it all. His speeches and editorials about Woodrow have all been *wonderful* and are among *my* very dearest treasures. In short, this matter involves something far more important than politics, viz: *friendship*. But I must close with many apologies for writing at such great length.[3]

With dear love to Cousin Hattie and all the family, I am,
            Affectionately yours,   Ellen A. Wilson.

TCL (WP, DLC).
    [1] Mrs. Wilson wrote the following letter to Judge Ewing because he was a brother-in-law of Colonel Watterson.
    [2] Wilson's erstwhile friend, James Calvin Hemphill, editor of the *Charlotte*, N. C., *Daily Observer*, whose report (it was actually written by Watterson) appeared in that newspaper on January 5, 1912. Again, see Link, *Road to the White House*, p. 367.
    [3] Ewing's account of the Manhattan Club meeting, based on Mrs. Wilson's letter, appeared, among other newspapers, in the *Nashville Banner*, Jan. 19, 1912.

To Henry Morgenthau[1]

My dear Mr. Morgenthau: [Trenton, N. J.] January 13, 1912.

Mr. McCombs as well as Mr. Tumulty mentioned to me your kind desire that I should speak some time early next month before the Real Estate men. I have asked Mr. McCombs to take the matter up with you. I talked it over fully with him, and he can tell you just how I feel tied up and overdriven, so that you can judge for yourself how difficult, if not impossible, it is for me to do what you suggest.

I am particularly distressed about this because I should so love to do anything you wanted me to do.

            Very cordially yours,   Woodrow Wilson

TLS (photostat in WP, DLC).
    [1] New York realtor; chairman of the finance committee of the Democratic
National Committee, 1912, 1916; Ambassador to Turkey, 1913-16.

To Mary Allen Hulbert Peck

Dearest Friend,   Princeton, New Jersey 14 January, 1912

I wonder what you *do* with yourself, these days? Apparently you do not go out, as you used to. Whom do you see? Have you put your evening gowns into camphor balls? Do you never go to Government House or see any of the people at the hotels? It is delightful to know that you are well, that you have until April to rest; but I fear sometimes, as I read your delightful letters, that you brood too much, and let your thoughts run on things that may never happen, instead of doing with them what would make you strong and happy. You have now a chance to clear your thoughts of the years that diverted you from your true development and recover the self that those long years overlaid. You can now come out of the shell in which you have hidden yourself,—in which you kept covert with the gay, enjoying, pure, and wholesome nature you were born with and which you have kept alive on poetry and out-of-doors nature and old furniture and silver and china,—on the beautiful things to which you belonged but to which you could turn only sometimes, to escape from suffocation and starvation. Now you are free,[1]— free to live your real life, with the true people and things you really love. You are no longer obliged to live by the law of self-defence. You can put off your defensive armour and take up your life where you left off when you made your great mistake. That is what I meant when I said that you could now renew your youth. You *can*,—in a very real and deep sense. When I see you again I shall see (whatever her disguise) the young Mrs. Hulbert. And I shall be so glad!

The great Jackson Day banquet came off,—and was a great triumph for me. I was made the lion of the occasion,—to my great surprise; and the effect of it all (for it was a national affair) seems to have been to strengthen the probabilities of my nomination many-fold. Some thirty-two of the fifty-two members of the Democratic National Committee have now, I am told, declared themselves for me. It begins now to "look like business." I like it less than I did before!

The worst has happened at the University: Hibben has been elected President![2] I need make no comment!

I am *so* sorry about dear Mrs. Allen. Both Ellen and I have learned to feel a real affection for her and it distresses us that she should be failing. It may not be, after all. She is *not old*! And how can you say that old age is 'tragic'? There is only one thing about it that I dread, and that is, its loneliness. *She* is not lonely. She has *you*, and needs no one else. All join me in affectionate messages, and I am, as always,

Your devoted friend,   Woodrow Wilson

ALS (WP, DLC).
  [1] She had just instituted divorce proceedings against her husband, Thomas Dowse Peck, on the ground of desertion.
  [2] On January 11.

From Mary Allen Hulbert Peck

Dearest Friend: Paget West, Bermuda. Jan 15th, 1912.

I wrote a letter of invitation to Mrs. Wilson, hoping she would come to Bermuda for a little visit while Allen was away, and I had a guest room to offer. Will you let me know if the letter was received. I also never heard from Margaret about the de Pachman[1] concert. This all makes me feel that there may be some reason *why* there has been utter silence from both. It would cost me dear, but rather than have the least shadow of unpleasant feeling, I would never write to or see you again, save as chance brought us together. Be frank with me. You know that I will understand. I am well, and am always, *always*

Your devoted friend   M. A. P.

ALS (WP, DLC).
  [1] Vladimir de Pachman, pianist who specialized in the works of Chopin.

To Verner R. Lovell

My dear Mr. Mayor: [Trenton, N. J.] January 16, 1912.

I have been deeply interested to-day in having a long conference with my friend, Mr. Eckard P. Budd, who has just returned from the Dakotas, and who has been detailing to me his interesting conversations while there with the leading men of those States. I have been so struck with what he said of your own interest in the things that I ardently believe in that I am taking the liberty, which I hope you will pardon, of sending you this message of sincere thanks for your courtesy to him, and of deep appreciation of your interest in my own incipient candidacy. I should be very proud to receive the support of North Dakota.

Cordially and sincerely yours,   Woodrow Wilson

TLS (received from Roland Dille).

From George Brinton McClellan Harvey, with Enclosure

My Dear Gov. Wilson,   [New York] January 16, 1912.

Thank you sincerely for your most handsome letter. I can only repeat what I said before—that there is no particle of personal rancor or resentment left in me. And I beg you to believe that I have not said one word to anybody of criticism of you.

I *have* to print a word of explanation to the *Weekly's* readers, but it will be the briefest possible.

Very truly yours,   George Harvey.

E N C L O S U R E

To Our Readers:

We make the following reply to many inquiries from the readers of *Harper's Weekly*:

The name of Woodrow Wilson as our candidate for President was taken down from the head of these columns in response to a statement made to us directly by Gov. Wilson, to the effect that our support was affecting his candidacy injuriously.

The only course left open to us, in simple fairness to Mr. Wilson, no less than in consideration of our own self-respect, was to cease to advocate his nomination.

We make this explanation with great reluctance and the deepest regret. But we cannot escape the conclusion that the very considerable number of our readers who have coöperated earnestly and loyally in advancing a movement which was inaugurated solely in the hope of rendering a high public service are clearly entitled to this information.[1]

Printed in the New York *Evening Post*, Jan. 30, 1912.
[1] This statement was printed in the newspapers on January 17 and 18 and in *Harper's Weekly* in its issue of January 20, 1912.

A Statement By Henry Watterson

[[Jan. 17, 1912]]

Regretting that I must appear either as a witness or a party to the misunderstanding which has arisen between Colonel George Harvey and Governor Wilson, I shall have to speak with some particularity in order to be just alike to the public and the principals.

The conference between us in my apartment at the Manhattan Club was held to consider certain practical measures relating to Governor Wilson's candidacy. Colonel Harvey stood toward Governor Wilson much as I had stood five and thirty years ago toward Mr. Tilden. This appealed to me. Colonel Harvey had brought the Governor and myself together in his New Jersey home eighteen months ago, and as time passed had interested me in his ambitions.

I was hoping I might find in Governor Wilson another Tilden. In point of intellect and availability I yet think Colonel Harvey made no mistake in his choice of a candidate; but the circumstance leading to the unfortunate parting of the ways between them leads me to doubt whether in character and temperament —it may be merely in the habits of a lifetime—Governor Wilson is not rather a schoolmaster than a statesman.

I have from Colonel Harvey and Governor Wilson statements according to the memory of each touching what did actually happen, and was spoken on the occasion named. These do not materially differ. They coincide with my own recollection. Nothing of a discourteous kind—even of an unfriendly kind—passed during an interview of more than an hour.

From the first, however, there was a certain constraint in Governor Wilson's manner, the absence of the cordiality and candor which should mark hearty, confidential intercourse, intimating the existence of some adverse influence. His manner was autocratic, if not tyrannous.

I did not take this to myself, but thought it related to Colonel Harvey, and when Colonel Harvey, apparently overcome by Governor Wilson's austerity, put the direct question to Governor Wilson whether the support of Harper's Weekly was doing him an injury, and received from Governor Wilson the cold rejoinder that it was, I was both surprised and shocked.

I had myself, as far back as last October, suggested to Governor Wilson that, in view of his supposed environment, it might be well for Colonel Harvey to moderate somewhat of the rather aggressive character of Harper's Weekly in the Wilson leadership. I am not sure that I had not said as much to Colonel Harvey himself, but that Governor Wilson, without the least show of compunction, should express or yield to such an opinion, and permit Colonel Harvey to consider himself discharged from the position of trusted intimacy he had up to this moment held, left me little room to doubt that Governor Wilson is not a man who makes common cause with his political associates or is deeply sensible of his political obligations; because it is but true and fair to say that, except for Colonel Harvey, he would not be in the running at all. . . .

Printed in the *New York Times*, Jan. 18, 1912.

A News Report of a Luncheon Address to Businessmen in Detroit, Michigan

[Jan. 18, 1912]

WILSON OPPOSED TO TRUSTEE FORM OF GOVERNMENT
CANDIDATE TALKS TO BOARD OF COMMERCE MEN AT LUNCHEON AT WAYNE.

"The Patriotic Function of Commerce" was the topic of Gov. Wilson at the noon day luncheon in the Wayne Gardens as the guest of the Board of Commerce. The governor was introduced by M. A. McRae, president of the Detroit organization,[1] and when the New Jersey man stepped before the audience he was cheered for half a minute, many of the guests standing and waving handkerchiefs.

Gov. Wilson discussed broad principles of social and political philosophy, rather than details of government and administration. He showed the ability of an orator. He called himself a radical throughout his address; once in a while resorted to Latin quotations, was free with gestures and emphasis, and provoked laughter frequently by humorous references to himself, or thrusts at certain interests and groups of men.

"There is no mistaking the fact that the nation is not satisfied with conditions as they are at present," said the governor early in his speech. "It is a fact not disputable that the people are not satisfied. And such dissatisfaction is not good for business. Everywhere I go business men cast an eye on me as if to say, 'If you had the chance what would you do?' "

["]Present conditions are dangerous to business, if business does not understand them. As soon as business makes a study of conditions and learns them as they really are, the danger will disappear. The real danger is that busines dienies [denies] that there is anything wrong. Men have said to me, 'Don't drag business into politics.' Since when has business not been in politics? As I understand it, business came into politics. I think I can name some of the men who helped it to get in. Some of them are dead and I will not mention their names." . . .

Printed in the *Detroit News*, Jan. 18, 1912; some editorial headings omitted.
    [1] Milton Alexander McRae, one of the founders of the Scripps-McRae newspaper chain and president of McRae & Roberts Co., brass goods manufacturers of Detroit.

From William Gibbs McAdoo

New York, Jan. 18, 1912.

In view of Watterson letter it seems to me that you can with great effect and advantage issue statement of truth. The facts will show whether or not Watterson's mere impressions are of any value. He admits that nothing discourteous or unfriendly occurred and that Harvey asked the question and you simply replied to it. This wholly disproves injurious report circulated that you had voluntarily and offensively demanded cessation Harvey's support. Watterson admits that he had advised you and possibly Harvey that aggressive support of Harpers Weekly might be doing you harm. Naturally you were influenced by this view as well as that of other friends who heretofore have expressed similar convictions and you can state that you rightfully supposed these friends desired candid answer and you therefore gave it. I do not know contents of letters you and Harvey have exchanged but could they not be published with effect? Post interviewed Harvey this morning who declined to publish them but says will give copies with your permission. The serious phase of whole matter is the attempt your enemies are making to prove by this incident that you are willing to sacrifice friends or anything else to realize your ambition. This of course is utterly untrue and ought to be dispelled and it seems to me can be with full statement of truth. Understand Harvey declines to make further statement unless you make one. Please make it clear that they and not you sought interview. I do not advise issuing statement immediately, but get it ready so it can be used at right moment. Best regards.   W. G. McAdoo

(4 29 PM.)

TC telegram (RSB Coll., DLC).

An Unpublished Statement About the Harvey Affair

[Detroit, Jan. 18, 1912]

I must confess to being very much distressed that this matter should have taken such a shape as to involve me in an apparent ingratitude. I did not tell Colonel Harvey that the support of *Harper's Weekly* was apparently embarrassing me in many parts of the country, without having first been asked the question point blank by Colonel Harvey himself. Had he not asked me I should never have conveyed any such intimation to him. The question was asked at the close of a most friendly and cordial conference, which Col. Watterson had suggested, and was, I supposed[,] asked as a natural part of the discussion[.] It was very frank and generous of Colonel Harvey to ask it, and I was very much embarrassed in having to answer. I never dreamed that the frank truth would seem an ingratitude.

I have very sincerely admired Colonel Harvey's course. I have never doubted his editorial independence. In his support of me he has written in a manner singularly lucid and effective; and has always interpreted my opinions as I should wish to have them interpreted, often with a[n] adequacy which I sincerely envied. But the rest of the country did not give him credit for editorial independ[ence] as I did; and when Colonel Harvey asked me whether the support of the *Weekly* was embarrassing me or not, I thought myself bound in frankness to tell him that it was.

I did not suppose at the time that my answer to his question would result in the withdrawal of his brilliant support; because immediately after the question was asked and answered, we discussed means, if any there were, by which to remove the impression of the country that the editorial policy of Harper's Weekly was under the control of special interests. I did not need to be convinced that it was not, and I wished that means might be found to disabuse the whole country of that impression. I want to add that I retain a great admiration for Colonel Harvey and for his singular ability, and that nothing he feels obliged to do will alter my personal feeling in the least.

T MS with WWhw emendations (photostat in RSB Coll., DLC).

McHugh[1] to Walter Measday

Washington, D. C., Jan. 18th, 1912.

Following message telephoned, now repeating: Very much regret that the matter should have taken such a shape as to seem to call for a statement from me. I did not tell Colonel Harvey that the support of Harper's Weekly was apparently embarrassing in many parts of the country without first having been asked the question point blank by Colonel Harvey himself. Had he not asked me the question I should never have conveyed such an intimation to him. The question was asked near the close of a most pleasant and cordial meeting which Colonel Watterson had suggested and was I supposed a natural part of the discussion. It was very frank and generous of Colonel Harvey to ask me and I was very much embarrassed at having to answer him. When Col. Harvey had asked me whether the support of the Weekly was injurious or not I thought myself bound in frankness to tell him the truth as I saw it and I never dreamed that stating the truth to him would seem an ingratitude. Subsequently some further friendly discussion was had and when I left the meeting I had no idea that the answer to his question had been regarded in any other spirit than that in which the question itself had been asked. Personally I would rather have sustained the injury if any than to have wounded his feelings. I want to add that I retain a great admiration for Colonel Harvey and for his singular ability and nothing that he feels obliged to do will alter my personal feeling in the least.[2]

McHugh

T telegram (WP, DLC).
   [1] A code name, almost certainly that of Thomas Jones Pence, Washington correspondent of the Raleigh *News and Observer* and head of Wilson's newspaper bureau in the capital.
   [2] Wilson killed this release, apparently after reading Watterson's statement.

From Thomas Bell Love

Dear Governor Wilson: Dallas, Texas, January 18, 1912.

I am taking the liberty of enclosing you herewith carbon copy of communication which I have today written the Dallas News, and also clipping from the editorial page of the News to which the communication refers.[1]

My own judgment is that this episode furnishes the last and best evidence of your fitness to be President of the United States.

I have been extremely busy for several weeks, which has made it impossible for me to write many letters, but there has been no break in the lines in Texas.

Am writing hurriedly.

Very truly yours,   Thomas B. Love.

TCL (T. B. Love Papers, Dallas Hist. Soc.).
   [1] He referred to "Why Harper's Weekly Took Down His Name," *Dallas Morning News*, Jan. 18, 1912. This editorial characterized Wilson's behavior at the Manhattan Club conference as "'ungracious, to speak charitably" and added that most men would rather have endured any disadvantage than "repulse a friend who, however much misguided, was actuated by the sincerest of motives." The *Dallas Morning News* did not publish Love's letter.

From John Garland Pollard

My dear Mr. Wilson: [Richmond, Va.] January 18, 1912.

I know that you will be gratified to learn that I have just received a phone message from Hon. James W. Gordon, Richmond,[1] who was Senator Martin's manager here during his last campaign, to the effect that he has decided to support you.

I have been working on him for some weeks, and am very much gratified to know of his decision, as he can be very helpful to you on account of his influence and intimate acquaintance with party workers.

I am writing you direct in this matter because I want to suggest to you that you write directly to Mr. Gordon, telling him that I have informed you of his decision to support you, and thanking him for whatever influence he may exert in your behalf.

If such a letter is in accordance with your best judgment, kindly write same.

Very truly yours,   [John Garland Pollard]

CCL (J. G. Pollard Papers, ViW).
[1] James Waddell Gordon of the law firm of Smith and Gordon, president of the Gordon Metal Co. of Richmond.

News Reports of Two Political Addresses in Detroit

[Jan. 19, 1912]

Woodrow Wilson Introduced by Osborn to Michigan Editors

Gov. Woodrow Wilson, amid difficulties, succeeded last night in indoctrinating the newspaper editors of Michigan with the Wilson creed of Progressivism.

It was Gov. [Chase Salmon] Osborn, of Michigan, however, who, though a republican, flashed his sword brashly into the midst of the democratic conflict over the Wilson presidential candidacy. . . .

Nothing less than oratorical steam could have warmed the thoroughly chilled company who gathered at the banquet of the Michigan editors in the Wayne pavilion. Besides the cold, the speakers struggled against the rumble of the roller rink below, the noise and clatter of chairs and tables dragged over the floor and the rattle of dishes—this after the banqueters had fled for warmth from the pavilion to the octagonal sun parlor. There the sizzling steam pipes and close quarters encouraged the speakers to warm to their task. While Gov. Wilson delivered his ad-

dress, Secretary L. E. Wilson, of the Board of Commerce,[1] tried
to keep the waiters outside quiet. . . .

"The people of New Jersey," began Gov. Wilson, "are supposed not to be progressive, but they never had the chance to
be progressive; they have been ruled by a government privately
owned. Now they are being released from their fetters.

"The west, however, is the real seat of progressive policies.
You newspaper men are charged with the sacred duty of creating an atmosphere needed for the growth of progressive ideals.

"I am not a reformer, one devoted merely to change, but I
cannot forget how our government policies lag behind the popular advance in other directions.

"The knife of the surgeon is a radical instrument, but its object is to save, not destroy. Newspapers should clear the air,
define terms and show men what is conservative and what is
radical." . . .[2]

[1] Lucius Edward Wilson, vice-president of the Warren Motor Car Co. of Detroit.
[2] Here follows Wilson's advance text on the meaning of the progressive revolt.

❖

WILSON GREETED BY HUGE GATHERING IN ARMORY; HITS TARIFF

When Woodrow Wilson, the governor of New Jersey and progressive democratic candidate for president, faced the most magnificent "off-season" political meeting ever held in Detroit, at the
Light Guard armory last evening, and told the assemblage that
a schoolmaster was a man "trained to find out all about things
and then tell the people," he was evidently thinking of the criticism leveled at him by Henry Watterson earlier in the day, that
he is a schoolmaster rather than a statesman. . . .

Gov. Wilson dealt rigorously with the bi-partisan bunderbund
in modern politics and arraigned a high protective tariff as a
powerful aid in wresting government from the people and making it a sort of trusteeship for "big business."

"For the first time in America recent years have disclosed
the conditions most favorable to serious debate, to the very
thorough consideration, with perfect candor, of questions which
may divide parties simply because they classify opinions, but
which do not constitute the groundwork of passionate party
differences; and when I try to sum up for myself in a single
phrase what it is we are all interested in, it seems to me that
I cannot better express it than by saying that we are interested
in establishing a people's government in America," began Dr.
Wilson.

"I believe that the fundamental difficulty in America is that these words have different meanings in different minds. When I ask myself what I mean by the people, I can candidly answer that I mean everybody; but when they say the people, I am aware that they don't include themselves.["]

Gov. Wilson said he understood a republican to be a person who really believed that the best qualified to judge of the true interests of the country are those who have the largest material stake in the country; that government is a sort of trusteeship for big business.

"And so I deem a democrat to [be] a man who utterly dissents from this opinion," continued the governor. "The democrat when he speaks of the people includes everybody, even including the special interests. We are more gracious than they. They do not include us. We do include them."

"To give the people a man they don't want, no matter how much he wants the place, is not representative government," continued Gov. Wilson. "Not being able to get the sort of man they want, American voters simply go on voting the ticket their father[s] voted and let it go at that.

"I believe in the judgment of the people because I feel safer in the great common judgment than I do in the specialized judgment. There is a great tide of rising public interest in this country which breeds [bodes] ill for unpopular government.

"I look with confidence to the future. There is no dignity in America which lies in her wealth. There is no strength which lies in her size. America is great because she has dreamed dreams, because she has seen visions and beheld the naked soul of man. This is a land of equality, not so much of power or talents as of opportunity.

"When I look at that flag I see written in it the history of our nation. Its strips of white are parchment whereon are written the rights of man. Its strips of red are the blood of her sons through which those rights have been defended."

Printed in the *Detroit News*, Jan. 19, 1912; some editorial headings omitted.

A News Report of Two Speeches
in Ann Arbor, Michigan

[Jan. 19, 1912]

GREAT RECEPTION GIVEN GOVERNOR WILSON TODAY

Gov. Woodrow Wilson arrived in the city one hour late this morning, and for that reason the proposed reception to him in

Memorial hall, which the faculty of the university and the students had planned to give him before his speech at the Whitney, had to be dropped from the program.

However, Governor Wilson, learning that President Emeritus James B. Angell was among those who were to have received him there, expressed the desire to drive to the campus before making the public speech. Arriving there, he grasped the hand of the venerable ex-president of the University of Michigan, and complemented him upon his years, and his apparent good health, while Dr. Angell was also complimentary to Governor Wilson upon his looks.

The audience that greeted Governor Wilson at the Whitney was one that taxed even the standing room, and packed the house to the eaves. It was an audience of representative business and professional men of the city, and of faculty and students from the university.

When the curtain rolled up, the student element was noticeable by its shouts and cheers, which evidently pleased the candidate for the Democratic nomination for the presidency, and after he was introduced, he referred to it as demonstration that made him feel as though he was at home and among friends. . . .

It's possible that men of more personal magnatism have addressed Ann Arbor and university audiences, but it is doubtful if any other man more firmly impressed his audience than did Governor Wilson.

Gov. Wilson is nothing if not optimistic regarding the future of politics. He believes the time has come when the people realize that they are not bound by any party ties formed by their forefathers. He believes they realize that they are facing today problems never faced by their ancestors, and that while the fundamental principles of party politics might have been and may be now, noble principles, that they do not entirely fill the needs of the issues of today. Said he:

"In the past two years in my campaign I have met all sorts of audiences, and I have found the typical ones were not partisan audiences, but audiences of men who felt that a new breath was abroad in the land, and the questions to be discussed were the questions necessary to the fundamental life of the nation. Such audiences are there to hear and to demand words of history. There is no mistaking the temper of the country at the present time. America is wide awake, and the time has come when no party organization can determine what the American people shall do. The last thing a man does now-a-days is to wear gum shoes," and then he added that he had left his outside the stage entrance, which brought shouts of laughter from the student section of the audience. Continuing[,] Governor Wilson said:

"People today resent private arrangements, secret session frame-ups, pre-arrangements of politicians, that have been a part of politics in the past."

He told the students that they were approaching the time to take an active part in the government of the country, and that they were entering life in its fullness, as problems were rising to be solved that had never been confronted before. He told the students that they, like scientists, should be constantly ready to accept new discoveries and new conditions, and like scientists they should give their best study to these conditions, accepting or rejecting them not because their ancestors had embraced such and such policies, but because, after their careful study, they, as men, believed in certain policies and in certain men and certain changes necessary for the greatest good of their country. He begged them to approach these questions without prejudice. He said that when a man was old enough to have a son in college, he had arrived at that age when his life was more or less a specialized one, and he was seeing but a special part of the world. The object of a great university, he said, is to take a young man out of specialized families and fit them for a generalized life, to give them a map of life in its entirety. "The thing that is needed today is community of interest, and comprehension, and you can't serve a nation till you comprehend it. It is like that part of the misguided public, who want to do for the poor. You can't do for the poor, but you can do with the poor. No amount of pity and condescension can do anything for them. That's the rule of life. You can't do anything for the people of the United States, but always remember that with them, you can do anything. The government of the United States was so conducted in recent years that small groups of men did the thinking and planning for the entire nation. They cannot do it longer. We must look into the face of each other, and tell ourselves that it is time for us to act together as a nation, and not be content to sit back and let a few men act for us in such manner as they choose. Patriotism is not a sentiment, but a principle by which a man realizes there is something greater than his own interests.

"Scientists change their opinion over night," said he, "they are ever ready to drop their theories if they can be shown testimony against their accepted theory. The university man, in politics as in everything else, ought to be open to arguments. He ought to be the least bound by prejudice of any body of men, ready at all times to recognize changing conditions and the necessities which these changes bring."

Governor Wilson thinks progressive Republicanism is but another way of spelling Democrat. He told a story which he said illustrated his theory of progressive-Republicans. "Once there was a dear old lady, very deaf. Her son brought to her a man by the peculiar name of Stickpin. He tried to introduce her. 'Mother,' said he, 'I want to present to you Mr. Stickpin.' 'I can't hear you,' said the old lady. Time and again the son tried it, each time in a louder voice, and finally the old lady said 'It's no use, Jamie, try as I will to hear, it sounds exactly like "Stickpin" to me,'" and the governor allowed that when a progressive Republican introduced himself, even though he repeatedly said he was a progressive Republican, it sounded exactly as though he had admitted he was a Democrat. "We are at a stage," said he, "when real men, no matter what party they once were affiliated with, are bound to get together sometimes. It's a hard thing to do. Once get a party label stuck to a family, and it's hard to get it off. Men are having great difficulties in getting the label off today. They feel the spirit of adjustment of new things, and the label bothers them. We are re-forming the life of America, by adjusting it to conditions that never existed before. We can find plenty of principles of old masters of state craft, but they do not fit the conditions of today. If you don't like the way your government is conducted, how are you going to remedy it by party labels? When you go to the polls, if your fundamental interest is for the greatness of your nation, you are going to make the basis of your thoughts something beside party labels."

He gave a very pretty figure of speech. He told of a great rise of waters, which he likened to American sentiment, a great body of progressive sentiment, from every source of the great country, all gathered in a great flood, piling higher and higher behind the "stand-pat dam a solid body of masonry as susceptible to reason as any other mixture of stone and mortar." He said he saw the dam holding back those great waters from the sources where they would normally dispose themselves. "The men forming this dam tell you that the country is on the brink of utter destruction if they give an inch, but," said Mr. Wilson, "the dam is not going to break or slide. It shows no signs of crumbling seriously. But we are thinking men, and while the waters have risen, the sediment of passion has settled to the bottom of the waters. There is, and there will be no excitement, but men are clearing their thoughts, while they have been studying the dam, and they have mapped out the course these waters must ultimately take. They will not break the dam, these progressive, sane, calm thinking and reasoning men; they will puncture that dam here and there; there will be no stopping of industry; there will be no panic. We have come to the period of our greatest statesmenship; we are here to see that no man muddies these waters by political argument. If the undesirable politician undertakes to meddle with these waters he will be drowned.

"This is the enterprise in which America challenges our attention now. There has been but little genuine reform. We must comprehend the country in which we live. We must abolish absolutely all special and private interests from our political life."

In closing, Governor Wilson said, "Let us go forth to serve a great nation in the spirit of a new age."

Decided enthusiasm and a big crowd marked the dinner given for Governor Wilson at the Allenel hotel at noon, and several times the enthusiasm of the students present burst out in yells for the governor which evidently pleased him mightily.

Just before the close of the dinner Mayor William L. Walz asked Governor Wilson to say a few more words to the crowd and he gladly did so.

The diningroom was decorated with the colors of Princeton, orange and black, and Governor Wilson began his speech by saying, "These colors make me feel very much at home, but there is something deeper which also makes me feel at home. It pleases me to learn how united this country is. No part of it now seems radically unlike any other part, and the country seems to be moving as a unit. I suppose there is no better omen for the future of the country than that the sectional feeling, the sharp antagonistic feeling of one region against another, is disappearing. I know of nothing more extraordinary than the rapidity with which things change in America. Is there any other country in the world except America where the same man has worn two uniforms?

"In political matters there used to be sharp sectional lines, but thank God geography is going out of our politics and a man no longer votes a certain way just because he happens to live in a certain part of the country. In every part of the country we speak the same language, discuss things from the same point of view, and everywhere we find the independence and freedom of expression.

"I am looking forward to an era of unprecedented national action. We are now coming to an era where there will be but one single expression and but one common thought. I protest against speaking of German-Americans, or Irish-Americans or

Jewish-Americans, for these nationalities are becoming indistinguishable in the general body of Americans. Drop out the first words, cut out the hyphens and call them all Americans. When I meet a bunch of boys as I did this morning, although their names may represent all nationalities, you can't tell their nationality from the cut of their jibs—they are all Americans. And so we are, in my judgment, building up an American politics, we are building up an American art and an American literature such as we've never had before, and I know of nothing more delightful than the prospect which is before our beloved country."

Governor Wilson's speech was received with great applause, and a call began for Mr. Maloney,[1] one of the private secretaries to the governor, who finally responded with a witty speech during which he told several good stories. He declared that Governor Wilson possessed one of the most lovable personalities in American life.

Three cheers were given for "Woodrow Wilson, the next president of the United States," as he was being escorted from the diningroom.[2]

Printed in the Ann Arbor, Mich., *Daily Times News*, Jan. 19, 1912; some editorial headings omitted.

[1] Dudley Field Malone.

[2] On his Michigan tour, Wilson spoke next in Grand Rapids on January 19 at the Soldiers' Home, to the Ladies' Literary Club, and in Press Hall to a general audience in the evening. News reports of these speeches appeared in the *Grand Rapids News*, Jan. 20, 1912. He spoke at Jackson on January 20. A stenographic report of this speech is printed in the Jackson *Patriot*, Jan. 21, 1912.

From Mary Allen Hulbert Peck

Dearest Friend,   Paget West, Bermuda. Jan 19th [1912].

Just a line to tell you we are well and that I received a letter from Mrs. Wilson by last mail in answer to my invitation, and am very sorry she can not come. I immediately cabled Mrs. Wayland[1] who accepted my invitation by the same means, as it seemed a pity to have a vacant room in this lovely place when so many are longing to enjoy it. We have had rather bad weather of late, but not too bad the last day or two for my swim, and I shall enjoy it still more when Mrs. Wayland can go in with me. I shall have to go up in April for the final settlement, and until it is all over, I shall shrink and shiver, and put on a bold front. I read of you and the hateful things they say of you, and rage inwardly, and sometimes laugh, it is so absurd. I am careful to say *nothing*, for the world is the world, and I know it. The "Bedfords" have gone, and the new Regt. is here—the Queens—something, a rather smart one, I hear. There is a garden party at Govt. House the 24th from 3 to 6—"Dancing." I am going but dancing in the afternoon is *too* frivolous for *me*. There are not many interesting people here so far. No really "classical people" as Ethel says. And *Jews* innumerable. Our dear islands are being spoiled by our own people, and I could weep over it. I am secure here in my little corner from all intrusion, and long to have you see it. It is so dear and bright and pretty, without & within. I hunt furniture steadily, and sold some today I did not care for at a very good profit. Write me as often as you can. I need my friends.   M. A.

ALS (WP, DLC).
1 Mary Isabel Scovill (Mrs. John Elton) Wayland of New York.

From Josephus Daniels

Dear Governor: Raleigh, N. C. 1/19/12

I did not know what to say with reference to the Harvey-Watterson statements and at first I thought I would not say anything, but I knew if I said nothing that it might be interpreted in North Carolina as feeling that there was no effective answer to make from the Wilson standpoint, and therefore I wrote the enclosed editorial[1] which I hoped would be the best way to handle it.   Sincerely,   Josephus Daniels

TLS (WP, DLC).
1 "Wilson—Watterson—Harvey," Raleigh *News and Observer*, Jan. 18, 1912. "Colonel Watterson," Daniels wrote, "was right when he called Governor Wilson 'a second Tilden,' and Colonel Harvey's earnest advocacy of his election to the presidency was based upon Governor Wilson's great ability, rare statesmanship and courage." Wilson might have been more tactful, the editorial continued, but the regrettable incident at the Manhattan Club did not change Harvey's and Watterson's just estimate of the Governor. The two men should "forget and forgive and lead in putting this 'second Tilden' in the White House."

From Oswald Garrison Villard

Dear Governor Wilson: [New York] January 22, 1912.

May I have your permission to print your letters to Col. Harvey bearing upon the Manhattan Club incident, if I can obtain them, and also Col. Harvey's letters to you? I shall be very grateful if you will give me permission to do this for I am sure that the publication of the letters will result in much good.

With kind regards,
                    Faithfully yours,   [Oswald Garrison Villard]

CCL (O. G. Villard Papers, MH).

Two News Reports

[Jan. 22, 1912]

WILSON WATCHES HIS WEDNESDAYS

"Bring on the Letters; I'm Getting Used to Them," He Says.

TRENTON, N. J., Jan. 22.—Gov. Woodrow Wilson was on the job in his office here to-day and received many callers. Asked to make his promised statement regarding the Col. Watterson-Col. Harvey affair the Governor laughed heartily.

"All a tempest in a teapot," said he; "as fine a lot of publicity work as I have ever seen."

"Is it true," the Governor was asked, "that the cause of your break was that Col. Harvey wanted you to arrange a conference with Thomas F. Ryan?"[1]

"Absolutely nothing to say on that," replied Gov. Wilson.

Wall Street, said the Governor, didn't interest him much, and in fact he has never thought of the interests there since "all this big boom for me started."

At first the Governor declined to make any statement whatsoever upon the Harvey-Watterson matter. Asked by newspaper men for the statement he had been expected to make to-day, Gov. Wilson declared he was not ready just yet to have the public know his views. He declined to say when the long promised statement would be made, saying that he has really not thought much of the matter and will take it up after he attends to some State affairs. Later he changed his statement and said that he didn't know whether he would ever make any statement at all.

Speaking of the Ryan story, Gov. Wilson wished it to be understood that he would neither deny nor affirm it. From his general talk, however, it was gathered that he was perfectly willing to have the story circulated provided he was not made responsible for it.

Gov. Wilson, commenting upon an amendment to the Geran law, said that if the amendment is passed by the State Legislature it would play the opposition party right into his hands. The amendment proposes to place the names on the ballots in alphabetical order, contrary to the methods used on the Australian ballots.

"And God help 'em if they do make the change," concluded the Governor.

---

[1] Stories were already circulating to the effect that, at the Manhattan Club meeting, Watterson (not Harvey) had tried to persuade Wilson to accept money from Thomas Fortune Ryan. The first such report had appeared in the *Atlanta Journal*, Jan. 19, 1912. Later ones were printed in the New York *World*, Jan. 23, 1912, and the Raleigh *News and Observer*, Jan. 25, 1912.

The Governor was in a discursive mood. He shifted quickly from one subject to another.

"I am anxiously awaiting the arrival of Wednesday," said the Governor, "it seems that I have something handed me every Wednesday and on no other day of the week. I can't imagine what is coming this time, and it will probably be my letters concerning the Cleveland-Wilson affair, as it is called. That, however, merely deals with some matters at the university when I was there. I sided with the poorer boys while Cleveland sided with the richer ones. This matter, should it be aired, would not be unfavorable to me anyhow. In fact I think it would do me a world of good. Bring on the letters. I'm getting used to 'em."

"Will you name the day upon which you will name the day [*sic*] your statement concerning Col. Harvey and Col. Watterson will be given out?"

"Ha, ha," laughed the Governor, "there you are again, trying to twist me up and make me say something, aren't you? Well, I won't do it. I don't want to talk, and you wouldn't have me do anything I don't want to do, would you?"

"What do you think of the whole affair, anyhow?"

"I refuse to talk. It is all a tempest in a teapot anyhow. That phrase suits the situation exactly. I can think of no better one. Wait until after Wednesday. Maybe I'll have something to say then. No, it is hardly probable that I'll make up my mind to talk later in the evening. I can't tell what will happen to-morrow. I am a busy man these days and I do not know what I am going to do from one day to the next."

"Do you think the attacks that have been made upon you about the manner in which you treated Col. Harvey were warranted?"

"I will not talk. I refuse to be interviewed."

"Did you ask the Colonel to take your name out of *Harper's Weekly*?"

"I positively refuse to be interviewed upon the subject." The Governor then went off into a discussion of some of the newspaper cartoons that have appeared concerning him and Col. Harvey. Then he told a story about a cartoon of several years ago concerning Col. Roosevelt at the time the sage of Oyster Bay was busy with his simplified spelling bee. "Well," said the Governor, "the cartoonists are funny. First they get after Roosevelt and then me. However, boys will be boys, and that's a pretty good excuse for almost any offence.

"Nobody reads my books but students," said the Governor at

another stage. "One of them is a history, and the other one is a story of the life of George Washington."

"You mean of his politics and the politics of his day?" was suggested.

"Not at all. It is a history of his life. The idea of this press agent stuff is very foolish. But you are trying to make me talk of Harvey and Watterson again, and I simply won't do it."

The Governor arrived at his home yesterday evening. It has been his intention to pass through New York a little after the time he really reached home. Because he wished to get away from being interviewed in New York, however, he took an entirely different route than the one announced and arrived at his home several hours ahead of time.

"Not a newspaper reporter caught me the whole way," said the Governor. "You are the first I have seen. I have been dodging 'em all morning."

It is stated by good authority that a long statement explaining his whole connection with Col. Harvey and his doings with Col. Watterson may be looked for at any time. And when it does come it will be a hot one, said the Governor's friend, who gave out the information.

Printed in the New York *Evening Sun*, Jan. 22, 1912.

❖

[Jan. 23, 1912]

GOVERNOR IN ANGRY MOOD

Orders from His Office Reporter Who Had Misquoted Him in an Interview.

PROTEST SENT TO NEWSPAPER

TRENTON, Jan. 23.—The wrathiest Governor the New Jersey State house has seen in a long time strode back and forth in the executive chamber last evening with a copy of the New York Evening Sun in his hand.

Now and then Governor Wilson would stop and read a paragraph of the article in the first column. But he couldn't read long —each line increased his anger.

Shortly afterward the Governor issued this statement:

"I want to denounce in the strongest terms the action of a representative of the Evening Sun in sending to his newspaper today an alleged interview with me, which was false from beginning to end. I cannot of course hold the paper itself responsible, but I feel that the reporter was guilty of a genuine outrage. I have just sent to the editor of the Evening Sun the following telegram:

" 'Editor Evening Sun, New York City.

" 'I wish to protest warmly against the alleged interview with me published in this evening's Sun. It is absolutely false from beginning to end, and the man who wrote it ought to be discredited. I, of course, hold him and not you responsible.

" 'WOODROW WILSON'

"I want to add that this is the first time I have ever been treated in this way by a representative of the press. I hope, and believe, that there are very few men who would be guilty of such conduct."

The newspaper article, which roused the Governor's anger, purported to be an interview with him. The subject matter covered was up for discussion at a ten-minute seance between the Governor and a half dozen newspaper men early in the afternoon. When the Sun story appeared, all the newspaper writers who had been present at the seance declared emphatically that the article so far as it purported to quote the Governor was a fabrication in all its important features.

The Sun man who wrote the story appeared in Governor Wilson's outer office a short time after the Governor saw the printed story. When Governor Wilson discovered him, he was ordered out with a curtness and vigor that made "Jim" Nugent's famous exit[1] look like a triumphal procession.

Printed in the *Newark Evening News*, Jan. 23, 1912.
[1] About this episode, see the statement printed at March 20, 1911, Vol. 22.

To Oswald Garrison Villard

Trenton, N. J., January 23d, 1912.

Sincerely appreciate your kindness. I certainly have no objection at all to the publication of my letters to Col. Harvey, but with regard to his letters to me, I have the strong feeling, which I cannot overcome, that I should hate to join the ranks of the men who are publishing private letters. There is, of course, nothing in them that I should not be glad to see made known.

Woodrow Wilson.

Printed in the New York *Evening Post*, Jan. 30, 1912.

To Thomas Bell Love

My dear Mr. Love: [Trenton, N. J.] January 23, 1912.

Thank you heartily for your letter of January eighteenth, and for what you are so generously doing to put me in a true light with regard to this regrettable Harvey-Watterson matter. I never dreamed that it would be considered ingratitude to return a frank and true answer to a question put to me by a friend in my own interest, and I cannot help believe that the whole country will in the long run see the thing in the right light.

Cordially and sincerely yours,   Woodrow Wilson

TLS (photostat in the T. B. Love Papers, Dallas Hist. Soc.).

To Francis Griffith Newlands

My dear Senator Newlands: [Trenton, N. J.] January 23, 1912.

I want to give myself the pleasure of telling you how extremely generous I think you have been. I think I have never known an instance of more handsome public spirit than you have shown,[1] and that I should be the beneficiary of it makes me feel a particular obligation not to disappoint the expectations of men who have so generously looked to me for the right kind of representation of the thought of the country. I think everybody must feel that you have shown an uncommon quality of patriotic principle.

Cordially and faithfully yours,   Woodrow Wilson

TLS (F. G. Newlands Papers, CtY).
[1] Senator Newlands, who had been endorsed as a favorite son candidate for the presidential nomination by his home state of Nevada, announced his support of Wilson's candidacy on January 18, saying: "It is evident that the big interests have isolated Wilson from all the other candidates and have made him the special object of attack. There is all the more reason, therefore, that the Democrats of Nevada and the West should recognize him as the true progressive leader and rally to his support." Raleigh *News and Observer*, Jan. 19, 1912.

To Josephus Daniels

My dear Friend: [Trenton, N. J.] January 23, 1912.

Thank you for your letter of the nineteenth with its enclosure. I feel that I can always depend upon you to do the wise and generous thing, and it reassures me very much. I believe that the country as a whole is rapidly coming to view the Harvey-Watterson matter in its true light.

Always cordially and faithfully yours,

Woodrow Wilson

P.S. Let me thank you for the letter, "Wilson and Progressive Democracy" from Washington.[1] It is bully.

TLS (J. Daniels Papers, DLC).
[1] It is missing in the Wilson Papers, but he referred to Thomas J. Pence's column in the Raleigh *News and Observer*, Jan. 18, 1912. Pence noted that Senator Thomas P. Gore of Oklahoma had declared that Wilson was the only Democrat who could command the support of progressive Republicans and independents, as well as Democrats, and he quoted from Gore's Jackson Day speech: "We want no wolves in sheep's clothing, no reactionaries in progressive clothing, no Harmon men in Clark's clothing. . . . The Democracy cannot conquer in the sign of the double cross."

From Ira Remsen

My dear Governor Wilson: [Baltimore] January 23, 1912

If you will need a house in Baltimore during the Democratic National Convention I should be glad to place a part of mine at your disposal. Mrs Remsen[1] will leave about the middle of June, but I shall stay on until after the Convention and shall be the only occupant. My servants will be in the house and everything will go on as usual. I think I can make you comfortable. You may have a double bed-room and bath, and the use of rooms on the lower story, as far as you may care to use them.

I hope this invitation may appeal to you, for I can assure you that your acceptance will give me pleasure.

                              Yours sincerely,   [Ira Remsen]

TLS (I. Remsen Papers, MdBJ-Ar).
[1] Elisabeth Mallory Remsen.

To Mary Allen Hulbert Peck

Dearest Friend,   Princeton, New Jersey 24 Jan'y, 1912

It was literally impossible for me to write last Sunday,—indeed until to-day,—and now I am afraid that I have just missed a boat. I am *so* sorry, because from your recent notes it is evident that you are "low in your mind" and need cheering and reassurance. Our dear little Margaret is an absent-minded, harum-scarum young person whose omissions mean nothing, except heedlessness,—and Ellen *did* write, almost immediately after she received your letter. There was evidently some delay in the mails, —as I fear there will be with this epistle, because it may not catch an early boat. And so you see how clear my proof is that your sensitiveness has been made a bit morbid by your suffering. I wish I could help! If understanding perfectly and with deep and constant sympathy is helping, I *can*. May I not beg that you will write me *real letters*? I think I know what it would do for you. It would release your spirits again. These little, almost constrained, notes that I get from my dear friend can mean only one thing. They mean that, out of sheer sensitiveness,—out of an exquisite, subtle pain in the thought of what she must go through with in April,—she is drawing into her shell,—turning away even from those who perfectly understand and perfectly sympathize,—depriving herself of the only comfort and relief she could get,—the comfort and relief that a loving friend is given to her to supply. And how does your friend feel, the while? As if he were of no use or service,—as if he were an intruder when he insists on knowing and sharing her thoughts. And so she cheats him as well as herself of one of the sweetest things in life,—the only wholly sweet thing, indeed—the comradeship and communion of those whose hearts would fain keep company in this fitful journey.

And *he*, meantime, the friend, what does *he* want so much as such a release from the strains he is under? It is *terrible* to stand in such a blaze of publicity as I now stand in,—and as the target of all attack. Every assault they make upon me ('they' are now becoming clearly defined as the men who dominate Big Business) strengthens me; every weapon they use proves a destructive boomerang,—but it is an awful ordeal. It needs steady nerves to stand it,—and every possible release into the dear company and *confidence* of friends. If I ever needed your confidence, a thousand times more do I need it now. It is a privilege and a blessing to me to be your trusted friend.

I was in Grand Rapids last Friday and spoke at a big evening meeting got up to give me an audience! How I wished that I had inquired of you more particularly just *where* you were born there,—I should so have liked to look it up and imagine you a child there. Of course it was of you I thought all the while I was there,—with a special poignancy. All goes well with us. We are all well. Democratic politics seems more and more to centre on me,—but what I am more conscious of that [than] that is, that I am   Your devoted friend   Woodrow Wilson

ALS (WP, DLC).

To Robert Bridges

My dear Bobby,   Princeton, New Jersey 24 Jan'y, 1912

The cheque came.[1] Thank you for sending it. It is delightful to think what it means.

I wish I could see you more often, my dear Bobby. I am very unhappy about Princeton—and feel that I am daily in need of the advice of my friends about larger matters.

Affectionately,   Woodrow Wilson

ALS (WC, NjP).
¹ See WW to R. Bridges, Jan. 2, 1911, n. 2, Vol. 22.

A News Report of Remarks to the Newark Board of Trade

[Jan. 25, 1912]

TRADE BOARD ORATORS SPLIT ON CURRENCY

Former Senator Aldrich and Congressman Kitchin Arrayed in Forensic Clash.

Currency reform, national finance, business conditions and the need of closer co-operation between the business men of the country and their legislative representatives were some of the topics considered by speakers at the annual banquet of the Board of Trade last night.

To many of the hundreds of diners the most interesting feature of the proceedings was the clash of views on currency problems presented by former United States Senator Nelson W. Aldrich, of Rhode Island, chairman of the National Monetary Commission, and Congressman Claude Kitchin of North Carolina.

Mr. Aldrich did not hear Mr. Kitchin's counter-argument, as he left the hall immediately after finishing his speech. But the diners stayed, and cheered the Tar Heel State man to the echo. The turn the debate took came as a complete surprise to most of them.

Nor was the oratorical jousting of Messrs. Aldrich and Kitchin the only matter of interest. Governor Wilson made an address on present business conditions that made the merchants and manufacturers present lend attentive ears, and Congressman Henry T. Rainey, of Illinois, made a few remarks about Presidential candidates that caused his hearers to wonder whether he was aiming his shafts at Governor Wilson or Colonel Roosevelt. Mr. Rainey later declared he was referring to the latter. The context of his speech backed up this assertion.

As far as Governor Wilson was concerned there was no indication that he might have been in "the enemy's country." On the contrary, when President Curtis R. Burnett,¹ in an opening talk as toastmaster, made a reference to "Governors who may be President of the United States," there ensued an ovation for the Chief Executive. . . .

Nor did it detract from Governor Wilson's popularity with the audience that in his talk, eschewing politics, he enacted the role of "schoolmaster." Colonel Watterson wasn't there and the following of his pedagogical bent by the Governor seemed to please his hearers. . . .[2]

Printed in the *Newark Evening News*, Jan. 25, 1912; some editorial headings omitted.
[1] Secretary of the American Oil and Supply Co. of Newark.
[2] Here follows a report of remarks very similar to those embodied in the following news report.

A News Report of an Address to the Jersey City Board of Trade

[Jan. 25, 1912]

GOVERNOR GETS OVATION AT TRADE BOARD DINNER

It was nearly 11 o'clock when Governor Wilson, accompanied by his private secretary[1] and State Comptroller [Edward Irving] Edwards, arrived at the Jersey City Club by auto from Newark to address the Board of Trade banquet. As the Governor entered the gaily decorated hall he was given a rousing reception. Red fire was set blazing on the tables, a coterie of singers at Table 4, under the direction of Benjamin E. Farrier,[2] sang this parody on Mr. Dooley:[3]

"Oh, Governor Wilson; Oh, Governor Wilson,
You're the greatest man that Harvey ever knew;
Oh, Governor Wilson; Oh, Governor Wilson,
As President of our country you will do."

The diners rose as one man and cheered their distinguished guest. The Governor, who was introduced in a few fitting words and referred to as "Our Illustrious Governor" by President Arthur C. Stratford,[4] the toastmaster, said in part:

"I am pleased to find myself again in such a familiar place in such good company, and where I have so often been forgiven the speeches I have made." The Governor then spoke of the Lincoln dinner at which he spoke here some years ago,[5] and

[1] Walter Measday.
[2] President of the W. W. Farrier Co., a large plumbing and contracting firm of Jersey City.
[3] About this popular melody, see n. 1 to the news report printed at Dec. 13, 1902, Vol. 14.
[4] Arthur Chazotte Stratford, president of the George Stratford Oakum Co. of Jersey City.
[5] A fragmentary report of this speech is printed at Feb. 13, 1902, Vol. 12.

said he did not think there were many Republicans in his present audience. At this there were several cries of "No!" succeeded
by much laughter when the speaker said that "there is no political campaign on now, and though our political campaigns
are like a continuous performance, this is an interval between
the acts." Continuing: "This is not a political body, but an organization with no color of partisanship, but devoted to the
bettermen[t] of the community, and for the relating of trade and
manufacture to the real social interests of the community. The
attitude of our business men toward our public men often causes
me some uneasiness; they seem critical and as if waiting for
something to happen, as if anticipating changes in politics that
will not be helpful. But they do not disturb themselves to take
part in and guide politics. Many of you feel no just reason why
extended changes should take place in our economic conditions,
and look upon the intervention of politicians as unjustifiable.
Indeed, many of you would no doubt like to shut politicians in
some institution, thinking then that business would be safe.

"Are the present conditions of business satisfactory—the conditions as a whole? I ask you to withdraw the veil from your
eyes and to see things as they are. Radicalism is a tearing away
of things detrimental to our welfare. Every man ought to be a
radical in tearing away these things, in making a diagnosis
from facts, looking at them as they are. Such radicalism is desirable. Undesirable radicalism is following up the disclosures
with too rapid alterations. We must act with the entire revelation of facts; must investigate and probe just as the surgeon
probes. A just diagnosis is most necessary to a cure. For my
part, I am afraid of a physician who acts without knowing what
is the matter with us. The radicalism of disclosures is not to be
feared, but only the revolutionary changes. Many brave men are
against covering things up, and upon this kind of radicalism
depends our salvation."

Gov. Wilson went on to the effect that it was not so much
combination that caused monopoly, but the secret any [and]
covert use made of combination. We should have these secret
methods disclosed and then dealt with. Business men, he declared, owed it to themselves first to see things as they are and
to call a spade a spade. Having got the facts as they are, we
can do something prudent and not destructive for the correction
of abuses. "But we must not only see things as they are, but we
must foresee them as they are going to be. Are you preparing
for the future? There is universal suspicion, distrust and unrest
as to the present condition of business, and these must be re-

moved." The Governor then spoke of the increasing consumption of grain in this country, which was no longer the granary of the world. "Our exports of grain are falling off. Our exports of manufactures are increasing in spite of ingenious measures to impede them. And we are not studying foreign markets. Long ago we deliberately and stupidly destroyed our merchant marine, not appreciating the fact that the nations that carry the goods can secure the markets of the world. We are more likely to see the Greek flag on the seas than the American flag. The English and German ships are everywhere, and America ships goods under every flag but her own. Yet when we were a little nation we dominated the carrying trade of the world on the seas; to-day we hove [have] no foreign carrying trade at all—all through sheer stupidity. We have got to have foreign markets and our seamen and merchant marine. The tariff is going to break down of its own dead, dull weight. America has got to burst its bonds."

The Governor then referred briefly to the Panama Canal and the changes its operation would bring, illustrating the point by showing how fifteenth century Mahomedan supremacy led to the discovery of America. He predicted that something was going to happen—that the centres of trade gravity would be shifted and the arteries of travel be changed, probably with results that would "jolt" some of his hearers. "Are you ready for that?" he queried. "I'm willing to stand still if you will guarantee that the world will stand still, but the blooming thing is getting away with us. Conditions are continually changing under our very noses. Our public men are the only ones who are trying to do anything. Why not get into the game? It is the old story—you must 'put up or shut up.' If things are done without your help, they may be done badly, and then you will only have yourselves to blame. You must cultivate a spirit of law. Thousands of dollars are spent in trying to get around the law. Business men should accommodate themselves to the law and get their lawyers to square their business with the law. Why not try that for a change?" The speaker made it plain that he did not accuse business men of criminal practices. In concluding, the Governor with matchless rhetoric said that the spirit of the times was altruistic, that men should see a vision of greater things and work for the ultimate realization of the ideal of universal human brotherhood.

Printed in the Jersey City *Jersey Journal*, Jan. 25, 1912; some editorial headings omitted.

To Richard Heath Dabney

My dear Heath: [Trenton, N. J.] January 25, 1912.

I know that you will understand why I do not write more frequently to acknowledge your notes which always delight me with their evidences of active and thoughtful friendship. My days are one continual absorbing rush.

I am very sorry to hear what you report of the effect of the Harvey-Watterson affair on the opinion of some of my friends in Virginia, but I cannot help hoping that this is only temporary because surely Virginians are not going to be the only people in the country who do not understand. I, of course, had every reason to suppose that Harvey asked me the question in good faith and the [for] the purpose of serving my own interests, and when he asked it, I answered it as frankly as he had propounded it, for the fact was certainly as I stated it.

I am glad that Gibboney has been down with you and cannot help believing that this particular thing is going to straighten itself out.

I am very much puzzled by hearing that I have been invited to come to Richmond, both by the City authorities and by the State authorities, for no invitation has reached me.

In haste,
Faithfully and affectionately yours,   Woodrow Wilson

TLS (Wilson-Dabney Corr., ViU).

From Richard Heath Dabney

Dear Woodrow: [Charlottesville, Va.] 25 Jan., 1912.

I am just back from a most delightful trip to Richmond, where I went to dine with Mr. McAdoo last night. The occasion was a most interesting one, Mr. McAdoo making a very strong impression on us all. Besides Smith[1] & G[eorge]. Bryan, the Pres. & Sec'y of the [Wilson] Club, there were present Speaker Byrd, Gov. Montague, Byrd's son,[2] Montague's brother,[3] Lewis Aylett,[4] Wyndham Meredith,[5] Archie Patterson[6] and Mum Gordon[7] & Davis,[8] in addition to Mr. McAdoo and his Sec'y, Mr. Martin.

We shall organize our Club here on Monday, & I hope it will start off with a large attendance & big enthusiasm.[9]

From what Mr. McAdoo said, I judge that you are still considering whether you will make a statement about the Watterson-Harvey incident.

If you ever get the time, you can assist me by letting me have

answers to the questions I asked about the Carnegie pension &
the recent election in New Jersey. But I know how great are the
demands upon your time.

Faithfully yours,   R. H. Dabney.

ALS (WP, DLC) with WWsh notation: "Invitation came. Am off to Richmond tonight."

¹ Henry Marston Smith, Jr., partner in the Richmond law firm of Smith and
Gordon. Wilson and Smith sat at the same dining table when they were law
students at the University of Virginia.

² Harry Flood Byrd, at this time engaged in journalism, fruit growing, and
highway construction.

³ Robert Lynch Montague, campaign manager for his brother and later his
law partner.

⁴ Lewis Dandridge Aylett, a Richmond lawyer. He was living in Atlanta when
Wilson began his law practice there in 1882.

⁵ Wyndham Robertson Meredith, corporation lawyer of Richmond, fellow-
student of Wilson's at the University of Virginia.

⁶ Archibald Williams Patterson, another old friend from the University of
Virginia days, lawyer with the firm of Courtney and Patterson of Richmond.

⁷ James Waddell Gordon.

⁸ Westmoreland Davis, large-scale farmer of Leesburg, Va.; Governor of Virginia, 1918-22.

⁹ Disaster struck Dabney's plans when Senator Thomas S. Martin, a few days
later, passed around the word that he desired the favorite son endorsement of
Virginia and expected support from his home county of Albemarle. Wilson's
friends in Charlottesville had counted on a large number of recruits from the
administration and faculty of the University of Virginia. However, Martin's
favorite son candidacy—an obvious anti-Wilson move—placed university people
in a difficult position, since Martin, the most powerful politician in the state,
was a strong supporter of the university. *Charlottesville Daily Progress*, Jan. 30-
Feb. 5, 1912. The Wilson club of Charlottesville was never organized.

From Oswald Garrison Villard

My dear Governor: New York January 25, 1912.

After getting your kind telegram we wrote to Col. Harvey as
follows:

"Pursuant to our conversation I am authorized to say for
Governor Wilson that he has no objection to the publication
of his letters to you, and of yours to him if you so desire."

In reply to this we have the following telegram from Col.
Harvey:

"Authorization does not insure me against possible criticism
either for publishing private correspondence or for virtually
forcing Governor Wilson's consent in response to my initiative. Are you authorized to say that Governor Wilson
thinks that, in justice to all concerned, the letters ought to
be made public. If so I will give them out as you suggest.
Answer to me care of W. O. Ingliss."

We are writing him that we are not authorized by you to say

that "in justice to all concerned the letters ought to be made public." We realize fully that there is a delicate question here as to where the initiative should seem to rest. Mr. Ogden and I, and others on the Staff are very strongly of the opinion that the letters ought to be published in justice to you and we hear some criticism of the failure to bring them out, since you have always so wisely insisted on doing everything in the open and with complete frankness to the public. If you feel that you could authorize us to say anything else to Col. Harvey beyond what we have already said, we shall be glad to hear from you. For the present the matter rests.

With kind regards,
                    Sincerely yours,   Oswald Garrison Villard.

TLS (WP, DLC).

To Oswald Garrison Villard

Personal.

My dear Mr. Villard: Trenton, N. J. January 26, 1912.

I thank you for your letter of yesterday. I find myself in a position in which it is very difficult, indeed, for me to judge what is right. I do not think that Colonel Harvey has entitled himself to the "justice" of having the letters published because his initiative statement about this matter in the Weekly was itself so incomplete as to be virtually untrue and very unjust, indeed, to me. Only Colonel Watterson's statement enabled the public to see the thing in some of its true aspects. I do not feel, therefore, that the initiative should come from me in regard to the publication of these letters. The action of both Colonel Harvey and Colonel Watterson was unjust and ungenerous. I do not feel that, in this matter, I owe anything to them whatever. I feel, therefore, that my methods to you must remain the expression of my judgment. I am perfectly willing that Colonel Harvey should give out my letters to him for publication, if he desires to do so, and I will, of course, give out his letters to me at any time that he requests it. I think that the country now fully understands this incident and, if anything is to be done, it must be done upon the initiative of the other party, not on my own.[1]

I must confess that I am rendered uneasy by the fact that your judgment in the matter seems to differ from mine, because I so highly value your judgment and feel under such real obligations to you for the generous support you have given me. But

I am bound, of course, in this case as in all others, to tell you what I really think.

With warmest regard, both to yourself and Mr. Ogden,
                    Cordially yours,   Woodrow Wilson

TLS (O. G. Villard Papers, MH).
    [1] The New York *Evening Post* published the Wilson-Harvey correspondence on January 30, 1912.

An Interview

[*Jan. 26, 1912*]

Post Representative Meets Presidential Candidate in Princeton Home

BY ROBERT L. NORTON

PRINCETON, N. J., Jan. 26. . . . In company with Dudley Field Malone of New York I called on Governor Wilson in Princeton tonight. Mr. Malone is the son-in-law of Senator O'Gorman of New York State. If he was a betting man he would wager life against a plugged nickel that Woodrow Wilson is the next President of the United States.

The visit to the Governor was unexpected. The "cabby" volunteered the information that the Governor was home[1] and that he had walked the mile from the station to his home.

The home of the "maybe President" is an ordinary cement structure, the average type of a simple country home. It sets back from the road.

The door was opened by a pretty light haired girl[2] who announced pleasantly that "father was in." "Father" walked into the reception room from his library, shook hands warmly and relieved us of our overcoats.

Simplicity was radiated from the moment that I struck the threshold of the Wilson home. It is the keynote of the personal character of the Governor of New Jersey. There was no formality whatsoever. The Governor advised a comfortable chair of which there were many in the cosey library.

He pointed to a mahogany desk heaped up high with papers and explained that he was getting ready for tomorrow's work. In the centre of the desk was an ivory miniature of Thomas Jefferson. The room had well selected oil paintings and books, plenty of them.

Mr. Wilson looked pleased when he was told that he was not

[1] At their rented house at 25 Cleveland Lane.
[2] Jessie Woodrow Wilson.

expected to be interviewed, but that I had called on him simply
to get a personal impression.

He explained that he did not like to be interviewed and conveyed the impression that to bask in the limelight was anything
but pleasant to him.

The Governor, with knees crossed in a big chair, talked of the
issues of the campaign. He had a way of making one feel at
home right away.

If Governor Wilson is elected President someone will say that
he looks like Abraham Lincoln. He does. He will be the home-
liest President since Lincoln, but his homliness is of the rugged
sort which radiates character and attracts.

Mr. Wilson stands over six feet. The most prominent feature
of his face is his jaw. It's of the steel variety, long and square.
You notice the jaw immediately and then forget it as quickly
when the Governor talks. His face softens up when he talks and
radiates humor of the keen, dry kind.

His forehead is broad and high, surmounted by iron grey hair
characteristically ruffled. There is only one man in public life
whom I know that has as large ears, and that is Senator Murray Crane.[3] . . .

When the Governor gets time, which is not very often in these
days, he plays golf for exercise.

I suggested that he and President Taft might settle the question of the presidency by playing an 18-hole course.

"Well, I guess that if we play the game it will be over a 48-
hole course," he retorted. Incidentally, there are 48 States in
the Union.

On the subject of golf the Governor told about the wonderful
playing of a fat man that he met in Florida once.[4] This man as
the Governor expressed it had not seen his knees for many years.
He could not see the ball over the "curvature," so the Governor
said. The man would stand off so he could see the ball and then
getting the idea of position firmly in his mind would take three
steps forward and aim at the ball without seeing it, always making good on the drive.

Governor Wilson explained that he experienced a somewhat
similar difficulty. A year ago he injured the ball of his eye.[5]
Through one spot in the right eye his sight is not very good.
"Therefore," he said, "when I aim for the ball my nose persists

[3] Winthrop Murray Crane, Republican senator from Massachusetts, 1904-13.
[4] When he recuperated in Palm Beach from a phlebitis in January and February 1905.
[5] Wilson was also still suffering from the effect on his left eye of the stroke
of 1906, about which see WW to J. D. Greene, May 30, 1906, n. 1, Vol. 16.

in getting in the way of my right eye and I have experienced much the same trouble in hitting the ball that this man did."

Speaking in a serious vein on the question of the presidency the Governor said that he disliked to be called a candidate for that office. "It means to any man a fight, a great fight," said he.

He said that he would willingly give way to any man that represented progressive policies and the people in the coming election.

Governor Wilson explained his experience in politics with this expression: "God gave me eyes and I only use my eyelids at night time."

Years ago Governor Wilson was called familiarly "Tommy." In fact this was one of the names which he was christened, although it is not generally known. Last year he made a trip to Carolina, where he has an aunt living who is over 80 years of age.[6]

"Tommie" was a pet of his aunt in boyhood, and she had not seen him for many years. After he had leaned over her chair and kissed her affectionately, she asked that he draw up a chair and sit beside her.

" 'Tommie,' dear, what are you doing now?" she asked.

Mr. Wilson looked a bit embarrassed, and his friends smiled. "Auntie, dear," he said, "I am now Governor of New Jersey."

Mr. Wilson carried the conversation on in this manner, illustrating his points with stories. There was nothing of the pedagogue in him, nothing of the suggestion carried in the scornful appellation of "schoolmaster," made by Colonel Watterson.

Rather there was the impression of a man versatile, modest, filled with human sympathy, understanding men and conditions. The Governor talked of the situation facing big business in this country in earnest fashion.

He said that a few men controlled business and that the thousands of smaller business men thought their success depended upon the bigger men. He deprecated the fact that big business seemed to be influenced more by what it couldn't get from the government than by what it could get by co-operating in the solving of the great problems of the country.

The Governor believes that the business conditions of the country can only be solved with the co-operation of business men with the President. He talked [about] the currency problem and gave his indorsement to a measure making it obligatory to publish the names of the men who seek to influence appointments

6 See the news report printed at June 2, 1911, n. 1, Vol. 23.

in order that the people might know the influences that are controlling appointments.

The talk turned to the books that Governor Wilson had written.

I told him of a reporter who had been instructed by Mr. Pulitzer of the New York World to take two weeks off and read everything that he had written.

The Governor smiled and said that he sympathized with the man who had the assignment. He said that it was satisfying to know that some men in New Jersey had learned what he knew about American history when they read his books, not with the intention, however, of absorbing knowledge, but hoping rather to find something which could be used against him politically.

Mr. Wilson referred to his friendship with President Lowell of Harvard, which he said was one of years' standing, and related a story of a controversy which he had many years ago with President Lowell on the subject of government.[7]

The speech of Wilson is scholarly but so simple that every idea goes straight home.

The Governor doesn't own an automobile. He shaves himself and polishes his own shoes.

Mrs. Wilson is a great companion of the Governor in his literary pursuits and takes a keen interest in his public life. She is a very pretty woman with a sweet, motherly sort of voice.

The Governor has four daughters.[8] Mrs. Wilson and her daughters sat in the room next to that in which I met the Governor.

The four Wilson girls are boon companions of their father and are frequently seen with him in his long walks which he likes to take.

In the State of New Jersey Governor Wilson has made 81 appointments, all of them Democratic. He has revolutionized political conditions. The efficiency test was applied to every man who was a candidate for office. He believes in political leaders rather than political bosses.

Governor Wilson refused to discuss the Harvey incident. He made no reference to it in his conversation.

The friends of Mr. Wilson in New York say, however, that the meeting between the Governor, Colonel Harvey and Colonel Watterson was a "frame-up" pure and simple.

At the proper time the Governor is to give out a statement on the matter. It was stated to me by close friends of the Governor that the withdrawal of the support of Colonel Harvey and his

[7] About this friendly controversy, see the essay printed at Feb. 10, 1886, Vol. 5.
[8] The reporter mistook Margaret Axson Elliott for Wilson's daughter.

weekly and of Colonel Watterson is due to the fact that Governor Wilson turned down offers of money support from the Morgan-Ryan interests.

In fact it is claimed that there was a suggestion of a meeting between Governor Wilson and Thomas Ryan. It is claimed that Colonel Watterson wished also to interest J. Pierpont Morgan in Wilson.

Printed in the *Boston Post*, Jan. 27, 1912; some editorial headings omitted.

From Joseph R. Wilson, Jr.

My dear brother: Nashville, Jan. 26, 1912.

It is time to get busy in Tennessee.[1] The Harmon people have commenced organizing clubs with a parent organization and headquarters in this city, and the Underwood people will soon start their campaign. The Harmon people, as evidenced by advices today from the Third or Chattanooga Congressional District, will endeavor to give local instructions to their delegates to the National Convention so as to insure the state for Harmon and the supporters in the state of the Ohio man are openly declaring their purpose to carry the state for him. While the two state Democratic committees have on the surface adopted a harmony plan providing for a joint primary to nominate candidates for all state offices, no provision is made in the general primary plan for expressing presidential preferences. One Democratic state convention will be held, May 16 being the date fixed, to elect delegates to the National convention and delegates to the state convention will be elected in each of the ninety-six counties. Although, as stated, there is harmony on the surface, the plan adopted by the state committees is meeting with wide opposition in the ranks of the independent Democrats and even many of the independent committeemen declare they have not officially ratified the harmony plan and are endeavoring to secure another meeting of their committee to reconsider what has been done. It may develop, therefore, that there will be two state primaries and conventions yet, for if the present state independent committee does not act further, prominent independents may take the matter in hand and continue their organization. Hence the situation continues to be considerably complicated. Your friends in the state should get to work at once and in earnest so we can make a strong effort to control the state convention by electing Wilson men from the different counties. There is no doubt of the fact that the masses of people in this state are for you, but the politicians at the head of the "regular" organization are doing all they can for Harmon. I suggest that your headquarters take the matter up at once with the organizations in this state and if possible have an organizer placed in the field as the Harmon people have done to form local clubs in every county of Tennessee, clubs composed of men who will work for the control of the state convention. Of course I will do all in my power, but if this movement was started by another, some one officially connected with your campaign, it would have greater force for the opposition would charge selfish motives at once if I should take the initiative and thus possibly weaken the cause. Please take this matter up without delay for it is important that immediate action be taken along progressive lines if we would carry this state.

The general opinion seems to be that the Watterson-Harvey affair has done you great good with the masses. How about that Ryan story? I would like to know, confidentially of course, the truth of the whole affair. You told me but little about the incident while I was at Trenton.

We have not heard when to expect Nellie and are counting fully on her stopping here enroute home.

Much love to all.   Your aff. brother,   Joseph.

How about that photo. of Sister Ellie?

TLS (WP, DLC).
    1 For the background, see J. R. Wilson to WW, Aug. 22, 1911, Vol. 23, and accompanying notes.

From Richard Heath Dabney

Dear Woodrow: [Charlottesville, Va.] 26 Jan., 1912.

I was considerably "flabbergasted" to learn from your letter this morning that you had received no invitation from either the Richmond City Council or the Va. Legislature. The newspapers announced that both of these bodies had passed resolutions to invite you, and I supposed the whole thing was settled. I have written to Geo. Bryan, Sec'y. of the Richmond Wilson Club, asking him to look in the matter immediately.

Have you received *no* invitation from *anybody*? none from the Woodrow Wilson Club of Richmond? I begin to feel dazed about it all. Gibboney said you were to arrive at Richmond at 7:50 A. M. on Feb. 1st & go to the Jefferson hotel, where you would be all day to receive visitors. Is all this a myth? I have never heard *directly* from you that you were to speak in Rich-

mond on Feb. 1st. It has been my expectation to go down to
Richmond on the afternoon of the 31st & to go to see you the
next morning as soon as I think you have finished breakfast.
There is a plan on foot to run a special train from Staunton &
Charlottesville on the 1st. It would be a huge fiasco if it went
down & found you wanting. So please send me a line & let me
know whether you are to be there or not, & when I can see you.
I expect to stay with Lewis Aylett at Ginter Park a little north of
the city. He has a phone.

Hastily but faithfully,   R. H. Dabney.

ALS (WP, DLC).

A News Item

[Jan. 27, 1912]

UNTRUE, SAYS WILSON.

Never Authorized Any One to Ask Watterson
to Solicit Funds.

Gov. Woodrow Wilson was in the city last night and took a
midnight train for Boston. At the Grand Central Station he was
met by a TIMES reporter and a copy of the correspondence between Col. Henry Watterson and Senator B. R. Tillman[1] was
shown to him. Gov. Wilson was greatly interested in the letters,
and smiled broadly when he read certain passages.

When he came to that part of Col. Watterson's second letter
to Mr. Tillman which stated that Col. Watterson had undertaken
to assist in raising money for Gov. Wilson's campaign, the Governor suddenly grew serious. Banging his suit case with his fist,
he said:

"Great Scott! What do you think of that? It is absolutely untrue."

He then issued this formal statement:

"So far as I am concerned the statement that Col. Watterson
was requested to assist in raising money in my behalf is absolutely without foundation. Neither I nor anyone authorized to
represent me ever made any such request of him."

When Gov. Wilson reached that passage in which Mr. Tillman refers to Col. Watterson as a "self-confessed expert groomer
of Presidential candidates," the Governor laughed heartily.

"Who is Swager Shirley?"[2] he asked. "Isn't there another 'g'
in the name?"

The Governor again laughed when he came to the mention
of the name of Thomas F. Ryan.

"Will you comment upon Mr. Ryan's connection with the controversy?" the Governor was asked.

"Not a word," he replied. "I knew nothing about it until I read these letters. I know nothing about it, and, anyway, my statement covers everything."

"Will you take this opportunity to clear up the Harvey-Watterson controversy, Gov. Wilson?"

"Does it need any further clearing up?" was all he would say.

Printed in the *New York Times*, Jan. 27, 1912.
   [1] H. Watterson to B. R. Tillman, Jan. 25, 1912; B. R. Tillman to H. Watterson, Jan. 26, 1912; and H. Watterson to B. R. Tillman, Jan. 26, all printed in the *New York Times*, Jan. 27, 1912. Watterson demanded that Tillman explain upon what authority he had charged that "Marse Henry" had concealed the crucial facts relating to the Harvey-Watterson-Wilson incident. Tillman replied that Watterson had published a description of the rupture without stating the cause. Watterson countered with a denial of the rumors circulated, he said, by "recognized spokesmen" for Wilson to the effect that Harvey had tried to bring Thomas Fortune Ryan into the Wilson camp. Harvey, Watterson said, had had nothing to do with this matter. While raising money for Wilson, the Kentuckian explained, he, himself, had broached the possibility of obtaining Ryan's support, and Wilson's managers had been delighted over the prospect. Wilson's spokesmen were making a hero of the Governor at the expense of his friend, Harvey.
   [2] Joseph Swagar Sherley of Louisville, Democratic congressman, 1903-19. Watterson had sent him to receive Tillman's reply.

To Edward Mandell House

My dear Mr. House: [Trenton, N. J.] January 27, 1912.

I am so glad to hear through Mr. McCombs that you are at last about to get out and feel like yourself again, physically. I have been very much distressed in thinking of your long illness, and it cheers me to thank [think] that you are not [now] about to be released. Pray, take care of yourself. If you will permit me to say so, I have come to have a very warm feeling toward you, and hope that in years to come our friendship will ripen.

Cordially yours,   Woodrow Wilson

TLS (E. M. House Papers, CtY).

To John Garland Pollard

Personal.

My dear Mr. Pollard: [Trenton, N. J.] January 27, 1912.

Thank you sincerely for your letter of January eighteenth, which I should have acknowledged sooner. I shall take great pleasure in writing to Mr. Gordon and have to thank you for your very generous friendship.

In haste,   Cordially yours,   Woodrow Wilson

TLS (J. G. Pollard Papers, ViW).

To Verner R. Lovell

Personal

My dear Mr. Lovell: [Trenton, N. J.] January 27, 1912.

I am very much obliged to you for your kind letter of January twenty-second.[1] I fear from one passage in it that you think I was unwise to write as I did concerning my desire not to appear as an opponent of Governor Burke's in North Dakota. I simply followed an instinctive personal impulse.

I have every reason to believe that Governor Burke is sincerely interested in the cause of Progressive Democracy and I fear that my fellow Democrats in North Dakota would think it very bad form on my part to contest with him the vote for Presidential preference.

I warmly appreciate your kindness in writing me so fully as to the circumstances and wish that I might have put myself earlier into communication with you, if you think that I have made a mistake. I wish only to act in the spirit of entire generosity and harmony.

Cordially and sincerely yours,   Woodrow Wilson

TLS (received from Roland Dille).
[1] It is missing.

To Robert Bridges

My dear Bobby,   [Boston] 27 Jan'y, 1912

This is to acknowledge yours of the 25th with its enclosure,[1]— which I am sure you know how much I appreciate.

Of course I will drop in on the very first opportunity,—alas that it should be so hard to find!

Affectionately Yours,   Woodrow Wilson

Hurrah for the Cumberland Valley partisan![2]

ALS (WC, NjP).
[1] Another check.
[2] Robert R. Henderson.

To Ira Remsen

My dear President Remsen: [Trenton, N. J.] January 27, 1912.

You are very gracious and I am very much obliged to you. Both my friends Doctor Charles W. Mitchell and General Riggs[1] have been kind enough to offer me the hospitality of their homes during the convention in June, but I am not at all sure that I shall attend the convention and, if I do, I foresee only too clearly that it will be necessary for me to live in public and not run to cover anywhere. I shall be obliged to lodge at the Belvidere.

I am denying myself the pleasure and I want to thank you again very cordially.

Faithfully yours,   Woodrow Wilson

TLS (I. Remsen Papers, MdBJ-Ar).

¹ Lawrason Riggs, Princeton 1883, Baltimore lawyer, brigadier general in the Maryland National Guard.

An After-Dinner Address to the Real Estate Men of Boston

[[Jan. 27, 1912]]

*Mr. President, Your Excellency, Your Honor,*¹ *Gentlemen of the Real Estate Exchange:*

I am not going to talk about politics. I am simply going to discuss public questions. And there is a difference, a very great difference, between discussing politics and talking about public questions. Indeed, it is very difficult to talk politics in America now, because you cannot be certain where any man you are talking to belongs.

There is what a football man would call a very broken field, and it is almost impossible to classify men any longer in America, at any rate, after you get them out of the field of their own businesses.

You cannot classify a man about other things until you have talked to him for a long time; and it is incredible that a thoughtful man in this State should really be a standpatter, because the penalty of being such is that the whole of your generation and your civilization will run away from you if you don't move with it.

The theme of my thought to-night as I came here is that we are now at the beginning of a new age, not at its immediate beginning, but near its beginning, and that everything, whether we wish it to do so or not, wears a new aspect for us. Almost every question which it is imperatively necessary we should consider and discuss is, if not a new question, now developed in such a new aspect for America that we must treat it as if it were a new question.

For example, it seems to me that the most pressing thing in

¹ Charles Francis Adams, Jr., Governor Eugene N. Foss, and Mayor John F. Fitzgerald. Former Secretary of State Richard Olney had introduced Wilson effusively.

America is the question of conservation, not merely the conservation of so much as remains of our unwasted resources—I do not mean the mere renewal of our forests; I do not mean mere preservation and a more economical use of our water power —I mean the preservation of our energies and of the genius of our people.

Questions of sanitation to me are questions of conservation; questions of morals are questions of conservation. You cannot conserve the energy of America unless you give to its exercise the proper moral environment. You cannot get the best work out of your workmen unless you make them by honest operations to believe that you regard them, not as your tools, but as your partners; and the whole conservation of America is a question of the supremacy of America, of her right thinking, and of her righteous action. We owe it to future generations that we should not waste or destroy our resources, and we owe it still more to future generations that we should not lower the vitality of our workingwomen, check the vitality of our children, demoralize the processes of our life at any point. And yet how long is it since America troubled herself with questions of conservation? How long is it since we felt in the heyday of thoughtless youth, with so much youth at our hands, that we did not have to be careful in the economy of it; and how constantly did we rejoice that we had put ourselves in a position to be wasteful.

Almost every time public questions are discussed in this day somebody asks the question: "What is the leading question of the approaching political campaign?" Now, I don't know what is the leading question, but I know what is the central question, or at least I think I do, because I find that every road leads to that question, and that is the question of the tariff. The question of conservation leads straight to that same radical origin, to this road of the tariff, because by protecting ourselves from foreign competition—from the skill and energy and resourcefulness of other nations—we have felt ourselves at liberty to be wasteful in our own processes. I believe that it is one of the most serious consequences of the protective tariff that it has made it unnecessary that we should be careful and saving in our own industrial enterprises. I am going to return to that presently, but for the time being let me point out simply this: That we can afford behind the wall of our tariff to pay for business that we are not doing.

What I mean is this: Take almost any modern combination. Suppose that twenty factories are drawn together in a single organization. Those twenty factories are not all of them similarly equipped for efficiency and economy of action, and it constantly happens that after the necessary money is put into the capitalization for the union of those factories under a single organization a number of them are put out of operation rather than brought up to the highest point of efficiency and thereafter are carried as dead enterprises. Now, you could not afford to do that, if you had to make every part most efficient in action. You could not afford to carry cold furnaces; you could not afford to carry silent looms; you could not afford to put up shutters and make people to whom you sell your goods pay for what you paid to put up the shutters.

We can afford to carry dead business in this country because we have not exposed ourselves to universal competition with live business. And so finding it possible to do things of that sort we have gone further—we are paying for things we have not yet used.

There are combinations in this country, for example, in which men have bought mines which they have never opened and which they are carrying, and probably will carry, until the next generation, while we pay the piper. They don't want anybody else to use the mines, and we are paying for what the next generation will use.

Have you realized the loads, the dead weights, that American business is carrying? You may not have analyzed it in this way, but whether you have analyzed it in this way or not, the prices we are paying for manufactured goods in this country tell the tale of what we have been trying to do. And when we swing our thought back to the question of conservation we see nothing less than this: That now we have got to the point where we have got to do something very different because the question of trade is a new question in this country.

I have no doubt that the explanations which Gen. Bancroft[2] offers for the falling off in the export business of Boston is one of the explanations for that decrease nationally. I have no doubt that the differential rate in favor of Baltimore has a great deal to do with it, but there is something else that has to do with it.

Have you looked at the general course of the export trade in this country? Don't you know that the export of grain is steadily going down from natural causes? We used to produce so much more grain than we needed ourselves that we could afford to export enough to feed the greater part of the rest of the world.

But with the increase in our population at a greater rate than

2 Hugh Bancroft, Boston lawyer, retired major general of the Massachusetts National Guard, and chairman of the board of directors of the Port of Boston.

the productivity of our soil, or rather the use of our soil after the productive fashion, the exports of grain are falling because we need more of it ourselves, and during the same period when this has become marked, our exports of manufactured articles have been increasing almost in spite of us by leaps and bounds.

While we have been producing less and less grain in proportion to our power of consumption, we have been producing more and more manufactured goods in proportion to our power of consumption until now we have a surplus of manufactured goods of which we must get rid or else do an unprofitable business.

At this point we discover that we have done something very singular, considering we are Americans. In the first place, by processes which you know just as well as I do, we destroyed our commercial marine.

I am not going to try to distribute the blame or to consider whether the measures which produced this effect were well-considered at the outset or not. We can afford to be indifferent as to whether they were or not, because we are considering the present or future.

The point is now that you are more likely to see the flag of the little kingdom of Greece on the seas than the flag of the United States. History shows, and this particular part of the country will bear witness to the statement, that whereas we were once noted as the common carriers of the Atlantic, whereas we once furnished the seamen and ships for a very considerable proportion of the commerce of the ocean, we have, for one reason or another, lost that carrying trade, and you also know, if you are merchants, that the nation which carries the world's goods can generally see to it that its merchants get the markets.

When we need markets, therefore, now that we are needing them, we have not the hands by which to reach out and take them. Our merchant seamen are gone. Our ships have disappeared from the sea, our registry lists are short and insignificant and by the same token while we had surrounded ourselves with this wall of the tariff and were rejoicing in the great area of free trade which we could enjoy in America under our own vine and fig trees, we were becoming ignorant of the markets of the world.

Where are the great East India merchants who used to have offices in Boston? Where are those men who understood the tastes and the needs of the ends of the earth? Where are the men who knew exactly what to send to India in order to exchange for what India could send to us to satisfy our tastes and needs?

The great trading nations of the world are not those who understand only domestic needs and tastes. They are those who understand the foreign needs and tastes. I heard it quoted from a great cotton manufacturer to-day that if we only had 200,000,-000 instead of 100,000,000 people in this country, we would have enough people to take up the full capacity of the cotton factories of the United States.

Well, lacking the additional hundred million, what are we going to do with our surplus goods? We have got to do something we do not know how to do now[—]to make cotton goods of the kind and pattern that are salable in all quarters of the world, and then to place them there.

But the tariff has made this extremely difficult and at the same time, we are preparing transformations for ourselves. What is the completion of that great ditch now being dug through the Isthmus going to mean to some of the Atlantic seaports? When you take the differential off which will even things between you and Baltimore how are you going to see your way out—how are you going to prevent the great blood of the economic life of the Nation from running down the Mississippi Valley? Where are you going to be when the arteries run north and south instead of east and west?

And after you have got your dock frontage, how are you going to bring the ships of the world here if the currents of trade are shifting, shifting, shifting in spite of you?

Stand pat when the world is changing? Sit still when everything is altering, whether you want it to alter or not? Tell your politicians to let you alone to the enjoyment of your false security when you are not secured at all? When the world itself is being transformed will you refuse yourselves to alter your thinking?

There is no such lack of intelligence in this great city of Boston as to dream of the possibility of an inconceivable thing like that. You have got, in order to relieve the plethora, in order to use the energy of the capital of America, to break the chrysalis that we have been in. We have bound ourselves hand and foot in a smug domestic helplessness by this jacket of a tariff we have wound around us (Applause). We are not about to change the tariff because men in this country have changed their theories about the tariff. We are going to change it because the conditions of America are going to burst through it and are now bursting through it. You cannot fight a Spanish war and join the family of nations in international affairs and still keep your gaze directed inward upon yourself, because along with the singular change that came upon us, that notably altered or affected the very character of our government, the nation itself began to be a different thing. Have you ever thought of the history of our government, of the history of the Executive part of it? Do you not know that down to the period when we began to shut our doors tight against foreign commercial intercourse the Executive was the most important part of the government of the United States and then we went through a long period when, except for the Civil War when there was concentrated energy to be found, the Executive counted for almost nothing and the Congress for almost everything, because every question was a neighborhood question. It was our own. We had not any national spokesman such as the Executive is, prepared to serve us. And then came the Spanish War, and since then do you think it is a question that the Executive has again become a conspicuous part of this government. So soon as a nation must act, you must have a body through which it can act. So soon as it becomes a single will you have to have a lodgement for the guiding intelligence, a single will in every nation that is important in international relations—a strong guiding Executive, not because it deliberately chooses to have it, but because it has no choice, it must have it. And so while we have waited and drifted in altruistic fashion into a war for the sake of the Cubans, we altered the centre of gravity of our government. Will we never learn this fact; that you do not make governments by theories? You accommodate theories to the circumstances. Theories are generalizations from the facts. The facts do not spring out of the theories. If they did we would have a very symmetrically ordered series of facts, but the facts break in and ignore the theories—contemptuously smash the theories, and as our life is, as our thought is, so will our government be.

Very well, our thoughts are concentrated upon ourselves. Now we are changing our point of view and looking abroad upon the face of the earth, seeking to allow ourselves an outline into the general field of competition, which includes the whole round globe. In the meantime, what have we done? Do you really think that the tariff has produced efficiency? Do you believe that combinations, most of which have been made possible by the tariff, have had as their chief effect efficiency and economy? Every tyro knows that, up to a certain point, combination produces economy. But it does not necessarily produce efficiency. That depends upon who runs the combination and on the amount of brains invested, not on the amount of capital pooled; and after you have got your combination, what do you do with it? I don't

mean what you say you do with it in public discussions. What
do you actually do with it? You have only to ask to look into the
testimony before the Stanley Committee; you have only to look
into the testimony in the trial of the meat packers;[3] you have
only to look in the public records to find what is done with some
combinations. There are private understandings with regard to
prices. Everybody knows that and that the penalty of not observing those prices and keeping to them is to be put out of the
combination, and it looks—I will not make this as assertion, but
I will venture to say—as if the object of some combinations was
the price, not the efficiency, not economy, but the avoiding of
the very things that make economy and efficiency absolutely
imperative. I don't have to be efficient over and above the point
that the men I am in competition with makes it necessary that
I should be efficient. If I know enough to know more than the
fellow that I am competing with I don't have to increase my
knowledge. If I understand the game well enough to checkmate
him, I don't have to understand it any better, and if I can enter
into an understanding with him, I don't have to understand it
at all (Laughter). So that my conviction is, and I think that the
admission of every candid mind will be, that in recent decades
we have been decreasing our efficiency.

There is only one thing upon which efficiency depends and
that is the whole thing. You cannot get efficiency out of your
workmen if your [you] overdrive them, any more than you can
get it out of your machines if you overdrive them. Did you ever
notice how much more tender and considerate of their machines
some American manufacturers are than they are of the human
beings they employ? Don't you know that every thoughtful manufacturer studies what his machinery will bear and he will dismiss an employee who puts more on that machine than it can
bear or than he ought to put on it? Very well, does he dismiss
the same superintendent who puts more on the human muscle
and spirit than it can bear? Not often. When you find a manufacturer who is considerate of the strain on his men and who
makes them feel that he is taking as much care of them as of
his machinery you find the most efficient establishment in the
trade (Applause).

Would it not be a good idea to draw your cost sheets after a
new fashion? Would it not be a good idea to have a cost sheet
to show the strain put upon the men in every respect—not merely

[3] He referred to the trial, then in progress in Chicago, of ten executives of the
major meatpacking companies for violation of the Sherman Act. They were
accused of forming a pool to fix meat prices by limiting the supply and shipment
of meat to particular regions.

the physical strain, but a sheet which would show the strain put on them by lack of ventilation in the factory, by the lack of opportunities of amusement, by the absence of the feeling on the part of the workmen that they are really regarded as essential partners in a mutual undertaking which makes every man just as eager to make the product good as his employer could possibly be! It would be a moral balance sheet of the whole industry of the nation. Don't you see how I am traveling in a circle? It is a question of conservation. Conservation is a question of efficiency. Efficiency depends upon those finer economies which assemble all the elements of energy, and economy is simply another way of spelling the word honesty, thriftiness, getting out of every ton of coal every unit of energy that there is in it without waste, throwing nothing away, making profit out of everything, but particularly out of your relations with your fellowmen.

We have this question to answer, therefore, gentlemen, and this is the central question of all politics and it is a perfectly non-partisan question—What do you want?—the economical adjustment, the moral adjustment, the physical adjustment which will produce these results, or do you want a fetish, called protection, behind which there will be waste, plus security? Do you really want to admit that you cannot make the American nation more efficient than any other nation in the world? The only reason that America is efficient is that American brains are capable of entering into any competition that you can conceive of. The central thing is that so long as we keep American life relatively what we intended it to be, we have only to import a workman who earns thirty cents a day on the other side of the water and find him in an employ earning two dollars a day on this side of the water. A man cannot change the dexterity of his fingers or his physical make-up in a month, but he can change his point of view. He can catch the infection of the factory in which he works. He can recognize under the intelligent supervision of the superintendent that through his participation and because he has become a constituent part of the great throbbing American machine that we call civilization, he can be an infinitely better workman than he is anywhere else.

When you want to cut down your working force, which of your workmen do you dismiss first? Those that get the smallest wages. You don't dismiss the high-priced men first. If you did you would dismiss the president and secretaries and superintendents and you cannot get on without those who earn the larger salaries. You don't dismiss from the top but from the bottom, which is your admission that the most economical labor you have is your highest priced labor. That is what you cannot dispense with. It is high priced not because of the tariff. O, I wish I had time to explode that ancient myth. No thoughtful economist in the world knows so little as not to be able to explode it. Only business men who will not take the pains to become economists believe it and some of them do not believe it.

A friend of mine who travels all over the world and sells a certain kind of American machine tells me he can sell $350 machines in competition with an $80 machine that does the same work because the $350 machine is more economical, it produces more in a given time and better goods in a given time, yields more to the intelligence of those who use it in a given time than the $80 machine, and the $350 machine is cheaper, produces a smaller labor cost than the $80 machine.

And the man who earns $10 a day, if he really earns it, is cheaper to you than the $1 a day man. And you can afford nothing so ill as to turn away from the idea, from the conception, that American labor is supreme because it is intelligent and not because it gets higher wages. That is a false reasoning; you are putting the cart before the horse. American labor gets higher wages because it is more valuable. Now, any intelligent labor can compete with any pauper labor and the intellectual absurdity of "protecting" intelligent men from unintelligent is too patent to need explanation. When I hear the reports that tell of protecting the American laborers that I know against the pauper labor of Europe I can only smile that my fellow voters are so gullible.

Now, gentlemen, you cannot afford to be narrow in the presence of change and you cannot afford to think that your legislators and your executives are bringing change upon you. Neither can you afford to think that you can take no guiding part in the change. We are facing a new age, with new objects, new objects of American trade and manufacture, because the minute you begin to make models for foreign sale you have to change the machinery, the whole point of view. We are facing new objects with new standards, the standards of cosmopolitan intelligence instead of provincial intelligence, and with a new conception of what it means to produce wealth and produce prosperity. The prosperity of America has often been checked but it has seldom been aided by legislation. I wonder how any man can keep the red corpuscles in his blood from getting up and shouting when he realizes the age that we are entering upon.

I was saying to-day to some of the fellows out at Harvard that

I wished I had been born twenty years later so that I could have had twenty years more of this exhilarating century upon which we have entered, a century which greets the challenge to originative effort. This is no century for any man who looks over his shoulder; it is no century for any man who has no stomach for the facts that change even while he tries to digest them; a century in which America is to prove once more whether she has any right to claim leadership in the world of originative politics and originative economic effort. This is a century just as worth living in as was the eighteenth century, better worth living in than was the nineteenth century.

When I hear men say that you are attacking American civilization by proposing, not rapid but slow, steady—if necessary, organic—changes, to meet the facts, I wonder what they think of when they look at the flag of the United States. The flag of the United States stands for the biggest kick on record.

The flag of the United States, in my imagination, consists of alternate strips of white parchment upon which are written the aspirations of men, and streams of blood poured out to verify their hope, and in the corner of that flag sparkle the stars of those States that have one after another swung into the fir[m]ament to show that there is a God in Heaven, that men will not abandon hope so long as they have confidence in the God of Righteousness, the God of Justice, the God of Liberty. (Loud Applause.)[4]

Printed in *Woodrow Wilson on Efficiency* . . . *January 27, 1912* (n.p., n.d.). A copy of this pamphlet is in WP, DLC.
[4] There is a WWhw outline of this address, with the composition date of Jan. 24, 1912, in WP, DLC.

Two News Reports

[Jan. 28, 1912]

WILSON'S BUSY DAY

Meets Governor, Mayor and Introduced at City Club by Richard Olney

Governor Wilson spent a busy day yesterday, arriving in Boston at 6:30 a.m. and going to the Hotel Somerset. He was accompanied by Dudley Field Malone of New York. He was met by Mayor Fitzgerald after breakfast. Edward A. Filene also called.

A call was made on Governor Foss at the State House, at which no politics were discussed. Governor Foss personally showed Governor Wilson over the State House.

At noon the Boston City Club gave Governor Wilson a luncheon which was presided over by Richard Olney.

In introducing Governor Wilson, Mr. Olney said in part:

"I am about to present to you a man whose life work thus far is a conspicuous exhibit of the traits and convictions and accomplishments to which I have briefly referred.

"I am presenting him, not as a high official, nor as a candidate, nor as a Democrat, but as American citizen entitled to the respect and esteem of men of whatever political faith; as a man who has made good wherever he has been tried; who has proved his possession of the inestimable gift of leadership; who has vindicated the claims to regard of the 'scholar in politics'; who, sensible of the abuses which have come to disfigure the administration of popular government, has lost not a jot of faith in popular government itself; and who is of the type of men in whom lies the best hope for the country's future. I may add that he has a capacity and propensity for telling the truth which is not always to the advantage or satisfaction of those who ask for it."

About 300 attended the dinner. Governor Wilson said in part:

"Business men have been saying, 'Keep your hands off.' They seem to fear that their chief peril is that the legislators will interfere with their business. Business men stand off, defiant, and seem to dare the public men to do something. They take the attitude of mere spectators.

"This is wrong. The business men should co-operate with the legislators. Do you business men believe that economic conditions are fixed, immovable? Do you really want them to leave you alone?

"If you know there is something wrong, why not get together with your public men and try to have them adjusted?"

❖

Glad He's a Schoolmaster
Wilson Tells Harvard Men He Thanks God He Is a Free Man

Twenty-five hundred students and members of the faculty of Harvard University packed practically every available inch of space in Sanders Theatre, Cambridge, yesterday afternoon to hear Governor Woodrow Wilson state the principles upon which he is a candidate for the Democratic nomination for the presidency and to listen to a severe but humorous arraignment of the tariff.

The demonstration that greeted Governor Wilson's appearance on the stage, which is usually reserved for commencement and strictly official functions, was unusually vigorous and lasted several minutes.

The New Jersey executive was accompanied by R. W. Stewart of the Harvard Democratic Club and introduced by W. M. Mc-Dermott of the Harvard Wilson Club,[1] under whose auspices the meeting was held.

The Governor won his crowd immediately and swept the theatre with a gale of laughter by attributing a dizziness, not to his liver, as his physician had inferred, but to the eminence attributed to him by his introducer.

"The disturbances today," said Governor Wilson, "are mainly evidence that everybody has neither the same nor the right point of view. I am sometimes very much surprised when educated men state to me as their opinion that this is a period of strife stirred up by violent agitators who are striking at the very fundamentals and attacking the very structure of our government. I have never learned that the structure of a government determined its fundamentals."

Inquiring into the fundamentals of the American government, Mr. Wilson stated that they were generally understood to be "liberty and equal opportunity, self-government and action in the common good. This is a government in which no one group of men is supposed to have the power to say 'you must,' but one in which the government says to all men alike 'you may.'" He then likened the best government to a locomotive, the power and freedom of which, he declared, were dependent upon the adjustment of the parts so as to eliminate friction.

"No man is free, however," continued Mr. Wilson, "when all his time, all his energies of mind and body must be directed to providing for himself and those dependent upon him for a living. He then becomes a slave to necessity. You cannot submerge a mass of men completely in a rigid economic order and then expect them to find the leisure to carry on government for themselves.

"The men whom I most respect today are the men who are fighting to put the government back into the hands of the people. Suppose you have a government in form representative, and in reality not; suppose it has a vast machinery and you are a legislator who goes to a State capital for legislative deliberation, at the same time having a business which necessitates going to a bank for funds to carry on that business, what condition of government have you if the bank will not loan you funds unless you allow it to dictate your policy? Much the same government as we were having when a member of the New Jersey Legislature came to me and said: 'Governor, I wish to God I could be with you, but they have my notes.'

"The whole aspect of these things changes when they are dragged out into the light. My course in New Jersey has been likened to that of a schoolmaster. My course in New Jersey, gentlemen, has been that of playing the schoolmaster, for it is easy for a schoolmaster to find out all about things and then tell all he knows, and I thank God I am merely a schoolmaster and a free man.

"Our grasp on the fundamentals of the American government," Governor Wilson concluded, "has been weakened in the strain of our economic development in the past century. But Americans are making ready to reclaim their birthright, and the evidences of the awakening are in the present day disturbances. The nation is bethinking itself of its fundamentals and is ready to re[e]stablish their fame and majesty."[2]

Printed in the *Boston Post*, Jan. 28, 1912.
[1] Roscoe Winfield Stewart of Forsyth, Mo., LL.B. Harvard 1912; Malcolm Mallette McDermott of Knoxville, Tenn., Princeton 1910, LL.B. Harvard 1913.
[2] There is a WWhw outline of this speech, dated Jan. 27, 1912, in WP, DLC.

To Nathan Straus

My dear Mr. Straus: [Trenton, N. J.] January 29, 1912.

Thank you sincerely for your letter of January twenty-sixth.[1] I have marveled, as you have, at the extraordinary change that has taken place in Colonel Watterson. I cannot even conjecture the cause of it. At the conference which has been so much talked about, he was eager to act in my interest, and everything was done and said in apparent friendliness.

I value very highly your generous approval. It is very delightful to have such friends.

Cordially yours,   Woodrow Wilson

TLS (N. Straus Papers, NHpR).
[1] It is missing.

From Richard Heath Dabney, with Enclosure

My dear Woodrow: [Charlottesville, Va.] 29 Jan., 1912.

For very important reasons I decided last night to postpone the organization of the Wilson Club that was advertised for tonight. I will explain these reasons when I see you on Thursday. It was a sore disappointment to me, and it required a great inward struggle on my part, but I feel even more confident today than I did then, that I did what was best for your interests. I didn't get to bed till 4 o'clock.

I shall spend Wednesday night with Lewis Aylett at Ginter Park in the environs of Richmond. We shall breakfast about eight Thursday morning, and I expect to get to the Jefferson shortly after nine and hope you can arrange for a conference with me soon after I get there. What I have to tell you may influence your entire policy with regard to Virginia, & not simply with regard to Charlottesville.

But I will now speak of another matter. I enclose a letter from Stewart Bryan. The editorial to which he refers was in the *World* of Jan. 25 & is entitled "Woodrow Wilson's Weakness." Be sure to get it, and to consider whether you will comply with the request to explain the reasons for your change of opinion on several matters. For fear you may not see the paper, I will briefly state its gist. It considers Bryan as your "most conspicuous weakness among the thoughtful Democrats of the country." It does not wish you to repudiate his support, but wishes to know why, after wishing to have him knocked into a cocked hat in 1907, you now eulogize him as "the one man whose broadened mind has been able to see what is the matter and to point it out to the public." It desires to know *when* & *how* Mr. Bryan's mind "broadened." Likewise it demands reasons for your change of view on the initiative & referendum. The last two paragraphs are:

"Gov. Wilson's greatest political assets are not the support of Col. Harvey or the support of Mr. Bryan or the support of any man or any faction, but his own brilliant abilities & his reputation for straightforward sincerity, for intellectual as well as financial & political integrity.

"This is a heritage that he cannot afford to place in jeopardy, regardless of any man's political favor. It is a heritage that he should conserve by the clearest & most forceful explanation that he can make of every change in his political beliefs. Otherwise he will have sold his birthright for a mess of pottage—and Bryan pottage is no better than any other pottage."

I shall not undertake to advise you to turn your speech into the line indicated by this editorial—in other words, into an explanation of the evolution of your opinions on Bryan & the initiative & referendum—but I thought you ought to have the chance to consider it. I know that your attitude to Bryan is what disturbs many Va. conservatives.

Well, *au revoir!* and good luck!

Affectionately & faithfully   R. H. Dabney.

P.S.—30 Jan.—I have been invited by Archie Patterson to break-fast with you at the Jefferson Thursday morning.   R.H.D.

ALS (WP, DLC).

E N C L O S U R E

John Stewart Bryan to Richard Heath Dabney

Dear Uncle Dab.:   Richmond, Virginia January 26, 1912.

I was in New York on Tuesday and Wednesday, and while I was there I took upon myself to go down to the N. Y. World office and talk to their chief men about Woodrow Wilson. That paper admires Wilson, and thinks he is the best man that can be nominated by the Democrats, but is not committed to him. After a consultation with the Editor of the World,[1] he agreed to write an editorial intended to bring out Wilson's real convictions, and I am enclosing you this editorial herewith for your inspection. Please return.

When Governor Wilson comes to Richmond, which I hope he will do on February 1st, he will have an opportunity to tell Virginia exactly how and why he is in his present position. I believe a statement of this sort from him will be worth more to his cause than any other single thing that could be done.

Do not give all your time to Lewis Aylett.

Faithfully yours,   J.S.B

P.S. We will print your interview about Woodrow Wilson.[2]

TLS (WP, DLC).
    [1] Frank Irving Cobb.
    [2] "Wilson Honest and Truthful," Richmond *Times-Dispatch*, Jan. 27, 1912. Anyone really knowing Wilson, Dabney said, was convinced of the absurdity of the notion that "he could possibly treat any friend with cold, heartless, over-bearing ingratitude." Watterson's statement was on the face of it self-contradictory.

A News Report

[Jan. 30, 1912]

"ADMITS OF NO COMMENTARY"

Governor Wilson Declines to Make Any Further Answer to Watterson's Statement.

ONLY REGRETS FRIENDSHIP

TRENTON, Jan. 30.—When Governor Wilson walked into a group of newspaper men waiting in his office at the State house this morning upon his arrival from Princeton, he smiled broadly as they rushed toward him with copies of the latest Watterson statement[1] in their hands.

"Good morning, gentlemen, I'm glad to see you," he said, as he waited, expectantly.

A dozen questions were thrown at him all together.

"This is what I will say," said the Governor, "and I wish you would take it down exactly. 'A statement like that admits of no commentary from me.' "

"Why?" asked one of his interviewers.

"I hoped that was evident," responded Governor Wilson.

"How do you like the idea that Colonel Watterson has upheld your version of Senator Smith's attitude toward the United States Senatorship?"[2]

"I find that story interesting," parried the Governor.

In answer to questions, Governor Wilson made it definitely plain that he was absolutely willing that Colonel Watterson should make public anything and everything he had touching on the situation.

The Governor made it plain, too, that while his relations with Colonel Watterson had been of a very friendly nature, he intended to recede not a whit from his statement that neither he nor any one authorized by him had ever asked Colonel Watterson to raise funds for the Wilson campaign. The Governor's face became sober as he added: "I am only sorry that I have to regret a friendship which, while it lasted, I found interesting and enjoyable."

Asked if he did not mean to say the loss of friendship, the Governor replied that he preferred to have the statement stand as he had dictated it.

The Governor said there would be no further statement on the subject.

Printed in the *Newark Evening News*, Jan. 30, 1912.

[1] "To the Democrats of the United States," a 2,000-word statement published in the newspapers on January 30, 1912.

[2] The reporter referred to Watterson's comment about the meeting at Deal, N. J., on June 26, 1910, attended by Wilson, Harvey, Watterson, and James Smith, Jr. "Mr. Smith," Watterson wrote, "declared that he wanted nothing for himself; only to see the State redeemed; that no one but Dr. Wilson could redeem it and the like." New York *World*, Jan. 30, 1912.

To Mary Allen Hulbert Peck

Dearest Friend,   Princeton, New Jersey 31 Jan'y, 1912

My last letter *did* just miss the *Bermudian*; no doubt this one will join it and go by the same steamer. But you will not *mind* getting two at once, will you? It's 'write when I can' *now*,—things

move faster and faster and with an ever thickening plot and I
am caught by some new turn of the play almost every day. What
you may be sure of is, that, whether I think of this or that, go
here or there, I never forget, even for a little interval, the dear
friend to whom my thoughts go, whether my words do or not.
I am mortified, none the less, when my letters miss, because
I know what it means to you,—particularly just now,—to know,
by visible token and spoken word, that your friends are thinking
of you,—thinking *with* you. Ever since that little note came in
which you showed how sensitive you had grown to every sign,—
and ever since I perceived, or thought I perceived, that you were,
in a way at least, shunning the society you used to enjoy and
so shine in that you took it with zest even when it was dull and
unpleasing, I have realized what you were suffering, and it has
moved me to the deepest sympathy. You are very proud; you
have carried your trials off hitherto with a sort of triumphant
concealment; no one has been permitted to see that you were
mortified! Now that your unhappy marriage is about to be acknowledged and talked about you shiver. Your pride is hurt.
Moreover, your principles are outraged. You have talked, sometimes, like an insurgent; you have pretended that you despised
conventions; but I, for one, have never been deceived. I have
always felt in you, and deeply admired, your essential reverence
for obligations undertaken; your indomitable *integrity* of thought
and action,—the thoughtful, serious, noble, faithful woman underneath the gayety and sometimes reckless *professions* of the
brilliant lady of fashion and of pleasure. The tastes that displayed themselves in *action* were always innocent and generally
elevated and sharply distinguished from those of many of the
people about you, whom you laughed with and at. You used to
seem to me obviously lonely in their company. But you have
found *some* who comprehended,—comprehended entirely and
with a thrill of admiration, confidence, and affection. They *still*
comprehend, and sympathize and admire,—ah so deeply. Cannot
they cheer and steady and suffice you. Oh! I *hope* they can!

What is happening to me? Nothing new. Constant bitter
attacks, winning me new friends. A constantly growing and
strengthening boom. I am well, though every fibre of me is tried
out every day. In the midst of the growing hurly-burly, calm
thoughts turn to you,—and now, in words, go to you with affectionate messages from all

Your devoted friend   Woodrow Wilson

ALS (WP, DLC).

To Robert Bridges

My dear Bobby,   Princeton, New Jersey 31 Jan'y, 1912
    The third cheque received, with the same feelings,—and with the warmest affection for the sender.
    Always   Faithfully Yours,   Woodrow Wilson

ALS (WC, NjP).

From Edith M. Whitmore[1]

My dear Mr. Wilson: [Staten Island, N. Y., Jan. 31, 1912]
    You may remember at the Staten Island fair[2] you were decorated with a Woman Suffrage Party sash, which we hoped expressed your sentiments, or at least expresses them now.
    As many thousands of women are going to vote for you in the West may I ask for publication in our New York papers if those votes are not legal according to our Federal Constitution? If so why are they not legal if cast in New York? I have voted in Colorado; am I constitutionally disfranchised in New York?
    Also I wish to ask if you favor woman suffrage and if elected will you openly do so?
    I ask this information for publication and shall deem it a favor to your admirers if you will let us know your stand on this, the issue of the year.
    Cordially for the betterment of the country,
                                    Edith M. Whitmore.

Printed in the New York *Sun*, Feb. 10, 1912.
    [1] Chairwoman in Richmond Borough of the Woman Suffrage Party.
    [2] Actually, the Richmond County Fair, on September 3, 1911. Trenton *True American*, Sept. 4, 1911.

From Emmett C. Davison[1]

Sir,   [Richmond, Va.] Feb. 1, 1912.
    As the representative of organized labor and the organized farming interests of Virginia, I have been directed to address you as a representative of progressive Democracy as to your position on the following questions:
    Should convicts be employed in competition with free labor?
    Is road-making practical employment for convicts?
    Is the manufacturing of articles for state use a practical way of employing convicts? If not, how, in your opinion, should convicts be employed?

What is your opinion as to the advisability of leasing the most desperate element of a state's prison population to private contractors?

Do or do you not believe that such leasing would add to the viciousness of the desperate element by bringing it in direct competition with the working men and women of a state?

I would greatly appreciate an early reply, and beg to remain,

Yours very truly,   E. C. Davison

Printed in the Richmond *News Leader*, Feb. 2, 1912.
[1] Lobbyist in Richmond for the Virginia Federation of Labor, later secretary-treasurer of the International Association of Machinists.

An Address to the General Assembly of Virginia and the City Council of Richmond[1]

[[Feb. 1, 1912]]

Your Excellency, Mr. Speaker, Your Honor,[2] Gentlemen of the General Assembly of Virginia, and of the Council of the City of Richmond, Ladies and Gentlemen:

I face this great audience to-night with a mixture of emotions. I am glad to feel like a boy who has come home to report in some degree to his neighbors, not about myself, but about the things that I have seen, or tried to see clearly, happening in the great communities of which we constitute a part.

I am not going to hold the distinguished gentlemen who have introduced me[3] responsible for the terms in which they have presented me to you. I am ready to believe, if anything should happen to me that is untoward, that they have uttered not a critical judgment, but have spoken according to the dictates of their hearts. They have been welcoming me home—they have not been telling you exactly what I am.

And yet, the voice of a friend melts the heart, and I, for my part, feel it very difficult here to-night to make an address from which the sentimental emotions that rise in me are left out. I have on my lapel a badge which, if I followed the dictates of good taste, perhaps I should not wear, for it bears my own name; but it was pinned on my coat by one of the delegation from Staunton[4]—my native place—(applause)—and I know that you

[1] Delivered in the evening in the city auditorium.
[2] Governor William Hodges Mann, Speaker Richard E. Byrd, and Mayor David Crockett Richardson.
[3] Richardson, Mann, and Byrd.
[4] A special train had brought some three hundred Wilson supporters from Staunton and sixteen from Charlottesville.

will indulge me in the sentiment which has led me to leave it there, not as a token of egotism, but as a token of my appreciation of the welcome which has been extended me.

You have been told to-night that the eyes of the nation were centered upon me. I hope not. That is very awkward. (Laughter.) I do not like to believe that the eyes of the nation are centered upon me. I do like to believe that the thoughts of the nation are centered upon the great questions which I, among many others, have tried honestly and fearlessly to expound—(applause)—because we are just now seeking to show our devotion, not to persons, but to a cause—a fundamental cause, a cause to which the whole history of America has been a commendatory example.

I could not stand before this audience of my one-time neighbors—for there are a great many men behind me, at any rate, if not in front of me, who have known me ever since I was a boy —and try to pose myself as an important figure. They would see through it. (Laughter.) I remember the story of an innocent old woman who went into the side-show of a circus and saw, or supposed that she saw, a man read a newspaper through a two-inch board. She got up in great excitement and said, "Here, let me out of here; this is no place for me to be with these thin things on." (Laughter and applause.) I fear that the disguise of greatness would be too transparent; and yet I do feel that every man should, who believes in the great ideals of this country and in their translation into action, stand up in every company and proclaim the faith that is in him, so that by common counsel and by common action we may achieve something for this great nation.

I have heard men complain of the changes of the times. I have heard men counsel that we stand still and do nothing. How futile the counsel is! Do you remember the quaint story of the Scottish highlander who went into the market at Edinburgh, followed by his dog? He went to a fishmonger's stall and the dog incautiously dropped his tail into a basket of lobsters, and one of the lobsters nipped his tail. Whereupon the dog went yelping down the street, with the lobster bouncing after. The fishmonger said, "Hoot, mon; whussle to your dog!" "Hoot!" said the Scotchman, "whussle to your lobster." (Laughter and applause.)

Now if you think some of your leaders are going too fast a pace, don't whistle to them. Whistle to the spirit of the age. Whistle to the questions that have whipped their consciences and dominated their understandings. They cannot stop if they are going to keep up with the great transmutations of affairs. For, gentlemen, whether we have realized it or not, we have entered a new age, and I have comforted myself with the thought as I journeyed towards Virginia again, that Virginia had never been daunted by a new age; with however debonair and young and confident a genius, Virginia led a great nation and helped to create a great nation in a new age. (Applause.)

I have heard men say that it was un-American to criticize the institutions we are living under. I wonder if they remember the significance of the American flag—the first insurgent flag that was flung to the breeze—the flag that represented the most colossal "kick" that was ever taken in political transactions; a flag that I can not look at without imagining that it consists of alternate strips of parchment upon which are written the fundamental rights of man, alternating with the streams of blood by which those rights had been vindicated and validated. (Applause.) In the blue sky of the corner there are swung star after star of commonwealths of free men who were setting up their own homes upon the principles of those vindicated rights.

Do you suppose that I will believe, or that any one knowing the history of America or the history of Virginia will believe, that it is inconsistent with being an American and a Virginian to propose that you construct liberty for each successive age, and that if necessary you reconstruct liberty for each successive age? If I had happened to get that breath out of my lungs in my absence from the Old Dominion, it would enter them again as I came back to her. (Applause.) I have not lost it elsewhere. The handsome contagion has infected the whole of the great nation. Do not suppose that the people of New Jersey have not seen visions, and dreamed dreams. Some gentlemen in some initial quarters wanted to suppress the dreams. (Laughter and applause.) It made the sleep of some men, in some quarters, uneasy that they should be haunted by those visions, but they never went out of the thought or the sleepless eyes of those great multitudes of men for whom happiness depends upon freedom, for whom self-respect depends upon freedom and principle, and in New Jersey as everywhere else they have drunk of those fountains which first began to flow in Virginia, those fountains by which we constantly renew our youth, and devote ourselves generation after generation to the preservation of the institutions of America.

I want, if possible, to explain to this great body of thinking persons the age in which we live, as it seems to me to present itself. Why, ladies and gentlemen, in our age every question is new. Every question that faces America is just as new now as were the questions that faced America in 1776. I do not mean that we are upon the verge of a revolution. I do not mean that passion is stirring which will upset the ancient foundations of our political order; but I do mean that life has changed under our very eye, so that what we do will have to be adjusted to almost absolutely new conditions, and I want that you will bear with me to point out just what I mean.

You know that one of the great questions that faces this great country is the question of conservation. Now just what do you mean by conservation? Do you mean the big thing, or do you mean the little thing? The little thing, though big in itself, but little by comparison, is the renewal of our forests, the protection of our great water powers against further depletion, the safeguarding of our mineral resources against waste and extravagance, the keeping in store as long as may be of those things which can not be renewed, and may even within a generation, some of them, come to the point of exhaustion.

That is the question of conservation as most men discuss it; but is that all? It seems to me that the fundamental question of conservation in America is the conservation of the energy, the elasticity, the hope of the American people. (Applause.) I deal a great deal with friends, for I have had such friends all my life, who are engaged in manufacturing in this country, and almost every one of them will admit that while he studies his machinery, and will dismiss a man who overtaxes the machinery so that its bearings get heated, so that the stress of work is too much for it, so that it is racked and over-done, not a man of them dismisses a superintendent because he puts too great a strain upon the souls and hearts of his employees. (Applause.) We rack and exhaust and reject the man machine, and we honestly, economically, thoughtfully preserve the steel machine; for we can get more men—we have only to beckon to them; the streets are full of them waiting for employment; but we can not, without cost, get a new machine.

Now that kind of conservation is a great deal more than the question of overstraining the factories. If I knew my business and were a manufacturer, what would I do? I would create such conditions of sanitation, such conditions of life and comfort and health as would keep my employees in the best physical condition, and I would establish such a relationship with them as would make them believe that I was a fellow human being, with a heart under my jacket, and that they were not my tools, but my partners.

Then you would see the gleam in the eye, then you would see that human energy spring into expression which is the only energy which differentiates America from the rest of the world. (Applause.) Men are used everywhere, men are driven under all climes and flags, but we have boasted in America that every man was a free unit of whom we had to be as careful as we would be of ourselves. America's economic supremacy depends upon the moral character and the resilient hopefulness of our workmen. So I say, when you are studying questions of conservation, realize what you have been wasting, the forests, water, minerals and the hearts and bodies of men. That is the new question of conservation. I say new, because only in our day has the crowding gotten so close and hot that there is no free outlet for men. Don't you remember that until the year 1890, every ten years when we took the census, we were able to draw a frontier in this country? It is true that in what is called the golden age, 1849, when gold was discovered in California, we sent outposts to the Pacific and settled the further slope of the Rocky Mountains. But between us and that slope, until 1890, there intervened an unoccupied space where the census map makers could draw a frontier. But when we reached the year 1890 there was no frontier discoverable in America.

What did that mean? That meant that men who found conditions intolerable in crowded America no longer had a place free where they could take up land of their own and start a new hope. That is what that meant, and as America turns upon herself her seething millions and the cauldron grows hotter and hotter, is it not the great duty of America to see that her men remain free and happy under the conditions that have now sprung up? It is true that we needed a frontier so much that after the Spanish War we annexed a new frontier some seven thousands miles off in the Pacific. But that is a long cry, and it takes the energy of a very young man to seek that outlet in the somewhat depressing climate of the Philippines.

So we now realize that Americans are not free to release themselves. We have got to live together and be happy in the family. I remember an old Judge who was absolutely opposed to divorce, because he said that a man will be restless as long as he knows he can get loose—(laughter)—but that so soon as it is firmly settled in his mind that he has got to make the best of it, he finds a sudden current of peace and contentment. Now there is no divorce for us in our American life. We have got to put up with one another, and we have got to see to it that we so regulate and assuage one another that we will not be intolerable to each other. We have got to get a *modus vivendi* in America for happiness, and that is our new problem. And I call you to witness it *is* a new problem. America never had to finish anything before; she has been at liberty to do the thing with a broad hand, quickly, improvising something and go on to the next thing; leave all sorts of waste behind her, push on, blaze trails through the forest, beat paths across the prairie. But now we have even to stop and pave our streets, we are just finding that out. I suppose it was good for the digestion to bump over the old cobble stones, but it was not good for trade, and we have got to pull up the cobble stones and make real sidewalks that won't jolt the life out of us. Let these somewhat whimsical comparisons serve to illustrate what I am talking about.

Now there is another new thing in America, and that is trade. Will you laugh at me and say, "Why, America has been supreme in trade ever since she was created." Has she? We have traded with one another, but we have traded with nobody else in proportions worth mentioning. Yes, we have in grain, in the great food stuffs, but do you know what is happening? Our food stuff exports, our grain exports are falling, falling, falling, not because we produce less, but because we need more ourselves. We are getting nearer and nearer to the point where we will ourselves consume all that our farms produce. Then we will not have anything with which to pay our balance, will we? Yes, we will, because while our exports of grain have been falling, our exports of manufactured articles have been increasing by leaps and bounds.

But under what circumstances? Long ago, after we had forgotten the excellent things that the first generation of statesmen had done for us in America, we deliberately throttled the merchant marine of the United States, and now it is so completely throttled that you are more likely to see the flag of the little kingdom of Greece upon the seas than the flag of the United States. And you know that the Nation that wants foreign commerce must have the arms of commerce. If she has the ships, her sailors will see to it that her merchants have the markets. I am not arguing this to you, I am telling you, for the facts, if we look but a little ways for them, will absolutely demonstrate this circumstance, that we have more to fear in the competition of England, Germany and France, because of the multitude of English, French and German carriers upon the sea than we have to fear from the ingenuity of the English manufacturers or the enterprise of the German merchants.

Anybody who has dealt with railroads knows what I am talking about. Railroads in America have made and unmade cities and communities, have they not? They would do it now if they were not watched by the inter-state commerce commission. We are obliging them to work without discrimination now, but they at one time discriminated as they pleased, and they determined where cities were to grow and where cities were to decay.

Very well. The same thing is happening upon the high seas. The foreign carrier can tell you where you can go and where you cannot go. He can discriminate against you and in favor of his own merchants and manufacturers, and he will, because he does.

And while all this is going on, and we lack the means, we are fairly bursting our own jacket. We are making more manufactured goods than we can consume ourselves, and every manufacturer is waking up to the fact that if we do not let anybody climb over our tariff wall to get in, he has got to climb to get out; that we have deliberately domesticated ourselves; that we have deliberately cut ourselves off from the currents of trade; that we have deliberately divorced ourselves from world commerce; and now, if we are not going to stifle economically, we have got to find our way out into the great international exchanges of the world. There is a new question.

I was speaking in Boston the other evening at a real estate exchange, and I asked those gentlemen what is going to keep real estate values in Boston steady? I asked them if they realized what was likely to happen after the year 1915. You know that in that year it is likely that the great ditch in the Isthmus will be open for commerce. We are not opening it for America, by the way, because we haven't any ships to send through it; we are opening it for England and Germany. (Applause.) We are pouring out American millions in order that German exporters, English exporters and French exporters may profit by our enterprise; and when that is done, of course something is going to happen to America. I asked those gentlemen in Boston if, after that was done, the arteries of trade in this country would continue to run east and west. Some great arteries are going to open north and south. The great valley of the Mississippi is to be the home of teeming industries and of a ceaseless commerce. And then I wonder sometimes if it will not be colder still in the northeastern section of this country where Boston is situated. Those east winds, of which they are fond, will not bring them increasing commerce, perhaps, but they will hear the throb of that great heart in the center of the continent, which is shifting the center of gravity, which is throwing into different arteries the course of the blood of the great commercial world. Does that strike you as something happening in America that you cannot sit still and neglect? Hadn't you better "whussle to the lobster?" Don't whistle to the dog, but whistle to the lobster, if you think it will do any good, but I have never enticed a lobster by whistling.

There is another new question in America, and that is the question of business. Business is in a situation in America that it was never in before; it is in a situation to which we have not adjusted our laws. Our laws are still meant for business done by *individuals*; they have not been satisfactorily adjusted to business done by great *combinations*, and we have got to adjust them. I do not say we may or may not, I say we have got to, there is no choice. If your laws do not fit your facts, the facts are not injured; the law is damaged; so much the worse for the law, because the law, unless I have studied it amiss, is the expression of the facts in legal regulation. Laws have never altered the facts; laws have always necessarily expressed the facts, adjusted interests as they have arisen, and changed to one another.

When before, in the history of America, were the Congress of the United States and the Legislature of every State called upon in every session to intervene in the regulation of business? Never before our own age.

Now why is all this happening? Why has business taken on a new aspect in America? Why does it wear a face with which we are only by degrees becoming familiar? For a very interesting reason. An ever diminishing circle of men exercise a control in America with which only the Government itself can compete.

I am not one of those, ladies and gentlemen, who speak of the interests in big letters as if they were enemies of mankind. I know the natural history of the interests, and they grew just as naturally as an oak grows; some of them grew just as naturally as a weed grows. (Laughter.)

I am not here to enter an indictment against business. No man indicts natural history. No man undertakes to say the things that have happened by operation of irresistible forces are immoral things, though some men may have made deeply immoral uses of them. I am not here to suggest that the automobile be destroyed because some fools take joy rides in it. I want to catch the fools. I am not here, in other words, to suggest that the things that have happened to us must be reversed, and the scroll of time rolled back on itself. To attempt that would be futile and ridiculous. I am here to point out as clearly as I can what I believe to be the facts, and what most of you *know* to be the facts, because some of you have been considering these things longer than I have, and I have no doubt that you have seen things clearer in twenty years than I have seen them in twenty months.

I am not talking about things distant; I am talking about things that I have seen with my eyes and handled with my hands.

Now these things, if you will allow me to express them briefly —and to express them briefly means to express them imperfectly —these things amount to this, that a comparatively small number of men control the raw material of this country; that a comparatively small number of men control the water powers that can be made useful for the economical production of the power to drive our machinery almost entirely; that that same small number of men, by agreements handed around among themselves, control prices, and that that same group of men control the larger credits of the country.

Do you know that nobody can undertake the larger kind of undertakings without their approval and consent? There are very few men who can afford to stand up and tell you that, because there are very few men in my happy condition. I haven't any note in bank. (Applause.) I live within my income and I cannot be punished for what I say. (Applause.) But I know perfectly well, and I have been told by men who dared not speak above their breaths with regard to it for fear they would be punished, that I could not start a great enterprise in this country that needed a million or more of money to start it unless I made an agreement and combination with certain gentlemen who control the great credits of the country.

Now I am not hot in my mind against these gentlemen. They used the opportunities which we accorded them, and they have got us. Some of them are just as patriotic, just as public spirited, just as honest as any man in America. But when you have got the market in your hand, does honesty oblige you to turn the palm upside down and empty it? If you have got the market in your hand and believe that you understand the interest of the country better than anybody else, is it patriotic to let it go?

I was trying to analyze the other day what a republican is. (Laughter.) I do not want to say anything about that great body of my fellow countrymen in various parts of America who have formed the bad habit of voting the republican ticket. They are not the men I am talking about, but the republican leaders, the men who establish the ideals and policies of that party, how would you describe them? Why, I would say that they are men who actually believe that the only men whose advice it is safe to take with regard to the happiness and prosperity of America are the men who have the biggest material stake in the enterprises of America. They believe, therefore, that America ought to be governed by trustees—(applause)—and that those trustees are the managers of the oldest and greatest "vested interests" of the country. That is a workable theory, that is a theory that has obtained time out of mind. It happens, though these gentlemen have forgotten it, that America was established to get rid of it, but, having forgotten that, reading only the older books, I dare say, reading back of the birth of America, they say that there are only a few men with grasp enough of affairs and knowledge enough of what are the bases of prosperity to run a big, complicated government like this.

Now, as a Democrat—(applause)—I define myself by absolutely protesting against that view of public affairs. I will not live under trustees if I can help it. (Applause.) No group of men less than the majority has a right to tell me how I have got to live in America. I will submit to the majority, because I have been trained to do it, though I may have my private opinion even of the majority; but, being a dyed-in-the-wool Democrat, I am proud to submit my judgment to that majority of my fellow citizens.

I know that there are some gum-shoe politicians in both camps who do not agree with that theory at all. They say, "You need not say much about it out loud, but we have got to run these people; this enterprise of free government has to be personally conducted—(applause)—that the people want this or that we do not deny, but they do not know what is good for them."

So there are two theories of trusteeship, a trusteeship of the big interests and a trusteeship of the machine. I do not see my way to subscribe to either kind of trusteeship. Not that I am an insurgent, because I believe in organization; I believe that party success is impossible without organization; but I make this distinction between organization and the machine—organization is a systematic co-operation of men for a common purpose, while the machine is a systematic co-operation of men for a private purpose. (Great applause.) I know what I am talking about, because we have a perfect specimen in New Jersey.

Now I know what supports the machine, because I have seen them eat out of a spoon. It is a golden spoon, and I have seen the nurse that fed them, and I have seen that nurse absolutely impartial as between the Republican machine and the Democratic machine—(laughter and applause)—and the price of the food, the price of the nutrition, is that the machine will be good, that it will see that nothing is done that will hurt the nurse, that nothing is done which will interfere with the private understanding that is established in the nursery.

Now, this is our problem. We have got to set to work now systematically to conserve every resource and every energy of America. We have got to realize that an absolute readjustment of trade is necessary, and that that is an irresistible battering-ram that is battering at the wall of the tariff.

The tariff is not the question it was a generation ago. I hear gentlemen make speeches now who do not know that, but it is not. They talk as if it was a question of protecting us from external competition, while internal competition keeps prices down; and I happen to know that there is not any internal competition. (Applause.) And I happen to know that this great, irresistible energy of America is doing more than it can keep within its own shops and limits, and therefore it has got to be released for the commercial conquest of the world. Say what you will, whether you are abstractly for protection or against it, you have got to legislate for the release of the energies of America.

Then, in the next place, there is the whole matter of business adjustment. Our laws are just about a generation belated, as compared with economic conditions not only, but as compared with what other advanced nations have done to bring about adjustment. Progressive America is belated, has lost its leadership in the handsome competition to show the world the way out of its difficulties.

That is the problem, and that is the reason I say that the Twentieth century is better worth living in than any century that has turned up in our recollection, and that is the reason I return with confidence to Virginia and say: "You remember that your men saw such an age when this government was set up; is she daunted now to see another age that calls for constructive statesmanship; has she less vision now; has she lost courage now; has she lost the indomitable integrity now that she had then?" I wonder what will happen when Virginia sees these things with the veil withdrawn from her eyes. She will rejoice as a bridegroom coming out of his chamber; she will say, "Here is an age for Virginia again."

Now, what are we going to do about it?

A Voice—Elect Wilson. (Applause.)

Mr. Wilson—I hoped that you would not hear that. What is our problem? First of all, in order to move carefully, we have got to move by standard[s], have we not? You cannot launch out and trust to the currents. You have got to have something to steer by. You have got to know whither you are bound.

You know that curious expression, that very erroneous expression we have, when a man has lost his way in a forest or a desert. We say he has lost himself. Did you ever reflect that that is the only thing he has not lost? He is there, but what is lost is all the rest of the world. If he knew any fixed thing in his neighborhood and knew whether it was east of him, or north of him, or south of him, or west of him, he could steer; but he has lost even the points of the compass. He does not know how he is related to the universe. Now unless you have a standard to steer by, you are lost; how would you know in which direction to steer, and where you are going? If I want to go in that direction, this way is not my road. I have got to know whither I am bound and what landmarks to guide myself by.

Do we lack landmarks in America after all those ancient principles which we have set up like secret temples in which to go and worship and compose our spirits?

In the first place, we have the standards of liberty and equal opportunity. In the second place we have this standard that the people are entitled to a government which represents them—(applause)—and in the third place they are entitled to government by that government which is in the common interest and not in the interest of special privilege.

Are not these the temples of liberty in which we have worshiped? Will any man be charged justly with trying to upset the institutions of America who works in the spirit of the worship of those principles?

What is liberty? You say of a great locomotive engine that it runs free. What do you mean? You mean that its parts are so assembled and adjusted that friction is reduced to a minimum, and that it has perfect adjustment. What do you mean by saying that a boat sails free? Do you mean that she is independent of the great breath that is in the heavens? Do you not mean that she has accommodated herself with graceful obeisance with the winds? Throw her up in the wind and see her shiver in every stick and stitch of her, while, as a seaman would say, she is held in irons. But let her fall off, let her bow to the majesty of nature, and then she is free in her adjustment. Let these serve as images.

Human freedom consists in perfect adjustment of human interests to one another. The whole problem is a problem of adjustment, reducing the friction; not reducing it by mere lubrication—(applause)—not reducing it by merely pouring in the oil of money and persuasion and flattery, but by so adjusting the parts that they love to co-operate, that they never buckle up, that they never grow so hot that we cannot move the machine at all without danger. And unless there is this perfect adjustment there will not be given that opportunity without which men cannot draw a full breath or live a day without despair. Let any group of men have the right to say to others, "You must come to us before you can do anything," and see how long America will be considered a place worth living in by free men.

Our standards, therefore, are these, and we must fearlessly use them—we must say to ourselves, "We are going to reject everything that does not square with those things."

Now, what is the fact? I am happy to believe that Virginia has so far been spared the mortifying experience that has come upon some other States. A great many of the States of this Union, ladies and gentlemen, have been privately controlled. There has not been an adjustment, there has not been free opportunity, there has not been government that represented the people, there has not been government in the common interests. When changes are proposed in those commonwealths, do not fall upon those who propose them and say they are changing the character of our government; or, if you do, admit they are changing it back from what it has become to what it was originally intended to be. (Applause.) No man that I know of and trust, no man that I will consent to consort with, is trying to change anything fundamental in America. But what means have we of change? Suppose that every time you try to change your government, you have the experience that the enterprising people of New Jersey had for sixteen years together, when to choose between one ticket and another ticket was to choose between tweedle-dum and tweedle-dee. Suppose that every time public opinion unmistakably expressed itself, something invisible, something intangible, something that you could not get at, intervened between you and the action upon which you had determined, then what image would arise in your mind? That you are disappointed in your institutions as they were established? No. That you are mortified because of the change that has come over your institutions by the extent to which they have been debased.

Now you have got to choose between one of two things. I never saw this as I see it now until I came into actual, practical contact with the administration of a great State. I thank God that I have learned something in the last eighteen months, and what I have learned is this—that you have got to choose between two courses, either construtive leadership which you will stand behind to the limit, or else a resort direct to the people themselves. There are no other ways.

What does it mean, ladies and gentlemen, that all over the United States people are demanding of their Governors and of their President that they take the affairs of those people in their own hands, demanding of them leadership, not satisfied that they are honest, merely, not satisfied with their good intentions, merely, but demanding of them that they shall translate their intentions into such persuasive government that nothing can withstand them as spokesmen of the people? That is what America is demanding.

I want to tell you a story, if you will allow me; I have told it very often, but most of you probably have not heard it. While Mr. Roosevelt was President, I boarded a train near my home one day and I found one of the gentlemen who were then Senators from New Jersey on the train. I dropped into the seat beside him. I found him in a very bad humor. I said, "Senator, what is the matter?" "Oh," he said, "I wish the Constitution had not given the President the right to send messages to Congress." "Why," I said, "Senator, you are barking up the wrong tree. That is not what is the matter. The trouble is that the President publishes his messages, and if the country happens to agree with him it does not stop to hear what you have to say." The President is the only member of the government of the United States elected by the whole people of the United States; he is the only one whose utterances go into all the newspapers of the United States; and inasmuch as he has a universal audience and nobody else has, nobody can answer him; and if he happens to speak the opinion of the country nobody can resist him. (Applause.) America has got the zest for that in its imagination, and it is unquiet if it does not get a President that will do that sort of thing; and I will tell you, having ridden a restive State myself, that the people in most of the States are very uncomfortable, and full of protest if their Governors do not do it. They do not want their Governors to exercise any unconstitutional power; but what is a more constitutional power than the power of public opinion? What is more persuasive and irresistible than the voice of universal conviction? That is the force that can bring back representative government in America where it has been lost. Thank God there are a great many places where it has not been lost. It is a local question which each community can settle for itself.

But if you cannot get constructive leadership, then what? If, every time you try it, somebody defeats the puropse which your leader expresses, what are you going to do about it?

I want to read you a passage from the Virginia Bill of Rights, that immortal document which has been a model for declarations of liberty throughout the rest of the continent.

"That all power is vested in and consequently derived from the people; that magistrates are their trustees

and servants, and at all times amenable to them."
Did you ever hear the doctrine put more flatly?

"That government is, or ought to be, instituted for the common benefit, protection and security of the people of the nation or community; of all the various modes and forms of government, that is the best which is capable of producing the greatest degree of happiness and safety and is the most effectually secured against the danger of mal-administration; and, when any government shall be found inadequate or contrary to these purposes, a majority of the community hath an indubitable, inalienable and indefeasible right to reform, alter or abolish it, in such manner as shall be judged most conducive to the public weal."

I have heard that read a score of times on the Fourth of July, but I never heard it read where actual measures were being debated. (Applause.) Now I am willing to come back to Virginia and stand with George Mason on the Bill of Rights. When I do that, I have got native soil under my feet, soil more fertile for the growth of liberty than any soil that can be compounded. (Applause.) And I say that if we cannot get constructive leadership, and we can if we will, then we have our solution in the Bill of Rights, "A majority of the community hath an indubitable, inalienable and indefeasible right to reform, alter or abolish it as may be judged most conducive to the public weal." I do not propose anything of that sort, I do not believe it is necessary, but I do like a gun behind the door. (Applause.) I do like to say to people, "Well, if you can't bring the game down any other way, go and get your gun."

There are wise and unwise ways of shooting. I had rather pepper the animal than kill him, I had rather touch him once than deprive him of vitality. But you can load your gun according to your own taste; you do not have to put buckshot in it, you can put the smallest birdshot in it that you can find, and then at your leisure afterwards pick it out of the hide. But always remember that behind you like a bulwark is that Bill of Rights, that you have the right to any kind of government you please to have. That is the kind of insurgent I am, because all the while I remember the temper of America. I honestly believe that a better nation, more long enduring, more patiently suffering, more conservative people does not exist upon God's planet. I am not afraid of the American people getting up and humping themselves; I am only afraid they will not; and when I hear of popular vote spoken of as mob government, I feel like telling the man who utters that that he has no right to call himself American. (Applause.) Just picture to yourselves, ladies and gentlemen, the great voting population of Virginia, from the sea to the far borders in the mountains, going calmly, man by man, to the polls, expressing their judgment about public affairs, and ask yourselves if that is your image of a mob.

What is a mob? A mob is a body of men in hot contact with one another, moved by a single, ungovernable passion upon doing a hasty thing that they will regret the next day. Do you see anything resembling a mob in that voting population of the countryside, men tramping over the mountainside, men going to the general store up in the village, men going in little conversing groups to cast their ballots—is that your notion of a mob, or is that your picture of free self-governing people?

I am not afraid of the judgments so expressed, if you give men time to think, if you give them a clear conception of the things they are to vote for; because the deepest conviction and passion of my heart is that the common people, by which I mean all of us, are to be absolutely trusted. (Applause.) The peculiarity of some representatives, particularly of the Republican party, is that when they talk about the people, they obviously do not include themselves. Now if, when you think of the people, you are not thinking about yourself, then you do not belong in America. I, on the other hand am liberal and generous enough, when I speak of the people, to include them. (Applause.) They do not deserve it, but then I cannot, if I am true to my principles, exclude them, they have got to come in. You know that delightful expression Horace Greeley, who was one of the generous advocates of a general amnesty to the Southern people, made use of in an eager argument one day. He said, "You know, we have got to forgive them, damn them." (Laughter and applause.) That is the only working program. You cannot have the people unless you include everybody, and therefore I am ready to admit everybody.

When I look back at the processes of history, when I look back at the genesis of America, I see this written over every page, that the nations are renewed from the bottom, not from the top; that the genius which springs up from the ranks of unknown men is the genius which renews the youth and energy of the people; and in every age of the world, where you stop the courses of the blood from the roots, you injure the great, useful structure to the extent that atrophy, death and decay are sure to ensue. That is the reason that an hereditary monarchy does not work; that is the reason that an hereditary aristocracy does not work, that is

the reason that everything of that sort is full of corruption and
ready to decay.

So I say that our challenge of to-day is to include in the partnership all those great bodies of unnamed men who are going
to produce our future leaders and renew the future energies
of America. And as I confess that, as I confess my belief in the
common man, I know what I am saying. The man who is swim-
ming against the stream knows the strength of it. The man
who is in the melee knows what blows are being struck and what
blood is being drawn. The man who is on the make is a judge
of what is happening in America, not the man who has made;
not the man who has emerged from the flood, not the man who
is standing on the bank looking on, but the man who is struggling for his life and for the lives of those who are dearer to him
than himself. That is the man whose judgment will tell you what
is going on in America, and that is the man by whose judgment
I for one wish to be guided—(applause)—so that as the tasks multiply and the days come when all will seem confusion and dis-
may, we may lift up our eyes to the hills out of these dark valleys
where the crags of special privilege overshadow and darken our
path, to where the sun gleams through the great passage in the
broken cliffs, the sun of God, the sun meant to regenerate men,
the sun meant to liberate them from their passion and despair
and to lift us to those uplands which are the promised land of
every man who desires liberty and achievement.[5]

Printed in *Address of Governor Woodrow Wilson to the General Assembly of
Virginia and the City Council of Richmond, delivered on February 1st, 1912*
(n.p., n.d.). A copy of this pamphlet is in WP, DLC.
[5] There is a WWhw outline of this address dated Jan. 31, 1912, in WP, DLC.

A News Report of Three Talks in Richmond

[Feb. 2, 1912]

STUDENTS CHEER GOVERNOR WILSON
Tells Them Not to Have Judgment Swayed
by People Who Call Names.

Before an audience which crowded the chapel of Richmond
College, Governor Woodrow Wilson yesterday morning spoke
briefly on the opportunities of young manhood, his remarks being
mainly addressed to the student body of Richmond College and
Richmond Academy, which filled the greater part of the hall.
While no direct reference was made to practical politics or to the
discussions now raging, one sentence in which he urged his

hearers not to let their judgment be influenced by "people who call names" was evidently construed by the audience as having a practical bearing on the Watterson-Harvey-Wilson controversy.

Governor Wilson reached the city yesterday morning about 7:40 o'clock, accompanied by Stuart G. Gibboney, of New York, an active leader of the Wilson campaign; Dudley Field Malone, of New York, and his private secretary, Mr. Meadsday.

He was met at Elba Station by George Bryan, secretary of the Woodrow Wilson Club, of Richmond, and a number of others, and escorted to breakfast at the Jefferson Hotel. During the hour after breakfast Richard Evelyn Byrd, Speaker of the House of Delegates; former Congressman Harry St. George Tucker and a number of others were callers.

Shortly after 10 o'clock Governor Wilson motored with his escort and members of the reception committee to Richmond College, where the chapel was already well filled with those desiring to hear him. On account of the illness of President [Frederic William] Boatwright, who is confined to his home with cold, Professor Metcalf[1] met the distinguished visitor and former president of Princeton University, and escorted him to the platform amid the cheering and singing of the students.

Dr. Metcalf introduced Governor Wilson as "the man Virginia claims, the man New Jersey owns, and the man whom the whole country wants." The New Jersey executive was given a typical college welcome, cheering, singing and hurrahing greeting him as he arose.

"There never was a time," said Governor Wilson, "when the realization of the dreams, hopes, ambitions, aspirations—call them whatever you may—of Democracy were nearer realization.

"I believe that the twentieth century will witness a new epoch —a new political era—or rather a recovery of the older days of self-possessed originative power that has distinguished public men of America in the past. We have no less originative power now, though we have allowed it to lie dormant."

He urged young men to take an interest in politics, to analyze issues and determine for themselves; to keep abreast of the times and be informed on public matters.

"I urge you," he said, "to make up your own minds on the questions which now confront us as a nation, and not to let your judgment be disturbed by the people who call names.

"I believe radicalism is necessary, for it means a stomach for facts. To my mind what some people term an objectionable radicalism is in reality the tearing of the veil of deception from our eyes so that we may see things as they are. Surgical operations are radical, but they are sometimes necessary."

Governor Wilson referred to having before spoken at Richmond College,[2] and impressed on the young men the great opportunities of the age in which they are living, and the wonderful prospect opening to men of the coming generation. At the conclusion of his address he shook hands with most of the members of the faculty and student body. Later, escorted by Mayor Richardson, Mr. Bryan and a number of others composing the committees of the State and city, he motored to the State Capitol, where he went at once to the office of Governor Mann, being presented by Edwin P. Cox, of the Richmond delegation in the House. After a brief call on Governor Mann in his private office, the two Governors led the way to the Senate chamber, where Lieutenant-Governor [James Taylor] Ellyson provided seats for both of the Governors on the platform, and where Governor Wilson was the recipient of much attention.

[1] John Calvin Metcalf, Professor of English at Richmond College.
[2] News reports of these lectures are printed at Oct. 28 and 29 and Nov. 1, 2, 4, and 17, 1898, Vol. 11.

❖

TAKES A SHOT AT BAD NEWSPAPERS

"I feel like a freshman standing before a body of seniors," said Governor Woodrow Wilson to the Senate of Virginia yesterday, acceding to the invitation of Lieutenant-Governor J. Taylor Ellyson to speak a few words to that body. . . .

"This unexpected demand upon me," said Governor Wilson, "is a positive test of my self-possession. I did not come with the intention of making a speech, and as a son of Virginia I cannot help feeling a sense of modesty when confronted suddenly with Virginia's most exalted legislative body.

"I have just been talking to a crowd of college students," said Governor Wilson, ["]and telling them about the tasks which lie immediately ahead of us. I always go away from such meetings with increased confidence in the future. The large body of thinking men that our colleges are sending out every year lead me to hope that the problems which shall confront us from time to time will not lack for men to meet them.

"I have been attending political meetings all of my life, and I cannot help observing that the meetings of to-day betray a seriousness and insight into political matters which ought to remove every fear or apprehension for the future. I can remember distinctly the time when political meetings were got up purely for the purpose of arousing enthusiasm and for making as much noise as possible. That time has passed. They are no longer solely a means of effervescence. Their purpose has become serious, and they are providing a means for sane discussion of the problems of the day. The great uneasiness which, we are told, is in progress in America to-day in all lines of activity should give us no apprehension because of the increasing seriousness with which the people are addressing themselves to the solution of their problems.

"In my recent trip across the American continent and back again," said the Governor, "I was impressed everywhere I went with the unity of feeling shown by the people on the really important questions which are confronting us to-day. The great readjustment which has been in progress the past score of years has resulted in a genuine community of feeling. Much of this is due to the quality of the modern press.

"The modern newspaper has had much to do with it, but I am inclined to place the greatest credit elsewhere. While I have no quarrel with most newspapers, and believe that as a rule they give us a mirror of the times, I believe that there are bad ones among them, particularly a few of them owned by certain men. These, I think, ought to be discriminated against.

"The weekly reviews and the monthly periodicals, in my opinion, have been chiefly instrumental in spreading abroad an accurate knowledge of measures and problems. They are performing a valuable service in creating an intelligent and impartial public opinion."

The present gathering, said Governor Wilson, carried him back to the time when Washington, Jefferson and other great Virginians were assembled in these very halls. Virginia, he thought, more than any other single State, has been rich in great individuals, and this he attributed to the common individuality which all Virginians have in comparison with the residents of other States, but which, in these particular individuals, was raised to its highest power.

The speaker apologized for the disjointed nature of his remarks, and said that he would feel more at home if he could join one or two of his college mates, whom he saw before him, in a song which they used to sing together at the university.

"I am glad to have had an opportunity to appear before you," concluded Governor Wilson. "I have wanted to come. I have wanted to let you see that I at least appear to be an honest man."

The Governor's last words took on an eloquent meaning for a

number of those present, who saw in them an allusion to present political disturbances, but nothing beyond this was said to lend color to that interpretation.

✧

HOUSE GIVES HIM WARM WELCOME

Obliteration of Sectional Feeling His Theme—
Jokes of University Days.

Immediately upon leaving the Senate chamber, Governors Wilson and Mann were taken in charge by the House reception committee, headed by Chairman Cox, and repaired to the hall of the House. A debate was in progress, but was halted by Speaker Byrd upon the appearance at the door of the distinguished guest.

"Mr. Speaker," shouted Doorkeeper S. M. Newhouse, "the Governor of Virginia and our distinguished guest, the Governor of New Jersey."

"The House of Delegates will arise and receive the Governor of New Jersey and the Governor of Virginia," said the Speaker. All arouse [arose], and the applause was hearty and spontaneous.

Advancing partly down the middile [middle] aisle with Chairman Cox, Governor Wilson halted, while the Speaker presented him to the House. On motion of Alden Bell,[1] the chair was ordered vacated for fifteen minutes, and Governor Wilson was escorted to the Speaker's chair.

"I know you don't want to hear a speech," began the guest. "There are so many good speeches made in this chamber, which is so celebrated for them, that I will not presume to enter into competition. It is with pleasure that I express my appreciation of being your invited guest.

"I am especially pleased that my introduction should have been by my old friend, the distinguished Speaker of this House. But I am glad he did not give me a full introduction. At the University of Virginia a good many things go on from day to day."

"And from night to night," interpolated Mr. Byrd amid the laughter of the House.

"I recall the days of the old athletic field, which used to be at the other end of Charlottesville from the university," said Governor Wilson, "and the place of popular resort where the fellows used to stop on the way through the street. While living at Princeton I was asked to act as a judge on some occasion at the University of Virginia, and while occupying a conspicuous place inside the oval some fellow shouted, 'Look at Wilson; he's as full as a tick.' Yet on that occasion I was entirely sober."

"My chief pleasure in coming here," pursued Governor Wilson, "is that of a boy coming back home. I cannot take myself seriously in this Capitol; I feel as though thirty years had fallen away as a garment. I wish, indeed, that thirty years would fall, so that I could have more years in which to experience the new era upon which we have entered. The period which we now face is fuller of hope and of achievement than any other time. I often think of what we might call the new character of America.

"I don't find sectional feeling, for instance, anywhere. There is no prejudice of North, or South, or East, or West. The time is at hand when our country will enjoy her greatest strength, because of the conglomeration of bloods and nationalities. There is a general protest against the use of the terms Irish-American vote, German-American vote, Jewish-American vote—all are American voters. All are being united in one blood of a common interest and a common purpose. The country rejoiced in grand old Joe Wheeler, who showed that a soldier could worthily wear the blue who had worthily worn the gray. We are coming to obliterate the divisions which once stood in the way of national united action.

"This assures the future of our land. And the impulses which arise are always lifting, lifting, lifting."

At the conclusion of his remarks, which were loudly applauded, Governor Wilson descended and stood in front of the clerk's desk, where the members and visitors were introduced to him one by one by Mr. Cox. He had a pleasant word for all, and was especially interested in those who hail from the Valley of Virginia.

When he retired from the hall, a motion was made and carried to have a group photograph on the south portico of the Capitol of the Senate and House, with Governor Wilson and Governor Mann. This done, the guest of Richmond was carried away to other scenes of the day's activities.

Printed in the Richmond, Va., *Times-Dispatch*, Feb. 2, 1912; some editorial headings omitted.
1 Lawyer of Culpeper.

An Address in Philadelphia to the Periodical Publishers' Association of America[1]

[[Feb. 2, 1912]]

Gentlemen, I am reminded very forcibly of a suggestion that a friend of mine made out West. He ventured the opinion that

1 Delivered in the grand ballroom of the Bellevue-Stratford Hotel.

if he could add the petition to the litany, it would be "From all introducers and traducers, Good Lord, deliver us," and yet I have been usually very fortunate, and I am very grateful to Providence for my traducers. I could not have chosen them more providentially myself. I face this audience with mingled feelings, because I remember how much I used to respect publishers, before they published anything for me, and I knew how far they could be imposed upon. I used to be afraid that they would not publish what I offered them, but now I am afraid they will.

Honestly, I don't see how some of you men can look one another in the face when I see some men here cheek by jowl. One gentleman had the courtesy to approach me just now with great good zeal and say that he was going to say just as ugly things about me as he could find. He was as modest about that as his good nature and his audacity would allow, and I can see how after that you can get along with one another.

You evidently mean it all in a perfectly Pickwickian sense. It is all in the day's work and in the business, and yet after all if one looks at a body of men like this and the seriousness of their vocation, it is perhaps the most serious that the nation experiences because it is through your medium and through the medium of what you do and what you write that the thought of the country is made up, and a singular circumstance of our time as it seems to me, gentlemen, is this.

There is no longer a literary caste in any country. That caste is broken. Anybody can write a book nowadays, and almost everybody does write a book. Everybody can find the corner in a newspaper where to express himself, and if he doesn't express himself something is said about him, and one way or other he gets into print, and the literary medium has become as common as the conversational medium. . . .[2]

Now the political caste is broken also. The old molds are broken up. It is necessary that they should assume some universal fashion of dress, instead of wearing those garments of a trade which they formerly professed. Everything is being broken open; everything is being exhibited to the public gaze; everything is being submitted to the public standard; everything is being universalized; the processes of politics along with the processes of literature; all our shelves are being broken, all our peculiar fashions are being merged.

The world is coming to think in common terms about everything, and everything is becoming common in the touch, and so I am the more astonished that there are some gentlemen who

[2] A brief garbled paragraph has been omitted.

find it impossible to think in the terms of actual facts. I am more astonished to hear gentlemen expressing themselves in formulas which no longer wear the color of reality. I am surprised to hear men thinking in the form who have opportunity of access to the substance.

This is a day of realities, because it is a day of exposure, and in this day of exposure, how is it that some men don't see that the world has changed, while that birth has been altered under their eyes, when they supposed that they were watching for it? What strikes me about our day is, gentlemen, that everything is new. Some men haven't discovered it, but the fact is so.

Everything is new and, therefore, every question that we touch wears a new aspect and must be approached from a new angle and, naturally, with new men. Now, gentlemen, it seems to me that the present day idea of conservation about which we talk so much is too limited in our view. Because we have been a spendthrift nation, we think that conservation means that we shall preserve the forests or create them anew, keep our water supply protected against further depredation, and see that our mines are not wasted and exhausted.

But that is not the question of conservation for America. That is only the obvious superficial part of the problem of conservation. The real thing that we have to conserve in America is the American people, their energy, their elasticity, their originative power, their capacity to hope and to achieve. Our task is to see that a great and ardent people are not depressed by conditions intolerable to the muscles and the nerves and the spirit.

Sometimes when I talk with manufacturers I realize how true it is that they study every piece of machinery that they are dealing with except the human machine. A man will dismiss an employee if he overdrives a delicate machine; he will see to it that it does not suffer a too great strain of work and motion. Yet he will not dismiss a superintendent who places a burden too hard to bear upon the muscles and the nerves and the spirits of the man whom he employs. He doesn't realize that we can throw machines upon the junk heap and make new ones.

But we cannot make a new people if we once sap them of their energy and their hope; and the real problem of our time, the real problem of production in America, is that human beings in America should be at their best when they produce, that they should be so treated with the processes of sanitation, that they should be so treated in the process of employment that they not only shall breathe like normal human beings, but they shall realize that they are not tools but partners.

If men want to make money, if they have hearts under their jackets, they will study these things, because only by these processes are the productive capacities of a nation raised to their highest point. And so I say the whole question of conservation in America is a new question, a big and far-reaching problem, because the intolerable pressure of economic conditions never rested upon America before. It now rests upon it, and we have got to lift and relieve that pressure in order to release America again for the kind of achievement that has made her distinguished.

We think we are a nation old in trade, but trade is a new question with America. When I hear gentlemen discuss the tariff question as if it were the tariff question that Mr. Blaine discussed, for example, I know they have been asleep ever since Mr. Blaine's day.

There are two circumstances to which I want to call your attention, and only two out of a great many that might be dwelt upon. You know that in the past we have paid the balances of trade principally by our vast exports of grain. Have you watched the grain exports recently? If you have, you will see that they have fallen, and fallen, and fallen, until we are just about to reach the point where we consume all of our own grain. It isn't that we are producing less, but we are consuming more, and the world will have to look elsewhere for its food than to America in the very near future unless we vastly increase by scientific processes the product of our fields.

At the same time have you noticed that the exports of our manufactured products have been increasing by leaps and bounds, and that has created an absolutely new situation for America? We have got to do what we never did before. We have got to know and we have got to take possession of foreign markets if we are to sell the surplus of our manufacturers. We don't know them save by deliberation. We have cut ourselves from them.

I don't know whose genius it was that led us to destroy our merchant marine, but we have destroyed it, as you are more likely to see the flag of little Greece upon the high seas than to see the flag of America, and you know that no nation can take possession of foreign markets unless it has arms to reach out and possess them (applause), and that the nation whose sailors carry the trade of the world will have merchants dominating the markets of the world, and only those who have a great part in the carrying trade can have a great part in the commerce.

We haven't observed these things, and we haven't been concerned about them, because of that vast experiment[3] that was going on when Mr. Blaine used to discuss the tariff question. It was the theory of that old declaration, and, although I myself do not favor it, I admit that it is arguable that although we were cutting ourselves off from foreign competition, there was so vast an area of free trade inside of America that competition in our domestic markets regulated prices and kept our trade and exchanges upon a normal basis.

To a certain extent that was true, but it isn't true now. What disturbs this nation most today is the slow, steady, as it were, inevitable disappearance of the elements of competition which regulated prices and at the same time so great a similarity of manufactures, that we have got vastly more than we can use ourselves, and must, unless we suffer severe contraction, have relief in foreign markets. And so our trade is fairly bursting its jacket, and the value is mounting until they have to find an outlet over the wall of the tariff, and it is very difficult to make an outlet without making an inlet (applause).

We have been ignorant and negligent of foreign markets, we have been a grand provincial experiment. Now the experiment worked to a certain extent and may be expanded to domestic trade, but we have got to the limit now, and whether you are a protectionist or a free trader, or an advocate of tariff for revenue only, you can't hold the tariff policy in this country where it is. (Applause.) It isn't the mere question of prices. It is the inevitable force of the exchange prices of the world.

We are going to break your tariff wall down. Now that is an entirely new thing, and not one man out of ten that I meet has considered it at all. He supposes that this pestiferous agitation against the tariff has again come to be beseiged, and again theoretical persons, chiefly out of universities, are going to upset the established order of things.

None of us can afford to sit still and see the forces of nature confounded, for they are the forces of human nature. In the meantime, what else has happened or is going to happen? I attended a dinner of the Real Estate Exchange of Boston the other night and, of course, those gentlemen were chiefly interested in the value of real estate in the city of Boston, and real estate has somewhat enhanced there since Benjamin Franklin[4] left. (Laugh-

[3] That is, the very high protective tariff.

[4] The after-dinner speeches had been opened by James Stetson Metcalfe, drama critic of *Life*, the humor magazine, dressed as Benjamin Franklin. The speakers following Wilson were Mayor Rudolph Blankenburg of Philadelphia, Senator Robert M. La Follette, and William John Burns, the detective.

ter.) I asked them if they supposed there would be the same element of value in the real estate of Boston in the next decade that there had been in the last century.

At present almost all the great arteries and movements of trade in this country are east and west, but wait until that big ditch is completed down on the isthmus, and then the currents of trade are going to sweep around and some of the greatest arteries of all are going to open to the northward and southward and then there is danger that that northeast corner where Boston is will be more cold and isolated than it is now. (Applause.)

The merchants of Europe must regard us a very philanthropic people, for we are building that ditch for England and Germany, not for ourselves. We haven't any ships to send through it. It will be very convenient for Germany and for England, and I have no doubt that the far-seeing merchants of these countries are very much obliged to us. But it will be a long time before America uses that canal for the carrying trade of the world.

While we are shifting our own currents we are not preparing ourselves to take advantage of the changed conditions of the world and here we sit crying out against the change when the world is changing under our feet. The spirit of the age has nipped you and you've got to run. Progressiveness means not getting caught standing still when everything else is moving.

Another thing that is changed is the whole business system of the country, and our laws have not been changed since it began changing (applause). Here are some nice processes of readjustment that the ghost of Mr. Franklin just now suggested, that the Constitution of the United States had got old-fashioned. The men who made the Constitution of the United States were all so single and farseeing geniuses that the Constitution of the United States can't grow old-fashioned (applause).

But some men can show themselves hopelessly incapable of guiding and interpreting the Constitution of the United States, and some gentlemen forget that we are not steering by forms of government, we are steering by principles of government. (Applause.) I am not afraid of steering by the principles that are shut through that great constructive generation of the dead. They believed in certain fundamental things which we have pushed into the background in order to worship their temporary and ephemeral forms of expression. I would a great deal rather be devoted to the inherent principles of the Constitution of the United States than any one of the forms of that Constitution, and when America once gets so in love with the way in which it has been doing things that it forgets what it was she intended to do, then I shall be with those who worship the form rather than the substance.

I happen to know what flag I live under. I happen to know what the flag of the United States typifies. I never look at it that it doesn't seem to me to consist of alternative strips of parchment, upon which are written the rights of man and little streams of blood shed to vindicate and validate those principles. (Applause.) And unto that little heaven in the corner swung star after star typical of rising communities of men who knew how to take care of themselves and live anew upon the principles which that flag illustrates.

I tell you, gentlemen, men have forgotten the history of America who have forgotten to be progressive and fight for principles. What are the principles which we want to fight for?

In the first place, we believe in liberty, do we not? We believe in the kind of liberty which provides free individual adjustments between man and his fellowman, to dominate them or to be dominated by them, but you establish freedom by putting an image of such relations that there is the utmost kindness and ease of co-operation. Similarly you say of a boat that she sails free not when she is resisting the great breath that is brought from the heavens, [but] when she is falling back with infinite grace; but throw her up into the wind and see what she does. Let her fall off and God's breath is gone in her sails, and so I say that these are the images to my mind of liberty.

These are the principles of obedience underlying the sacred laws of human nature and the great adjustments of human establishment. These are our standards, and we will get them by establishing governments that represent them. Nobody has a more profound and reverent belief in representative government than I have, but I haven't the least sentiment or regard for government that is not representative. (Applause.) But just so long as it ceases to be representative then I am bound by the representative principles to see to it that the representative character is not destroyed. Our fundamental principle is that we shall have a government representative of whom? That is the parting of the ways: representative of whom?

There are two theories of government. We don't lie back in vague regions of theory which we think we are carrying along with us in action. There are some men in this country, and they have been the guiding hands of this government, who believe that the only people whose judgment it is safe to take in regard to the policy of government are the people who have the biggest interests at stake in the industries and trade of America, and that we are not safe except in the hands of these people as trustees. And I heard many a speech in recent months when it was evident that the orator in speaking at all wasn't including himself; he was not including the little coterie of men of whom he sought counsel, from whom he received funds for the support of campaigns.

These were the guardians and the people were the beneficiaries. You want representative government, do you? Well, whom do you want this government to represent—this class of guardians, business trustees, or the great rank and file of human beings working their way by their strain of muscle and good of heart toward the modest goal of their own self-support and the support of those whom they love and who are depending upon them? Who do you want to represent them?

When you speak of representative government and of the people, do you include yourself? Are you of those who stand apart? Do you want to speak for or with the people? Do you want to feel the throb of their hearts under your own jacket? By that test it will be known on which side of the water you belong; by that test you shall know whether you are an American or not an American. And I challenge every man to that test, and I challenge every man to deny that in recent years this country has been privately, not publicly controlled (applause).

Do you comprehend the signs of the time? Don't you see how the people are insisting upon a change in the center of gravity of our institutions? What is happening? Why, I can tell you that a Governor is made very uncomfortable who does not undertake to insist upon the realization of the judgment of the people of his State as against everybody, including the legislators.

The Governor is the only man in the State whom every voter votes for; he is the only general representative and spokesman. (Applause.) And he is the man to speak our thoughts; and if he doesn't, what is their verdict?—a verdict of disappointment or condemnation or contempt.

A President of the United States is not now tolerated if he follows, if he listens, to little groups of men. He is expected to hear the unspoken voice of a great mass of people, be their servant and their leader, else there is universal discontent, universal criticism.

Am I mistaken in the signs of the times? What do they mean? They mean that the people are seeking means of recovering the direct power of the common judgment. (Applause.) And if they don't get that, what are they going to ask for? They are going to ask for the return of this power. It has been done in State after State, and now, in one of the great "conservative" States of the country, Ohio, a body of men[5] is sitting who mean to have that power established in their Constitution.

Is this revolutionary? Let me read to you from the Virginia Declaration of Rights which preceded the Declaration of Independence and on a part of which that declaration is based. To my mind the things that are said in that Declaration of Rights are sacred and they mean business.

(The Governor read the second article, referring to the unalienable character of the people's rights and the fact that "magistrates are their servants," following with the third, which declares that all government must be conducive to the good of all the people.)

Come and square yourselves by these ancient standards and then we shall have a basis for discussing what is to be done in America at all times amenable to the people. They mean that the people have a right to do what they blank please with the Government.

The American people are the most good natured, the most honest, and most liberal, the most patient and the most just in the world. You may point out to me a few mobs here and there. That is not the picture of the American people. At least, it is not the picture in my mind.

Where did we learn such self-possession? It is because the American people had a reverence for the laws they themselves had made. Once convince the people that the Government is not their own and you will see a changed people.

I have not the least fear that there will be a revolution in this country. It is the peculiar genius of the American people that they avoid revolution. I find nowhere among thoughtful men a desire to "get even," but everywhere among them do I find a determination to "be even."

There is no disease in this country. There is blindness, but the people are not blind; there is the sure sign of determination, the inclination to stand pat. There are many of the guiding minds of this country today sitting at the stern and looking at the course of the vessel behind.

But, gentlemen, there is a road before that leads upward. We may be in the shadowed valley, but if you will look ahead you will see the cleft in the hills. You will see that the road goes upward without a break. True, there are the crags of special

---

[5] The Ohio constitutional convention.

privilege, but the prophecy of America will be fulfilled, not withstanding them.

Let us not try to keep the people back from their true upward way. Let me say again, let the prophecy of America be fulfilled.[6]

Printed in the Philadelphia *North American*, Feb. 3, 1912, with extensive corrections and additions from the nearly full texts in the *Philadelphia Record*, Feb. 3, 1912, and the *Philadelphia Inquirer*, Feb. 3, 1912, and the partial text in the Philadelphia *Public Ledger*, Feb. 3, 1912.

[6] There is a WWhw outline of this address, dated Feb. 2, 1912, in WP, DLC.

From Edward Mandell House

My dear Governor Wilson: [Austin, Tex.] February 2nd, 1912.

Thank you so much for your letter of January 27th.

Your kindly expressions as to our future relations touches me deeply for I have come to have a regard for you that is akin to affection.

I hope that your recent experience has not made you altogether distrustful of friends and that you will believe there are some who are entirely unselfish in their devotion to you and the cause which you represent.

I regret that my recent illness has caused me to lag behind others in endeavor but I am rapidly gaining strength and I shall soon be doing my full share.

Mr. Bryan is now on his Rio Grande farm and I have asked him here before he leaves. In the meantime I will continue to keep in touch with him by correspondence.

Please let me know if there is anything you would like to have suggested to him for there can be no better place to do this than by the quiet fireside.

I am, my dear Governor,

Yours very sincere,   [E. M. House]

CCL (E. M. House Papers, CtY).

From Francis Ignatius Drobinski[1]

Honorable and Dear Sir: Brooklyn, Feb. 2, 1912.

I have the honor of forwarding to you a copy of resolutions[2] which have been acted upon at a meeting of the Polish citizens of South Brooklyn, New York, held January 31, 1912. The motive which actuated the passing of these resolutions is a feeling of injury and resentment at your opinion concerning Polish immigrants as expressed in the fifth volume of your "History of the American People."[3]

Since a copy of these resolutions has been given to the public press it is also very probable that any answer which you might kindly give to this communication will be diverted into the same channel.

Hoping that you will understand that the action as taken by the Polish citizens of South Brooklyn is not one of animosity against your person, but only a firm stand for what we consider a principle, we remain, with expressions of respect,

United Polish Societies of South Brooklyn.
Per F. Ig. Drobinski.

Printed in the *New York American*, March 25, 1912.
  [1] Physician of Greenpoint, Brooklyn.
  [2] Opposing Wilson for the presidential nomination.
  [3] He referred to the following passage: "Throughout the century men of the sturdy stocks of the north of Europe had made up the main strain of foreign blood which was every year added to the vital working force of the country, or else men of the Latin-Gallic stocks of France and northern Italy; but now there came multitudes of men of the lowest class from the south of Italy and men of the meaner sort out of Hungary and Poland, men out of the ranks where there was neither skill nor energy nor any initiative of quick intelligence; and they came in numbers which increased from year to year, as if the countries of the south of Europe were disburdening themselves of the more sordid and hapless elements of their population, the men whose standards of life and of work were such as American workmen had never dreamed of hitherto. The people of the Pacific coast had clamored these many years against the admission of immigrants out of China, . . . and yet the Chinese were more to be desired, as workmen if not as citizens, than most of the coarse crew that came crowding in every year at the eastern ports." *A History of the American People* (5 vols., New York and London, 1902), v, 212-13.

To Mary Allen Hulbert Peck

Dearest Friend,   Princeton, New Jersey 4 Feb'y, 1912

It seems a long, long time since a letter came from you to cheer me. The wretched steamers seem to have lost their way on the sea. Perhaps they dread to plunge back into this savage winter. If I could get away from it, you may be sure I would never come back if I c'd help it. It fills me with a great longing when I think of dear Bermuda and its release from the strain and confusion of the life we poor devils are condemned to lead here,—for Bermuda means to me, not only sweet airs and the beauty of a land meant for pleasure, but also sweet friends and the leisure to enjoy them,—which America cannot afford amidst the rush and fever of its life. It rests and refreshes me merely to send my thoughts down the seas to the other side of the Gulf Stream where the bright little islands lie in their sea of jewels,— and to think of the dear people I know there who do *not* rush

their days away but have time to sit and share each others'
thoughts and ease each others' anxieties and quicken one the
other's hope and courage. Do not think of me as one who has not
time to recall the days of renewal he has spent there. My days
are refreshed at all sorts of odd intervals by giving them leave
to follow in imagination and in intimate sympathy friends far
away, and so bring them near and enjoy something very like the
delight of being actually with them. But they will help mightily
by writing me full and frequent letters, for I never feel so near
them as when I am thinking *their* thoughts, putting myself in
their places, placing my mind and heart at their disposal. Moral:
write to me as you would talk to me,—and as leisurely as possible!
As for me, I have no leisure! I have to write these poor makeshift
letters at all odd hours. I would not be happy if I did not. Since
I wrote last I've been to Virginia, my own, my native land; and
they gave me a royal welcome. A special train from Staunton, my
birth-place, brought some two or three hundred men down (with
the local band) some hundred and forty miles to greet me and
cheer for me at Richmond and (after speaking to each house of
the Legislature) I had, in the evening, an audience of about four
thousand in a huge auditorium, and won them to me, everybody
said. The next night I spoke to some six hundred men at dinner
who represented the chief newspaper and magazine men of the
country. It is very stimulating; but it takes everything out of me,
and I have little that is worth writing for my dear friend, to
whom I so long to send cheer and comfort and diversion of
thought. We all send most affectionate messages, and I am,
amidst every distraction,

Your devoted friend   Woodrow Wilson

ALS (WP, DLC).

To Joseph A. Di Silvestro[1]

My dear Sir: [Trenton, N. J., c. Feb. 4, 1912]

Allow me to thank you for your very courteous letter of February 3, which I warmly appreciate.

I beg that you will judge the passage in Volume V of my "History of the American People," to which you allude, in connection
with its full context, and not by itself. I yield to no one in my
ardent admiration for the great people of Italy and certainly no
one who loves the history of liberty should fail to accord to Italians a great place in the history of political freedom.

I should be very much pained if I thought I had been guilty

of an injustice. I was, in the passage alluded to, only deploring the coming to this country of certain lawless elements which I had supposed all thoughtful Italians themselves deplored. I was thinking only of the men who have once and again threatened to give to that whole, fine body of Italians, who have enriched American life, a reputation which they did not deserve. Certainly, the Italians I have known and honored have constituted one of the most interesting and admirable elements in our American life.   Very sincerely yours,   Woodrow Wilson.

Printed in the New York *Evening Post*, March 22, 1912.
  1 An editor of *La Voce del Popolo* of Philadelphia and secretary of the Italo-American Publishing Co.

To Edward Mandell House

My dear Mr. House: [Trenton, N. J.] February 6, 1912.

It was the greatest pleasure to learn that you are really getting thoroughly well again, and I want to send my most hearty congratulations. I thought of you with real anxiety and solicitude and have been at times anxious that I did not hear of your more rapid improvement.

What you are doing is being done with the usual instinct of friendliness not only, but also for doing the right thing, and I have at present nothing to suggest, only my warm and cordial thanks.   Faithfully yours,   Woodrow Wilson

TLS (E. M. House Papers, CtY).

To Francis Ignatius Drobinski

My Dear Dr. Drobinski: [Trenton, N. J.] February 7, 1912.

Your courteous letter of February 2d does you honor. I wish to thank you for it very warmly and to say that I respond with pleasure.

I do not believe that the passage in my history to which you refer, if read with the full context, can possibly be interpreted as an attack upon the Polish people or upon those fine Polish elements which have added strength to the already large variety of American life. I yield to no one in my admiration of the Polish character. I have received the greatest stimulus from my reading of Polish history. If my terms were too sweeping, they must be attributed to my clumsiness in expressing myself.

What was in my thought was only a reference to some lawless elements which had recently been added to our population, by drawing from the poorer sort, certainly not from the great sound body of a people which, like all others, has its lawless elements.

I was simply pointing out the coming to America of those elements out of several countries which the several countries themselves might be supposed to be glad to get rid of. If I did not speak of the fine elements which had also come, it was only because I thought that everybody would take that for granted.

Cordially and sincerely yours,   Woodrow Wilson.

Printed in the *New York American*, March 25, 1912.

To Agostino De Biasi[1]

My Dear Sir: [Trenton, N. J.] Feb. 7, 1912.

Allow me to thank you for your courteous letter of Jan. 29,[2] which I warmly appreciate, and to which I would have replied sooner had I not been absent from my office.

I beg that you will judge the passage in Volume 5 of my "History of the American People," to which you allude, in connection with its full context, and not by itself. I yield to no one in my ardent admiration for the great people of Italy, and certainly no one who loves the history of liberty should fail to accord to Italians a great place in the history of political freedom.

I should be very much pained if I thought I had been guilty of an injustice. I was, in the passage alluded to, only deploring the coming to this country of certain lawless elements which I had supposed all thoughtful Italians themselves deplored. I was thinking only of the men who have once and again threatened to give to that whole, fine body of Italians, who have enriched American life, a reputation which they did not deserve. Certainly, the Italians I have known and honored have constituted one of the most interesting and admirable elements in our American life.   Very sincerely yours,   Woodrow Wilson.

Printed in the *New York Times*, Feb. 10, 1924.
[1] Editor of *Il Carroccio* of New York.
[2] It is missing.

To Marcus Braun[1]

[My dear Mr. Braun: Trenton, N. J., c. Feb. 7, 1912]

It pains me very much to be accused of injustice to so great a country as Hungary, whose role in the world has been great and honorable, and I do not think that any quotation from anything that I have written, if taken in connection with its context, can fairly be judged as derogatory to that great people.

I was not speaking of a nation, but of certain elements which had recently disclosed themselves among our immigrants. I am perfectly willing to abide by any fair reading of the passage in my history, to which you probably allude.

I pride myself on knowing something of the great history of Hungary; that history displays a struggle for liberty which all the world must admire and applaud. I know as well as any man can know what elements of strength and of energy the Hungarian people have contributed to the variety and richness of the American people. I do not distinguish Americans in my mind, but the country from which they come.

If I have at any time deplored certain elements that have come to us in our later immigration, I count myself very unfortunate if I have been so awkward in my way of expressing what I had to say as to bring injustice to a people whom I admire and respect.

[Sincerely yours,   Woodrow Wilson]

Printed in unidentified clipping (WP, DLC).
[1] New York City port warden, publisher of the *Hungarian American* and the *Oesterreichisch-Ungarische Zeitung*, both of New York.

To Emmett C. Davison

My dear Mr. Davison: [Trenton, N. J.] February 7, 1912.

I sincerely regret that I did not have the time to reply while in Richmond to your letter of February first.

In answer to your general question, "Should convicts be employed in competition with free labor," I should answer No.

From the experience of several states, I should say that the making of roads was a practicable employment for convicts.

The manufacturing of articles for State use is also, I think, practicable. A law was passed in New Jersey last year, with the entire approval of representatives of organized labor, to put that system in operation here.[1] The system of leasing criminals' work for manufacturing purposes to private contractors has been tried in recent years here, and we think the effects have been most undesirable. I was glad to take part in the abolition of the system.

Cordially yours,   Woodrow Wilson

Printed in the Richmond *News Leader*, Feb. 9, 1912.
[1] *Laws of New Jersey, 1911*, Chapter 372.

To Verner R. Lovell

My dear Mr. Lovell: [Trenton, N. J.] February 7, 1912.

Absence from my office has prevented my replying sooner to your kind letter of the thirty-first of January.

I am glad you do not think I made a mistake in writing as I did to the chairman of the State Central Committee.

Since I wrote to you, Mr. Budd has shown me your very interesting and, as I think, wise letter written to him. My own judgment is that the thing to do is to see that the delegates instructed for Governor Burke are also sincere friends of ours so that we may be sure that when they find the nomination of Governor Burke impossible, they may be counted upon to turn to us.

Nothing would please me better than to see you yourself a delegate.

With warm regards,

Cordially yours,   Woodrow Wilson

TLS (received from Roland Dille).

A News Item

[Feb. 8, 1912]

THE LA FOLLETTE INCIDENT.

In the train on the way to this city[1] Governor Wilson captivated the members of the committee and talked freely on the questions of the day. He gave a graphic description of the La Follette incident at the Publishers' banquet in Philadelphia last week and expressed the opinion that the great insurgent leader was suffering from what seemed to be a nervous breakdown.[2] It was a most tragic event, he said, and additional pathos is presented in the unseemly haste with which the leader is being deserted by the followers he had, most of whom held to be supporters of the great principles represented by La Follette rather than mere followers of the man.

Speaking of Col. Roosevelt, in response to a query, Governor Wilson marvelled at the apparent midway position being maintained by the former president on the question of his candidacy[3] and when one of the members of the party ventured the guess that he would be the strongest candidate the Republicans could name, there was no answering conjecture as to the possibility of the outcome on the part of the guest of the day.

Printed in the *Allentown*, Pa., *Morning Call*, Feb. 8, 1912; some editorial heading omitted.
    [1] Allentown, Pa.

2 La Follette spoke for nearly two hours after Wilson in a faltering, rambling, and repetitious manner and ended his speech with a bitter attack against the press, which he said had been bribed by corrupt business. Rumors that he had suffered a nervous breakdown immediately swept the country. His spokesmen, saying that he was tired and overworked, canceled all his engagements for the next two weeks.

3 Roosevelt declared his candidacy for the Republican presidential nomination on February 24.

A News Report of a Political Address in Allentown, Pennsylvania

[Feb. 8, 1912]

A ROYAL WELCOME FOR DR. WOODROW WILSON

Notable Outpouring of Leading Citizens to Hear Aspirant for Presidential Honors

Whatever Governor Woodrow Wilson, of New Jersey, thought about Allentown before his visit here last evening he certainly will leave to-day impressed with the cordiality of the reception accorded to him; impressed with the underlying sincerity of his welcome; impressed with the immense outpouring of citizens to hear his message and impressed with the fact that there is a live hustling city called Allentown which with Reading shares the honor of being located in a Democratic oasis in a state noted for its Republican strength.

When Governor Wilson rose in the Lyric Theatre last evening, as the speaker at the annual Jackson Day celebration, he addressed by far the largest audience that ever congregated in this city for a similar occasion. Not only was the theatre packed to the very roof, but enough people were turned away to fill another theatre comfortably.

Not only was the audience the largest that ever listened to a political address in this city, but the old timers, those who attended meetings of this nature for years, agreed that it was the finest and most intelligent audience that has ever assembled in this city.

The balcony and gallery were open to the public and these were jammed before those for whom seats had been reserved arrived. The Lehigh Democratic club was escorted by the Allentown Band and the Youny [Young] Men's Democratic Club of the Sixth ward was escorted by the First ward drum corps.

While the band played "The Star Spangled Banner," the curtain rose and the audience rose like one man and every one waved an inspiring American flag. When District Attorney Rupp[1] introduced Governor Wilson, the audience tendered him an ovation such as is seldom tendered, even to a president of the United States. It was several minutes before the applause subsided.

Just before the speaker was introduced two bodies of college students who were seated in the wings gave their college cheers and cheers for Wilson. First of all fifty Muhlenberg men cheered led by Herbert Frederick and then followed the Lehigh crowd, under the direction of cheer leader George Shurts adding three lusty "Wilsons" on the end. . . .

It was a glowing introduction that had been accorded the New Jersey governor and as he arose amid cheering of the crowd that continued for minutes and minutes he appeared flushed with pleasure, almost embarrassment and when the applause had subsided and he had addressed the audience he said: "It sobers a man to be introduced in such terms." Then in a happy vein he added "If you folks were a grand jury, it would be very embarrassing to be introduced in this manner by the district attorney." He followed this pleasantry with another that provoked as great laughter: "I certainly hope that he has evidence of the allegations which he has made."

Explaining the reason why the celebration of Jackson Day had come so late for Allentown, he referred to the fact that on the day that Allentown Democrats would like to have celebrated the day, he had been in attendance at a Jackson Day dinner where there were fifteen speakers and he concluded that it is pleasanter to listen to speeches than to be compelled to deliver them. He quoted the English author who said: "The best way to enjoy your works is to have other people write them for you."

He did not dwell long on Jackson Day or Andrew Jackson either. . . . He said:

"It is significant that the great Democratic party has drawn much of its inspiration and its strength from two widely dissimilar characters, the first, the philosophical Jefferson, and the other the downright, plain Jackson, the man who was of the blood of the people's blood and bone of their bone. It is a wonderful combination, thoughtfulness inspiring action and philosophy which inspires action, and action which inspires thoughtfulness. I think it fine that the Democratic party is associated with these two men. It is significant, too, that both of these men could not make speeches. Jackson could formulate a militant toast, but he could not utter a platform address."

From this point on, the governor drifted to the problems of the day, discussing them in an incisive, penetrating way that sought for principles. It was a speech marked by oratory of the highest type. There were periods that provoked not so much applause as they did thought. The lecture was one directed at thought not at emotion. Everywhere that Wilson has gone, according to his own statement, he has been met by thoughtful audiences.

The people of the United States are thinking, he says. The audience that jammed the Lyric Theatre last evening did some long thinking. Many a time when the governor diverted for the moment to some anecdote to illustrate a point that he wished to make, it did not provoke the laughter of the kind that is shown at the ordinary political gathering where men gather to be amused. Wilson had been advertised as the school-master. Last night's audience sat, as it were, at the feet of Gamaliel, while the wisdom of the school-master in politics was being given out. . . .

Printed in the *Allentown*, Pa., *Morning Call*, Feb. 8, 1912; some editorial headings omitted.
[1] Lawrence Henry Rupp, district attorney of Leigh County, 1912-16.

To Edith M. Whitmore

My Dear Madam: [Trenton, N. J., Feb. 8, 1912]

Allow me to acknowledge with real appreciation your letter of January 31 in which you put me a very difficult question. I can only say that my own mind is in the midst of the debate which it involves. I do not feel that I am ready to utter any confident judgment as yet about it. I am honestly trying to work my way toward a just conclusion.

Cordially and sincerely yours,   Woodrow Wilson.

Printed in the New York *Sun*, Feb. 10, 1912.

From Edward Mandell House

My dear Governor Wilson: [Austin, Tex.] February 8th, 1912.

I am enclosing you a copy of a letter which I have just received from Mr. Bryan and which may perhaps be of interest to you.

Among the clippings which I sent to him and which he says that he will use was the one from the February issue of Current Literature showing your natural evolution from a Conservative to a Progressive.[1]

It absolutely answers your critics on that point and I wanted Mr. Bryan to read it.

I also sent him clippings from the Saturday Evening Post, Colliers and other papers giving the main source of the opposition to you. This of course is Wall Street and its allies.

Please treat Mr. Bryan's letter in confidence and oblige,

Your very sincere,   [E. M. House]

CCL (E. M. House Papers, CtY).
1 "The Political Transformation of Woodrow Wilson," *Current Literature*, LII (Feb. 1912), 153-57.

A News Report of Two Addresses in Frankfort, Kentucky

[Feb. 9, 1912]

GOV. WILSON AT FRANKFORT

Speaks Before Assembly On Democratic Policies.

Frankfort, Ky., Feb. 9.—(Special.)—What he believed the Democratic party should do to win in the next national election was told the members of the Kentucky General Assembly here this afternoon by Woodrow Wilson, Governor of New Jersey, and candidate for the Democratic nomination for President. The first essential, he said, is to win the confidence of the people by letting them know that the Democratic leaders are conversant with true conditions, and then recommend remedies that, while not radical, will bring about the desired effect. The speech was delivered in the House of Representatives, and at its conclusion Gov. Wilson was given an ovation. Every seat, both on the floor and in the gallery of the chamber, was occupied, and standing room was at a premium.

Gov. Wilson was the guest of honor at a banquet given here to-night at the Capital Hotel. He arrived aboard a special train from the East in Frankfort at 9:12 o'clock this morning, and was met at the station by a special legislative committee, headed by Senator L. W. Arnett, of Covington. This committee escorted him to the Capital Hotel, where he was called upon a short while later by Gov. [James Bennett] McCreary. He accompanied the latter to the Capitol building at 10:30 o'clock, and after greeting various members of the General Assembly in one of the retiring rooms, went to the home of the Rev. J. R. Ziegler, graduate from Princeton,[1] where he took luncheon.

He began his address to the General Assembly at 3:30 o'clock.

"I feel as if political business was being transacted in this country at present," he began, "and therefore I am going to speak to you this afternoon as a Democrat. I know there are Republicans present, but I have come to believe there is no Republican who is hopeless.

"I am not aware of any partisan prejudice on my part, but I am a believer in party allegiance. I believe in a close union of men to accomplish an object. The only thing of which we need feel jealous is not the party organization, but the party machine. The party organization is formed for public purposes, while the party machine is formed for personal purposes. No man can act with party efficiency if he does not act as an integral part of a party organization.

"The United States is dissatisfied with the rule of the Republican party as at present controlled. I do not need to prove this. I am not arguing with you, but I am telling you.

"There is a widespread dissatisfaction. Not a dissatisfaction with the professed principles of the Republican party, but with the policies of the Republican party. The country is profoundly dissatisfied with the leaders of the Republican party. They believe, many of them honestly, that this country cannot enter upon a course of action without the approval of men who control the largest financial interests of the country. It is a theory of trusteeship.

"When they speak of the people of the United States they do not include themselves. They are in the attitude of guardians. Their idea is that every election must be personally guided. Whenever there is a campaign it is made to turn upon the question of prosperity doled out by the material-controlled interests.

"They do not trust the general judgment of America, and the people realize this. They are demanding that in Federal affairs they have a government of their own.

"This isn't an indictment against their characters. It is an indictment of their ignorance of the United States. I am not surprised at it. These gentlemen have been so absorbed in vast undertakings that they have never had time to lift their eyes to the horizon.

"We have come to a time when the country is looking around for a substitute for the Republican party.

"Now there are candidates and candidates in the Republican party, referred to by some as 'insurgents,' who say the present policies of the Republican party are wrong, and who want to bring that party to a realization of its duty. These gentlemen have swung around until there is only one difference of any consequence between us, and that is that they still adhere to a protective tariff. That may be all right, but I have never had a feeling of piety for it. My heart has never been touched by the principle of protection. And so they are candidates to be substituted for the present Republicans in power.

"Why has the country hesitated to substitute the Democratic party for the Republican party? America is a business country, dominated by practical men of affairs. They do not tolerate interference with the normal course of their business. You know what the lawyer's argument is for following precedent. It is a great deal better for him to know what is going to be done in court to-morrow than to be in doubt. The same is true of the business man. He wants definite points by which he may draw his orbit.

"Therefore, I say that America is intolerant of experiment and uncertain change. The indictment against the Democratic party is that it is a party of experiment and change. Is not that true? Is not that the argument that has been used against us? The truth of it is neither here nor there.

"Business has undergone such changes that merely standing and letting things alone will not serve the interests of business itself. The field of business is not free as it used to be, but is bound by certain central controlling influences in the financial world giving privileges and artificial advantages. Not many business men are speaking out about this. Many a man knows if he complains there are men who can jeopardize his success more than now.

"The questions of business of this country have become new questions. The processes of our law are not true to the new processes of business. The judges are a bit at sea.

"Privilege governs unrestrained. These combinations in business are disclosing themselves as coincident with combinations in politics.

"The problem to my mind, therefore, is how to commend the Democratic party to the confidence of the nation. How can we show the people of the United States that they can trust us? By showing that we know the facts when we see them. We are getting knowledge by the investigations of the Stanley Committee, and by the meat packers investigation. We now know how the price of meat is fixed. The biproducts of the carcas[s] are the great profits of the meat concerns. The price of meat is made to cover the whole operating expense.

"With regard to the Steel Corporation, we now know something of its operations, but not all. We will know in time.

"All that I'm interested in is how can I best get the crowbar under these locked gates to open them."

To illustrate his point, Gov. Wilson here told a story of a young woman and her sweetheart. She was just in her teens, he said, and her mother always made it a point to be present when her daughter's sweetheart called.

The young man arrived at the house one afternoon before the

mother had completed her toilet, and he and the young woman were in the parlor alone when she began to bleed at the nose. He, wishing to do something for her relief, and having heard that cold steel at the back of the neck was a good remedy, stepped over to the door for the key. In his excitement he inadvertently turned the lock in extracting the key, and then hurried over to the young woman and held it to the back of her neck. Just then the mother arrived at the door, and finding it locked, rapped for admittance. Adding to the embarrassment of the situation, the young man dropped the key down the young woman's back.

"What is to be done?" Gov. Wilson asked, and his hearers began to laugh. When the merriment had subsided somewhat, he added: "My solution is to get the key at any cost."

Becoming serious, Gov. Wilson said:

"We must be willing to deal with one thing at a time. We must undertake to stop that way of fixing prices that establishes and maintains a monopoly.

"I'm not afraid of the size of a corporation. Bigness, associated with privileges, is extremely dangerous. Without privileges bigness is not dangerous at all.

"I believe the business of America is conducted by honest, patriotic men, and that the dearest wish of these men is to have these errors of business removed that have brought business into disrepute.

"The thing for the Democratic party to do is to show that it is more familiar with the business of this country than the Republican party. The Democratic party is saturated with certain ancient principles which underlie the whole structure of political society.

"Every nation is renewed out of the ranks of the unknown men. A democratic nation is richer in genius than any other nation because it releases genius. The fine proof of the principles of Democracy is that you can't predict from which class the leaders are to come. These giants more often come from cottages than palaces. The genius that rises out of that is genius that will not be denied.

"The Democratic party has the enormous advantage of having that principle to work upon. The additional principle of the Democratic party is that no one group of individuals has the right to judge for the whole. The business of the Democratic party is to translate the old into the new; the old principles into the new principles. The body politic changes just as truly as the physical changes.

"I believe the Democratic party still pulsates with these old pulses of life. If that be true, then certain things are necessary. Clear-sightedness will enable us to prove to the business world that we do know what we are doing; that we are going to act from the standpoint of expediency.

"Some men are going to try to make us afraid. If certain groups of men can accomplish almost anything they set out to accomplish, then they can threaten us with the spectre of financial disaster. We shall be cowards if we so much as regard such things.

"I utter these things in tones of defiance, perhaps, but I feel no defiance. It's no fault of mine, if I was born with Scotch-Irish blood. I don't carry a shillalah, but I have a great interest in those who do. I describe myself as an arch conservative.

"If you were a surgeon and found your patient suffering from a malignant growth how would you prove your conservatism? By the use of the knife, or course; but as you insert it you must be wholly sensible of the sensitiveness of the nerve centers.

"I think, after the operation, there need be no trained nurse. I don't think the patient will even have to go to bed. Nothing is going to hurt except the parts removed. It isn't a large part, but creates a considerable disturbance while it is there.

"Various ways have been suggested as to how we are to get what we are after. Every programme I am interested in is a programme to open the channels. The courses of business are clogged. The channels can be opened without interfering with navigation.

"How are we now seeking to control monopoly? By taking monopoly and dividing it into pieces and leaving the same men in the pieces that accomplished the monopoly. You can't make such a puzzle out of these pieces as to keep them from fitting them together. The only way to check the genius of anybody is to imprison the genius.

"The world consists of individuals. Motive originates from individuals. You don't exercise government unless you reach suggestive origins. Let us deal with corporations only when they are operating honestly. When operating otherwise, let us lift off the cover and expose the people composing the corporation. If the trouble is beyond this circle, then let us go outside and deal with it there."

Lieut. Gov. [Edward John] McDermott presided over the meeting. He was introduced by Representative Francis Douglas, of Boyle county. In introducing Gov. Wilson, Lieut. Gov. McDermott referred to him in high terms.

Gov. Wilson entered the House chamber with Gov. McCreary, and the moment they entered the door they were greeted by waves of applause. Students of Georgetown College occupied seats in the gallery and cheered Gov. Wilson, following this with their college yell.

More than two hundred men from all parts of the State were at the banquet in Gov. Wilson's honor. At the banquet to-night only three speeches were made besides the address of Gov. Wilson. Henry S. Breckinridge, of Lexington, presided as toastmaster and the welcome address was delivered by Gov. McCreary. The diners thought that the Governor was going to declare for Gov. Wilson for the Democratic nominee, but he put it that hundreds of thousands of Democrats want Gov. Wilson to be the nominee. Gov. McCreary predicted a Democratic victory in 1913, and said if the man elected happened to be Gov. Wilson every Kentuckian would be proud to go to Washington and shake his hand.

Senator Claude M. Thomas, of Bourbon, accepted the office of president of the Woodrow Wilson Association in Kentucky, and pledged himself to work and use every honorable means to send from Kentucky a delegation instructed for Gov. Wilson. Representative Francis B. Douglas spoke only a minute, but started a laugh which lasted for a longer time than the speech. In his speech at the banquet Gov. Wilson discussed the development of this country and the hopes and aims that are before it. He denounced the idle rich as those who spend without pleasure. Gov. Wilson will go to Louisville to-morrow morning and from there to Chicago.   CLAUD W. PERRY.

Printed in the Louisville *Courier-Journal*, Feb. 10, 1912; some editorial headings omitted.
[1] Jesse Reinhart Ziegler, Princeton 1896, pastor of the First Presbyterian Church of Frankfort.

From Charles Henry Grasty

My dear Governor: New York, 9 Feb 1912

You may be interested in the within, which I send you in confidence, of course. Please return it to me care The Sun, Baltimore, after reading.[1]

Would it be possible for you to adapt, or have adapted, your Philadelphia speech, for use in *The Sun* as a statement of your views? I think if it appeared as an article fresh from your pen, or an interview, it would be carefully read in the Sun territory,—Maryland, the two Virginias & the two Carolinas.

Sincerely yours   Charles H Grasty.

ALS (Governors' Files, Nj).
[1] See WW to C. H. Grasty, Feb. 14, 1912.

From Eugene Lee Crutchfield[1]

My dear Sir: Baltimore, Md., Feb. 9th., 1912.

I desire to tender to you my sincere thanks for your kindness and courtesy in granting an interview to my friends and myself on Tuesday, the 6th. inst. To me it was the occasion of much pleasure to have the opportunity of once more greeting an associate in the Johns Hopkins Glee Club after the lapse of so protracted a period. Twenty-eight years have rolled around since those agreeable gatherings, but when I consider the usefulness of your life to the present time and the benefit which it seems you will continue to be to your country and the human race, I can but wish for you (with a slight amendment as to nationality) what Flaccus wished for his illustrious friend:
                    "Serus in coelum redeas, dinque
                    Laetus intersis Populo Americano."
With best wishes and high esteem believe me to be
Yours very sincerely,   Eugene Lee Crutchfield, M.D.

ALS (Governors' Files, Nj).
  [1] Physician of Baltimore; undergraduate at the Johns Hopkins, 1880-1881, 1882-84; M.D., University of Maryland, 1887.

Ellen Axson Wilson to Richard Heath Dabney

My dear Mr. Dabney,   Princeton, New Jersey Feb. 9, 1912.

We were speaking recently of your repeated requests to know more in detail about the Carnegie pension affair.[1] Woodrow has tried in vain to find time to go into the matter more fully, and so now at his suggestion *I* shall give you what seems to us the right point of view about it.

To our mind the one all-important fact which has never been brought out even by his defenders is that before the recent change of rule the[re] were in effect *two* sorts of Carnegie pensions,— one an *old age* pension given to all who were sixty-five years old and otherwise eligible, and the other a *distinguished service* pension, given after twenty-five years of teaching in specially selected cases.

At first the 25 year pension was given very freely by the board, but when the number of colleges under the foundation was so greatly increased, it became clear that the money would not suffice to make that so general a rule. Then it was decided, (Woodrow being on the committee and largely instrumental in the reaching [of] the decision,) to make the 25 year pension *exclusively* and *conspicuously* a question of distinguished service, and in *no* sense one of superannuation. It was thought that to have such pensioners on the list would not only benefit scholarship in America but give to the "Foundation" a dignity and prestige which it has not secured so far,—for the way in which the pensioners are invariably spoken of in the papers is an insult to many noble gentlemen.

It was distinctly intended that the select ones should while *still* in the *fullness of their powers* be set free to devote those powers to the public service, either as scientific investigators, writers or speakers; and it was, of course, intended to be a badge of honour, as such pensions are regarded in other countries.

That it should be considered disgraceful or humiliating to receive it is a monstrous perversion of the idea. Woodrow himself being not only on the board but on the *committee* from the first can speak with authority of all this. There would have been no question of concealing the matter if he had received it, and indeed he made no secret of his application. His friends here were merely amazed and indignant that there should have been any question about granting it. Possibly the refusal was due,— as the publicity *certainly* was,—to the personal animosity of Nicholas Murray Butler. He it was who gave the "Sun" its "story."

Of course, though honorable to receive it, it is more or less humiliating to anyone to be refused, and hence it was regarded as a point of honour (or rather of *decency!*) to keep all applications secret, a rule invariably observed except in Woodrow's case. So far Butler has escaped the punishment visited on Joline —(and I personally would be greatly obliged to you if you should let his name *leak* out in this connection!)

Such as I have described them were the rules when Woodrow resigned from Princeton and from the Carnegie Board. But when he sent in his application to the committee he was told that they had just come to the conclusion that no more 25 year pensions should be granted for any cause,—that they should in the future be exclusively old age pensions; and that such a change of rule was to be proposed at the next meeting of the Board.

In answer to another of your questions I will add that when he applied he had *not* been elected Governor and had no means of support, for he refused to take anything from Princeton after the *day* on which he sent in his resignation. We were utterly without income for three months,—and people were declaring his election impossible!

Of course he could easily get another "paying job," but that would force him to give up, in large measure, his leadership in the reform movement. What he had in mind to do was to devote his time and his voice to the cause of the people. The three years of office-holding as Governor,—if it came to him,—was a mere episode designed to gain more completely the public ear and the public confidence as one who knew what he was talking about. The urgent appeals to him for speeches have for many years numbered from four to eight a day,—a perpetual cry to "come over and help us." I need not say that there is no money in such work, often not even his travelling expenses,—and his income from his books averages less than $1000 a year,—all of which goes for life insurance. You see I am talking to you now as a *very* intimate friend, because I think it will be of service for *one* person to know *just* how it stands with him. He is the most unselfish and generous of men, and has for twenty years supported in large part his widowed sister[2] and her family and my young sister,—(now married)[3] as well as his own.

When he was a mere professor he could and did make some money writing and lecturing, so that we even built a home for ourselves,—but for the past ten years he has given his pen and his voice to the public service absolutely free, gratis, for nothing!

I don't know what he would do to me if he knew I was writing all this, but I am sure I can trust your discretion, and fortunately he is in the West!

With warm regards to Mrs. Dabney and yourself I am,

Yours very cordially,   Ellen A. Wilson.

ALS (Wilson-Dabney Corr., ViU).
[1] About this matter, see WW to H. S. Pritchett, Nov. 11, 1910, Vol. 22.
[2] Annie (Mrs. George, Jr.) Howe.
[3] Margaret Randolph Axson (Mrs. Edward Graham) Elliott.

Ellen Axson Wilson to John Grier Hibben

Dear Mr. Hibben,   Princeton, New Jersey Feb. 10, 1912.

I beg to acknowledge your note with regard to seats in the college Chapel;[1] and at the same time to offer my congratulations on your recent success.[2]

All who know you will feel that you have fully earned it, and that you are ideally fitted for what is expected of you; since conditions which to others would be a burden too grievous to be borne will be to one of your temperament a source of unalloyed pleasure. Still in an imperfect and ungrateful world it does not always follow that even such useful, unwearying and conspicuous service as yours is so promptly and fully rewarded. Your friends are therefore the more to be admired in their unhesitating recognition of your very unusual loyalty and availability.

It is unfortunate, of course, that in the hour of your triumph you should have cause for anxiety, because the circumstances of your "election." will not bear the light. But since for the credit of Princeton all parties are equally determined to bury those facts in oblivion, you need have no serious concern on that score.

In the full confidence that you will continue as prudent and successful in the future as you have been in the past, and that you will enjoy, as always, the satisfaction of a conscience void of all offense toward God and man, I remain

Very sincerely,   Ellen A. Wilson.

ALS (photostat in WC, NjP).
    [1] It is missing.
    [2] That is, his election as President of Princeton University.

To Mary Allen Hulbert Peck

Woodburn House[1]

Dearest Friend,   Spring Station, Ky 11 Feb'y, 1912

I was *so* much obliged for that delightful kodak of yourself in your last letter:[2] it had so much of your brightness and charm. It was like a fresh glimpse of you. The letter that came with it sparkled with *some* of the old enjoyment of simple things that I used to look for in your letters; but the shadow of April is still there. Do you know what occurred to me,—I *hope* it's true. It occurred to me that perhaps you are more blue and feel more of that sort of sinking fatigue that goes with depression when you are writing to me than you are conscious of, or give way to, at other times,—just as the teachers at boarding schools say that boys who all the rest of the week are gay and careless, grow suddenly, deeply, genuinely homesick on Sundays when they sit down to write *home*. You know that I want to know what is at the bottom of your heart. In your generous confidence, and in your certain knowledge that I will wholly understand and perfectly interpret and sympathize, you let the undercurrents of your thought and mood come to the surface. Is it not so? I hope so, with all my heart! It would distress me very, very much to think that you were constantly depressed and worn out with sadness and anxiety. Because it is so unlike you. You are not of that kind.

(14 Feby, '12) I began this letter in Kentucky and am finishing it in my office in Trenton! I have to take such scraps of time as I can catch on the fly! I went down to Ky. to address the Legislature (at their invitation, I hope I need not add) and had a mighty good time. I wrote the first part of this letter at a country

house where I was supposed to be resting. But one cannot rest *and* be 'entertained,'—as hospitably as the Kentuckians entertain. They are a virile and entertaining lot who speak with vigour and all the necessary expletives. I seemed to 'get' them with my speech. From Kentucky I went to Chicago and was entertained by the Iroquois Club (the Democratic club of the city) at a whopping big midday affair where I was received by a company, made up of all sorts and conditions, as an old and admired friend would be received. It was fine and stimulating. To-night I start for New Hampshire!

We are very anxious because Nellie is in Mexico on a visit, where revolutionary disorder has broken out again. Train service is interrupted and we do not know when she can get out. An occasional telegram relieves our immediate fears.

I hope Allen got back in good shape. I am perfectly well. All unite in affectionate messages.

Your devoted friend   Woodrow Wilson

I am afraid my letters do not cheer you. What sort shall I write?

ALS (WP, DLC).
  [1] An inn near Lexington, Ky.
  [2] It is missing, as are most of Mrs. Peck's letters during this period.

An Address in Chicago to Democrats on Lincoln's Birthday[1]

[[Feb. 12, 1912]]

Mr. President,[2] Mr. Toastmaster,[3] and Fellow Citizens:

I feel it a great honor to stand here in the presence of this distinguished body of men in order to speak once more the faith that is in me. I have many times spoken in the City of Chicago and I want to say with commiseration for them, that many gentlemen here present have often heard me, and yet it is always delightful to be able to speak again to those with whom I have been brought in close association, on those principles which I know to be sound and patriotic, upon a theme which invites any man to speak the truth. For the thought that is uppermost in the minds of all of us is, of course, that this is Lincoln's birthday, and I know of no example which more provokes than his, simplicity, sincerity and truth.

  [1] Delivered before the Iroquois Club at a luncheon meeting in the Hotel La Salle.
  [2] Alexander Frederick Reichmann, president of the Iroquois Club, 1912-14, lawyer with the firm of Judah, Willard, Wolf and Reichmann.
  [3] William Emmet Dever, judge of the superior court of Cook County.

I sometimes think it is a singular circumstance that the present Republican Party should have sprung from Lincoln, but that is one of the mysteries of Providence, and for my part I feel the closest kinship in principle and in political lineament to that great mind. I wonder if we appreciate, gentlemen, just how apposite his example is to the present moment. Here was a case where the nation had come to a critical turning point in its history, where it had to make a choice whether it would divide or remain united upon a fundamental question of social structure —a question which was all the more difficult to approach and more difficult to solve, because it involved so much passion, because it involved some of the deepest feelings that men can acquire. There is nothing so solid in our present social structure as was exhibited in the old social structure of the United States for at that time there were roots that had run back generation after generation, and to disturb them seemed almost to disturb the foundation of the life of the people. At that critical juncture what happened? Was a man picked out who had become experienced and sophisticated among the ruling class of the community? Is it not an interesting circumstance that a man should have come almost untutored from the mass of the people, who had the wisdom, who had the vision as well as the courage and sagacity to handle a great crisis with a steadiness which made it possible to save the nation? I do not know any life which more illustrates the fundamental faith of democracy. The fundamental faith of democracy is that out of a mass of uncatalogued men you can always count upon genius asserting itself, genius suited to mankind, genius suited to the task. The richness of a democracy is in this—that it never has to predict who is going to save it. It never relies upon those of established influence. The gates of opportunity are wide open and he may enter who is fit. And when you look back to that rugged, almost ungainly figure, like the gnarled oak of the forest, that suddenly arose and showed itself to be head and shoulders not only in physical but moral stature above its fellows, and then see the sad and wistful eyes with which he moved among his fellowmen, not as a man who works revolution, but as a man who interprets the thought of his own and insists also upon all classes listening to this fundamental voice of the people themselves—is not that a vindication of democracy? We don't have to train men to interpret the United States. They are born with the largesse of Providence, a Providence that has always tried to teach mankind that only God can classify man and that men cannot.

What produced the birth of Freedom in the modern world?

It was the conception that every man stood naked and individual in his responsibility before his God and Maker and that the only test was the test of native worth and native principle. That's what has been the foundation of liberty, and so far as we have forgotten and obscured it, so far as we have impaired its operation, we have gone astray and found ourselves in a jungle from which we do not see any way of extrication. Therefore, I do not know of any better day upon which to explain what seems to me to be the duty of the Democracy than the Birthday of Lincoln.

I heard a story about Lincoln the other day—a new one—which had such a distinctive flavor of authenticity that I am sure it was true. I believe it was told by Mr. Horace White, who was a young reporter at the time of the debates between Lincoln and Stephen A. Douglas. As I was told the story, at one of the very best of those debates he was sitting on the platform in an open space near Lincoln. Lincoln was seated, as usual, in his long linen duster and alongside of him was a lady whom Mr. White did not know. Mr. Douglas spoke first and when he had sat down Mr. Lincoln leisurely got up, slowly removed the linen duster, carefully folded it up, placed it in the lap of the lady who was sitting by and said, "Won't you be kind enough to hold this garment until I go stone Stephen?" Now, Stephen Douglas, as the men of Illinois need not be told, was a very astute and very admirable figure in our politics, but just at that moment Douglas stood for an order of things, a process of reasoning in politics, about to be rejected and this man of the people used as the missiles with which to stone Stephen not any words of personal bitterness, nothing but the words of common, homely reason and a fearless analysis of the existing situation of affairs in the United States. He uttered, you will remember, that immortal sentence, "I do not say that the Union will be destroyed, but I do say that it cannot continue to exist half free and half slave." He predicted a peaceful outcome, he predicted an outcome that would save the unity and integrity of the Nation, but he also fearlessly stated the fact that as it stood it could not go on. And, gentlemen, that statement ought to be made now—that *as our economic affairs are now organized they cannot go on*. There is no such deep division as existed in Lincoln's day: it is more intricate, it is more difficult to-day than the division which existed in Lincoln's day, but it is not of the sort that invites the passions of whole populations, thank God. It is something that can, by clear thinking, be dealt with and successfully dealt with, and no man who is a friend of this country predicts any of the deeper sorts of trouble, any of the revolutionary processes which

destroy and do not restore. Our task is one of restoration, of refreshment, of rejuvenation, of the recovery of things which we
all revere but which are overcast and overweighted with all sorts
of things which we wish, by slow and prudent stages, to rid ourselves of. But, notwithstanding that we wish this, that we have
the time and we have the temper in which to solve these things,
we ought to be perfectly radical in our statement of the fact that
as at present organized the thing cannot go on. That is really
not debatable. What is debatable is the wise thing to do.

As I have looked about me and as I have traveled from one
part of this country to the other I have been struck by nothing so
much as this—the unity in the thinking and in the temper of the
people of all parts of the United States. Not long ago I had the
pleasure of visiting the city of Madison, Wisconsin, and then
proceeding directly from there, without interruption of journey,
to Dallas, Texas,[4] and if I had not known that I had not been
transported in my dreams, had not known the space I had trav-
ersed between Wisconsin and Texas, I should have thought I
was in the same state, for there was the same point of view, the
same purpose in politics, the same desire for emancipation from
the old connections that will allow men to argue and also to act
the way they feel instead of acting the way they are labeled, the
same determination to pick out men and measures as they please,
and not to be satisfied until they had picked out the right men
and measures according to the purposes they had framed in their
hearts, the determination to see to it that they did not get fooled
by anybody any more. And there are various ways of getting
fooled. You can get fooled by people who think they mean what
they say and don't; you can get fooled by people who know they
don't mean what they say and yet say it. You can even get fooled
by people who earnestly mean what they say and don't know
what they are talking about. And the people are out to catch all
kinds of fraud in respect of the man who is a fraud upon himself
as well as the man who is a fraud upon them. And in the circumstances it is a most interesting and exhilarating field in
which to play ball, because you feel that the combination of politics that is about to take place is going to take place with an impulse gained from a new generation. It is a very interesting fact
that the harness of modern politics sits most lightly upon the
youngest men. The young men of this country are now about to
take a serious part in the plot and they are determined that they
are going to make the plot, not such as it was theoretically repre-

4 See the speeches and news reports printed at Oct. 25, 26, 28, and 29, 1911,
Vol. 23.

sented to them to be when they were in school and college, but such as they have found it is. I myself contributed to deceive them at one time in some respects, but I know more than I did then; I have found some gentlemen out. Distance and perspective make a great deal of difference. When you get on the inside things look somewhat different from the way they looked on the outside, and you can always test a man by the very simple rule, put in very plain language, which we generally express when we say "put up or shut up." *Do* the thing you profess to believe or else get out of the game. I used to take a somewhat active part in advising men younger than myself about the game of football, and we always knew when we were picking out promising material for behind the line that it did not prove a man was a good halfback because he would take the ball and start with it instantly. You had to wait until he approached an opening and see how he struck the line, and if he hesitated to go through there was no more time wasted on him. The way you tell a man is whether he still has his head down and steam on when he strikes the line, because most of them will go down very finely and then check and stop and wonder what is going to happen when that mass of men come in his way. There is the same thing in politics. We need a great many men to forge through the line.

I am going to speak very frankly to you to-day about what I conceive to be the opportunity of the Democratic Party. That's the opportunity I am interested in. I am not responsible for the Republican Party. I would wish to mention men in my prayers to a higher authority who are, because the Republican field is singularly broken and what really needs to be expounded in order to explain the Democratic opportunity, is why the Republican Party *is* so broken. Why is it that you cannot for the life of you calculate which are in the numerical ascendency, the Standpatters or the Insurgents? Of course the Insurgents make more noise than the Standpatters. Most of the Standpatters wear gum shoes and it is impossible by the assistance of your ear to count the number of men with gum shoes on, whereas it is quite possible to reckon the host of their opponents, for they all shout and there is a great deal of noise among the allies of war on the Insurgent side of the Republican camp, but nobody quite knows who is in command of the camp. All of that is due to the fact that the so-called Insurgent Republicans know something has happened to the Republican Party; that it has lost its way. But whether it has lost its way or not every man with a weather eye must perceive that it is not bound for any accommodating haven, that the country is out of humor with those who recently administered its affairs; that it does not believe they are bound for a definite enough goal and does not believe they know how to get there even if they believe they know they do. I am not saying this by way of harsh criticism but by way of analysis. I am not arguing with you; I am telling you. Now, on the other hand, you have an extraordinarily stubborn tradition and that tradition is that every man of business standing and of business foresight will naturally ally himself with the Republican Party, because that's the businessman's party. That is the proposition that has been established in this country by those elections which have time out of mind been personally conducted. These people have had expounded to them so long and forcibly the idea that nobody understands the prosperity of America except Republicans that a good many intelligent people have actually come to believe it and it is expected of young men, if they are going to get into the ranks of solid persons, that they will ally themselves with the Republican Party.

Now, the business of America must be taken care of. Nobody denies that. America is a business country and the particular thing of which business is intolerant is ill-considered and rapid change. It is profoundly distrustful of everything that it regards as experimental. It believes that sure perdition lies in the direction of a theoretical program and therefore it shrugs its shoulders with regard to any such out and out doctrine as free trade, and to say a man is a free trader is almost as much as to say that his credit is not good at the bank, that he does not understand business, that he does not understand all those interests which have been built together and become vested by reason of the advantages which have been founded upon a protective tariff. When I talk with Insurgent Republicans and we lay our views frankly before one another, the only difference I can find between myself and them is this: they have a profound reverence for the theory of protection. They are willing to let down the bars of the tariff a good deal, willing to reduce it if it don't go down very far, but even to take down a single bar seems a concession. They say, "The fence was higher when the old man was living and I don't know what the old man would say if his son should take down a bar. The cattle might get out. I recognize the spirit—the cows are free agents, but I am not going to take the fence down. I would do it with a bad conscience and if I took it down I wouldn't dare join the old man in the next world."

Now, I have not the least feeling of piety on the question of protection. The whole question is one of expediency pure and simple. Either it is or it is not good for the country. If it is good for the country we ought to have it. If it is not, we ought not to have it and if it is good in some degree for the country we ought to have it in that degree and no more. Everything you say about it must be proved by data and facts and not by any theory. I have no feeling of piety with regard to the doctrine of free trade or any political doctrine except the political doctrine of the equal rights of men. The standard is the actual good of the country, not any theoretical measure of that good nor anything taken out of theoretical books.

Now, we are in the presence, therefore, of a state of mind and a state of mind is a very serious thing, I can tell you. A panic is a state of mind. When a panic comes on there is just as much money in the country as when it started and there is just as much credit; that is to say, men are just as much deserving of credit as they were before it started, but it is a state of mind where nobody any longer knows it is safe to trust, where everybody is looked upon with distrust and every enterprise is supposed to be overworked. There is therefore universal timidity, and inasmuch as states of mind in a crisis can ruin men's fortunes, a state of mind is a very serious thing. And this present state of mind of the country at large is a very serious thing, which the successful party must understand and arrest. The fortunate circumstance is that business is finding out for itself that something is the matter. It does not have to be told by politicians; it knows something is the matter, for business is aware that privilege has lifted its ugly head in the organization of business and that in order that the average businessman should have the free opportunities of his own occupation something has got to be done to stop the domination and tyranny of privilege. In other words, business itself is aware that it is in bondage and it is determined to break out of bondage.

The pathetic thing to my mind, gentlemen, is this: I make it my business to talk to as many men engaged in large affairs as I can get access to, to lay my mind frankly before them and induce them to lay theirs frankly before me, and what strikes me is the extraordinary number of men who absolutely agree with me as to what ought to be done but beseech me not to use their names or to quote them. In other words, something exists in this country of which businessmen are afraid, and if there is something to make the businessmen of this country afraid it ought to be removed at any cost. And so business is getting a little more tolerant before the proposals of change. Business is saying, "After all there is something the matter. We are perfectly willing to sit down and work out an analysis of what it is that is the matter and we will assist in correcting it if you will only deal temperately with it and in the terms which we can understand." And business is beginning to realize, also, that the combinations—and I am not now speaking of individual trusts, for the problem is much bigger than that, but with the combinations of personnel, the understandings, private tips; of those things which I need not describe to this body of men, that hold you together or else make it dangerous for you to break out; that the very privilege that is dominating business is seeing to it that politics is dominated by its purposes and that most of those processes of politics of which we have grown suspicious are allied with processes of business of which we also have grown suspicious. When I hear you say to me let business alone, I say I will do it upon one condition; that you will let politics alone. Politics did not enter business. Let me tell you that business entered politics. Now if you want this thing remedied take business out of politics. Take your own condition—and I am now talking on the chance that I am addressing some people who hold the opinion I have just quoted—if you want the politician to give business a chance, then all I have to say to you is, give politics a chance to act independently of the influence of money and of privilege. These are some of the things, gentlemen, to which my eyes have been opened since I got on the inside. I have seen men with my own eyes, in at least one state legislature, who did not dare to vote the way they thought and who clearly disclosed to me in private that they wouldn't dare say it in public, and for their sakes I wouldn't dare use their names for they would be ruined—who disclosed to me in private those business connections which had them in their grip. They told me if they voted the way they thought they could not renew their notes at certain banks. This is terrible. It is disgraceful. It is the grip of business on politics, and I say, let the throat of politics go, withdraw this iron hand and let the wholesome blood get into the brain again. Mark you, gentlemen, I know just as well as you do that this is not what most businessmen do. I am honored by the friendship and confidence of scores of businessmen who study and understand the interests of this country just as well as any man of my acquaintance; but what sometimes makes the heat come into my blood is to realize how a small number of men have put their comrades in business in a false attitude toward public affairs by the things they ventured privately to do. No man of conscience or who knew anything would enter a protest against the honest businessmen of this nation, but it is because we are fighting the old thing that I am so much interested in the cause we are fighting—the old thing of privilege, of little groups of men, the thing we have been fighting time out of mind ever since the conception of liberty was born.

Such is the state of mind of the country, and now the question is, will the country trust the Democratic Party to undertake the solution of these difficulties? I say that it is not a question of individual leaders—it is a question of the disposition and methods of the Democratic Party. Upon what terms will they trust the Democratic Party? Why, in the first place, they will trust it just so soon as they make sure that the Democratic Party knows what's the matter, that it does not see phantasms, that it does not see unreal things, that it has gone to the bottom of the items which constitute the process that we should correct; that it has the intimate knowledge of the actual things to be done which will make the touch of its hand definite when it comes to the cure. I am fond of using a figure of speech in this connection which I think is a very useful figure. If a man is ill, the whole of whose system is sound except that in some one place there is a malignant growth, what does the surgeon do if he wants to save his patient's life? He cuts out the malignant growth, but he cannot do so until he knows just where the growth is, and it is not safe for him to approach it unless he can tenderly and delicately separate the intervening muscles and nerves and vital fibres and touching nothing else, finds the exact spot, and with a skill, bred of knowledge, extricates the one thing that interferes with the wholesome course of the blood. And the country is going to judge the Democratic Party by its prognosis and diagnosis. It has got to show that it knows just where and what the malignant growth is and then it has got to show that it can produce surgeons who can cut that thing out without hurting anything else.

Now, the diagnosis is going on. It is somewhat unpleasant. It is very embarrassing to have your interior structure inquired into. There is an intimacy about the inquiries of the surgeon which is in one sense highly unconstitutional. It invades the very intimacies of the individual structure, but there is this inquiry going on. The Stanley Committee has been conducting a part of the diagnosis. There are inquiries going on which are inquiring into the particulars item by item of the processes by which prices are determined irrespective of the demand in the market; the processes by which the product is controlled and competition excluded, the processes by which the output is limited and thereby the income determined; the processes by which free competitors are thrown out of competition or pushed to the wall. These things are being, item by item, disclosed.

Now, when we get these items—we don't have to wait for all of them, we can go after them one at a time—having discovered your item then get your cure. You know if you want to make a rabbit pie, first you get your rabbit—and so with these; having discovered them, then see that the Democratic Party is wise enough to suggest a way in which the remedies can be matched with the details. We have got the principles. We did not have to have statutes to forbid monopoly in the United States. The immemorial principles of the common law forbid monopoly. It needed only the genius of those who could blaze a way into new territory, to make statutes unnecessary in stopping the processes and methods of monopoly. We are not debating monopoly. We are debating the very much more difficult problem of how to stop monopoly; and whenever we see monopoly showing its head there is the place for your shillalah. I withdraw the analogy because I don't look upon politics as a Donnybrook Fair, but with that apology I would not further amend the indictment.

We know the items. Now it is perfectly possible to direct the processes of your law against the items without disturbing anything that is honest and natural and inevitable in the development of modern business. The enemy of business is a man with a program which goes further than he can see, or with a program the items of which are not based upon the indisputable evidence produced in the examination. Just so long as you feel your way in politics you are unreasonably disturbing business, but so soon as you know your way, go the whole length without stopping to ask anybody's leave. Correct the mistakes, correct the errors, check the things that are wrong, and you cannot make a mistake in checking anything that is wrong. Now I, for my part, feel that the Democratic Party is better qualified to do these things I will say than any other party, because the Democratic Party keeps its connections and has kept its connections time out of mind with those things fundamental in our political conceptions. I always remember, gentlemen, that America was established not to create wealth—though any nation must create wealth which is going to make an economic foundation for its life—but to realize a vision, to realize an ideal. America has put itself under bonds to the earth to discover and maintain liberty among men, and if she cannot see liberty now with the clear, unerring vision she had at the outset, she has lost her title, she has lost every claim to the leadership and respect of the nations of the world.

If she is going to put her material processes before her spiritual
processes, then all I have to say is she has ceased to be America
and should withdraw the name in order to withdraw the promise, because that name has always shone here in the West
like a beacon of hope and confidence for all the nations of the
world. Men have turned their eyes towards America in order that
they might release themselves from the very kind of privilege
which we have permitted in some places to grow; and if we discover that we ourselves have fallen into the slough, that we ourselves have not taken the ways that lie upon firm ground, the
ways that lift themselves up the long slopes that are the slopes
of ultimate emancipation, then how will the hope of the world
subside, how will men cry out in despair that the great light in
the West has gone out. Unless, gentlemen, we once more get
in our hearts the passion for what America stands for we shall
accomplish nothing. And in this age of difficulty and perplexity,
how does any man relieve himself from perplexity? If he goes
to bed at night arguing upon the grounds of solvency and expediency he will toss all night long on his bed, but if it is proof
he desires, there is only one rule, and that is the rule of right
and justice, and if he says, "I am going to stand by that, cost
what it may," then sleep will come to him as it came to him when
a little child and he imagined that angels were about his couch.
That is the temper that makes America and I, for my part, am
confident with the confidence of youth that this spirit has come
back to America. I don't profess its coming. The great hurricane
with which comment moves from one part of this country to
another is to realize that it has come, that men are ready to make
sacrifices in order that the public weal may be served and that
there is henceforth to be a common council into which men will
enter, not only that they and their individual fortunes may be
served but that the great fortunes of America may also be served;
I am not speaking in my interest. No, gentlemen[,] you knew
when you came here that you were not going to listen to a man
who was going to commend himself to you. You knew you were
going to listen to a man who whether he was right or wrong was
going to tell you what he thought and leave it to the jury and
not the private councils held with men of understandings. In
this country I am aware of the coming on of a new spirit—that
old subtle cunning and sagacity that used to be the rule in America. The old idea of lie low and let the thing work itself out is
disappearing. You can't lie low any more, because there is a
searchlight moving everywhere. You know the old quotation,
Heaven lies about us in our infancy, and the cynical modifica-

tion of it is that in old age we lie about ourselves; but we have not reached the stage of senility as yet in which we do lie about ourselves. Frankness has come to be the law of life amongst us —amongst those of us who respect ourselves and respect our communities and hope for the best things in politics, and that's the reason the lines of party are being obscured; that's the reason men are about to treat them according to their right temperaments and purposes; that's the reason the standpat dam that has been built so high but of such stolid, stupid masonry, is going to give way. Nothing is more solid than the solidity of the [un]willingness of men to think. After twenty years of teaching I was greatly comforted by a professor at Yale who told me that after an equal length of time he had come to the conclusion that the human mind had infinite measures of resources [for resisting knowledge]; and these resources are not going to give way, but what is going to happen is this: Engineers are coming to the front. They say you don't have to break that dam down; it would flood the country. You have to penetrate it, and let this great body of water piled up behind run through those great courses, alongside of which we can build mills and happy homes and see that the future generations of America know what the power is amongst them and can guide it and trust it. That's what is going to happen and then we will be thankful; and I am thankful the standpat dam was so long unpenetrated. It gave us time to think. That's the only thing I have to say in favor of chewing tobacco; it gives you time to think between sentences. We have had time to think and examine and we have concluded we cannot break the "dam" thing down, but we can penetrate it and take control of these great forces which have been built up behind it; and so far as I am concerned the future is a future of hope for the Democratic Party, because it has a prospect of vision, of ideals applied, of knowledge soberly acted upon, of purposes indomitably applied, until nothing can resist the steady impact of its force. And so in the Twentieth Century we shall renew the distinction which came upon America at the end of the Eighteenth Century, where, looking upon our own affairs without excitement, without revolutionary impulse, we altered the processes of our life to suit the sober processes of our law and America has come again upon a constructive age of politics where her statesmen shall talk business and her business consent to the processes of liberty and achievement.

Address of Woodrow Wilson Governor of New Jersey Before the Iroquois Club Chicago, Ill. Lincoln's Birthday February 12, 1912 At the Hotel La Salle (n.p., n.d.).

To Charles Henry Grasty

My dear Mr. Grasty: Trenton, N. J. February 14, 1912.

Thank you for your letter of the ninth of February. I had heard about the affair at the University of Virginia. I doubt whether Senator Martin is to be personally held responsible for what happened, but men who were supposed to be his representatives certainly were, and it made a very bad impression. I think things have a bit cleared up since.

I have not yet received any such report of my Philadelphia speech as would enable me to judge whether it was correctly taken or not. I am very much interested in your suggestion that it might be worked up. If I can get hold of a copy, I will look at it with that in view.[1]

With haste and cordial thanks,
          Sincerely yours,   Woodrow Wilson

TLS (WP, DLC).
[1] He did not "work up" his Philadelphia speech for the Baltimore *Sun*.

To Edward Mandell House

My dear Mr. House: [Trenton, N. J.] February 14, 1912.

Thank you sincerely for your letter of the eighth with its enclosure. It is fine to feel that you are actively on the watch. I wish you were not so far away.
          In haste,   Faithfully yours,   Woodrow Wilson

TLS (E. M. House Papers, CtY).

From Thomas Bell Love

Dear Governor Wilson: Dallas, Texas, February 14, 1912.

After receiving your telegram from Allentown I decided to go to Philadelphia the next morning for the purpose of meeting you during your brief interval there. During the night I was taken ill, and a physician, called at the instance of my friends, stated that I must not leave my hotel the next day, and yielding to his admonition, I reluctantly wired you that it was impossible for me to meet you, addressing the telegram in care of the Bellview Stratford Hotel, Philadelphia.[1] From the press dispatches I have seen since, I assume that this telegram was not received by you, and this I very much regret. On Thursday and Friday of last week I endeavored repeatedly to get Mr. Measday, or someone of your staff, by telephone, but was utterly unable to do so, and as I was unable to definitely ascertain where you would be on Saturday and Sunday, and as it was imperative that I should be in St. Louis on Monday, it became impossible for me to see you before returning home.

What I wished to say to you was: That I am keeping in close touch with the situation in Texas and that I am convinced without doubt that the Texas delegation will be instructed for you.

Because of a malignant and widespread epidemic of cerebro spinal meningitis which has been prevailing in this State for some two or three months past, it has been practically impossible to get men together, or to promote any organized public interest of any kind, but, notwithstanding this situation, I am convinced by my correspondence that the Wilson sentiment in the State is predominant and is growing stronger.

It seems to me that an excellent opportunity is afforded by the present agitation, pro and con, of the matter of investigating the money trust,[2] to forcefully illustrate your very excellent and undeniably sound idea of the benificence of pitiless publicity.

While in New York I was struck with the widespread sentiment, practically unanimous outside of Wall Street and Big Business, in favor of a thoroughgoing investigation and exposition of the existing facts, whatever they may be, relative to the source and method of control of the money of the country, and it seems to me unanswerable to say that the people are entitled to know what power of control exists, who exercises it, and by what method, and that the claim that a disclosure of these facts will hurt business unnecessarily implies the confession that there is something radically wrong in the premises.

If the people are to run the Government then they must know the facts before they can intelligently exercise their powers and duties as citizens. I believe that a clear-cut and unmistakable declaration of your views upon this question at this time would be of great value to the country and to the progressive cause. There can be no doubt that Wall Street and Big Business are determined to leave nothing undone to prevent your nomination. I do not believe they will succeed. They will have little chance to succeed if the lines are in some way sharply drawn so that they will have to fight in the open and so there will be as little excuse as possible for division among those who claim, sincerely or otherwise, to stand for progressive principles and on the peoples' side. In my judgment, this could not be done better than by calling widespread attention to the fact that the existing conditions of the finances of the country are such that those in control of them and responsible for their existence admit that they would be seriously interfered with if the light of day were turned upon them.

For what it may be worth, my diagnosis of the situation is this. President Taft will undoubtedly be renominated. Roosevelt will probably take himself out of the contest. If not he will be defeated in the convention. There is no hope for Governor Harmon's nomination by the Democrats. Wall Street would prefer him, but does not think much of his chances. They have chiefly in mind at this time Champ Clark, or possibly Underwood, of Alabama, holding in reserve a movement for some dark horse, most likely Kern of Indiana.[3] Clark and Underwood have both been instrumental in soft-pedaling the money trust investigation. They are both clinging to the delusion that no man can antagonize Big Business and win the Presidency. From the standpoint of sheer expediency, this may have been good politics in the past, but my judgment is that 1912 is not that sort of a year. The interests are desperately against you and I am thoroughly convinced that your opportunity for usefulness to the American people lies in causing these facts to be known of all men in some proper way, and as quickly as possible.

Trusting that you will pardon me for this lengthy communication, and again expressing my sincere regret that I was unavoidably prevented from seeing you while in the East, I am

Very truly yours,   Thomas B. Love.

TCL (T. B. Love Papers, Dallas Hist. Soc.).

[1] Wilson spent two hours in the late morning of February 8 in the Bellevue-Stratford waiting for Love. He left for Frankfort at 12:10 P.M. Philadelphia *Evening Bulletin*, Feb. 8, 1912.

[2] After much controversy between Bryanites, led by Robert L. Henry of Texas, and conservatives, led by Oscar W. Underwood, House Democrats, on February 7, 1912, had instructed four standing committees to investigate the so-called money trust—Underwood's method of preventing any serious inquiry. The Bryanites wanted a special committee dominated by themselves.

[3] John Worth Kern of Indianapolis, Democratic vice-presidential candidate in 1908; United States senator, 1911-17.

A News Report of a Political Speech in Concord, New Hampshire

[Feb. 16, 1912]

WILSON ON THE ISSUES.

It was an audience of good size that listened on Thursday evening[1] to an exposition of the principles for which he stands by Woodrow Wilson, governor of New Jersey and prominent candidate for the Democratic presidential nomination. It was an audience that no more than comfortably filled the floor and first gallery of the Auditorium, however, and the second gallery was nearly empty. The overflow meeting for which preparations had been made proved to be unnecessary.

Besides the humbler members of the Democratic party, with the curious ones of other political faiths, or no well defined faith at all, who occupied the body of the house, there was a considerable assemblage of prominent party members on the stage.

It was a friendly and interested audience to which Mr. Wilson talked, though not a markedly enthusiastic one. There was laughter and clapping of hands when a point was scored and close attention was giveen [given] throughout, but had Mr. Wilson been addressing a national convention of his party he would not have stampeded it.

Before proceeding to the stage, Mr. Wilson held a reception and cordially greeted the people as they passed into the hall. . . .

Printed in the *Concord*, N. H., *Evening Monitor*, Feb. 16, 1912; three editorial headings omitted.
1 February 15, 1912.

An Address in New Haven, Connecticut, on Civil Service Reform[1]

[[Feb. 16, 1912]]

Mr. Toastmaster, Mr. President,[2] gentlemen of the association, it is a real pleasure to be here and to associate myself, if only for a very short time, with the work of this association. It is also a pleasure to be at a meeting where it is not necessary to talk politics. I must add this, that just because it is not necessary, I am tempted to do it all the more because I see so many men who would make promising converts. When again shall I have the opportunity to say to so many substantial republicans what would do their souls good?

I want to say that some of you have never heard a real out and out democratic speaker bred in the bone and thereby committed by the very constitution of his system.

But when I think of the theme of the evening and of the business of this association, I cannot help recalling that civil service reform was the first reform that was put into working force in America by independent action. Nothing is venerable in America,

1 Delivered at the annual banquet of the Connecticut Civil Service Reform Association in the Hotel Taft.
2 The toastmaster was Edward Bliss Reed, Assistant Professor of English at Yale; the president of the association was Henry Walcott Farnam, Professor of Political Economy at the same university.

but if there is a venerable reform, it is civil service reform. This takes precedence of all the movements which have resulted in substantial action, and when I think of the contribution that this movement has made to what I might call the public citizenship of the country, it fills my imagination. You have only to think of one figure, the figure of George William Curtis,[3] to see how this movement has brought out some of finest types of citizens, men who have done their work without any expectation or desire for public office, without any ambition for public distinction, but have done it with the idea that they were bound in conscience to put into words, and into words that would affect opinion, the thoughtful views of men everywhere engaged in business, standing outside of political circles and looking on at things that were tended to debauch our political practices. For after all, the vitality of the nation, politically speaking, is to be judged by this. How many movements for civic betterment originate outside the circles of public officials, and how many of those movements result in substantial action? For all the reforms that amount to anything must come from the body of the thoughtful people of the community. The government is theirs, and their opinion must impose upon the government the standards which they think ought to be observed.

This spreading out of the independent thought of men who had no axes to grind, had nothing but a public conscience with regard to the things that were being done. And so it seems to me that there is a sort of distinction in connecting one's self with the movement for civil service reform, that it is an expression of the desire to connect one's self with the best kind of citibens [citizens]. I do not think that we have always acted very wisely in our agitation for civil service reform or that we have always thought very clearly as to our objects. Neither do I think that we have always been quite aware of the limitations of what we might accomplish by this movement. I have known so many men who thought that they would have brought on the millennium with respect to the government if they could only see civil service reform.

As I look back on the various things we have tried to do in this country, there are two lines of reform. The object of one has been purification of the government. The other has been to give the government efficiency. I believe for my part that civil service reform does purify the government but it does not of itself give the government efficiency. You will say "Why that is

3 (1824-1892) author, editor of *Harper's Weekly*, 1863-92; long-time leader of the civil service reform movement.

the very object of it." I dare say it is the object of it, but there is something more than the mere elimination of the principle that to the victor belongs the spoils necessary before you will have a business administration that will carry out the object of government with the proper organization and efficiency, for efficiency is a matter of co-ordination in large part. It is not a matter so much of the character and the integrity and the knowledge of the individual public servant as it is of his relation to other public servants and to his subordination in the scheme of superintendence which will bring about what the business man would regard as efficient results.

Civil service reform of itself does not accomplish these objects. They yet remain to be accomplished. But it does take a first step and until that step is taken, efficiency is out of the question. Until you have purified the government, until you have put it beyond the misuse which can be made of it by the improper employment of patronage, efficiency cannot be debated, for it is beyond our reach.

If offices are to be filled merely as personal rewards, generally for personal rather than for public service, then efficient government is out of the question. It is a mere and large political machine.

Now we are, all of us, interested in breaking up the machine. You can always kill a thing by starving it. The primary object of civil service reform is to starve the machine, to take away its food. It lives upon patronage. It has got to have patronage in order to live, and the object of civil service reform is to take patronage away from it.

The interesting thing is that civil service reform has had very much more complete success in the national field than in the local field. Long ago these ancient principles of civil service reform were enacted into law by the federal statutes, but our statutes have gone at a very irregular pace and it is very surprising if you will canvass the country from one side to the other, in how few places the principles of civil service reform have been put into operation. And it is also interesting to note how easy, for the most part, it is to put them into operation if you once get the proper basis of the law.

I have been much interested in examining the pamphlet which was laid at every place, containing the Connecticut statute. I note it corresponds fairly closely with the legislation which we passed some years ago in New Jersey. Ours is, if the subject were a different one, what we would call a local option bill. The several political units or organizations of the state are authorized to adopt the provisions of the act as the provisions of their local government and to establish civil service reform. That is to say, the principles are civil service examination and appointment. And almost in every instance where the people have been given a chance to vote upon it, they have adopted it; not only in the quiet counties, not only in the little towns, but in big populous miscellaneous cities, where one would suppose that the work of the political machine man, who is always opposed to this, could be most effectually carried out in order to block and prevent it. What is interesting to me in New Jersey and every other state is this, that the moment you give the people a chance to effect a reform, they effect it, and I have found that the political machine man is always opposed to letting the people have a chance. He does not want the thing submitted to the public vote. He does not want men acting independently of the machine to get up a petition which will make it necessary to submit it to a vote. If you will notice, the machinery is this. Each is independent of the organization. A body of citizens with a sufficient body of signatures can set the things in motion and can make it absolutely necessary that the citizens of the locality concerned shall vote upon it. And I venture to predict that in most localities just as soon as any sort of agitation is set and any sort of agitation made, the provisions of the act will be adopted.

But I consider it my duty to tell you that the results will not entirely satisfy you. They do one thing, but they don't do everything. For example, you take a great city and generally the fire department and the police department are the most effectual parts of the political machine, all the policemen being dependent for their tenure of office upon the boss or men in office who represent the boss, all the men in the fire department being in the same position and these departments being spread in that personnel like a net throughout the community so that in every neighborhood there is a fire engine house and a police station. Whenever an election takes place these men dare not disobey an order to man the polls—the police, under the guise of watching the polls, but really as watchers for their party and their bosses. Not only that, but before the election these men are used as canvassers who in the greatest detail canvass every precinct in the city.

Now you can stop all of that practically by civil service reform. Once let these men know that they don't have to take orders and they won't take them. But after you have done it, see what you have done. After that there will certainly be an association of firemen and an association of policemen, and these men, with their continuing to exercise their detailed local influence, will be able to control votes with regard to their own salaries, with regard to the selection of men to go to the city council, and they will send very influential delegations to lobby in the state capitol for legislation for their benefit. I say very influential, for they still have the power to control a very considerable number of votes, and it is votes that count in politics.

We have to face the whole of this situation in order to intelligently deal with any part of it. If you only regard civil service reform as a way station, then in my opinion, it is a way station that is worth hurrying. But don't forget that it is a way station. Don't forget that you have then just begun, that you have cleared the field, that the field is before you to conquer and feel that it is absolutely necessary that public opinion should dominate political process. And so long as you leave your political machinery complicated, you can't do that. We have given the American voter a practical thing to do. We have made the boss almost an indispensable part of our political machine. To make up a ticket to select men all the way from sheriff down to pound-keeper, from mayor down to pound-keeper, from governor down to the smallest local office, requires time and thought, and you have to go about and pick out the men who are willing to run, for there are hundreds and thousands of men in America who are not willing to take public office. You have got to get the willing men and the fit men and the responsible men, and the voter generally comes in only after the slate is made up. He votes for the slate that the republican boss has picked out or for the slate that the democratic boss has picked out, and if you will be particular in your inquiries, you will usually find that these two gentlemen have been in consultation, so that it is heads I win and tails you lose. It is tweedledee and tweedledum, and the real force in politics lies not in the election, but in the selection. If you will allow me to select the candidates, then I am perfectly willing that you should go through the motions of electing them, and that is about all you have been in the habit of doing. And the only way to overcome that is to reduce, as far as you possibly can reduce, the number of offices to be filled by election and therefore by preliminary selection. Then, don't you see, your civil service will begin to amount to something, because then the number of appointed officers will increase. The number of officers taken out of the temptations of politics will be increased and the possibility of the control of public opinion by the selection of those who are elected will be very much facilitated. Don't forget that the whole electoral process lies back of this. What difference does it make to you, except that you have removed temptation in some respects, that you still leave your government to private management? The whole difficulty of government does not lie in the fact that it is corrupt. It centers in the fact that it is private, and so long as it is private it is going to be corrupt in one direction or another. It is its privacy that renders it corrupt.

I don't think the rest of us realize how much that is moral depends upon publicity. I daresay that you have had the experience that I have had of finding yourself in a foreign city where you supposed there wasn't a living soul that knew you, by sight, and then felt an awful temptation to adjourn your morals and have a fling. And then you realize that when you get back home the eyes of your neighbors, the comments of your friends, the standards of your circle, buttress you in your morals more than you conceived would be possible. And if you debate things and if you would make up all determinations in private, that would less often square with the standards which you profess to set. I was asked the other day, for example, why on the principle of the short ballot it would not be the best thing in a city, for example, to elect only the mayor and to let the mayor appoint everything. I said: "Because the mayor would not have to debate his decisions out loud, and it is necessary to have enough men to make agreement necessary and to go the further step of making the agreement public so that the votes have to be public and the debates have to be public. In other words the processes of choice have got to be taken out of the private lines and displayed to the public gaze in order that they may be free from corruption." Now when you come to widen into this field you will see that you have got an absolutely unlimited thing to do.

Civil service reform? Why, of course, civil service reform. I don't see how any honest and intelligent man can hold off from it, but after you have got your civil service reform and have put your men in without partisan purpose, have put them in after examining them as to their fitness and character, what are you going to do with them? How are you going to conduct the government?

I will go further than one of the speakers that preceded me went. I don't doubt that any group of fairly capable business men could take the government of one of our states and run it for one-half what it is being run for and make a profit of twenty per cent. If you would give them the contract, they would be foolish if they didn't jump at it. Why? Because of the enormous waste in the mere organization of the government. Every time you want to do anything, you have to have a new commission to do it and pay a new set of salaries. Why there are so many commissions in New Jersey that I have to count them up about once a week to find the men I have to appoint because the governor of New Jersey appoints nearly everybody and I can't keep track of the various commissions. Why, every oyster bed in New Jersey has a commission of its own and every county that borders on the sea or any important river has some fish or game commission of its own and there is no pretense of any kind of standardization of accounting. There is no means of finding out what the various departments of a complicated machine cost, and there is no means of checking the cost of one as compared with another. It is truly said to-night that if any business was run in that way it would go bankrupt, and the only reason the government is not bankrupt is not that we do not permit it to be run economically or efficiently, but we depend on the taxation and the taxation in nine cases out of ten is drawn from the men who can least afford to pay it. I don't know if you are unfortunate in that respect here in Connecticut but in New Jersey we have no means of standardizing the taxes. They differ in neighboring communities.

We have boards of taxation but they can act only when applied to act, so the property in one neighborhood will be assessed at forty per cent. of its value and in a neighboring place at seventy-five per cent. of its value, and everything is based in this way. If you live in a house that costs $500,000, the assessor will very kindly say, "Well, that is a house that very few persons can afford to buy, and therefore if you had to sell it you couldn't sell it for anything like $500,000, because the customers will be so few." But if you live in a house that cost $500, if there are any such houses left, then you can easily sell it for $500, because there is a great competition for cheap houses, and therefore the man with a $500 house is assessed for $500 and the man with a $500,000 house is assessed for about $250,000. That is true all over any community that I have made inquiries in. That is the way we do the public business, and do you suppose that civil service reform is going to touch that? You might elect every tax assessor and every official. You might select him by civil service process and you would not have touched the process of taxation. You would not have made them any more efficient or any more business-like.

What I want to say, therefore, tonight is not to argue in favor of civil service reform, because I would be ashamed of myself if I argued so obvious a thing as that. It would be an insult to the intelligence, it seems to me, of any body of men like this at any rate, to try to prove to them what is evident upon its face, that you have got to take patronage away as a temptation from politicians or else make the business of purifying your politics absolutely hopeless. That is the basis of civil service reform. But I wish that our civil service reformers could conceive their business in a wider scope. You don't reform a civil service merely by purifying its personnel. What we need right now is an agitation that would carry this along with it, an agitation for the study of business with scientific efficiency. Suppose that this association, for example, composed so largely of business men, should set itself to this task without being guided by [the] legislature of Connecticut. Suppose that it should take the government of the state of Connecticut, study it as any citizen can study it, by getting the documents, and then suggest a real reorganization of it upon such lines as the business men of Connecticut could approve of and then publish a pamphlet explaining the thing in such wise as any taxpayer could understand and then put the whole force of the association back of a systematic agitation to bring the thing about. Don't you think that would be more interesting than the thing that you are doing now? Because you meet all sorts of objections to what you are doing now, you are asked now if it is a reasonable thing to ask a man the names of all the rivers in Asia to find out if he is fit to occupy a public office. Of course you never do ask him to name all the rivers of Asia, but it is always assumed by the critics of civil service reform that the most impractical questions are asked.

Now if you could fill the minds of the people with this idea that we are not merely interested in pestering the applicants for public office with teasing examinations, [then] we are putting the business of the state of Connecticut on such a footing that they will have to have qualified men to conduct it. As a matter of fact, gentlemen, if your business is conducted as the business of most states is conducted, you don't have to have men of very much qualification to conduct. Any man of ordinary intelligence could do the job in most of the minor posts. If you make it evident that you are agitating for a thing so big that the little parts of it have to be looked into in order to be effective, you will put behind civil service reform the spirit of this particular age. Whom are men most regarding now in the business world? They are regarding the experts in business reorganization, is it not so? If it is worth the while of a comparatively small insurance company in the state of New Jersey to pay experts $10,000 to tell them how they can improve the organization of their force, isn't it worth while for the state of New Jersey to spend, say $100,000 to find out the same thing for its own activities? And if business men find the advice of experts good investments won't the public find the advice of experts good investments, and if they are indeed experts, can't they make it evident that what they are saying entails good sense and good political economy? I believe and I want to say with the utmost fairness the civil service reform associations in this country have languished because they did not have a big enough conception of their job.

It is not worth your while if you are going to stop there, to waste a good deal of time upon the obvious thesis that a man of good character and some ordinary capacity disconnected from politics should occupy your minor offices. That is the reason you cannot often get men to come to meetings of civil service reform associations. The topic isn't big enough. They have got bigger topics every day in their own offices than that. Moreover you haven't got the real dynamics of civil service reform until you concede [conceive] it as a great scheme for redeeming your government from inefficiency.

I remember when I was a youngster, I was easily diverted by the writings of Mr. Eaton[4] who was one of the first Americans to devote himself to the American system of politics, and I was somewhat bored while I waded through that book of his on civil service reform[5] because by the time I had read one paragraph in each chapter I knew what it was going to contain because it was so painfully obvious. But if I had only seen that this was the best view of the modern conception of what a government ought to be, I would not have been bored, but I would have seen for each community, provided each community had its individual problems, there was a scheme of civil service reform necessary as an introduction to the great scheme of reorganization. One of most humiliating things to my mind in America is the knowledge that almost all of the best governed cities in the world are on the other side of the water and the things that we have been debating have long ago been done in those countries which we speak of as effete monarchies. And in America, where there is in my judgment more natural political capacity than anywhere in the world, that capacity has not been organized up to and kept up to the standards of those things which we boast that we invented, that we set up the standards for, for the whole world. And if we are going to have real vitality in this country

4 Dorman Bridgman Eaton (1823-99), lawyer and leader in the movements for civil service reform and the reform of city government.
5 *Civil Service in Great Britain: A History of Abuses and Reforms and their Bearing upon American Politics* (New York, 1881).

in the things that now agitate us, we have got to conceive our tasks very largely and do them with the indomitable spirit that ought to quicken the blood of every man. So that what I have ventured to conceive as my duty to-night in coming here is to preach the idea that you have only begun and that you have it in your power now to set an example to the rest of the country in conceiving your task so largely and executing it so broadly that men will turn to Connecticut and see how government ought to be organized and say "Yes, they have built upon this foundation which we used to stop short in calling civil service reform but they were men of vision and knowledge and they knew that that was only the foundation, that that was only the beginning." For, gentlemen, the interesting, and I hope I am not going to venture upon your politics, in what I am about to say, the important thing about our time is this: We are rediscovering the principles of America. We have forgotten that they have become overshadowed by the efficient business which we have undertaken in so great a spirit in exploiting the new continent. We are rediscovering the principle that while everything has been efficiently organized in America, that government has not been. And the result has been that special interest has grown and government did not, and what we have got to do all over again is to get the general community into the game by irresistible organization.

Government, to my mind, is nothing more nor less than organizing the general interest so efficiently that no special interest can dominate it. And we have no doubt that in America we have let our governments become so disordered in respect to their organization, that special interest could break in and we not be aware of it.

I will illustrate what I mean. I was out in Oregon a few months ago, last May, and in Oregon there is a very interesting person, a Mr. Uren, who has been perhaps the most active man in the state in bringing out the reforms which we do not regard as characteristic of Oregon. It happened that the day I reached Portland, Oregon, the Oregonian, the most important paper in Oregon, had a little sneering paragraph in it which said that there were two legislatures in Oregon, one at Salem, the capital of the state, and the other going around under the hat of Mr. Uren.[6] And I took occasion that evening to say that while I was very far from being an advocate of government in the hands of a single man or body

[6] See n. 4 to the news report of Wilson's address to the Commercial Club of Portland, Ore., printed at May 19, 1911, Vol. 23.

of men, nevertheless if I had to make a choice I would rather have a government going around under the hat of Mr. Uren than going around under God knows whose hat.

Now if you were asked under whose hat the government of Connecticut goes around, would you know? There are railroad offices where you might find out.[7] But could you know and could you point out to the state? Some of you could. You could, many of you, point out to the state in whose offices important statutes are generally written. Nobody supposes, I take it for granted, that the statutes are ever written by the members who introduce them. I don't suppose anybody is innocent enough to think that. Now if a member of the legislature introduces a bill in the legislature of great consequence to the state, who knows who wrote that bill? Sometimes you can guess, but you can't know, and then who knows what happens to the bill? You know it takes a dive and disappears in a certain committee and you know that sometimes it gets drowned and never comes up again, but you don't know what happens in the committee, you don't know what arguments prevail there to choke it or to alter it, or what arguments prevail to bring it out by report to the assembly again. All these things are done under cover—I don't say purposely under cover—but as a matter of fact, under cover, and you haven't the least idea who originates nine-tenths of the legislation of Connecticut, and until you have a distinct idea how are you going to hold anybody responsible? . . .

The tendency toward democracies, the tendency toward republics, is everywhere one of enlightenment. You can't have light and keep narrow lines in government. You can't have a place and keep privilege unless privilege owns the place. You can't get the general solution of those things and have a narrow concentration of power, and, as the light spreads, special interests find it more difficult to go abroad and they can't go abroad five minutes after the light is turned on.

Now I say that the object of associations like this is not attained unless they use a larger lamp than office by examination. That is part of what the light discloses, but it is another part for our enterprises as Americans, gentlemen, are nothing else than the service of humanity. Our enterprise is nothing else than to purify and rectify and energize anything that represents the common interests. To see that we have some surplus of energy that we care to spend outside of the narrow circle of our own individuality. That is the problem of government, and I see in the

---

[7] A reference to the alleged domination of Connecticut politics by the New York, New Haven and Hartford Railroad.

signs of the times the certainty that reforms are going to grow easy that were once conceded to be too big to undertake.

I was asked to-day by somebody what I understood the insurgency of our times to signify. The questioner seemed to think that it was some kind of a pleasure that a man had in making trouble that brought on insurgency and that it was just a grand rejoicing in the opportunity. And I said: "Why, it seems to me that what we roughly term insurgency, which obtains everywhere except where providence has prevented it penetrating, this universal phenomenon that we call insurgency is simply the rising of the sap, of the old sap in America.["] I used to say that a sophomore had the sap of manhood in him, but it hadn't got to his head, it was rising, and we have the life sufficiently, we have had the sap in us, but it has not until recently got to our heads, and now insurgency means that it is getting to our heads, that it is setting something growing in our thinking boxes, and that is stimulated by what created America and the vision of the greater rights of mankind and the knowledge that only the gates of opportunity afford the egress from the difficulties that we now face. The gates of opportunity are all but closed in some directions in America, and we have got to open them—somewhere and some places that are absolutely closed to the individual. I was saying the other night that we have either got to find the key or get a crowbar. I don't want to get a crowbar. I believe I can find the key and we have got to get the key. . . .

Now, just to go out with reform in your eye isn't going to accomplish anything. It will accomplish something if you know what you are after, if you make it your business to find out the things that are wrong and go after them, and I think I can see a rising spirit in America in this new age, for which we are no longer bound and no longer waiting. While we are sitting now in the consciousness of our own superiority we nevertheless are awake as we never were awake before to the necessity for systematic effort and systematic reform. That always precedes an age of achievement. God give us grace to see our way and courage to hesitate never a moment.

Printed in the *Hartford*, Conn., *Daily Times*, Feb. 17, 1912.

To Mary Allen Hulbert Peck

The Bellevue-Stratford
Dearest Friend,   Philadelphia 18 Feb'y, 1912

Even on Sundays, nowadays, I am on the go. Here I am in Phila. to-day to address a *peace* society,—I do not even remember what its name is, exactly! But, two more weeks of this nonsense, and I am done,—at least for the present. I am going to stop this unending round of speech-making and return to the simple life! I am well, perfectly well, but I do sadly need rest *and recreation.* Writing to you is one of the few I have left,—I mean one of the few recreations. And when I turn to it I fear that I am getting more pleasure than I give. For I am a dull cuss in my moments of release from the constant rush and strain I am under. It gives me the keenest pleasure to write to you,—to have those few minutes of direct speech with you and intimate thought of you, while other things are all put aside and I am no "public man" but just a loving friend; but my pen catches none of the life that is in my thought! All the vivacity of my mind seems to be exhausted in the interminable conferences, the exacting business, the daily framing of public speeches. It's a shame to give a beloved friend only what is left in the moments when the stress is relaxed. Sundays, besides, seem, by life-long habit of our minds, to be days of reaction, when all the tides are at ebb. If I could only put into words what is really there! but the words lag and turn out to wear a dull face when they are actually put down! As I write the kodak picture you sent me the other day of yourself talking to Mr.—Somebody,—and as I look at it it is impossible to realize that you have a care in the world (I think I shall look at it every time I think of you!): it is so natural, so graceful; you are so at ease and are smiling as one does when one is easily pleased,—in a holiday spirit. And therefore it delights me. I can believe when I look at it that you are *not all* the time tired and sad and heavy with hidden cares,—that the theory of my last (very scrappy) letter is a shrewd guess,—in short, that you are a bit of a humbug (you always were delightful in sweeping, without notice, from one mood to another) and only let your troubles come to the surface when and where you find, like an indulged child, that you can always get sympathy[.] And you certainly can! I always read on the page more than you write—comprehend and sympathize with all my heart. Remember that after April your sky will be *wholly* clear! If they were here all the home folks would join me in affectionate messages. I hope all are well.

            Your devoted friend   Woodrow Wilson

They are *still* searching for every scrap I ever wrote, public or private, to find something that will embarrass me.

ALS (WP, DLC).

To John Wesley Wescott

My dear Judge: [Trenton, N. J.] February 18, 1912.

Thank you sincerely for your interesting letter of February fourteenth.[1] It was better than a valentine. I probably am over-taxing myself, but by the end of another week my distant engagements practically come to an end, and I shall behave more sensibly. I am particularly happy by reason of your motive which led you to give me the warning.

Thank you for letting me see the letter from Mr. Harris.
                    Faithfully yours,   Woodrow Wilson

TLS (J. W. Wescott Coll., NjP).
[1] It is missing.

A News Report of After-Dinner Remarks
[Feb. 19, 1912]

SUSSEX SOCIETY TENDERS WILSON HEARTY GREETING

NEW YORK, Feb. 19.—Governor Wilson of New Jersey might well have been considered one of Sussex County's sons if the reception accorded him at the fourth annual gathering of the Sussex Society at the Hotel Astor Saturday night,[1] meant anything. It was a home gathering for many of the natives of the northernmost bailiwick of New Jersey who had sought other fields in which to labor. And to them the New Jersey Executive gave a little family talk.

Just returned from his New England tour, Governor Wilson laid politics aside with one brief exception, when he accounted for the solid Democratic vote of Sussex. He saw in the country store gatherings and the old-fashioned neighborhood controversies the best method of arriving at a comprehensive viewpoint on current affairs.

"Back to Sussex," was the Governor's theme, for there, as might obtain in other rural districts, the proper poise was to be gained. The speaker took occasion to refer to the ancient bill of rights of Virginia, which he said was the true example of democracy. . . .

Mr. [Job Elmer] Hedges undertook to have some fun with the Governor. He started off by saying that he wished Dr. Wilson every success—socially.

"He will not expect any political assistance from me," added Mr. Hedges, and the Governor joined in the laugh.

Continuing, the speaker commented on the large number of women present, for whom he begged the Governor's consideration. Referring to the recent effort to secure an expression regarding the woman's suffrage movement from the Governor and their reception thereat accorded, Mr. Hedges expressed his pleasure in the fact that the women might again "corner" the Executive, and he could not evade the question with the same diplomatic skill. This brought another laugh, but it was noted that none seemed inclined to follow the speaker's suggestion.

When it came Governor Wilson's turn, he was greeted enthusiastically, the diners rising and applauding as Mr. Bennett[2] ended his introductory remarks.

Disposing of Mr. Hedge's facetious flings with the comment that "such a genial personality overcame all thoughts of bitterness," he proceeded to explain the Democratic unanimity of Sussex County.

"In looking over this assemblage," the Governor said, "I can understand why Sussex County holds its almost unanimous Democratic vote. It appears that the Republicans of Sussex have all moved out of the county, but they have not forgotten the place from which they came." It was a comfortable thing, the Governor continued, to meet and think of the simple life back at the old home, and he wondered if it were not true that one recovered poise in the regions of greater quiet. There was no "neighborhood" in New York, he said, and unless it were possible to get the old neighborhood point of view, the sophistication of Manhattan would be overwhelming. No nation, he declared, could solve its great problem save the people approached the issues from the point of view of one just "getting into the game." It was necessary to go back, and from a distance to focus the mind from the point of old beginnings.

The absolute ultimate of democracy, the Governor went on to say, was contained in the bill of rights which Virginia adopted many years ago. In that bill, he declared, it was set forth that the magistrates were the servants of the people, and must at all times be amenable to them, this in the face of the opinion held by some that the common judgment of the people could not be trusted.

In this connection, the Governor said that the hope of the country lay in the people who have yet to achieve, not those who have achieved, and therefore it was important that there should be a system of laws by which the gates of opportunity should always remain open.

"I don't mean to say," he continued, "that the gates of opportunity are closed. The key is somewhere. I don't know where it is, but the solution is obvious; get the key at any cost. No scruple of delicacy ought to stand in the way. The key of the gates has got to be found, no matter if some 'special interest' should be shy about a personal search."

Printed in the *Newark Evening News*, Feb. 19, 1912.
1 February 17.
2 William Stiles Bennet, president of the Sussex Society, Republican congressman from New York, 1905-11, 1915-17.

A News Report of an Address in Philadelphia to the Universal Peace Union

[Feb. 19, 1912]

PROGRESSIVES ARE DOING WORLD WORK, DECLARES WILSON

Governor Woodrow Wilson, of New Jersey, presented forceful views on international peace, amity and good feeling among nations before the Universal Peace Union in the ballroom of the Bellevue-Stratford last night.

Only at one time in his epigramatic address did he strike a note of politics, and that was when dealing with the enlightenment necessary for a perfect understanding of national and international good will.

"We are hearing," he said, "a great deal these days of disturbance. These are radical processes and thought by timorous persons to be processes of change. They are not of change, but of thought. There are not enough radical persons. The only radical thing I see is that men are standing up in the meeting and are telling just what is going on. Nothing has been done yet, and, as Kipling would say, 'that is another story.'

"After we really find out what is happening we must get hardheaded men together and without fear or favor know what is going on in the economical, moral and social world. When we have the facts we must call in the physician. We can't kill the patient; can't tie up his arteries or suffocate him or stop the irresistible forces of nature. These things we can't alter, but we can lay them before the jury of experts.

"Many things are wrong in this country. Many a man does not know he has stolen and is much mortified when he finds he is a thief. Stealing is so ingenious and the man who receives the article is so far from the man from whom it is stolen that it seems that he paid for value received. Our life is complex and our morals are simple. What we must do is to bring up our moral bookkeeping to the complexity of business."

In discussing peace, he said:

"This is not a domestic matter, but an international one, for the same exploitation and injustice within our borders applies to international questions. Just so soon as we are just to the people in the United States justice and equity in China and in Manchuria will follow. This mote must be removed from the international eye, as must be the beam from our own eye. How are we going to do justice to other nations if we don't know justice?

"I believe the cause of peace is being advanced, not only by Doctor Love[1] and his associates, but because the world is more and more awakening to the details and ramifications of moral responsibilities. This great country of America has had a long heedless youth of material enterprise. We have now come to the time of second thought, when we must see that our own house is in order, and that we love and do justice.

"America is not great because she is rich, not because of her great population and possessions; her only title of distinction is that she has a play on the boards which realizes the rights of man. All are welcome, the doors are open, and all may share the freedom, sympathy and justice.

"If we have lost these things, it is our duty to recover the title deeds. Let us turn back and begin where we began, and then make no mistakes. Let us change that which is wrong. Let us place our eyes to the horizon and here again raise lights as beacons to mankind, once more to serve the people of [with] justice and the cause of peace."

In the first part of the address Governor Wilson said that it was necessary to carefully study the whole question and to endeavor to ascertain whether we could clearly advocate peace. He said that countries must first have industrial peace and justice within the confines of the country before the question of international peace should be discussed. He said that war was "clumsy and brutal," and that we were steadily outgrowing such methods of righting wrongs, but that all must gravely consider the question of concession and equality before war could be abolished. He characterized peace as a perfectly running machine with friction practically eliminated, due to the perfection of construction.

The whole keynote of the address was the need of righting wrongs, securing justice for the laborer, equity and right in each country and international good will would necessarily follow.

"We have courts," he said, "to stop private warfare. Once people took the law in their own hands, families fought for vengeance against a family who slew a son, and then men took the rectification of ordinary rights of business in their hands and courts sprang up only as a means to protect private peace.

"Public courts are only the same to protect international peace. When there is a wrong it must be fought out. Often this is just, but war is clumsy and a brutal method to get at justice."

Here Governor Wilson pictured the glory of the man dying for his country, but spoke of the greater glory of a just and reasonable understanding which would prevent such catastrophes. In closing this portion of his address he said:

"You can't stop the inevitable, slow grinding to set things right."

Publicity and enlightenment—knowing what the world is doing in every corner—is a potent factor of peace, as outlined by the speaker. He said it is necessary to know what is occurring in the Congo, and that the acts of the nations should be held up before the public—"the great jury" which is steadily righting wrongs.

Printed in the Philadelphia *North American*, Feb. 19, 1912; some editorial headings omitted.
    1 Alfred Henry Love (1830-1913), woolen merchant of Philadelphia and a radical pacifist who had refused to serve or procure a substitute when drafted during the Civil War and was an outspoken opponent of the War with Spain. Founder in 1866 of the Universal Peace Society (later the Universal Peace Union) and president of that organization until his death.

A News Report of an Address in Trenton

[Feb. 20, 1912]

JERSEY HARBOR DEVELOPMENT

TRENTON, Feb. 20.—Vast opportunities are being neglected by New Jersey through its failure to take advantage of its natural harbor facilities and develop them for trade and commerce, according to the views expressed by several speakers at the conference held in the Assembly chamber yesterday afternoon to consider various inland waterway propositions in their relation to this State.

The two chief topics under consideration were the proposed ship canal across New Jersey and the improvements which are contemplated as the result of investigations made by the New Jersey Harbor Commission.

Governor Wilson was one of the speakers, who expressed himself as impressed by the importance of the subjects under consideration as affecting the commercial and industrial developments, which, he said, are immediately ahead of us in America. He predicted that great changes are about to be accomplished in this country, which, when they begin, will operate very rapidly. New Jersey, he said, should not be caught unprepared to take advantages of the opportunities when they are presented.

These changes, Governor Wilson explained, will come from two sources, and he said the commerce of this country, so far as international exchanges are concerned, is "about to burst its jacket." He declared that our exports of grain are rapidly falling off, while exports of manufactured articles are increasing by leaps and bounds. He said that it meant that every harbor of consequence must be repaired and united with each other wherever possible. It means that mere seafaring traffic can no longer be depended upon, but that there must be intracoastal deep waterways.

"You know that we are building the Isthmian Canal now for the rest of the world," continued the Governor, "not for our own use because we haven't got the ships to send through it. By a policy singularly consistent in its stupidity, we have destroyed the carrying trade of the United States.

"There might be a very large roll of the names of gentlemen who contributed their lack of intelligence to this process. They have contributed to it with diligence and the result is that it is commoner to see the flag of the little kingdom of Greece upon the seas, so far as commercial vessels are concerned, than the flag of the United States.

"At the same time it is probable that the country will adhere to its ancient policy that carriage between port and port of the United States shall be in American bottoms; but unless you can find these bottoms the trade has struck bottom. It is all very well to say these things must be carried in American bottoms, but it takes a lot of bottom to stand the race if you have to run it with only two or three ships. We have got to develop a great carrying navy and along with that development we have got to give that carrying navy a great body of facilities which now simply do not exist. Look at the port of New York with the present trade of the port of New York, and you will see a thing congested and embarrassed by lack of development; and when you consider that the only development has been on the Manhattan side, I mean almost the only developments, and that the Jersey side has been almost absolutely neglected, and yet when you look at any one of these maps and see the great areas available on the Jersey side and the enormous expansions that may be made of the real harbor in and by the port of New York, you will see the things that wait to be done. When you add that to the project that must be carried out of making access easy from the lower Bay down to the Delaware River you see some of the things which haven't yet been touched, but which must be done within the course of three or four years if done in time to meet these great changes."

Printed in the *Newark Evening News*, Feb. 20, 1912; some editorial headings omitted.

A News Report of a Busy Morning in Kansas City, Missouri

[Feb. 22, 1912]

HIS "HAT IN THE RING," TOO
"AND MY HEAD IN IT," GOVERNOR WOODROW WILSON SAYS.

Woodrow Wilson came to Kansas City this morning, ate breakfast, shook hands with several hundred persons in the lobby of the Hotel Baltimore, made a 5-minute talk to the Grain Dealers' Association at the Coates House and left at 11:15 o'clock for Topeka where he is to speak tonight.

Surrounded by a crowd as soon as he stepped from a motor car at the Hotel Baltimore the New Jersey governor was compelled to hold an impromptu reception before he could get to his room. The only statement he made to a crossfire of questions was when a copy of The Star was handed him containing Colonel Roosevelt's declaration that his hat was in the ring.

"Well, so is mine," the governor said, laughing, "and my head is in it."

But something else in The Star caught his eye and by the expression on his face he was making a mental calculation.

"The combined Democratic progressive vote—that is Bryan, Wilson and Folk—is double that of Clark and Harmon," volunteered an onlooker who saw that the governor's attention had been attracted by The Weekly Star's poll.

"Ah, that is very gratifying," said the governor with a broad smile. "I have had fragmentary reports of The Star's poll from time to time, but I have not before seen the exact figures. Is it finished?"

He was told the votes were still coming in.

"I should like very much to see the result when the figures are collated," he said.

Governor Wilson was almost dragged from the crowd in the Baltimore by a committee from the grain dealers' association and had reached the Coates House in a motor car before the crowd waiting to shake hands with him learned that he had gone.

The grain men received the candidate with cheers. "Trade," he told them, "is one thing in this country that is not standpat. Its currents cannot be controlled. They have put a straitjacket tariff on it, but it will burst from it sooner or later and release itself. Politicians and platforms bind it in vain—it cannot be controlled. The world, like trade, moves on with little regard for the men who pretend their standing still keeps the world standing still, too. My idea of a progressive is a man who keeps up with the world. If he just keeps up he is progressing. A standpatter, on the other hand, is one who stands still with his eyes shut and his ears stuffed with cotton and refuses to concede that the world is moving under him."

Governor Wilson's stop in Kansas City was the result of a "holdup" as was explained to him by Judge H. C. Gilbert,[1] who invaded his car at the yards at the Union Depot. The governor had not been made aware that he was to stop here.

"Here is a bunch of highwaymen who are going to take you uptown and let some people shake hands with you," Judge Gilbert told the governor. "Being a good roads advocate I have a double right to call myself a highwayman," Judge Gilbert explained further.

The other highwaymen were Newton Gillham, William H. Wallace, Henry Koehler and Charles A. Sumner.[2] They took the governor to the Hotel Baltimore and told him they had planned a reception to take place after he had breakfasted, but the plan miscarried. The reception was held before, during and after breakfast. As soon as the crowd caught sight of the visitor he was surrounded and the handshaking began. There were a number of Missouri Democrats in the lobby fresh from the convention at Joplin,[3] and they were presented to the governor. Among them were Attorney General Major, Judge James Cowgill, Joseph B. Shannon, John P. Gordon, state auditor, and Harry J. Simmonds, a member of the legislature.[4]

Governor Wilson took off his overcoat and the hat that he had announced was in the ring and handed them to Walter Measday, his secretary, and went at the handshaking in a business-like manner. The line was kept moving in front of him by Judge Wallace, but nearly every man who grasped the governor's hand had something to say in passing. "Good luck to you," "I like a fighter," "You're among friends here," "Don't let up on 'em, governor," and similar greetings accompanied the outstretched hands, and to each the governor made a cordial response. One white haired man couldn't shake the governor's hand long enough.

"I want to shake hands with the next President," he said, as he hung on.

"Well, you've done it, now give us a chance," the man behind him urged, and the laugh that followed saved Governor Wilson the embarrassment of making any reply.

To all inquiries about the situation in Missouri, Governor Wilson made the same reply: "I am not going into any state that has a favorite son or that has instructed its delegation for another."

Printed in the *Kansas City*, Mo., *Star*, Feb. 22, 1912; some editorial headings omitted.
    1 Hugh C. Gilbert, presiding judge of the county court of Jackson County, Mo.
    2 Newton Cloud Gillham, lawyer of Kansas City; William Hockaday Wallace, lawyer of Kansas City; Henry Koehler, cashier of the Western Exchange Bank, Kansas City; and Charles A. Sumner, secretary of the City Club of Kansas City.
    3 The Democratic state convention, which had just endorsed Champ Clark as a favorite son.
    4 Elliott Woolfolk Major of Jefferson City, Attorney General of Missouri, 1908-12, Governor, 1913-17; James Cowgill of Kansas City, state treasurer; Joseph Bernard Shannon, lawyer of Kansas City and chairman of the Democratic State Central Committee; John P. Gordon of Lexington, state auditor; and Harry J. Simmons, state representative from Shelby County, editor of the *Clarence*, Mo., *Courier*.

A News Report About Wilson's Arrival in Topeka, Kansas

[Feb. 22, 1912]

WARM WELCOME FOR WILSON HERE

New Jersey Governor Given the "Glad" Hand.
Democrats Receive Presidential Aspirant Joyfully.

Governor Woodrow Wilson of New Jersey, Democratic candidate for president, arrived in Topeka at 1 o'clock this afternoon and was driven in a motor car direct to the residence of Governor Stubbs.[1] The New Jersey governor visited a few minutes with the Kansas executive and then drove to the Throop hotel, his headquarters while in the city. The New Jersey statesman received the newspaper men in his rooms at the hotel a few minutes before he went to lunch.

Governor Wilson is not an easy man to interview. He admits this fact himself. "I am the poorest timber in the world for an interview," he said, "because I won't talk about myself."

"Well, then, how about Roosevelt? Will T.R. make the race?"

"I would rather not talk about him, either," was the reply.

When asked about the issues of the campaign and his message to the west, the governor replied: "You will get that in my speech tonight at the banquet."

But Governor Wilson had one message to give, and it is the keynote of his campaign for the presidency.

"The political party that wins this year must serve the people," he said. "Its issues must be plain and it must keep close to them always. The people can no longer be deceived."

The Throop was thronged with Kansas politicians this afternoon when the governor arrived and they crowded his reception. Several offers to address gatherings had to be declined by the distinguished guest. He talked a few minutes to the Democratic Editorial association, received a long line of visitors and then tried to get a few minutes of sleep before going to the banquet.

The governor is slight of build and has a thin, ascetic face. He wears eyeglasses constantly. Is quick and alert in his movements and speech and is pleasant and affable. He joked and parried with the reporters in their efforts to make him talk and was good natured under all kinds of questions.

The governor is pleased with his reception in the west and declared he had many warm friends far from home. He talks entertainingly about his tours and told the funniest kind of a story about an introduction speech he received in a Nebraska town.

"Three local men were required to make the introduction speech," said Governor Wilson, "and then I thought they had not enough. The third man made a good start and then stopped dead. He turned to me and said: 'What the d——l was I going to say?' I told him and he finished up with a rush. I had a great time there and received a fine reception."

Printed in the Topeka, Kan., *State Journal*, Feb. 22, 1912; some editorial headings omitted.
1 Walter Roscoe Stubbs, insurgent Republican Governor of Kansas.

A News Report of an Address in Topeka
to the Kansas Democratic Club

[Feb. 23, 1912]

FULL OF GINGER

Democratic Annual Love Feast a Rousing One.
Many Unable to Find Places at Tables.

WILSON IS WELL RECEIVED

More than 1,000 Democrats sat at the annual love feast in Masonic hall last night and applauded every mention of the names of their party chiefs—it was the largest political banquet ever held in Topeka. Until nearly 11 o'clock they waited for Governor Woodrow Wilson of New Jersey to begin his talk. But the reception accorded Wilson in no man[n]er exceeded the demonstrations at the mention of the names of Bryan and Clark. . . .

Wilson's modesty, his candid, apparent straight forward manner of handling his argument, appealed to the men and the enthusiasm that had all but gone to sleep in the breast of banqueters arose and responded to the speaker's climaxes. He was introduced as the George Washington of the Democratic party and the 1,000 men and women in the big hall greeted the New Jersey governor with the best that Kansas can give. For an hour Wilson urged his doctrine. He criticised the manner of handling the trust investigations and Kansas Democracy yelled. Once he mentioned William J. Bryan as a man whom the people trusted and loved;[1] and again Kansas Democracy went wild. In the very midst of Wilson's talk, an electric gong in the banquet hall began ringing. For a minute the crowd feared the building was afire. Wilson himself restored quiet. He said the gong was a Republican gong—that it didn't mean anything.

From the ranks of the Clark following, from the hearts of Wilson enthusiasts came generous applause throughout the speech. Perhaps it was Wilson's lack of fire in his speech. Perhaps it was the lack of punch behind the big adjectives that made an impression with the crowd. Possibly it was just the plain, ordinary manner of putting over his arguments that made Wilson stronger as his speech progressed. When he offered to sacrifice himself, if necessary, that the people might have a man they trusted, the sentiment hit a responsive chord and Wilson stock took a new grip on the crowd. After his speech, he was surrounded for more than half an hour by men and women and an informal reception was held in the big dining hall. . . .

Printed in the Topeka, Kan., *State Journal*, Feb. 23, 1912; some editorial headings omitted.

[1] "Men wince when you touch them on the raw, they don't wince when you touch them where the flesh is sound, and if you want to know if what you are saying is true, just wait and see them wince.

"I want to say in my judgment, there is one man who has won the undying affection of this country by having performed that great service and that man is Mr. Bryan. His greatness and influence does not consist merely of the fact that men believe in him, but consists in the fact that men love him and trust him because he has kept his own life untainted by improper influences and his own heart absolutely true to Democratic interests. That is the reason no man can displace him."

Ellen Axson Wilson to John Wesley Wescott

My dear Judge Westcott,   Princeton, New Jersey Feb. 23 1912

Your kind, though necessarily disturbing letter, is at hand,[1] and I thank you deeply for writing it, and for all your interest in Mr. Wilson's health and work. He has frequently spoken to me of your watchful friendship in respect to his health. I am the more grateful to you because it is my own special grievance that few of his friends seem to realize that he is even *mortal*. They are pitiless in their demands upon his time and strength.

Of course my own anxiety, though concealed from him, is constant and intense. He is, as you say, "very willful," but he assures me that after this month he will do much better. In the meantime I can only "keep guard" & save him from friends, cares and anxieties,—in short make of his home, when he *is* in it, a place of peace.

I must add one reassuring circumstance. He went some ten days or so ago to Dr. Stengal,[2] the great Phila. diagnostician, and was exhaustively examined—as to blood-pressure and everything else—and the doctor was able to give him a perfectly clean bill of health! He said he was actually in *finer* condition than he was when he last examined him, some fifteen months ago. So we have reason to trust that the symptoms you observed were due to nothing more than fatigue and a rather heavy cold. But as you say, he absolutely *must* have more rest! With kindest regards, I am,   Yours most cordially,   Ellen A. Wilson.

ALS (J. W. Wescott Coll., NjP).
  [1] It is missing.
  [2] Alfred Stengel, M.D., Professor of Medicine, University of Pennsylvania, distinguished pathologist and specialist in internal medicine.

From J. Robert Gillam[1]

Oklahoma City Okla. Feb 23-12

Wilson forces captured convention[2] on harmony agreement and instructed delegation to vote one half of delegation for you and one half for champ Clark   a most splendid victory for progressive democtracy   will write you fully after I return to ardmore.   J. Robert Gillam

T telegram (WP, DLC).
  [1] Real estate dealer of Ardmore, Okla., president of the state organization of Wilson clubs.
  [2] The state Democratic convention, which met in Oklahoma City on February 22 and 23.

A News Report of Remarks at a Reception in Nashville, Tennessee

[Feb. 24, 1912]

RECEPTION HELD.

At 10:30 o'clock a committee representing the Woodrow Wilson Club called for Gov. Wilson and went with him to the Hotel Hermitage, where a larger committee was holding a reception for Gov. Wilson and his friends who desired to meet him.

Nashville is the last stop on a trip that Gov. Wilson has made during a recess of the New Jersey Legislature, which is now in session. "Our Legislature meets annually," said Gov. Wilson this morning, "but it only meets the first three days of the week. As the state is small the members are able to return to their homes on the day of adjournment and spend the last half of the week there.

"Next week, however, is the last week that I will make one of these long trips while the Legislature is in session. So far only about a dozen bills have been passed, as the session is still young, and I have had very little work to do in connection with the Legislature. However, my work will soon be beginning. The Legislature will remain in session until about April 1, March 22 having been fixed by the caucus as the date of adjournment.

"This has been a splendid trip. I spoke at Topeka to the Kansas State Democratic Club on Washington's birthday. It was a great annual occasion with Democrats there from all over the state. There was a big banquet that night, and there must have been a thousand persons present. It seems to be a very vital organization in the state.

"On the way to Topeka I was waylaid at Kansas City between trains, and made a short address there. Yesterday morning I had to be back in Kansas City at 10 o'clock to make the connection for Nashville, and they got me up at 6:30 and took me over to Lawrence, twenty-six miles from Topeka, where the State University is located. They have a great school there, beautifully situated. I spoke in the gymnasium for about twenty minutes. The crowd in the hall was said to be 4,000, and while that may be an exaggeration, there was certainly a large audience.[1]

"They had a special train to make the trip from Lawrence to Kansas City, and then the 10 o'clock train that I was to catch had to be held thirty minutes for us to make the connection. From Kansas City I came direct to Nashville, and must leave here to-night, so as to arrive in Trenton by Monday morning." . . .

Printed in the *Nashville Banner*, Feb. 24, 1912.
[1] A news report of Wilson's visit to the University of Kansas appeared in the *Kansas City*, Mo., *Star*, Feb. 23, 1912.

A Political Address in Nashville[1]

[[Feb. 24, 1912]]

The introduction[2] to which I have just listened certainly puts me under a great obligation for the generous judgment which

[1] Delivered in the Hermitage Hotel to the Woodrow Wilson Club of Nashville.
[2] He was introduced by Thomas E. Matthews, judge of the first circuit court of Davidson County, Tenn.

it embodies. But I am very much afraid that it will be very difficult for me to play up to the rôle, and I want to say at the outset, while I appreciate most profoundly all that has been said, that I do not come here as a Wilson man. I think I can say most sincerely that what stirs my blood in the present contest is not that it may affect me, but that there is a great thing to be done, which intelligent men can combine to do successfully and triumphantly; that there is an opportunity now immediately awaiting the Democratic party such as has never awaited it before. I was saying just now to Mr. [Lee] Douglas that it was an interesting thing to me that there was one lesson that some men never seemed to learn, and that was that whenever they tried to serve themselves and made it obvious that they were trying to serve themselves, the thing they least succeeded in doing was serving themselves; that the only way in which you can connect yourself with the forces of success is by connecting yourself with the forces of society, because every man will be as little as himself if his thought is centred upon himself. (Applause.)

You know that we are sometimes laughed at by foreigners for boasting of the size of America, and they naturally suggest that we didn't make America, that we didn't make the physical continent we tread upon, and therefore it is hardly to our credit that it is so big. But it seems to me they do not discriminate. Men are just as big as the things they dominate, and we have dominated a continent and therefore have reason to be proud of its size. Our greatness, the elasticity of our institutions, the adaptability of our life, is measured by the scale of a continent. Having covered that continent with happy homes and successful institutions, we have the right to be proud of its size. And so it seems to me with the individual. In proportion as he can cover with his activities and with his imaginations a great plan, so is he himself enlarged, and in proportion as a party can conceive a great opportunity and forget the things that may come to individuals in the struggle, in that proportion is it noble and in that proportion is it in the road to success. No party that centres its view upon itself can ever be serviceable to the United States. The United States can be served only in its own humour, and according to its own facts and circumstances. What moves my imagination is this, that the circumstances are not now what they ever were before in the United States. For example: we all of us agree that the central issue in the next campaign will probably be, as so often before, the question of the tariff. But the tariff is not now the question that it was a generation ago; the tariff is not now the question it was ten or fifteen years ago.

Nature, and the development of our enterprises, the change in the circumstances of the world, would have taken charge of the tariff question. Take this single fact, for example—what made it very difficult to answer the old arguments of the advocates of a protective tariff was this. They pointed out what was perfectly obvious, that within the United States, with its great size and infinite variety, there was an unparalleled area of absolute free trade. The Constitution was set up in order that there might be free trade. There would have been no Constitution of the United States if it had not been that the colonies that had become states were determined to pull down the economic barriers between themselves. That was what led to the Annapolis Convention, and the Philadelphia Convention. They first met to make a commercial arrangement and upon that commercial arrangement built the institutions of the Nation. The Constitution was made in order that there might be free trade between all the states, and that was the object of the power over interstate commerce that was granted to the Congress. And so, because there was domestic competition it was very difficult to answer the arguments of the protectionists, that protection does not directly govern price and therefore was not directly a burden upon the consumer, because the price was kept down by domestic competition upon the vast scale of a continent. All that has been altered in the last decade. In field after field of our economic exchanges competition has ceased to determine price. Monopoly in one form or another has taken the place of competition, and now, without competition, these gentlemen who lie so snugly behind the high wall of protection are determining arbitrarily what the prices of everything, from foodstuffs up, are to be.

It is not the old question. Senator La Follette, for example, in his interesting autobiography,[3] calls attention to this fact, that the old argument so prominent on the lips of McKinley and Blaine, for instance, is absolutely obliterated by change of circumstances. Not only so, but in those old days we did not have such a surplus of manufactured articles as we have now. An interesting fact is, that our exports of grain with which we used to feed the world have been steadily falling off until the grain dealers tell me that we are within sight of the vanishing point, not because we are producing less, or because it is harder to sell our grain, but because we are needing more ourselves. And the proportion of grain to the domestic demand is very much smaller

[3] Robert M. La Follette, "La Follette's Autobiography: A Personal Narrative of Political Experiences," was serialized in the *American Magazine*, LXXI-LXXIV (Oct. 1911-July 1912). Wilson referred to remarks in LXXIII (Dec. 1911), 146, 148.

than it used to be. We are, therefore, coming to the point at which we do not export grain and cannot pay our international exchanges except by other products.

At the same time these tremendously stimulated manufacturers of ours have piled up their output to such an extent that they must have an outlet in foreign fields, or else there will be a congestion that will operate calamitously upon the economic conditions of the country.

But what has happened in the meantime? By the most stupendous stupidity on record we have obliterated our merchant marine. We haven't got the ships in which to carry these goods. We are not allowed to have the ships in which to carry these goods upon any terms by which we can afford to own them. So that we are very philanthropically digging a ditch through the Isthmus to the south of us for the use of the ships of all the world except American ships, for there aren't any American ships to go through. And we are told that the railways of the country are so jealous of their carrying trade that they are trying to prevent the loans necessary in order to build up new lines of ships to reach to the South. I don't know whether that is true or not, but it would be just like them for stupidity.

The trouble with our time is not so much selfishness as ignorance, inability to see what is going on under the eyes of the world. Now these are the things that are going on, and the nation that has the ships to carry her goods has the hands with which she can reach the foreign markets, and if she hasn't got the ships she has to go there under such disadvantages as the owners of foreign ships, owned by competing nations, choose to impose upon her.

Not only that, but we haven't a banking system which enables us to set up satisfactory exchange with foreign markets. Our national banks are actually not allowed to deal in accepted bills of lading, so that Canadian bankers come down to New York, San Francisco and other ports and set up branch banking houses which can do this absolutely essential function of international trade. We have been so rooted in our provincialism, so unaware of the very processes of our own industrial life, that we have cut ourselves off from the means of making ourselves supreme in the world from an economic point of view.

All this has been going on without the leave of the gentlemen who have established and maintained a protective policy. It has been like a great underground body of creeping waters, destroying the very foundation of the citadel which they thought they had built so stout. At the same time what is about to happen?

Why all the threads are going to run in other directions; because the minute you cut that canal through the Isthmus then the great arteries of trade are not going to run exclusively East and West as they run now, they are going to sweep around to the South; they are going to fertilize that great valley of the Mississippi as it never was fertilized before with industry and commerce; and all the railroads instead of shipping outward to the ports are going to find their lines running inward. There are going to be more carrying problems than ever before, but not in the same parts of the country as before. No one can stay the change. And these gentlemen want to stand pat, are standing pat, while the tide is rising around them. You can see by their disconcerted manner that it is almost getting to their breathing apparatus. (Applause.)

In other words, what fills me with confidence in the future is this, that the world is not waiting upon the stupidity of Republican politics. The world has an awkward way of taking things into its own hands. The life of the people must in the long run express itself in its politics, and it does not now express itself in this country in the politics we have been accustomed to in the last decade. (Applause.)

These gentlemen may sit tight and hard as long as they please but they will be hoist by powers they cannot control. The whole query of the future is, does the Democratic party understand the job and does it know how to do it?

We all feel the inflation of pleasure as Democrats that this is a Democratic year, but it isn't going to be a Democratic year if the Democratic party does not understand the job. (Applause.) Democratic enthusiasm isn't going to do it. Democratic confidence of success isn't going to do it. The selection of the right candidate isn't going to do it. People of this country know what they want and what they are after is not the candidate but the goods. If the candidate is suitable for their purposes, and the party puts him upon a platform that expresses those purposes, then they are for him, otherwise they will wait. They would rather bear the ills they have than fly to others that they know not of.

That is the temper of America. There is a great deal of talk in America, but it is, when all is said, one of the most inveterately conservative people in the world. Americans talk much more freely than they act, particularly in the field of politics. And in a country knitted together with the most delicate and intricate fibres of business, the one thing that is most dreaded is ill-considered experiment. America is not afraid. America is not afraid of acting on principle, of moving, of changing, but is afraid of changing by uncalculated courses. It does not want schemes the operation of which it cannot foresee the effect of, and therefore it always wants a bill of particulars, and we are getting ready to present a bill of particulars. For example, round about this core of all questions which lies in the tariff, lie all these other questions, many of which we sum up under the general term of the corporation question, the trust question.

Nobody can fail to see, no matter how clearly you perceive the evils that have come upon the country by the use of them,— nobody can fail to see that modern business is going to be done by corporations. The old time of individual competition is probably gone by. It may come back; I don't know; it will not come back within our time, I dare say. We will do business henceforth when we do it on a great and successful scale, by means of corporations. But what we are afraid of, as we have said in the Sherman Act, is such use of corporations as will be in restraint of trade; that is, such use as will establish monopoly. Very well, we have got to know what particular things do establish monopoly; because if we merely say "this concern is so big that it looks to us like monopoly" that isn't satisfactory. I am not afraid of any corporation, no matter how big. I am afraid of any corporation, however small, that is bad, that is rotten at the core, whose practices and actions are in restraint of trade. So that the thing we are after is not reckoning size in measuring capacity for damage, but measuring and comprehending the exact damage done. Very well, we are getting details. For example, in the Stanley investigation, in the investigation connected with the trial of the meat packers, and in the investigation I hope will be pushed forward in connection with the so-called money trust (great applause) we are going to find out how the thing is done.

For example, take the meat men, I have some friends connected in a subordinate way as employees of that great industry, some college men who are quick to see and intelligent to comprehend, and once or twice when I have made remarks that did not seem complimentary to the meat trust these gentlemen have written to me and asked if I was aware of the fact that the operations were as a matter of fact yielding this concern only a very minute fraction of profit, and there would be no profit in it at all if they didn't command so large a proportion of the product as to make the sum total considerable.[4] And I didn't know what to say until I read the testimony taken in the trial of the meat

---

[4] About this correspondence, see n. 1 to the address printed at May 12, 1910, Vol. 20.

packers at Chicago, and then I found out that these gentlemen buy cattle on the hoof, as everybody knows, and they charge up all the expenses of all their operations to the meat; and they sell the hides and the hoofs, and the parts, whatever they may be, that yield very valuable glue, and all the by-products, which in their sum total are extremely profitable, without any charges being entered against them in their books. So that we are paying for meat in order to enable them to sell hides and determine the price of shoes. (Applause.) Now that is a valuable inside piece of information. They can't any longer impose upon us by show-ing us their books upon fresh meat (or meat that isn't fresh that comes out of cold storage). That is what I call one of the items in the bill of particulars. We know also by their own testimony it isn't necessary for them to combine themselves in a corpora-tion in order to fix prices; it is only necessary to have a gentle-man's understanding, and have correspondence through a sec-retary agreed upon, and that this secretary, once every so often, shall send out a circular suggesting a price for meat, and this suggestion be taken kindly and acted upon. (Laughter.) That suggestion is perfectly arbitrary; they can establish the price of meat upon an absolutely non-competitive basis.

Very well, we know what the meat packers are doing and what the steel men are doing, and what all these other men are doing. We have got now some of the transactions and the form in which they are carried through. It seems to me that now, therefore, we are ready to proceed to business, so far as we see what we are about. We are not going to lay about us in any blind and vague way, but we are going to do something like this, not proposing this as a measure but merely as an illustration. If you want to cure men of joy riding you won't break up their automo-biles, but catch the men that do the joy riding and see that these very useful and pleasant vehicles of our modern life are left for legitimate uses. If you want to stop joy riding in corporations—for that is what is being done (laughter and applause)—you will not break up the corporations; we may need to use them; but you will break up the game, namely, that use of corporations. I dare say the judges and other lawyers present,—if it is true that judges are still lawyers (laughter) will agree with me that this is at any rate feasible; with the necessary legislation, we can say that a corporation, so long as it acts within its charter, or is within the limits of the law, is something we won't look inside of. We will regard it as long as it is within its legitimate uses as a body corporate that has its own separate entity, and into the de-tails of whose organization we won't pry. We will hold it responsible so far only as a body, an unbroken body, but the minute somebody inside begins to use it for purposes he has no right to use it for, then we are going to turn it inside out and see who is inside. And we are going to establish this principle that with regard to breaches of the law we will deal not with corporations but with individuals, that we don't know corporations, that we never heard of them, when we are dealing with breaches of the law. We can oblige every corporation to file with the proper officer of the law a sworn analysis of the way its business is done, which will be conclusive—not merely presumptive evidence—upon any trial, an analysis which it cannot controvert upon trial; which will show that such and such transactions are ordered by the president, such and such transactions are ordered by a committee of its board, certain other transactions are ordered by the board as a whole, others by its first vice-president, and so on down through the analysis. Then when a wrong is committed we will turn to the analysis and find the officer who according to that analysis ordered that particular thing done, and we will indict him not as an officer of the corporation but as an individual who used that corporation for something that was illegal. Then you say, we will find out he was a dummy. Very well, go on, push the trial, draw in all the collateral evidence and find whose dummy he was, then amend the indictment and include the gentlemen whose dummy he was, whether it happens to be an official connected with that corporation or not, because in this process we have nothing to do with corporations, we are finding men. You know the old cynical French maxim, when any man is running an incalculable course "cherchez la femme" (find the woman). Now we must establish the maxim "find the man." Anything that is wrong must have originated with some person in particular. When you have found that person and given him a season to think it over in the penitentiary (applause) the thing will be stopped, and business will be relieved of the embarrassment of breaking up its organization in order to stop these practices.

Do you see any other way to avoid interrupting the natural and normal processes of American business? If you will do this then all the prohibitions of your law will work, no man will use corporations in restraint of trade; and item by item we can put in our statutes what constitutes restraint of trade, not leaving it to courts for generalizations which may fit some cases and not others. Then we shall have a programme which need disturb no honest man, and will begin to see the map of the thing. I want to see the map of our corporate life. You don't know the high-

ways of it, you don't know any of the intricacies of it. The difficulty in this country is not altogether that we have big corporations, but that these big corporations are combined with one
another, not by law, but by the fact that their directorates interlace in every direction and that the same combinations of men
control the majority of the stock in corporation after corporation.

No corporation can ever get big enough to make the Government of the United States afraid, but all of them combined
might in some sinister and fateful day make the Government of
the United States subserve them. So that you have got to disentangle this puzzle; you have got to find where the lines of
personal responsibility interlace; you have got to lift these persons up and put them under cross-examination as to what they
are doing with the business of the country, not for the purpose of
gibbeting them, not for the purpose of putting them under contempt and mortifications, but for the purpose of saving the country and saving its business.

I am not aware that I cherish in my heart any bitter feelings
toward any individual concerned in these matters. Many of these
men do not see the consequences of the thing they are doing.
They are just as patriotic so far as they have examined their
own consciences as either you or I. They don't comprehend. We
have got to wake them to the things that are to be feared, and
then devise the particular methods by which they are to be corrected. We are not vindictive, but determined men, with open
eyes.

For in the meantime what is going on? When I hear gentlemen say that politics ought to let business alone, I feel like inviting them to first consider whether business is letting politics
alone. It is a two-sided matter; if you will quit, we will. If you
will stop trying to determine elections by campaign contributions; if you will stop encouraging bi-partisan political machinery, so that it is worth your while to contribute to both campaign funds; if you will stop making the control of legislatures
a business proposition, then you will find that in the most complete and only effectual way you have disentangled business
from politics.

The initial steps are taken in lobbies, they are not taken in the
councils of statesmen; they are taken in those secret and whis-
pered conferences that go on in almost every legislative lobby
in this country, where men are shown that it is to their material
interest—whether directly or indirectly—that they shall vote as
interested parties desire them to vote. These great leagues of
business, in other words, are not merely leagues to command

markets, but they are often also leagues to command legislation.

And so the view widens, does it not? So the country is asking itself, who is represented in our representative assemblies? In some states the people are represented, thank God, but in some states they are not represented. In some states the legislatures are secretly and privately controlled. Now, are you going to stir the blood of those people in those states by preaching a eulogy on representative institutions? If they have found out election after election that to vote one ticket or the other is to choose between tweedledum and tweedledee; if they know no matter how they vote things don't get better at the State capital, how are you going to stir their patriotism with the tradition of the great representative institutions in this country? They will laugh in your face, they will say: "Are you so young, so unsophisticated as to suppose you know what you are talking about? Show us representative institutions to worship and we will be the first to fall on our knees, but we want to know who are represented."

There are two or three theories of government in this country. Don't deceive yourself by supposing all the people in this country believe in democratic government, because they do not. You have only to listen to the utterances of very distinguished Republican speakers to see that they do not believe and do not pretend to believe in popular government. They will tell you they do not believe the judgment of the people can be trusted. Are you going to take counsel from these gentlemen as to the preservation of our representative institutions when they don't want them to represent the great body, the rank and file of the people? I don't know whether I was born so, or learned so, or what happened to me, but I know this, that the deepest conviction I have, arising out of observation and experience is this, that I would rather take the judgment of the rank and file than the judgment of the men who have become absorbed and successful as the leaders in great undertakings. (Applause.)

I want to ask these gentlemen this query: What sustains business in the United States? What is it that makes the United States prosperous? Is it that we have great captains of industry? What would they do without the cunning and skill, the muscle and the indomitable aspiring hope of the American people? If these people were to find hope dying out of their hearts, they will be dumb-driven beasts, and your enterprises will fail for lack of the very breath that sustains them. (Applause.)

If you want to find whether a nation is prosperous or not, ask the men who are on the make what they hope and what they fear. Go to the country districts and ask anxious fathers who are looking for openings for their sons where they expect to get them in, where they find doors open and where they find doors shut. Go to the places where men are making earnings and see whether they dread or confidently look forward to the future, and then you will find whether America is waxing or waning, for if these men are confident, full of hope, if they know they are going to have free chances, if they know that the doors of opportunity are open to them, if they know they are going to get fair treatment wherever they go, then America can conquer the world of enterprise by means of their hope. But if you find, what you do find, men everywhere asking themselves whether the doors of opportunity have not been locked in their faces, then you will have to take a new reckoning as to the future of America.

What was it that they proposed to investigate in Congress the other day? Not a money trust in the ordinary sense that anybody is hiding or hoarding money anywhere. Men who have money are not fools enough not to want to use it, because it does not yield them anything if it is not used. What is suspected is this: that nobody can get large loans in this country to start those large enterprises by which alone our industry thrives, unless he will consent to take certain gentlemen in with him who furnish the money; that the privileged circle is closed, and that while you can get all the little credits you please in your local banks you can't get your big credits where the reserves of the country are kept, except on the terms of the gentlemen who stand guard over these reserves. (Applause.) That is what is charged. And it is not charged without evidence. It is not charged without abundant evidence. Therefore, if only those who are chosen at the top have the right of way in, what is going to happen to America? Did you ever hear of a nation that was renewed from the top? Did you ever hear of a nation that was not made virile, that did not account for its youth by renewal from the bottom? Did you ever hear of a tree that drew its sap from its flowers? Does it not draw it from the dark and silent places of the soil? Does not a nation draw its power of renewal and enterprise, and all its future, from the ranks of the great body of unnamed men? And if you are going to discourage these men; if you are going to put the chill of fear in their hearts, then American captains of industry can whistle for their future, and they will whistle in a wilderness. (Applause.)

I am the friend of American business, because I know where

its foundations are laid, and where they are weak; and those foundations are solid only when laid in the confidence of the common people. (Great applause.)

A democrat? Why a man does not understand history who isn't a democrat. A man doesn't understand enterprise who isn't a democrat. And let me tell you this: democracy is not merely a matter of programmes, it is a matter of sympathy and insight. It depends upon whether your heart is in connection with the great heart of the people or not. It does not depend upon whether you can cunningly devise a platform that looks firm and good or not. You can build a flimsy platform and stand on it successfully, provided its basis is in the right kind of spirit. It is a matter of seeing—not from your eyes out, but from the eyes of other men in. Getting the vision that is in the back of the other man's head is the thing; getting the hope that is the universal hope; getting that impulse that is the common human impulse, forward. This world has been swept by wave after wave of democratic impulse. It is being swept by it now. The great waters are rising, rising, and nothing prevents their fertilizing the valleys except that stubborn, stupid stand-pat dam. (Great applause.)

What fills my imagination, therefore, gentlemen, is this, that we are at the threshold of a great enterprise, the enterprise of retranslating the liberties of America into the terms of our lives as we now actually live them. The party that can do that first is the party that will rule this country for the next generation, and the party that misses it, that doesn't do it, won't rule it now and will never rule it. There are competitors. We aren't the only candidates in the field, we Democrats. Illumination has penetrated the Republican ranks. You don't describe a Republican by merely calling him a Republican. There are various kinds of Republicans; some of them are so attenuated in their doctrines that you can hardly recognize them as such, but all of them still stubbornly cling to that old name, for this reason—I believe in my heart this is the real reason—these men don't come over and call themselves Democrats because they believe the Republican party is the only party that has shown practical genius in understanding and administering the affairs of the nation; that is the reason they claim the title. They say, yes, we agree with the Democrats but the Democrats don't know how to do it. Yes, our programmes are the same, but do you suppose they know how to carry them out? That is the basis of it, and the deuce of it is that so much of the country agrees with them in it. They agree that they haven't yet sufficient evidence that the

Democrats know how to carry that programme out, or clearly know what the programme is.

When I sit down and compare my views with those of a Progressive Republican I can't see what the difference is, except that he has a sort of pious feeling about the doctrine of protection, which I have never felt. (Applause and laughter.) He will always insist, "Oh yes, I am a protectionist, but the tariff needs revision." Now, I don't say anything about protection. I don't care anything about protection. The only thing I want to know is which duty and how much of a duty is serviceable to the country? That is all I want to know. I don't care a rap about the doctrine of protection. It isn't a scientific doctrine; neither is the doctrine of free trade. But the administration of the government of a nation is a very practical thing, and we intend to do, without any feeling of regret or piety of any kind, that which is necessary to do for the promotion of the prosperity of the United States. That is all. (Applause.)

Now they think that is profane. They say: "Just suppose I should vote the Democratic ticket, what would the old man say?" I don't like to say anything unparliamentary about the old man, but I would let the old man take care of himself and vote the way the country seemed to demand in the year 1912 without reference to what may have been thought to have been demanded in the year 1846, for example; for I don't happen to have shared any of the responsibilities of the year 1846, but I do happen to share some of the responsibility for the year 1912, and, therefore, it is that year, and that year alone, which at present interests me.

Very well, then, we have got to show the Progressive Republican that he can come over without being ashamed of it and without being uneasy about the consequences. He is ready to come over if you will only give him polite language and the right sort of encouragement and a hospitable reception. But try to push him over the line and he balks; he balks at the label. If you ask him why, he says, "The Democratic Party hasn't in the past stood for the things I believe in." He will assert, foolishly I think, but nevertheless he will assert it, that it has not been a sufficiently practical party. That is what he will tell you. That is why I am so intensely interested in having the country understand that we know what we are about, and mean to do those things we have specified. That will remove some obstacles, some questions.

Mr. Louis Pettigrew, of Charleston, S. C., a very commanding figure of a past generation, was a man of humour, as well as force of character. He lost a case one day in court and his client followed him out of the court house and abused him for everything that was vile, called him a thief and a liar, but the old man didn't pay any attention to him until he called him a Federalist; then he knocked him down. Somebody asked him why he did that, and pointed out that that was the least offensive thing he had said. "Yes, damn him," he said, "but it was the only true thing he said." (Laughter.)

Now I went quietly on my way with smiles from many quarters, until on a certain day, in the city of Harrisburg, I happened to let it slip that I knew there was a corner in credit. I said that the most serious trust of all was the money trust. And I know that was so, because it drew blood. They hadn't winced until then, and ever since then they have said, this man ought to be put out of business, and I dare say from their point of view he ought. I quite agree with them. Because if those things are true they must be stopped, but nobody need fear anything who is not implicated and engaged in them. Therefore, let every man who doesn't want them touched stand up and get counted. It will shorten the process of identification later on.

When you get your specific programme, these gentlemen are going to balk. They are going to say you will destroy business. You are not going to destroy business, you are only going to break up monopoly of enterprise, you will be letting in new men, new light, new energy and new prospects of achievement. I am interested in nothing so much as releasing the energy of the country. That, to my mind, is the whole task of politics, to release the honest energy of the country.

When I think over what we are engaged in doing in the field of politics, I conceive it this way. Men who are behind any interest always unite in organization, and the danger in every country is that these special interests will be the only things organized, and that the common interest will be unorganized against them. The business of government is to organize the common interest against the special interests. (Applause.) That is the reason it is worth while going around and trying to expound—no matter how imperfectly—what the situation is, so that you may draw these threads of common thought into one pattern, so that you may organize the general mind for the comprehension of the situation. As soon as the common mind is organized then no special interest can hold its own against it.

This is the thing to which we must challenge ourselves; this is the enterprise of the so-called radicalism of our time. If I am informed correctly as to the meaning of the word radical, it has something to do with roots. Now the false radical pulls up roots to see if the thing is growing; the true radical goes down to the roots to see that the soil is wholesome (applause) and that the tap-root is getting the pure nutriment that ought to come from the soil. That is the kind of radicalism I believe in, recultivation, thence reformation of the whole process.

In the presence of such things, gentlemen, what ought we to do? Why we ought, above all things else, to get together. (Great applause.) This is a national conception, a national enterprise, a national opportunity and a national hope. Will any man dare thrust his individual ambition in the way? Will any man dare, because he would be the leader, say that unless he is the leader he will not coöperate? Will any set of men say that unless they can have their way in doing the thing they will not coöperate? Ah, gentlemen, the stake is too big, the condemnation for failure is too overwhelming. We shall be judged for a generation as we act in 1912. If we allow ourselves to fall apart by reason of any jealousies, if we put any obstacle in the way of the universal movement towards this happy goal, then all the rest of our lives we shall know that we made it impossible for democracy to have a fresh fruitage in America.

And what would that mean? It would mean the old vision gone. It would mean that those old days were forever gone when men forgot their own fortunes in order to promote the common interest; those days gone by when America lifted her head so blithely and so bravely among the nations, and drew the gaze of mankind to her own fair countenance; that this countenance now wears the mask of self-interest; that men find covert behind it, and dare not display their passion for self-interest; and that America has taken the common road of the nations that go down because they have forgotten the destiny of man. (Great applause and ovation.)

Printed in Ray Stannard Baker and William E. Dodd, *The Public Papers of Woodrow Wilson: College and State* (2 vols., New York and London, 1925), I, 405-23; with typographical corrections from the complete text in the *Nashville Tennessean*, Feb. 25, 1912. The Baker and Dodd text, taken from a pamphlet which cannot be found, is a revision of the text in the *Tennessean*.

An Address in Nashville
on Behalf of the Y.M.C.A.[1]

[[Feb. 24, 1912]]

Your Excellency,[2] Ladies and Gentlemen:

I did myself notice that the elephant bore the label March 4,[3] and I have no doubt that the elephant will be there on March 4, but not in the main tent; he will be in the side show. (Laughter.) I am extremely honored by the two introductions[4] I have received. I suppose that nobody cared to take the entire responsibility (laughter and applause) for turning me loose upon this unsuspecting company.

One can't come to an occasion like this, or face an audience gathered for a purpose like this, without very serious thoughts indeed. I listened with a great many reflections to the interesting exposition by Mr. Lewis[5] of what the Young Men's Christian Association has done in some of the great cities of this country. I know, and you know, other stories equally remarkable that might be added to these, and the only disappointment that I had in Mr. Lewis' speech was in the closing part of it. Mr. Lewis said this is what can be accomplished by organization. But is that all? Is there nothing back of the organization of the Young Men's Christian Association that distinguishes it from other organizations? I know that very thing was in Mr. Lewis' thought; perhaps it was reserved for me as a special privilege that I might bring it into explicit statement.

The Young Men's Christian Association[s] of this country have not prevailed to assist their communities to higher things because they were effective organizations. They prevailed because back of their organization lay a spirit advancing the interests that had nothing to do with advancing the interests of individuals or of groups of men. Nothing less than the all-prevailing spirit of Christ. (Applause.)

I am not a preacher, ladies and gentlemen, and unhappily I have not the endowments of the great preacher from whom I am sprung; but it does seem to me that upon an occasion like

---

1 Delivered in the gymnasium of the new Y.M.C.A. building in Nashville.
2 Ben Walter Hooper, Republican Governor of Tennessee, 1911-15.
3 There were a number of Republican campaign signs in the gymnasium. In his speech introducing Wilson, Hooper said: "Have you noticed that all of the blue republican elephants hung around the walls have turned white? I have wondered whether this is due to fright, since I have arrived. I also notice that the big one at the end has the date 'March 4.' Just how those talismanic words happened to be there, I do not know, or what the significance is, if any, I am not prepared to say." *Nashville Tennessean*, Feb. 25, 1912; see also the *Nashville Banner*, Feb. 26, 1912.
4 By Senator Luke Lea and Governor Hooper.
5 Robert Ellsworth Lewis, general secretary of the Nashville Y.M.C.A.

this we should go back to the fundamentals and ask ourselves what it is that we depend upon for the salvation, not of our individual souls, for sometimes that seems to me rather a petty business, but for our salvation upon the earth and the lives of the communities to which we belong.

I have never thought it a very handsome enterprise for a man to devote himself to the salvation of his own soul, and one of the greatest apostles of Christ said that for his brother's sake he would be willing to be damned, thereby exhibiting that ultimate spirit of Christ which the cross typifies.

The thing that runs in my thought, as I think of the Young Men's Christian Association, and as I have been privileged to speak in behalf of its work elsewhere, is this, that men do not rise to the best energy that is within them unless the standard to which they conform is external to themselves. It is an interesting thing to my mind that we have an expression in our language which we do not often enough speak and analyze. We note some youngster who has sowed his wild oats; he has been reckless of the mandates of his own conscience and of the example of his leaders, and has had a fling in the world; then when he comes to a soberer consideration, when he comes to see what all of this means for him, for those who love him and depend upon him, that we say that "the lad has come to himself." And it is a great inspiration to me to realize what that expression means; it does not mean that he has come to center his life upon himself; it does not mean that he has come to realize what deterioration this will work upon him; it means that he has come to realize his relations to his fellow-man; he has come to realize that he is not pulling himself down merely, but pulling the whole delicate, lovely fabric of a family and of a community down with him, and he has found himself when he has found his relations, his moral relations to his fellow-man. I like to picture it in this way: We have a saying which we perhaps thoughtlessly use when a man has lost his way in a desert; we say that he has lost himself. Do we never reflect that that is the only thing he has not lost? He is there, and if he could determine any known and fixed points of the universe he could get out. What he has lost is his relationship to the rest of the physical and social world, and the minute he knows the points of the compass, the minute he knows where any human habitation lies, then he has found himself, hasn't he? He has found his necessary direction; he has found his human relationships again, and he has found the way to join the ranks of his fellows in the world. Let that serve as an image to our thought, to interpret what we mean when we say a man has morally found himself; he has found himself when he has re-established the right moral relation between himself and his fellow-man. And then for the first time he begins to take on a new size. A man is as big as his conception; as big as his imagination; as big as the scope of his plan; as big as his knowledge of the world in which he lives, and you are measured according to your conception of the universe, you are not judged according to your conception of yourself.

My dear father used to tell me that the old casuists said that all sin could be reduced to the terms of selfishness, that when a man came to imagine that he himself was the pivot of the community, or of the world, when his egotism reached such a point that he supposed that affairs centered upon him, then he had lost the whole moral perspective of the universe, was essentially sinful, because he was acting, not according to the light that shines out of the scriptures, or out of an enlightened conscience, but according to the light that shines out of his own conception of self-interest and self-advancement, and no man could be moral who was the object of his own actions. There is something profoundly and movingly true in all of that. The Young Men's Christian Associations would not have been the power they have in modern communities, the extraordinary power they have been, if it had not been that their compass was set to that pole; that they laid the map of life out with those courses marked upon it that led to the haven of achievement and of rest.

The career and record of the Young Men's Christian Association has been an extraordinary one. Do you realize what the international committee of the Y.M.C.A. does? It presides over some of the most radical educational and spiritual processes of the world. When Mr. John R. Mott, who acts for that committee, travels about this round globe, in every country in it men flock by the thousands to sit at his feet and learn the message of light, and whole communities, and now apparently whole nations, are taking their cue and initiative from the suggestions of the representatives of the Young Men's Christian Association. The governor was, of course, partly playful when he said that Mr. Lewis had started the revolution in China, but it is true. It is probably true that the Young Men's Christian Association in China has had a great deal to do with the political revolution there, because nothing is so revolutionary as the light; nothing is so revolutionary as those rays that disclose the moral relationships of men, and things that are wrong cannot stand the intense illumination of that light.

The Young Men's Christian Association of China has gone where the ordinary missionaries of the church were not permitted to go. Before the missionaries the Young Men's Christian Association got access to the upper classes of China, to the literati, to the men who were leading and doing the thinking, and had social position from which they could command the course of the times. I remember hearing a somewhat amusing story of a reception given to Mr. Mott in Peking, where some of the highest officials of the empire were present for the first time at a function which bore the name of Christ, and when they poked gentle fun at one another, and one old man would say to another, "old man, you are a nice member of a Young Men's Christian Association," seeing the humor of how under that designation the oldest officials of an ancient empire had been drawn in to greet an international character, the representative of the Young Men's Christian Association.

The other day I heard it suggested[6] that Mr. Mott should be asked to take the presidency of a great university, and I said Mr. Mott can't afford to take the presidency of a great university; Mr. Mott occupies a certain spiritual presidency in the spiritual university of the world.

And so it is in foreign countries as well as in America, and through such processes we are not merely organizing our life; we are standardizing it; we are standardizing it by the only standards that are eternal, the only standards that are universal, the only standards that have borne the test of long experience, the standards that underlie the very processes of civilization and furnish the genius of human liberty. It is Christianity that has produced the political liberty of the world, gentlemen (Applause.) Political liberty is based upon this proposition, not that one man's brain is of equal value with another man's brain, but that one man's soul is of equal value with another man's soul. And that was the discovery of Christianity. Christianity is based upon this proposition, that every man stands directly responsible to his Maker, and that therefore his standard of right is external to himself and eternal in the heavens, being independent of creed, independent of race, independent of national organization, and that it is his binding duty to serve his conscience before he serves his king. (Applause.)

Every man, everywhere, who holds a Christian belief is bound

6 Undoubtedly by Cleveland H. Dodge.

to prefer his convictions to his political allegiance. Did you ever hear of anything more revolutionary than that? That is the foundation of all revolutions. That means that no one anywhere is pledged to stand for what is wrong, is pledged to stand for imposition, is pledged to stand for anything that negatives the proposition that one man's soul is as good as another man's soul. And so throughout the leven that has levened the house, that is the leven that has brought energy into the world; that is the leven that has produced this unconquerable thing. When a man can stand up in the presence of his government and say this, you can take my property, you can take my life, but you cannot command my soul, and I will go into the next world happily if you will but send me there upon an errand of duty, governments cannot stand against that. No wrong anywhere in the world can stand against that. And that is the moral of the story you have been hearing from Mr. Lewis, that these gentlemen who made these inquiries, that forced the needs [hands] of the public officials, that made it possible to clean places that were foul, kept themselves in the background; they were unadvertised mediums of change. They were willing to be unknown provided the souls of their fellow-men might be given a chance to thrive in an atmosphere that they could breathe. (Applause.) Set any set of men with such a motive and such a standard in the midst of any community, and that community can give it money or withhold money from it, but it will conquer the community.

This association does not depend upon whether you give it the additional eighty thousand dollars it wants or not. It will conquer your spirits. It is the old story of the fable of the wind and the rain and the sun that compete to remove a man's cloak from his back, how he held his cloak grimly about him when the rain beat upon him, and the wind tried to snatch it, but when the genial sun poured its soft rays upon him his heart expanded and he threw the coat back and welcomed the light. That is what this community will do for you. You may seal their purses with adamant, and this sun will dissolve the adamant, because you will find that there is something, some little thread of connection somewhere between your money and your soul. Some men don't find that out for a long time. (Applause.)

But at the bottom of every man's nature, no matter how he may fool you, from one generation to another, there gleams a fountain which will sooner or later be uncovered. I have seen men who pretended that they didn't have any religious feeling at all, but who went listlessly, sullenly to church every Sunday, and they said they didn't go to church because they believed in anything particular, but the old folks used to go to church, and that had been their pew for a long time. Don't believe a word of it. They have sealed the fountain over with concrete, but underneath that concrete in depths which they are ashamed to uncover gleam the eternal waters, and only those waters keep those men from dry rot.

These are the fountains of the renewal of youth, these spiritual fountains.

You know how Benjamin Franklin, with that uncanny shrewdness of his, whenever he went to hear Whitfield preach, always left his purse at home, because he said he knew he could not keep anything in it that was there if he had anything in it, but if he could only get off in the cool distance and lose the ardor of Whitfield's speech, then he might keep a penny or two. And it is so everywhere; these are the avenues by which you reach men's souls. And therefore it seems to me in a community that has any vision it is a word of supererogation to come and recommend to them that they support the Young Men's Christian Association, to recommend to them that they support their own souls, to recommend to them that they support the only things that will keep them young in their souls. I am not contrasting the Young Men's Christian Association with the churches. On the contrary, I am the champion of the churches, but I want you to realize this thing is an offshoot of the churches, and I don't want you to be hypocrites enough to think you can subscribe to this association and then say you are not subscribing to religion. You can withhold your subscription from the churches and subscribe to this, and, if I may say so without impiety, the Lord smiles behind his hand. However you pretend that you scorn creeds, that you are not led by priests, that you are not imposed upon by religion, this you know, that somewhere you have got to cast an anchor, inside the veil, inside the veil that hides from your too impertinent scrutiny the profoundest secrets of the human heart and of human society.

Why should men, therefore, support a Young Men's Christian Association? There are a good many foolish things done in Young Men's Christian associations. I have attended meetings from which I went away with distaste, because the thing was done without dignity, and a sort of attempt to make horse-play out of it. But that couldn't conquer it because I have sometimes thought—and I have had the pleasure of sitting under some of the most distinguished preachers that ever preached—I have sometimes thought that the supreme proof of living Christianity was the preaching that it has survived.

You couldn't kill it by yourself being foolish in the comprehension of it, because it is so much bigger than anything you could touch; it is something you will have to swing around to no matter how eccentric your orbit is. Our instinct in supporting the Young Men's Christian Association therefore is this, that we have got to plant seed somewhere in ground which is not our selfish acre, plowed for our own benefit. That is the point of the whole matter. If you haven't got a seed planted that will bear a perfect fruit of unselfishness, then you have nothing to depend upon in this world but the compounding of interest, and you know perfectly well that the compounding of interest will not bring you the ideal results which you desire. You will not suppress things on the mere basis of compounding interest; you will not seek to relieve the pressure of human hearts upon any calculation of interest whatever. There are a thousand things of which you would relieve your conscience if you could reckon only upon the basis of self-interest, and therefore you instinctively feel that there has got to be an additional organization in society, an organization which is not commercial, not a manufacturing organization, not an organization for mere philanthropy, even not a political organization, not an organization that lifts anybody to positions of distinction, but an organization based upon the interests of the human heart, and unless you have got that there is no kindly gleam in the eye; there is none of that enthusiasm upon which you can sleep every night with the quiet of an infant. I don't know how some men sleep at night at all. I should think the wheels would keep going around in their heads; the wheels do keep going around in their heads, and they are wheels which ring out with a discordant note of machinery that is ill-adjusted and has no motive power except some clanking chain, self-interest connecting it with cupidity.

It is a very interesting circumstance that Dante in his Inferno peoples the lower regions with men who were still living when he wrote the book. (Laughter.) He knew exactly where they were going, and more than that, he knew that they had got there already, because men are impatient, they don't wait for hell to die, they carry it around with them; and some men, upon whose faces you can see the thing written, prefer to carry heaven around with them while they live, to experience that utter release of spirit which they hope will come to them in some distant day when they shall have cast off the temptations that now make their heaven imperfect, but other men walk in the obscurity of time.

They walk there because they have already filled their souls with blackness and decay, and feel at home nowhere but in hell. They have got to have a hell to go around in. They can't breathe anything else but sulphur. I don't know whether there is anybody here who can testify to that or not, but I have never seen a company of men as large as this that there were not some individuals who could. But fortunately the bars to the roads that lead upward are never finally closed, and the very fact that a man is in some place like this indicates that he is interested in these doors, at any rate. He wants to have a look at that road, he wants to see how pleasant its slopes can be made, and therefore he comes and says he will invest for a little while in something that won't bring us any money at all.

One of the great universities of this country was founded upon a very interesting thought. Mr. Johns Hopkins, who founded the university in Baltimore that bears his name, was a man who devoted himself with increasing passion as the years went on to making money, and some of his friends, knowing he was without family and without near relations, thought he ought to be advised what to do with his money when he came to die, since even he did not suppose he could carry it away with him. And so they bethought themselves of what had happened to George Peabody, whose munificences in an earlier age in Baltimore everybody has heard of. Mr. George Peabody was a man who made money in what always seemed to me the most attractive field that the imagination can conjure. He was one of the men whom we used to call the East India merchants. Almost every sea saw some ship of his going upon some quest of commerce. He could dream, as the merchants in the Merchant of Venice dreamed of their argosies coming from every quarter to make port at Venice. That has always seemed to me the most imaginary form of making money, to feel that your threads of thought and purpose are spread out like a great net all over the world, and you are gathering in the energy of men and the profit of business from every quarter. That was the kind of thing that George Peabody did, and it fascinated him. Men, after a certain amount of money is raked into their coffers, don't go on for the sake of the money; the thing that fascinates them is the power that goes with it, to know that sitting in their offices they are commanding the activities of the world. It is the instinct of the general and sometimes the capacity of the statesman that rises in them. It passes the point where it is sordid, and comes to a point where it is a great plan flung out over the world. Now George Peabody couldn't imagine any use of money that didn't bring power, and when it was proposed to him to subscribe to some philanthropy he didn't see anything in it at all. It was suggested to him that he should do, what he afterwards did, found a great library—and not merely put up a library building, mark you—but filled [it] with books. (Applause.)

The library is on the inside, not on the outside, and he said that that seemed to him like throwing his money away; nothing would come back from it. But the gentlemen who approached him said, why Mr. Peabody, don't you see all sorts of men, young and old, who can't go to college, will resort to that great collection of books, and will garner out of them new careers, and that will be a permanent investment, whose usury will be in the thought and energy of men. And for the first time Peabody began to see the thing in the terms of interest, and he understood the terms of interest, coming back on the money, and that this interest was incalculable and interminable, because, while his interest account in the bank would be so lost at his death that nob[o]dy could trace it, this interest account would never stop so long as the investment was safeguarded by conscientious trustees, and that generation after generation this amount would be enlarged by what they draw out of his library. And what had been endeavors turned to enthusiasm.

And this story of George Peabody was laid before Johns Hopkins, and this shrewd, calculating, vulgar old man, whose pleasures had been chiefly sensual pleasures, was caught by the magic of the idea that he could render his own energy and his own money immortal by investing it in these invisible, intangible, endless things.

And so every soul is sooner or later touched by this idea that the real increment of human interest is built up in this way.

When you are dead and gone, how would you wish to be remembered? In the first place, would you wish to be remembered at all? (Laughter.) You will not be remembered for having a lot of money, because there are hundreds of thousands of men in this country now who are millionaires. It is commonplace to be rich in America. Two or three years ago I went to a school so expensive that I was told there was nobody there except the sons of rich men, and I told those youngsters that I looked upon them with commiseration; that boys who were certain to have money generally didn't do anything, and they would only be rich men and were foredoomed to obscurity; and I said, you youngsters have got to do something else before you will rise a single inch above the dead level of your generation. If you want to be remembered at all you will do something besides get money.

Now, how would you prefer to be remembered? Did you ever know a monument erected to a millionaire just because he was a millionaire? Did you ever know a monument to be erected to a man because he was successful in his own business? To whom are the monuments erected? They are erected to the men who spend their money and their energy upon something else than themselves invariably, and their only distinction comes by hitching their wagon to a star, by hitching their wagon to the spiritual forces of the world, which alone lifts things into the empyrean. Then, if you will see that your star gets high enough for people to see it, you will be remembered; but if your star is never going to glimmer outside of your own counting-room or your own factory, then you will have to do a good deal of furbishing to make people think it is a star at all. There is no firmament for it.

You are not being asked, therefore, to do a favor to anybody but yourself, but being asked to subscribe to the Young Men's Christian Association, you are approached with the interesting suggestion that you should cease to be quite so obscure as you are now; that you should join the only nobility that there can be in America; that you should take out a patent of nobility which it is open to any man to take out, who will serve his fellow-man unselfishly, in the United States. Come up, therefore, and file your patent, come up and put in your claim to be inscribed upon the roll of honor, of honor because the only standard of honor is external to yourself. Honor does not come to the man because he seeks to please his fellow-man for the sake of his own comfort and gratification. Honor comes to the man who is willing to offend his fellow-man in order to serve something that is greater than he is, and greater than they are, something that they will ultimately honor.

Do you never reflect upon the singular course of heroism in this world? Heroism is not originated in doing popular things. Heroes have been bred out of those men who were willing to do what they thought was right before anybody agreed with them or thought it was right. And, though they have gone to the stake, whether they knew it or not, those fires kindled at the stake have never gone out. Men see their glow in the sky. Yet men, these were the immortals.

We do not build fires in our day with faggots; we build them with slander; we build them with depreciation; we build them with sneers. But they are of no avail. They will illuminate the fame of the man at whom we scoff and we will be ashes under the embers.

America ought not to need to be taught the lesson that greatness is spiritual; that it is in the vision; that it is in what men devote themselves to in the spirit of self-sacrifice; and that human liberty, human appreciation of the truth, is elevated higher than anything else in this world. When America devotes her money to the ends that are everlasting, then America will have secured her permanency in the world, and there will never come a time of decay; there will never come a time when the breath of inspiration has gone out of her lungs; there will never come a time when she cannot have all the heroes, all the leaders, all the ministers, that she needs to accomplish to the utter end the thing that she set out to do, namely, to erect a beacon which will guide the feet of mankind always in the paths of purity and self-sacrifice and peace and achievement. (Great applause.)

Printed in the *Nashville Tennessean*, Feb. 26, 1912, with corrections from the partial text in the *Nashville Banner*, Feb. 26, 1912.

To the Legislature of New Jersey

To the Legislature: [Trenton, N. J.] February 26th, 1912.

I take the liberty of calling your attention to the pending amendment to the Constitution of the United States, which grants to the Congress of the United States the right to impose a tax upon incomes. It seems to me of the utmost importance that this power should be bestowed in unmistakable terms upon the Congress of the United States. The jurists who first interpreted the Constitution of the United States believed that this power might legally be exercised by the Congress of the United States, under the terms of the Constitution as it stands, but later decisions have so embarrassed the exercise of that power by restrictions as to render it practically nugatory. The limitations which under these decisions are imposed upon the taxing power of the Federal Government, practically deprive the Congress of a free choice of the sources from which the income necessary to support the government is to be derived. They put the taxing power in a straightjacket.[1] Every argument of expediency seems to speak in favor of this amendment, by which some part of the limitation is sought to be removed.

I urge it upon your attention as a subject worthy of the most thoughtful statesmanship. The confirmation of a large majority of the States has already been secured. It would be a conspicuous service to the country if New Jersey might add her vote to the number of States who are willing thus generously and in ungrudging public spirit to complete the necessary powers of the general government in the field of taxation.[2]

    Respectfully,   Woodrow Wilson, *Governor*.

Printed in the *Minutes of the N. J. House of Assembly*, 1912, p. 408.
  [1] See WW to the legislature of New Jersey, March 20, 1911, n. 2, and WW to the Senate of New Jersey, April 4, 1911, n. 2, both in Vol. 22.
  [2] As has been noted earlier, the New Jersey legislature did not approve the Sixteenth Amendment until February 4, 1913.

To William Gibbs McAdoo

                    Trenton N J Feb 26 [1912]

    I have just returned and have only just now heard the terrible news of your bereavement[1] you have my deepest warmest and most affectionate sympathy. Woodrow Wilson

T telegram (W. G. McAdoo Papers, DLC).
  [1] His wife, Sarah Fleming McAdoo, died of heart disease on February 21.

To Richard Heath Dabney

My dear Heath: [Trenton, N. J.] February 27, 1912.

    I have been knocking about from place to place, utterly unable to sit down and tell you what is really in my heart about your tragical loss.[1] I cannot tell you, my dear fellow, with what affectionate sympathy my heart has gone out to you in the loss of your daughter. Everything that you tell us about her makes more vivid my impression of how inconsolable you must be. I hope you realise, my dear Heath, how intimate my feeling of affection and sympathy is. It has given me great pleasure to feel that anything I might say would convey to you the least solace. You bear the whole thing so nobly yourself that it shows that you were worthy to have such a daughter. I shall always remember her as one of my own dear friends, after what you have told me of her.

    With warmest affection,

              Faithfully yours,   Woodrow Wilson

TLS (Wilson-Dabney Corr., ViU).
  [1] His daughter, Lucy Davis Dabney, born April 23, 1903, died of diabetes on February 11, 1912.

To Mary Allen Hulbert Peck

Dearest Friend,   Princeton, New Jersey 28 Feb'y, 1912

It was literally impossible for me to write on Sunday,—I was on the train coming back from Kansas and Tennessee—and now here I sit by four noisy (and, what is worse, witty) persons playing Euchre and I, poor wight, am very poor at *not* hearing what is said at my elbow. To-morrow I start for Iowa,—to spend another Sunday on the road and get back on the 4th. Enough of the trips! This is the last one,—at any rate for the present,— I am tired of taking them and of talking of them! Indeed I am tired of politics just at this momentary writing (there is a lot of meanness in it, and of weary futile things which disgust sooner or later) and I want to change the subject,—to something as far from myself as possible (*what* a tiresome subject that has become since *every*body began talking of it!).

Suppose we make it Mexico. Our precious Nellie has just got out of the wretched, unstable place. You remember she went down there just before Christmas, to Chihuahua (the northern province which we are forever obliged to sit on the border and watch). When the present disorders broke out she was in the tight interior, at a lumber camp, and before the world realized what was going on the insurrectos were all about the place, the trains were stopped, the wires down, and a bridge or two destroyed. The dear little sport (so far as we can learn) enjoyed it all, and was loath to come away! By dint of kindness and management she was got from stage to stage of the 270 miles to the border (some newspaper men finally rushing down in an automobile and fetching the little party breathless into El Paso[)]. Juarez, next door, was taken next day. I was *very* anxious, to tell the truth, and could not get my darling out of my head until she was safe on this side that imaginary line that means so much. She is now on her way to Denver, but will not be at home again for some eight or nine days yet[.] How happy I shall be to see her. She shall never go into Mexico again until we get guarantees from both the Mexican government and all possible leaders of revolution. When will the poor land know what it can expect, and have comfortable to-morrows? Margaret, meanwhile, poor girlie, was robbed, at her rooms in New York, by a sneak thief, of all her trinkets *and* her watch. We are certainly having all the experiences there are. Being a scattered family, we are in a position to pick them up with a wide dragnet. I, poor chap! move around, a very public character, while longing for nothing so much as private chats with dear friends, where there are no expediences to consider, but only frank avowals, real thoughts lying deep, where the springs of the heart are. What would I not give for a stroll on the South Shore with a dear, dear friend who loves it as much as I do.

We are all well, and all send affectionate messages to the dear Pecks, Allens, and Hulberts, who, if they love us, will keep well!   Your devoted friend   Woodrow Wilson

ALS (WP, DLC).

From Francis Ignatius Drobinski

Honorable Sir: [Brooklyn, N. Y., Feb. 29, 1912]

At a meeting of the delegates of the Polish Societies of South Brooklyn, held on February 23d, I had the honor of reading your communication bearing the date of the 7th inst.

The assembly expressed its appreciation of the kindness of tone and the breadth of view that characterized your letter. However, while judging from your letter that you are on the right road yourself in the estimate of the Polish character, still it was felt that you have sent the readers of your volumes on the wrong path. Something it was thought should in fairness be done by you to return your misguided readers to the proper way of measuring Polish immigrants, who in the main have been a welcome addition to the social life of America.

An erratum slip in the yet unsold volumes, a promise to bring your meaning out of the cloud of ob[s]curity, and this in the next edition, a statement to the public press, these are the means that if taken will, I believe, bring your friends and well-wishers from the Polish peoples who still are unconvinced that they or any other immigrant elements which had recently been[1] deal from you, if you were lifted into the office of President.

Letters, because of the economy of writing, are not the best method of conveying one's impressions; consequently if your excellency thinks it advisable and wishes to appoint the time, a committee from the Polish Societies of Brooklyn will wait on you and discuss and adjust the matter satisfactorily.

Awaiting your kind answer, Believe us to be, Honorable Governor, Respectfully yours,
                    United Polish Societies of South Brooklyn.
                              [Per F. Ig. Drobinski]

Printed in the *New York American*, March 25, 1912.
1 The printer dropped a line at this point.

A News Report of Two Addresses in Des Moines, Iowa

[March 2, 1912]

GOV. WILSON MAKES DIRECT APPEAL TO IOWA REPUBLICANS

Only one man ever attracted more people to the Coliseum than did Governor Woodrow Wilson of New Jersey last night. The one man was Colonel Roosevelt.

By accurate estimate, 4,000 men and women heard the eastern candidate for the democratic nomination for president relate his views of how to get the government of the United States "back to the people."

More interest was manifest in the Wilson meeting than in any political meeting held in Des Moines in recent years, so seasoned campaigners said. Republicans pointed to the marked difference between the careless reception to President Taft on the occasion of his visit here last fall and the spontaneous enthusiasm of the state for the former president of Princeton university.

Leaders in the Iowa Wilson league were jubilant over the success of their enterprise.

The distinguished visitor himself was highly elated over his reception.

"I had ex[p]ected an interested crowd in my visit here," he remarked, as he stood on the platform at the Coliseum after his address and smiling all over his big face, gripping the hands of the citizens with real enthusiasm as they crowded to pay their respects. "This audience certainly is one to be proud of. I know I will never be sorry that I came. This is great."

Neither before the University club at its banquet at the Savery, nor before the Coliseum audience, did Governor Wilson speak from manuscript.

Instead, he spoke in the free and easy conversational manner for which his platform work is famous.

Although at times he sprinkled the language of the university class room in his verbal dishes, for the most part his address was in words of the street, one and two syllables. Many a listener commented upon the fact that Wilson's education and refinement appears to advantage in the simple construction of his arguments. To many, the plainness to which his knowledge was turned in arguments, and the pleasant similes and metaphors fitting into the entire theme with such nicety, was a revelation.

The speaker's reference to his sincere belief in the initiative,

the referendum and recall as instruments with which to restore
the rule of the separate states to the body politic, fell upon an
enthusiastic house, which demonstrated its attitude by noisy
seconds. No mention was made of the recall of judges as advanced by Theodore Roosevelt. All he said about the recall was
that he favored it as concerning state government.

As to the national political problem, the speaker said the
business of the people is "to lay out a programme, to decide
what you are going to lay out and who is going to carry it out."

Governor Wilson chided the republicans who vote the republican ticket because "they wonder what the old man would think
about it if they voted the democratic ticket."

There is only this one difference between the insurgent, or
progressive republicans, and Governor Wilson, he says. "You
speak of a protective policy with a certain air of piety and I
don't," he asserted, addressing the progressive republicans in the
audience. "I do not think either a protective policy or free trade
is the only principle to steer by. I consider what fiscal policy it
is best to adopt for the good of the country. We are brothers in
principle."

No caustic words were spared by Governor Wilson in dealing with the "standpatters." His reference to the "standpatters"
echoed in many a chuckling face. . . .

In the wake of Henry's band, Governor Wilson was hurried
to the Savery. In the automobile with him rode his secretary,[1]
Jerry B. Sullivan, chairman for the evening, Earl Bronson, manager for the Iowa Wilson league, Henry Riegelman and Judge
E. M. Carr of Manchester.[2]

Disappointed by the unavoidable delay of the governor's party,
the 175 members of the University club proceeded to get the
courses out of the way.

When the governor's party arrived, the banqueters were well
along in the dessert course, but not too busy to quit their chairs
and raise the roof with applause for the visitor when he bright-
ened the banquet hall doors.

Without any formality, Governor Wilson fell to, to annihilate
the grape fruit in front of him. He was a hungry governor. He
had had nothing to eat since noon. He thanked the waiter at
his elbow for a second baked potato. After he had fortified himself with a regular meal he talked.

James B. Weaver, Jr.,[3] introduced the guest of honor.

"I recognized the cut of your jibs the minute I came into this
room," he said at the outset, and for thirty minutes he talked

across the table like he was a guest at a fraternity dinner party.

"The business of university men is to find out what is true and then proclaim it without fear."

Such was the keynote to his frank, homely illustrated after dinner speech. Governor Wilson is a story teller. His anecdotes settled well with the diners, whom he complimented as being of most discriminating appearance.

Telling of the transformation from a university head to a governor, and telling of the function of the university man in politics, he said: "The whole problem of society is to transform learning into action, to transform knowledge into a constructive programme.

"University education should endow every man with a habit of inquiring which is impartial, a sight which is undimmed, should enable every man to see things as they are.

"A schoolmaster is a man whose business it is to find out the facts about everything he deals with and then to tell the people what they ought to know," he said.

Governor Wilson related that his practice has been to talk until he reached a sore spot on somebody. "Then that person metaphorically knocks me down and I know what I have said is so. Every time you probe the truth the patient cries out.["]

Printed in the Des Moines *Register and Leader*, March 2, 1912; many editorial headings omitted.

1 Walter Measday.

2 Bronson cannot be further identified; Riegelman was a dealer in real estate and commercial loans in Des Moines; Edward Michael Carr was a lawyer, businessman, and newspaper publisher of Manchester, Ia., never a judge.

3 James Bellamy Weaver, lawyer of Des Moines, Republican, son of James Baird Weaver, Greenback and Populist candidate for President in 1880 and 1892.

A News Item

[March 3, 1912]

GOVERNOR WILSON SPENT BUSY DAY
Called on Governor Carroll at Capitol.

Yesterday was a busy day for Gov. Woodrow Wilson before his departure shortly after noon for Davenport[1] over the Rock Island. Beginning with a reception at the Savery early in the morning, the governor later visited Highland Park college, where he delivered an interesting talk to the students,[2] and wound up the morning with a fifteen minute visit with Gov. B. F. Carroll[3] in his office at the state house.

The two governors talked about a number of topics of interest, but politics was not mentioned directly, though the governor from New Jersey gave the governor from Iowa an opening to take up the burning issues of the day politically.

A little sermon on life was given to the Highland Park students at 10 o'clock by Governor Wilson, who spoke on the high rank taken by vocational education and its bright future in this country.

Governor Wilson told his auditors that they did not have to die to go to hell and that they could live in such a state while on earth. Living and thinking rightly, he said, would bring heaven on earth.

Printed in the Des Moines *Register and Leader*, March 3, 1912.
[1] Wilson spoke on the tariff to the Commercial Club of Davenport, Ia., during the evening of March 2. A report of his speech is printed in the Des Moines *Register and Leader*, March 3, 1912.
[2] There is a typed transcript of this speech in WP, DLC.
[3] Beryl F. Carroll, Republican Governor of Iowa, 1909-11.

To Francis Ignatius Drobinski

Dear Dr. Drobinski: [Trenton, N. J.] March 4, 1912.

Thank you for your kind letter of February 29. I think with you that it would be best for me at the earliest possible moment to rewrite the passage referred to in my history. I shall get into communication with my publishers and ascertain the feasibility of doing this at an early date in case a new edition should be in contemplation.[1]

With much appreciation for your kindness,

Sincerely yours,   Woodrow Wilson

Printed in the *New York American*, March 25, 1912.
[1] Wilson's letters failed to mollify Drobinski and the United Polish Societies of South Brooklyn. In an interview in the *New York American*, March 24, 1912, Drobinski declared that Wilson's "half-retractions" in letters were not enough; only a public retraction of his comments on the Polish people in his *History of the American People* would suffice. Since Wilson had had "ample time" to correct his error, but had "practically refused," the United Polish Societies would henceforth strive with all their power "to spread the anti-Wilson movement."

To Harper and Brothers

My dear Sirs: [Trenton, N. J.] March 4, 1912.

I write to ask if a new impression is soon to be made of the Fifth Volume of my History of the American People? There are one or two passages in that volume which I should like to reconsider and re-write in order to remove the false impressions which they seem to have made, and I should like to know what occasion I might look forward to to altering them.[1]

Sincerely yours,   Woodrow Wilson

TCL (RSB Coll., DLC).

[1] Further correspondence on this subject is missing, but the offending passages were not changed.

A News Report

[March 5, 1912]

GOVERNOR CHATS WITH ISLANDS COMMISSIONER

TRENTON, March 5.—Manuel E. Quezon,[1] one of the resident commissioners from the Philippines in this country, representing the islands, with one other associate, on the floor of Congress,[2] was a visitor to Governor Wilson yesterday afternoon. He came to pay his respects, said Senor Quezon, but during a conversation that lasted about fifteen minutes the Governor and commissioner found Philippine matters a subject of mutual interest.[3]

The Governor acknowledged that there was much concerning the islands with which he was not acquainted, and it is probable that he and his visitor will have another meeting.

"You know the next President of the United States will be inaugurated a year from today?" said a News reporter, interrogatively.

"Yes, I know," answered the commissioner. But he would not go any further in a statement, though he smiled appreciately.

Printed in the *Newark Evening News*, March 5, 1912.

[1] Manuel Luis Quezon, Philippine nationalist leader, Resident Commissioner to the United States, 1909-16.

[2] Benito Legarda.

[3] Quezon wrote to Erving Winslow, the anti-imperialist leader of Boston, on March 5, 1912, that Wilson had told him that he believed that the Filipinos lacked sufficient cultural homogeneity to live amicably with one another and govern themselves responsibly. He added that he was open to persuasion on this matter. Peter W. Stanley, *A Nation in the Making: The Philippines and the United States, 1899-1921* (Cambridge, Mass., 1974), pp. 179, 300n1.

From William Jay Gaynor

Dear Gov. Wilson: New York, March 6, 1912.

We have in this town a proprietor of several newspapers,[1] including one in Yiddish, who thinks himself fit for any and every office that comes along, including the Presidency. Once every four years he is a violent candidate for that office, to the amusement of the nation, more or less. He sometimes gets in the convention the votes of the delegates from the States which we ordinarily call "purchasable." He is now puffing himself up in his publications and crying down every one else whom he thinks may be in his way as a candidate.

His method is like that of some hogs in a fire or a like emergency, namely, to jump upon all others in his way and bear them down and trample the hobnails of his shoes into their flesh in his efforts to save his own carcass. That is his way of striving for a nomination or an election. Not until the human heart generally becomes as cold and base as his will that way succeed. The average human heart is kind and true.

Some one has sent to me an attack of his on you.[2] He wants to get you down and get the hobnails of his shoes into your flesh. The more fit you are the more he wants to trample on you, because you are in his way. He ridicules and denounces you for saying somewhere that Washington did not write the "Farewell Address."

As usual, he seeks to excite passion and prejudice by appealing to the ignorant. It is no discredit to Washington that he had the "Farewell Address" written by others. As I remember Jefferson's account, Madison prepared a farewell address for Washington, at his request, when the end of his first term was approaching, and Hamilton revised it at the end of Washington's second term, and it was used in that form by Washington.

But I write to you only to say that I am glad that you do not pay any attention to this common libeller. He can neither add to nor detract from a man like you.

Sincerely yours,   W. J. Gaynor, Mayor.

Printed in the New York *World*, March 13, 1912.
[1] William Randolph Hearst.
[2] Hearst's editorial in the *New York Evening Journal*, March 5, 1912. For an account of his campaign against Wilson, see Link, *Road to the White House*, pp. 382-84.

From Edward Mandell House

Dear Governor Wilson: [Austin, Tex.] March 6th, 1912.

I am pleased to tell you that we now have everything in good shape in Texas and that you may confidently rely upon the delegates from this State.

We may or may not have a Presidential Primary but the result will not be changed.

In two or three weeks our organization will be perfected and then I shall leave for the East where I shall have the pleasure of seeing you.[1]   Faithfully yours,   [E. M. House]

CCL (E. M. House Papers, CtY).
[1] House was grossly exaggerating his role. See Lewis L. Gould, *Progressives and Prohibitionists: Texas Democrats in the Wilson Era* (Austin, Tex., and London, 1973), pp. 58-84, and Arthur S. Link, "The Wilson Movement in Texas, 1910 1912," *Southwestern Historical Quarterly*, XLVIII (Oct. 1944), 169-85.

To John Arthur Aylward

My Dear Mr. Aylward: [Trenton, N. J.] March 7, 1912.

Wha[t] you tell me about the use that has been made of quotations from my History distresses me very much, because it confirms my feeling that a malicious attempt is being made to misrepresent me in the eyes of a class of my fellow-citizens for whom I have the most genuine respect.

No man who candidly and honestly examines the passages referred to can find in them anything except what I meant to put into them. That was, of course, not a condemnation or even a criticism of the great nations I there mentioned. He must be a very ignorant man who does not know the distinction attaching to the history of the great Italian people and of the Hungarian and Polish nations, which, through so many generations have made a gallant struggle to maintain the rights of man, and who have in the process developed so many qualities that entitle them to the profound respect of the world. I have never for a moment regretted that our great composite nation was enriched by the blood of these people.

All that I commented upon was the undoubted fact that during the years of which I speak some of the baser elements out of these nations—elements such as might have come out of any of the nations of the world—had been brought in undesirable numbers into our ports to the embarrassment of their former compatriots as well as to the detriment of some of the communities into which they went.

Clearly the class to which I refer in my history is not the intelligent, liberty-loving class which came of its own volition, seeking a home and a land of freedom. I refer to the class of laborers which was brought here under pauper labor contracts by some of the great protected industries. During the times mentioned the peoples referred to happen to be the ones drafted upon. This vicious practice became so offensive and dangerous that Congress, yielding to a strong demand from the laboring classes which included Hungarians, Italians and Poles alike, passed a stringent law against the abuse.

No well-informed man can question these facts or censure the criticism which was based upon them, and I am sure that the leaders of the Polish, Italian, and Hungarian citizens of this country will be the first to recognize the malicious injustice which has been done me by putting my views in any other light.

Cordially yours,   Woodrow Wilson.

Printed in the Madison *Wisconsin State Journal*, March 12, 1912.

An Address to the General Assembly of Maryland

[[March 7, 1912]]

Mr. Speaker,[1] Mr. President,[2] your Excellency,[3] gentlemen of the Senate and Assembly of Maryland, ladies and gentlemen:

It is a great pleasure and a real privilege to stand in this presence and be able to say something of the faith that is in me. The Speaker has just informed me that it is a very rare thing for the privileges of this House to be extended to a Governor, especially, may I venture to say, to the Governor of the State of Maryland.

From my own experience at Trenton, the place where I am least expected to be is near the chambers where the Legislature sits.

I remember a singular incident which struck me even as a boy, when Mr. William M. Evarts was Secretary of State. One day[4]—one would suppose innocently enough—he wandered into the gallery of the Senate,[5] and a member of that body[6] called attention to the fact that an effort was being made to overawe that Assembly, and the motion was made not to proceed until he had withdrawn.[7] It is undoubtedly true that it is a very rare thing for an Executive and a Legislature to come face to face in America, and yet what strikes me as most singular in the history of such matters from first to last is that America of all places in the world should be the place where this is true.

Practical, common-sense America makes punctillious division between the executive and the Legislature, in that the one body and the other person are not expected to stand in the presence of one another. I make this introduction because it seems in a way to me pertinent to the matter which I want to discuss before you tonight.

If I may say so without breach of taste, we are talking too much about persons and too little about principles. We are too much engaged in discussing personalities and personal possibilities that we are, I am afraid, in danger of forgetting that we stand in the presence of public questions, which will not long wait to be settled, and that while we stop to choose a man we may forget to promote a cause.

[1] James McConky Trippe of Baltimore.
[2] Jesse Dashiell Price.
[3] Governor Phillips Lee Goldsborough.
[4] March 29, 1879.
[5] Actually, into the House of Representatives.
[6] Joseph Clay Stiles Blackburn of Kentucky.
[7] No such motion was introduced; Blackburn spoke on April 3, 1879.

I will tell you frankly I am not interested in men, except as the instruments of causes, and I call you to witness that America is not in an ordinary frame of mind just now. There is everywhere, while no threat of serious disturbance, profound discontent and uneasiness. America is not satisfied today with her public affairs and she is not satisfied either with the means or the spirit in which they are administered.

Perhaps it would be interesting to ask how well founded these feelings are, but it is not possible to deny their existence. America has determined that she will conduct her affairs after a different fashion, and we who are for the time being responsible for those affairs must study her mind and see what our duty is read to be in the light of her disposition and purpose.

What is government for? Government is nothing else than a means of organizing what would otherwise be a disorganized people, to resist the force of every competitive organization. Do you know that we are fond of saying that the object of our government was expressed more fundamentally than by anybody else, by Thomas Jefferson when he said that it must be a government where there must be "equal opportunities for all and special privileges for none."

And yet, by common consent, special privilege has sprung up in this country. Special privilege will spring up in any country, but what created our present state of mind is that special privilege does not merely exist, but is organized, and we are not certain that the Government is sufficiently organized against it. Is it not true, gentlemen, whether the question be debatable or not, that we are not certain that organized privilege cannot govern unorganized public opinion?

Are we not uncertain as to whether there are forces smaller than the forces of public opinion which are determining what the policies of our State and national governments should be? That is the fundamental question which makes a breath of uneasiness stir everywhere in America and creates a condition which business men above all others should wish to see an end put to, because there cannot be solid business upon a basis of suspicion.

Confidence is the very breath of life to business. Confidence is the condition precedent to every sort of stability, and if there be not universal confidence there cannot be universal prosperity. Is there universal prosperity? On the contrary, is there not universal suspicion? And is it not our business to resolve that suspicion into its elements in order to see if it cannot be dissipated, for in wholesome-minded people like those of America suspicion is not the natural thing.

Suspicion, then, is the abnormal thing. America has not often suffered from it. America has suffered more commonly from optimistic confidence than suspicion. Therefore we must see what it is that has crept like a malady into the thought of this country. In my judgment it lies where I have already stated it lies, in the fear that the common opinion is not sufficiently organized against the special interests.

You will say that is what representative assemblies are for. But are the people of America contented with their representative assemblies? In some States they are. But in many States they are not, and I fear that the States in which they are not outnumber the States in which they are.

There are some States in which the people are satisfied that their representative assemblies represent them and speak their minds, but there are not many such States in the Union. In most there is a feeling that the representative body does not speak the public voice, but is apt upon occasion, at any rate, to speak some private purpose.

We speak about "lobby," but there are different kinds of lobbies. There are lobbies of the old sort made up of the men who wished to press special purposes, and there are lobbies of the new sort sent by the great civic societies to watch legislation and to see that the public interests are represented while private interests are being pressed, and Legislatures are put under surveillance by the representatives of civic societies as if they needed watching in the public interest. Another evidence of the instinctive feeling that there is not sufficient organization through which public opinion can express itself.

Why do you suppose that is the case? I believe that it has something to do with the machinery of legislation in this country. The streams of legislation in this country, whether they are so by intention or not, are underground. The minute a little bill appears it is at once submerged in committee. Committee meetings are not public. Committees upon occasion will hold hearings, but after the hearing the deliberations of the committee are private. Some bills never come out of committee, and nobody ever knows why they do not. Some bills do come out upon an apparently whimsical choice, and nobody is told why they come out.

It was supposed, ladies and gentlemen, at the last session of the Legislature of New Jersey that I did some kind of coercion.

I want to tell you that the only kind of coercion I ever felt just-tified indulging in was this: I said:

"If certain measures do not come out of committee, what I am going to do is to go down in the county from which the chair-man of the committee comes, ask the people there to organize a public meeting and invite the chairman down to tell them why they did not come out of committee." And I offered to go down at the same time and engage in debate with the chairman of the committee. Is not that a perfectly fair proposal? And the singular thing was that the bills did not stay in committee.

Why didn't they? Don't you see the answer that everybody can give to that question is a comment upon the very subject I am discussing? The people want to know, but don't know what are the real moving influences in the committees of their representative bodies. They feel that whether there is anything sinister about it or not they don't know; but just because it is all private, they suspect that it may be sinister, and instances might be cited where it has been obviously sinister.

Instances might be cited where certain definite interests are known to have been instrumental in the make-up of committees where it can almost be proved to demonstration that it never was intended that these bills should come out. And therefore one fundamental feeling of Americans today is that they are not sure that they have an organized and public voice in their own affairs. They feel that it may be that the special interests are more effectively organized than they are themselves, and you cannot beat organization except by organization.

Diffused public opinion cannot beat concerted co-operative purpose. For one thing, arguments don't tell according to their full weight. Suppose that when a hearing is held only the parties specially interested in the bill bestir themselves to be present by counsel or representative and that nobody speaks for the gen-eral interest, then the committe[e] is hardly to be blamed if it does not itself conceive the subject matter it is dealing with in the largest view in which it might conceive it. So that the or-ganized influences at work are not public but special.

And that is the problem of government in America. For my part, I do not believe anybody is to blame. I am one of those who do not believe that any essential corruption has got into our blood politically. Americans are naturally the frankest, the most direct people, but they have tied themselves up in processes so complicated that they have constituted themselves a jungle and nobody but an expert knows the trail.

And there are in some localities beasts in the jungle and if you don't know the trail you had better keep out in the open. That is the reason for such movements as the movement for commission government in our cities. People say let's cut down the jungle and see what is inside of it. Let's have just a few persons talking in open converse before us so that we can over-hear their conversation, and know what it is they are saying with regard to the public business.

The slogan of modern reform is simplification, because we have the thing so complicated that nobody knows how the thing is worked. A great many honest men are by that drawn under suspicion. Many a man who acts in the public interest has no means of letting it be known by demonstration that he did act for the public interest, and if he dared upon some legitimate object to confer with a representative of a private interest and then made the right decision, he is tainted by his conference. That is certainly an unwholesome state of affairs.

There is no citizen of the Commonwealth to discuss with the Governor or with members of the Legislature, but if some members of the Commonwealth were often to consult with him, the Governor's chances for remaining long in the public service would soon be at an end—an absolutely poor state of affairs, for which we are to blame and which we must remedy.

Well, what are we going to do about it? And what are we trying to do about it? In the first place, we say that we don't know who chooses our representatives, because all we know is that somehow before election slates are made up and the slate on one side contains just as many names that we don't know as the slate on the other side, and as far as we are concerned, busy men, earning their bread from the rising of the sun to the going down thereof, the choice is really between the tweedledum and tweedledee.

In other words, the people are beginning to see that the process of selection is fundamental and the process of election is not. If I am at liberty to select the man you can vote for, then you can vote as you please and I am master of the situation, and I could cite instances not very far from the Capitol of New Jersey where the gentlemen who selected the two tickets sat in the same room.

So far as the result was concerned, they had you coming and they had you going. The process of selection was the final determination of who should control the government of that State. It was well known from season to season who owned the Governor of New Jersey, and through none of those seasons did it happen to be the people of New Jersey. That was largely because almost entirely they did not select the persons who were to represent them in legislative and executive capacities.

That is at the foundation of our eager demand everywhere in the United States for direct primaries. The people are saying, "We do not intend that little coteries and cabals of men sitting in private conference shall determine whom we shall vote for. We want to do the selecting as well as the electing, and we are going to be very much more particular at the primaries, where the selecting is done, than at the election, where the electing is done. We know we want to beat the bosses at the primaries, because that is where they have always got us."

Did you ever think of the difference between a machine and an organization? I believe in a party organization. I don't know how a party could be held together without an effective, closely knitted organization. But an organization is as wide as the party; a machine is not. A machine consists of two or three self-elected gentlemen who by sagacity and staying on the job day and night have managed to collect all the threads of the organization in their own hands and have determined not for the interests of the organization but for the interests of themselves or for someone whom they represent what the organization shall do.

I am for the organization; I am against the machine. But after you have got the direct primaries the same thing is going to happen. I mean that after you have chosen the threads, the threads are going to be lost in the pattern. You select your legislative representatives, you select your executive officers and then send them on their jobs and they get so mixed up in what they are doing that you don't know any more then than you did before.

It is very well to collect them at the polls and say, "Now, gentlemen, the thing has been personally conducted, and we have picked you out, and you are to do our work. Go your ways and be good boys"; but suppose you lose sight of them afterward, then you don't know whether they are being good or not.

That is the basis of another very singular movement in the United States. It is a movement which is bearing very hard on Governors. A Governor is expected to take charge of the whole job. The people say "we can't follow the intricacies of this business; only some of us voted for any of these gentlemen; one county chose this group; another county chose that group, and if the county watches its men it is not going to control things. There is only one person in the State that we all choose and that is the Governor and we are going to insist that the Governor be eyes for us, that he watch what is going on and keep us informed and keep his grip upon things."

That condition is getting to be abnormal. For one thing it is not fair. I do not mean it is not fair to the Governor, but I do not think it is fair chiefly to the Legislature.

There is a story which I have told many times, but it is so applicable that I must tell it again.

Some years ago, when we had a President who sent more messages than our present President sends, I boarded the train at a junction near my home and found one of the Senators from New Jersey on the train, who was an old friend of mine, and it was very hard that day to draw him into conversation. Finally, I knew him well enough to say "Senator, what is the matter?" and he said:

"I wish the Constitution had not given the President the right to send messages to Congress."

I said:

"You are on the wrong trail. The trouble is he publishes his messages for everybody, and if the public agrees with him it does not stop to hear what you have to say. The trouble is his opinions are published everywhere and yours only some places. And the trouble is you can't answer him. The newspapers won't take it up when you reply. Your voice does not reach where his does. He has the whip hand on you always. There is no forum where you can reply to him. Is not that true?"

And the same with the Governor. He being the head of the Commonwealth, everybody is interested in what he says and does. What difference does it make if somebody else in somebody else's county gets up and replies to the Governor? You don't know much about that person, and you don't know whether he "cuts much ice or not," and therefore you don't pay any particular attention to it, and the Governor then is not answered.

Nor is it not wholesome for the Governor not to be answered. It is not wholesome for anybody to have such an obstructed forum. A man should be brought to book for what he says and yet every Governor in the United States has that advantage, particularly when the people cheer the more loudly the more he baits the Legislature.

I am simply stating things within your own knowledge and I am not criticising any particular part of our system, but I am expounding a very extraordinary situation. What do the people demand of the President of the United States? Chiefly this—I had almost said, only this—that he constitute himself their leader.

They don't care which way he leads, providing he will only hump himself and lead.

They expect that. They like the spice of it. They feel that he is the only servant of all of them, the only man not localized, and they say to him, "Stand up and say what ought to be done and keep on saying it until we can find out whether we agree with your [you] or not." They are demanding, in other words, that the President show Congress the way and that every Governor show the Legislature the way. Don't you see that involves some very interesting [s]uggestions? They are looking for a simplification of the process and they are looking for a spokesman.

Why should they look for a spokesman if they thought their legislative assemblies always afforded them a spokesman? To put the thing in brief, they are not sure that they are represented. When I hear gentlemen say that they will stake their lives and political fortunes on our representative systems, I reply:

"So will I where you show it is representative, but I will not where it can be shown that it is not representative. If you like representative institutions, produce specimens and let's look at them."

There are specimens, very handsome and ancient specimens in the United States; but you can't find them in every State. It is notorious that you cannot find them in every State, and the people are aware of that. That is the reason they are not stopping with insisting that their Governors lead and that they have the selection of men who are going to constitute the assemblies to which they look for legislative action. That is the reason, gentlemen, why there is one insistent issue constantly arising in our public discussion, and that is the issue in initiative and referendum and recall.

Now mark you, it is a man's duty in this day to state very clearly just where those questions come in and just what their significance is. In the first place, they have nothing to do with national politics. There is no central body of opinion in this country demanding the initiative and referendum or the recall with regard to national representatives, and the call for these things is acute only in those States where the people feel that they must have what they have somehow lost and wish to recover—a control over their own representatives.

I have not heard men of thoughtful wisdom in this matter anywhere propose that direct legislation should be substituted for elective representation. Nobody who knows the tedious and long way in which representative institutions were built up and tested can ever make a proposal of that sort.

The object of these things is control. They are not constructive. They are not meant to create a new system of government. They are meant or necessary to recover a lost control, and in many places where they have been used the interesting thing is that they have recovered control and that the men who have made the most active use of them and engaged in the most active advocacy of them are men who speak of them as a reserve power to be resorted to when it became necessary to resort to them. Have you ever noticed how comfortably America gets on with its disengaged view of the Fourth of July and the actual process of affairs?

What was the soil out of which our constitutions grew? I can show you a very rich and fertile piece of that soil in the Virginia Declaration of Rights. Have you read that document recently? If you have, I am afraid that some of you who have grown unfamiliar with it would think it was a plank out of a Populistic platform. It says that public servants are the trustees and agents of the people and shall be amenable to them at all times. It says that whenever the people find their institutions not suited to the purposes of their life, it is a fundamental principle of our government that they may alter or abolish as they please.

Don't these phrases remind you of something you have heard on the Fourth of July? These are the principles upon which the constitutions have been built, and only when built upon these principles are they in conf[o]rmity with the real underlying convictions out of which American institutions grew.

Does it follow that I individually for example, advocate the adoption of the initiative and referendum everywhere? Of course not. It is a question for each State. It is a question for Maryland, for Virginia, for New Jersey, whether she has control of her affairs in satisfactory fashion and whether, if she has not, she wishes additional means of recovering that control. That is all. Nobody can decide it for Maryland. Nobody can decide it for New Jersey. It is her own domestic problem. If she be fortunate, if her public men have resisted temptation, if they have always drunk from the undefiled waters from which our forefathers drank, then they need not debate these questions.

I may be indulged if I express a personal conviction. I have never been able to bring my own judgment to the point of believing that a prudent means of control would be proper with anything but administrative offices.

I do not believe in the recall of judges, but only because I believe that the recall of judges is treating a symptom instead of treating the malady.

If judges are unsatisfactory they are unsatisfactory because they were chosen by processes which public opinion did not govern. They were selected by somebody in particular instead of by everybody in general. Therefore the way to purify the judiciary is to purify it at its roots, if it needs purification, in the process of selection, because after the process of selecting them you require the training of lawyers to discriminate what the law is, for the layman cannot determine what the law is.

There is many an instance in which the judge must utter an unpopular decision for the very reason that the people have not come to realize what the actual principles of the law are sufficiently to have them changed. There are some principles of the common law which are shocking to the modern sensibilities. To base the damages for the death of a child as nearly as possible upon how much that child might have earned for its parent in its nonage is very shocking to modern sensibilities, but that is the principle of common law.

The judge is not responsible for the opinion. That is the law. You ought not recall him because of the history of the common law. If you do not like the history of the common law, you can change it, and if you don't trust the judge there is a process by which you can get another. So that I accept that evil, not because I do not believe in the idea that the people ought to control their instrumentalities, but because I do not believe that is the way to apply in that field.

If a people is not to control its own life, then I see no point in American institutions. So that we must never forget what we are for. We are for this: That the nation and the Commonwealth should determine its own life. If it determines it wrong, it is no business of coteries of sensitive persons to criticise, and so we have to face this, that, under the pressure of the necessity, if we wish to change the law that is our business. . . .[8]

America was set up to realize the things which I have told you tonight. Sometimes we have been blind and sometimes we have been deaf. But with one common voice let us hail men back to the old road that goes up the long steeps that lead to the heights of political righteousness and the welfare of the people.[9]

Printed in the Baltimore *Sun*, March 8, 1912; the final paragraph from the partial text in the *Baltimore American*, March 8, 1912.

[8] Here follow remarks about the need for tariff reform, expanded foreign trade, and the rebuilding of the merchant marine.

[9] There is a WWhw and WWsh outline of this address dated March 7, 1912, in WP, DLC.

From William Gibbs McAdoo

Dear Governor: [New York] March 8, 1912.

I send you the last four pages of a very interesting letter from Hon. M. G. Cunniff, from Prescott, Arizona[1] (who will be the President of the new Arizona State Senate) and wish you would read what he says about his talk with Mr. Bryan and Governor Marshall. I also enclose three letters from Mr. Gonzales, of the "State," Columbia, S. C., which I wish you would take the time to read, as I think you will find them very interesting, particularly the one of February 1st, which may give you some information about the Watterson-Harvey affair which you do not now possess. This throws new light on that affair, which seems to me to be replete with treachery and insincerity towards you.

What Mr. Gonzales says about Mr. Bryan is exceedingly interesting, and the latest news I get from the South is that there is a great revival of Underwood activity in several of the States, North Carolina and Mississippi particularly. Vardaman's attitude in Mississippi is the only thing which causes me concern there.[2] I get fine reports from Georgia and Virginia. Your friends seem better organized in those two states than anywhere else in the South. The only thing that gives me concern about your prospects is the lack of organization everywhere.

I wish Mr. Bryan could be induced to openly express his preference for you, so that the Bryan organization throughout the country could get actively to work. I am sure it would be a great help.

I will be much obliged if you will return all of these enclosures to me. I have been anxious to see you to tell you about my observations and experiences in the South and West, but you have been away most of the time and I have had no opportunity on the days that you have been at home, but I hope to see you on my return from Bermuda.

I am sending this letter to you at Princeton, hoping that you may find time to read it quietly there.

With kind regards, always,

Sincerely yours,   W G McAdoo

TLS (LPC, W. G. McAdoo Papers, DLC).

[1] Michael Glen Cunniff, progressive Democrat and Wilson supporter. Formerly managing editor of *World's Work*, he was at this time engaged in the mining business in Arizona.

[2] James Kimble Vardaman supported Underwood. For the preconvention situation in Mississippi, see William F. Holmes, *The White Chief: James Kimble Vardaman* (Baton Rouge, La., 1970), pp. 262-66.

A News Report of an Address to the Brooklyn League

[March 10, 1912]

WILSON'S ONE FEAR AMERICA WILL NOT
"HUMP ITSELF"

Jersey Governor Tells Brooklyn League that the Country
Needs to Adjust the Tariff.

Two hundred members of the Brooklyn League pounded their tables in approval last night when Gov. Woodrow Wilson told them that he wasn't "afraid of the American people getting up and humping themselves" in a legislative way, but that he was only afraid they wouldn't.

Gov. Wilson was the chief guest and speaker of the fourteenth annual dinner of the league, which was held at the Masonic Temple, Lafayette and Clermont avenues. Congressman E. B. Vreeland, Vice-Chairman of the National Monetary Commission,[1] shared honors with Dr. Wilson, and in an hour's address urged the adoption of the commission's plan for a national reserve association.[2]

President Charles H. Fuller[3] introduced the two speakers, with an assurance that neither of them would talk politics. Dr. Wilson smiled at this when he had acknowledged the very cordial welcome given him, for the address he had prepared was strongly political in tenor, although not partisan.

"I am sure that what your chairman means," Dr. Wilson suggested, "is that we are not to lead you politically. I suppose he said it because most of you are Republicans and I am a Democrat. A good old fashioned Democratic speech wouldn't hurt you a bit, but I'll be obedient, and instead of talking politics, I'll just suggest it.

"And that, by the way, will be quite in keeping with the present situation. Most of our leaders are following erratic orbits just now, and when any of us set out to follow them we have no notion where we will land. So when I suggest a line of thought to you I'll not concern myself with where it may lead you, I will only hope that it will not land very far from where I'd like to se[e] you land."

The leaguers liked this immensely, and let Dr. Wilson know it. Seventy-five women who had come into the balconies to hear the speeches joined in the applause. Then Dr. Wilson set out upon his prepared address, in the course of which he said: . . .[4]

Printed in the New York *World*, March 10, 1912; two editorial headings omitted.
  1 Edward Butterfield Vreeland, Republican congressman from New York, 1899-1913.

² About this, the so-called Aldrich Plan, see n.3 to the interview printed at Aug. 26, 1911, Vol. 23.

³ Charles Humphrey Fuller, lawyer of New York, Democratic leader of Brooklyn, brother-in-law of William C. Redfield.

⁴ Here follow portions of the address to the General Assembly of Virginia and the City Council of Richmond printed at Feb. 1, 1912. The *Brooklyn Daily Eagle*, March 10, 1912, reprinted the Richmond address almost in full as the text of Wilson's address to the Brooklyn League.

To Mary Allen Hulbert Peck

Dearest Friend,   Hotel Astor New York 10 March, 1912

It's a long time between treats,—I have had no letter from you for many, many days! I hope that it means that you are happily busy about something, and not that you are ill. I am sure there is nothing to make you ill, except worry,—and why should you worry? Everything is going to come out right with you not only (if you will consent not to suffer from the things that never happen) but, in the mean time, as I can prove by your own letters, whenever you give me a chance to see what you are doing for others, you have grounds for deep content. You brighten and cheer and guide everybody you come into contact with. Your own splendid spirit infects them, with the fine infection of courage and initiative and quick sympathy with others, and life brightens about them with the light that has come from you. I do not have to go to your letters to prove it: *I have met you myself,*—and in Bermuda, where you seem to interpret the very spirit and charm of the islands themselves—their brilliancy and beauty and stimulating power, as if of Nature herself! *I* am a witness to what happens, and to what you add to the meaning of life when you have turned with quick comprehending sympathy to the stranger. I have *seen* others come within your circle of radiation, and have heard them again and again render you homage for what you have done for them. It is a great, a very noble power, my dear lady, and its effects should make you very happy,—even in those hours of reaction when, having spent yourself and become utterly fagged because you have spent so much, you—write to your friends! But do not spend yourself utterly, *please!*

I was very much shocked to learn of the death of the Governor General.¹ It must have upset the little colony completely.

The chief event of the week with us has been the return of our darling baby, Nell, from Mexico. We were desperately anxious until she was this side the border, as you know—much more anxious than she was, for she is a sport if there ever was one and came away with genuine reluctance. For she found the "revolution" a most diverting, opera bouffe affair and brings back some delicious stories about the motley insurrectos. She came leisurely home, the wretch! by way of relatives in Colorado and friends in Indiana, so that we were blessed with her only last Friday. She is well and had a deeply delightful time in a strange and very beautiful country amidst strange 'doings.' How happy it made me to see her, my blessed little chum! She's the life of the house. And so many male creatures are trying to steal her![2]

Nothing new is happening in politics, except Mr. Roosevelt, who is always new, being bound by nothing in the heavens above or in the earth below. He is now ra[m]pant and very diligently employed in splitting the party wide open—so that we may get in!

All join me in affectionate messages. I wish they might make you well! Love to Allen and Mrs. Allen.

Your devoted friend   Woodrow Wilson

ALS (WP, DLC).
[1] Lieutenant General Frederick Walter Kitchener died on March 6, 1912.
[2] The successful suitor was Benjamin King of Weyerhaeuser, Wisc., who was in charge of a lumber camp near Madera, Chihuahua. He and Eleanor became engaged in early 1913.

To William Jay Gaynor

My Dear Mayor Gaynor: Trenton, March 11, 1912.

I am deeply sensible of your kindness in writing me your letter of March 6.

Misrepresentation is the penalty which men in public life must expect in the course of their effort to render service. The unfortunate fact is that there are probably hundreds of men in America of first rate intellectual force, of genuine public spirit and broad patriotism, who would be of immeasurable value to public service, but who are deterred from entering it because they shrink from this particular penalty. They prefer to pursue private careers, rather than expose themselves and their families to unfounded criticism and attack, and the country is thereby impoverished. Such attacks, moreover, create personal feeling and party factions, which render the task of government infinitely difficult for any one who undertakes it. It is the more necessary, however, as I look at it, that these things should be borne with fortitude, if not indifference, in order that our duty may be rendered without regard to our personal feeling.

Your defense of the historical accuracy of the statement attributed to me was very generous and I trust that I may have the pleasure of seeing you soon to thank you in person.

I have often sincerely sympathized with you in the complex and burdensome duties of your high office. The country sometimes does not adequately appreciate the grave problems of city government that are being solved in a great city such as yours. May I not congratulate you on the character of the administration you have succeeded in giving the greatest metropolitan city of the country?

Cordially and sincerely yours,   Woodrow Wilson.

Printed in the New York *World*, March 13, 1912.

From Nicholas L. Piotrowski[1]

Dear Sir: Chicago March 11th, 1912.

My attention has been called to the following excerpt from the text in your History of the American People:

"Now there came multitudes of men of the lowest class from the south of Italy and men of the meaner sort out of Hungary and Poland, men out of the ranks, where there was neither skill nor energy, nor any initiative of quick intelligence, and they came in numbers, which increased from year to year, as if the countries of the south of Europe were disburdening themselves of the more sordid and hapless elements of their population

["]The Chinese were more to be desired as workingmen, if not as citizens, than most of the coarse crew that came crowding in every year at the Eastern ports."

I have followed your career for a number of years, and have regarded you as a man of the highest attainments and of the broadest views. I, therefore, cannot believe that you intended to convey the meaning that the Poles are less desirable than the Chinese. However, your language is susceptible of that construction.

As writers do not create history, but simply record it, the merit of their work consists mainly in the fidelity of their statements, and the judgment with which they are selected, grouped and recorded, and it may be that you were misadvised when the above was written.

Permit me, therefore, on behalf of the 3,000,000 Polish people resident in the United States, to call your attention to facts which may possibly have escaped your notice.

The Polish immigration to this country is of comparatively recent date. Prior to 1870 but few were here. Since then large numbers have settled in every State in the Union and they have established large and prosperous settlements both in cities and in the Country.

Chicago, with over 300,000 Poles, has thirty Polish churches and as many schools where the same studies are taught as in the public schools. A number of hospitals, orphan asylums, and other charitable institutions, sufficient to properly take care of the needs of our people, are supported and maintained by our own voluntary contributions. The same general conditions prevail in all the Cities where Polish residents are found, and the Polish farmers are as thrifty and as honest as any,—they own their land, pay taxes, support their families, and are known as law abiding and respected citizens.

The Pole on his arrival here, hampered by his inability to speak the English language, and his unfamiliarity with our methods and manner of life, is willing to work in the lowly, but none the less useful and essential fields of labor, which the average American is loath, or will refuse to do. He saves his money, and when sufficient has been accumulated, he sends for his wife and children and supports them when they arrive. There are not many cases of wife abandonment and divorces among the Poles are very rare. A Pole is never a tramp or vagabond.

This class of men is not only useful and desirable, but is essential for the development of the resources of our Country.

In honesty, integrity, thriftiness and respect for the laws, the Poles in this Country rank as high as any other nationality, and the percentage of criminals among them is less.

It is true that among the 3,000,000 Poles in this country, there will be found undesirables; but the same is true of all nationalities; Americans of English descent not excepted.

Now a great many of our people have taken exception to this excerpt from your history, and it might be fitting if you so desire, and deem it expedient, to explain or amplify it so that none of our people may have any misconception of the meaning you intended to convey.

Very respectfully,   N L Piotrowski

TLS (Governors' Files, Nj).
1 City Attorney of Chicago, 1911-15.

To Nicholas L. Piotrowski

Personal.

My dear Mr. Piotrowski: Trenton, N. J. March 13, 1912.

I remember with pleasure meeting you when I was in Chicago and esteem it a privilege to reply to your frank and interesting letter of March eleventh.

My history was written on so condensed a scale that I am

only too well aware that passages such as you quote are open to misconstruction, though I think their meaning is plain when they are fairly scrutinized.

No one who knows anything of the history of Europe can fail to be familiar with the distinguished history of the Polish people, and any writer that spoke without discrimination of members of that nation as constituting undesirable elements in population, would not only be doing a gross injustice, but exhibiting a great ignorance. I did not know all of the facts you so interestingly set forth in your letter, but I did know in a general way of the honorable and useful careers of the Polish citizens of America, and the self-respect and steady achievement of the Polish communities which have been established in various parts of the country. In the passage quoted from my history, I was speaking of a particular time when it had become the practice of certain employers on this side of the water to import large numbers of unskilled laborers, under contract, for the purpose of displacing American labor for which they would have been obliged to pay more. They were drawing in many cases upon a class of people who would not have come of their own motion and who were not entirely representative of the finer elements of the countries from which they came. It was, of course, never in my mind to compare the normal immigrant from Europe with the Chinese laborer. Indeed, I had no discrimination in mind, which involved anything more than to call attention to the fact that whatever might be the merits of the question as to the admission of Chinese into this country from the point of view of general public policy, the labor of the Chinese had been intelligent and extremely useful in many fields which they had been permitted to enter.

I know that just and thoughtful men like yourself will pay no attention to the miscellaneous misinterpretations which have been put upon the passage referred to, and that you will have already interpreted my meaning as I have here endeavored to interpret it. Your letter has very graciously afforded me an opportunity of making this explanation.

Cordially and sincerely yours,   Woodrow Wilson

TCL (RSB Coll., DLC), with minor corrections from the text printed in an undated clipping from the *Milwaukee Journal* in WP, DLC.

Ellen Axson Wilson to Richard Heath Dabney

My dear Mr. Dabney,   Princeton, New Jersey March 13, 1912.

For a reason which I havn't time to explain just now a copy of my letter to you about the pension is wanted, and I of course did not keep a copy. Would you be so very good as to have it copied for me? I am sorry to trouble you!

I hope you have found an opportunity to print the true facts about the pension as I stated them. They want to use it here, but I think for some reasons it would be better for the true version to be started in Va.—or anywhere a little removed from Woodrow himself.

Please excuse great haste,
                    Yours very cordially,   Ellen A. Wilson.

ALS (Wilson-Dabney Corr., ViU).

Two News Reports

[March 13, 1912]

FITZHERBERT SCANDAL CALLS OUT HOT WORDS
WILSON MAY TAKE A HAND

TRENTON, March 13.—The case of Senator Fitzherbert came up in the Senate this morning.[1]

Senator Fielder bitterly attacked as a villifier and a liar the author of an article in the New York Sun containing innuendoes against Senator Fielder and other Democratic Senators.

During the recess of the Senate, Senator Fielder and Governor Wilson had a conference on the Fitzherbert case at 1 o'clock. The Governor told the Senator he would take no action without conferring with the other Democratic members.

Governor Wilson later arranged for a conference between himself and the Democratic Senators in his office, at 2 o'clock, for the discussion of the case.

When the Republicans learned that the Democratic conference with the Governor was to take place, they were in doubt as to their own course of action. They quickly came to the conclusion, however, that the conference was an indication that the Governor was planning to urge the Democrats to vote for expulsion.

In arriving at this conclusion they figured that Governor Wilson would have no reason for a conference if he was satisfied that the action of the Democratic Senators was right.

At 2:10 o'clock the nine Democratic Senators filed into the

Governor's inner office and the conference began behind closed doors.

Meanwhile, the Senate, which was scheduled to begin its afternoon session at 2 o'clock, took a recess of half an hour.

At 3:08 the conference ended. At its conclusion the Governor said he would issue a statement. He would give no information as to what it would contain.

All the information that could be gained concerning the conference was that the Democrats would proceed in the Fitzherbert case just as if they had not seen the Governor.

Printed in the *Newark Evening News*, March 13, 1912; some editorial heading omitted.

1 Richard Fitzherbert, Democrat of Morris County, was implicated in a case of bribery involving the Commercial Acetylene Co. in a hearing before the Judiciary Committee of the New Jersey Senate on February 20, 1912. After a brief investigation, that committee, on February 26, recommended that Fitzherbert be tried by the full Senate with a view to his expulsion. The trial took place on March 5 and 6, 1912. The testimony in the case was not conclusive, and Fitzherbert's own testimony was muddled. Senators from both parties later agreed that, at best, Fitzherbert's conduct had been foolish and indiscreet. On March 7, by a strict party division of eleven Republicans to nine Democrats, the Senate declared the Morris man guilty of "an offense inconsistent with the trust and duty of a Senator." As the news report printed at March 14 reveals, the Senate on March 13 failed by another party vote of eleven to seven to expel Fitzherbert, a two-thirds vote being necessary. For a running account, see the *Newark Evening News*, Feb. 20-March 14, 1912, *passim*. A transcript of Fitzherbert's trial before the Senate is printed in *Journal of the Sixty-Eighth Senate of the State of New Jersey* (Trenton, N. J., 1912), pp. 1105-1262.

❖

[March 14, 1912]

REFUSE TO VOTE FOR EXPULSION

But Democrats May Ask Fitzherbert to Resign.
Governor Wilson Holds a Conference with Senators
that May Bring About Change.

TRENTON, March 14.—The Democratic members of the Senate are making plans to get together quickly and ask Senator Richard Fitzherbert to resign in case he does not voluntarily resign before that time. This is in spite of the fact that the Democrats voted yesterday against his expulsion.

This afternoon the Democratic Senators spent much time peering over copies of a document which, it is understood, is a letter from the Democrats to Fitzherbert, requesting him to resign.

It has been learned that a large part of the time at the conference in Governor Wilson's office yesterday was taken up with a discussion of the fitness of Senator Fitzherbert to retain his seat.

The result of the discussion was a practically unanimous expression of opinion that the Morris Senator had done things which had brought his usefulness as a Senator to an end.

The Democrats are thoroughly convinced that they were justified in refusing to expel the Senator. They believe that he was not wilfully guilty of wrongdoing, but they are of the opinion that he ought to quit his seat, and that if he does not resign voluntarily his Democratic colleagues should tell him that he ought to quit.

The fact that this subject was discussed at the conference with the Governor has been closely guarded, and only the most meager details have reached the public. Rumor has it that Governor Wilson urged that the strictest secrecy be maintained until the Democrats were ready to act.

By requesting the Senator's resignation the Democrats expect to end with one sweep the charge that they have been playing party politics in refusing to expel Fitzherbert. By asking for his resignation they will demonstrate that they are not so anxious for a seat in the Senate that they will tolerate improper conduct.

That there was to be further Democratic action in the case was forecasted by Governor Wilson in the statement issued by him yesterday, following his conference with the Democratic Senators. All inquiries as to what this action was to be brought no response from the Governor. But he made it plain that he was to act, not as Governor, but as leader of the Democratic party, to help the Democratic Senators solve a difficult problem.

This morning several Democratic Senators admitted individually that they believed Fitzherbert's usefulness was ended and that he should be asked to resign.

The Republicans, who were unaware of the plans of the Democrats, were preening themselves this morning, because they believe the Democrats had got themselves into a deep political hole by supporting Fitzherbert. The Republicans said that the incident was closed so far as the acetylene bills were concerned, but that it was not improbable that some notice might be taken of certain charges that Fitzherbert was involved in some unsavory way with another bill.

The absentees at the roll call on expulsion yesterday were Senators Silzer and [John Wesley] Slocum. Both explained today that they were necessarily absent and that had they been present they would have voted against expulsion.

It was at the close of a long and at times overheated debate that the Senate late yesterday afternoon divided on strictly party lines on the Fitzherbert case. The question was on the resolution by Senator [Carlton Brownell] Pierce that Senator Fitzherbert, having been found guilty of "an offense inconsistent with the trust and duty of a Senator," be expelled.

All of the eleven Republicans voted for the resolution. Two of the Democrats, Senators Silzer and Slocum, were absent, but the other seven cast their votes against expulsion. As a two-thirds vote is required to vacate a Senatorial seat, the resolution failed.

The vote on the question of expulsion in the Senate was a far less impressive ceremony than the vote on his guilt or innocence last week.

After the vote was announced the Senate ordered the printing of 5,000 copies of the testimony in the case.

As told in the News yesterday, Governor Wilson had a conference with the Democratic Senators in the afternoon. After it closed the Governor issued the following statement:

"I conferred with the Democratic Senators in order to inform myself as fully as possible of every aspect of the charges against Senator Fitzherbert, of Morris County, and of the action of my party colleagues on those charges. I am convinced that when the vote was taken on the question of 'Guilty' or 'Not Guilty,' the Democratic Senators voted with a solemn consciousness of their obligation as judges on a question of personal guilt, and without regard to any party purpose, such as saving a seat which might in certain circumstances be vacated. I wished for my own information and guidance to be fully apprised of what the basis of their judgment had been and of all circumstances that might throw light on the case itself.

"In view of the fact that I was not myself a member of the court, I have at present no personal judgment to express in the case. I did not call the Senators together for the purpose of suggesting any action to them, but only for the purpose of determining whether there was anything that I myself ought to do. This I cannot finally determine until the case is concluded. I should no more feel at liberty to attempt to influence the judgment of the Senate as a tribunal than I should deem myself at liberty to influence the judgment of one of the regular courts."[1]

Printed in the *Newark Evening News*, March 14, 1912; some editorial headings omitted.

[1] Democratic leaders continued to press Fitzherbert to resign, as the best solution of an embarrassing situation. Indeed, the *Newark Evening News*, March 26, 1912, quoted Wilson himself as hinting strongly that, during a brief meeting on March 25, he had urged the Senator to resign. Wilson stated that Fitzherbert had promised to place a "communication" in his hands later that day and added: "But if I do not get it, I shall be forced to say something." However, neither Wilson nor anyone else was able to persuade the stubborn Fitzherbert to withdraw. He served out his term, which ended in 1914.

From Thomas Bell Love

Dear Governor Wilson: [Dallas, Tex.] March 14, 1912.

As I am leaving the city on a business matter which may take me as far as New York, I am writing to say that the prospect for an overwhelming victory for our forces in Texas have never been so good as they are at this time. The reports from all sections are the very best possible, and I think that a solid Wilson delegation from Texas is practically assured.

I shall endeavor to make certain to see you if I get to New York on this trip.

With kind regards, I am

Very truly yours,   Thomas B. Love.

TCL (T. B. Love Papers, Dallas Hist. Soc.).

To Edward Mandell House

My dear Mr. House,   Princeton, New Jersey 15 March, 1912

Your kind note of the 6th brought me great cheer when I most needed it. I have been a good deal discouraged by the news from Kansas and from Michigan, where we *ought* to have won,[1] and thought of what you are doing puts me in heart again,— as does also the knowledge that we are soon to have your counsel here.

Signs multiply that there is a combination of Clark, Underwood, and Harmon (with a division of territory quite after the manner of the industrial combinations) and the evidence that the combination is being financed from Wall St. falls short only of legal proof. It saddens me to see things done and alliances formed which may render the dear old party utterly unserviceable (as a free unit) to the country.

With warmest regard,

Faithfully Yours   Woodrow Wilson

ALS (E. M. House Papers, CtY).

[1] In Kansas, although supporters of Wilson in the congressional district conventions had elected fourteen out of twenty delegates to the Democratic national convention, the Clark men succeeded in electing a majority of the delegates to the state convention. It met in Hutchinson on March 14 and instructed the Kansas delegation to vote as a unit first for Clark. However, the convention also decreed that, whenever two thirds of the delegates should deem it expedient, the delegation should vote as a unit for Wilson. The bad news from Michigan was the outcome of a meeting of the Democratic State Committee in Detroit on March 2. The Wilson leaders had sought to have the state convention postponed until after the legislature enacted a presidential primary law. The supporters of Clark and Judson Harmon in the committee combined to name a definite place and time for the state convention—Bay City on May 15. When the convention met, the combine succeeded in defeating Wilson instructions, and the Wil-

son men elected only twelve of the thirty delegates to the national convention. *New York Times*, March 3 and 15, 1912; Link, *Road to the White House*, pp. 407, 418.

To William Jennings Bryan

My dear Mr. Bryan   Princeton, New Jersey 15 March, 1912

I greatly appreciate your note of the 11th.[1] I altogether subscribe to your view, that the publication of pre-nomination subscriptions should be made obligatory by law,—and the subject is just now being pressed home to me in a way that gets beneath the skin. Signs multiply that the nomination will again be determined by money,—the indications of a combination are palpable; and there is danger that things are being done which may render the use of the party, *as a unit*, in the free service of the people impossible. Alliances are being made that I would have thought impossible and which may rise up to discredit us.

But here is a thought I wish to suggest to you (how often I would like to take counsel with you on such matters in these critical times!). We are engaged in a war for emancipation,—emancipation of our institutions and our life,—from the control of the concentrated and organized power of money. There are men—many men—who have come by their money perfectly cleanly and honestly—who are as keen to be emancipated as we are and who would gladly subscribe the money absolutely needed to organize opinion and the scattered force of the people. They dare not subscribe, if their names are to be published. They would be squeezed and put out of business. I know such men. They are victims of the system,—are caught in its toils,—and cannot get free without our assistance and guidance, for which they are eager. Shall we make any temporary abatement of our programme for their sake?

My own managers have not been able to obtain the sums needed for an adequate campaign—and I have refused to promise rewards. They know that *we* must hold ourselves ready to open everything.   Faithfully Yours,   Woodrow Wilson

ALS (W. J. Bryan Papers, DLC).
[1] It is missing.

To Mary Allen Hulbert Peck

Princeton, New Jersey
Dearest Friend,   17 March, 1910 [1912].

It was as I feared,—you *were* ill! I knew it instinctively. You do not know even the rudiments of how to take care of yourself,—and yet who with a heart can blame and scold you? The *way* in which you wear yourself out and make yourself ill is mere proof and demonstration of why your friends love you so deeply. You *spend* yourself with reckless generosity and presently are, of course, absolutely spent. How can one of those who have been the chief beneficiaries of your largess chide you? And yet it is a serious business! You ought to think of it in this way: Will it really serve your friends to snuff yourself out utterly? Will it not be the deepest disservice you can do them to fail them altogether? It is indispensable to their happiness that you should *not*[.] You should live and keep well and give them the joy of knowing that you are all right. Of course it is easy to understand why, though you are so superb a creature, sound and sweet to the core, you are apparently so weak and prone to collapse now. It is the reaction from an entire *life*-time of moral effort,—years upon years of struggle to keep up to some standard of duty and fidelity and efficiency despite the desperate load at your heart,—despite the fact that all hope had gone except the hope of keeping your own self-respect and winning out without flinching or repining. All the tides of life are now feeling the ebb, the reaction. So be careful, dear friend; *please* be careful! Do not put any unnecessary strain on a heart that has already carried, for years together, more than any heart can bear. Indulge yourself in every way you can think of,—and write me *soon* that you are *well*! For I have been, and am, very anxious indeed, and cannot hear the reassuring words too soon for my thought's ease.

Every day is, with me, a sort of melée,—trying to get through with more things than one day can contain; but I am well and my spirits are as equable as such circumstances permit. Last night I spent on the road! Yesterday was observed as St. Patrick's Day and I spoke at two dinners of the Friendly Sons of St. Patrick,—one at Elizabeth, the other at Montclair (I grow more talkative every day!). I left Montclair at 12.45 A.M., to come home by motor, and reached Princeton at 4.50, just as the dawn was showing itself,—having taken the wrong road twice and wandered through the sleeping country for four hours, to make 50 miles!

All join me in affectionate messages—Love to A[llen]. and your mother.   Your devoted friend   Woodrow Wilson

ALS (WP, DLC).

A News Report of an After-Dinner Address in Elizabeth, New Jersey

[March 18, 1912]

WILSON SAYS BIG PROBLEMS FACE AMERICA
Governor Gives Address at Dinner of Friendly Sons of St. Patrick.

Governor Wilson spoke of his Irish ancestry at the eighteenth annual dinner of the Friendly Sons of St. Patrick held at the Y.M.C.L.A. Hall, in Rahway avenue, Saturday night. . . . Before Governor Wilson arose to respond to the toast "America, Our Country," the diners sang Champ Clark's "Houn' Dawg" song.[1] It seemed to fit in the festivities nicely. Everybody joined in singing it, even the Governor. Along with the others present he applauded for encores.

The famous Missouri ballad raised the enthusiasm several points and set the audience in a receptive mood for what the Governor had to say.

"All the Irish that is in me arises to greet you," he declared in opening his address. "My father's parents were born in Ireland; born farther north, perhaps, than most of you would approve of. But there was no one with more Irish in him than my father." The Governor's opening remarks struck the chord of sentiment that pervaded the banquet. . . .

Just one little unpleasantry cropped up to mar the genuine spirit of friendliness and good fellowship. Governor Wilson made reference to it in bringing his address to a close.

"I met a gentleman here to-night who reluctantly arose to shake hands," the Governor said. "Ordinarily I would have passed off the incident and speedily. But it did sadden me because this man was not willing to keep his eyes forward. Are you going to nurse sore places, are you going to harbor grudges because you did not win? You can have political paralysis any time you choose by sitting down and brooding over bygones.

"But if you want to have red blood, if you want to show yourself a man who can take defeat, then you will not look to what has passed, you will keep your eyes forward. You are American in proportion as you show your capacity to get together."

The guest referred to by Governor Wilson was Peter Egenolf, former Democratic State Committeeman.[2] He was seated in an arm chair in the parlor of the hall when General Collins brought Governor Wilson over to introduce the Executive. Mr. Egenolf was reluctant to shake hands. It is said that he did not arise from his chair to greet the Governor.

It is known that Mr. Egenolf was opposed to the nomination of Governor Wilson and that he has never been in sympathy with the Executive nor his policies. This, coupled with the fact that General Collins introduced the Governor, in the estimation of many present accounted for Mr. Egenolf's action. He and General Collins have been at odds for a long time. . . .

"America is surely the most interesting country in the world," said Governor Wilson. "It is vitality in analysis. We have drawn from the strongest and best part of the stock of which we are made. There is an added vitality in keeping touch upon our variety. We are constantly being refreshed by new streams of virile blood.

"Some people have expressed a fear that there is too much immigration. I have the least uneasiness as to the new arrivals all being gripped as we have been gripped. The vast majority who come to our shores come on their own initiative and have some understanding as to what they want and a definite object in view.

"The country should be divested of all prejudices. I do not like to hear the Irish referred to as the Irish-Americans, nor the Germans as the German-Americans, nor the Jews as the Jewish-Americans. We are all Americans when we vote. There is a common Americanism which is gripping the composite race which peoples this Republic. We have not gotten together as yet, but when this nation once gets together it is going to be irresistible.

"America is just now in a very disturbed state of mind. The next four years are going to be years of peculiar significance. In our present state of mind we are all self possessed and I pray God that we may keep so. America is longing for a change. Not many are certain what the change is, but they know that it should come promptly. The next decade is going to determine some of the most important questions in the national life of America. America has got to prove her title deeds in the next ten years."

In speaking of the Irish people Governor Wilson declared that one thing about them that always interested him is that they display their capacity everywhere else better than in Ireland. He declared that they had a gift for affairs, a gift for government and a mastery of national life. "Once set this nation free," he declared, "and it displays the very things those who put it into thraldom thought it did not possess."

Printed in the *Elizabeth*, N.J., *Daily Journal*, March 18, 1912.
 [1] It became popular in 1912 when the Clark supporters adopted it as their campaign song. They usually sang only the last of the six stanzas:

"Every time I come to town
the boys keep kickin' my dawg aroun',
Makes no difference if he is a houn',
They gotta quit kickin' my dawg aroun'."
The song's provenance is obscure, some students claiming that it originated before the Civil War, others that it made its appearance after 1910. For the complete text, the tune to which it was sung, and a summary of what is known of its history, see Vance Randolph (ed.), *Ozark Folksongs* (4 vols., Columbia, Mo., 1946-50), III, 278-79.

2 Egenolf, born in Germany and a Civil War veteran, had for many years been superintendent of the New York City agency of the Prudential Life Insurance Co. He lived in Elizabeth.

A News Report of Remarks to the Friendly Sons of St. Patrick of Montclair, New Jersey

[March 18, 1912]

GOVERNOR POINTS OUT AMERICAN REQUISITES

Governor Wilson was greeted by 150 diners at the first annual banquet of the Friendly Sons of St. Patrick, of Montclair, held Saturday night in the Hotel Montclair, that town. He made an address in the course of which he touched upon the mental equipment essential to being an American. . . .

"American patriotism is enhanced and heightened by events of this sort," Governor Wilson said in his address. "The word 'American' does not express a race—it expresses a body of men pressing forward to the achievements of the human race.

"It's an intellectual venture to be an American. You've got to have a mind that can adjust itself to many kinds of processes to be an American. If you're adjusted to one kind of tunes only, you're not an American."

Printed in the *Newark Evening News*, March 18, 1912.

To William Frank McCombs

My dear McCombs,   [Trenton, N. J.] 18 March, 1912
This will introduce to you Mr. Harvey Thomas, editor of the Atlantic City Review, a generous friend of mine, a true man, and worthy of all consideration.

Faithfully Yours,   Woodrow Wilson

ALS (WC, NjP).

From Thomas Bell Love

My dear Governor: Indianapolis, Indiana, March 19, 1912.

I arrived here this morning on a very pressing, professional engagement, which will keep me in Indianapolis for some days. The situation in Texas is in first class shape and is improving, decidedly, all the time. The State Committee will meet within a few weeks, probably about April first, and we are going to present a strong memorial requesting a presidential preference primary. They may turn this down but if so that will only make it easier for us to carry the precinct and County Conventions, which we can carry anyhow. Under the Law, Conventions will be held in all the voting precincts on the first Saturday in May, at which delegates will be elected to a County Convention in each County to be held on the second Saturday in May, at which delegates will be elected to a State Convention to be held on the fourth Tuesday in May, at which delegates will be elected to the National Convention. We have a good organization, which is in touch with all portions of the State, Judge Sells being in active charge of the headquarters and campaign, and there is no doubt about our success.

The main purpose of this letter, however, is to make a suggestion, which I think of paramount importance. In the last few weeks my professional duties have called me to Oklahoma, Kansas, Missouri, Indiana and Michigan and though for twenty years I have been a student of political affairs and have endeavored to keep in touch with political matters, I have never before seen such evidences of the general and generous use of money to influence political results. I have no doubt, whatever, that the forces behind both Taft and Roosevelt and those behind Harmon, Clark and Underwood are plentifully supplied with campaign funds, of which they are making lavish use. In fact this is scarcely denied by their adherers.

In a clipping from the Indianapolis News, which I am enclosing,[1] I note that Mr. Niblack[2] quotes a letter sent out by the Clark people in which, referring to your candidacy it said: "We democrats will demand of him to know who is furnishing the money for him to conduct his campaign." In view of the situation and of the suggestion above quoted, I am firmly convinced that it would be the part of wisdom for you to, in some appropriate way, publicly and at once express your desire for an authoritative investigation by a Congressional Committee of the subject of contributions to campaign funds of all candidates for the nomination for President now before the people, in both parties, and the use to which such funds have been and are being put and their sources. This might be the most effective if it took the form of a letter to Sen. Martine or to Sen. Culberson or to some other known supporter of yours. Undoubtedly the people are entitled to know how much money has been contributed to further the candidacy of every man whose name has been mentioned in connection with both the Democratic and Republican nomination for the presidency, who contributed and how it is being spent. In view of the fact that the National Conventions are some three months off it is entirely practicable for a Congressional Committee to be raised which can give all these facts to the public before the Conventions meet. I believe such a Resolution could be passed in the Senate. In any event, I am sure that the suggestion of your desire to see the action taken would be helpful and timely.

I will be here at the Claypool Hotel for several days. Will probably go to New York before I return to Texas and in that event will arrange to certainly see you while in that vicinity.

With kind regards, I am

Very truly yours,   Thomas B. Love.

TCL (T. B. Love Papers, Dallas Hist. Soc.).
[1] A news story in the *Indianapolis News*, March 19, 1912, about the vast quantities of Wall Street money allegedly being used in Iowa to defeat Wilson and carry the state for Clark.
[2] William Caldwell Niblack, vice-president of the Chicago Title and Trust Co., and chairman of the Wilson League of Illinois.

From Patrick C. Anderson[1]

Dear Governor Wilson,   New York. 19th March 1912

Please accept a sample of "Scotch" which I send you today by Adam's Express. It is a product of Brechin, where at one time—a good many years ago—your predecessor at Princeton, Dr. McCosh, lived. I hope, when you try it that you can say "well, with all due respect to the worthy Dr., he was not the *only* good that came out of Brechin."

I wish you the very best luck in your campaign and remain

Yours truly   P. C. Anderson

ALS (Governors' Files, Nj).
[1] Liquor dealer of New York.

To Richard Heath Dabney

My dear Heath: Trenton, N. J. March 20, 1912.
  You are quite right about the pension question.[1] Both Mrs.
Wilson and I agree that it is too late now to take the matter up
again. It seems to have quite lost its significance.
  I cannot tell you how constantly my thought and sympathy
go out to you, my dear Heath, but I know that you will know
how to live through even this time of infinite pain and depression and will come out right in the end.
  That you should be working and thinking of me at this time
touches me more than I can say.
                    Affectionately yours,   Woodrow Wilson

TLS (Wilson-Dabney Corr., ViU).
  [1] Dabney's letter, to which this was a reply, is missing.

Walter Measday to Thomas Bell Love

My dear Mr. Love: Trenton, N. J. March 20, 1912.
  Your letters of the fourteenth and eighteenth instant to Governor Wilson have been received. The Governor directs me to
say that he considers the matter you mention of the greatest
importance, and will take it up as soon as possible. This, however, probably will not be until the early part of next week because Mr. McCombs is in the South at the present time and on
Friday morning the Governor leaves for Wisconsin where he is
to speak at Appleton and Milwaukee on Saturday.
  Will you kindly keep in touch with us, and let us know when
you are coming this way?
                    Cordially yours,   Walter Measday
                        Asst. Secretary to the Governor.

TLS (photostat in the T. B. Love Papers, Dallas Hist. Soc.).

To Frank L. Mayes[1]

My dear Mr. Mayes: Trenton, N. J., March 21, 1912.
  Mr. Vick has handed me your letter of March eighteenth, and
I thank you for writing it.
  It is extraordinary how persistent long lived lies are. I did, of
course, vote the Democratic ticket in 1908. There has been so
much question of the matter that I have had the records here
looked up and one of our local papers will, presently, publish

the whole thing,[2] though I must admit that it is a little mortifying to me to have my word backed up by legal proof.

It was an act of real courtesy on your part to write me, and I thank you sincerely.

Cordially yours,   Woodrow Wilson

Printed in the *Pensacola*, Fla., *Journal*, March 26, 1912.
  [1] Editor of the *Pensacola*, Fla., *Journal*, Wilson's leading editorial supporter in Florida.
  [2] No local newspaper published this story.

To Wade Edward Eller[1]

My dear Mr. Eller: Trenton, N. J. March 21, 1912.

Permit me to thank you for your letter of March twentieth,[2] notifying me of the result of your recent mock convention.[3] It is very delightful to find I have so many supporters among the young men of North Carolina, a State whose endorsement I should most highly value.

Cordially yours,   Woodrow Wilson

TLS (NcD).
  [1] A senior at Trinity College (now Duke University).
  [2] It is missing.
  [3] Wilson had been nominated for the presidency at a mock national Democratic convention held by the students of Trinity College on March 12.

A News Item About Wilson's Arrival in Fond Du Lac, Wisconsin

[March 23, 1912]

WILSON IN DENIAL

Smiles at Misrepresentation of Views on Union Labor.

FOND DU LAC, Wis., March 23.—A score of candidates gathered to greet Gov. Wilson in an informal reception at the Palmer house after his arrival here at noon. The governor was met at the station by a committee headed by D. F. Blewett, Mayor F. C. Wolf,[1] and other prominent Democratic leaders. . . .

While the reception was in progress, the governor made some inquiry about Gen. E. S. Bragg, leader of the Iron Brigade.[2] The governor insisted upon meeting Mr. Bragg, and he was taken in an automobile to the Bragg residence where he remained a short time.

The Wilson meeting began at 2:30 P.M., in the armory. The governor and his party made some inquiries into the nature of the campaign being waged against him in Wisconsin. The governor smiled when he was told that he was being pictured as an enemy of union labor and the critic of immigrants.

"That opinion is based on misrepresentation," was his comment. "They are welcome to any victory they can get in that way. I don't care to make use of such weapons."

Printed in the Milwaukee *Journal*, March 23, 1912.
  [1] Dennis Francis Blewett, lawyer of Fond du Lac, chairman of the Fond du Lac County Democratic Committee; Frank J. Wolff, Mayor of Fond du Lac, 1911-16.
  [2] Edward Stuyvesant Bragg (1827-1912), prominent Wisconsin Democrat and Union officer, whose "Iron Brigade" fought in many of the major battles of the Civil War and led the assault on Petersburg on June 8, 1864. A congressman, 1877-83, 1885-87, a Cleveland Democrat, and a Gold Democrat in 1896, he supported McKinley in 1900 and Taft in 1908.

A News Report of a Busy Afternoon in Wisconsin

[March 24, 1912]

ALL GREET WILSON
New Jersey Governor Makes Friends at Fond Du Lac.

FOND DU LAC, Wis., March 23.—Gov. Woodrow Wilson spent a busy day in Wisconsin Saturday. He made one speech here, and one at West Bend, in the return trip to Milwaukee. Beside that, he shook hands with several hundred citizens, talked with farmers, mechanics and politicians, and called on Gen. E. S. Bragg, commander of the famous Iron Brigade. His visit was a big success.

The meeting in the armory was declared to be the biggest afternoon political me[e]ting ever held in Fond Du Lac. There were many Republicans in the crowd, mostly of the Progressive stripe.

D. W. Bluett was at the head of the local committee. He introduced P. H. Martin,[1] one of the Wilson delegates at large, who introduced the governor. Mr. Wilson had nearly an hour between the time his speech was ended and when his train left, and he proved a ready campaigner. In the hall he held an informal reception. As a hand shaker, the governor was a success. There is no affectation in his rather dignified greeting and the smile that goes with it, and there is no lack of Democracy. Bluett, who accompanied the governor, knew nearly everybody. Once the keeper of a small shop rapped on the window to attract the party, and came out bare-headed.

Two men in the spacious entrance of a livery stable were summoned to the sidewalk and presented. A farmer driving home in a sleigh who had been watching the party stopped and yelled that he wanted to meet Gov. Wilson, who walked out into the street to where the sleigh stopped.

Gov. Wilson's interest in historical matters prompted the interview with Gen. Bragg. Politics were not mentioned, Gen. Bragg informing the governor that failing eyesight had prevented him from keeping track of political affairs as he would like to do.

Gov. Wilson discussed the tariff in the Fond Du Lac speech.

"If the protective tariff theory was once defensible, it has now been carried to a point far beyond which it is even debatable," he said. "We have long since passed the station. One reason was that we did not see the station. It was passed more than a decade back. We are in the hands of those whom we invited to serve us. It is the result of the development when we were so anxious to get money and capital that we were willing to give anything in return for the building of railroads and industries. So our creatures became our masters—those who should have been the servants are the economic dictators.

"The Democratic party is free to undertake the task of taking the government back to the people. I do not know whether it will, but it is free to go ahead. It is not tied by allegiance to those who are seekers of special favors."

The West end crowd had been gathered into a hall opposite the depot. In spite of short notice, several hundred citizens were present.

Printed in the *Milwaukee Journal*, March 24, 1912.
¹ Patrick Henry Martin, lawyer of Green Bay.

1 Patrick Henry Martin, lawyer of Green Bay.

A News Report of Three Addresses in Milwaukee

[March 24, 1912]

GOV. WILSON ADDRESSES TWO BIG AUDIENCES
New Jersey Candidate Gets Warm Reception
From Milwaukee People.

"We are engaged in the difficult but handsome undertaking of bringing the government back to the people."

These words, repeated in various forms, were the foundation of the speech that Gov. Woodrow Wilson, chief hope of the Democracy for 1912, delivered before an enthusiastic audience in the Pabst theater Saturday night. The speech marked the beginning of the real Wilson movement in Milwaukee. From the moment the New Jersey leader stepped upon the stage, and, hidden from the audience by the wings, he was gretted [greeted] by the guests seated upon the stage. Until he finished he was applauded again and again.

The tall, spare figure of the former college president won his audience. The quiet delivery, with the touch of the scholarly dignity, made an impression that gestures and fervid oratory never would have gained.

Gov. Wilson made it plain to his audience that he was talking business. "This is a business speech," he said. "There is no politics in these questions. We have got to have sense, label it, and call it political sense. But we must first get sense and hard facts."

He was introduced by J. L. O'Connor,[1] former attorney general of Wisconsin, as "that distinguished Democrat, champion of the people's cause, the hope of the people, whether they be Democrats or not—the Hon. Woodrow Wilson of New Jersey."

For nearly five minutes the applause and cheering continued, and then the speaker began.

First he apologized for what he termed his lack of beauty, with a limerick. The audience laughed. The next moment he began a serious discussion of the conditions of today. . . .

Gov. Wilson, addressing an audience of 2,000 in South side armory composed largely of Polish citizens, discussed the immigration and labor questions, and Americanism. In a general way he made reference to the strains of immigration that have contributed to the upbuilding of the country. He gave special recognition to the service of Pulaski and Kosciuski, as Poles who stood for the genius of their country. There was in his speech no note of impatience or anger toward politicians who have warped quotations from his history to suit their necessities in the campaign.

August M. Gawin[2] opened the meeting. His introductory address was twice delivered, once in Polish and once in English.

"When we think of Americans we do not think of a race, we think of a people," Gov. Wilson said. "I was protesting the other day against those who speak of the German, or the Polish, or the Irish or the Jewish-American vote, because when you get through with that vote, whom will you have left as Americans? The original stock came from Great Britain, Scotland and Ireland, and when you speak of them you are speaking of the minority. When you speak of those who came from the other European countries, you are speaking of the majority. Is it not about time to stop the practice of prefixing some race before the names of these Americans? I somehow feel that America is bigger than the continent on which it has been placed.

"The problem, my friends, is what will become of the immigrant after he comes here. We promise them freedom and opportunity. What will their lives be?

"We must keep the promises we have made them. The first Americanism is that we must love one another—forget race and creed. That is why I protest against referring to the Irish, or the German, or the Polish, or the Jewish vote.

"Now, what does America do for her people—not the leaders, not the captains of great enterprise, but the people, who are the heart, the muscle, the mind of the country? If they hope, the country hopes; if they despair, the country despairs.

"The United States consists of its people, not of its politicians. You are justified in judging your public men by their ability to think your thoughts and judge of your interests. You can't afford to have a government that hears one who speaks out and cannot hear the almost inarticulate murmur for justice. The greatest American was Lincoln—great because he knew what the people thought."

The governor also paid his respects to the Standpatters in terms similar to those he used in his Pabst theater speech.

"Don't abuse these Standpatters," he said. "Pass them by, like ghosts or corpses, and go about your business. We are interested in the issues and achievements of today."

Following his speech at the Pabst theater, Gov. Wilson addressed a meeting of the Travelers' Protective Association at the Hotel Blatz. The governor left at 7:30 Sunday morning for Chicago.

Printed in the *Milwaukee Journal*, March 24, 1912; many editorial headings omitted.
  1 James L. O'Connor, Attorney General of Wisconsin, 1891-95, lawyer of Milwaukee.
  2 Manufacturer of stained glass, Democratic leader of Milwaukee.

Three Veto Messages

To the Senate: [Trenton, N. J.] March 25th, 1912.

I take the liberty of returning, without my signature, Senate Bill No. 177, entitled "An act to amend an act entitled 'An act regulating the granting of municipalities of consent to the use of streets, avenues, parks and other public places,' approved March twenty-seventh, one thousand nine hundred and six."

This act deals with one of the most difficult and perplexing subjects now connected with the administration of government. The existing law of the State, limiting to twenty years the period for which franchises may be granted to public service corporations, is unquestionably most unsatisfactory. The period is so short that it is seldom worth the while of investors of money to embark upon expensive enterprises of that kind. In certain localities the term may be extended to forty years, if the proposal be ratified by a vote of the people of the municipality, but this referendum has seldom, if ever, been made use of, and there is everywhere a feeling that the law of the State should be thoughtfully reconsidered, and that at a very early date.[1]

The situation in the southern portion of New Jersey is particularly unsatisfactory. In the northern portion the people are reasonably well provided with means of transportation, but in the southern part of the State settlement and expansion and the conveyance of produce from the farm is seriously hampered and restricted by the lack of trolley lines and other facilities of inter-communication. It is a situation which ought to be relieved at once. There is, in particular, a pressing necessity that favorable terms of investment should be made possible in order that a tunnel may at as early a date as possible be constructed under the Delaware river between Camden and Philadelphia. Such means of communication between the two cities has become imperatively necessary, but is out of the question, in view of the immense cost of the enterprise, so long as only a twenty-year franchise can be granted.

But inasmuch as under the constitution of the State, local relief in matters of this kind cannot be afforded, and every act must be of general application and embody a general and universal policy, it is imperative that the measures adopted should be suited for permanent use, rather than wear the character of temporary accommodation. Everywhere that this question of public service franchises is being liberally dealt with, in the light of general experience, it is being recognized that no fixed period for such franchises can wisely be established. The period must differ according to circumstances, according to the undertaking, according to a great variety of conditions, which it is impossible to foresee in a general statute, or provide for beforehand. Where public service enterprises are going forward with the least embarrassment, and with the greatest energy, it has been found that a system of indeterminate franchises is the only system that can be called a system at all. That system grants franchises to be enjoyed so long as adequate and satisfactory service is rendered, with an option of purchase by the State or the municipality at the end of a stated period of years at a definitely assessed valuation. It is elastic, it is permanent, it is fitted to an infinite variety of local conditions, and yet it safeguards the public against the abuse of long term contracts, which cannot be altered or violated, and which leave the public service corporations free to do much as they please.

The most pressing need of South Jersey could have been met by a statute providing special terms for tunnel franchises. To attempt to remedy the present law by fixing at a guess another maximum period in place of the twenty-year guess is not to move forward at all, but to stumble along according to the same archaic system which now embarrasses us and our public enterprises. Relief must be found, but surely this is not the way to find it. It is neither suited to permanent investment nor to the adequate and constant protection of the public. It is to run a great risk without any adequate compensating benefit.

One of the features of this bill most to be regretted is that it entirely discards the safeguard of the present law which consists in the necessity of a *referendum* to the people in case of all long-term franchises. Much as I regret standing in the way of any pressing necessity, it seems to me to be my duty to utter my strong dissent to legislation of this demonstrably dangerous and unsatisfactory kind.

Respectfully,   Woodrow Wilson, Governor.[2]

Printed in the *Journal of the Senate of N. J.*, 1912, pp. 814-16.
  [1] Senate Bill No. 177 set a limit of fifty years on franchises and repealed the sections of the law of 1906 requiring referenda.
  [2] The legislature overrode this veto.

✧

[Trenton, N. J.]

To the House of Assembly: March 25th, 1912.

I take the liberty of returning, without my signature, Assembly Bill No. 218, entitled "An act to authorize the board of chosen freeholders of any county in this State to acquire, improve and maintain roads lying within the corporate limits of any of the municipalities of said county, except cities; to authorize the straightening, widening, changing of location of and vacation of any such road so acquired, and to authorize the acquiring by gift, grant, or purchase or condemnation of lands necessary therefor."

This is a very dangerous and objectionable piece of legislation. It not only gives unprecedented powers to boards of freeholders in respect of establishing systems of county roads, but it eliminates all of the protective and prudent provisions of the existing road laws which were designed to prevent extravagance and dishonesty in the expenditure of public moneys.

Under this bill a board of freeholders may at any time, without any public notice of their intention to do so, and by a mere majority of a quorum of their number, vote to establish a system of county roads, and thereafter by a similar vote, determine to improve the same and to bind the people of the county to financial obligations to the extent of one-quarter of one per cent. of the ratables of the county each year.

Under the existing law the State Road Commissioner is required not only to approve the road improvement program of the board of freeholders, but every contract for such improvement must be submitted for his approval. This bill abolishes that requirement.

Under the existing law, the contractor bidding for public work of this sort must make a substantial deposit by certified check or otherwise as an evidence of his good faith and responsibility. This bill eliminates that requirement.

Under the existing law a contractor is required to give bond in an amount equal to the amount of his contract. Under this bill it is provided merely that he must furnish such security as is deemed satisfactory by the freeholders.

Under the existing law a contractor is required to allow five per cent. of the contract price to be retained by the county for one year after the completion of his work to guarantee maintenance and repairs. No such guarantee is required under this bill.

Moreover, it so reduces advertisement for bids as almost to eliminate it. Taken altogether, these objections seem to me overwhelming.

Respectfully,   Woodrow Wilson, *Governor*.[1]

Printed in the *Minutes of the N. J. House of Assembly, 1912*, pp. 1287-88.
[1] The legislature overrode this veto.

❖

[Trenton, N. J.]
To the House of Assembly: March 25th, 1912.

I take the liberty of returning, without my signature, Assembly Bill No. 283, entitled "An act to amend an act entitled 'A supplement to an act entitled "An act regulating the employment, tenure and discharge of certain officers and employes of this State and of the various counties and municipalities thereof, and providing for a Civil Service Commission and defining its powers and duties," approved April tenth, one thousand nine hundred and eight,' approved April seventh, one thousand nine hundred and ten."

Where, as in the case of the Commissioner of Labor, additional duties of an extensive and onerous sort have recently been imposed upon a public officer, it seems to me to be clearly justifiable to increase the salary which he is to receive. But there are no such reasons for the increased salary proposed in this bill; and I feel that it is not improper for me to call the attention of the Legislature to the very numerous increases of salary which have been proposed during this session, either in the case of officials of the State itself, or in the case of officials of localities. Extravagance becomes so easy when indulged in item by item that I feel justified in urging my objections to a bill like this very earnestly and very seriously.

Respectfully,   Woodrow Wilson, *Governor*.[1]

Printed in the *Minutes of the N. J. House of Assembly, 1912,* pp. 1288-89.
[1] The legislature overrode this veto.

To George Foster Peabody

My dear Mr. Peabody: Trenton, N. J. March 26, 1912.

I thank you warmly for your two letters and for the enclosures.[1] I shall be hungry to read them when I get a moment's leisure after the distracting rush of the closing hours of our legislative session.

I hope I need not tell you how warmly I appreciate your expression of confidence. You need not fear that your radicalism alarms me in the least degree. It is a mere frankness of thought which does you the utmost honor.

Apparently everywhere in the West the Clark people are making great inroads upon my strength, or rather upon my strength with the people, or upon the possibility of my controlling delegations through the politicians. The campaign they are conducting is of the most unfair and malicious sort, and I cannot help believing that there will be a receding when the true facts are known, but for the time they are gaining delegates and causing my friends great anxiety. I wish with all my heart that Mr. Bryan were at liberty to render some positive assistance in these unusual circumstances.

It is a real disappointment to me that I must turn away from your gracious invitation, but I am sure you will believe that it is only because I am straining my physical powers to the utmost and see no way to turn aside.

Cordially and faithfully yours,   Woodrow Wilson

TLS (G. F. Peabody Papers, DLC).
[1] They are all missing.

To Cleveland Hoadley Dodge

My dear Cleve: Trenton, N. J. March 26, 1912.

You need never hesitate to bother me about anything.[1] It is delightful to get into communication with you if only on business.

I understand how important the matter of the Palisade Commission[2] is, and you may be sure that I will act very slowly and very prudently in the matter, so as not to touch anything essential. It just happened that Mr. DeRonde[3] was out of the question because his most intimate business associations are with a Republican leader who did not leave behind him in Trenton the best reputation, and he has been perhaps connected with certain irregular things in Bergen County itself.

You may be sure that when I can get free, I will look you up at the earliest possible time.

In haste,   Affectionately yours,   Woodrow Wilson

TLS (WC, NjP).
  [1] Dodge's letter is missing.
  [2] Created by New York and New Jersey in 1900 to develop an interstate park along the Hudson River from Fort Lee, N. J., to Piermont, N. Y., boundaries greatly extended in 1910 through private donations and public funds.
  [3] Abram De Ronde, chemical manufacturer and banker of Englewood, member of the Palisades Interstate Park Commission, 1900-1912.

Two Veto Messages

                                                    [Trenton, N. J.]
To the House of Assembly: March 26th, 1912.

I take the liberty of returning, without my signature, Assembly Bill No. 166, entitled "A supplement to an act entitled 'An act providing for the formation, establishment and government of towns,' approved March seventh, one thousand eight hundred and ninety-five, providing for the licensing and regulating of pool and billiard rooms and of persons conducting the same."

This bill seems to me to involve a clearly unreasonable, because excessive, exercise of public power. The licensing and regulation of pool and billiard rooms is no doubt in the interest of public order and morality, but to give the governing authorities of towns the right to regulate prices to be charged by the promoters or keepers of such places for the amusements they offer, seems to me to be entering upon a field of public regulation which is without definable limit, and a questionable invasion of private right.   Respectfully,   Woodrow Wilson, *Governor*.[1]

Printed in the *Minutes of the N. J. House of Assembly, 1912*, p. 1289.
  [1] This veto was overridden by the Assembly but sustained by the Senate.

To the House of Assembly: March 26th, 1912.

I take the liberty of returning, without my signature, Assembly Bill No. 261, entitled "An act to regulate the location by municipalities of this State without their territorial limits, of sewage receptacles or sewage disposal works, or stations or plants for the treatment or rendering or disposal of sewage."[1]

A very careful consideration of this bill convinces me that it is based upon a most unsafe and unscientific principle. The question of sewage affects whole regions of the State. It cannot be dealt with community by community without regard to the topography of the country, the method and closeness of its settlement, or the natural facilities for disposing of sewage. Political divisions are in no sense natural divisions when this most difficult matter is to be handled. To adopt the principle of this bill would be to embarrass engineering undertakings connected with the public health in the most serious way, and in some instances might render them impossible.

Any careful consideration of the great urban areas of the northern part of the State will convince a careful student of this subject that those areas must be studied as wholes and dealt with as wholes, and that it is not safe to put the settlement of neighborhood questions with regard to drainage in the hands of any authorities having a smaller jurisdiction than that of the State itself.

It would seem that the present powers of the State Board of Health are sufficient to safeguard the several political divisions of the State against the deleterious influences resulting from sewage disposal within their limits, and if the Board has not now powers sufficiently comprehensive to accomplish this object, such powers should certainly be conferred upon it, rather than allow questions of drainage to be settled by neighborhood preferences and jealousies, instead of by the scientific rules of sanitary engineering. I think the establishment of the principle involved in this bill would be a most unsafe experiment.

Respectfully, Woodrow Wilson, *Governor.*[2]

Printed in the *Minutes of the N. J. House of Assembly,* 1912, p. 1290.

[1] According to the *Newark Evening News,* March 27, 1912, this bill was specifically intended to prevent the construction of a sewerage disposal plant in Bloomfield and Belleville which would chiefly benefit Montclair, East Orange, and Orange.

[2] This veto was not overridden.

From William Gibbs McAdoo

PERSONAL AND CONFIDENTIAL.

Dear Governor: [New York] March 27, 1912.

Mr. Stovall, of the Savannah Press, President of the Woodrow Wilson Club of Chatham County, Georgia, has been urging me to speak in Savannah some time before the 15th of April. You can, of course, understand how reluctant I am to appear in public at this time, and, for that reason, I cancelled some time ago all of my engagements, and have been obliged to decline his invitation. What Mr. Stovall says about Georgia I am quite sure is true. The Underwood people are going to make a desperate fight there, backed by Hearst, quietly if not openly. It is going to be necessary for you and your friends to put forth every effort.

Will it be possible for you to make a speech in Savannah before the 15th? I think you ought to do this. I do not know what your programme is for the immediate future, but I certainly should, if I were you, include Savannah in my plans. It would never do for you to fail to carry Georgia, and I know it can be carried if the proper effort is made.

Please let me hear from you as soon as possible about your plans, so that I may write Mr. Stovall.

Believe me, with warm regards,

Very sincerely yours,   W G McAdoo

TLS (LPC, W. G. McAdoo Papers, DLC).

A Veto Message

To the Senate: [Trenton, N. J.] March 28th, 1912.

I take the liberty of retur[n]ing herewith, without my signature, Senate Bill No. 8, entitled "An act to amend an act entitled 'A supplement to an act entitled "An act to regulate elections" (Revision of 1898), approved April fourth, one thousand eight hundred and ninety-eight, which supplement was approved April twentieth, one thousand nine hundred and eleven'".

This bill seems to me to open the way to many corrupt practices which the Legislature cannot have had in mind when the bill was passed. The object of the bill, I understand, is to reach certain legitimate cases of neighborly courtesy in the transportation of voters to the polls, but it opens the door to so much more than this that I feel justified in returning it with my very urgent protest. It seems to me to destroy, to a large extent, the efficiency of the Corrupt Practice Act of last year, which the whole State has accepted as a deliverance from some of the most debasing practices in our politics.

It seems to me evident that under the guise of a volunteer arrangement, vehicles in large numbers can be provided in such a way as practically to renew some of the most demoralizing practices of the old régime at elections. It is easy to see in how many ways vehicles ostensibly provided without pay could be paid for subsequent to the time of the election. This bill, therefore, seems to me to be an attempt to remedy a very small inconvenience by creating again a very great danger.

Surely it is the duty of all those who are interested in the purity of elections to safeguard at any cost the admirable legislation of last session, which was accepted by the voters of the State, without regard to party, as an emancipation from what has brought discredit and demoralization upon us, and had created a doubt as to the genuineness of every popular vote. Individual citizens will undoubtedly be willing to put up with any inconveniences rather than to break into the principle which we must maintain.

Under the Corrupt Practice Act of England, which is regarded as one of the most stringent, it is indeed true that vehicles may voluntarily be offered for use on election day without remuneration of any kind, but there every volunteer must go and be registered. A description of the vehicle is taken, along with a description of the driver also, and the whole matter is so restricted and safeguarded that the very inconveniences complained of under our present law must be suffered there for the sake of the principle involved.

Respectfully,   Woodrow Wilson, *Governor.*[1]

Printed in the *Journal of the Senate of N. J., 1912*, pp. 940-941.
[1] This veto was overridden.

Thomas Bell Love to Walter Measday

Dear Mr. Measday: [Dallas, Tex.] March 28, 1912.

I am sure you have all seen the statement recently issued by Hon. George Fred Williams, of Massachusetts, in which he refers to what Gov. Wilson has said in his books about the Poles, Italians, and various other classes of people.[1] I think this should be answered promptly and effectively.

It occurs to me that the most effective way would be to have some one go through the history of the American people and collate full extracts showing the opinion expressed by Gov. Wilson as to each of the classes of people he, Mr. Williams, has him denouncing. It might be advisable to have this take the form of an open letter to Gov. Harmon and Messrs. Clark & Underwood, or to Clark alone, which would be in the nature of a challenge to him to express his views on the same subject, or to say whether or not he dissents from the view expressed by Gov. Wilson.

The more I think about the suggestion I made to you when I first met you on Sunday, relative to platform pledges, etc., the better I think of it. I am confident that if you can get this done and give it quite wide publicity, it will be valuable.

With kind regards, I am

Very truly yours,   Thomas B. Love.

TCL (T. B. Love Papers, Dallas Hist. Soc.).

[1] Williams' statement was in the form of a public letter to Richard Franklin Pettigrew, senator from South Dakota, 1889-1901, at this time a lawyer and businessman of Sioux Falls.

"This week," Williams wrote, "I have been shocked at the reading of the fifth volume of his story [history] of the American people, published in 1902. It is Toryism of the blackest type. It is not a history of the American people, but a history of Woodrow Wilson's admiration for everything which the radical democracy now seeks to change, and a series of sneers and insults to every class of men who have sought to alleviate the injustices of capitalism. The worst is that there is no note of sympathy for any suffering and protesting class, but he seems to search for phrases to show his contempt for them.

"Gov. Wilson has undoubtedly changed materially his old point of view, but his book proves that a revolutionary change of heart is also necessary."

While again avowing that he did not doubt the sincerity of Wilson's change of heart, Williams elaborated his opening charge. It was clear, he wrote, that Wilson had had profound contempt for the Farmers' Alliance, Populists, greenbackers, bi-metallists, trade unionists, Italians, Poles, Hungarians, pensioners, strikers, the armies of the unemployed, etc. "The vital question is, 'Has a year destroyed all these impressions and put mercy, charity, love, and nationality into a hardened heart?' I am eager to believe it, but I rely on faith for justification."

In a parting shot, Williams condemned Wilson for applying for a Carnegie pension: "I cannot understand how a real Democrat could touch such money. It is steeped in the human blood of Carnegie's workers, shot down by his hired Pinkertons, while struggling for a decent wage out of the hundreds of millions which their labor was rolling into the Carnegie coffers." *New York Times*, Feb. 2, 1912.

Walter Measday to Thomas Bell Love

My dear Mr. Love: Trenton, N. J. March 30, 1912.

The George Fred Williams statement about Governor Wilson's History has been answered by the Governor several times. In a recent public letter to Mr. Aylward of Wisconsin, he set forth his position very clearly and when he was in Milwaukee he went down to the Polish district and made a speech which was very well received. The Wilson Headquarters is very active in circulating literature to offset this attack, which is inspired by Hearst. The

Governor is taking up your suggestion about the publicity of campaign funds, and I have no doubt some definite action on it will be taken within the next day or two.

  Cordially yours, Walter Measday

    Asst. Secretary to the Governor.

TLS (photostat in the T. B. Love Papers, Dallas Hist. Soc.).

To Mary Allen Hulbert Peck

Dearest Friend,   Princeton, New Jersey 1 April, 1912

 I fear, I fear you are ill again. I have learned to dread long intervals between your letters as *always* meaning *that*. You are so kind and so thoughtful of my pleasure that I know the letters would come if you were well enough to write them. A long gap between my letters to you means nothing of the kind. It means only that this inexorable business I am caught in has demanded of me every waking hour and every pulse of energy that my will could keep going in me. Sundays are the only days I can *ever* write to my friends, it is now clear, and all of last Sunday I was on the train, hurrying, not to say scurrying, back from Wisconsin, to be "on my job" early Monday. And *what* a day Monday was,—what a *week* it turned out to be! It was the closing week of the legislative session: Monday was the last chance candidates for appointive offices had to persuade me to put their names on the list that was to go in that night for confirmation by the Senate! This has been a petty and barren legislature. It has done nothing worth mentioning except try to amend and mar the wonderful things we accomplished last year. Small men have ignorantly striven to put *me* in a hole by discrediting themselves! It is a merry world—for a cynic to live in. For a normal man it is not a little sad and disheartening. And what shall we say when we find the leader of the petty partisan band a learned and distinguished professor in a great University (Prince of Columbia), with plenty of independent means and plenty of brains, of a kind, but without a single moral principle to his name! I have never despised any other man quite so heartily,—tho. there are others whom I have found worthier of hate and utter reprobation—in *another* university!

 But now both the session and (it would momentarily appear) the winter are over, Heaven be praised! and we can settle to a more normal, if no less strenuous life. Now I must rush out again in search of delegates,—shy birds more difficult to find in genuine species than the snark itself! I keep singularly well, and some of my adventures I enjoy thoroughly. Last night, for example, I spoke at a chamber of commerce dinner in Plain-field[1] and then came the twenty-seven miles back through the midnight in a motor, speeding amidst misty moonlight full of ghosts and mysteries,—everything still and asleep except the creeping chilly vapours. It does not sound very wholesome, does it? but it was good for a weary, jaded mind within the thinking box of a tired governor!

All join me in affectionate messages. You will work through this winter of weary reaction and be better and stronger than ever, to the deep relief and contentment of
Your devoted friend   Woodrow Wilson

ALS (WP, DLC).
[1] There is a report of this speech in the Plainfield, N. J., *Courier-News*, April 1, 1912.

To Homer Stillé Cummings[1]

Trenton N J April 1, 1912.
Would greatly value an opportunity to confer with you   Could you meet me Hotel Knickerbocker N Y Wednesday evening? Am also inviting Reed,[2] Brown[3] and Greene.[4]
Woodrow Wilson

TC telegram (RSB Coll., DLC).
[1] Lawyer and former Mayor of Stamford, Conn., member of the Democratic National Committee since 1900.
[2] Eugene Elliott Reed, Mayor of Manchester, N. H., 1903-11, member of the Democratic National Committee since 1908.
[3] Thomas H. Browne, lawyer of Rutland, Vt., member of the Democratic National Committee since 1908.
[4] George Wellington Greene, lawyer and former Mayor of Woonsocket, R. I., member of the Democratic National Committee since 1900.

To Francis Griffith Newlands

My dear Senator: Trenton, N. J. April 1, 1912.
I should very much value an opportunity to confer with you personally with regard to the National situation. I feel that I very much need your counsel with regard to the whole situation.

Hitherto I have been tied hand and foot by our legislative session, but that is now at an end and by Wednesday of this week I hope to have finished my work on the bills remaining to be acted upon by me. I am writing to ask if it would be possible and convenient for you to confer with me Thursday forenoon next the fourth. I am planning to go to Washington by night train, getting me there by early morning, and, therefore, would find any part of the forenoon convenient. I suggest this on the assumption that that is the part of the day when you are most apt to be free.

I am also asking our friends Senators Hoke Smith and E. B. Smith, Gore, Gardner, Lea, Bryan, Tillman, Williams, Culberson, Chamberlain, Martine, O'Gorman and Overman,[1] in order that we may all get the benefit of common counsel.

I would very much appreciate a reply by telegraph.

With warm regard,

Sincerely yours,   Woodrow Wilson

P.S. I would appreciate it very much if you would suggest what in your judgment is the best place to hold the conference.

W. W.

TLS (F. G. Newlands Papers, CtY).
[1] The previously unidentified senators were Ellison DuRant Smith of South Carolina, Nathan Philemon Bryan of Florida, and Lee Slater Overman of North Carolina.

To Carter Glass

My dear Mr. Glass: Trenton, N. J. April 1, 1912.

I am expecting to be in Washington on Thursday next the fourth of April, and am wondering if I might have the pleasure of seeing you at my rooms at the New Willard Hotel sometime in the afternoon before one-half past three o'clock.

Unfortunately I am bound to take a train at 3:40 for Chicago but although I am sharply limited in time, I do not want to forego the advantage of seeing you while I am in the city, if it is possible for me to do so.

Cordially and sincerely yours,   Woodrow Wilson

TLS (C. Glass Papers, ViU).

From William Jennings Bryan

My dear Gov. Wilson: Lincoln, Neb., April 1, 1912.

Letters are pouring in here reiterating the charge that you have a large campaign fund. The enclosed is a sample.[1] I only call your attention to it to emphasize the importance of publicity.

I wish you would telegraph me for publication your views on the Aldrich currency scheme. Someone wrote me that you had attended a meeting at which Mr. Aldrich spoke and at which you are quoted as discussing the subject in a general way but your remarks were capable of being construed as an endorsement of the bill. I think that it is necessary that you should express yourself on this, because the money trust which you have been denouncing is back of the Aldrich scheme. A straightforward declaration against the Aldrich scheme, or any measure looking to a central bank or any other consolidation of the banking interests, would be a great help.[2]

Very truly yours,   W. J. Bryan

TLS (WP, DLC).
    [1] The enclosure is missing.
    [2] The Editors have been unable to find Wilson's reply, if there was one. However, three quotations from Wilson concerning the money trust and the Aldrich Plan appeared in *The Commoner*, xii (April 19, 1912), 2, 5. The first was Wilson's remarks on the money trust in his speech at Harrisburg, Pa. (see the news reports printed at June 16, 1911, Vol. 23). The second was his statement, in an interview in the *Outlook* (printed at Aug. 26, 1911, *ibid.*), that he had not studied the question of currency reform in detail but was dubious about any plan proposed by Senator Aldrich. The third was a brief comment on the money trust taken from a news release and printed in the *Chicago Record-Herald*, April 7, 1912.

From William Gibbs McAdoo

PERSONAL AND CONFIDENTIAL.

Dear Governor: [New York] April 1, 1912.

I enclose a letter just received from Col. Gray.[1] I presume that you have similar advices from him, but I thought you had better see this. I also enclose copy of my reply. I hope you are going to bring about the conference we discussed yesterday at the earliest practicable moment. No time should be lost.

With warm regards, I am,

Sincerely yours,   W G McAdoo

P.S.: Since writing this I have just received the enclosed cheerful letter from Mr. Spearing,[2] of New Orleans. Please return it to me at once so that I may answer it.

TLS (LPC, W. G. McAdoo Papers, DLC).
    [1] James R. Gray, editor of the *Atlanta Journal*. His letter is missing.
    [2] James Zacharie Spearing, lawyer of New Orleans.

From Henry Dallas Thompson

My dear Governor Wilson: Princeton, N. J. April 1, 1912.

The public inauguration of President Hibben will take place on Saturday, the eleventh of May. On behalf of the University,

I have the honor to convey to you our invitation to be present on that occasion and also to make one of the few addresses of welcome to President Hibben at the luncheon. The Committee on the Inauguration requests that these addresses be not more than eight minutes in length. The favor of an early reply is requested.   Very respectfully yours,

H. D. Thompson,
Secretary,
Inauguration Committee.

TCL (M. T. Pyne Coll., NjP).

From Francis Griffith Newlands

My dear Governor: Washington, D. C. April 1, 1912.

I understand that the Legislature has taken a recess and write to ask whether you cannot come down to Washington towards the end of the week, any time from Thursday to Sunday, and stay a few days with me. I could have your Senatorial friends to dinner, and then it might be well for you to visit the Capitol and meet your friends there. It would give Mrs. Newlands[1] and myself great pleasure if Mrs. Wilson could accompany you. Next Monday I will leave for Nashville and New Orleans, and if this week is not convenient, we might arrange for the second week following.

Very cordially yours,   [Francis G. Newlands]

CCL (F. G. Newlands Papers, CtY).
[1] Edith McAllister Newlands.

From William Henry Murray[1]

Dear Mr. Wilson: Tishomingo, Oklahoma, April 1, 1912.

I am a bit tardy in replying to your telegram sent from Des Moines, Iowa, nevertheless I thank you most sincerely for the same. What I was enabled to do for you was done in the interest of the country. Of course one appreciates recommendation of services well performed, such as your telegram evidences. . . .

Yours sincerely,   Wm. H. Murray

TLS (Governors' Files, Nj).
[1] Rancher, prominent Oklahoma Democrat, and a leader of the Wilson forces in that state.

To Francis Griffith Newlands

My dear Senator: Trenton, N. J. April 2, 1912.

Your gracious letter of the first crossed mine to you yesterday.

I warmly appreciate your generous invitation to be your guest. I am fearing that in the circumstances, since I have written our friends in the Senate requesting a conference with them in the forenoon on Thursday, and to our friends in the House requesting a conference in the early afternoon, that I should only be overwhelming Mrs. Newlands and you by making your house a convenience and meeting place, which, of course, I should not like to do.

Perhaps you would be gracious enough to arrange the morning conference at your house, and let me meet the gentlemen from the House of Representatives in the early afternoon. Apparently, I am obliged to take the 3:40 train for Chicago.

With the warmest appreciation of your thoughtful kindness,
        Cordially and faithfully yours,   Woodrow Wilson

TLS (F. G. Newlands Papers, CtY).

Thirteen Veto Messages

To the Senate: Trenton, April 2d, 1912.

I take the liberty of returning, without my signature, Senate Bill No. 206, entitled "An act to authorize cities and boroughs of this State to fill in or drain any swamp, meadow or low lands within the corporate limits of said city or borough, and providing for the payment of the expense thereof and the assessment of benefits therefor."

This act is a revision and an extension of an act entitled "An act to authorize the corporate authorities of cities and towns to drain meadow and swamp lands lying within their corporate limits," P.L. 1876, page 375; Compiled Statutes, page 3284 and following. The original act applied to cities and towns. The proposed act applies to cities and boroughs. The old act contemplated drainage of swamp or meadow lands lying within the corporate limits. The proposed act applies not only to swamp and meadow lands, but to "low land on which water stands, runs or collects." The proposed act, therefore, would include the diversion of a water course and the filling of its bed. The general provisions of the act relating to the contract, assessment of benefits, payment of benefits, payment of assessments, collection, bond issue, are practically the same as in the old act, with this exception: in the old act there is this clause: "No contract, however, shall be entered into under the provisions of this act if the total net indebtedness of such municipality shall be increased thereby to a sum greater than twelve per centum of the ratables of the previous year." This clause is omitted in the proposed act, and since the act contains no other limitation whatever upon the amount of indebtedness which may be created thereby, if approved, therefore, subsequent to acts limiting bonded indebtedness, it would in all probability operate to allow the creation of a bonded indebtedness to any extent the common council or other governing body of a city or borough might for any reason whatever desire. The interest on such a debt would necessarily, under the act, be raised by taxation. The act contains no provision whatever for the creation of a sinking fund for such bonds.

Respectfully,   Woodrow Wilson, *Governor*.[1]

Printed in the *Journal of the Senate of N. J.*, 1912, 1003-1004.

[1] On April 11, 1912, Senator Robert Edmonds Hand of Cape May County introduced another bill with the same title, presumably meeting Wilson's objections, as a substitute for the vetoed Bill No. 206. The substitute passed the Senate but died in committee in the Assembly.

✧

To the Senate: Trenton, April 2d, 1912.

I take the liberty of returning, without my signature, Senate Bill No. 224, entitled "An act to amend an act entitled 'An act providing for the employment of inmates of penal, correctional or reformatory institutions of this State, and creating a board for the control, regulation and supervision of the labor of such institutions, and for the disposal of the products of the labor of such inmates,' approved June seventh, one thousand nine hundred and eleven."

This bill provides that the present commission shall be elected by the Legislature in joint session. It thus places the responsibility for the administration of the laws with regard to the labor of prisoners where it cannot be traced or made obvious. No better plan could have been devised for making of the present commission a political agency.

It is not necessary to conjecture what would be the result. In several states the commissions charged with the administration of matters of this kind have been habitually elected by the Legislature with the result that the most extraordinary network of political influences were set at work and the election of the Legislature itself sometimes turned upon the activity of the various applicants for a position upon such commissions. I think that the enactment of this measure into law would have very serious, and perhaps scandalous consequences.

Respectfully,   Woodrow Wilson, *Governor*.[1]

Printed in the *Journal of the Senate of N. J.*, *1912*, p. 1005.
[1] The legislature overrode this veto.

✧

To the Senate: Trenton, April 2d, 1912.

I take the liberty of returning, without my signature, Senate Bill No. 229, entitled "A supplement to an act entitled 'A supplement to an act entitled "An act to regulate elections" (Revision of 1898), approved April fourth, one thousand eight hundred and ninety-eight,' approved April twentieth, one thousand nine hundred and eleven."

This bill, perhaps unintentionally, makes it mandatory upon the judge upon whom jurisdiction in such matters is conferred to grant the right of filing the statement of election expenses with the necessary result of relieving the person at fault of all consequences of his dereliction, notwithstanding that his failure to file the statement may have been deliberate and wilful. Surely, such a provision is against public policy.

Respectfully,   Woodrow Wilson, *Governor*.[1]

Printed in the *Journal of the Senate of N. J.*, *1912*, pp. 1005-1006.
[1] The legislature overrode this veto.

✧

To the Senate: Trenton, April 2d, 1912.

I take the liberty of returning, without my signature, Senate Bill No. 276, entitled "An act to amend an act entitled 'A supplement to an act entitled "An act relating to courts having criminal jurisdiction and regulating proceedings in criminal cases (Revision of 1898)," ' which act was approved June fourteenth, eighteen hundred and ninety-eight, and which supplement was approved March sixteenth, nineteen hundred and nine."

This bill is one of the many bills which create an additional office,—in this case in connection with the courts,—and so increases the burden of taxation without any clear or sufficient justification.

Respectfully,   Woodrow Wilson, *Governor*.[1]

Printed in the *Journal of the Senate of N. J.*, *1912*, pp. 1006-1007.
[1] The legislature overrode this veto.

To the Senate: Trenton, April 2d, 1912.

I take the liberty of returning, without my signature, Senate Bill No. 285, entitled "An act to authorize the formation of corporations for the construction of electric traction lines known as trackless trolleys, and to operate the same by motor devices on highways or private ways, to regulate the same, and to provide for the consolidation with or the leasing to or by other corporations."

The object of this bill is most interesting, and drawn in other terms the bill might be a great public service, but it seems to me to be open to three fatal objections. In the first place, it grants certain very valuable franchises absolutely freely, contemplating no payment for them in any case, and permits franchises thus freely granted to run for one hundred years. In the second place, it confers apparently unlimited powers of condemnation of private property upon the corporations thus set up; and in the third place, by providing for a lease of the lines established under it to existing trolley lines or steam lines of railway, it seems to provide for mergers which might put these unlimited franchises within the right of corporations, which might not operate them in the spirit or for the purpose contemplated.

Respectfully,   Woodrow Wilson, *Governor*.[1]

Printed in the *Journal of the Senate of N. J., 1912*, p. 1007.
   [1] Wilson's veto was sustained. The Senate repassed this bill on April 11, but the Assembly failed to act before adjournment.

✧

To the Senate: Trenton, April 2d, 1912.

I take the liberty of returning, without my signature, Senate Bill No. 306, entitled "An act to divide the State of New Jersey into districts for the purpose of electing members of the House of Representatives of the United States, and prescribing the boundaries of said districts."

I have studied with close attention the geographical relations and the composition of the districts proposed in this bill, and feel constrained to send the bill back with my very emphatic dissent. The districts are arbitrary and even whimsical. The bill does not effect a redistricting of the State, but a veritable gerrymander.

I am aware of the extreme difficulty of a task such as was set the authors of this bill. It may be that the result of their labors was unsatisfactory to themselves. The outcome of what appeared to be inevitable compromises and concessions to the various interests and forces always to be found contesting in a matter like this. But, whatever the difficulties, however insuperable they may have seemed, I think I will be sustained by the public opinion of the State in saying that they did not justify the formation of districts so manifestly manufactured, not out of real neighborhoods or units of population, but out of mere spaces forced to conform, whether they were natural or unnatural, to the interests of those concerned. I earnestly hope that some arrangement at once more fair and more reasonable can be hit upon.

Respectfully,   Woodrow Wilson, *Governor*.[1]

Printed in the *Journal of the Senate of N. J.*, *1912*, pp. 1008-1009.
[1] The legislature overrode this veto.

✧

To the House of Assembly: [Trenton, N. J.] April 2d, 1912.

I take the liberty of returning, without my signature, Assembly Bill No. 272, entitled "An act relating to, regulating and providing for the government of cities of the second class."[1]

This is a bill for the government of cities of the second class, which has the distinction of conforming with none of the best considered ideas with regard to the reformation of our city government. Responsibility is divided by this act in such a way as to make it impossible for the voters to alter the personnel of the government or get at the root of any evils that may arise at a less cost than the patience of three years' waiting, and the effort of three distinct elections. It provides that the council, the mayor, the comptroller, the treasurer, and the tax receiver shall all be elected, but for different periods, ranging from two to three years. Moreover, it reduces the opportunity for a referendum upon matters connected with the bonded indebtedness of the city, and so again removes the government just so much further away from the people and the public opinion which control it.

It sets up, in short, one of those hide-and-seek governments in which responsibility is centered nowhere, and in which popular control can hardly be obtained, except by the most elaborate and intricate political action. It is in no sense a step forward in the reorganization of city government.

Respectfully,   Woodrow Wilson, *Governor*.[2]

Printed in the *Minutes of the N. J. House of Assembly*, *1912*, p. 1469.
[1] Cities with a population of not less than 12,000 or more than 150,000 inhabitants.
[2] The legislature overrode this veto.

✧

To the House of Assembly: [Trenton, N. J.] April 2d, 1912.

I take the liberty of returning, without my signature, Assembly

Bill No. 309,[1] entitled "A further supplement to an act entitled 'An act relating to courts having criminal jurisdiction and regulating proceedings in criminal cases (Revision of 1898),' approved June fourteenth, one thousand eight hundred and ninety-eight."

This act would practically place the release of prisoners under the political control of the board of inspectors. It takes away from the judges the very wise and necessary discretion now exercised by them in sentencing convicts. It, moreover, cuts down all sentences to the State Prison made before the act of 1911 by one-half, thus giving to the offenders affected by this provision a peculiar advantage over all others, and an advantage which is clearly unfair.

Respectfully,   Woodrow Wilson, *Governor.*[2]

Printed in the *Minutes of the N. J. House of Assembly, 1912*, p. 1471.

[1] It provided that all prisoners confined in the New Jersey state prison who had been committed there prior to October 21, 1911 (the date on which a previous supplement to the law of 1898 had become operative), who had not previously been convicted of felony in New Jersey or any other state and "who shall, immediately from the date upon which this amendment becomes a law, have served two-thirds of their full respective sentence as prescribed by the trial judge less such commutation time as has been earned during confinement shall be eligible to make application to the board of inspectors [of the state prison] for release on parole; *provided*, that one-half a life sentence of any such prisoner, coming within the terms of this provision, shall be construed as amounting to twenty-five years." The granting of such paroles would be at the discretion of the board of inspectors. *Laws of New Jersey, 1912*, Chap. 384.

[2] The legislature overrode this veto.

❖

To the House of Assembly: [Trenton, N. J.] April 2d, 1912.

I take the liberty of returning, without my signature, Assembly Bill No. 344,[1] entitled "A further supplement to an act entitled 'An act to regulate the sale of spirituous, vinous, malt and brewed liquors, and to repeal an act entitled "An act to regulate the sale of intoxicating and brewed liquors," passed March seventh, one thousand eight hundred and eighty-eight, approved March twentieth, one thousand eight hundred and eighty-nine.' "

There is a very strong argument for the range proposed in this bill, in the fact that the policy of the federal government in respect of interstate commerce permits liquor dealers outside of the State to deliver their wares at pleasure inside of the State, thus unquestionably working a hardship upon their competitors within the State, but it does not seem to me a mistaken and hurtful federal policy justifies an imitation of that policy by the State itself. It seems to me imperative upon the principle of self-government to preserve the integrity and autonomy of the several licensing districts and that that autonomy is seriously impaired by this act.

Respectfully,   Woodrow Wilson, *Governor*.[2]

Printed in the *Minutes of the N. J. House of Assembly, 1912*, pp. 1472-73.
 [1] It permitted liquor dealers to sell liquor in other areas than those in which they had their licenses.
 [2] The Assembly repassed the bill on April 11; however, the Senate sustained the veto on the same date.

❖

To the House of Assembly: [Trenton, N. J.] April 2d, 1912.

I take the liberty of returning, without my signature, Assembly Bill No. 535,[1] entitled "An act to amend an act entitled 'An act to regulate elections (Revision of 1898),' approved April fourth, one thousand eight hundred and ninety-eight."

This bill strikes at the very heart of what was sought by the election legislation of last winter. It virtually prevents independent nominations within the ranks of the two chief political parties.

Respectfully,   Woodrow Wilson, *Governor*.[2]

Printed in the *Minutes of the N. J. House of Assembly, 1912*, p. 1475.
 [1] It prevented independent candidates defeated in the primaries from running as independents at the ensuing general election.
 [2] Wilson's veto was sustained. The Assembly repassed the bill on April 11, but the Senate narrowly sustained the Governor on the same day.

❖

To the House of Assembly: [Trenton, N. J.] April 2d, 1912.

I take the liberty of returning, without my signature, Assembly Bill No. 582, entitled "An act fixing the compensation of directors of boards of chosen freeholders in counties of the first class in this State."

This is one of the large number of bills affecting a specific increase of salary. I think that the general opinion of the State condemns acts of this sort as not only of questionable policy, but as clearly operating against local rights of self-government.

Respectfully,   Woodrow Wilson, *Governor*.[1]

Printed in the *Minutes of the N. J. House of Assembly, 1912*, pp. 1476-77.
 [1] This veto was sustained.

❖

To the House of Assembly: [Trenton, N. J.] April 2d, 1912.

I take the liberty of returning, without my signature, Assembly Bill No. 603, entitled "An act to amend an act entitled 'An act to authorize the construction and establishment of public docks and the shipping facilities connected therewith, and the purchasing and acquiring of riparian lands and rights and other lands and rights in lands necessary therefor or incident thereto, and for the regulation of the same in cities fronting on navigable waters of this State,' approved October twenty-first, nineteen hundred and seven."

If this bill merely authorized a larger expenditure for the purpose of the very extensive and important improvements begun and contemplated in the city of Newark, there could be no valid objection to it, but it does much more than that. It very greatly and vaguely extends the power of acquiring the meadow lands and does not restrict the purpose of the acquisition of the use contemplated in the original act. Neither does it authorize any process of condemnation. It would practically put the city at the mercy of those who now own the meadow lands, because the purchases could only be made at prices they would accept.

Respectfully,   Woodrow Wilson, *Governor*.[1]

Printed in the *Minutes of the N. J. House of Assembly, 1912*, pp. 1478-79.
[1] The legislature overrode this veto.

✧

To the House of Assembly: [Trenton, N. J.] April 2d, 1912.

I take the liberty of returning, without my signature, Assembly Bill No. 678, entitled "An act to defray the incidental expenses of the Legislature of New Jersey, for the session of one thousand nine hundred and twelve."

I feel that I am assuming a very grave responsibility in returning this bill without my approval. I do so only because I have not the data at hand for determining just wherein its evident extravagance lies. Ever since the law of 1900 was passed, which constitutes the latest legal regulation of the official and clerical force of the Legislature—assistants, stenographers, filing clerks, door keepers, gallery keepers, and sub-assistants of every kind—have been added to the pay-roll of the Houses, until the expenditure has mounted from $30,150, the amount required under that law, to the sum of over $67,000.

I am convinced that there can be no justification for this great increase, but I am unable to pick out the items which could be omitted without embarrassing the Legislature in regard to the actual work of the session, and, therefore, I have no choice but to return the bill as a whole, without my approval, in the hope that it may be reconsidered and the unnecessary items cut out by the Houses themselves, upon a basis which will reduce the expenditure to the real exigencies of business.

Respectfully,   Woodrow Wilson, *Governor*.[1]

Printed in the *Minutes of the N. J. House of Assembly, 1912*, pp. 1480-81.
[1] The legislature overrode this veto.

To William Jennings Bryan

Hotel Knickerbocker New York.
My dear Mr. Bryan,   3 April, 1912

About the enforced publicity regarding pre-nomination campaign funds you misunderstood me.[1] I must have expressed myself obscurely. I was not taking a position: I was stating a problem and seeking your advice.

But that is no matter. My conviction is clear as to what ought to be done. The full disclosure of pre-nomination (as of all other) campaign funds ought to be made obligatory by law. No doubt you are right,—that the consideration I urged might be *alleged* as against *any* provision of the kind.

I shall write to Mr. Henry at the earliest opportunity expressing my unqualified approval of the measure I understand, and hope, he will propose.[2]

With warm regard

Faithfully Yours,   Woodrow Wilson

ALS (W. J. Bryan Papers, DLC).
[1] Bryan's letter, to which this was a reply, is missing.
[2] For the text of the Henry bill (the second of its kind), see *Congressional Record*, 62nd Cong., 2nd sess., p. 5049; amendment, 5059-60. The bill was never adopted.

To Henry Dallas Thompson

My dear Professor Thompson: Trenton, N. J. April 3, 1912.

It is with genuine regret that I find myself already pledged to engagements on the eleventh of May, which will make it impossible for me to be present at the public inauguration of President Hibben.[1] I have been particularly unfortunate in being prevented from joining in University functions this season, by public engagements.

Cordially and sincerely yours,   Woodrow Wilson

TCL (M. T. Pyne Coll., NjP).
[1] Wilson spoke to the Reform Club of New York during the evening of May 11; however, as WW to Mary A. H. Peck, May 11, 1912, reveals, he left Princeton early in the day to avoid being in town during Hibben's inauguration.

To Benjamin Palmer Axson[1]

Personal.

My dear Palmer: Trenton, N. J. April 3, 1912.

I am afraid that my trip[2] must be a very hurried one, but I am going to try and bring Ellen with me, and you may be sure that we shall look forward with the deepest pleasure to being your guests.

In haste,   Affectionately yours,   Woodrow Wilson

TLS (received from B. P. Axson).
  [1] Mrs. Wilson's first cousin of Savannah, Ga.
  [2] A campaign tour through Georgia.

From Francis Griffith Newlands

Washington, D. C., April 3, 1912.

Have arranged with Pence to bring you and your companions to my house for breakfast. Will thence go to Willard to meet Senators at ten, as distance to my house would be inconvenient to Senators.   Francis G. Newlands.

CC telegram (F. G. Newlands Papers, CtY).

From Willard Saulsbury

Dear Governor: [Wilmington, Del.] April 3d, 1912.

It has just occurred to me in looking over the Senate list that you omitted from among your friends in the Senate Senator [Henry Lee] Myers of Montana and I thought I had better write you at once, calling your attention to that lest you might overlook him in writing to your friends in the Senate.

From the morning papers, I fancy you have had a sweep in Wisconsin,[1] but I am hoping to hear from Mr. Nieman, of the Milwaukee Journal,[2] so I am not giving away to too much public enthusiasm until I get exact results.

Yours very truly,   Willard Saulsbury

TLS (Saulsbury Letterpress Books, DeU).
  [1] Wilson carried the Wisconsin Democratic presidential primary on April 2 by a state-wide vote of 45,945 to 36,464 for Clark. Wilson men elected twenty of the delegates to the Baltimore convention, Clark men, six.
  [2] Lucius William Nieman, proprietor and editor of the *Milwaukee Journal*, strong Wilson supporter.

From William Gibbs McAdoo

PERSONAL AND CONFIDENTIAL.

Dear Governor: [New York] April 3, 1912.

I enclose two letters[1] about the North Carolina situation which I think will interest you. I have great hopes of getting Col. Osborn[2] with us. You will observe he expects to be here next week.

I congratulate you heartily on the Wisconsin result, although I see, as usual, that the New York papers have not featured it as it deserves. I am writing Mr. Spearing, of New Orleans, again to-day, and urging him to take hold of the state for you. I wish he would do this.

The more I think about Georgia the more I am inclined, if it is agreeable to you, to go down there with you, although I would not, of course, undertake to make speeches under the existing circumstances, even if that should be desired by our friends in that state, but I believe I can help you a good deal by merely talking privately with the people in the different cities that you visit. What do you think about this? Georgia is essential, and we must not lose it.

Always,   Sincerely yours,   W G McAdoo

TLS (LPC, W. G. McAdoo Papers, DLC).
[1] They are missing.
[2] William Henry Osborn of Greensboro, former mayor and president of the Keeley Institute, a hospital for alcoholics.

A News Item

[April 4, 1912]

WILSON SEES NEW ENGLANDERS

His Manager Pleased by Their Report—
Wilson Starts West.

Before starting on his speaking trip through Illinois, Gov. Woodrow Wilson conferred last night at the Hotel Knickerbocker with H. S. Cummings of Connecticut, a member of the Democratic National Committee, and Eugene E. Reed of New Hampshire. Thomas H. Browne of Vermont, another member of the Democratic National Committee, hunted around the Knickerbocker lobby in a vain attempt to find the Governor, who was closeted upstairs with the two other men and his campaign Manager, William F. McCombs.

Mr. McCombs left the conference first. Gov. Wilson followed him in a few minutes. The Governor was in a hurry to catch a train for Washington where he will stop on his way to Illinois. He said he could not wait to tell about his talk with the New Englanders. Mr. McCombs said that he had brought them to meet the Governor, whom they had not seen before.

Printed in the *New York Times*, April 4, 1912.

A. News Report

[*April 4, 1912*]

NATIONAL LEADERS AT CAPITAL GATHER ROUND GOV. WILSON

Senators and Others Confer With Candidate

WASHINGTON, April 4. Governor Woodrow Wilson stopped off in Washington today on his way to Illinois where he is to make several speeches. From the moment of his arrival until his departure late this afternoon he was surrounded by prominent Democratic senators and members of the house of representatives.

He was a breakfast guest at the house of Senator Newlands immediately after his arrival, and following that was in close conference with Democratic leaders representing many states.

Some of those with whom he talked were Senators John Sharp Williams, of Mississippi; Hoke Smith, of Georgia; Culbertson, of Texas; Representatives Burleson, the chairman of the Democratic house caucus, and Henry, the chairman of the rules committee; Senators Myers, of Montana; Chamberlain, of Oregon; Newlands, of Nevada; Martine, of New Jersey; Bryan, of Florida; Smith, of South Carolina, and Representatives Talcott and Kinkred, of New York; Carter, of Oklahoma; Taylor, Hughes, Scully, Tuttle, Kinkead and Hamill, of New Jersey; Difenderfer, Lee, Donohoe, Wilson and McHenry, of Pennsylvania; Johnson, of South Carolina; McGillicuddy, of Maine; Riley, of Connecticut; Smith, of Texas, Jones and Glass, of Virginia; Kitchen, Small, Stodman and Godwin, of North Carolina, Cravens, of Arkansas; Stone, Foster and Evans, of Illinois; Covington, of Maryland; Peters and Murray, of Massachusetts, and Ferguson, of New Mexico.[1]

From every one of these the governor learned of rapidly increasing sentiment in his favor in each of the states represented and of active efforts by the men present and their friends to obtain delegates for him.

One of the immediate results of the conference is that Governor Wilson will visit Georgia soon after his return from Illinois and will make several speeches there. Senator Hoke Smith, the progressive Democratic leader of the state, who has carried the state in the last two elections, will go to Georgia at once to aid the Wilson campaign.

The state is already well organized for Wilson, and the Wilson supporters are confident he will have the delegates. Underwood, of the reactionary Clark-Harmon-Underwood combination, is the candidate in Georgia against Wilson, and is backed by all the reactionaries and the special privilege railroad interests.

Governor Wilson had little to say respecting his campaign, but is apparently confident of success. He was greatly encouraged by the enthusiastic reception accorded him by leading Democrats here and by what they told him.

"Our campaign is one depending on friends and their brains," said Governor Wilson. "We have no money; our campaign has been bankrupt four times, including the present time, and we must depend altogether on our friends." His friends appear to be decidedly reliable.

Printed in the Philadelphia *North American*, April 5, 1912; two editorial headings omitted.

[1] Their full names and states are given herewith for convenience, even though many of them have been identified before: John Sharp Williams of Mississippi, Hoke Smith of Georgia, Charles Allen Culberson of Texas, Albert Sidney Burleson of Texas, Robert Lee Henry of Texas, Henry Lee Myers of Montana, George Earle Chamberlain of Oregon, Francis Griffith Newlands of Nevada, James Edgar Martine of New Jersey, Nathan Philemon Bryan of Florida, Ellison DuRant Smith of South Carolina, Charles Andrew Talcott of New York, John Joseph Kindred of New York, Charles David Carter of Oklahoma, William Hughes of New Jersey, Thomas Joseph Scully of New Jersey, William Edgar Tuttle, Jr., of New Jersey, Eugene Francis Kinkead of New Jersey, James Alphonsus Hamill of New Jersey, Robert Edward Difenderfer of Pennsylvania, Robert Emmett Lee of Pennsylvania, Michael Donohoe of Pennsylvania, William Bauchop Wilson of Pennsylvania, John Geiser McHenry of Pennsylvania, Joseph Travis Johnson of South Carolina, Daniel John McGillicuddy of Maine, Thomas Lawrence Reilly of Connecticut, William Robert Smith of Texas, William Atkinson Jones of Virginia, Carter Glass of Virginia, Claude Kitchin of North Carolina, John Humphrey Small of North Carolina, Charles Manly Stedman of North Carolina, Hannibal Lafayette Godwin of North Carolina, William Ben Cravens of Arkansas, Claudius Ulysses Stone of Illinois, Martin David Foster of Illinois, Lynden Evans of Illinois, James Harry Covington of Maryland, Andrew James Peters of Massachusetts, William Francis Murray of Massachusetts, Harvey Butler Fergusson of New Mexico. There was no Taylor from New Jersey in Congress at this time. The Taylor referred to was Edward Thomas Taylor of Colorado.

To Josephus Daniels

En Route THE PENNSYLVANIA SPECIAL
My dear friend: New York-Chicago April 4, 1912.

There are many penalties for being absolutely absorbed in necessary work and one of the chief of them is that one does not know what is happening to one's friends. I actually did not know until today that you had been ill. It shocked you [me] very much that you had undergone an operation,[1] though I was immensely relieved to hear that it had been entirely successful and that you were now happily recuperating. May I not send you with my warmest regard my congratulations upon your recovery and my sincere assurances of distress that you have suffered at all.

Cordially and faithfully yours,   Woodrow Wilson

HwLS (J. Daniels Papers, DLC).
[1] The operation was a hemorrhoidectomy.

To Harvey Thomas

Personal and Confidential.

En Route THE PENNSYLVANIA SPECIAL

My dear Mr. Thomas: New York-Chicago April 4/1912.

When you were in Trenton on the generous errand of asking me if contributions to my campaign fund from some of the hotel men in Atlantic City would be acceptable, we parted with the understanding that I was to let you know when it would be most useful for them to act.

That time has come now. We are at the crisis of this preliminary campaign and it will break down unless we have very considerable additions to our exchequer.

I would not have taken this liberty had you not made me free to do so, but now that the critical moment has come I feel that I can, without impropriety, urge that these gentlemen lend us their utmost assistance.[1]

I cannot close without expressing my admiration and gratitude for your own unprecedented personal generosity in refusing to be paid for the admirable edition of the Review you issued in my behalf.[2] Such things are as admirable as they are rare and words are very inadequate to express my deep appreciation.

Cordially and faithfully,   Woodrow Wilson

HwLS (received from Bruce Gimelson).
[1] Thomas contributed $6,000 to Wilson's preconvention campaign, most if not all of which presumably came from some Atlantic City hotel men. See the testimony of William F. McCombs, Oct. 14, 1912, in *Campaign Contributions: Testimony before a Subcommittee of the Committee on Privileges and Elections,* United States Senate, 62nd Cong., 3rd sess. (2 vols., Washington, 1913), I, 868.
[2] A "Special Woodrow Wilson Edition" of the *Atlantic City Review* came out on March 21, 1912. It contained a front-page story analyzing Wilson's chances of winning the Democratic nomination; a photograph of Wilson and an editorial on the editorial page; and another full page of articles about Wilson and his political prospects.

A News Report of a Busy Day in Illinois

[April 6, 1912]

WILSON GREETED BY HUGE CROWDS IN FIVE DISTRICTS

Terms Hearst a Slanderer and Stone a Tool
Wielded by the Editor.

BY H. M. LYTLE.

PEORIA, Ill., April 5.—Governor Woodrow Wilson not only booted Champ Clark's "houn' dawg" over five Illinois congressional districts today, but he took a resounding kick with hob-nailed shoes at a pestiferous pup owned by one William Randolph Hearst.

Hearst he charged with being a slanderer. Senator William J. Stone of Missouri, the Clark manager, who aroused the New Jersey presidential candidate's ire by the spoken charge that he was a traitor to the Democratic party, he disposed of under the category that he was a tool wielded by Hearst.

As to Hearst Governor Wilson, before 6,000 people in the Arsenal at Springfield, said:

"Senator Stone is coming here tonight as an antidote in answer to a hurry-up call sent out by the man—a man who has newspapers all over the country—who so far has managed to attack the character of every man who has spoken in favor of the Democratic party."

As to Senator Stone's charges that he was a traitor and that he did not vote the Democratic ticket in 1900 and 1908, he said:

"In 1908 I voted the whole Democratic ticket. In 1900 I did the same. I never voted anything but the Democratic ticket in my life." . . .

Governor Wilson in his speech [in Peoria] made thinly veiled references to the attack of Senator Stone. He spoke on preferential primaries and said the people are straining at the leash to get into the running. When they do, he declared, Illinois will have no more election scandals,[1] because United States senators will be nominated and elected by popular vote.

On the preferential primary score the presidential aspirant was especially enthusiastic. Before a dozen audiences, in halls, en route from the back end of the special train which raced from town to town in the whirlwind finish of the preliminary campaign, and finally at the large mass meeting at night in the Coliseum here, he praised the wisdom of the legislature in passing the preferential primary bill.

"The conventions in Chicago and Baltimore will be the last of their kind," he declared. "Four years from now every state in the Union will have laws of this character. The President then will be nominated by the people and not by slate makers. Delegates will go to these conventions under strict orders from the voters and their choice will be nominated. It will mark the end of boss rule in national politics."

Referring to the scandal connected with the election of Senator Lorimer, before a crowd of 1,500 at Joliet, he declared:

"You people of Illinois have had experience in electing senators; selecting in back rooms means election of unworthy candidates regardless of the wishes of the people.

"I'm ready to argue the rights of the people to have a say in the nomination of their candidates seven days a week. I'll argue it on Sunday as well as weekdays, because I believe politics to be a semi-religious duty."

At Bloomington he was escorted to the courthouse by former Vice President Adlai Stevenson. There he attacked the tariff.

"I've learned a lot of things since I entered public life," he said. "I've learned some things about tariff and I'd like to expose everyone behind the various schedules.

"Numerous Republicans advocate my views. The trouble is that they hold Republicanism sacred, are sort of afraid of the old man in the grave."

At Jacksonville he turned loose on those who have accused him of being the Wall street candidate. He branded them as falsifiers.

"If I knew that any individual or individual interest were behind my candidacy or that my campaign expenses were coming from such sources I'd be ashamed to show my face before you," he declared with considerable warmth. "I wouldn't be traveling on a special train if I knew such to be a fact, but I'd take the first fast express west and make sure it didn't stop any place I was known."

Mr. Wilson took occasion to express his views of William J. Bryan at Jacksonville, the latter's birth place. Senator Stone had accused Governor Wilson of having played traitor to Bryan.

"William J. Bryan is one of the greatest leaders the country has ever produced," Mr. Wilson said. "He is one of the greatest friends the common people ever have had. That he never reached the presidency in the long battle he waged does not d[e]tract from his glory, but rather adds to the honor for the fight he made."

At Peoria Governor Wilson spoke before a tremendous crowd in the Coliseum. George T. Page and Mayor D. H. Woodruff introduced the governor.[2] A committee composed of seventy-five admirers met him at Pekin and acted as escort into the city.

Governor Wilson had several unique experiences during the day. At Pontiac 100 school-teachers greeted him when he made a talk from the rear end of the train, and at Jacksonville an interpreter translated his speech in sign language to more than 300 pupils of the deaf and dumb institute.

If Governor Wilson's popularity may be gauged by the crowds he attracted enroute on the first lap of his two days' journey, it may be safely said that he carries with him the well wishes of Illinois Democrats. At every stop of the special, crowds ranging from 500 to 6,000 were on hand to greet him.

At Lincoln and Springfield the demonstrations were especially enthusiastic. While the latter city cannot be construed as "in the enemy's territory," there is a touch of Clark sentiment there with which the New Jersey governor had to reckon. . . .

Governor Wilson visited eleven places on his first day's journey. He spoke at Joliet, Dwight, Pontiac, Bloomington, Lincoln, Springfield, Jacksonville, San Jose, Petersburg, Mason City and Peoria. The total number of his auditors is roughly estimated at 25,000.

Printed in the *Chicago Record-Herald*, April 6, 1912; several editorial headings omitted.

1 A reference to the scandal caused by the election of William Lorimer to the United States Senate in 1909. About this matter, see G. L. Record to WW, Oct. 17, 1910, n. 11, Vol. 21.

2 George True Page, lawyer of Peoria, and Edward N. Woodruff, Republican Mayor of Peoria.

A News Report of an Address in Springfield, Illinois

[April 6, 1912]

HEARST, CLARK AND STONE ARE LINKED TOGETHER BY WILSON

Vast Audience at State Arsenal Hears Presidential Candidate.

Eloquently and emphatically declaring his faith in the ability of the American people to govern themselves; repudiating boss domination and condemning "personally conducted conventions"; exploding what he termed deliberate falsehoods uttered against him by Hearst and Senator William J. Stone in behalf of Champ Clark, Governor Woodrow Wilson, democratic candidate for president, electrified an enormous audience at the arsenal yesterday afternoon. . . .

Governor Wilson was deeply impressed by his initial visit to Springfield. He spoke often of the home of Lincoln as he approached Springfield on the train. He insisted before arriving here that he be taken to the Lincoln tomb. At the conclusion of his address he went to the Lincoln monument and impressively placed a great cluster of American Beauty roses upon Lincoln's sarcophagus, and for a few moments stood with bared head in silent meditation. He then asked that he be taken to Lincoln's old homestead, and there he viewed with interest the relics recalling the life of the emancipator. . . .

At Springfield Governor Wilson was met by the members of the local reception committee and two thousand people who were with difficulty prevailed upon to stand back so the distinguished guest could be escorted to the automobiles which were in waiting to convey the party to the arsenal. The procession of automobiles went immediately to the arsenal where Chairman Patton[1] introduced Governor Wilson who delivered a forceful, genuinely democratic, dignified and intensely interesting address punctuated alternately by laughter and applause. . . .

Following is the address in full as delivered at the arsenal:

Mr. chairman, ladies and gentlemen: It is a great pleasure to come to Springfield. I am almost ashamed to say it is the first time I ever visited Springfield.

I suppose that everybody who comes here must feel descend upon him the inspiration of coming to the place so closely identified with the name and fame of one of the greatest of the presidents of the United States. (Applause.)

I am impatient to have the honor of doing what I shall presently have the pleasure of doing—visiting the grave of Mr. Lincoln, and paying my tribute to his memory.

It seems to me that nothing is more inspiring in a country like this than to reflect upon the career of a man like Lincoln, who perhaps more clearly than any other American who reached a conspicuous post of honor, sprang from the very loins of the people themselves.

It is astonishing to me, ladies and gentlemen, that any man should miss the point of the history of great free peoples like this of America.

There is a theory of government in this country which has persisted ever since the time of Hamilton. Some very great statesmen have entertained it, but they can hardly be characterized as characteristically American statesmen. It is exemplified in some of the policies and some of the party points of view of our own day.

I have nothing to say that is in the least disrespectful of those

[1] James W. Patton, lawyer of Springfield and president of the Woodrow Wilson Club of that city.

great bodies of my fellow citizens who have habitually voted the republican ticket, but I do want to call their attention to one circumstance of the leadership of their party which I think is worth their serious reflection.

Sometimes I wonder how the leaders of that party can claim any kind of spiritual lineage from Abraham Lincoln, because in these later days of tariff privilege there has sprung up again and no where more conspicuously than among them, the theory that it was not safe to trust the judgments of politics to the great body of the people, but that the only way in which it was possible prudently to conduct a great government was through a sort of board of trustees, consisting of those who had the greatest material stake in the prosperity of the country.

I do not want to misrepresent those gentlemen, and I dare say I am putting into words what has been only vaguely in their consciences; but I believe that many of them rely upon the principle that there is only a small body of men in this country who know how to make the country prosperous, and that it is not safe to govern the country except according to the judgment of that small body of persons.

I do not believe in any principle of trusteeship for a great people. Either the people of America can take care of themselves, or the government of the United States is a failure. (Applause.)

I note, because I have been in contact all my life with the study of history, that there never has been a nation in the history of the world that was renewed from the top, but that every nation has in the course of beneficent nature been renewed from the bottom.

Only that nation is vital which keeps all the courses of its blood open so that unknown men may discover themselves to the common use and service.

Therefore, I have often dwelt with a great deal of pleasure upon the history of a particular part of the people of the world. Did you never reflect upon the history of the Roman Catholic church? I myself need not remind you, I suppose, that I am not a Catholic; but I want to point out to you the indispensable service, the typical service, which the Catholic church has rendered to mankind.

For the sake of example, in the middle ages, when all the world was organized upon the principle of aristocracy, and would have gone to seed, the Catholic church was the open door of democracy. There was not a peasant so obscure that he might not become a priest. There was not a priest so humble that he might not become the pope of Christendom, and every chancellory in Europe had its blood constantly renewed out of the ranks of the Catholic priesthood.

I do not hold a brief for any church, but I hold that to be one of the most extraordinary examples of how democracy, the open courses of the blood in every great people, is necessary in order to maintain the purity and the strength and the vitality of the governing forces of the world.

The governing forces of this country are not going to come from well known families. They are not going to come from men whose names we now know. Somewhere in obscure little cottages, somewhere in remote farms, somewhere among the multitudes who throng the mills, somewhere among the men who are in the mines, it may be, is welling up the future strength and vitality of America.

I have learned many things, but nothing so deep and permanent as this—that the sources of strength, whether physical or spiritual, are in the great bodies of a free people. (Applause.)

Now I say that this is the question which we are facing at this moment in America. Are we or are we not to carry government back to the people themselves?

My past record has served a very useful purpose. It has been an indispensable part of my education. I have learned a great many things and there are a great many men who are hoping and praying that I will never tell anybody what I have learned. (Laughter.) Through the habit of a lifetime I have been so talkative that I am afraid sooner or later it is going to come out. I find it constantly upon the tip of my tongue. I met a gentleman, who is sitting not far behind me, who said, "Governor, the first time I took a fancy to you was when you assisted to defeat James Smith, Jr., for the United States senate." I said, "Why so?" And he said, "I know James Smith." (Laughter.)

That contest interested me, not because I was personally opposed to James Smith, as that is neither here nor there. It is none of a governor's business to say who shall be a senator from his state. That may seem strange because you may think I made it my business, but I did not. I simply insisted, in my innocence and inexperience that when the democrats had said at a primary whom they wanted, it was none of my business to want anybody else. (Applause.) I will say that again and again and again. It does not make any difference whether he is my choice or not. It is when the people have spoken, nobody else, if I can prevent it, shall break in and get ahead of him.

I am interested all along the line in nothing but this—in restoring the government to the people. You say, "In nothing but that? I thought that the tariff was the chief issue in this campaign and have you not said so yourself?" Yes, I have said so and it is. How are you going to settle the question unless you can get at it yourselves? How often have you settled the tariff at the polls and how much good has it done you? During the last presidential campaign you voted on the tariff question and everybody knew how you voted, but did you get what you voted for? What is the use of discussing the tariff until we give the people of the United States a seat inside the committee rooms where the whole game is put up? (Applause.)

Do you suppose it disturbed Mr. Aldrich in the least degree that the people of the United States had voted that the tariff be revised downward? Mr. Aldrich had again and again succeeded in doing what he did again, of putting into any schedule he picked out things that nobody would understand, except himself and the people who were in his confidence, and so Schedule "K"[2] and every other schedule was packed with things concerning which he said to the senators of the United States that the details were none of their business. He refused information to the minority members on his own committee, and the representatives of the people were not allowed to know what the tariff contained.

Now, I say, until we get the government back into our hands, what is the use of making orations about the tariff? We are going to get the government back into our own hands. (Applause.)

I want you to read the speeches of some of the chief standpat republicans and carefully reflect upon the context whenever they speak of the "people" and you will see that they don't include themselves. They speak as if they were in a position to dispense prosperity to the people, but not as if they constituted part of the people.

Now, a man who does not think in the terms of the people themselves can not think in the terms of America.

So, I say, it is an inspiration to stand in a place identified throughout the world with the memory of a man who slowly grew into the stature of a statesman, with no sap in him except that sap of indomitable American manhood, which is sufficient to raise any man to the highest place of a great nation.

We are picked and chosen of all the people of the world. The best initiative, the best strength and the best vision of all the nations makes its way across the Atlantic, season after season, and we are renewed out of all the fountains of hope that spring anywhere in the world; fountains of hope because there towers here and there in our history a rugged figure like this, of a man

[2] That is, the wool and woolen products schedule of the Payne-Aldrich Tariff Act.

made out of the pure stuff that God himself implanted in us, the stuff of life and of conscience.

Now, I am reminded by someone behind me that the train starts in a few minutes and I must get away to give myself the pleasure of visiting the tomb of Mr. Lincoln. In order that you may not be deprived of what I know will be a pleasure, I am going to introduce a substitute, a very dear friend of mine from New York, where he is assistant corporation counsel, and he comes of the best guaranteed fighting Irish block and his name is Dudley Field Malone. I thank you. (Applause.)[3]

I congratulate you that among the first of the states you are to have the opportunity next Tuesday to express a preference, not as to who shall be president of the United States, but of who shall be nominated for the president of the United States. (Applause.)

I want you to realize the significance of that particular choice. It is a great deal more important to select the candidates than to elect the officers, because unless you can do the preliminary selecting, you can have two slates presented to you which, so far as your interests are concerned, offer you the choice between Tweedle-dum and Tweedle-dee. (Laughter.)

The conventions that are to meet in Chicago and Baltimore in June next are the last conventions of their kind that are going to meet in America. (Applause.)

The leaven that is going to leaven the lump in those conventions is the leaven that is going to come out of Wisconsin, Illinois (Applause), Nebraska and Oregon, and that series of states, already long, which constitutes the first honor roll of those who are carrying the government back to its sources.

I feel a sort of exhilaration in having been permitted to come into politics at this particular time. I am not going to quarrel with the judgment, whatever it may be, provided it is an untrammeled judgment, not dictated to or personally conducted by anybody. (Applause.)

I have lived in a state where politics were personally conducted. I have had the pleasure of knowing the small groups of gentlemen who have "personally conducted," some of them very likeable men, some of them very honest men, but not one of them a man who had the slightest suspicion as to what constituted a democratic government. I have known the trustees, in short, who were running the government of the state of New Jersey. As trustees they did pretty well. I for my part am for rejecting all trustees.

I suppose from what I have heard within the half hour that I

---

[3] Someone evidently told Wilson that he had more time. He continued.

am regarded as a dangerous person, because I have heard that it was necessary, when it was learned that I was to pollute the air of Springfield, to telegraph for a certain well-known senator of the United States from Missouri, to come here tonight and offer you an antidote for the poison I was to distribute. (Applause.)

I am very much interested in the chemist who compounded the antidote. (Laughter.) I do not know how they get the elements for such a compound in newspaper offices, but the chemist who compounded this particular antidote owns a great many newspaper offices throughout the United States. It has been his particular pleasure to destroy so far as he could the reputation of every man who spoke for the democracy of the United States. (Applause.)

I am sorry that a senator of the United States should distribute his wares. The same senator asked me a question, which he may want to hear answered to-night. I wish I could wait and tell him. It has been stated again and again, and the statement, I understand, has been supported by affidavit, sworn to by gentlemen who are willing to swear to anything, that I not only did not vote for Mr. Bryan in 1900 and in 1908, but that in 1908 I did not vote at all.

Now, there is one thing I have never done, and that is that I have never run away. I have never stayed away because of the impossibility of making up my mind. I have mind in manageable quantities and I can always make it up. (Laughter.)

In 1900 and 1908 I was in the first case a professor and in the second case the president of a university. It is considered very bad form for the members of the university faculties to take an active part in politics and though I will admit I was straining at the leash, I did not take an active part in politics until 1908, when I was,—let us say, released from academic seclusion.

In 1908, if Senator Stone is interested to hear the thing repeated for the one hundredth time, I had the pleasure of voting for the whole democratic ticket and also in 1900. Indeed, I never voted anything but the democratic ticket in my life. (Applause.) I have had the pleasure recently of stating so often, not only that I voted the democratic ticket, but that that ticket contained Mr. Bryan's name, that I am surprised that Senator Stone has not been reading any of the things that have been printed. He is a man of limited information.

I am not interested, gentlemen, in these personal questions, I am not interested in my own past record. I am very much interested in my future record. (Laughter.)

Printed in the Springfield *Illinois State Register*, April 6, 1912; many editorial headings omitted.

A News Report of Another Busy Day in Illinois

[April 7, 1912]

WILSON CHARGES DEAL TO BEAT HIM

Charges Frameup and Says He Won't Bargain for a Political Office.

Charges of an existing frameup by the Clark-Harmon forces to defeat him for the Democratic presidential nomination were made yesterday by Gov. Woodrow Wilson.

His sensational statement first was made at Sterling, near the end of the second and closing day of his tour by special train. At four night meetings in Chicago he made thinly veiled references to an alleged alliance under which Harmon's name is omitted from the primary ballot in Illinois, centering the opposition to Wilson upon Champ Clark.

Along other lines, too, the governor made aggressive remarks. Usually suave and delicate of speech, he overstepped his past habits.

"Big business men who resort to illicit methods," he asserted, "should be sent to the penitentiary the same as chauffeurs who recklessly drive automobiles disregardful of the rights and lives of others. Put a few men who misuse the great corporations in prison and the illicit business will stop with a dull thud.

"William R. Hearst has 'decided' I am not to be nominated. What an exhibition of audacity. What a contempt he must feel for the judgment and integrity of the American people. But it is delightful to realize the people of Illinois on next Tuesday will decide who is to be nominated and Mr. Hearst—a nonresident—can only have his say in his newspapers.

"In attacks made upon my history (chiefly by the Hearst interests) I have been lied about, but lies take care of themselves. I am merely stating a few facts to set myself right before the Poles and other foreigners."

In his closing speech, the governor excoriated the Lorimer-Lincoln league[1] for using the name of Lincoln.

"How men who have things to conceal try to hide behind Lincoln's name as a mask," exclaimed the governor. "Don't let any man use that name to conceal purposes not in the interest of the great body of the people. We should not have any games worked on us by any men who, in their eagerness to conceal their real aims, use Lincoln's name.

---

[1] In July 1911, William Lorimer and some of his friends, in an effort to bolster his sagging political fortunes, formed an organization called the Lincoln Protective League. The press promptly dubbed it the "Lorimer-Lincoln League."

"But nobody is deceived by a masquerade; it is sometimes useful, though never effective. The strange thing is how men in a partisan fight dare to take unto themselves the name of the man they must know never supported any special class in all his policies. They must have heard his voice always lifted in the interests of the great body of the people. There ever was to be heard Lincoln's tramp, tramp, for the great multitude of the people."

Members of the Wilson party held that it was a great day for the Governor. From his start, early in the morning in Galesburg, where some 1,500 tramped in the rain to the station to hear him, until his closing Garrick Theater meeting in Chicago near midnight, the governor was greeted by big crowds. His reception everywhere was enthusiastic.

After speaking in his old time conservative fashion in Galesburg and Moline, Gov. Wilson opened the throttle when he reached Sterling and spoke under the cover of the station protecting the crowd from the rain.

"There are all sort of rumors floating around," he said, "rumors of combinations; rumors of understandings; rumors that make one feel very lonely. I don't much care if these rumors are true or not. They have nothing to do with my speech at this moment, but there is a very strong suspicion in the minds of a great part of the voters of the country that there is a game being framed up.

"Now you can't do business properly when there is suspicion about and there is no doubt that there is great distrust in the minds of the people at this time with regard to the action of certain of the men whose names are very frequently mentioned wherever politics is discussed."

The governor gave notice he would not enter into any deals or make any personal pledges to gain office.

"For the last eighteen months," he said, "I have wielded considerable influence in New Jersey, and it is because I have been talking right out just as I am talking now. I would not condescend to bestow a political job or to make a pledge for the sake of obtaining political power or advantage. My record will show that never have I bestowed or promised to bestow a political office in the state of New Jersey for the purpose of affecting the enactment of a law or for any political advantage whatever."

When he got to De Kalb he spoke of "big business," giving assurance that he would not tear down or destroy any property, but would compel obedience to the laws under penalty of jail terms.

"I am not afraid of business," he asserted, "because it is big any more than I am afraid of an automobile because it is powerful. But I am afraid of the chauffeur. I do not want to break up the machine, but I do want to get at the man who has no regard for the rights or the lives of his fellow men.

"I believe it is just as possible to find out who it is who misuses the great corporations as to find out who it is that drives the automobiles. I believe the place for them is the penitentiary. There they will have time to think of the acts that put them there. There is nothing so curative as the prison. And I believe that if a few were sent to the prison the illicit business would stop with a dull thud. A new social conscience would result and all the problems of big business be solved."

In Rochelle the governor mentioned Mr. Hearst by name for the first time.

"I find myself a good deal embarrassed because I have just heard Mr. Hearst has decided I am not to be nominated, but that somebody else is. I regret I did not find it out sooner; I should have been spared a long journey.

"What a commentary it is upon our affairs when one man should suppose he can frame the affairs of the nation. What an exhibition of audacity. What an exhibition of the contempt he must feel for the judgment and independence of the American people."

During a day of speeches from a special train in half a dozen Illinois towns he declared existing political conditions are "intolerable."

"The people," he said, "are tired of government by the special interests for the specially interested. They are so tired the situation is becoming fraught with danger. The people are determined to get back the control of the government. They will take the first decisive step in Illinois on Tuesday next when they pick their favorites for the presidential nominations."

"My record as governor of New Jersey is entirely fair to labor," he said. "I do not say it, nor do I like to have it said that I am the laboring man's special friend. I am his friend in the sense that he is a part of the country and I am the country's friend. I do not like to draw class lines, but prefer to consider the laboring man in the get together spirit, with no interest attempting to hog it all, but all pulling together for the good of the common country."

Dudley Field Malone, Tammany Hall orator from New York City, the governor's companion campaigner, presented Wilson's labor record in detail and offered a resolution adopted by the

New Jersey Federation of Labor as proof that the educator has been "fair."

Though giving lengthy attention to the tariff, the governor argued that it does but little good to discuss the tariff, for the people are not represented in the committee rooms at Washington. The primary step, therefore, is to restore the government to the people, then the people's representatives may go about solving the tariff problems.

On his arrival in Chicago in the evening the governor was taken to Lincoln Turner hall in South Chicago, where he talked to a crowd largely composed of Polish-Americans.

Without delay he branded as false, using the short and ugly word, the charge that he had attacked in his historical reviews, the good citizenship of immigrants from Southern Europe.

He was met as he approached the South Chicago hall by a committee of Democrats representing every nationality in the city, and was escorted to the auditorium. Julius [F.] Smietanka, a member of the board of education,[2] presided.

"When we speak of America," he said, "we speak not of a race, but of a people. After we have enumerated the Irish-Americans, the Jewish-Americans, the German-Americans, and the Polish-Americans who will be left?

"Settlers and descendents of the settlers constitute the minority in America, and people of all the races of Europe a majority. The term America is bigger than the continent. America lives in the hearts of every man everywhere who wishes to find a region somewhere where he will be free to work out his destiny as he chooses."

At the Garrick theater, where the governor was introduced by Clarence N[orton]. Goodwin,[3] he spoke in regard to the "money trust."

At the St. Anne's auditorium meeting, Fifty-fifth street boulevard and La Salle street, Judge William E[mmett]. Dever[4] introduced the governor. Here he advocated publicity as one of the purifying elements of politics.

Gov. Wilson will have a dinner at noon today with Father Peter J. O'Callaghan of the Paulist Fathers, St. Mary's rectory. He will depart in midafternoon for Buffalo and Syracuse, to make non-political speeches next week.

Gov. Woodrow Wilson received two cheering telegrams last night. One was from Detroit, Mich., bearing the information

2 Lawyer and influential Polish-American leader of Chicago.
3 Judge of the Superior Court, Cook County.
4 Judge of the Superior Court, Cook County.

that Ingham county had instructed its forty-six delegates to vote for him at the state convention. The other telegram was from Des Moines, Ia., notifying the governor that Polk county had instructed its thirty-eight delegates to vote for Wilson at the state convention.

Printed in the *Chicago Daily Tribune*, April 7, 1912; two editorial headings omitted.

A News Report About an Incident in Chicago

[April 8, 1912]

ROB GOV. WILSON OF PRIVATE DATA;
PLOT IS CHARGED

Papers Relating to Candidate's Campaign
Stolen from Hotel Room.

Thieves, believed to have been employed by political enemies, stole a big suit case containing wearing apparel and important private correspondence and papers from the apartments of Gov. Woodrow Wilson at the Hotel Sherman yesterday afternoon. He departed for Syracuse, N. Y., in the evening with only the clothes he wore.

The presidential candidate was disturbed when he discovered his loss, but asserted there was nothing in the case that he would fear to show to any interested person or to the country at large.

"The robbery will greatly inconvenience me," asserted the governor, "but whoever obtained the papers and correspondence will be greatly disappointed. While the correspondence is of a nature which necessarily should be considered private between the writers and myself, there is nothing but may be published without doing me harm.

"A great deal of the correspondence deals with the campaign I am waging, as do the other documents which were stolen. As a matter of fact the most valuable things which the burglars will find in the suitcase are my dress suit and clean linen."

Gov. Wilson hesitated to suggest that any political antagonist was back of the theft, although conceding its disappearance was "suspicious." Others in his party, including his Illinois managers, however, were not so considerate.

"It has political earmarks," said Walter Measday, traveling secretary to the New Jersey executive. This opinion was echoed by Dudley Field Malone, son-in-law of United States Senator

O'Gorman of New York and Gov. Wilson's companion campaigner.

William C. Niblack, president of the Wilson Club of Illinois, was even more emphatic in his charges.

"It's nothing more or less than a political trick," was his comment. "It is in line with the campaign of lies and vituperation which has been waged against Gov. Wilson."

The governor himself missed the traveling bag when he returned to suite 214 after dining with the Rev. P. J. O'Callahan [O'Callaghan] and other Paulist fathers at St. Mary's church. Mr. Malone accompanied him.

The governor left his rooms, shared with him by Secretary Measday, at 10:40. He worshiped at the Fourth Presbyterian church, after which he kept his dinner engagement. A maid who straightened up the apartments at 11:30 said the suit case was then on a chair.

Mr. Measday was in the rooms afterwards and when he left at about 2:10 p.m. said the suit case in the governor's room had not been disturbed. He had misplaced the key and went to the office to tell the clerk to have the door locked.

The clerk misunderstood him and thinking he wanted the door of the Wilson headquarters on the parlor floor unlocked sent a bellboy to these rooms. The boy did not visit the governor's private suite.

Gov. Wilson returned to the hotel at 2:55 p.m. and hurried to his apartments to finish packing. He found his toilet articles, including silver backed brushes, on the dresser, but the suit case was gone.

A few minutes afterwards his visitors called and they joined in the fruitless search. The hotel management was notified and house detectives got busy.

Gov. Wilson considered it strange that the thieves had taken only his suitcase and had left his toilet articles on the dresser. They also ignored a smaller traveling bag in Mr. Measday's room.

Besides the correspondence and papers in the suitcase were Gov. Wilson's evening clothes, an assortment of linen, and several scarf pins, which he said had a sentimental as well as intrinsic value.[1]

Printed in the *Chicago Daily Tribune*, April 8, 1912; three editorial headings omitted.

[1] As the result of an anonymous telephone call to the Hotel Sherman, Wilson's suitcase was found in an alley on April 16 with its contents apparently intact. *Newark Evening News*, April 17, 1912.

To Robert Lee Henry

[Syracuse, N. Y., April 8, 1912]

I am heartily in favor of legislation requiring publicity of contributions to presidential campaign funds, including both the
contests for nomination and the contests for election, and their
publication before the contests. Indeed, I think such legislation
absolutely necessary to the purification and elevation of our politics. It would absolutely open to public view the field in which
sinister influences are most apt to lurk and control.

[Woodrow Wilson]

Printed in the Syracuse, N. Y., *Post-Standard*, April 9, 1912.

To Mary Allen Hulbert Peck

The Onondaga
Dearest Friend,   Syracuse, N. Y. 8 April, 1912

It was impossible to write yesterday and I fear this will not
reach you before you get away on the 13th,—but I write on the
chance. You seem to feel that, for some reason, this is your last
trip to Bermuda. I do not know why it should be. It is your only
real haven,—and another year,—when your ordeal is over and the
dread and sensitiveness are gone and your nerves have surrendered to your really splendid natural energy and self-command (you are naturally the *most* normal person, if that is not
nonsense, that I have ever known)—your mind and heart will
turn toward "Glencove," or, maybe, Somerset, again with, I daresay, an irresistible longing,—like a bird in the season of migration,—and you will obey and go. At least I hope you will,—I trust
you will,—I *believe* you will. I somehow feel easier and more content about you when you are in Bermuda than when you are in
this country amidst scenes and persons who remind you constantly of what, for your heart's ease, you would fain forget. As
I have said to you so often before, you seem to me to belong
in Bermuda,—and Bermuda seems to belong to you. To me the
place seems a sort of extension and embodiment of your personality it is so full of colour and variety: its moods vary so
whimsically and so rapidly and carry with them so individual
and piquant a charm it is never dull, never monotonous, never
what you *expect* it to be,—always something so much better and
more interesting! And so you have the proper *setting* there. When
you shine elsewhere I seem to lack the corresponding brilliancy
of air and water and scene. Alas! that there should be a possibility that I may never be free to visit the place of enchantment

again! But *you*, at least, need not keep away from it. *It* need not be deprived of *you!*

I have just finished a big job,—a swing of six hundred miles through middle and western Illinois in which I made twenty odd speeches,—from the rear of the train, from benches in railway stations, from the steps of courthouses, and from the stages of crowded halls,—ending with *four* speeches in Chicago—one in each of the four distinctly marked sections of the conglomerate town! I am here to-day to dine with the Chamber of Commerce, and am *very* dull and sleepy with the physical reaction from the fatigue and excitement. I keep wonderfully well and strong. I suppose I am like a man living on strong stimulants. How I wish I might command that most delightful of all stimulants, a talk with you.

Love to Mrs. Allen and Allen

Your devoted friend   Woodrow Wilson

ALS (WP, DLC).

From William Gibbs McAdoo

PERSONAL AND CONFIDENTIAL.

Dear Governor: [New York] April 8, 1912.

Please note the enclosed from our friend McGaffey,[1] of Albuquerque. He seems to think that New Mexico is all right. I did not tell you about my meeting with him and the speech I made to a lot of representative Democrats in Albuquerque when I was there in February. I have written McGaffey to "stay on the job" and not to be guilty of over-confidence. I am sure that he and his friends can hold New Mexico if they are active and vigilant.

I also enclose a copy of an editorial from the Savannah Press,[2] which Mr. Stovall has just sent me, which is based upon a paragraph in a letter I wrote to him a short time ago. Also enclosed you will find a letter from National Committeeman Ewing, of New Orleans.[3]

Always,   Sincerely yours,   W G McAdoo

Please note the enclosed from Col. Gray & tell me if you would like me to go with you. I am not sure that I can but will try if you wish. Had a most important talk with Col. Osborn of Greensboro N. C. today. He is going to help and can be very effective. Please return Col. Gray's letter.

TLS (LPC, W. G. McAdoo Papers, DLC).

¹ Amasa B. McGaffey, president of the McGaffey Co. and active in other business enterprises in Albuquerque.

² "Georgia for Georgians," *Savannah Press*, April 6, 1912. It quoted a letter from "a prominent citizen of New York" [i.e., McAdoo] arguing that Georgians should support Wilson, "the only Southern man in the race who has a chance for the nomination," rather than Oscar W. Underwood, "who has no real show for the nomination." McAdoo also emphasized that Wilson, "although born in Virginia, was brought up in Georgia and is essentially a Georgian, as is also his wife." As McAdoo suggested in the above letter, the remainder of the editorial was an amplification of these two points.

³ It is missing.

A News Report of a Day in Syracuse, New York

[April 9, 1912]

GUEST OF HONOR AT BANQUET

New Jersey's Chief Executive Speaks Before Chamber of Commerce

With Governor Wilson of New Jersey, aggressive candidate for the Democratic nomination for president, as the principal speaker, the Syracuse Chamber of Commerce last night held the largest and most brilliant annual banquet in its history in the ballroom of the Onondaga.

There were 320 guests, not including a hundred Syracuse society women, who occupied the large balcony at the east end of the hall and helped in applauding the striking passages in the Governor's address.

"Politics in Its Relation to Business" was Dr. Wilson's theme.¹

Except the new president of the Chamber, Robert Dey,² and the toastmaster, Dean J. Richard Street of the Teachers College at Syracuse University,³ the only speaker of the evening in addition to Governor Wilson was Prof. Max Eastman of New York, formerly of Columbia University.⁴ He gave a humorous talk which brought forth a great deal of applause and laughter.

It was 8.25 o'clock when Governor Wilson, with others assigned to the table of honor, walked to his place. He was greeted with a hearty round of applause, which quickly gave way to the Princeton locomotive cheer, with "Wilson! Wilson! Wilson!" tacked on at the end.

The cheer came from sixteen Princeton alumni seated at two tables opposite the place occupied by Princeton's former president.

Governor Wilson wore a dress suit—but it was not his own. His was stolen from his room at the Sherman House in Chicago on Sunday. Arriving in Syracuse yesterday morning minus his evening clothes, the Governor was confronted with the necessity of buying, renting or borrowing, and finally accepted the latter alternative.

W. A. Mackenzie, jr.,[5] who headed the Princeton delegation which met the distinguished visitor upon his arrival here, came to the rescue and furnished the apparel for the banquet. The Governor will be measured for a new dress suit when he reaches Trenton on Thursday. That which he wore last evening seemed to fit all right. . . .

Governor Woodrow Wilson put in a busy afternoon yesterday with his secretary attending to New Jersey state affairs and mapping out future political speeches. Following a luncheon in one of the private dining rooms at the Onondaga, at which he was the guest of the Princeton alumni of Syracuse, he secluded himself in his room.

"I regret not being able to see more of Syracuse," he said to a Post-Standard reporter. "It is one of the penalties of traveling about the country under circumstances such as surround me that one has little or no time for sightseeing." . . .

Printed in the Syracuse, N. Y., *Post-Standard*, April 9, 1912; three editorial headings omitted.
[1] There is a WWhw outline of this speech, dated April 8, 1912, in WP, DLC.
[2] Founder and president of Dey Brothers and Co., a department store of Syracuse.
[3] Jacob Richard Street.
[4] Formerly an Associate in Philosophy at Columbia University, Eastman was at this time earning his living as a professional lecturer and advocate of woman suffrage. He later recalled having a long and friendly conversation with Wilson on woman suffrage and other subjects during the banquet. He also recalled that the program chairman had offered him a dollar a minute in addition to his regular fee as long as he could keep Wilson laughing during his (Eastman's) speech and that he earned forty dollars extra. Max Eastman, *Enjoyment of Living* (New York and London, 1948), pp. 385-87.
[5] William Adams Mackenzie, Jr., Princeton 1892, lawyer of Syracuse.

A News Item

[*April 9, 1912*]

Surprise to Gov. Wilson.

BUFFALO, N. Y., April 9.—"The result of the primary in Illinois, showing a substantial victory for Speaker Clark, comes as a great surprise to me. I fully expected to carry the State."[1]

This was all that Gov. Woodrow Wilson, candidate for the Democratic Presidential nomination, would say on the returns from Illinois.

Printed in the *New York Times*, April 10, 1912.
[1] In the preferential primary on April 9, Wilson lost to Clark by a vote of 75,527 to 218,483. Wilson carried only the sixteenth, or Peoria, district. For a

discussion of the preconvention campaign in Illinois, see Link, *Road to the White House*, pp. 408-13.

A News Report of a Speech to the University Club of Buffalo, New York

[April 10, 1912]

WILSON BELIEVES IN ELIMINATION
OF ALL CLASSES

By JOHN R. BALL.

BUFFALO, April 9. . . . The governor believes the present situation has grown up to a great extent through a misunderstanding between classes. He advocates the elimination of all classes and a general "Get-together" spirit. He holds that there has been too much class feeling; that is, that the men of education and "that inexplainable thing, refinement" have held themselves aloof from their fellow men and have not been willing to give the "other fellow" credit for what he knows. He declared today that it was amazing now [how] much the man in the mill could teach his fellows of life.

"We think we know all sometimes, but get down with the man in the mill and you will learn more than you ever knew," declared the governor.

This sentiment was brought out forcibly by the Governor in a short address at the University club here today. He scored the university men for their exclusiveness and advised them to get out and share life with the ordinary working man. "It will be surprising," said the governor, "how much you can learn. You are living in a narrow circle. It is not enough to discuss the things of life with those who have not had your advantages. You must get out and share it with them. You will be broadened and will bring about a better understanding. You will find that the practical man can teach you things you never dreamed of. Those who hesitate about touching unrefined things are not fit to live in a democracy," declared the governor.

"After dealing with university men," said the governor at the University club, "the men I am striving with appear as amateurs. I fail to find the same subtle political games that I found in the university. When I draw the regular politician into the open he did not know how to handle himself. He was unaccustomed to the open.

"I find there is a great deal of difference between academic and practical views. The academic is narrow and built on theories. I have always tried to look at policies from a practical standpoint. Books are constructed immorally. You start out with enough knowledge to write a chapter but as one chapter would not satisfy the publisher you then write all but one chapter borrowed from some other person.

"Life is not systematic. It has no complete pattern. It should not be foiled by books nor duped by men. The academis [academic] is bound by hard and fast theories; [there is] no one standard of what is or ought to be. The academic is the intellectual barrier of caste. It shuts you off from minds not developed. Caste is the enemy of Democracy. You can't get others point of view because you start out with a false conception of what he knows. Most philanthropy is imparted by [con]descension. Wealth endeavors to bestow blessings. You can't bestow 'blessings'; you must share them. There must be that human sympathy which draws men together.

"The so-called refinement is one of the fundamental difficulties of Democracy. Many men feel a repulsion against common things. Life is a gross reality and those who hesitate about touching unrefined things are not fit to live in a Democracy. I have felt this repulsion and I had to overcome it and by overcoming it I have learned more than I ever did any other way. Those who do not overcome this live in a narrow circle.

"No person can 'condescend' to others. The same things are in all. We are only putting up a huge bluff. Put on rough clothes and go where you think those of your own circle will not find you and see what you do. Then when you meet one of your own class you will start to apologize. No man should ever apologize for anything except that which is morally wrong. I think much of our morality is found in the watchful eyes of our neighbors. We do many things when we think there is no person around to see.

"There is a great deal in policies [politics] that excite distaste in men of so-called refinement. You come in contact with all kinds of men but you can soon learn much from them; you are greatly enriched by seeing things from their point of view. Any nation which is governed by any class or by men with a common point of view will break down. No single class of society can see the truth round and whole. We must let all into the game. That is why I am a Democrat. Anything that teaches otherwise is no Democracy. All my life I have been an insurgent against the class in which I was born."

Printed in the *Pittsburgh Post*, April 10, 1912; two editorial headings omitted.

A News Report of a Political Address
in Buffalo, New York

[April 10, 1912]

WILSON SCORES BOTH PARTIES

Governor Blames Broken Pledges
for Present Political Unrest.

HE IS CONSERVATIVE

Woodrow Wilson, Governor of New Jersey and Democratic candidate for the nomination for president, gave his views upon present conditions in this country to an audience of 300 men and women at the Ellicott Club[1] last night. He spoke as if giving instruction and much as might be expected of him were he addressing a class at Princeton.

Orange and black, the Princeton colors, and American flags were the decorations of the banquet-room. The spirits of the diners had been enlivened by music and song until it came time for the oratory. . . .

Governor Wilson was warmly applauded. He spoke calmly and as an instructor, from the start and seemingly made no play for applause. But during the speech there were outbursts of handclapping at word pictures, notably when he touched upon Lincoln as working his way out of the masses with a message and one that had to be heard. The whole trend of the speech was that the government had to be brought back to the control of the people.

He had a pleasing, a convincing delivery and had his audience with him after a few minutes of talk. . . .

"Some standpatism does greatly resemble a vacuum."

"I can't conceive of a legitimate privacy for anything concerned with government."

"Government, as I see it, is simply the organization of all of us so no organization of some of us can boss all of us."

Are samples of apt phrases in Governor Wilson's speech last night. He arrived in Buffalo yesterday afternoon at 2 o'clock from Syracuse. He was met at the station by a committee of Loran L. Lewis, Jr.; Sherrill N. McWilliams and Thomas B. Lockwood, representing the University Club, and Newton E. Turgeon, Charles N. Armstrong and Jacob J. Siegrist, representing the Ellicott Club.[2]

[1] A men's social and dining club of Buffalo.
[2] Loran Ludowick Lewis, Jr., lawyer of Buffalo; Shirrell Norton McWilliams, Princeton 1894, commissioner of jurors for Erie County; Thomas Brown Lockwood, lawyer of Buffalo; Newton E. Turgeon, insurance agent of Buffalo; Charles

The reception given to Governor Wilson was non-political, as shown in the makeup of the committees. He was taken to luncheon at the University Club and afterwards given an automobile ride about the city. From 5 o'clock to 6 o'clock a reception was given to him at the University Club and he was introduced to a large number of Buffalo men.

He declined to be interviewed upon the political situation and had no comment to make upon last night's returns, giving the result of the Illinois primaries. Governor Wilson remained in Buffalo last night and this morning will go to Pittsburgh with the members of his party.

His speech last night was in part as follows:

Mr. President,[3] Mr. Toastmaster,[4] ladies and gentlemen—I do not think I will let Mr. Malone speak before me again. He has forgotten how to make anything but a nominating speech. I do not like to get up before a company like this and have you think the moment I get up and as long as I stand, that I am desirous of the suffrages of my fellow citizens.

When I was casting about in my mind what I should talk to you about tonight I was brought into a leading frame of mind by being associated today with one of your most interesting and distinguished citizens who asked me a question which I was able at the time only very briefly and hurriedly to attempt to answer.

This gentleman asked me if I thought that the legislators of America, particularly the members of Congress, were making their assaults upon business, as he deemed them, merely in order to protect themselves; merely in order to play a game of advantage; merely to gain the applause of the populace and the discontented, or whether I thought there was something deeper underlying the whole thing, something more rational; more manly, more public spirited. Now, I want to say that I do think that there are very substantial reasons why these should be the signs of the times. It is manifest to everyone that the land is full of what may not inappropriately be called discontents. I do not suppose that any man in this room, for example, though you are of a chosen and particular class, supposes that our affairs now rest upon a foundation which should not be changed. I suppose you all feel the breath of anticipated alteration in the

Newton Armstrong, insurance agent of Buffalo; and Jacob J. Siegrist, partner in a department store in Buffalo, unsuccessful Republican candidate for mayor in 1910.

[3] Charles Mercer Heald, president of the Ellicott Club.

[4] Robert Rodman Hefford, coal dealer, banker, and Republican leader of Buffalo.

life of the country, and in seeking around for the causes of that, I think we ought to be very frank and candid.

In the first place we ought to get out of our minds any disposition to attack anybody or to upset anything that is legitimate. I believe, ladies and gentlemen, that in the first place, these discontents are due to the repeated disappointments of the voters of this country. I will not say that these disappointments have come from one party more than from the other, except that one party has had more opportunities to disappoint the electorate than the other. If you take the things upon a smaller scale in the area of each individual state, both parties have again and again broken their pledges. If you narrow the circle still further to municipalities, how often have the people of our cities sought, now in this direction and again in that, for some satisfactory administration of their affairs, and found at last that they did not get it? . . .

Men want results; they want to know why it is useless and futile to vote in this country; they want to know why they cannot find somebody who will do something; they want to know why every campaign is a mere forensic exhibition and nothing ensues. And there is underying that, something which produces the uneasiness more than mere disappointment could.

Disappointed? Yes, and fighting in the dark, with foes they cannot grapple with; foes they cannot find; so that they look with suspicion upon honest men as well as upon dishonest men. Nobody has dreamed and no responsible person has ever said that the business-men of this country were not honest, or that its business was not sound. But how are you to know which business-men to suspect, when you know that some of them somewhere are doing things that will work to the damage not only of business, but of politics and to the life of the whole country?

Because we have not found the men, honest men are suffering the disadvantage by the suspicion, and so you have what so many men deplore and do not understand.

Now, this discontent manifests itself in two things, in two ways. The extreme revolt against the existing condition of affairs, we call socialism. When you do socialism justice, ladies and gentlemen, when you read as it were the heart of the socialistic doctrine, it is hardly different from the heart of Christianity itself. But this heart, this abstract heart of socialism, is one thing and the socialistic programme is a very different thing. I must say very frankly that I have never read a socialistic programme which I thought practical men could so much as debate.

Moreover, my mind revolts from programmes. I do not know enough, it goes without saying, to reconstruct society, and in my egotism I suspect that nobody else knows enough to reconstruct society.

Not that I have the least fear of anything revolutionary happening in this country. America has the most lively mind and the most conservative disposition in the world. You can get an American to talk about anything, but you sometimes have to put dynamite under him to make him do anything.

Progressiveism is the adaptation of the business of each day to the circumstances of that day as they differ from the circumstances of the day that went before. That is what I understand progressiveism to be. And if you are not a progressive you better look out, because the world is not standing still and if you insist upon standing still the world is going to run over you. You can stand pat if you want to, but you will regret it, because there is nothing that nature abhors so much as the things that stand still.

Have you heard of no spheres of our economic life in which competition has been checked and limited? Do you think that competition has the free play that it once had in America? Have you not heard of circulars and understandings and gentlemen's agreements and all sorts of things which absolutely determine prices? I am not saying that they determine them unjustly —I do not know whether they do or not. I simply say that they are not determined by competition and that the very reason they are not determined by competition is that somebody can regulate and sup[p]ress and constrict competition inside of America because they need not be afraid of competition outside of America and that therefore that alters the whole aspect of the tariff question. . . .[5]

Printed in the *Buffalo*, N. Y., *Express*, April 10, 1912; three editorial headings omitted.
  [5] There is a WWhw outline of this address, with the composition date of April 9, 1912, in WP, DLC.

A News Report About Wilson's Arrival in Pittsburgh

[April 11, 1912]

WILSON'S FRIENDS VERY CONFIDENT

Meet Governor at Reception and Many Predict His Triumph at Polls.

The arrival of Governor Woodrow Wilson in the Pittsburgh & Lake Erie depot on the Southside at 4 o'clock yesterday afternoon was the occasion for a display of hearty good-will on the part of a considerable number of Pittsburghers assembled. During more than three hours which he spent at the Fort Pitt hotel previous to the great mass meeting of that night the same desire to speed him on his way toward a presidential nomination was in evidence.

The train which brought Governor Wilson and his party from Buffalo was on time, pulling into the Lake Erie train sheds at 4 o'clock. Samuel J. Graham and Joseph F. Guffey[1] had accompanied the party from Buffalo. . . . The train was heavily loaded and many of the disembarking passengers waited in the train sheds and joined with others in cheering and greeting the candidate and his party as they passed through on their way to a line of waiting automobiles in front of the depot.

No time was afforded for street demonstrations, the party proceeding rather hurriedly to the Fort Pitt hotel, where a reception, to permit the supporters of Governor Wilson in this and adjoining counties to meet him, had been arranged to begin at 4:30 o'clock. The reception took place in the big English room of the hotel, where for an hour and a half the leadership of the Democracy of Western Pennsylvania streamed in and out giving and receiving a word of pleasant greeting from the leader and exchanging with each other cheering expressions of confidence in the outcome next November.

Charles A. Fagan[2] and Joseph F. Guffey took turns in introducing those who came to the candidate. . . . There were a number of ladies among Governor Wilson's callers and he had at least one narrow escape from capture by the suffragettes. Miss Mary Bakewell[3] came in, accompanied by one of her lieutenants, and proceeding straight to where Governor Wilson was standing, asked for a declaration of his position on the equal franchise question. He pondered a minute and then replied that he had not fully considered it and must ask to be excused from making a positive answer. Miss Bakewell suggested that he lay jokes aside and come to the point. To this Governor Wilson replied:

"I spoke in all sincerity. It is a big question and I am only about half way through it. My mind works somewhat slowly and on this subject I really have not come to any conclusion."

The suffrage leader found it impossible to either argue the matter or be displeased. She and her companion departed apparently impressed with Governor Wilson's courtesy and with his ability to meet difficult situations. With equal tact he handled a number of Democrats present who were not his supporters but who shook his hand with as much apparent good will as those who came to pledge support to the finish. Near the close of his afternoon of neighborliness with the Democrats of Western Pennsylvania, Governor Wilson said to a representative of The Post:

"I am highly encouraged by the reception I have met in Pittsburgh and Western Pennsylvania on this trip. Of course I see only the outside of things, but it certainly appears that a great many Democrats wish me to believe that they are well disposed. It could not have any other effect than to give me the deepest gratification." . . .

Following the reception, Governor Wilson took a rest of about an hour in his room and then sat down to dinner with a small party of his supporters. . . .

After an hour spent at dinner, Governor Wilson and a party, composed for the most part of those who had shared his meal, repaired in automobiles to the Exposition music hall for last night's meeting. Previous to leaving the hotel, however, he was obliged to pause for a little time in the lobby and meet a number of his admirers who had failed to arrive during the afternoon.

Printed in the *Pittsburgh Post*, April 11, 1912; two editorial headings omitted.

1 Samuel Jordan Graham, lawyer of Pittsburgh, and Joseph Finch Guffey, Princeton 1894, general manager of the Philadelphia Co., a public utilities operating company of Pittsburgh. Both were leaders of the reform or "reorganizer" faction of the Pennsylvania Democracy.

2 Charles Aloysius Fagan, lawyer of Pittsburgh.

3 Mary Ella Bakewell, secretary of the Free Kindergarten Association of Pittsburgh. She later claimed that she afterward served as the rector of a small Episcopal church in the Far West. Mary E. Bakewell, *What Woman is Here?* (New York, 1949), pp. 12-13.

A News Report of an Address in Pittsburgh

[April 11, 1912]

WILSON AN ECHO OF TEDDY

New Jersey Governor in Many Respects Seems to Repeat Roosevelt Speech

There were sentences of Governor Woodrow Wilson's speech at Exposition Music Hall last night that sounded like echoes of former President Roosevelt's speech that had been hiding in the nooks and crannies of the big hall for 24 hours. There was a remarkable similarity in the two speeches demanding that "big business" should take its hands off politics, that the Government is not to blame for the wave of discontent that is sweeping the country, but the men who are administering the Government and the forces back of them.

Governor Wilson's first political address in Pittsburg was impressive. He spoke deliberately, forcefully, academically. The music hall was full of people, and they listened attentively, though some of his logic seemed to be over the heads of his hearers. When he fell back into his friendly, conversational style and hit a climax, the crowd was quite as enthusiastic as when the band played "Dixie." In his scholarly manner he showed a keen sense of wit that was pleasing. Had it not been for the great outpouring to hear Colonel Roosevelt on the previous evening, the Wilson meeting would go down into local political history as a big one, for though he addressed but one audience, it was a good sized one, and included hundreds of Democrats from the surrounding counties, who paid their respects to the candidate at a public reception tendered him at his hotel shortly after his arrival here. . . .

Governor Wilson's speech at Exposition hall last night follows in part:

Mr. Chairman,[1] Ladies and Gentlemen—It is a great privilege for me to stand before this great company of my neighbors of Pennsylvania and enjoy expounding some of the things which engage our common thought. I know that it is not any reputation of mine that has drawn this great company together, neither is it any mere curiosity that has brought them to this place. Certainly I have no pretensions to personal beauty that would entitle me to be looked at by such an audience.

I know that you must think that there is something inside of me which is worth sampling; and I have thought in recent months that it would not be a bad plan, at any rate, for our Republican friends to adopt some of the practices prescribed under the pure food law, because the mere label, "Republican," does not now "display the contents," and it would be just as well to have a sworn to and guaranteed analysis of what the package contains; because I have been very much surprised in sampling the contents of the minds of some of my Republican friends to find very little difference between their contents and what I supposed my own think-box to contain.

I have urged a great many of my Republican friends to consider very seriously the question whether they could not be accused of lurking in a masquerade, because Republicans are

[1] David Thompson Watson, lawyer of Pittsburgh, participant in several important antitrust cases and a counsel for the United States in the Alaskan boundary dispute with Great Britain in 1903.

showing many signs of awakening intelligence, and I cannot
help suspecting that there are a great many Republicans present
here tonight who are drawn here by the desire to be converted.

There are a great many things, ladies and gentlemen, that
ought to be discussed in our day—with the greatest possible candor—at the same time that they ought to be treated with scru-
pulous fairness. It is the general impression that there are a
great many radicals, myself among the number, who are going
about the United States attacking somebody and something,
and I find the impression prevailing on the part of a great many
men—that what is being attacked is the Government—the form
of government under which we live, and that when we stop
talking about politics, we begin talking business, and so are
running amuck amid all the questions which concern the most
fundamental things of our life, our means of support and our
means of common activity.

Now, I want to ask you when you feel a discontent with the
politics you are living under and analyze the basis of your discontent, what is it that you find yourself discontented with—
with the Government, or with the way in which it is being conducted? Are you displeased with the operations of your institutions because there is some radical defect in them, or are you
displeased because somebody is making such mystery of them
that you feel that they are not being used as you had intended
that they should be.

It is particularly significant to me that tonight I stand in the
presence of a great body of Pennsylvanians. I have been near
neighbor to Pennsylvania a good many years. I am happy to
say that I enjoy the friendship and the confidence of a great
many thoughtful men in the great Commonwealth of Pennsylvania, and I am also happy in the thought that I have been able
to learn a great deal from them.

One of the things that I have learned is this: that there is
not any body of people in the United States more intelligent
or more intelligently set toward progress than the people of
Pennsylvania, and that the significant circumstance of our day
is that they are suddenly awakening to the fact that they have
been purposing and purposing and purposing these things, and
always being cheated, somehow, by somebody.

You are not unlike the people of New Jersey—I don't mean in
appearance—but in principle. The people of my own State for
years have been throwing themselves against bars in their effort to liberate themselves from conditions which they knew
to be intolerable, and again and again they have been disap-

pointed bitterly. They have voted every time they got a chance that they wanted certain policies carried out, and they have voted how they wished them carried out, according to the explicit platform promises of both the political parties; and, nevertheless, after the promising is over, and after the voting is over, nothing whatever ensues; and the people of New Jersey came at last to ask this question: Were they a self-governing Commonwealth? Were they in command of their own affairs? Did they have a representative government?

Nobody that I have met has any hard words against representative government, but everybody is raising this searching and fundamental question: Have we got representative government in all the States of this Union.

Have you had representative government in Pennsylvania? Not within my recollection. For half my lifetime I have known whom I ought to go to if I wanted anything done by the Legislature of Pennsylvania, and you have known whom you ought to go to if you wanted anything done by that Legislature. You know that it was not determined at the polls; you know that your resort was not to your fellow citizens, but that your resort was to a little group and sometimes to a single person, by whom the whole process of selecting your representatives and the whole process of using your representatives was determined.

This is not single to Pennsylvania. You need not suppose that you have been a unique bad example, because there have been a great many other cases. We had the same situation exactly in New Jersey. Why, it came to be a matter mentioned with a smile among newspaper man in New Jersey that New Jersey was under the care of a board of guardians.

Everybody knew who constituted the board of guardians. No one of them was a member of the Legislature. Most of them had not been elected to any office whatever, but throughout the legislative session they held weekly conferences in the State house in Trenton, and determined what should and what should not be done by the Legislature of New Jersey. Have you known nothing like that on this side of the border? And has it not been uttered as a reproach against you that you were living submissive, silent, contented, almost under an autocracy, of which you were perfectly clearly aware?

Very well then, I am happy to see the evident signs that the time is up, and that Pennsylvania has determined to get rid of this farce that has been enacted on her great soil.

We did get rid of it in New Jersey; not by any complicated process, merely by permitting the indiscretion from the political point of view of choosing a few men who knew what was going on and did not hesitate to talk about it. . . .

We are dissatisfied in this country because a small number of persons are running our politics and a relatively small number of persons are running our business. For instance, your banks here in Pittsburg carry only enough money to meet the demands of your wonderful payrolls. The rest of it is sent to New York for investment and the inauguration of new enterprises. If you want to start anything you must go to New York for the money, and it is unfortunately true that you have to consult a remarkably few persons.

Truly we are at the point of infinite danger that will not have passed until we have broken up these circles that bind and hamper us and are responsible for the discontent that is abroad.

This is only a preliminary campaign in which an individual, like myself, is unimportant. The question is whether the people are going to nominate and elect their President, or whether the politicians are to make the choice. There is no use discussing the tariff, the trusts or other questions they would have us consider, until we have decided this one important one. Are the conventions to be held at Baltimore and Chicago to give us the popular choice, or are they to be made by the messengers sent there by the cliques, after deals and intrigues? . . .

If the nominations are to be made that way it would be better to adjourn for four years, for, thank God, these will be the last conventions of their kind. I solemnly believe that within the next four years every State in the Union will have adopted the preferential primary system—that the people will have insisted upon and received it. . . .

In conclusion the Jersey Governor expressed the belief that "we are on the eve of a new age of creative politics" and retired amid great applause.[2]

Printed in the *Pittsburg Dispatch*, April 11, 1912; many editorial headings omitted.

[2] There is a WWhw outline of this address, with the composition date of April 10, 1912, in WP, DLC.

To Alexander Mitchell Palmer

My dear Mr. Palmer: Trenton, N. J. April 11, 1912.

Thank you for your letter of April fifth.[1] I quite understood the circumstances which kept you away from the meeting in

Washington.[2] As the papers will have informed you, I spoke in Pittsburgh last night and had a very gratifying reception from a splendid audience. I feel a good deal cheered by what my friends there told me of the situation and I am looking forward with a certain amount of confidence to results next Saturday. Whatever may happen, however, I am quite confident that every honorable effort has been made by you and my other Pennsylvania friends in my behalf.

Cordially yours,   Woodrow Wilson

TLS (WP, DLC).
  [1] It is missing.
  [2] That is, Wilson's conference with his supporters in Washington on April 4.

A Veto Message

To the House of Assembly: [Trenton, N. J.] April 11th, 1912.

I take the liberty of returning, without my signature, Assembly Committee Substitute for Senate Committee Substitute for Senate Bill No. 14, entitled "An act to amend an act entitled 'An act concerning public utilities; to create a Board of Public Utility Commissioners and to prescribe its duties and powers,' approved April twenty-first, one thousand nine hundred and eleven, by adding a section concerning the safeguarding and removal of railroad crossings and the payment of the cost thereof."

I know the seriousness and great consequence of the question affected by this important measure. There is a demand, well grounded and imperative, throughout the State that some practicable legislation should be adopted whereby the grade crossings of railways which everywhere threaten life and interfere with the convenience of both city and rural communities, should as rapidly as possible be abolished. But there is certainly not a demand in New Jersey for legislation which is unjust and impracticable.

The first part of this bill,[1] which provides for the handling of this difficult question of the elimination of grade crossings by the Board of Public Utility Commissioners, is excellent both in method and in purpose and suggests a way by which the whole matter can be successfully handled; but that portion of the bill which arbitrarily provides that every railroad of the State shall every year eliminate at least one grade crossing on its line for every thirty miles of its whole extent, the commission to determine which crossings shall be dealt with first, seeks to accomplish an impossible thing. It is not possible thus to lay down a hard and fast rule, and enforce it without a likelihood of bringing on conditions under which the whole undertaking would break down and result in utter disappointment.

The circumstances which surround this problem are not the same for any two railways of the State, but what might be a reasonable enough requirement for one of the railway systems of the State might be a very unreasonable requirement for another, leading to an impossible situation and breakdown of the law, and that is certainly not the purpose of the people of this State. The bill does not forbid the creation of new grade crossings, neither does it attempt any classification of those already in existence. I take the liberty of quoting the following from the "Comments of the Board of Public Utility Commissioners on Grade Crossings," in the report of the Board for the year 1911:

"After a classification of crossings has been made on the basis of the relative danger they create, there arises the engineering problem of the cost of elimination. This will, of course, vary widely in different localities. It is equally true that a great difference exists in the financial ability of the different carriers to provide funds for defraying the requisite expense. This is wholly apart from the question whether the carriers, including trolley companies, are to be required to bear the whole cost or only part thereof. Moreover, many other factors enter to complicate the matter. The elimination of grade crossings may adversely affect adjacent property. If, for example, tracks are elevated in eliminating a crossing at grade so as to transform a street into a blind alley, the loss of immediate accessibility may result in depreciating the property on the street in question. Similarly the construction work might often require a relocation of sewers or pipe system to the financial detriment of a municipality, a public utility or an individual. These things tend to increase the cost of grade-crossing elimination, which, as a State-wide proposition, must be very great."

This quotation makes very clear the possible complexity and engineering difficulty of the whole matter.

What is needed is an adequate enlargement of the powers of the Board of Public Utility Commissioners. The Board can be empowered, and should be empowered, to push the elimination of such crossings as fast as it is possible to push it without bringing hopeless embarrassment upon the railways. The law could easily establish a principle by which it might be determined when it was equitable that the several communities affected should participate in the expense, and to what extent, if any, they should participate. In this way all the results that could possibly be attained by the present bill would be attained without the risk and perhaps the discouragement and discredit of attempting a thing, in itself inequitable and impracticable.

The non-enactment of this bill into law will, of course, be a serious disappointment to the people of the State, but it will only concentrate their attention upon the just and equitable way of accomplishing the end in view. I do not believe that the people of the State are in such haste as to be willing to work a gross injustice, either to the railroads or to private owners of property or to the several communities affected.

Respectfully,   Woodrow Wilson, Governor.

Printed in the *Minutes of the N. J. House of Assembly, 1912*, pp. 1518-20.

1 The history of the grade crossing bill subsequent to its passage by the Assembly on March 27, 1912, and the Senate on the following day, is almost as complex as its title. By error Wilson first sent the above veto message, *mutatis mutandis*, to the Senate on April 2. Republican leaders immediately claimed that the bill had become law because Wilson had not returned it to the Assembly, the house of its origin, within the five days (excluding Sunday) which the constitution allowed the governor for consideration of bills. However, Attorney General Edmund Wilson, in an opinion handed down on April 11, called attention to the further proviso of the constitution that a bill not returned within five days became a law "unless the legislature by their adjournment prevent its return, in which case it shall not be a law." He ruled that the two houses, by adjourning from March 29 to April 10, had brought this proviso into play and, hence, that Wilson could still send this veto message to the Assembly at any time up to and including April 15, 1912 (*Journal of the Senate of N. J., 1912*, pp. 1022-1025). Wilson withdrew the message from the Senate and sent it to the Assembly on April 11.

The Assembly, by a resolution adopted on April 16, avowed its belief that the bill was already law. However, "to avoid if possible unnecessary technical legal questions," it repassed the bill by a vote of thirty-three to eighteen (*Minutes of the N. J. House of Assembly, 1912*, pp. 1544-46). The Senate upheld Wilson's veto on April 16 by a vote of nine to six (*Journal of the Senate of N. J., 1912*, p. 1066). Thereupon, the Assembly, in a final burst of bravura, resolved that its clerk should file the bill with the Secretary of State, "as the same is now a law" (*Minutes of the N. J. House of Assembly, 1912*, p. 1566). This was done and the document, together with several "jurats" explaining its tangled history, is printed as Chapter 412 of the *Laws of New Jersey, 1912*.

Cooler heads subsequently prevailed, and no effort was made to implement this "law." A revised version of the grade crossing bill, one embodying Wilson's recommendations, was passed by the legislature in 1913 (*Laws of New Jersey, 1913*, Chap. 57).

A News Report

[April 12, 1912]

FORTY VETOES START FIGHT

Republican Members of Legislature Bitterly Attack Governor.

HIS STINGING REPLY

Nearly a Riot in Yesterday's House Session—Sergeant-at-Arms Was Called Upon to Restore Order.

That 42 vetoes in one bunch was too much for the equanimity of even a conservative Legislature became apparent yesterday morning when, soon after the opening of the sessions in Senate and House, a storm of partisanship broke loose, and Republicans and Democrats soon found themselves arrayed against each other in the bitterest controversy of the session.

The Republican members of the Legislature produced a statement in which they set forth their views of the Governor's action in vetoing the forty-odd bills. . . . Further fuel for the flames was contained in a petition from the Board of Trade, of Paterson, in which the Governor was attacked for his veto of the grade crossing elimination bill. This petition, which asked for the passage of the bill over the Governor's veto, was extremely uncomplimentary to the Chief Executive,[1] and its reading brought forth a storm of protest from the Democratic members. For many minutes during the reading of this petition the House of Assembly was in an uproar. Assemblyman Taylor[2] characterized the communication as "dirty and contemptible." Assemblymen Davidson and Donnelly[3] expressed their minds in a similar strain.

[1] The petition was actually a letter (it is spread upon the *Minutes of the N. J. House of Assembly, 1912*, pp. 1486-87) from the Paterson Board of Trade signed by its president, George Arnold, and dated April 10, 1912. The most accusatory part was the second paragraph:

"The Board of Trade of Paterson has been a strong advocate of grade crossing separation legislation, and it regrets that after the passage of the bill that would insure mandatory relief that Governor Wilson departed from the usual course heretofore practiced by Governors of the State, to give a hearing on important legislation upon intimation that their intention was to go contrary to the action of the Legislature. The Board of Trade believes it is unfortunate that the demands made on the Governor's time very recently, outside of New Jersey, made it impossible for him to arrange a hearing on this important measure, for his veto would appear to indicate that he had no time to familiarize himself with the provisions of the proposed act as he says it is unfair in a particular which it lacks, while the truth of the matter is the Public Utilities Commission already has the power which Governor Wilson says it ought to have under this bill. This alludes, of course, to the establishment of new railroad grade crossings."

[2] Leon R. Taylor of Asbury Park.

[3] William Stewart Davidson and Thomas Marcus Donnelly, both of Jersey City.

Wilson in Governor's office, Trenton

Wilson and William Frank McCombs

William Randolph Hearst

William Gibbs McAdoo

Francis Griffith Newlands

Willard Saulsbury

Judson Harmon

Oscar Wilder Underwood

Champ Clark

William Jennings Bryan

Convention Hall, Baltimore

Wilson greeting visitors at Sea Girt, New Jersey

Attempting to still the uproar, Speaker McCran[4] beat a thunderous tattoo with his gavel, but the row continued until the speaker at last called upon the sergeant-at-arms to compel the three Democratic Assemblymen to take their seats.

Feeling ran high all through the morning session. The Democratic members charged Speaker McCran with having a hand in the preparation of the Paterson communication, and did not hesitate to express their displeasure.

Later in the day Governor Wilson made public his position in the controversy in a formal statement. . . .

The statement of the Republican legislators follows:

"The veto messages transmitted to the Legislature by Governor Wilson, taken as an entirety, demonstrate such a deplorable lack of study of many of the measures that it brings prominently into light a situation, covering which we believe a public statement should be made.

"The Legislature has no desire to pass measures over the Governor's veto simply because it is of opposite political complexion, but the office of a veto, as defined in the constitution, is to call attention to objections to proposed legislation, that a reconsideration may be had. Of necessity, this means specific objections, founded in fact, in order that the re-examination may be intelligent.

"It is a plain case. In passing upon the legislation recently submitted to him, the Governor has not performed this duty. Many of the measures were important, all were entitled to careful study. Given 10 days in which to do the work, the duty was met by crowding the work of 10 days into two, approving ninety-odd measures and vetoing 38, and then hurrying from the State.

"During the session, aside from general recommendations in the annual message, a special message urg[ing] the adoption of the Federal income tax, and a message just received requesting the continuance of the employment of the railroad valuation expert,[5] not a single policy has been submitted or suggestion made to the Legislature, looking to the good of the State. The initiative throughout has been with the Legislature.

"The crudity of the recent veto messages is illustrated by the following cases:

"Senate 306—The reapportionment bill. This is vetoed with the general statement that it is a gerrymander. Not a single specific defect is pointed out.

[4] Thomas Francis McCran of Paterson.

[5] This message was not printed in either the House or Senate Journal, and the New Jersey newspapers are silent about it.

"House 678—The incidental bill. Dismissed as extravagant. Not a single item is pointed out as extravagant.

"Senate 14—the grade crossing bill. Objected to because not forbidding the creation of new crossings—the fact being that a law containing such a prohibition, signed by the Governor last year, is already upon the statute books[6]; objected to further as 'unjust and impracticable,' without stating why, though hints are given that different roads should be differently treated, which would make the law invalid, and that the expense should be apportioned, which would be a violation of party pledges and of the Governor's personal pre-election promises.

"Senate 285—The trackless trolley bill. Three 'fatal defects' are alleged—that the bill gives franchises for 100 years without consideration, that it gives the power of condemnation, and permits mergers and consolidations.

"The fact is, the bill gives no franchises at all.[7] Under the constitution, general laws must be passed upon such subjects, under which specific companies may incorporate. Senate 285 is such a general act, and the three 'fatal objections' are in substance the same powers contained in similar general statutes.

"Senate 224—The bi-partisan prison board. Objected to as creating a political agency.

"The fact is, the Governor sought by nominations submitted to make the board political, and the bill was passed to prevent this and keep the board bi-partisan.

"Senate 229, permitting a judge to extend the time to file statements of that year's election expenses. Objected to as mandatory when it should be permissive. The fact is, the bill is permissive and is not mandatory.[8]

"Senate 276, vetoed because it created an additional office and increases the burden of taxation. The fact is, the bill simply gives more work to one already in office without any additional compensation.[9]

[6] The act creating the Board of Public Utilities Commissioners included a provision stating that no new grade crossings could be created without the board's permission. See Chap. 195, Sect. 21, *Laws of New Jersey, 1911*.

[7] This was sheer obscurantism. Wilson's veto of Senate Bill 285, printed at April 2, 1912, did not imply that it granted specific franchises or that it was not intended to be a general act. As n. 1 to Wilson's veto states, the Senate repassed the bill on April 11, but the Assembly failed to act upon it before it adjourned.

[8] This statement was correct. Chapter 403, *Laws of New Jersey, 1912*, stipulated that the judge, after hearing all the evidence, *might* issue an order permitting the late filing of a statement of expenses.

[9] This statement was correct. The law contained a specific proviso that "the person so designated shall not be entitled to any extra compensation for his services." *Laws of New Jersey, 1912*, Chap. 409.

"Assembly 309, the indeterminate sentence bill. Objected to because it cuts down sentences to one-half. The fact is that the bill as passed distinctly reads 'two-thirds,' demonstrating that the bill has not been read.[10]

"The above enumeration is sufficient to show the general character of the vetoes. Had the time-honored custom been observed, of conferring in each case, instead of occasionally, with the introducers of bills before veto, many of the blunders the Governor has made would have been avoided.

"This statement is issued because the inaccurate work of the Governor, his failure to give the requisite time to and properly perform his constitutional duties, has reflected upon the Legislature and embarrassed it in the performance of its duties."

The statement of Governor Wilson, in reply to the foregoing, is as follows:

"Ordinarily I would remain entirely silent under partisan attacks of this kind, but feel that it is due to the people of the State that I should speak my very emphatic protest against an uncalled for grossly discourteous attack upon my official career, proceeding as a manifesto from a conference of Republican members of the legislature.

"Of my vetoes, I shall say nothing. They speak for themselves and are justified by the bills against which they were uttered. But the statement that I have by frequent absences from the State in any degree neglected my duties as Governor, is absolutely false. No important matter of business has been allowed to fall in arrears in my office. Every bill has been read and acted upon within the time prescribed by the constitution. I have been absent from the State only two of the session days of the legislature.

"Not ten days, but five days only,[11] under the explicit prescription of the constitution, were available for the consideration of the more than one hundred and fifty bills which were sent to my office just before the temporary adjournment of the legislature on the 29th day of March. I devoted to these bills the full five days allowed me. They received my careful attention. The legislature had, by deliberate arrangement of its Republican lead-

10 The Republican leaders misunderstood Wilson's veto of Assembly Bill 309 (printed at April 2, 1912). What he meant, but did not say clearly enough, was that the stipulated reduction in sentences plus the commutation time already coming to prisoners would have the effect of cutting their sentences in half.

11 Wilson wrote this before reading the Attorney General's opinion of April 11, 1912.

ers, determined to reassemble the following week, so that I was not permitted, under the constitutional provision, to take more time than I did take in the consideration of the bills.

"It is a noteworthy circumstance that, although a great many of the important measures sent me at the end of the session were introduced early in the session, they were delayed in their passage until the very end. The bills that came to me while the session lasted were for the most part of an incidental and trivial importance. Almost all the bills of capital consequence were reserved until the last. Among these none were more conspicuous than those which attempted to break down at one point or another the best legislation of the session of 1911, to the maintenance of which both parties were explicitly pledged in the campaign of the autumn of 1911. Bill after bill was introduced to weaken the force of the corrupt practices act and of the Geran act. This, that and the other door of loose practice was deliberately opened. It was my duty to stand guard against these things, and I have done so. Against the bills to this effect which have been passed over my veto, I wish to utter my earnest protest in the name not only of party obligation—an obligation fairly resting upon both parties—but in the name of the people of the State. The session has been fruitful of nothing so much as of legislation tending to impair rather than to increase the efficiency of the laws of the State.

"In my annual message I called attention to the great matters to which I understood both parties to be committed. I did not deem it wise or courteous to avow, as the session advanced, by repeated messages, my fear that these matters were to be neglected, and that the whole force of the session was to be spent upon measures of another sort and of questionable expediency. If the session has been barren and disappointing, as it has been, the people of the State will know where to bestow the blame. It is not yet too late to retrieve the record, if the Republican leaders are themselves aware of the failure. It might reassure the voters of the State to see them turn anew to the task in a new spirit. I am at their service."

Printed in the Trenton *True American*, April 12, 1912.

To Mary Allen Hulbert Peck

Dearest Friend,
The Waldorf-Astoria New York.
13 April, 1912

Here I am in New York the day you sail from Bermuda, and the day you arrive here I shall be on my way down to campaign in Georgia. What hard luck!

Your recent notes have made me deeply uneasy. They indicated illness without telling me anything about it that my mind could take hold of,—and so my apprehensions have wandered over many sad fields of anxious conjecture. I comfort myself as best I *can* by saying to myself that I understand,—that it is all due to the nervous apprehension of what you have to go through, —your whole nature turning back from it as from the culmination—and the open culmination at that—of all that has made you miserable and at odds with the world and with yourself these twenty long years,—and that when it is all over the great and happy reaction will come, as I have tried to expound to you a score of times. God send it may be so! You are entitled to happiness along with your freedom now!

This is just a message of welcome and cheer—from all of us. Since it cannot be delivered in person, it must be sent as it is, in all its inadequacy. Even a friend's handwriting may seem like a greeting,—like a reminder of the manner and the voice,— and you know with what heartiness this greeting comes. Welcome back! Welcome to the home and the new environment you *are to make* for Mrs. Allen, for Allen, and for yourself, in whom their happiness centres. I shall be gone a whole week; but we would be very grateful for a memorandum of your movements, so that we may keep in touch with you. I am here to attend a big banquet to-night and go down to Princeton early to-morrow (Sunday) forenoon.

Your devoted friend   Woodrow Wilson

ALS (WP, DLC).

From Willard Saulsbury

Dear Governor: [Wilmington, Del.] April 13th, 1912.

I send you a copy of a letter I have just written to Sir Wilfrid Laurier[1] which please destroy after you have read it.[2] It explains the reason for my writing him and I hope I may be able to get something from him or through him from some prominent Canadian Liberal. I send you the letter because some inquiry may be made as to the good faith of the request, as probably Sir Wilfrid does not know me or remember me sufficiently well to be certain I am not trying to get some embarrassing statement from him.

I think the result in Pennsylvania[3] will help us greatly.

I am endeavoring to hold our friends in Illinois and Kentucky who are connected with the mechanical end of politics and I hope Mr. McCombs and I will be able to develop something in Washington, where I expect to meet him to-morrow. It may interest you to know that I think I have the Porto Rico Delegates absolutely nailed down, details of which I will give you when I see you.   Yours very truly,   Willard Saulsbury

TLS Saulsbury Letterpress Books, DeU).
[1] Prime Minister of Canada, 1896-1911, at this time leader of the Liberal party in opposition.
[2] W. Saulsbury to W. Laurier, April 13, 1912, TLS (Saulsbury Letterpress Books, DeU). The object of this letter was to secure from "some high Canadian official or exofficial" a statement regarding Champ Clark's indiscreet remarks on the annexation of Canada during the congressional debates over reciprocity, with a view to showing the Speaker's unfitness for the presidency. For the reciprocity question and a sample of Clark's remarks, see WW to Mary A. H. Peck, March 5, 1911, n. 3, Vol. 22.
[3] The results of the Democratic presidential primary in Pennsylvania on April 13 were Wilson, 97,585 votes; Clark, 710; Harmon, 394; unpledged, 53,953. At least forty of the sixty-four delegates elected were Wilson men. Twelve more pro-Wilson at-large delegates were named by the state convention in May. See A. M. Palmer to WW, May 11, 1912.

A News Report

[April 14, 1912]

TARIFF REFORM THE KEYNOTE AT JEFFERSON DINNER

Honoring Thomas Jefferson and reavowing the principles on which he founded the Democratic party, five hundred prominent Democrats gathered at the annual Jefferson Day dinner of the National Democratic Club at the Waldorf-Astoria last night and heard party leaders of national eminence lay down the lines upon which the forthcoming Presidential campaign shall be fought.

Tariff reform is to be the paramount issue. This was made clear in speeches delivered by William J. Bryan, Senator James A. O'Gorman, Gov. Woodrow Wilson of New Jersey, Mayor Gaynor and Gov. Dix. The latter, in fact, spoke almost entirely on this subject, while Senator O'Gorman bitterly arraigned President Taft's tariff policy, declared that the Republican party was split in two and that the people were tired of broken Republican promises. . . .

Gov. Wilson of New Jersey, speaking to the toast, "What Would Jefferson Do?" spoke first of the difference in the circumstances that exist to-day and those of Jefferson's time; then paid a glowing tribute to the writer of the Declaration of Independence, and declared that had Jefferson lived to-day he would, with his clear-sightedness, have acted on the facts as they actually are; therefore, to determine what Jefferson would have done, it is necessary to find out what the facts are. He continued:

"Monopoly, private control, the authority of privilege, the concealed mastery of a few men, cunning enough to rule without showing their power—he would have at once pronounced the rank weeds which are sure to choke out all wholesome life in the fair garden of affairs. He would have moved against them, sometimes directly, sometimes indirectly, sometimes openly, sometimes subtly; but whether he merely mined about them, or struck directly at them, he would have set systematic war against them at the front of all his purpose.

"As regards the economic policy of the country it is perfectly plain that Mr. Jefferson would have insisted upon a tariff fitted to actual conditions, by which he would have meant not the interests of the few men who find access to the hearings of the Ways and Means Committee of the House and the Finance Committee of the Senate, but the interests of the business men and manufacturers and farmers and workers and professional men of every kind and class. He would have insisted that the schedules should be turned wrong side out and every item of their contents subjected to the general scrutiny of all concerned.

"It is plain, also, that he would have insisted upon a currency system elastic indeed and suited to the varying circumstances of the money market in a great industrial and trading nation, but absolutely fortified and secured against a central control, the influence of coteries and leagues of banks to which it is now in constant danger of being subjected. He would have known that the currency question is not only an economic question but a political question, and that, above all things else, control must be in the hands of those who represent the general interest and not in the hands of those who represent the things we are seeking to guard against.

"In the general field of business his thought would, of course, have gone about to establish freedom, to throw business opportunity open at every point to new men, to destroy the processes of monopoly, to exclude the poison of special favors, to see that, whether big or little, business was not dominated by anything but the law itself, and that that law was made in the interest of plain, unprivileged men everywhere.

"Constitutions are not inventions. They do not create our liberty. They are rooted in life, in fact, in circumstances, in environment. They are not the condition of our liberty, but its expression. They result from our life: they do not create it. And so there beats in them always, if they live at all, this pulse of the large life of humanity. As they yield an answer to that they are perfected and exalted."[1]

Printed in the New York *World*, April 14, 1912.
[1] These paragraphs are taken from Wilson's advance text, which was published in the *Cong. Record*, 62nd Cong., 2nd sess., Vol. 48, pp. 4747-48. There is no record of what Wilson actually said. There is a WWhw outline of this address, dated April 13, 1912, in WP, DLC.

From Edward Mandell House

My dear Governor Wilson: New York. April 14th, 1912.

Will you not lunch or dine with me some day next week?

I have had a talk with Mr. Bryan and I am to breakfast with him Sunday the 20th, and it is important that I talk with you before that time.

I want to again thank you for the pleasure you gave us last night.

If your voice could reach the people they would do the rest.

Faithfully yours,   [E. M. House]

TCL (E. M. House Papers, CtY).

From Henry Skillman Breckinridge

My dear Governor Wilson: Lexington, Ky., April 16, 1912.

For once I can sing with perfect sincerity "Hail, Hail Pennsylvania."

I have not been writing lately as it wastes both your time and mine. We have been doing our best with the means at our disposal,—travelling around making speeches and organizing Wilson clubs.

The pronouncement of Ollie James for Champ Clark[1] has caused a considerable defection, but I think it will be impossible for the Clark forces to instruct Kentucky for the Speaker, as the movement is merely a political play of local politicians to wrest control of the State organization.[2] The State Administration stands for an uninstructed delegation and will fight the Clark instruction to the bitter end. What I look for in the State Convention is that the Wilson forces will hold the balance of power and that the State Administration will have to come to us to carry through their plan with regard to local matters. It looks as if we now control the Second and Eleventh Congressional Districts with a good strong hold on the Sixth, Seventh, Eighth and Tenth. If we carry these Districts solid we can control the convention. We are working every minute, sending speakers where ever possible. I have just come back from the county-seat of Scott County where I addressed an organization meeting of the Woodrow Wilson Club, and Judge Samuel M. Wilson[3] is at this moment in Danville for the same purpose.

I am confident that you will be the next President of the United States, and you may rest assured that no stone will be left unturned in your interest in Kentucky.

   With great respect,

                Faithfully yours,   Henry S. Breckinridge.

TLS (Governors' Files, Nj).
  [1] Representative (and Senator-elect) Ollie Murray James joined several other Democratic congressmen from Kentucky in coming out for Clark on April 5, 1912. James became state chairman of the Clark campaign.
  [2] The Democratic preconvention contest in Kentucky was badly entangled with state politics, in particular the running controversy over the liquor question. The faction in control of the state Democratic organization, headed by former Governor John Crepps Wickliffe Beckham, favored local option, while a rival faction, headed by Henry Watterson, advocated a hands-off policy. The former supported Wilson, for the most part; the latter, Clark. See Arthur S. Link, "The South and the Democratic Campaign of 1910-1912" (Ph.D. dissertation, University of North Carolina, 1945), Chap. xvii.
  [3] Samuel Mackay Wilson, lawyer of Lexington, who served many times as special judge of various circuit courts in Kentucky.

A News Report of a Reception in Gainesville, Georgia

[April 17, 1912]

WOODROW WILSON RECEIVES WELCOME
TO GEORGIA HOME

By W. T. Waters, Jr.

At Gainesville, Tuesday afternoon, the first real Georgia ovation awaited Governor Wilson. . . . It was at Gainesville that Mrs. Wilson vied with her distinguished husband in the popular eye. She was besieged by ladies, and numbers of bouquets were sent aboard to her and delivered on behalf of Georgia women, after the train had gone on its way. . . .

From Gainesville to Atlanta the ride was in the hands of Governor Wilson's numerous friends from Atlanta and other parts of Georgia, who crowded aboard the train at Gainesville and practically assumed possession of it.

The party all had supper in the dining car.

The train arrived in Atlanta at 7:30 o'clock.

Following was Governor Wilson's speech at Gainesville:

"I am very sorry that our train was so much delayed that I could not have the pleasure of greeting my friends in north Georgia at the time appointed. I suppose that is another illustration of the way the trains interfere with politics. (Laughter.)

"I very much wanted to speak a few minutes at Gainesville because I have many delightful memories connected with this place. This happens to be the birthplace of two of my daughters,[1] and I wonder if there is some gentleman here who will be kind enough to send a telegram to my daughters—collect["] (Laughter). (A telegraph messenger was called and dispatched.)

Just at this moment a flash light picture of the governor was taken, following which he said:

"Now, I will try and turn myself inside out and show you what is inside of me as well as what is outside." Then he continued:

"It seems to me that an occasion like this is important because we are in the presence of very great changes in this country. It seems to me that the great force, the primeval power of the south is going to be put into politics again with the accession of the Democratic party to the control of the government of the United States.

"I suppose that there is no serious doubt but that the Democratic party will win in the approaching campaign, and with the winning of the control of the government by the party there will be added to the councils of the nation, as they have not been added in many years, all the thoughtfulness, all the reserve power that there is in this great southern country. Because I believe that no part of the country has preserved its force in greater purity than this southern part. I mean that we have stood off by not taking part in the affairs of the nation. We cannot take part without being concerned in these things we are trying to remedy. In many parts of our country generally the government of our states, and in some degree the government of the United States, has fallen into the control of small groups of interested men, but now I believe the control of our affairs is to come again into the possession of the people in general, and that what is done will be for the common interest.

"The south has not hitherto participated in the government of the nation as its wealth and greatness have entitled it to take part, but I believe that time has passed and that it will now rise to the full measure of its responsibility and opportunity." (The train began moving and Governor Wilson's last remark expressed his regrets that he was not permitted to say more.)

Printed in the *Atlanta Journal*, April 17, 1912; one editorial heading omitted.
[1] That is, Margaret (in 1886) and Jessie Woodrow Wilson (in 1887).

A News Report of a Campaign Address in Atlanta

[April 17, 1912]

Wilson Is Choice of Georgia

OVER 7,000 HEARD HIM IN SPITE OF
HEAVY DOWNPOUR

While a remnant of the afternoon's downpour pattered on the roof and fell in a drizzle in the streets, the citizens of Atlanta and Georgia gathered in thousands at the auditorium Tuesday night to hail Woodrow Wilson as the next president of the United States. . . .

Judge George Hillyer, J. R. Smith,[1] and Senator Hoke Smith preceded Governor Wilson in addressing the large audience. . . .

Each speaker received the applause of the enthusiastic crowd, but the greeting to Governor Wilson and Senator Smith was particularly cordial. As they entered the hall, accompanied by an escort of prominent citizens, the band struck up "Dixie." The crowd rose as one man to its feet, and cheers filled the auditorium in wave after wave of sound. Throughout the address of both Governor Wilson and Senator Smith repeated applause marked their forceful expressions.

Applause, however, fully as enthusiastic, greeted Mrs. Wilson on her entrance into the auditorium. She arrived before her husband, and was escorted to a box near the platform. As she appeared, the band broke into the merry strains of "Dixie," and the audience rose eagerly to do her honor.

At the conclusion of Senator Hoke Smith's introductory speech, Governor Wilson, who received an ovattion almost unparalleled in Georgia, said:

Mr. Chairman,[2] and Fellow-Citizens of the Great State of Georgia:

I am very deeply honored by the reception you have so gra-

[1] Judge Hillyer, retired, had presided at Wilson's examination for admission to the bar in 1882 and signed his license to practice law; James R. Smith was a dry goods merchant and real estate dealer of Atlanta.
[2] That is, Judge Hillyer.

ciously given me. I could not help wishing, as Senator Smith drew to a conclusion of his remarks, that these interesting gentlemen whom we have just heard might do all the speaking, because they can commen[d] me to your favor very much better than I can commend myself. (Applause.)

It was particularly interesting and touching to me to find Judge Hillyer presiding here tonight. It was under him as judge that I was admitted to the bar of Georgia. (Applause.) And he was as kind and indulgent to me then as he has been tonight. I remember that when I came up before the court for an oral examination he assigned the duty of examining me to a young lawyer of that day who was, fortunately, a friend of mine,[3] and who, after asking me a few questions, which I readily answered, pumped at me a question in equity practice which I could not answer. I promptly said, realizing my helplessness at once, that I didn't know, and then Judge Hillyer showed how big a man he was. He said: 'Well, Mr. Gadsden, I am afraid the court itself couldn't answer that question.' (Great applause.) And I have felt a strong affection for Judge Hillyer ever since that moment.

My thoughts naturally, ladies and gentlemen, turn backward tonight because I remember with a great deal of pleasure the years that I spent in Georgia. I remember how I was stimulated by the already rapid growth of this great city at that time, and how Georgia then as before and since showed that extraordinary vitality which has given her a supremacy in this part of the south. And I remember a great many associations which are so private that probably it wouldn't be in good taste to me to recall them, but nevertheless which seem to lift me in spirit with this happy state, and yet I do not feel that I stand here tonight privileged to recall the past, but in duty bound to turn your face to the future.

There are reasons why I should prefer to turn away from the past in order to relieve myself of embarrassment. One of the speakers has said that there are a great many college men, Princeton men among them, here in Georgia who remember me in years gone by. Now those young gentlemen, some of them no longer as young as they were, remember me in a very intimate way and they have long been "on to my curves." (Laughter and applause.) . . . I feel that in the presence of these former college associates of mine the disguise of greatness may be all too apparent. And yet, after all, where could I look for greater indulgence than among my old friends and my old neighbors, and

---

[3] Edward Miles Gadsden.

what better sort of audience could I expect to address with the thoughts to which I wish to direct your attention tonight.

Ladies and gentlemen, the south has had very little direct share in the immediate past. There is a sense in which ever since the civil war the south has stood aside and looked at a development in which she took no guiding and leading part. I don't need to tell you that the south has felt a great industrial stimulation in the years that have intervened between us and the sad time of the civil war. But you know what the circumstances here for participation in the development of the nation have been.

You know that she has looked to another region of the country to send her the means by which she might dev[e]lop her own unexcelled resources and make use of her own neglected genius. And that while the rest of the country has guided and dominated in the industrial and economic development of the nation, she has only shared modestly upon a scale that did not compare with the scale upon which other regions of the country shared the common life, and that while there was a development going on in the north which was changing not only the whole economic aspect of affairs but the whole political aspect of affairs, the south held off. The south didn't take a leading and guiding part. So that there remained here in the south what I may call a great unexhausted reserve of unused thought, of unemployed power. Just as some of our great water courses for a long time did not drive the wheels of industry, so for a long time our own native genius did not touch the springs of enterprise except upon a local and limited scale. Now the south by that token is much more interested in the future than she is in the past. And what the south is now invited to do is to take her part and share in the things that this nation is henceforward to accomplish.

Senator Smith said to you, and said very truly, that the circumstances that some of us who have had to work in the northern states have had to deal with in the field of politics have not been duplicated in the south.

The state of Georgia, for example, has never been owned by the special interests, but the state of New Jersey has been owned by the special interests. The state of New Jersey has suffered for a generation under a reputation which her people did not deserve, all over the country. It has mortified those of us who lived in New Jersey that we should be looked upon as a state which nursed, originated, nurtured the trusts that were dominating the economic life of this country, and that New Jersey was content to be ridden by the power of the bosses.

New Jersey was no more content under those conditions than the most progressive people in the United States. But this was happening in New Jersey, that no matter how people voted, no matter which party they voted for, nothing was changed. The same men dominated, the same influences were in the saddle, and so, in a desperate moment, in a moment well-nigh reaching the point of despair, she turned to an humble schoolmaster and asked him if he could see any way out of the situation. (Applause.)

There were some gentlemen very accomplished in politics in the state of New Jersey who were foolish enough to advocate the nomination and election of that schoolmaster. (Applause.) I hope that they did not doubt his principles—I believe that they did not doubt his purposes. But they thought that he was so innocent and inexperienced a person that they could "get him," no matter what he tried to do. (Applause.)

I carefully and candidly explained to my fellow citizens that I wanted them to vote for me, if they did vote for me, with a full knowledge that I was a schoolmaster, and that a schoolmaster was a person who was trained to find out everything that he could and then tell everything that he knew. (Prolonged applause.) The most dangerous thing that could have happened to New Jersey at that time was to put anybody in that was accustomed to find out how things stood, and the next most dangerous was to find somebody so inveterately talkative that he would give it all away. (Laughter and applause.) And all that was necessary to do, in order to summon the people of New Jersey to the exercise of a novel supremacy, was to reveal everything that was going on at the state-house and everywhere else. . . .

Now, while these things have been going on, while states have been owned, in what direction has the thought of the people turned? You have heard a great deal about radicals and conservatives, you have heard about men who were standing pat in order to preserve those institutions.

What institutions were there to preserve in New Jersey, for example? There was no representative chamber there, there was no executive there who could be counted upon to guide the legislative chamber in the way of popular legislation, and the conditions in New Jersey were duplicated in every part of the country. Men, therefore, looked around for new instrumentalities. They said, "Here, right in front of us, is a jungle, with an infinite intricacy of coverts and marshes, and full of cunning beasts who inhabit the jungle. And there are only two things to do—either to burn the jungle down or else to fence it in and go around it.["] Now, I believe that the thing to do is to burn the jungle down. (Applause.) And the way to burn it down is to shed upon it that fulminating light of publicity which burns where it touches, which burns everything that is false, everything that is unfair, everything that is fraudulent and corrupt.

But if you won't apply fire, there is another thing that you may do. There are two words that send cold shivers down the backs of some people, but which are not calculated to chill the prudent, and those are the words, "Initiative" and "Referendum." You don't have to discuss initiative and referendum in Georgia, because, as I understand it, there is no jungle to burn down in this state. But suppose that you were convinced that you didn't have a representative chamber to pass legislation in accordance with your will; and suppose it were suggested to you that occasionally, when it was necessary, in order to bring these gentlemen to a realization of what the government consisted in, you should take legislation into your own hands. Would that be very shocking? Ah, gentlemen, the south is a conservative region; but the south has operated on the fundamental principles upon which these very measures rest.

I had the pleasure of speaking, not long ago, before my fellow citizens in the city of Richmond, Virginia.[4] I knew that Virginia was conservative—as Georgia is—and I took the liberty of asking how long since it was that they had thoughtfully read the great Virginia Declaration of Rights, written by George Mason, and the very soil out of which all of our declarations of rights sprang; and I took the liberty of reading some of the sentences from that great declaration to them. I wish that I carried those immortal sentences accurately in my memory—but I can only approach them.

One of the first principles laid down there is that all magistrates, all elected officers, are trustees of the people, at all times responsible to them. Does that sound as if the responsibility was confined to certain revolutions of the seasons when elections come around? At all times amenable to their direct responsibility to the people. In the next sentence it goes on to say that the people have established our governments in order to promote their own convenience, happiness and prosperity, and that whenever, in their judgment, those institutions do not promote these purposes they can alter or abolish them.

Did you ever hear any more radical doctrine than that? Now, we don't want to abolish things, we don't want radical altera-

4 This address is printed at Feb. 1, 1912.

tions, but we do want every public servant to realize that his masters are not private groups of special interests, but the great masses of the people, of the commonwealth of the nation. (Applause.)

This is a preliminary campaign. This is a campaign which has to do with the question who shall be chosen as the representatives and spokesmen of the people. During this campaign it is not worth your while to discuss the great economic problems now pressing upon America.

Why should you discuss the tariff until you know whose judgments are going to settle the tariff question?

Why should you discuss the trusts until you know what body of the nation is going to settle the question of how we are to deal with the trusts?

Don't you see that the fundamental question, the only question worth discussing, is whose government is this? For I tell you that for the last generation it has not been the government of the people. (Applause.)

When I look at the utterances of some of the most conspicuous Republican leaders, I read a very ominous thing in their utterances. I read that they hold that theory of government which is at the antipodes from the theory which can sustain a wholesome democracy. They maintain that only those are able to judge what will promote the prosperity of America who have the biggest material stake in that prosperity. And if you want to know how to govern America, you must resort to the men who are at the head of the great enterprises by which great fortunes have been accumulated here. I say that that is turning the whole doctrine of government upside down.

Who constitutes the strength of America? The little handful of men who have succeeded, the little body of men who have accumulated great fortunes and led in great enterprises? Are you going to fertilize the tree out of the blossoms and its fruits? Do you not know that you must fertilize and renew the tree out of its roots—out of the silent soil? Do you not know that the future of America rests not with the men who have succeeded, but with the men who are going to succeed? (Great applause.) And that no man can predict whence those sources of youth and renewal are going to be drawn? Does any man know where the leaders of the next generation are going to come from? Can you pick out the sort of house they are going to be born in? Do you know whether they are coming from the mines, or the farms, or the factories, or the palaces—or not? Do you not know that America has proved not only the virility, but the validity, of democracy, by opening wide all those avenues of success which are absolutely necessary for the stimulation of individual genius?

When I preach the doctrine of the rule of the people I repudiate absolutely the suggestion that there is any touch of the demagogue in the suggestion; because if I hadn't read history, I might dream of the leadership of a little coterie of men of specially trained genius. But I turn, with ever renewed admiration, to that great founder of the Democratic party, Thomas Jefferson, and remember that he, bred an aristocrat and scholar, and companion of men of learning; a man who loved to delve into the secrets of science and philosophy, nevertheless looked forth upon the masses of the people with that divination which is the divination of knowledge, knowing that out of these great masses of his fellow men were to come the hope and salvation of the great commonwealth with which he was connected. So that he wished every man to know that his fame was to be linked with the foundations of universities, with the carrying of learning to the people, with the cutting off of all class distinctions, with the philosophy that the government belongs to the great body of the people themselves.

Every thoughtful man, every man to whom the vision of humanity has been revealed, must hold this vital philosophy: He must know that these are the sources and these only are the sources of great power in politics.

Now the thought which is uppermost in my mind tonight is not the thought connected merely with this general setting forth of the conditions that obtain in our time. The fundamental thought, as I look into the faces of this company, is this: The south has been touched by the stimulation, but she has not been touched by the corruption of the age in which we live. (Applause.) Democratic victory will mean, no matter who the leader is—for I want you to know that my thoughts are not concentrated tonight upon myself—no matter who the leader is, the success of Democracy will mean what?

It will mean the enlistment for the first time in 16 years of scores of southern men in the service of the nation. It will mean that this quiet force, which has not been touched by some of the more baleful influences of our time, which has stood apart, which has kept deep-rooted its vital connection with the past, which has been sobered by some of the most tragical experiences that any nation can go through, is going to come forward to take council with regard to the future. And the future is not going to be like the past. . . .

That is the center of our whole situation as a nation. Those who control the great credits, those who control the great masses of capital in this country, constitute a little closed circle, and unless the laws and enterprise of this country can break that circle, we are enslaved, and the enterprise of any one man is checked and forbidden. No thoughtful man, no responsible man, has ever said that the business of this country was unsound. No such man has ever said that the business men of this country are dishonest. But many responsible persons have said, including the representatives of the government of the United States, in the papers they have filed in important suits, that the credits of the United States are being so controlled and concentrated that the business of this country is being dominated by small bodies of selfish men, and we have now to contrive a thoughtful policy and to contrive a government which will emancipate this country from private control, and put it back into the hands of the people. (Applause.)

This is the enterprise to which I, whether I occupy office or not, shall devote the rest of my life. (Applause.) I know how to find out what is going on. I know what is going on, and I mean to describe what is going on, not in order to upset or disturb or to throw out of balance of this country. On the contrary, to emancipate it, to make it wholesome, to make it free, to base it upon the only thing upon which business can rest—the good, universal confidence.

Do you business men not know that there is universal distrust and suspicion in this country with respect to the foundations and methods of business, and do you suppose that business can rest upon suspicion? Do you know that the most delicate thing in the world is the faith, the confidence, upon which business rests?

But, you say, we are just beginning to come in to the benefits of national business, and are we to take the initiative in setting these things right?

Do you not remember the history of the country, gentlemen? Do you not remember the history of the south in particular? Let your thoughts run back to the great period of the Revolution.

Who led, who formulated the policy, who dreamed the dreams and saw the visions of that time? Men out of Virginia and her sister states of the south who did not have any material stake whatever in the things that were at issue between America and the mother country. Every policy of the mother country in that day which was hurtful to trade of America hit New England hard, and benefited the south. And yet New England was divided upon the question of liberty and independence, and the south was united. (Great applause.)

I say it is the most conspicuous case in history of disinterested, altruistic, statesmanlike vision that the south, that had the smallest stake in the matters in controversy, should have taken the initiative and made the prime sacrifice, and I believe that one of the great reservoirs of unselfish, irresistible, altruistic power lies right here in the unexhausted south. (Applause.) I don't know where else to find such continuity of tradition, such unbroken standards of public service, such a consciousness of connection between the individual and the service that he owes to his neighbor, and I know that the hope of the nation does not depend so much upon its thinking as upon its principles. And principles, gentlemen, lie, if they live, in the heart and not the mind.

I have heard it said that this is an age in which mind governs. If it is, I have a comment to make upon that—that mind is one of those modern monarchs that rules but does not govern. We are, in fact, governed by a great representative body made up of the passions, and all that we can manage is that the handsome, unselfish passions shall be in the majority. And, therefore, the thing we have to guard is our hearts, our impulses, our visions, and see to it that as we come to do our daily tasks we do not merely look upon the dusty roads which we are traveling, but lift our eyes to the horizons that light above us with some delectable ray which seems to lift our hearts and quicken our pulses as if they were like the radiance of justice and of the righteousness of God.

All that we can hope for is, in my generation, to hearten one another, to look in one another's faces and say: "Friends and fellows, this is not a hopeless matter, look back at the dark valley of human injustice out of which we have laboriously climbed by the blood and sacrifice of our ancestors; look at the light as it broadens about us; look at the accessible heights that are immediately in front of you; let us take heart for that work, that work that lives in our hearts, that connects us with everything that is sacred in the past, that throw[s] aside the trivial circumstances of our day—the little day in which our generation lives, and remember that the glory of America is the glory of the sacrifice for humanity."

I have sometimes thought as I entered the great port of New York and saw that majestic bronze effigy of Liberty lifting her unlighted torch, of how admirable a symbol it was, because an actual flaming light there would have cast its rays only a little way across the water, but the flame that burns there is an invisible flame; it is the flame of an everlasting spirit of liberty that gleams out unlimited in its illumination, casting its rays far over distant waters, distant lands where multitudes toil, and occasionally lift their eyes and see that fair gleam out of the west, and say: "Ah, there are men there who believe in common folks, who believe that every man has a right to live and to get justice and to enjoy hope. They are saying to us, come, brethren, come to this great land in the east, where we entertain all the enchanted and beautiful memories of liberty and let us show you the way to peace and achievement."

Printed in the *Atlanta Journal*, April 17, 1912; three editorial headings omitted.

Two News Reports of Campaign Speeches in Georgia

[April 18, 1912]

SOUTHWEST GEORGIA GREETS GOV. WILSON
WITH BIG RECEPTION

Great Crowd at Albany, With Every County in Section Represented, Hears National Evils Discussed

By W. T. Waters, Jr.

ALBANY, Ga., April 18.—South Georgia gathered here from a score of counties Wednesday night and saw and heard and was conquered by that great Democrat whom Georgia gave to the nation, Woodrow Wilson, governor of New Jersey. Over 2,000 people were in his audience. . . .

That Governor Wilson's audience was the greatest which has ever gathered in the chautauqua building is a statement repeated upon the authority of W. A. Duncan,[1] the superintendent of instruction in the chautauqua organization, who has been identified with it from its beginning. He so declared from the platform at the conclusion of Governor Wilson's speech, when he urged the whole audience to come forward and meet the distinguished visitor personally. Superintendent Duncan introduced Governor Wilson. From the moment when the latter began to speak he held his audience enthralled. Some members of it seemed hardly to move while he talked. "I have not been in this part of Georgia since I was a very little boy," declared Governor Wilson, "and yet the place seems familiar to me. It can't be

what I see around me. It must be the people themselves. I have
rarely seen anything more wonderful than the progress that
this part of Georgia has made."

He discussed the at[t]itude of the north toward the south and
reproached the south for its timidity, its backwardness in national affairs and said it is not to be excused by any lingering
prejudice against the south that he has ever found in the north.

"It is thoroughly understood in the state of which I have the
honor to be governor," said he, "that I am a southern man and
yet I have never heard anybody in the state objecting to a southern governor."

He declared that he is almost embarrassed at discussing the
subject of his presidential candidacy. "It must look to every one
as if I were going about to commend myself," he explained, "as
if I were on an individual errand. But I would be ashamed of
myself if I thought that was the moving impulse to the acceptance of invitations to various parts of this country. I would not
go if I did not think that we American people are engaged in
the difficult task of understanding one another. There never was,
in my opinion, any time in the history of America when we
people were more in touch with each other's thoughts than at
the present moment." And yet, as he showed, this sympathy of
conviction has until now been without result.

"How many times have the people of the United States voted
on the tariff?" he asked as an illustration. "How many times
have they voted a distinct mandate as to that tariff? and yet
have they ever been obeyed?" . . .

Turning to the money trust, which he regards as the real menace among trusts, he said: "I have heard a great many people
object, and I must admit that I am myself opposed, to the idea
of a central bank. But we have other agencies in the United States
that are much more powerful than a central bank. There is a
little group of banks in New York that practically dominate the
banking capital of this country. This same central control, which
is the control of business, has spread its unhappy influence until it has become the control of politics. We know that the very
men who are controlling business are controlling politics, and
that, therefore, we are in the control of a great system which
governs America's affairs from one end of the country to the
other."

Governor Wilson's audience followed him intently and was
quick to catch every point he made. "Have you noticed the
growth of Socialism in this country?" he asked. "Socialism does

not mean anything dangerous yet. Until Socialists unite upon a single program, it is not absolutely necessary for us to sit up and take notice. I am not afraid of reform, but I am afraid of programs. I know that I do not know enough to make a program of reform and I suppose that other men do not know enough.

"There is not any man who can determine by what formula men have become what they are and may be rendered what they are not."

He referred to the insistence of President Gary, of the United States Steel company, and George W. Perkins, the millionaire investor, that the government should legalize monopolies and fix prices.[2] "That is Socialism," he declared. "It is from those who are already our masters that we have to fear Socialistic suggestions, and not from the great mass of men who are seeking a way to liberty. Those other men are so absorbed in the great enterprises which they head they can not see the rest of the human world. I know that the only people who can save America are the people of America themselves."

He said that against the dangerous extreme of Socialism we must set off the program of progressive thought. He compared the standpatter to a great dam holding back accumulated waters from the valleys below. He said that the Socialist would break the dam and let the waters run riot and spread ruin and death in their course. The progressive, said he, would bore through the dam and with sluices and valves would control and govern the waters and make their force turn the whole of industry. . . .[3]

[1] William Alexander Duncan (1837-1916), for many years a leading figure in the Sunday School and Chautauqua movements; secretary and superintendent of the Chautauqua institution at Lake Chautauqua, N. Y.; founder of the Georgia Chautauqua assembly at Albany, Ga.

[2] For Elbert H. Gary's comments on governmental regulation and price-fixing before the Stanley Committee (about which, see n. 1 to the second news report printed at June 16, 1911, Vol. 23) on June 2, 1911, see n. 8 to the interview printed at Aug. 26, 1911, Vol. 23. George W. Perkins, in a public lecture at Columbia University on February 7, 1908, advocated close federal supervision and regulation of great corporations. He had reiterated this view since that time in many different media. In testimony before the Stanley Committee on August 10, 1911, Perkins partially dissociated himself from Gary's view on governmental price-fixing, as follows: "I agree that there should be something of a constructive nature done in regard to the supervision of our great corporations. If you refer to Judge Gary's statement as to governmental regulation of prices, I do not agree with him. That is, I should regard that as the very last thing to be done, and should much regret if it should become necessary. . . . But, as between even going to that limit and going on as we are now, I would prefer to go to that limit." House of Representatives, *Hearings before the Committee on Investigation of United States Steel Corporation* (8 vols., Washington, 1911-12), IV, 1526. See also G. W. Perkins, *The Modern Corporation, Address, Columbia University, February 7, 1908* (n.p., n.d.), pp. 12-16, and John A. Garraty, *Right-Hand Man: The Life of George W. Perkins* (New York, 1960), pp. 216-54.

[3] There is a WWhw and WWsh outline of this address, dated April 17, 1912, in WP, DLC.

WILSON ENTHRALLS WAYCROSS CROWDS
WITH GREAT SPEECH

By W. T. Waters, Jr.

WAYCROSS, Ga., April 18.—The vital difference between selection and election of candidates for offices was pointed out to
tremendous audiences of southeast Georgia voters here this
morning by Gov. Woodrow Wilson, of New Jersey.

"The Enemy of Private Control of Public Affairs," Governor
Wilson's speech, was delivered in the yard of the Waycross High
school, from a platform which left him exposed to a hot sun,
though his audience stood under the shade of the trees, but
notwithstanding this radical change of weather from the wet
rains of the past two days, Governor Wilson was so interested
in his subject that he seemed not to heed the sun and would
have spoken without any shelter whatever over the head, having
removed his hat, had not Jesse Mercer, Georgia chief game
warden, of Fitzgerald, held an umbrella over his head. . . .

Printed in the *Atlanta Journal*, April 18, 1912.

A News Report of a Campaign Address
in Jacksonville, Florida

[April 19, 1912]

VAST AUDIENCE HEARD WILSON'S ABLE ADDRESS.

STATESMAN GIVEN A SPLENDID OVATION

Truly one of the most magnetic speakers that a Jacksonville
audience has ever had the pleasure of hearing is Woodrow Wilson, governor of New Jersey and candidate for the Democratic
nomination for the presidency of the United States, who, in the
presence of approximately 2,200 people, a large percentage of
whom were ladies, delivered in the Duval theater last night one
of the most interesting and convincing speeches ever heard in
this city. . . .

Gov. Wilson then advanced to the center of the stage. In beginning his address he stated that the South is the only place
where nothing had to be explained to him—that he is a native
Southerner, and felt perfectly at home in this portion of the
country.

He directed attention to the fact that, at the present time, it
was not necessary to discuss platforms but to discuss candidates. In opening a discussion of himself, Gov. Wilson stated that

he hardly knew how to begin such a discussion and, with a few brief remarks in this connection, passed on to the next thread of his address.

He spoke of the arrangements made by several states of the Union in holding what he termed "preferential primaries," by which the will of the people might be expressed in regard to any candidate suggested for office. He complimented Florida on its wisdom and foresight in adopting this plan.

The vital thing was more the selection of a man than his election, was one of Gov. Wilson's most pertinent statements during the evening. He referred to sessions of conventions, "behind closed doors," when little or nothing was known of what transpired therein except to those on the inside; to the preparation of slates and to the use of a second slate in the event that the first did not, for any reason, go through as planned. . . .

He predicted that the conventions to be held in Baltimore and Chicago in June of this year would be the last of their kind and that before another four years have passed it will be known who will be selected, without conventions—this being the result of preferential primaries, by which the states which have already adopted them have indicated that they are Americans and believe in government by the people.

Whether in office or not, Gov. Wilson stated that as long as he could find something by which he could make a living he would be able to find out things and tell them and that he could make it very uncomfortable for the man whose position made him susceptible to publicity or comfortable for those whose actions were above reproach.

Gov. Wilson closed with a message containing sentiment most lofty in character and which left a most indelible impression on his hearers.

Upon the conclusion of his address, large numbers of people made their way onto the stage, where for a few moments the governor was kept busy shaking hands with men and women and acknowledging the numerous compliments and expressions of good will bestowed upon him.

Printed in the Jacksonville *Florida Times-Union*, April 19, 1912; two editorial headings omitted.

A News Report of an Address in Savannah, Georgia

[April 20, 1912]

Woodrow Wilson Enthuses Great Audience in Plea for Self Government on the Part of the People of America

When Governor Wilson arose to speak after being introduced briefly by Mr. [Pleasant A.] Stovall, who hailed him as the next President of the United States, there was prolonged applause. It was necessary for Governor Wilson to raise his hand as an appeal to the audience to discontinue the applause that he might speak.

In his characteristic manner, Governor Wilson humorously related the incident of his marriage in Savannah. When he entered the ordinary's office for the purpose of procuring a license, he said that little attention was paid to him until mention was made of the young lady's name. Then, he said, the official scrutinized him carefully as if to ascertain if the candidate was qualified.

"It seems a long time, in one sense, since this occurred," Governor Wilson said, "because so many things have happened since that time."

This narrative put the audience in fine spirits for the reception of the brilliant address delivered by Governor Wilson.

Frequently since arriving in Savannah, the speaker said, he had been cautioned by friends that "Savannah was the most conservative city in the world." They seemed to have an idea that he would say or do something that would startle Savannah. Governor Wilson asked if it was thought that his same creed would not be acceptable to the people among whom he was born. "It would be impossible for me to think in terms that Southern people could not understand," he said.

There is not is not [sic] a great difference in the people of one part of the country from another, he said. In traveling from one state to another Governor Wilson said he had been unable to find any great difference between the people. He declared that it was his intention to speak to the Savannah audience in the same terms and language as he would to Republicans. . . .

Competition in this country is disappearing, Governor Wilson said. The prices of commodities are now all arranged by private agreement, he said, and those who arrange them abide by the prices agreed upon. The affairs of the country are controlled by a few individuals. The names of a few persons will be seen as the controllers of the great corporations. The same names will be seen among those who control the banks and the railroads. Presently we will begin to see these same small groups of men governing, not only the present industries, but the future industry of the state. Governor Wilson said that it is possible to cite hundreds of instances to prove that this is true.

Continuing Governor Wilson showed that the control of financial affairs in this country is in the hands of a few. The same men who now control the large credits of the country also control politics. But, he said, it is slipping out of their grasp. These few who controlled the affairs have had the selection of the men who were to be the candidates for office. In New Jersey, he said, the few had arranged both tickets between them. The people of Georgia, he said, would recover control of their affairs when they expressed their [presidential] preference on May 1. . . .

The speaker said this country now has facing it the question, who will control it? He said the country was facing the issue of the interests against the masses.

"Whenever the same men control business and control politics, and determine whom we shall nominate, don't you think it is time for us to sit up and take notice?" he asked. "I tell you, ladies and gentlemen, the radicals of this age are the men who are doing these things. They are going to the root of the matter. They are gripping the sources of government and we must take cognizance of the consequent conditions and deal with them. We have confronting us now nothing less than this—who shall control the business of this country, and by the same token who shall control its politics?

"It is useless to discuss any question whatever until this question is settled. Do you suppose any thoughtful man would get up and discuss the tariff again if he thought Mr. Aldrich was going to settle it again? I shall decline to discuss the tariff question and the trust question and the questions connected with our changing trade conditions until I know who the jury is going to be and who is going to carry out the verdict. . . .

He passed from this to a discussion of the initiative, referendum and recall, on which he has repeatedly expressed his views. The topic seemed to be one in which his Savannah audience was particularly interested, for the first mention of it brought a ripple of applause. He therefore made his position very clear, emphasizing his well known opposition to the recall as applied to the judiciary, repeating that the remedy there lies in the selection

of the judges and not in their recall after they have been selected. . . .

Governor Wilson referred to the rising tide of Socialism. He
said the Socialists are reveling in Utopian dreams and their
theories are impossible but he could not help but admire the
spirit that was behind them.

He asked the audience if it had noted the rising tide of Socialism. "It means the despairful protest of thousands of our
people against the uses to which our institutions have been put,"
he declared. "They wish nothing more than to recover control
of their own lives. Their programs are impossible, but I understand and I honor the impulse which lies behind them."

In conclusion he said there is a way out of the unrest of the
people which was devoid of excitement and which had no trace
of passion. He said the simple restraint was to enter into a new
era of constructive statesmanship.

Printed in the *Savannah*, Ga., *Press*, April 20, 1912; several editorial headings
omitted.

From James Duval Phelan[1]

Dear Governor Wilson: [San Francisco] April 20th, 1912.

In your history of the United States, you refer to immigration and make mention of the Chinese. I have read your letter[2]
in which you state that as a historical fact, the United States
legislated against undesirable immigration, which many years
ago entered our ports; but that you entertained only the highest
esteem for the men of the several European Nations who have
showed themselves worthy of American citizenship. In this, we
are all agreed, but we on the Pacific Coast will be pleased to
know your views at this time on the subject of Oriental Immigration.

Permit me to briefly state the situation on this coast. The
Chinese have been excluded by legislation and are diminishing
in numbers. It is notorious, however, that parties of Chinese
are smuggled into the United States from time to time, and
recently, a shipload of contraband Chinese were taken in San
Francisco Bay. They come generally by way of Mexican ports
or across the border. By a "Gentleman's Agreement," the Federal
Government pretends to keep out the Japanese. Statistics will
no doubt show that under this agreement, Japan has kept its
coolies from shipping from Japanese ports to ports of the United

States, but the Japanese are also smuggled in over the border, and recently, a party of them actually fired upon inoffending farmers near San Diego, believing them to be officers seeking their arrest. There seems to be no restriction upon the immigration of Hindoos who are coming in considerable numbers.

I enclose you a copy of California's Memorial to Congress, dated 1901, which states the case against the Chinese. The same objection lies against the coolies of Japan. The fundamental objection to the coming of these people is their non-assimilability. They cannot become a part of our composite Nation. They remain foreign. Where there has been intermarriage, the issue is degenerate and the vices of both strains are exaggerated in the offspring. We do not believe that they can, by any stretch of the imagination, become a part of the American people, and, that ultimately, the same race question, which arose in the South, will arise—a possibility, which certainly should be averted. In order to preserve our State and protect American institutions, we must see to it that our's remains a white man's country.

I think you will appreciate the danger when you contemplate for a moment these circumstances: The Japanese have invaded the Central valleys of California. Take for example, one highly productive fruit growing valley known as the Vaca Valley. There, the Japanese, refusing to work for wages after the first year or so, bargained for a share of the crop, and finally ousted in many instances the tenant farmers by offering the land owner larger returns, and in some instances acquired the fee of the property by purchase. The white man is thus driven off the land to move farther away. The village stores, churches and cottages suffer and in many instances are left without patronage. In other words, the Japanese are a blight on our civilization, destructive of the home life of the people, driving the natives to the city for employment. To-day, in San Francisco, thousands of unemployed men are demanding bread and lodging from the public officials. When the Panama Canal is opened, a large immigration will flow to California to find the land occupied by an alien and non-assimilable people. The Hawaiian Islands are now practically a possession of Japan, as California will be unless the Japanese question is solved. In ten years the native Japanese population will outvote the whites in Hawaii.

President Taft last spring surrendered a clause in the Japanese treaty giving us the right to regulate immigration. No protest was raised by our Legislature, because San Franciscans were in Washington at the time seeking the President's support for the Panama-Pacific Exposition, and a part of the consideration

for the President's support was that California should be silent
on the Japanese question and allow the treaty to go through
without protest. I wrote a protest, however, in the National
Monthly, April, 1911, to which I beg to refer you. It is vital, I
believe, for our civilization and for the preservation of our domestic institutions, whose success and perpetuity rests upon the
character of the population, that Oriental coolies be excluded
from these shores.

In the campaign, this question will be raised and I would
like to be able to answer the allegations made against your
History, as reflecting your views, recently printed in the newspapers. I have come to the conclusion from reading your works
that as you are opposed to immigration of the dregs from
Europe, as distinguished from the better element, you would
logically be opposed to Oriental coolieism; but, even where
coolies are capable of doing a day's work, as they admittedly
are, the question is, should they be allowed, in a fierce competition, to lower the standards of living and wages of the members of the white race, who stand for home life, Republican
government and Western civilization. If you destroy the man,
you certainly destroy everything that he stands for. We cannot
segregate a labor class and regard it exclusively by its capacity
for work. In that event, California would be a plantation and
the white population would for a period of time, possibly, remain as overseers, but, indeed, with my knowledge of the Japanese, that would be for a very short time. The end would soon
supervene.   Yours very truly,   [James D. Phelan][3]

CCL (J. D. Phelan Papers, CU).
  [1] Wealthy banker and real estate dealer of San Francisco; Mayor of San
Francisco, 1897-1902; Wilson leader in California; United States senator, 1915-
21.
  [2] One of the several public letters written by Wilson to immigrant groups
which had protested against certain passages in his *A History of the American
People.*
  [3] For the origin and subsequent effect of this letter, see WW to J. D. Phelan,
May 3, 1912, n. 1.

From Willard Saulsbury

Dear Governor: [Wilmington, Del.] April 20th, 1912.

We had our 1st primaries here last night when 2/3 of the
wards of the city of Wilmington expressed themselves and
elected delegates. You will doubtless be glad to know that there
is only one fight over one delegate to be threshed out at the
polls and one other delegate whose personal attitude is some-

what undertain [uncertain] but I have the assurance of his nearest friends that he will be all right.

Yours very truly,   Willard Saulsbury

P.S. I enclose copy of a letter which I have just sent out here[1] in order to keep the fires burning, the substance of which I hope you will approve.

TLS (Saulsbury Letterpress Books, DeU).
[1] It is missing.

A Report of Remarks to College Students in Macon, Georgia

[April 21, 1912]

COLLEGE STUDENTS GREET GOV. WILSON

Governor and Mrs. Woodrow Wilson reached Macon at 1 o'clock Saturday afternoon[1]. . . . At 3 o'clock Governor and Mrs. Wilson paid a visit to Mercer University. They were received with college yells and cheers galore by the students, who gave full reign to their enthusiasm in the reception of their guests.

The stay at the college was brief, but long enough for a bit of oratory. . . . Gov. Wilson said he felt perfectly at home in facing a body of college boys.

"It is hard to put up a bluff and keep it up in the presence of the boys who have been onto my curves for a number of years," said he. The speaker attacked the theory that a boy begins life when he leaves college. He should begin it before, said he. He pointed to the fact that the undergraduate body in Europe is regarded seriously and plays an important part in worldly affairs. He compared the conditions there with those in the United States, where, he said, the undergraduate isn't taken seriously.

"It is time for the American undergraduate to do his own thinking," he said. "Instead of being the memory of a lesson he should be the beginning of a purpose. My appeal to you is this. Let's have done with the boyishness of undergraduate life, and let's begin the manliness of it," he said in conclusion.

The close of the spe[e]ch was a signal for another outburst of college yells.

From Mercer the party, accompanied by a great many of the students, motored over to Wesleyan, where a novel reception had been arranged for their delight. The young ladies of the college, scattered about over the lawn and terraces and porches, were singing an improvised campaign song when the Governor arrived.

In the reception hall were Dr. Ainsworth,[2] head of the Institution; Vice President C. R. Jenkins[3] and a number of ladies in the receiving line. After the young ladies of the school assembled in the hall, Gov. Wilson was formally introduced by Dr. Ainsworth, who spoke of him in the most eulogistic terms.

Turning his back to the students who had accompanied him from Mercer, Mr. Wilson laughingly remarked that he was glad to turn his back to the boys to address the girls. In a brief talk to the young ladies he said that, if that part of history were taught which was brought about by the influence of women, the rest would be worth reading.

"The most significant thing in modern life is the larger and larger role woman is playing in it," he said. "She is taking up now as she never took up before the things which concern the welfare of society. I have come to a rather unusual conclusion," the governor declared. "I have always heard men say women are illogical, but my observation is just exactly the opposite. I think women are the most truly logical people in the world."

At the conclusion of his speech Dr. Ainsworth introduced Mrs. Wilson, who had come in while her husband was speaking.

Printed in the *Macon*, Ga., *Daily Telegraph*, April 21, 1912; several editorial headings omitted.

[1] April 20.

[2] The Rev. Dr. William Newman Ainsworth, president of Wesleyan Female College, Macon.

[3] The Rev. Charles Rush Jenkins, vice-president, who succeeded Ainsworth in June 1912.

A News Report of a Campaign Address in Macon

[April 21, 1912]

PLEA FOR FREE BUSINESS AND FREE POLITICS MADE BY GOV. WILSON IN SPEECH

Says That Cure for Nation of Employes Is the Restoring of the Individual Initiative

MACON, Ga., April 20.—Preceded by the Macon drum and bugle corps that marched in the middle of the streets while Governor Wilson and his escort kept pace with them on the sidewalk, Macon's Wilson forces made their way to the city auditorium tonight and found it already packed to the doors in advance of their coming. Governor Wilson's entrance was received with enthusiastic cheers. . . .

Governor Wilson received an acclamation when he arose to speak.

"So far as I am myself concerned my interest tonight is not that you believe in me but in the cause I represent. I do not wish you to think of me tonight. . . .

"The control of our affairs has slipped away from general public opinion and is vested in small groups of interested individuals," he declared, reciting that as the central trouble of our government today. . . .

"We are becoming a nation of employes. As a remedy for this, we are after restoring individual initiative, which is at the very foundation of the prosperity of every nation. America is what she is because her men are prouder of founding families than of being born of families." Talking of the money trust, he declared that the same men appear upon the directorate lists of great corporations where business is associated.

"They make money and lend the money and spend the money," he declared. "Now, where are we going to get in? I am not jealous of the amount they make. I am jealous of the amount they handle, the amount they control, the amount they prevent us from handling. I am among those who are trying to recover free business and by the same token I am among those who are trying to recover free politics."[1]

Governor Wilson finished his speech at 9:45 o'clock, going immediately to the Volunteers' bazar. His audience at the auditorium numbered 2,500 at a close estimate. No more could enter the building.

Printed in the *Atlanta Journal*, April 21, 1912; some editorial headings omitted.
[1] There is a WWhw outline of this address, dated April 20, 1912, in WP, DLC.

To Willard Saulsbury

My dear Mr. Saulsbury: [Trenton, N. J.] April 22, 1912.

Thank you sincerely for your letter of April twentieth, which I received on my return today from a trip to Georgia. While, of course, I felt quite confident that Delaware Democrats would be found in our column, it is none the less gratifying to receive the positive news that everything is all right.

You will pardon the brevity of this acknowledgment; I am hastening away to keep an engagement in New York.[1]

Cordially yours,   Woodrow Wilson

Georgia looks fine,—and Fla. favourable.

TLS (W. Saulsbury Papers, DeU).
¹ To speak to the Methodist Social Union of New York. A news report of his speech is printed at May 2, 1912.

From Henry Skillman Breckinridge

My dear Governor Wilson: Lexington, Ky., April 22, 1912.

You have a splendid chance of being the next President of the United States, and we in Kentucky feel the heavy responsibility that rests upon our shoulders with regard to our contribution to the consummation of this desired end. We feel an interest in the situation at large, but our immediate interest is in Kentucky. It may not be possible for us to send an instructed delegation to the National Convention, but it is possible for us to send a delegation friendly to your candidacy if the proper work be done. The opportunity to clinch this State for you immediately after your trip here[1] was lost for lack of funds. A well supported organization could have nailed Kentucky. The opportunity to send a delegation friendly to your interests will be lost if funds are not forthcoming within the next week. The temper of the Kentucky delegation may mean victory or defeat in the National Convention for your candidacy.

The Clark movement in Kentucky is prompted by a desire of a certain faction to wrest the State Organization from the Administration and by one of the exigencies of politics we have the silent aid of the State Administration. The Governor stands for an uninstructed delegation, that is, he does not want instruction from the floor of the State Convention, but he is willing that we should dig for delegates; and is also willing that they be instructed for you by districts just so long as there is no instruction from the State Convention. We hold the balance of power in the fight for control of the State, and as we have no interest in the state fight the administration is forced to alliance with us.

Your friends are ready to make every sacrifice possible and have made every possible effort to insure your success. The work done in Kentucky has been done under the most miserably disheartening circumstances and with the most miserable means. We believe that Illinois, Kansas and Nebraska[2] were lost by poor organization of the country districts and Kentucky will just as certainly be lost unless Mr. McCombs gives us financial support.

The precinct conventions in the cities will be held May the twenty-fifth; the county conventions May the twenty-seventh and the State Convention May the twenty-ninth. Four weeks alone remain. We must not let victory go by default at this, the eleventh hour.

This letter is urged by scores of your friends in Kentucky who are doing every thing they can in the expenditure of time and money in lining up their localities. The Clark people are well supplied with funds and are making a desperate fight from their headquarters in Louisville.[3]

With great respect, I am

Very faithfully yours,   Henry S. Breckinridge.

TLS (Governors' Files, Nj).

[1] That is, when Wilson spoke to the General Assembly of Kentucky on February 9, 1912. A news report of this affair is printed at that date.

[2] In the Nebraska presidential primary held on April 19, 1912, Clark received 21,027 votes; Wilson, 14,289; Judson Harmon, 12,454.

[3] In the Kentucky Democratic county conventions held on May 25, Clark won 100 of the 120 counties. Thus his supporters controlled the state convention, which met on May 29, and instructed the Kentucky delegation to the Baltimore convention to vote "first, last, and all the time" for Clark. *Louisville Times*, May 30, 1912.

A News Report of an Address in Paterson, New Jersey

[April 24, 1912]

GOVERNOR SEES MENTAL MENACE

PATERSON, April 24.—Discussing the evils of privileged business in this country, Governor Wilson last night said there is something "worse than moral corruption, so far as politics is concerned, and that is a corruption of the mind itself, so that it thinks along lines along which progress is impossible."

The Governor was the guest of honor at the dinner of the Woodrow Wilson Club at Entre Nous Hall. More than 300 persons attended. Congressman Rufus Hardy, of Texas; Congressman William Hughes, former [State] Senator John Hinchliffe, Congressman William F[rancis]. Murray, of Boston, and a number of county officials occupied places at the speakers' table. Congressman Hughes was toastmaster.

The Governor spoke on "Progress and the Smallness of the Individual in that Progress." He said he understood that twenty-three directors of the United States Steel Corporation control fifty-five per cent. of the railroads of the United States, a large proportion of the finances of the country, many steamship lines and much commerce and industry.[1]

"It is important that we should ask ourselves how this came about," went on the Governor. "Did it come about by any malevolent design on the part of these gentlemen? No; it did not. It came about by the genius of these gentlemen."

The Governor said that, leaving out manipulations that have produced false worth, the undertakings are solid and represent good management and constructive ability. Now, he said, these men, finding themselves virtually with the country in their power, are scrutinized and questioned as to the honesty of their purposes.

"What does it profit the country if you cut the legal strings that bind a number of corporations together," queried the Governor, "if they are still bound together by being controlled by the same men; so long as the personal control is the same, the legal control is a matter of comparative indifference.

"Now, what renders these gentlemen open to suspicion is this: While this power has been built up, has been in process of being built up, they have thought it necessary at first for their protection and then found it necessary for their profit to control the political machinery of this country. If they had never laid hands on the political machinery of this country, I doubt if we would have this attitude of suspicion toward them that we have, but they have laid hands on the political processes of this country. The time has come when these gentlemen honestly believe that it is necessary that they should control the government in order that the United States shall be prosperous.

"They do not conceive it possible that the people of the United States should prosper without their management and control. So that my indictment against them is a deeper indictment than the indictment of dishonesty. Ever so many of these men are not dishonest.

"There is something very much worse than moral corruption so far as politics is concerned, and that is a corruption of the mind itself, so that it thinks along lines along which progress is impossible. These gentlemen have become absolutely unable to conceive government in the terms of democracy, and therefore they are instinctively and of necessity the enemies of democracy."

Asserting the hope of the people to be in the Democratic party the Governor assailed critics within the State. Mentioning no names, he said there are some in the State who are seeking to create "divisions and dissensions, so that it will be impossible to use the Democratic party as a single unit dedicated to the service of the United States.

"I tell you, when I think of some of the petty things that are being done and some of the deliberate misrepresentations [and] of some vile assaults upon character which are being undertaken to pull men down instead of to build the party up, I marvel how any man can be so blind as well as so stubborn."

Printed in the *Newark Evening News*, April 24, 1912; two editorial headings omitted.

¹ In his speech at Baltimore, printed at April 30, 1912, Wilson cited a recent circular of the United States Department of Labor and Commerce as his source of this information. The Editors have been unable to find this document. However, it was clearly based on the elaborate series of tables prepared for the Stanley Committee, showing the business concerns, together with their capitalization and bonded indebtedness, in which the directors of United States Steel were officers or directors. These tables were available at least as early as January 26, 1912, when they were printed in the *Congressional Record*, 62nd Cong., 2nd sess., Vol. 48, pt. 12 (Appendix), pp. 242-51, in a speech by Representative Charles Lafayette Bartlett of Georgia.

To Edward Mandell House

My dear Mr. House: [Trenton, N. J.] April 26, 1912.

I am so sorry that I received your note of the fourteenth after it was too late to comply with its helpful request.

In haste, with affectionate regard,
          Sincerely yours,   Woodrow Wilson

TLS (E. M. House Papers, CtY).

A News Report of a Campaign Address in Boston

[April 27, 1912]

WILSON CHEERED BY GREAT THRONG

Tremont Temple Jammed to Hear
The Democratic Candidate.

Gov. Woodrow Wilson of New Jersey enunciated last evening the principles for which he stands as candidate for the Democratic nomination for President before as great a gathering as has ever attended a political meeting in Tremont Temple. . . .

Occupying rows of center seats on the floor nearest the stage were members of the Harvard Woodrow Wilson Club. Provision had been made for 300, but the eagerness of twice that number to attend was responsible for the informal assembling of auditors in the choir loft and on the platform.

The students wore Wilson buttons and bits of crimson ribbon, and no matter how uncomfortable their seats—some sitting in the laps of others—were prepared to cheer and applauded every minute, which they did.

When the cheering, led by William S. McNary, had subsided Gov. Wilson waited until the enthusiastic throngs of young men before him sat down again and he then spoke substantially as follows, in a 40-minute address:

"I am conscious of standing here with a certain degree of embarrassment as if I were a sort of exhibit attached to this very interesting aggregation of speakers[1] here tonight. I am to stand up apparently in the very dangerous predicament of one who would if he could verify what they have said of him.

"I have been interested in nothing so much in recent months as finding out the men who were standing with me. Mayor Baker and I were fellow-students,[2] though he is a great deal younger than I am, at the Johns Hopkins University. . . . I tell you very frankly that it gives a man a very deep sense of personal responsibility to be trusted by those who have known him. I have been trusted by those who don't know me. (Laughter.) One of my quondam friendships has been mentioned tonight.

"Senator Smith's friendship was offered to me under a misapprehension. Senator Smith believed that I corresponded to the ordinary theory of a college man, that the minute I got out into the open I could be led about like a sheep. I remember hearing expressed the other day in a very quaint, though not a very parliamentary way, the ordinary idea of a college professor. The point of it may help me but it may be in bad taste to tell it. After I had made a speech in a Western city, this conversation was overheard by a man: 'That fellow,' one said, 'has got brains,' and the other fellow said: 'I can't see why a fellow with such good brains should spend 20 years of his life in college.' (Great applause.)

"Senator Smith evidently shared the general impression that a university is a place where brains go to seed, and if my brains were in the sere and yellow leaf he thought possibly I might be a very manageable governor of New Jersey. I took every means that the English language affords to undeceive him, but he supposed I was a master of nothing but language. (Laughter.)

"I feel, therefore, that the subsequent damage done to the friendship should not rest upon me by way of responsibility.

[1] The other speakers were William Sarsfield McNary, congressman from Boston, 1903-1907, at this time in the furniture business; Francis M. Carroll, lawyer of Boston; Newton Diehl Baker, Mayor of Cleveland; Robert L. Henry; and Dudley Field Malone.

[2] Baker, A.B., Johns Hopkins 1892, had been an undergraduate and a graduate student in history and political science while Wilson was a lecturer at the university.

"I did exactly what I said I would do. The only point was that he didn't expect that I would. (Laughter.) . . .

"The contest we are engaged in now is a contest which is very much greater than a mere choice among persons. I would if I could, at this stage of the contest, divest every audience I address of any consciousness that I myself am concerned, because I would not go before great audiences of my fellow-citizens if I thought the thing I was pleading for was that they should express their preference that I should be nominated for the office of President.

"The fortunes of this country do not depend on the particular choice we should make; do not center on any individual. The danger is that the thought of the country might be ready to suppose that they do center upon some particular individual.

"The United States is greater than any one man. (Renewed applause.) One of the distressing circumstances of our time—and I say it as a Democrat, who would like to see the Republican party utterly defeated—is that the Republican party is now rent asunder because, not of a contest upon principle, but of a contest with regard to the individual merits of two persons.

"What difference does it make to us which of these men is the honest man? (Laughter and applause.)

"When Mr. Taft and Mr. Roosevelt are dead and unexpectedly quiescent (laughter) we shall look back to this time as a time when we excited ourselves about nothing. (Laughter.) When I was on my way up here on the train I thought to myself: These people I am going to address have been living on spices and I have no spice to administer.

"I have nothing to talk about except the interests of the United States. I have nothing to discuss except public questions. I would not condescend to discuss persons (laughter and applause) except so far as it may be necessary to discuss persons who are standing in the way of the general interests.

"Now, I am going to take it for granted that every man here tonight either is or is going to be a Democrat (laughter). I am going to take it for granted because I wish to pay you the compliment of taking it for granted that you are an intelligent body of persons (laughter).

"I don't say that, desiring to intimate for one moment that the great body of my fellow citizens who in the past have been voting the Republican ticket, therefore, lack intelligence. That is not my point. My point is this: We are in the presence of great things that have to be done; we are in the presence of certain critical choices—critical because upon them depend in the immediate future at any rate—the character and the uses of our institutions.

"The United States has now to choose instruments by which to accomplish its purpose. It is not intelligent to choose an instrument which has destroyed itself and, therefore, it is not intelligent for us at this stage to choose the Republican party as the instrument of reform (applause). . . .

"We want to know how we are going to deal with the question of the tariff; with the question of trusts; how we are going to restore individual initiative, individual opportunity, to set free the energies of the United States upon the great field of foreign commerce.

"The preliminary question with regard to these matters is not a question of detail or of legislative measures, but of who is to be intrusted with the formulation of those measures—those who offer to the nation a united and concerted body, or those who are at war among themselves?

"The Democratic party has now an opportunity that it never had before within the recollection of the present generation. That opportunity is to offer itself united, unimpaired, zealous, eager to the common service of the country, without personal jealousy, without petty division, without factional contest, so that, setting an example to the other party and to the other parties of the nation, it may say: 'Here are we robed and ready with united front and purpose to be your servant in a great cause.' (Enthusiastic applause.)

"Up to this point in the campaign I have not spoken of individuals, but I feel it my duty and privilege to utter my very sober and serious and respectful protest against some of the things that are being done. I feel that it is my privilege and my duty to protest very earnestly indeed against the things that Mr. William R. Hearst is doing. (Tumultuous applause.)

"It is a matter of no concern whatever to me what Mr. Hearst thinks of me personally. That is a matter of indifference to me and it may be to the United States; but what does concern me is that I am a Democrat, and I protest against the disorganizing influences of a man who whenever the Democratic party did not take his command took the liberty of separating himself from the Democratic party and fighting the Democratic party. (Loud applause.)

"I do protest against the proposition of any man who says: 'If you pick out a candidate whom I do not like the party will not have my allegiance and support.' That, I say, is in the present juncture an act of absolute disloyalty to the United States, because if you divide the Democratic party upon petty lines of personal jealousy, as well as the Republican party, to whom is the country to turn?

"Where will it find a united body of men determined to do their duty in loyalty to one another as well as in loyalty to the country as a whole?

"Now, a gentleman in the gallery just now said that Mr. George Fred Williams had always been a good Democrat. I do not dispute that. I am not here to impugn the character of any man, for I have been taught ever since I was a boy that that is none of my business. (Applause.)

"But Mr. Williams also has taken the position that he will not stand by anybody, even his old friend, Mr. Bryan (applause), who dares to support a candidate of whom he, Mr. Williams, disapproves. Now, I say that Mr. Williams has been a good Democrat up to this point. When he does that and when he says that he ceases to be a good Democrat.

"The rest of us are ready to support any candidate whom the Democracy picks out (cheers), because whatever may be our judgment with regard to the person picked out, whether we think he is the most or the least efficient and available, our first duty is to see that the country has a united party to depend upon; and I believe this is the time when the country is looking as it never looked before to the Democratic party as the instrument of its success and rehabilitation.

"I will tell you why. I am not going to say that if the Democratic party had been in power for 16 years it might not have loaded itself with certain alliances and obligations which would make it unserviceable to the country at this time—for the temptations of power everybody recognizes and the processes of politics everybody recognizes.

"It requires a great deal of money to conduct any sort of campaign, even though every dollar of that money is properly and honestly spent. The rank and file of people of this country cannot afford to pay for a political campaign and therefore if you are going to have organization it seems necessary in order to get out the vote merely. . . .

"The temptation is to obtain the money where you can get it, provided you believe that the individuals who give it to you are personally honest, and sometimes whether they are or not, and every dollar you receive is apt to seem to you like an implication of obligation; it is apt to seem to you that you must create, that you must accept that final negation of an obligation and of a political responsibility, that you must be amenable to the claims of your friends, even over and above the claims of your nation. That is what has been at the bottom of politics.

"The Republican party has accepted the favors of the privileged interests of this country and is bound to them hand and foot. The Democratic party is free, thank God; and whether it be by fortunate circumstance or by moral superiority, it is not bound by the shackles that have bound this other party. . . .

"My single lesson tonight therefore is this: Something must be done, it must be done through some set of leaders. Let us concentrate our attention upon those leaders and upon no others. Let us ask ourselves which party, which way we ought to choose our leaders, which way they ought to lead this party, which leaders have the visions of these purposes in their mind, which leaders are intending not merely to serve the party, but to serve the nation, which leaders are absolutely ignoring the controversies and the factions of the past and turning to the discussion of future business. We are not interested in the past divisions of parties, but we are immensely interested in our own intricate and difficult present and our still more intricate and difficult past. These things we must turn to with determination and devotion. . . .

"I want to tell you that if both the regular parties of this country disappoint it, it will turn to the Socialists. I have nothing to say of the underlying motives and principles of the Socialistic party, because as they disclose these purposes they are the purposes which I hope all of us entertain, namely, to bring common justice and brotherhood to pass again. But the Socialistic programme I honestly believe to be an impracticable programme. I want to proclaim myself here tonight a disciple of Edmund Burke, who was opposed to all ambitious programmes on the principle that no man, no group of men, can take a piece of paper and reconstruct society. I believe that politics, wise statesmanship, consist in dealing with one problem at a time and the circumstances of each particular case. Burke once said, in an immortal passage, which I wish I could repeat, that the wisdom of every case consisted in the circumstances of that case, and no man's vision can go further than that, no man can see the next generation, no man can predict the recording [reordering] of society in an age not his own.

"Another interesting circumstance about the Socialists is that if there are half a dozen groups of Socialists there will be half a dozen programmes. There is no single Socialistic programme, and if there were I should be suspicious of it because it was 'a programme,' because it assumed to see further than I, for one, am capable of seeing, so that no matter what the impulse back of it, no matter what the voting spirit of men who have allied themselves with those parties, the great Socialistic vote in this country is not a vote for a programme; it is a protest, a vote in protest against the bitter disappointments that the country has suffered at the hands of both parties.

"Is the Democratic party going to redeem the situation? Is the Democratic party going to redeem the pledges that public men have made from generation to generation and neglected to redeem? Ah! what a vision of service presents itself to the great party which now has it within its choice to lead the nation; what traditions of statesmanship, what splendid memories of liberty, what fine chapters of history, constitute their inspiration! America, the nation which has bidden all nations to send their hopeful people to it, in order that they might be put in the school of brotherhood and of justice!

"This party, taught by Thomas Jefferson, taught by a man who had the only vision that is set to guide the feet of any people! The only lamp that we have for our feet, ladies and gentlemen, is the lamp of experience. Thomas Jefferson was not a man of the people. He was a man bred in the schools, he was a man bred among the ranks of those who called themselves cultured and refined; he was, from the top of his head to the soles of his feet, saturated in the aristocratic traditions of an ancient Commonwealth, and yet Thomas Jefferson, because he associated his mind with the thought of the world, saw the vision of the world; he saw that the world advances not by the principle of selecting the classes, but by the lifting of the general levels of humanity; he saw that mankind advances by the common instinct, the general illumination, the universal impulse which spreads far beyond the homes of those who are wealthy and cultivated, and puts the fire of stimulation into each cottage and mill and mine, so that all the nation burns from end to end with the energy which is bred only by the stimulation of liberty. This was what he saw and what every man must see who has read any of the pages of history that glow with this ancient history.

"I would consider myself an uneducated man if I did not believe in Democracy. I would consider myself a man who had shut his eyes to all the lessons of human experience if I did not believe that that principle was to come only out of the impulses, the intelligence of the great body of my fellow citizens. It is at these fountains that we drink; it is these and these only that are the fountains of eternal youth."

Printed in the *Boston Daily Globe*, April 27, 1912; several editorial headings omitted; with many corrections and additions from the text in the *Boston Post*, April 27, 1912.

A News Report of a Tour Through Massachusetts

[April 28, 1912]

GOV. WILSON CHEERED BY THOUSANDS

Tour of the State a Continuous Ovation

SPRINGFIELD, April 27.—Governor Woodrow Wilson of New Jersey was given a continual ovation from end to end of the Commonwealth today. From the time that he was cheered wildly by the students of Holy Cross College, Worcester, whom he addressed in the forenoon, until he closed his strenuous day in Holyoke City Hall late tonight, in his campaign for the Democratic nomination for President, he was received with enthusiasm everywhere.

Before an audience including some of the most prominent citizens of Springfield, which filled the auditorium of the Technical High School, he delivered tonight a scathing indictment of the small coterie of men in control of the Republican party.

Governor Wilson's scholarly address was cheered to the echo. As he warmed up to his subject, and for once departed from his rigid rule of discussing only the abstract problems awaiting the nation's decision, the crowd vehemently applauded him. They eagerly tried to encourage him to even more radical condemnation of those he indicted for the social, economic and political evils of the day.

"When I speak of the Republican party," he declared, "I mean a small coterie of men, so few in number that, although I live in a small house, I could invite them all to dinner. When these men speak of the people of the United States, they don't even include themselves. They believe in government for the people—not government of the people.

"This is not a question of personalities. I was bred in a theology which left that to the Almighty, and it makes no difference to us whether Mr. Roosevelt or Mr. Taft is the honest man.

The question is who is to govern the United States, a small coterie of men who control the wealth of the nation, or the people themselves?

"I have had some of the great business men of the country come to me secretly and behind their hands, with bated breath, whisper they were for the principles I am trying to represent, but were afraid. Their notes were held by the money trust. They knew that if they came out in the open, their paper would be called and they would be ruined.

"That is the way these few corrupt men control the officers we elect. They don't bribe them today. That would be too crude, and it would be too easy to find them out. They control the money, they choose the candidates of both the great political parties, and it makes no difference to them which candidates we elect.

"This is a war of emancipation. The only question is who shall be the emancipators. The label on goods is often very different from the contents. The progressive Republicans don't correspond with the contents. It is time to drop the labels and get together for our country." . . .

Printed in the *Boston Sunday Post*, April 28, 1912.

To Josephus Daniels

My dear friend: [Trenton, N. J.] April 29, 1912.

Thank you heartily for your letter from Washington.[1] I must steal a minute from my morning's work to tell you how deeply I appreciate it and all that it expresses and leaves unexpressed. It is delightful to know that you are gaining strength. You are certainly needed more than ever in the fight that is ahead.

In haste,   Cordially yours,   Woodrow Wilson

TLS (J. Daniels Papers, DLC).
[1] It is missing.

An Interview

[April 30, 1912]

BOOKS OPEN—WILSON

Says He Favors Henry Bill And Campaign Fund
Publicity.

Coming down on the train from Trenton yesterday afternoon, Governor Wilson, of New Jersey, who came to Baltimore to speak at the big meeting last night at the Lyric and at the earlier meeting at Towson, was asked about his attitude toward the Henry bill, which, if passed, will require the publication of the expenses of candidates for the Presidential nomination before they are nominated.

"I am heartily in favor of it," he said, "and have written Representative Henry, earnestly commending his bill. I hope it will pass. I believe the people have a right to know how the money with which campaigns for the nominations are waged is raised. They have a right to know just who feels enough interest in any candidate to contribute money for his nomination."

"Are you prepared to file a statement of the sources of your own campaign fund?"

"Most assuredly I am. If the bill should be passed and be signed before the conventions, the statement will be ready on the date specified. I would say we are prepared to make a statement at once, but I suppose things are a little mixed up. However, they could be straightened out in a day or so and the statement prepared with every cent accounted for, with the names of the persons who have contributed the money."

"You have been quoted as saying," he was told, "that your campaign fund has been bankrupt two or three times. Is that a correct statement of the situation?"

"Well, perhaps that was drawn rather strongly. But we have been pretty near to rock bottom, and money has been hard to raise. But we have always come through."

Then the direct question was put:

"Governor, what is the source of the Wilson campaign fund? Where has the money with which your campaign has been carried on been coming from? I do not suppose you have any objection to saying."

"None in the world," he answered. "I cannot tell you offhand just who have contributed to it; in fact, I do not know except in a general way, but Mr. McCombs could tell you. Of course, we have an understanding as to the kind of men from whom contributions would be accepted. But in a general way I would say that most of it came from my old Princeton friends, and it has been mostly in small amounts. Mr. McCombs has been a liberal contributor himself. But there is no contributor whose name we are ashamed of, none we would object to the people knowing. We have nothing to hide. We believe in publicity in this, as in other matters in which the people are concerned, and would have no hesitancy in publishing our lists of contributors.["]

"Are you still as great an advocate of publicity in public affairs as you used to be?"

"Oh, absolutely," Governor Wilson replied. "I have frequently said that I cannot understand why the business of the public should not be transacted in full view of the public. I can conceive of no situation in municipal, State or national affairs that the people should not be permitted to know all about, except possibly some affairs of the nation that might have an international bearing and the publication of which might cause international complications. But those occasions are not common. As a general principle, I have always said that the people have a full right to know everything that is being done in their name and by the men whom they have put in office to transact their affairs for them."

Governor Wilson was asked his opinion of the situation in the Republican party. He smiled, but would not discuss it.

"My opinion," he said, "is, I suppose, that of pretty much everybody else in the Democratic party. We are all very much amused. However, that is a matter that does not concern me."

It was suggested that it might be a matter that could concern him a good deal. If he should be the Democratic nominee, he might have a preference as to the man he would oppose in the general election. He only laughed and shook his head, as if it did not matter who might be his opponent—he would be satisfied with either.

Governor Wilson was sick with a severe cold, and tired from his trying trips of the last few days, when he came to Baltimore last evening, but he showed little of the distress he felt. He hurried through the business of his office at Trenton in the morning, ate a hasty luncheon just before train time and left Trenton at 2.25 o'clock for Baltimore. . . .

Printed in the Baltimore *Sun*, April 30, 1912; two editorial headings omitted.

A News Report of a Campaign Address in Baltimore

[April 30, 1912]

WILSON PLEADS NEED OF DEMOCRATIC RULE

Declares That The Party Is The Nation's Hope
For Better Things.

HAILED BY GREAT CROWD AT THE LYRIC

In spite of a sore throat that caused him intense pain, Gov. Woodrow Wilson spoke for an hour last night to an audience

that strained its ears to catch every word he uttered and which
he aroused to outbreaks of the greatest enthusiasm.

The Lyric was crowded. The main floor, the boxes, the galler-
ies and the stage all held as many persons as could get on and
in them, and the crowd was one such as is rarely seen at political meetings. . . .

Governor Wilson did not arrive at the hall until about 20 minutes after the time set for the meeting to begin. When he entered,
in company with State Senator Blair Lee, who was to preside,
Mr. William L. Marbury, chairman of the Woodrow Wilson campaign committee, Mr. George N. Numsen and a few others, the
crowd rose and cheered lustily.

As the party took their seats, Senator John Sharp Williams, of
Mississippi, entered from an opposite door, and there was another
demonstration which continued while Governor Wilson, Senator
Lee and Mr. Marbury shook hands with the gentleman from Mississippi. Some particularly enthusiastic applauding from a box
on the right-hand side of the hall attracted Governor Wilson's
attention and he turned and waved his hand to his old friend,
Dr. John M. T. Finney, who occupied it with a number of other
gentlemen and some ladies.

Mr. Marbury was cheered when, as chairman of the committee,
he "called the Democratic party in Maryland to order." He said
it was hardly necessary for him to do any introducing; that the
party had a candidate who spoke for himself and whose record
spoke more eloquently for him than anything he himself could
say. Then came more cheers. . . .

Governor Wilson spoke as follows as [at] the Lyric:

"Mr. Chairman, ladies and gentlemen, it is very delightful to
find myself in this town, where I feel so much at home and
know that I have so many friends, and it is perfectly embar[r]ass-
ing in facing a splendid audience like this not to have brought
with me the voice in which I could present my speech, because
I am well aware that it is what is inside of me and not what is
ouside of me that is important. (Applause.)

"I was taught, I thought with malice propense, by one of my
family a limerick which expresses the disability I suffer under
tonight:

> "For beauty I am not a star
> There are others more handsome by far;
> But my face I don't mind it,
> Because I'm behind it
> It's the people in front that I jar."

(Applause and laughter.)

"And so it seems to me that inasmuch as it is necessary for me to do something very much more than offer myself as an exhibit to be looked at, it is highly painful that I should come with so little vocal power to present it.

"With your indulgence, I do want to speak about some important matters, because, ladies and gentlemen, I would have you forget tonight that any part of the motive that brought this audience together was to consider me as a candidate for the Presidential nomination. That, in my own view, is of relatively small importance. What we have come together to consider is the immediate future and usefulness of the Democratic party and situation of America in respect to her public affairs.

"When I have read the papers in recent days I have thought that it might be useful after so much controversy as to personal merits and demerits, to remind the audience that I should face what are the public questions of America. They do not concern individuals. They do not concern the rival claims of persons to be considered by the voters of the country, but they do very deeply concern the state of the country itself.

"Senator Williams has said a great many things about me that I will not hold him responsible for as critical judgments, but he did remind you of one thing which was very true. I have been very close to some of the intimate operations of American politics in one of those States where those operations have been particularly intimate. I have seen a great party betrayed by the bargains and private understandings of a few self-constituted managers.

"Like Senator Williams, I profess myself a devoted partisan, devoted to the legitimate organization of my party as well as to the principles of that party, and one of the few things that I am proud of is having set the organization of the Democratic party in New Jersey free from a domination that was hateful to it. (Applause.)

"I have exercised as I best know how an unremitting loyalty to the men who have been faithful to the Democratic party in such fashion that they showed themselves willing and capable to make some kind of sacrifices for its benefit, but wherever I have found men who considered first their own private advantage and ambition I have been proud to array myself against them as enemies of the party as well as the State. (Applause.)

"Thank God, the organization of the Democratic party in New Jersey is free. It is free to act for whom and under whom it pleases. (Applause.) But why should we be devoted to a party organization? What is a party organization for? It does not exist for its own sake.

"It exists in order to advance principles for which that party stands. I need not expound in this great Democratic city what the Democratic party has professed to stand for, but I do need to remind you at this critical turn in our national politics that the Republican party in its present condition cannot stand for even the principles which it professes. (Applause.)

"It is rent asunder from top to bottom upon a personal, not upon a national, issue, and every day's press lays before us further particulars to sustain the very indictments that we have been bringing against this party for a generation. For the controversy between Mr. Roosevelt and the President is nothing less than a controversy upon this point: which of them was the least implicated in the alliances which have held the Republican party in thrall? (Applause.)

"We have maintained that the Republican party was guided in its counsels and in its policy by private influences which it would be dangerous for any man to discuss if he wished to maintain his personal credit, and now they are being disclosed. (Applause.)

"I found a very interesting thing that applies to politics as it does to the smaller spheres of human nature.

"If you believe a thing to be true, state it in public and see who winces, and just as soon as they begin denying they begin proving. . . .

"I took my course in politics rather serenely, under skies that seemed rather fair, until the day that will always be memorable to me. I happened to make a speech in the city of Harrisburg, Pennsylvania, in which I said that the real trust was the Money Trust. I did not know it. I suspected it. And the next morning I knew it (applause and laughter) because they knocked me down and ever since then I have been one of the most dangerous men in the United States. (Applause.)

"But fortunately for my credit, after telling the truth, the United States Government itself has been engaged ever since in proving my case. (Laughter.) Every time it institutes a suit against the meat packers, against the Steel Trust, against the Tobacco Trust, against the Standard Oil Company, it sets forth in the suit itself the details of the money power, and only the other day the Department of Commerce and Labor, I believe it was, issued a circular of information pointing out one of the most interesting series of conclusions that could possibly be dealt upon by the thought of the people of this country.

"It pointed out that the 23 gentlemen constituting the directors of the United States Steel Corporation owned or controlled 55 per cent. of the railways of this country, an enormous percentage of the available banking or lendable funds of this country, an extraordinary proportion of the industrial undertakings of this country, and when you reckon up the ownership of stock and the interlacing of directors and the power of holding loans, controlling something that looked like half the industries of America. Now, they are one group. There is another group centering, not in the directors of the United States Steel Corporation, but in the directors of the Standard Oil Company, and these two gentlemen —I mean these two groups of gentlemen—like the groups of gentlemen who constitute the political machine in some quarters, are not disconnected from one another. (Applause.) They overlap and have a *modus vivendi* which makes their co-operation extremely interesting.

"I am not setting forth these things in order to inflame any feeling whatever, for I myself have known most of these men. I know some of these men. I believe them to be perfectly honest. I believe most of them to be entirely patriotic, but I also believe that they have not the sympathies or the knowledge or the equipment to be the masters of the United States (applause), and I also know that they control the Government of the United States. (Applause.) Not, let me say again, with malevolent purposes, but on a theory as old as government itself and as false as anything that was ever entertained in connection with government. The leaders of the Republican party have in recent years allowed themselves to accept this theory, which was the theory of Hamilton at the outset, that the only safe guides in public policies are those persons who have the largest material stake in the prosperity of the country.

"They believe in a government by trustees, and they do not trust the judgment of the people with regard to great and complicated affairs. This is an honest theory on their part, but it is an absolutely false and unsafe theory. They believe in government for the people, but they do not believe in government by the people. (Applause.) They say they are willing to share their inordinate prosperity, though they do not often share it, and I dare say that their disposition is one of entire benevolence, but I have detected a very interesting thing in their speeches. I am subtly aware when I read their utterances that when they speak of the people of the United States they do not include themselves. (Applause and laughter.) They are thinking not from the body of the people, but for the body of the people. They believe that it is their function and privilege to determine with a larger view than the ordinary man can come on what is for the benefit of the people of this country. My indictment against them is that their view is not large enough, that they do not know enough. My indictment against them is that they are ignorant, not that they are corrupt. . . . I say in regard to these gentlemen that, being engaged in enormous undertakings which tax the genius of any man or any body of men, they become so immersed and submerged that they see no horizons whatever. They do not see the great struggling mass of mankind. They do not see where the mass heaves by the mere effort of men to gain a foothold.

"They do not remember the times when they lay awake the night through wondering where the food would come from the next morning for those who were dependent upon them. They do not remember the day when they went to bed with every muscle and nerve exhausted by the sheer effort and anxiety of the long hours of labor. They have forgotten those things. They do not know that a nation is great in proportion to those who are struggling for confident hope and expectation of the future. (Applause.) . . .

"I hear a great deal said by business men against the agitations of politics being inimical to business. Is this system not inimical to business? Are the business men of this country, the rank and file of them, contented with the conditions of affairs? Ah, I know what mask they wear. I have a very wide acquaintance among business men, and when I get them in a private room they tell me what their real opinions are and they dare not tell their real opinions out of doors. In some quarters I know that they dare not because I can name quarters in which if they did they could not get a single note renewed. I am not arguing these things, I am telling you. For I know how money is used in politics nowadays, and I know that back of all the bad politics in this country lies the control which little coteries of business men have over these politics, and when business men say to me, 'Why don't politicians let business alone?' I reply, 'Why don't business men let politicians alone?' (Applause). You are the influential members of the partnership. Withdraw the capital and the business will stop, for the whole capital of politics, so far as it is bad, is based upon the implications of campaign contributions. (Applause.)

"There again I deal with things which I myself have seen. I know the danger of accepting any man's money, no matter how public-spirited that man may think himself to be provided there is the slightest implication of political obligations lying behind the acceptance of the gift. That is the crux of the whole business in America.

"I am not intimating that money is used in the old crude way of bribery. Sometimes it is, but we are all so suspicious nowadays that that is hastily found out and men have grown virtuous through prudence. (Laughter.) . . .

"I tell you, ladies and gentlemen, there is a profound and universal discontent in this country, not with our institutions, but with the private manipulation of our institutions, and I want to tell you what is happening. If neither the Democratic nor the Republican parties qualifies to rectify these things, do you know what is going to happen? Have you noticed the rise of tide in the Socialistic vote?

"Have you noted the number of intelligent men you have met in your daily intercourse who are becoming subscribers to the Socialistic doctrine? Do you see no clouds upon the horizon with regard to the stability of our institutions themselves? We are a patient people; we are slow to act; we do not act in anger; we do not act in excitement, but we do think.

"I have taught young men for 25 years in the doctrines of politics, and the hardest thing I have ever had to do was to make them believe that it was worth while to vote, because they are not so young as not to know that nothing happens after election. (Applause.) If you let these gentlemen in private conference select whom you are to vote for and select them on both tickets, what difference does it make which ticket you vote? They get you coming and they get you going. (Laughter.)

"And so I say I have no quarrel myself with the fundamental impulse of socialism. I absolutely dissent from the socialistic program—I absolutely dissent from any program. I know that I have not sense enough to reconstruct society and I suspect that other people have not either. I do not believe that any man or any group of men know enough to lay down a program by which society is to be reorganized from top to bottom.

"The only thing I can see is the next step, the immediate evil, the necessary thing to do to cure that immediate evil. The only thing I comprehend is the thing I touch. The only way I have ever learned was by observation and experience. I have been suspicious of books all my life—partly because I have written some. (Laughter.) I know that there are so many weak parts that it will not do to stand on that. I do not believe more than one-third of what I read until it is corroborated and validated and made vivid for me by my actual experience and observation and my converse with men who have had wider observation than I have. I know that the game is too complicated for any man to forecast it in its completeness, but I also know that some men are willing to forecast it in its completeness. . . .

"The rise of the Socialistic vote is a sort of index of cynical despair; it is a sort of index that the people of this country are beginning to wonder if they really have the institutions that are written in their Constitution. Any institution professing to be popular and representative that represents a few special interests and not the great body of the people is a fraud in itself. But you do not have to destroy the institution to break up the fraud.

"The best thing to do is to turn the light on. That was the only mistake that those politicians made in New Jersey that Mr. Williams has referred to. They made the mistake of forgetting that I had spent a lifetime learning how to find out things and also a lifetime in talking about them. It was extremely indiscreet to have things in New Jersey talked about (laughter and applause). The people of New Jersey were just as enlightened, just as progressive, just as honest as the people of any other State of the Union, but they had never found a way to have their own purposes realized before. And they met the opportunity with a sort of joyous relief like a great force released after being pent up until it was almost in despair.

"Now I, for my part, subscribe to the doctrines of democracy wit[h] all my heart because I have learned, if nothing else, this fundamental lesson—I do not see how any man who reads history can fail to find it out; some men have not read history and therefore they have not found it out—the lesson of history is that every set of institutions and every nation is renewed out of the mass of unknown men, that you c[a]nnot predict a generation ahead who are to be the leaders, who are to be the saviors, who are to be the representatives of great people. And that the moment you shut off the avenues of individual initiative, the moment you check the processes by which obscure men assert themselves and rise to the top, you have checked all the vital processes of national growth. (Applause.)

"That is the reason aristocracies have gone to seed. Every little coterie goes to seed. It can not fructify under a single generation, and you and I know that trees are not renewed from the top, they are renewed from the bottom. All that fair flower, that luscious fruitage that comes out like quaint ornaments upon the bough has found its source in the operations of the soil, in the roots that you do not see, and the hopeful sap has been drawn up under the generous sun and at last expresses its joy. So it is with a nation. All its sap, all its energy, all its vitality comes out of the great mass of men. Here, there and elsewhere, out of each generation rise the leaders and saviours of mankind. (Applause.)

"Equal opportunity for all and special privileges for none! Why, of course the one is the way of life and the other is the way of death. Not that any man has contrived the destruction of America, but without knowing, by the growth of a system which has tempted men to put the reins into one hand, we have come to a situation where without putting class against class. Without trying to get even with anybody, we must nevertheless destroy the sources of false power and renew those institutions which for a little time because we slept we were about to lose. This thing which we call radicalism is respiration. I subscribe to every word that Senator Williams said in reply to the question whether he was a conservative or a progressive. Sometimes you have to be a progressive in order to save things. (Applause.)

"I remember when I was president of the university that I was somewhat touched with the reform spirit and the very conservative—that is to say, a standstill—friend of mine among the body of the alumni said: 'Wilson, can't you let any thing alone?' I said: 'My dear fellow, I will let anything alone that you will guarantee to me will stand still. (Applause.) But I am going to try to head off anything that I see going in the wrong direction.' (Applause.) And I said: 'That is, the only way to keep it standing still is to head it off.'

"If you want to keep a post white, don't let it alone, keep painting it. There is nothing that you can let alone that won't deteriorate. You have got to stay up nights and nurse it. Let your automobile alone, let any piece of machinery, let anything at all alone and it will collect dust, corrode and presently, when you try to move it, buckle up and defy every effort that you make to move it. . . .

"The country is looking for some instrumentality through which to act. Is it to have it, or is it not? The Democratic party is free to act. The Democratic party is united. (Applause.) The Democratic party knows its purposes. (Applause.) The Democratic party knows its duties. And if we disappoint the country this time, when again shall we ask for its sufferance? The Republican party cannot do it. . . .

A voice: "And Woodrow Wilson is the only man to do it." (Applause.)

Governor Wilson (continuing): "I wonder if you realize what

it means to have a tradition which runs back to the beginning of the republic! What was the republic formed for? It was not, among other things, formed for the inhabitants of the continent of America.

"From the very outset until now we have done what was typified in that dignified Statue of Liberty which stands at the entrance of the harbor of New York—we have lifted the light meant to guide the feet of men everywhere towards the land of freedom and opportunity. We have said to the world, We are not setting up a little selfish kingdom of our own.

"We have met here together as men and brethren to work out a common destiny, which no man can dominate for his private purposes, and we invite all men who love liberty, all men who have the energy to shift for themselves, all men who have the courage to join in enterprises of emancipation, to come to America and let us join together in these things which will bring mankind together to its day of hope and fruition.

"America now must vindicate this claim or cease to make it. America must recover her title deeds. She has forgotten how to be free. Shall she remember again? Shall she take the veil from her eyes? Shall she say, 'There is something else besides the material power? There is this great trusteeship for humanity which we have undertaken.' Shall we not lift our eyes from the dusty road, shut our ears to the harsh cries . . . and see the uplands upon which shines the eternal light of the justice of God himself, join the great visionary host that has marched thither in days gone by and will march thither in days to come, and press forward towards those regions where men will be masters of their own destiny again?"

Printed in the Baltimore *Sun*, April 30, 1912; many editorial headings omitted.

To Willard Saulsbury

My dear friend: [Trenton, N. J.] April 30, 1912.

One of the results of my being constantly off speaking is that I sometimes treat my best friends with apparent neglect. Your letter of April thirteenth, enclosing copy of your letter to Sir Wildred Laurier, is among a number of letters which have suffered neglect at my hands. I want to express my regret that this has happened and my warm appreciation of your kindness in sending me the letter. I shall be very much interested to know what reply, if any, you receive.

Always faithfully yours,   Woodrow Wilson

TLS (W. Saulsbury Papers, DeU).

To William Bayard Hale

My dear Mr. Hale: [Trenton, N. J.] April 30, 1912.

Thank you sincerely for your thoughtful kindness in sending me the copies of the book.[1] It certainly has been got up very nicely indeed, and I want to again express my warm appreciation of the spirit and generosity with which you wrote from a scant material, an admirable sketch.

Cordially and sincerely yours,   Woodrow Wilson

TLS (WC, NjP).
[1] William Bayard Hale, *Woodrow Wilson; The Story of His Life* (Garden City, N. Y., 1912).

From Josephus Daniels

Dear Governor: [Raleigh, N. C.] May 1st, 1912.

I am sending you a marked copy of today's News and Observer which is about the same sort of paper we print every day and you will see that it is pretty "Wilsonish," and I think is continuous of strengthening the sentiment in North Carolina for your nomination.

I trust and believe that Clark has gotten about all his votes and that from now on we will continue to gain votes. I dont believe Clark will ever be nominated and I believe that when the Convention comes seriously down to work they will feel that you can carry more votes than any other man in the country and that the Convention will be wise enough to see that. Your friends here think you will carry North Carolina and we are leaving no stone unturned.

With every good wish,

Sincerely,   [Josephus Daniels]

CCL (J. Daniels Papers, DLC).

A Brief News Report of an Address to the Methodist Social Union of New York

[May 2, 1912]

THE METHODIST SOCIAL UNION BANQUET

The annual banquet of the Social Union was held Monday evening, April 22, at the Hotel Astor. . . .

Governor Woodrow Wilson was given an enthusiastic welcome. Speaking on "Methodism and Progress," he declared that isolation makes progress impossible. The several units of society must be united by bonds of common interest in a homogeneous mass. Genuine sympathy with the people is essential to successful forwarding of a great cause. The real forces that move the world to better things are not intellectual, but heart forces —love, sympathy, enthusiasm. No revival, literary or religious, ever had its origin in a logical conclusion. These enthusiasms must be kindled in not the few, but in the multitude. The rise and growth of Methodism illustrate. John Wesley went out, not down, but went out among the people. The masses had been alienated and would not come to the church, so he took the church to the people, and they caught the spirit of life, and thus the great movement began. And it is the glory of the great Methodist Episcopal Church that it is a democratic church— democratic spelled with a little "d"—a church essentially of the people. And Methodism, with its honored past, is certain to have a future of splendid progress so long as it keeps alive in the multitudes its traditional enthusiasms and in the spirit of John Wesley follows in the footsteps of the Incarnate Christ.

Printed in the New York *Christian Advocate*, cxxxvii (May 2, 1912), 637.

From Henry Wilson Bridges[1]

My dear Dr. Wilson: New York May 2, 1912.

Needless to say I was greatly disappointed at the result in Georgia.[2] I am afraid it is the natural consequence of the combination against you. It is pretty hard to buck all the money and all the other candidates at the same time. Dont give up the fight. I still feel that you not only deserve to win but will win. I know you are over twice as strong with the independent republicans as any other man mentioned and the Democratic party needs a large number of such votes to pull through. I saw Dean Rogers of Yale[3] in New Haven last week, immediately after he had been chosen president of the United Democratic Clubs of Connecticut, and he told me to say to you he was for you first, last and all time.

Sincerely,   H. W. Bridges

TLS (Governors' Files, Nj).
   1 Princeton 1893, lawyer of New York.
   2 The vote in the Georgia presidential primary held on May 1 was Under-wood, 71,410; Wilson, 57,267; Clark, 692; Harmon, 189.
   3 Henry Wade Rogers, President of Northwestern University, 1890-1900, lec-turer and professor, Yale Law School, 1900-1903; dean since 1903.

From Willard Saulsbury

Dear Governor: [Wilmington, Del.] May 2d, 1912.

I have your note of April 30th, saying you would like to know what the result of my letter to Sir Wilfrid Laurier was. He wrote a very friendly letter of considerable length, in which he said that he thought he had better make no expression at all which would look in any way as though he desired to influence Ameri-can politics. I did not intend that such expression should come from him exactly but he either overlooked the suggestion that someone else should make the statement or avoided it in that way. I think however that his conclusion is probably a wise one from his standpoint.

I am very sorry the Georgia and Florida[1] elections have gone against us but hope we will have some better news soon. I was in New York yesterday with Mr. McCombs and came down with him on the train as far as Princeton Junction. I hope your con-sultation was productive of some conclusion as to what our next moves had best be. I expect to see him again on Monday and may hear from him at any time.

With best wishes,

Yours very truly,   Williard Saulsbury

TLS (Saulsbury Letterpress Books, DeU).
   1 The vote in the Florida presidential primary held on April 30 was Under-wood, 28,343, Wilson, 20,482.

To James Duval Phelan

Princeton, N J., May 3, 1912

In the matter of Chinese and Japanese coolie immigration I stand for the national policy of exclusion (or restricted immi-gration) The whole question is one of assimilation of diverse races. We cannot make a homogeneous population out of peo-ple who do not blend with the caucasian race. Their lower standard of living as laborers will crowd out the white agriculturist and is, in other fields, a most serious industrial menace. The success of free democratic institutions demand of our people education, intelligence, patriotism, and the state should protect them against unjust and impossible competition. Remunerative labor is the basis of contentment. Democracy rests on the equality of the citizen. Oriental coolieism will give us another race problem to solve and surely we have had our lesson.

Woodrow Wilson.[1]

T telegram (J. D. Phelan Papers, CU).

[1] This telegram was evoked by the campaign against Wilson then being vigorously waged by the Hearst newspapers. In the eastern states, they usually printed the passage from *A History of the American People* that sounded highly derogatory of immigrants from southern and eastern Europe (for this passage, see F. I. Dobrinski to WW, Feb. 2, 1912, n. 3). In California, the Hearst organs used the continuation of the same passage to allege that Wilson favored Oriental immigration. The full portion of the text relating to Chinese immigrants follows:

"The people of the Pacific coast had clamored these many years against the admission of immigrants out of China, and in May, 1892, got at last what they wanted, a federal statute which practically excluded from the United States all Chinese who had not already acquired the right of residence; and yet the Chinese were more to be desired, as workmen if not as citizens, than most of the coarse crew that came crowding in every year at the eastern ports. They had, no doubt, many an unsavory habit, bred unwholesome squalor in the crowded quarters where they most abounded in the western seaports, and seemed separated by their very nature from the people among whom they had come to live; but it was their skill, their intelligence, their hardy power of labor, their knack at succeeding and driving duller rivals out, rather than their alien habits, that made them feared and hated and led to their exclusion at the prayer of the men they were likely to displace should they multiply." *A History of the American People*, v, 213-14.

Chinese and Japanese immigration had been an explosive issue in California since it became a state. On January 27, 1912, the day on which Hearst's *San Francisco Examiner* first publicized Wilson's allegedly pro-Oriental stance, Phelan began bombarding McCombs with letters urging him to extract from Wilson a public statement opposing further Chinese and Japanese immigration. McCombs suggested that Phelan write directly to Wilson; Phelan finally did so on April 20 (see J. D. Phelan to WW, April 20, 1912). Six days later, Phelan again wrote to McCombs, this time including a draft statement. Wilson (or McCombs) used the statement as the text of this telegram. Phelan immediately gave it to the San Francisco newspapers, but only two of them printed it, and only one featured it on its front page.

The telegram came too late to have any effect on the vote in the California presidential primary on May 14; Clark swept the polls, with 43,163 votes to 17,214 for Wilson. However, Phelan and the state Democratic organization made extensive use of the telegram during the presidential campaign. The document also found its way into at least one national magazine in the course of the campaign, being printed in the New York *Independent*, LXXIII (Oct. 10, 1912), 863.

For detailed studies of this incident, see Robert E. Hennings, "James D. Phelan and the Woodrow Wilson Anti-Oriental Statement of May 3, 1912," *California Historical Society Quarterly*, XLII (Dec. 1963), 291-300, and Roger Daniels, *The Politics of Prejudice: The Anti-Japanese Movement in California and the Struggle for Japanese Exclusion* (Berkeley and Los Angeles, 1962), pp. 54-56.

From James Duval Phelan

My dear Governor   San Francisco May 3 12

I am in receipt today of your telegram on the question of Oriental immigration which will effectually serve to silence Mr Hearst.

Thanking you & with best *hopes*, I am

Very truly yours   Jas. D. Phelan.

ALS (Governors' Files, Nj).

From William Gibbs McAdoo

PERSONAL AND CONFIDENTIAL.

Dear Governor: [New York] May 4, 1912.

I am very sorry to learn that you are laid up with a cold; I am just getting over a similar attack.

I cannot tell you how sorry I am about Georgia. Col. Gray says that fully $100,000. was spent by the opposition in that state. I, myself, cannot explain the result upon any other theory than the prodigal use of money. You must not, however, let this discourage you. It disappoints me, but doesn't discourage me. What is needed now is to have, as quickly as possible, a conference of some of your leading friends from some of the leading states. Such a conference ought to come upon your personal invitation. I think you ought to take this up with McCombs immediately and agree upon the men who shall be invited to that conference. I hope, as soon as you are able, that you will give this serious attention.

I trust that you are much better and that you may soon be entirely well; also that the results in Maryland and Texas may be in your favor.

Please remember me to Mrs. Wilson, and believe me, with kindest regards,   Sincerely yours,   W G McAdoo

TLS (LPC, W. G. McAdoo Papers, DLC).

To Thomas Bell Love

Princeton, N. J., May 5, 1912.

Thanks for your generous message[1]   Texas puts me in heart[2] The work of my friends was a satisfaction as it was unselfish

Woodrow Wilson

TC telegram (T. B. Love Papers, Dallas Hist. Soc.).
  [1] It is missing.

2 Wilson supporters won an overwhelming victory in the Democratic precinct conventions in Texas on May 4. This assured a Wilson victory in the county conventions held three days later and hence in the state convention on May 28 and 29.

To Josephus Daniels

Trenton N. J. May 5th, 1912

Would gratefully appreciate any information or advise about North Carolina that you would be generous enough to give me.

Woodrow Wilson.

T telegram (J. Daniels Papers, DLC).

A Fragment of a Letter to Mary Allen Hulbert Peck

[Princeton, N. J., c. May 5, 1912]

delightful that she should be the right sort!

I have been losing States and gaining them,—and I have been in bed for half a week because I went to Baltimore and defied that cold,—but my spirits hold serenely and the consequences (one way or the other) do not give me serious concern, for myself,—and I am getting well and strong and rested. Providence will determine things better than we can foresee or arrange.

All join me in affectionate messages. Love to Mrs. A. and Allen.   Your devoted friend,   Woodrow Wilson

TCL (WC, NjP).

To Edward Mandell House

My dear Mr. House: [Trenton, N. J.] May 6, 1912.

I certainly had splendid and effective friends in Texas, and I want to express to you in particular my warm and deep appreciation of the intelligent work done. It is very delightful to have the support of the great old State.

I am enclosing a letter which I wrote almost a month ago, and stupidly addressed to Huston instead of to Austin.[1] I send it as an evidence that I was not as thoughtless as I must have seemed to you.

Your suggestion that I lunch or dine with you is most acceptable. I have lost a lot of time from my office by defying a cold and having to pay the penalty by four days in the house, but I am going to look you up at the earliest possible moment.

We can have a little celebration over the splendid result in Texas.

> Cordially and faithfully yours,   Woodrow Wilson

TLS (E. M. House Papers, CtY).
¹ It is missing.

From Josephus Daniels

Dear Sir: [Raleigh, N. C.] May 6th, 1912.

We have no primary in this State and no legal method at getting at the wishes of the people and we cannot tell with any certainty until the Congressional and State Conventions meet what the situation will be. The State Convention meets on the 5th of June and the Congressional Conventions in the ten districts meet from the 25th of May on to the 4th of June.

The Underwood people have been very busy doing in this State what they did in Georgia, issuing supplements with all the country press and they seem to be well supplied with the sinews of war. The Harmon people who are probably not so numerous are working with the Underwood people for an uninstructed delegation.

In most parts of the State the sentiment is largely for you and I believe we are going to carry the State. I have been doing everything in my power and my paper has had little else in it but interviews with Democrats in the State who favor your candidacy and presenting the issue.

Three weeks ago Mr. McAdoo induced Col. W. H. Osborne of Greensboro, who is a very active man, to enter upon the fight and to organize and before that, Mr. S. E. Williams¹ of Lexington, who is well known to Mr. McCombs, undertook the work of organization.

I am going to Greensboro tomorrow to have a conference with those gentlemen and with others and find out how far they have effected it and exactly what the situation is. The vote in Georgia and Florida tremenduously helped the Underwood people as you understand but the Texas vote helped us very much. I will write you Wednesday or wire you from Greensboro more fully.

> Very truly yours,   [Josephus Daniels]

CCL (J. Daniels Papers, DLC).
¹ Stevens Edwin Williams, lawyer of Lexington, N. C.

From Pleasant Alexander Stovall

Dear Governor: Savannah, Ga. May 6th, 12.

I have not had the heart to write you since our miserable primary and its result.

There is really nothing to say except that you carried every city in which you spoke and that the opposition spent money like water in the state. They poured it out heavily in Chatham County but we trimmed them in Savannah very neatly.

I simply write to congratulate you upon the splendid result in Texas. I believe that South Carolina and Maryland[1] will give good accounts of themselves to-day.

I notice in some southern states the opposition has withdrawn Clark and Harmon, and is seeking to get up "uninstructed" delegations which are really plays for Harmon. I notice this is the game in Virginia & possibly in North Carolina where in a square fight your friends would beat the other fellows easily.

There is something plausible and insidious about an "uninstructed" delegation. Sometimes good conservatice [conservative] men are won over by this plea, and we must expose it when ever possible.

With best wishes, I remain,

Yours very truly,   Pleasant A. Stovall

TLS (Governors' Files, Nj).
[1] In the presidential primary in Maryland on May 6, Clark received 34,510 votes; Wilson, 22,816; and Harmon, 7,157. In South Carolina on the same day, Wilson carried all the counties which instructed their delegates to the state convention (to be held on May 15) and was endorsed by several others as well.

Two Letters to Josephus Daniels

My dear friend: [Trenton, N. J.] May 7, 1912.

Your letter of May first would have been answered long ago had I not been in my beg [bed] struggling with a desperate cold. I am just back at my office and want to send you my warmest thanks for the cheer your letter brought me.

Faithfully yours,   Woodrow Wilson

❖

Personal.

My dear friend: [Trenton, N. J.] May 7, 1912.

Thank you warmly for your letter of yesterday. It has done me good to hear from you.

I do not for a moment doubt that you were doing everything

that was possible, and more than was generous, but I was no
[so] anxious to learn just what your letter tells me, that the
various friends of mine who are working in North Carolina
are getting together in conference. I did not like to suggest that
you see Colonel Osborne and Mr. Williams, because it would
seem impertinent to suggest anything to a man of your experience and knowledge of the State, but I am delighted that you
are to see them and shall await the result with the greatest interest. A letter recently received from Colonel Osborne[1] gave a
rather pessimistic hue to the outlook.

　　With warmest regard,

　　　　　　　　　Faithfully yours,　Woodrow Wilson

TLS (J. Daniels Papers, DLC).
　[1] It is missing.

To Francis Griffith Newlands

Personal.

My dear Senator:　　　　　　　　[Trenton, N. J.] May 7, 1912.

　　I feel that things might have gone better recently if I had had
the benefit of closer contact with you and my other friends in
Washington, and I am wondering if it would be possible for you
to run up to see me. I hope you will not think this presuming
upon your kindness.

　　If you would let me know what your liberty is in the matter,
I am sure we could arrange a time. There are many things I
feel I ought to talk over with you.

　　　　　　　　　Cordially yours,　Woodrow Wilson

TLS (F. G. Newlands Papers, CtY).

From Josephus Daniels

Dear Sir:　　　　　　　　　Greensboro, N. C., May 8, 1912.

　　In compliance as to my letter to you on Monday I came here
last night and had a conference with Mr. Williams, State Chairman Eller,[1] Speaker Justice,[2] Col. Osborn, and others advocating your nomination.

　　We find that the Underwood people have transferred the
Georgia and Florida nomination to North Carolina, and the con-
sensus opened by this and our conference last night was that it
was of the highest importance, if it was at all possible, for you
to come to North Carolina next week and make a speach at

Raleigh, Charlotte, and this place, and perhaps a few other speaches between times.

I sincerely hope you can come and hope you will telegraph if you can do so, and that you are well enough to do so. Will you please wire me at Raleigh that you can come.

Faithfully your friend,   [Josephus Daniels]

CCL (J. Daniels Papers, DLC).
    [1] Adolphus Hill Eller, lawyer and trust officer of the Wachovia Bank & Trust Co. of Winston-Salem; member of the North Carolina Senate, 1905-1907; chairman, North Carolina State Democratic Executive Committee, 1908-12.
    [2] Edwin Judson Justice, lawyer of Greensboro; member of the North Carolina House of Representatives, 1899 and 1907; speaker, 1907.

A News Report of Remarks in Trenton
to New Jersey Wilson Men

[May 10, 1912]

WILSON'S AIDES ARE OPTIMISTIC

Governor Hears Favorable Reports
from All Over the State.

TRENTON, May 10.—Addressing the gathering of Wilson workers from all parts of the State[1] who met here yesterday afternoon,[2] and presented favorable reports, Governor Wilson intimated that in the National Democratic convention at Baltimore he would receive for the nomination for President, the votes of many of the delegates from other States, who are classified as unpledged or pledged to Speaker Champ Clark or Representative Underwood.

The statement was not made by the Governor as a positive declaration, but it was so couched as to indicate that he was aware of conditions in the campaign that were unknown to the mass of workers. The Governor's remarks brought out enthusiastic applause. . . .

When Mr. Hinchliffe called on Governor Wilson to speak the Governor said that he had been hearing his name so much that it came to have a kind of impersonal significance to him. He regretted that meetings similar to the one in progress had not been held in other States.

Referring to the belief that delegates that are unpledged or are nominally for other candidates, he said that he believed many of them would be for him because the delegates realized that the sentiment of the people was for Wilson.

At the present time, said the Governor, it was impossible to accurately analyze the situation regarding the possible nominee, but he said that he did not want to be a candidate if he was to be a candidate of only a minority of the party.

Printed in the *Newark Evening News*, May 10, 1912; one editorial heading omitted.
  ¹ Democratic leaders working for a large Wilson turnout in the New Jersey presidential primary on May 28.
  ² At the "rooms" of the Democratic League, 144 E. State St., Trenton.

From Josephus Daniels

Dear Sir: [Raleigh, N. C.] May 10th, 1912.

I received the letter sent by your Private Secretary¹ and I am returning herewith the copy of the one you sent me.

I was in Greensboro Tuesday night and Wednesday and Mr. Williams and other friends there are very active and believe their situation well in hand. Of course, there is opposition and we cannot see matters as clearly as we ought to because of the high bridged sort of way we have of holding primaries and county conventions but Mr. Williams and others are hard at work and I am in touch with everybody I think I can reach in the State.

Mr. Craven² is a very good man but his judgment is not the best although it may be very well that he is that way—it may make Williams and others more alert.

Very truly yours,   [Josephus Daniels]

CCL (J. Daniels Papers, DLC).
  ¹ W. Measday to J. Daniels, May 8, 1912, TLS (J. Daniels Papers, DLC).
  ² Bruce Craven, lawyer of Trinity, N. C.

From Francis Griffith Newlands

[Washington] May 10, 1912.

I find myself under such pressure that it is impossible to get away. It would give us great pleasure if you could pass this or next week end with us. Would arrange for you to meet your friends.   Francis G. Newlands

T telegram (F. G. Newlands Papers, CtY).

To Francis Griffith Newlands

Trenton N. J., May 10 [1912]

Very sorry indeed   will seek an early opportunity to see you am tied for the present   Woodrow Wilson

T telegram (F. G. Newlands Papers, CtY).

From Francis Griffith Newlands

My dear Governor,   Washington, D. C. May 10th, 1912.

I regretted very much my inability to go to Trenton. But I am simply pressed to the wall. In addition to measures which I am daily pressing in Committee relating to the trusts, I have been urging my bill for river regulation, which has become a very live question in view of the Mississippi overflow. Within the last few weeks I have been on the cars for seven nights, attending Waterway Conferences etc. Then too I have a luncheon to about 30 members of the Senate and House on Sunday, at which the related questions of storage and drainage will be discussed. I was in hope that you might be able to come to us at the week's end and meet these gentlemen.

I have been in frequent communication with friends at Nevada. They state that Clark sentiment is growing there, the result of the general circulation of the [George Fred] Williams letter, the constant attacks of Hearst's [San Francisco] Examiner, which largely circulates there, the impression that Clark is gaining, and a factional fight that has been going on since the last election. I had my letter printed and generally circulated and my preference is well known. Ordinarily I think this would have weight, but there are elements of confusion which I dont quite understand and as I was away in Europe last Summer, I am not in such close touch as I could wish.

It looks as if Roosevelt would be nominated. If he is, I know of no one who could meet him before the public except yourself. It would be a pretty debate—the rapier against the club.

With kindest regards and warm wishes for your success, I am
          Most sincerely yours   Francis G. Newlands

TCL (F. G. Newlands Papers, CtY).

To Mary Allen Hulbert Peck

Dearest Friend,   Hotel Astor New York 11 May, 1912

I am here to-day to attend a dinner of the Reform Club[1] tonight and make a speech on the tariff (did you ever hear of anything less exciting!) but I need not have come over last night, as I did, merely to be early and get a seat. I really came when I did in order not to be in Princeton any part of to-day. Jack Hibben is to be (is being) inaugurated as president of the University to-day, and I could not be present or play any part without hypocricy. I am Governor of the State and, as such, president of the Board of Trustees of the University. I *could* not be in the town and not show myself at the ceremonies,— particularly as the President of the United States is to be there and I would be his official host. Why should I feel like a runaway, and as if I were doing an ungenerous thing? Because I love the University, I suppose, and many of the fine men who are connected with it,—and also because I am constitutionally averse from sparing myself anything hard and disagreeable,— and perhaps because it seems a less candid course to absent myself than to go there and speak out what is in my mind. *There's* the whole point of the matter! To be present and silent would be deeply hypocritical: to go and speak my real thoughts and judgments would be to break up the meeting and create a national scandal, to the great injury of the dear old place. No doubt I should stay away. But it is hard and it is mortifying. To be true to oneself and candid in the utterance of the truth is to live in a very embarrassing world. And yet what *man* would buy peace at the price of his soul.

Alas! my dear friend, it is a hard world to live in! I dare say no man is so humble as not to feel the jolts and jars and clashes of it. And who shall set an estimate, in such circumstances upon real, tested friendship,—friendship with insight and comprehending sympathy, that understands before the case is stated and sees as much as your own heart does? It is *that* that makes life noble and beautiful and good to live.

The cold that knocked me out last week has almost entirely disappeared, but has left me with a little less than my wonted vigour. I am more quickly tired than is usual with me. But that is nothing. I am quite fit and in excellent spirits—except for the particular thoughts of the day.

No letter from you yet since you sailed. I trust you are all right. All join me in affectionate messages to you all.

Your devoted friend   Woodrow Wilson

ALS (WP, DLC).
¹ A New York organization devoted to tariff reform, especially active during the Cleveland era.

From Alexander Mitchell Palmer

My dear Governor: [Stroudsburg, Pa.] May 11, 1912.

You have doubtless noticed the result of the Democratic State Convention at Harrisburg.

I was Chairman of the Committee on Resolutions and reported the platform of which I enclose herewith a newspaper copy. I also introduced in the Resolutions Committee a resolution "That the delegates to the National Convention, this day elected, be and they are hereby instructed to vote for the nomination of Woodrow Wilson for president, and to use all honorable means to accomplish his nomination."

Judge Gordon,[1] in the Committee on Resolutions, suggested an amendment, which should bind the delegation to vote for you "until his name shall be withdrawn from the Convention."

I objected to this language being inserted in the resolution because of the fear that it would go out to the country that we anticipated that your name might be withdrawn from the Convention, and I believed the language of the instruction resolution was sufficiently strong. The Resolutions Committee took my view and it was so reported to the Convention. After the resolution was adopted by the Convention, Thomas J. Ryan, of Philadelphia,[2] made the suggestion, in a speech in which he charged bad-faith to about everybody, that the resolution should contain a provision that the delegates should vote for you as long as your name remains before the Convention. I told him that would certainly be done.

We elected twelve delegates at large, all of whom are with you to the last ditch. In addition, at least forty of the sixty-four district delegates already elected are with us in our plans to oust the machine and I will have at least fifty-two votes for National Committeeman. The chances are that there will be no opposition to my election.[3] Those fifty-two men, who are unreservedly for me for National Committeeman, will never waver in support for yourself for the nomination. I can not speak for the others but having been elected as avowed Wilson men, I hope they will continue true to the finish.

We were somewhat disturbed at Harrisburg by the activity of Mr. [Henry E.] Alexander, of Trenton, who was working hard to secure the election of Judge Gordon as a delegate to the National Convention. Gordon sought this place only to advance his candidacy for National Committeeman, and for that position he was backed by the old Guffey-Donnelly machine. The election of Gordon as National Committeeman in our state would be a continuation of the present deplorable conditions, under which the state has been operated by a bipartisan machine. Alexander's support of him, coupled with his statements that he was making the fight in your name, mixed the situation somewhat; but I am glad to say it did not shake the confidence of any of the reorganizers in their assurance of your support of their cause. Yours truly, A. Mitchell Palmer.

TCL (WP, DLC).
1 James Gay Gordon, Sr., lawyer of Philadelphia, former judge of the Court of Common Pleas, Philadelphia County, a leader of the conservative faction of the Democratic party in Pennsylvania.
2 Thomas J. Ryan, a leader of the conservative faction of the Democratic party in Philadelphia.
3 The Pennsylvania delegation to the Democratic national convention elected Palmer national committeeman by acclamation in Baltimore on June 24, 1912.

A News Report of An Address to the Reform Club
of New York

[May 12, 1912]

WILSON ASSAILS TRUST DECISIONS
OF SUPREME COURT

Trusts in Control of the Country and
All Its Resources,—He Adds.

Gov. Woodrow Wilson, speaking last night at the dinner of the Reform Club at the Hotel Astor, said:

"I am opposed to the various and varying decisions of the United States Supreme Court in regard to the Sherman Anti-Trust law. Mr. Sherman intended to say that every kind of organization or industry or trade which interferes with competition should be illegal. But a very clever change of phraseology made it very easy to change it. The United States Supreme Court has been engaged in interpreting it so that it does not interfere with the operations that have strangled competition in the United States.[1]

"But the minds of lawyers are very unserviceable for reform. I know, for I was myself bred as a lawyer, and it took me thirty years to get out of the settled game.

"The leading financial minds of this country do not understand the United States. They do not see the muscles and brawn of the people who are carrying the burden. What is the truth in the United States to-day? A universal suspicion of big business, and there is no business that can exist on suspicion.

"We are constantly trembling on the verge of panic when we are in this state of mind. The country does not own its own government. That is my indictment against the tariff. The power of money comes before liberty."

Gov. Wilson went on to say that the centre of privileges comes from the tariff.

"The tariff prices were fixed by gentlemen who met in private conference," he said. "The names of these gentlemen I could give. That was the beginning of the special privileges from which has grown most of the tariff evil and the high prices."

The Governor declared that the United States Steel Corporation controls 55 per cent. of the railroads in this country and most of the lendable money. In view of this, he said, the corporation is able to say whether or not there shall be competition. He said the country is in the grip of the trusts and declared that since the Sherman Anti-Trust law has been passed more trusts and monopolies have sprung up than ever before.

Gov. Wilson proclaimed the tariff not only the chief issue of the coming campaign, but the issue upon which the settlement of practically all other important questions before the country at the present time depends.

In addition to listening with great attention to Gov. Wilson's declaration that the whole tariff policy of the country to-day is sham, about four hundred diners applauded three other speeches attacking the protective system[2] and unmistakably showed themselves in favor of substantial tariff reform, if not of free trade.

"The whole tariff policy has become a huge scheme of make-believe," began the Governor, and he went on to declare that while the whole economic life of the country had changed, the beneficiaries of the tariff had continued to maintain it along the old lines until it occupied an absurd position.

"It begins to dawn upon the whole country," he went on, "that the tariff is no longer a statesmanlike plan of protection, but a privately managed game for profits. A big game—a huge scheme —carried out through the votes of enormous numbers of men, who are deceived by the old phrases and do not face the new facts; a game in which the powerful, the subtle, the unscrupulous, are more likely to prevail than any others. It stands as ugly and as full of unwholesome secrets and hidden places to which the light has never penetrated, as the old Bastile."

Printed in the New York *World*, May 12, 1912; two editorial headings omitted.
[1] That is, the "rule of reason" enunciated in the Standard Oil and American Tobacco decisions of 1911 had sanctioned restraint of trade.
[2] By Senator Gore, Charles Sumner Hamlin, Boston financier, and Henry George, Jr., New York congressman.

To Josephus Daniels

Personal.

My dear friend:　　　　　　　　[Trenton, N. J.] May 13, 1912.

Thank you heartily for your letter of May ninth.[1] It was generous and characteristic of you. I find that I regain my physical tone slowly and it is evident that I shall have to go rather carefully and experimentally for a week or two.

I not only know that you and my other friends in North Carolina are working, but I know that you are working with the closest knowledge of actual conditions, and therefore in a way that nobody else could work, and I am pleased that after your conference with Colonel Osborn he feels encouraged.

It occurs to me that if the people of North Carolina could be thoroughly informed as to just what is happening in the transference of what you so properly call the "caravan" from the other Southern states in to Carolina in behalf of Underwood, it would cause a great revulsion of feeling and operate to our benefit. Surely, North Carolina will not like to be taken possession of in this way against the guidance of her own thoughtful men.

I need not tell you how deeply it gratifies me that you should be so interested in this campaign. I feel very much honored by your condifence [confidence], and shall do my best for the rest of my life to deserve it.

Give my warmest regards to Mrs. Daniels, and to all the family. I think of you all very often.

　　　　　Cordially and faithfully yours,　　Woodrow Wilson

TLS (J. Daniels Papers, DLC).
[1] It is missing.

Two Letters to Alexander Mitchell Palmer

Personal.

My dear Mr. Palmer:　　　　　　[Trenton, N. J.] May 13, 1912.

Your letter of May tenth has gratified me very much. I was hoping that I might presently get an inside account of what happened at the Convention, because I have grown very chary of crediting ehat [what] I see in the newspapers.

I felt the utmost confidence throughout in what you and my other friends would do and had not the least uneasiness, but your letter gives me the specific details, and I thank you for it very warmly indeed. It warms a man's heart to have such support, and I am particularly proud to have won the delegation from Pennsylvania.

I do not wonder you speculated about the activity of Mr. Alexander of Trenton. He is a very erratic person and I for some time past have lost sight of him. I do not know just what his connections are at present. He is a man of strong friendships and impulses, and means everything that he does for the best.

Cordially and sincerely yours, Woodrow Wilson

❖

My dear Mr. Palmer: [Trenton, N. J.] May 13, 1912.

One of the delegates from Pennsylvania[1] sent me a copy of a letter which I am asking my Headquarters in New York to have copied in order that you may see it.

It was from a certain Mr. Grover Cleveland Gladner,[2] claiming to represent Mr. Speaker Clark, asking of the delegate a secret pledge to vote for Mr. Clark, and even intimating the hope that he would vote for him on the first ballot. I thought that you ought to see this letter.

Cordially and faithfully yours, Woodrow Wilson

TLS (WP, DLC).
[1] Asher K. Johnson of Bradford, Pa., as the following letter reveals.
[2] Unidentified.

To Roland Sletor Morris

Personal.

My dear Morris: [Trenton, N. J.] May 13, 1912.

I greatly valye [value] your letter of May ninth.[1] It has given me deep pleasure, as your letters always do. And it makes me very proud that you should feel as you do about the opportunity to vote for me at the Convention. I do not know anything that has steadied or heartened me more than the confidence which so many generous friends have placed in me in these recent weeks and months.

I received a letrer [letter] this morning from Mr. Asher K. Johnson of Bradford, Pa., containing enclosures which disturb me. The enclosures showed that the Clark Managers are trying hard to get hold of our delegates from Pennsylvania, and are asking *secret* pledges of them. I find that these enclosures have been sent to our Headquarters, in New York, but I am going to ask them to send you copies of them.

Cordially and faithfully yours,   Woodrow Wilson

TLS (photostat in the R. S. Morris Papers, DLC).
    ¹ It is missing.

To Richard Heath Dabney

My dear Heath: [Trenton, N. J.] May 13, 1912.

I am all right again and the reports about my "break down" were absurd. I simply had to go to bed to cure a severe cold.

I am very much distressed to hear that you do not sleep and that your nerves are bad, and I am rejoiced to hear that you are going to the other side of the water to recuperate. This is exactly the thing to do, and I wish you all the strength in the world, my dear fellow.

I think that, politically, things are in fairly satisfactory shape. As a matter of fact most of the support of Clark and Underwood is perfunctory and on the surface, and underneath, if I am correctly informed, the purpose to nominate me is as strong as it ever was. These things cannot be depended upon, of course, but this is what is reported to me by men who ought to know.

The combination against me has certainly done wonders, and yet my chief disappointment in the primaries of various states is not that they did not result in my favor, but that they were so small in respect of the numbers who voted. The people did not take any interest in them. They were about equivalent to caucuses held through the polling places. Possibly the people will wake up later to the significance of the whole thing, but for the present there seems to be extraordinary lethargy and indifference.

I saw Dick Byrd in New York on Saturday night and he is very hopeful, not to say confident, of controlling the Virginia situation in my favor. At any rate, the fight there is by no means in bad shape.¹

With genuine affection,

Faithfully yours,   Woodrow Wilson

TLS (Wilson-Dabney Corr., ViU).
    ¹ The result of the Virginia state Democratic convention held on May 23, 1912, was, considering the circumstances, a considerable victory for Wilson's friends. Realizing that they could not defeat the anti-Wilson state machine headed by Senator Thomas S. Martin, the Wilson managers made a compromise agreement with the Martin leaders. Four of the eight delegates at large were to be Wilson men, and the delegation to the national convention would be uninstructed. However, the unit rule could be invoked after the first ballot

by a two-thirds vote. As it turned out, the delegation contained enough Wilson supporters to prevent the adoption of the unit rule. See Link, "The South and the Democratic Campaign of 1910-1912," Chap. XI, and Allen W. Moger, *Virginia: Bourbonism to Byrd, 1870-1925* (Charlottesville, Va.), pp. 277 and 277n39.

To Francis Griffith Newlands

Personal.

My dear Senator: [Trenton, N. J.] May 13, 1912.

Thank you sincerely for your letter of the tenth. I of course understand how necesarily you are absorbed. It was only in the hope that there might be a chance of your getting away that I took the liberty of making the suggestion I did.

For I am very anxious to have your advice, if there is any you can give me, as to what ought to be done to offset the unfortunate sentiment gathering in Nevada. You alone among the friends to whom I have access would know how this should be handled.

I need not tell you how warmly I appreciate your own interest and your own indifference, and it is hard for me to believe that your desires will not in the end be regarded.

With much regard and appreciation,

Cordially yours,   Woodrow Wilson

TLS (F. G. Newlands Papers, CtY).

From Josephus Daniels

Dear Governor: [Raleigh, N. C.] May 13th, 1912.

I am sending you a copy of yesterday's News and Observer and you will find that it is a very good Wilson number. For fear the paper may not reach your personal attention, I am enclosing you herewith an editorial from it.[1]

We were greatly disappointed that you could not come to North Carolina and I hope you are improving every day.

With sentiments of esteem and high regards,

Sincerely,   [Josephus Daniels]

CCL (J. Daniels Papers, DLC).

[1] "Come, Let Us Reason Together," Raleigh *News and Observer*, May 12, 1912, an editorial three and a half columns in length. It argued that Underwood was a sectional candidate with no chance to win the presidency; that Clark, although stronger, could not attract the independent votes so essential to election; and that Wilson was the only Democratic candidate who could possibly win.

To Cyrus Hall McCormick

My dear Cyrus,   [Trenton, N. J.] 14 May, 1912

I am glad you are going to confer with McAdoo. He is a true friend of right things and a real man, loving what is just and for the good of the country,—a sincere friend, too.

Affectionately   Woodrow Wilson

ALS (WP, DLC).

From William Elliott Gonzales

Dear Mr Wilson: Columbia, S. C., May 14/12

Yours of yesterday has just reached me and I hasten to write amid the bustle of the evening before the convention.

The man I refer to is C. W. Tyler, formerly of the New York Sun,[1] four years ago the publicity man for the Anti-Bryan men in Wall Street. That he handled their money I know, but I cannot make that public as it came to me confidentially.

He took Harvey's letter to Watterson at Atlanta, and Harvey's letter to Watterson at Richmond, Dec. 24 and 30th respectively —and Harvey placed "the utmost confidence" in him.[2]

I sent that editorial to Geo W. Perkins and asked if he was in position to indicate to me for publication that the outline of the formula was correct, but his secretary tells me he is out of New York and will be absent for some time.

Bankhead[3] is here today. I find that Tillman's opposition to instructions is standing in the way of hearty support, the local fight interfering with honest action. But earnest work is being done, and I expect to get instructions. In this case my first ultimatum has been issued to the organization in control.[4]

With best wishes,

Sincerely yours,   William E. Gonzales.

ALS (WP, DLC).

[1] Charles W. Tyler, journalist of New York, for many years on the staff of the New York *Sun*.

[2] Harvey's courier was (Isaac) Wayne MacVeagh, not Tyler. See Link, *Road to the White House*, pp. 365-67.

[3] Senator John Hollis Bankhead of Alabama, manager of the Underwood preconvention campaign.

[4] At the state convention in Columbia on May 15, the Wilson supporters lost a vote (178 to 162) to instruct the delegation, but by an overwhelming majority (241 to 91) they passed a resolution warmly endorsing Wilson's candidacy.

To George Foster Peabody

My dear Mr. Peabody,　　　Princeton, New Jersey 15 May, 1912

Your letters of May 6th[1] came to my office in Trenton, while I was ill in bed with a cold and, because of a bit of veritable stupidity there, neither Mrs. Wilson nor I had the pleasure of reading them until to-day. I am chagrined that I should have been made to seem so unappreciative by a long delay in replying.

I need not tell you that we enjoyed them, and appreciated them very deeply. Your friendship, your frankness, your generous estimate of us, your delightful gift for saying what cheers and strengthens,—and what clears both motive and object, made the letters have the effect upon us of water upon a parched land,—and we are very grateful.

After all, it was well for us that they seemed to drop out of heaven upon us to-day. For there has been a great deal to check our spirits lately. The support that seemed assured only a few weeks ago has been turned away, by one force and another, until there seems small chance of service on a large scale. There were things I was eager to set all my strength to which I must now, apparently, content myself to merely talk about from the outside. The Powers have shunted me. I do not repine; but I do feel like a man in leash,—and such confidence in me as you express was needed.

Mrs. Wilson and my daughters join me in every cordial message, and I am your debtor

　　　Cordially & faithfully Yours,　Woodrow Wilson

P.S. It seems that my stenographer in Trenton read part of your letter to me to Mrs. Wilson over the telephone while I was ill,—in explanation of the arrival of the flowers, which we enjoyed so much.　W.W.

ALS (G. F. Peabody Papers, DLC).
　[1] They are missing.

To Charles Henry Grasty

My dear Mr. Grasty:　　　Trenton, N. J. May 15, 1912.

The attitude of the Sun towards my candidacy has given me so much pleasure and encouragement that I cannot refrain from the pleasure of sending you a line of warmest thanks and appreciation. Papers such as the Sun can do a vast deal towards getting our party out of the confusion into which it now seems to have stumbled.

Cordially and faithfully yours,   Woodrow Wilson

TLS (WP, DLC).

From Cleveland Hoadley Dodge

Dear Woodrow   New York. May 15th 1912

You are constantly in my thoughts, but I couldn't help having an especially big "think" when I read last night this entry, in the office-notes of Lord Dalhousie, India's greatest Governor General:

"To fear God, and to have no other fear, is a maxim of religion, but the truth of it and the wisdom of it are proved day by day in politics."

It is so true of you, that I have not lost my confidence one whit. It is trying however to have to wait so long.

À Dios   Aff'ly   C H Dodge

ALS (WP, DLC).

To Cleveland Hoadley Dodge

My dear Cleve.,   Princeton, New Jersey 16 May, 1912

Bless you for your note of yesterday! You must have known that I needed it. I do not lose heart,—somehow I cannot, *dare* not, there is so much to do,—so much that affects the very foundations of life for every man and woman in the country. But sometimes when I see vast sums of money poured out against me, with fatal success, and it begins to look as if I must merely sit on the side lines and talk, as a mere critic of the game I understand so intimately,—throw all my training away and *do* nothing,—well, I do not repine, but I grow a little sad, and need such a message, of generous love and confidence, as this you have sent me!

God bless you!   Affectionately,   Woodrow Wilson

ALS (WC, NjP).

To Josephus Daniels

My dear friend: [Trenton, N. J.] May 16, 1912.

This is indeed a stunning Wilson number of which you have sent me a part, and you know how I feel about it.

My throat is still giving me a good deal of trouble. It does not regain its strength and tone. I feel it is merely the result of a great many months of overduing.

Always cordially and faithfully yours,

Woodrow Wilson

TLS (J. Daniels Papers, DLC).

From William Gibbs McAdoo

PERSONAL.

Dear Governor: [New York] May 16, 1912.

The Tennessee situation has panned out better than I hoped. I have just received a telegram from Hon. George F[ort]. Milton (owner of the Knoxville Sentinel and the Chattanooga News) saying that he had been elected a delegate at large, and that we would get from seven to nine of the delegates. Mr. Milton is one of our strongest friends. I have not, in any of my estimates, figured on getting anything from Tennessee.[1]

I have arranged that meeting for Saturday morning. Be sure to let nothing interfere with your keeping this engagement, as I regard it as of the utmost importance. I understand that you are to let me know, on arrival in New York, where I am to meet you Friday night.

Very sincerely yours,   W G McAdoo

TLS (LPC, W. G. McAdoo Papers, DLC).
[1] The results of the state convention held in Nashville on May 15, 1912, reflected the confusion and bitter factionalism in the Democratic party in Tennessee. In order to avoid a floor fight, the leaders of all factions divided the eight delegates at large to the Baltimore convention equally among Wilson, Clark, Underwood, and Harmon. The remainder of the delegation was also split into equal divisions. Each of the four candidates received six Tennessee votes on the first ballot at Baltimore. See A. S. Link, "Democratic Politics and the Presidential Campaign of 1912 in Tennessee," *The East Tennessee Historical Society's Proceedings*, No. 18 (1946), p. 122.

From Francis Griffith Newlands

My dear Governor: [Washington] May 16th, 1912.

I greatly regret the bad news from Nevada. To show you how difficult it has been to gauge the public sentiment, I will state that the Attorney-General and two Democratic members of the Railroad Commission of Nevada are here. All of them assured me that the State would go to Wilson. One of the Railroad Commissioners told me that at the recent Jefferson Day banquet at

Reno, at which more than a hundred Democrats were present from all parts of the State, a standing vote was taken as to presidential preference, and three-fourths were for Wilson. It seems to have been an unanticipated groundswell vote.

I received yesterday the following telegram from ex-State Senator James T. Boyd, of Reno who supported Clark:

> At presidential primaries yesterday State went overwhelmingly for Clark, Wilson carrying only Ormsby and White Pine counties. Clark probably carry State by more than four to one, which was ratio this county; Esmeralda twenty-five to one. Shall I make effort to have you go to Baltimore instructed for Clark?

To which I made the following reply:

> Many thanks. I preferred Wilson as Democratic nominee for President, thinking he would command more Republican and independent votes than any one else. I have not changed my view in this particular, but I have great regard for Clark and will support him cheerfully as Nevada's preference. Would have liked to aid on platform committee, but under circumstances think Clark's supporters should go as delegates and would prefer not to have my name urged.

Very sincerely yours,   [Francis G. Newlands]

CCL (F. G. Newlands Papers, CtY).

From Josephus Daniels

Dear Governor: [Raleigh, N. C.] May 17th, 1912.

I am in receipt of your esteemed favor of the 16th inst. and thank you very much for your expression. I trust your throat is soon going to be in good shape.

With best wishes,   Sincerely,   [Josephus Daniels]

CCL (J. Daniels Papers, DLC).

Three News Reports

[May 17, 1912]

ITALIANS GET WILSON'S REPLY

Governor Wilson's letter to the committee which waited upon him last week, representing the Italian-American Alliance, was made public today by Dr. Frederico Luongo of Orange. In it the Governor makes a full explanation of statements contained in his "History of the American People," which some of his antagonists have interpreted in a way calculated to prejudice Italian and other foreign-born citizens against him.

In making public the Governor's letter which was addressed to him, Dr. Luongo issued a formal statement expressing satisfaction with the explanation of the historian and confidence in his ability to recognize the importance of Italian immigration.

With Dr. Nicola Pernice, of Atlantic City, Dr. Luongo visited the Governor at the direction of the Italian-American Alliance, which met at Philadelphia, May 5. Governor Wilson promised to prepare a formal declaration of his views on the question of immigration which he gave the committee permission to make public.

It was in keeping with that promise that Governor Wilson wrote to Dr. Luongo.

His letter follows:

"Our conversation of yesterday affords me a very welcome opportunity to explain to you my judgment and feeling with regard to the whole matter of foreign immigration.

"The passage so often referred to in my history, and so grossly misrepresented, referred to a particular period of our history when certain practices were in vogue with regard to immigration which it had become necessary for Congress to put a stop to by legislation in the well-known prohibition of the importation of laborers under contract.

"If you will refer back to the newspapers and other annals of that date, you will find that the character of our immigration was very seriously affected at that time by the practices of the steamship companies and the employers of labor in the country, who were bringing over from the more shiftless classes in a great many of the European countries, great numbers of unskilled laborers intended to displace laborers on this side of the water, and lower the scale of wages. The immigrants thus brought over were of an entirely artificial kind and were not really representative of the countries from which they came.

"This is the only point of criticism I have ever found against the immigration from Europe into the United States. It has been my good fortune to know a great deal about the elements which the Italian and other southern peoples have contributed to our composite population, and I have reason to know how much the country has been enriched in every way by the elements thus added to it. I never at any time entertained any prejudice whatever against the immigration from the south of Europe, and recent years have shown a constant improvement in regard to the distribution of the immigrants and the influence they have exerted upon our life and industry.

"This has been partly due, in the case of the Italians, to the very intelligent organization and effort among thoughtful Italian citizens of America. They have taken pains to guide the settlement of new immigrants and to put them in the way of finding the labor best suited to their former occupation and development. Any anxiety the country may have felt in former years may, I feel confident, be now dismissed.

"Certainly neither I nor any other well-informed man was ever so ignorant as not to know the great elements of racial strength and character which is being added to our population by the immigration out of Italy, Austria, Hungary and the other countries of Europe which have so abounded in the spirit of our liberty, and which have given so many touches of ideal conception to the whole history of the race."

Dr. Luongo issued his statement in English and Italian. It reads as follows:

"Last week Dr. Pernice and I, as a Committee from the Italian-American Alliance, went to Trenton and were most courteously received by the Governor. Upon explaining our mission to him we were promised a formal declaration of his views to be made public if we so desired. Our interview with Governor Wilson not only makes clear the meaning of the historian, but also causes the Italian-American Alliance to be recognized as a defender of the Italian interests in this country.

"Governor Wilson's letter clearly shows that those sentences can only be deliberately misinterpreted for the purpose of stirring up dissatisfaction among the Italians. Let it be remembered that Governor Wilson's history was written many years ago and that it is hardly fair to apply to present conditions words meant to portray facts correct at the time of its publication.

"A historian worthy of the name owes it to himself, and above all to his readers, to be scrupulously exact in his statements, and the only person qualified to authoritatively pass judgment is he who has made a profound study of conditions as they were and as they are now.

"No further comment regarding the Governor's letter is necessary, and, personally, I am grateful to have had Professor Wilson's explanation at first hand.

"Whatever our political beliefs may be, we Italians may be certain that no man is less capable of damaging our interests even by a chance word, no man is better aware of the real position and importance of our countrymen in the United States, no man is better disposed and more capable of viewing the Italo-American citizen as he really is than our present Governor."

Printed in the *Newark Evening News*, May 17, 1912; two editorial headings omitted.

❖

[May 19, 1912]

CAMDEN'S DEMOCRATS HEAR WOODROW WILSON

Hailed as "the next president of the United States," Governor Woodrow Wilson, of New Jersey, was cheered for five minutes when he arose to speak at a reception given in his honor by the Camden Democratic Club, in the Temple Building, Camden, last night.

The meeting was the official launching of Governor Wilson's presidential boom in Camden county. In his address he rapped bossism, and told the people that they must be vigilant or the control of the state and nation will be bound up by the special interests.

Referring to the presidential fight in the Republican party, he said he deplored the effect of the contest between President Taft and former President Roosevelt. "The great problems of government," he declared, "are being lost sight of in the attempt of the president and ex-president to prove that each has done the more to bring discredit on the Republican party."

Governor Wilson rapped David Baird, Republican leader in south Jersey, and urged the people to throw off the shackles of bossism. He said that Camden county has not yet begun to free itself from the chains of the bosses, although other ecvtions [sections] of the state have made rapid headway in that line.

"But," said the governor, "if you can't elect good men here, I can appoint good ones, who will honestly represent you."

The governor said there is danger ahead if the people listen to the siren voices of the "harpies," who, he declared, make a business of harrassing the administration and the legislature. He said the "harpies" make capital of the fact that a governor is in office for only three years, and that they are laying their plans to elect a man who will do their bidding.

"Eternal vigilance," he said, "is the price of liberty, and if you are not vigilant you will be dominated all your lives by bosses."

He said the special interests have succeeded in getting control of the necessities of life; that they own the mines that produce coal and the food products that people eat.

"They have it in their power," he said, "to give people food-stuffs that will not let them think properly, to grapple with the problems that confront the nation. It is time for us to throw off the shahckles [shackles]."

Printed in the Philadelphia *North American*, May 19, 1912.

❖

[May 20, 1912]

GOV. WILSON AT CORNERSTONE LAYING
OF GERMAN HOSPITAL

The members of the German Hospital and Dispensary Association, who have been working for fifteen years for a new hospital, had their hopes realized yesterday when the cornerstone of the new $20,000 building at Warner Avenue and the Boulevard[1] was laid by Mayor H. Otto Wittpenn. Governor Woodrow Wilson was the principal speaker, and other speakers were United States Senator James E. Martine and Congressmen Eugene Kinkead and James Hamill. . . .

Gov. Wilson was the next speaker. He was given a warm reception. Gov. Wilson was cheered for two minutes.

"It is peculiarly pleasing for me to be here with you to-day," he said. "I have a rather familiar feeling every time I come to visit my friends of Hudson County.

"I was bred in a State where the Sabbath was observed. All the beneficent enterprises of history have been provided in the expression of Christian belief. There were no hospitals before Christ was born. His day could not be better employed than in the laying of the corner stone of a charitable enterprise. This enterprise represents to my mind the real vitality of the country. I believe in public hospitals built at public expense, but how much greater is an institution built out of the contributions of private individuals at their own expense. That is what this institution represents.

"The real test of the vitality of the community can be found in voluntary enterprises. When you have a public enterprise like this you have something even more vital. This hospital has grown, as I understand it, not by large gifts, but has been the result of small gifts. That means so much more. That means greater effort and self-sacrifice. The peculiarity of an endowment is that the donor thinks more of personal glory than of the object of his endowment.

"I have been president of a great institution and know that men who subscribe great endowments have often been thinking more of personal benefit and were more interested in the name to be carved over the door than they were of these invisible sources of which the public does not know.

"Why call it the German Hospital when all the people are in it?

"Some people might say that the Germans are getting the credit. Still I see no meaning in this. You would not be jealous of one family doing some great deed would you? This is an evidence of the German enterprise and principles in American life. The German is hard to describe. It is easier to describe an Irishman than a German. I have Irish blood in my veins and speak by the book. The Irishman plays across the board and you can see what is going on, but the German is peculiarly retrospective and meditative and has a poetry of nature which is beautiful. The Irishman is given to poetry too, but it is more outspoken than that of the German. The German, so to speak, consumes his own voice. Science has not been without imagination and poetry. The German has contributed more of this kind of poetry than he of any other country. We find this true in music. There is not a great deal of music among the English, Irish or Scotch, but when I think of the great stream of music which has come to us from German composers I wonder why that Germanic gift did not cross the English Channel. These Germans have worked untiringly for fourteen years to bring this enterprise into being and I esteem it an honor as Chief Magistrate of the State of New Jersey to take part in this ceremony today, when I know how they have striven for the people."

Printed in the Jersey City *Jersey Journal*, May 20, 1912, with an addition from the brief text in the Trenton *True American*, May 20, 1912.
    1 In Jersey City.

To Mary Allen Hulbert Peck

Dearest Friend,   [Trenton, N. J.] 20 May, 1912

Business has simply absorbed every hour—Sunday and all, and left nothing for the letter I wanted to write you. *Do* you come this Saturday, the 25th? Your last letter had a touch of your natural spirits, your natural self, in it, and made me easier about you.

I am well, and you may be sure that this letter carries as much *thought* of you as if it were twenty pages, instead of a dozen lines long.

All *would* join me in affectionate messages if I were in Princeton and they knew I was writing.
                    Your devoted friend,   Woodrow Wilson
I was *so* glad to hear of Mrs. A's improvement.

ALS (WP, DLC).

To Francis Griffith Newlands

My dear Senator: [Trenton. N. J.] May 20, 1912.
Thank you sincerely for your frank and cordial letter of May
sixteenth. I must admit that I was taken aback by the result in
Nevada, but I understand perfectly how impossible it has been
for you in Washington to gauge or anticipate what was happening there, and you may be sure that there is no crisicism in my
mind of you, and that I warmly appreciate the position you have
taken with regard to being a delegate from the State.
                    Cordially and faithfully yours,   Woodrow Wilson

TLS (F. G. Newlands Papers, CtY).

A News Report of a Campaign Address in South Jersey

[May 21, 1912]
WILSON LAUDED AT BURLINGTON

Governor Grills Politicians Who, Failing
to Get Berths, Deserted Him.

TAFT AND T.R. GET THEIRS

BURLINGTON, May 21.—If Governor Wilson has lost any ground
in Burlington County the fact did not manifest itself last night,
when he was cheered by 1,200 men and women in the Auditorium
Theatre, where he delivered a stirring speech, denouncing the
office-seekers who have turned against him in their disappointment, and condemning the alliance between politics and corrupt
business.

"I don't want any drummed-up sentiment for my nomination
for President," Governor Wilson said in the course of his speech.
"I want my fellow-citizens to come to the polls[1] and exercise their
best judgment. If they do not want me, let them reject me, and
watch me take my medicine.

"The verdict must be yours. If you reject me, I may question
your taste, but not your judgment. I would rather have the voice
of twelve men who would go interestedly to the polls than the

votes of 100 who would go there because the organization drove them out—and it is necessary, I am sorry to say, to have to drive some voters out."

United States Senators John Sharp Williams, of Mississippi, and James Martine, of this State, spoke at the meeting. . . .

Governor Wilson got a warm welcome when he was presented as the last speaker of the evening. He declared that he was embarrassed because the theme of the evening seemed to be himself and that he was never able to become eloquent over that theme.

The Governor then launched out into a criticism of the political methods of the two great parties and of the bosses who control them, declaring that the people had come to the belief that parties existed for the purpose of getting office and not with the object of serving the masses.

"Do I not see them turn against me, turn enemies because they have not received office?" Governor Wilson asked. "Do I not see them turn to other men and receive their money because they have not received office?"

The Democratic party had been the same as the Republican party in its office-grabbing methods, the Governor said he was sorry to say, and it was this that led to its being driven out of power.

"And the chief purveyor," continued the Governor, "was a man whom everybody knows, one who was the arch-conspirator in the wrecking of his party nationally."[2]

Then speaking of the allegiance [alliance] between politics and business, the Governor repeated the story of a legislator who told him he could not be with him because "they held his notes," and he told of this system of a politician in getting a hold on a man.

"I am speaking," the Governor said, "of the very man whose name I did not mention a minute ago, because it was not necessary," and some one in the rear of the hall shouted:

"You don't have to."

"I am not going to mince words," the Governor went on. "I am not going to live in a fool's paradise and believe all men are patriots who say they are. I have found some of these gentlemen out. They have showed me their credentials and I have discovered their character.

"Don't I know that there are some men in certain counties of this State that I could mention who would squeeze the blood out of me if they could," Governor Wilson declared. "Don't I know that if they dared they would falsely cause my arrest, have me indicted by a packed grand jury and convicted by a corrupt petit jury.

"We must not shut our eyes to the savage way that power has been used in this civilized State of New Jersey, and is still used today in some places. The only reason that some of these men are afraid of me is that they know I would turn the light on if I had the chance, and these same men do not want me to have more power, because they fear the light would be the keener."

Taking up national affairs, where he said the same evils existed as in this State, Governor Wilson made mention of the Republican contest between Taft and Roosevelt and asked what they were doing. They are debating, he said, which of them was more controlled by the same system.

"I do not want to do either of them an injustice," the Governor said, "because no man should be too severe upon another until he himself has been tried, but are they not producing letters showing the subtle system in which they both took part? It has been shown that they were receiving suggestions from men[3] who were to be indicted whether the law of the United States should be put into operation."

Patronage in the way of legislation is as great an evil, if not worse, than the patronage of office, Governor Wilson declared. He made mention of the large political contributions that have been made by the Public Service Corporation and he declared that the concern considered every contribution an investment.

The tariff was then taken a fling at by the Governor. The people are not the beneficiaries of this taxation, he said, but those who have owned and still own the government of the United States have been and are still protected by the tariff.

Returning to the affairs of his administration and the office-seekers, the Governor said that nine-tenths of his time at the State house has been taken up by those who have been seeking appointments for themselves or their friends.

Printed in the *Newark Evening News*, May 21, 1912.

[1] At the New Jersey presidential primary on May 28.

[2] That is, James Smith, Jr.

[3] Wilson referred to a recent development in the battle between Roosevelt and Taft for the Republican presidential nomination. On April 24, 1912, as the result of a Senate resolution, Taft sent to the upper house and also made public papers dated August and September 1907 relating to the proposed anti-trust prosecution of the International Harvester Company by the Roosevelt administration. The papers revealed that George W. Perkins had visited Roosevelt and other officials on behalf of International Harvester and the Morgan interests, stressed the good intentions of the company and the damage that would be done to it by an antitrust action, and requested that the Justice Department delay the threatened suit pending the completion of an investigation of the company by the Bureau of Corporations. Roosevelt in turn had requested the Attorney General not to file the suit until they discussed the matter further. In addition, the Commissioner of Corporations, Herbert Knox

Smith, wrote a lengthy letter to the President on September 21, 1907, generally defending the company and the Morgan interests and recommending postponement of the suit. The published documents carried the story no further, but no prosecution of the harvester company was instituted by the Roosevelt administration.

Roosevelt immediately denied any wrongdoing and asserted that Taft, as Secretary of War in his cabinet, not only knew about the matter but had urged that the prosecution be delayed. In a public statement on April 29, 1912, Taft flatly denied any previous knowledge of the affair and pointed out that he had been out of the country during the period when the subject might have been discussed by the cabinet.

For the papers made public in April 1912, see 62nd Congress, 2nd sess., Senate Document No. 604. There is a brief discussion of this contretemps in Henry F. Pringle, *The Life and Times of William Howard Taft* (2 vols., New York and Toronto, 1939), II, 790-793.

An Address to the Annual Banquet of the Economic Club of New York[1]

[[May 23, 1912]]

Mr. President,[2] ladies, and gentlemen, I listened with a great deal of interest to the very gracious introduction that you have just heard, but with some skepticism upon one of the statements. Mr. Milburn said that everybody here knew what I am, but that depends upon which newspaper he has read. Most persons are so thoroughly uninformed as to my opinions that I have concluded that the only things they have not read are my speeches.

But I want to say that it is with a great deal of pleasure that I find myself here to-night, turning out of the troubled paths of practical politics to come into a place where you have the purpose and the appearance of deliberation. I have never believed entirely that there was very much thinking upon general public questions done in the city of New York; not because there are not some of the finest thinking machines in New York that are to be found anywhere, but because the brains of New York are so devoted throughout long days to special undertakings that there is only the evening, when fatigue has conquered you, in which to think about the affairs of the country. And, therefore, it seems to me that men of eminent success in the fields of business are, above all others, under a moral obligation to get together and talk of things which do not concern their own private undertakings. It is refreshing at this particular time to have an opportunity to discuss not personalities but the questions of the day. I was in a New England city, not many weeks ago,[3] which

---

1 In the Hotel Astor. The Economic Club of New York, founded in 1907, was dedicated to the creation and expression of an enlightened public opinion on important economic and social questions of the day.

2 John George Milburn, prominent New York lawyer and president of the Economic Club.

3 Springfield, Mass., on April 27.

had just been visited on the two preceding days by two militant candidates for nomination. I had occasion at the opening of my speech to say: "After what you people have been through the last two days perhaps you would like to know what the questions of the day are." I was interested to find that instead of a mere smile I got out of that audience that had dropped in from the street a spontaneous cheer. They felt refreshed at the idea that they might hear something discussed which did not have the bitterness of personality in it.

And yet, it is a serious fact, ladies and gentlemen, that it is very difficult to discuss those very questions of the day without seeming to bring a touch of passion and bitterness into them. We talk a great deal about the radicalism of our time, but the radicalism, if you will analyze it, does not consist in the things that are proposed, but in the things that are disclosed. It is in the analysis of existing conditions that your public speakers seem to be radical. How shall our difficulties be settled after we have excited our minds by disclosing those conditions? We are so busy with the preliminary controversy with regard to what the real state of the facts is that we carry that extreme over into the other area, which should be an area of calmness, of deliberation, namely, the area of the discussion of what shall be done in the circumstances.

Very little has been said about that, but a great deal has been said, and sometimes intemperately said, about the real state of affairs. Nowhere, it seems to me, in the country more than in New York ought we to be very frank with one another, because in New York, taking you in the aggregate, you know what the facts are, and if you are frank with one another and take the public into your confidence you may be instrumental in instructing the country concerning what it must found its thoughts upon.

When you discuss the relation between government and business, you touch at once the seat of irritation. I have not found a single audience in this vicinity in which the business men were not up in arms at being interfered with by the action of the Government—in which there were not to be found a great many men who said, "If the politicians would only let us alone the country would prosper and all business would settle down to a sound and steady condition." They have been critics of Government because Government would not let business rest and be free. Now, no study of the history of the Government can be candidly made which will not lead to this conclusion—that the very thing that Government can not let alone is business, for business underlies every part of our life; the foundation of our lives, of our spiritual lives included, is economic.

I heard a very interesting preacher say several months ago, in preaching upon the sequence of the petitions in the Lord's Prayer, that it was significant that our Savior's first petition was, "Give us this day our daily bread," for no man can rationally live, worship, or love his neighbor on an empty stomach; and if he is in doubt where the food is to come from, if he fears he will be without work and sustenance, it is impossible that he should have a rational attitude toward the life of the community or toward his own life. Therefore it is the object of Government to make those adjustments of life which will put every man in a position to claim his normal rights as a living human being.

Government can not take its hand off of business. Government must regulate business, because that is the foundation of every other relationship, particularly of the political relationship. It is futile, therefore, to have the politicians take their hands off. They may blunder at the business, but they can not give it up. They may make fundamental mistakes—they will make a great many if you do not frankly assist and instruct them—but they must go forward whether instructed or not.

I think one of the few grounds of discouragement in our days —for I do not think there are many—is that business men and the lawyers who guide business men are jealously withholding their counsel from those who try to guide affairs, withholding it as those who withdraw in suspicion, as if they should say, "We can not parley with those men; their ears are not candidly open to us"; and so there has grown up on one side and on the other an attitude of distrust which does not augur well for a settlement of delicate questions.

The whole problem of life, gentlemen, is to understand one another, the whole problem of politics is to get together. Politics is not a mechanical problem, politics is not a problem of setting interests off against each other upon such a plan as that one can not harm the other. The problem of politics is cooperation. The organic cooperation of the parts is the only basis for just Government; unless we come to an understanding, there can be no Government. No man can hold off from affairs and count himself a faithful citizen of the Republic.

I have been interested in one piece of speculative explanation which, perhaps, I might turn aside for a moment to call to your attention.

One of the chief benefits I used to derive from being president of a university was that I had the pleasure of entertaining thoughtful men from all over the world. I can not tell you how much dropped into my granary by their presence. I had been casting around in my thought for something by which to draw several parts of my political ideas together when it was my good fortune to entertain a very interesting Scotchman who had been devoting himself to the philosophical thought of the seventeenth century. His talk was so engaging that it was delightful to hear him speak of anything, and presently there came out of the unexpected region of his thought the thing I had been waiting for. He called my attention to the fact that in every generation all sorts of speculation and thinking tend to fall under the formula of the dominant thought of the age that has preceded that.

For example, after the Newtonian theory of the universe had been developed, almost all thinking tended to express itself upon the analogies of the Newtonian theory, and since the Darwinian theory has reigned amongst us everybody tries to express what he wishes to expound in the terms of development and accommodation to environment. Now, it came to me as this interesting man talked, that the Constitution of the United States had been made under the dominion of the Newtonian theory. You have only to read the papers of the Federalist to see it written on every page. They speak of the "checks and balances" of the Constitution and use to express their idea the simile of the organization of the universe, and particularly of the solar system —how by the attraction of gravitation the various parts are held in their orbits, and represent Congress, the judiciary, and the President as a sort of imitation of the solar system.

No Government, of course, is a mechanism; no mechanical theory will fit any Government in the world, because Governments are made up of human beings, and all the calculations of mechanical theory are thrown out of adjustment by the intervention of the human will. Society is an organism, and every Government must develop according to its organic forces and instincts. I do not wish to make the analysis tedious; I will merely ask you, after you go home, to think over this proposition: that what we have been witnessing for the past hundred years is the transformation of a Newtonian constitution into a Darwinian constitution. The place where the strongest will is present will be the seat of sovereignty. If the strongest will is present in Congress, then Congress will dominate the Government; if the strongest guiding will is in the Presidency, the President will dominate the Government; if a leading and conceiving mind like Marshall's presides over the Supreme Court of the United

States, he will frame the Government, as he did. There are no checks and balances in the mechanical sense in the Constitution; historical circumstances have determined the character of our Government. While we were forming the Government—that is to say, down to a hundred years ago, when the War of 1812 was being fought, while we were finding our place among the nations of the world, while our most critical relations were over foreign relations—the Presidency necessarily stood at the front of affairs. You will find all the early Presidents directly forming the Government. But after we got our standing among the peoples of the world—from the close of the War of 1812 down to the beginning of the Spanish-American War, with the exception of the interval of the Civil War—the Presidents count for very little. There was then a free, miscellaneous domestic development that was insusceptible of guidance; it was spontaneous; it sprang up unbidden in every part of the country; the place of common counsel was the Congress of the United States; and the Congress overshadowed the President.

One of the things I have always felt that Webster and Clay did not see was that they would diminish their prestige and power if they left the Senate of the United States and entered the Presidency. Why the men who were leading the Chamber that was dominating the Nation should have wished to be in the chair which was overshadowed by that Chamber I have never been able to understand.

But then came the Spanish-American War. Since then America has stood up, looked about her, drawn the veil of preoccupation from her eyes, and beheld herself a great power among the peoples of the world; and ever since that moment the President has, of necessity, become the guiding force in the affairs of the country. It was inevitable and it now will, no doubt, remain inevitable because we are now in the same case with all other Governments. We can not shut our eyes to foreign questions—particularly now when we see some prospect of breaking our isolation by lowering the tariff wall between us and other nations; now that we see some possibility of flinging our own flag out upon the seas again and taking possession of our rightful share of the trade of the world.

We have found that the private debates of committees and the haphazard creations of legislation in bodies which no one leads do not suffice to clear our affairs. We must have some central points of guidance. This is the adjustment to environment; this is the Darwinization of the Government of the United States. There is no violence in the process; there is no violence to any principle of our Constitution; because, as has been said so often, the beauty of that Constitution is that it did not predict anything, but left everything possible by the very simplicity and elasticity of its make-up. If the Constitution of the United States had gone into the detail that some of our State constitutions go into, we would have to change it every 10 years, on the average, as we have changed them.

Now, all of this that seems pertinent to the matter which I would now bring to your attention is that there must be some guiding and adjusting force—some single organ of intelligent communication between the whole Nation and the Government which determines the policy of that Nation. And, inasmuch as that determination must turn upon economics—that is to say, upon business questions—it is absolutely necessary that we should analyze our present situation with regard to nothing but the facts.

Perhaps I may sum my idea up in this way: The question of statesmanship is a question of taking all the economic interests of every part of the country into the reckoning. Every time any change is to be made in economic policies it must be made by an all-around accommodation and adjustment. Is that possible? There is no man, there [is] no group of men, who comprehend the entire business interests of this country; it is inconceivable that there should be. At best we can make a very rough and ready approximation of it; and in order that you may make even an approximation, it is necessary that there should be a free play of opinion from every part of the country upon the sensitive center at Washington. Just as soon as one part begins to press harder than another, then the prospect of justice is uncertain, the task of statesmanship is rendered just so much the more difficult. All the sensitive parts of the Government ought to be open to all the active parts of it. So soon as a small group of the active parts organize for the purpose of seeing to it that the Government hears and heeds only them, then the task becomes impossible.

Let me illustrate it by the tariff, because every business question in this country, whether you think so or not, gentlemen, comes back, no matter how much you put on the brakes, to the question of the tariff.

I hear on every side that the tariff was [is] the "dominant" issue. Why, you can not escape from it, no matter in which direction you go. The tariff is situated in relation to other questions like Boston Common in the old arrangement of that interesting city. I remember seeing once, in Life, a picture of a man standing at the door of one of the railway stations of Boston and inquiring of a Bostonian the way to the Common. "Take any of these streets," was the reply, "either direction." Now, as the Common was related to the former winding streets of Boston, so the tariff question is related to the economic questions of our day. Take any direction and you will sooner or later get to the Common. In discussing the tariff, you may start at the center and can go in any direction you please.

Let us illustrate by standing at the center, the Common itself. You know as far back as 1828, when they did not know anything about politics as compared with what we know now, a tariff bill was passed which was called the "tariff of abominations," because it did not have any beginning or end or plan. It had no traceable pattern in it. It was as if the demands of everybody in the United States had all been thrown indiscriminately into one basket and that basket presented as a piece of legislation. It had been a general scramble, and everybody who scrambled hard enough had been taken care of in the tariff schedules resulting. It was an abominable thing to the thoughtful men of that day, because no man guided it, shaped it, or tried to make an equitable system out of it. That was bad enough, but at least everybody had an open door through which to scramble for his advantage. It was a go-as-you-please, free-for-everybody struggle, and anybody who could get to Washington and say he represented an important business interest could be heard by the Committee on Ways and Means. We have a very different state of affairs now. The Committee on Ways and Means and the Finance Committee of the Senate discriminate by long experience among the persons whose counsel they are to take in respect to tariff legislation, because there has been substituted for this unschooled body of citizens that used to clamor at the doors of the Finance Committee and the Committee on Ways and Means one of the most interesting and able bodies of expert lobbyists that has ever been developed in the experience of any countrymen, who know so much about the matters they are talking of that you can not put your knowledge into competition with theirs. Because they overwhelm you with their knowledge of detail you can not discover wherein their scheme lies. They suggest the change of a fraction in a particular schedule and explain it to you so plausibly that you can not see that it means millions of dollars additional for the consumer of this country. Again they propose to put the carbon in our electric lights in 2-foot pieces instead of 1-foot pieces and you do not see where you are getting sold, because you are not an expert and they are. They have calculated the whole thing beforehand; they have analyzed the whole detail and consequences, each one in his specialty. As compared with him the average unschooled, inexperienced business man has no possibility of competition. Instead of the old scramble, which was bad enough, you got the present expert control of the tariff schedules. Thus the relation between business and government becomes not a matter of the exposure of all the sensitive parts of the Government to all the active parts of the people, but the special impression upon them of a particular organized force in the business world; moreover, so far as deliberation is concerned, its action, its motions, its actual purposes are secret. Why, it is notorious, for example, that many members of the Finance Committee of the Senate did not know the significance of the tariff schedules which were reported in the present tariff bill to the Senate, and Members of the Senate who asked Mr. Aldrich direct questions for information were refused the information they sought, sometimes, I dare say, because he could not give it, and sometimes, I venture to say, because disclosure of the information would have embarrassed the passage of the measure. There were essential papers which could not be got at. Take that very interesting matter, that will-o'-the-wisp, known as "the cost of production." It is hard for any man who has ever studied economics at all to restrain a cynical smile when he is told that an intelligent body of his fellow citizens are looking for "the cost of production" as a basis for tariff legislation. It is not the same in any one factory for two years together. It is not the same in one industry from one season to another. It is not the same in one country at two different periods. It is constantly eluding your grasp. It does not exist as a scientific, demonstrable datum fact. But in order to carry out the extraordinary program proposed in the late national platform of the Republican Party it was necessary to go through the motions of finding out what it was. I am credibly informed that the Government of the United States requested several foreign Governments, among others the Government of Germany, to supply it with as reliable figures as possible concerning the cost of producing certain articles corresponding with those produced in the United States. The German Government, I understand, put the matter in the hands of certain of her manufacturers, who sent in just as complete answers as they could procure from their books. The information reached our Government during the course of the debate on the Payne-Aldrich bill and was transmitted—for the bill by that time had reached the Senate—to the Finance Committee of the Senate. But I am told—and I have no reason to doubt it—that it never came out of the pigeonholes of the committee. I do not know and that committee does not know what the information it contained was. When Mr. Aldrich was asked about it he first said it was not an official report from the German Government. Afterwards he said it was an impudent attempt on the part of the German Government to interfere with tariff legislation in the United States. But he never said what the cost of production disclosed by it was. If he had, it is more than likely that some of the tariff schedules would have been shown to be entirely unjustifiable.[4]

Such instances show you just where the center of gravity is— and it is a matter of gravity indeed, for it is a very grave matter. It lay during the last Congress in the one person who was the accomplished intermediary between the expert lobbyists and the legislation of Congress. I am not saying this in derogation of the character of Mr. Aldrich. It is no concern of mine what kind of man Mr. Aldrich is. Now, particularly, that he has retired from public life, it is a matter of indifference. The point is that he, because of his long experience, his long handling of these delicate and private matters, was the usual and natural instrument by which the Congress of the United States informed itself, not as to the wishes of the people of the United States or of the rank and file of business men of the country, but as to the needs and arguments of the experts who came to arrange matters with the committees.

The moral of the whole matter is this: The business of the United States is not as a whole in contact with the Government of the United States. So soon as it is the matters which now give you, and justly give you, cause for uneasiness will disappear. Just so soon as the business of this country has general, free, welcome access to the councils of Congress, all the friction between business and politics will disappear.

There is another matter to which you must direct your attention whether palatable or not. I do not talk about these things because they please my palate; I do not talk about them because I want to attack anybody or upset anyone; I talk about them because I wish to find out what the facts are; otherwise I will move like a man groping in darkness. If what I say is not true, then I am susceptible of correction.

You will notice from a recent investigation that things like this take place: A certain bank invests in certain securities. It appears from the evidence that the handling of these securities

4 About Wilson's misinformation on this matter, see n. 1 to the article printed at Sept. 5, 1909, Vol. 19.

was very intimately connected with the maintenance of the price of a particular commodity. Nobody ought, and in normal circumstances nobody would, for a moment think of suspecting the managers of a great bank of making such an investment in order to help those who were conducting a particular business in the United States to maintain the price of their commodity; but the circumstances are not normal.

It is beginning to be believed that in the big business of this country nothing is disconnected from anything else. I do not mean in this particular instance to which I have referred and have in mind to draw any inference at all, for that would be unjust; but take any investment of an industrial character by a great bank. It is known that the directorate of that bank interlaces in personnel with 10, 20, 30, 40, 60 boards of directors of all sorts, of railroads which handle commodities of great groups of manufacturers which manufacture commodities, and of great merchants that distribute commodities; and the reason that a bank is under suspicion with regard to its investments is that it is at least considered possible it is playing the game of somebody who has nothing to do with banking, but with whom some of its directors are connected and joined in interest. The ground of unrest and uneasiness, in short, on the part of the public at large is the growing knowledge that many large undertakings are interlaced with one another, undistinguishable from one another in personnel.

Therefore, when a small group of men approach Congress in order to induce the committee concerned to concur in certain legislation, nobody knows the ramifications of the interests which those men represent, and therefore it is not the frank and open action of public opinion in public counsel, but every man is at any rate suspected of representing some other man and it is not known where the connection ceases. The whole question, therefore, with regard to the relation of government to business is this, gentlemen, not whether there should be a connection, not whether economic legislation should be carefully, studiously, prudently considered, but through whom is the connection to be maintained? Are the contacts to be general or special? Are they to be in the nature of general public opinion or in the nature of private control?

I am one of those who have been so fortunately circumstanced that I have had the opportunity to study the way in which these things come about and therefore I do not suspect any man has deliberately planned these things. I am not so uninstructed and misinformed as to suppose that there is a malevolent combination somewhere to dominate the Government of the United States. I merely say that by certain processes, now well known, and perhaps natural in themselves, there has come about so extraordinary a concentration in the control of business in this country that the people are afraid that there will be a concentration in the control of government. That either is so or is not. If it is so, I beg you to observe that I am not a radical in frankly stating it. If it is not so, then I am desirous of your cooperation in order that I may be better informed; for I hold my mind open to every kind of information that I can get; and I have sense enough to know that no one man understands the United States.

I have met some gentlemen who professed they did. I have even met some business men who professed they held in their own single comprehension the business of the United States; but I am educated enough to know that they do not. Education has this useful effect, that it narrows of necessity the circles of one's egotism. No student knows his subject. The most he knows is where and how to find out the things he does not know with regard to it. That is also the position of a statesman. No statesman understands the whole country. He should make it his business to find out where he will get the information to understand at least a part of it at a time when dealing with complex affairs. What we need more than anything else, therefore, is [to] experience meetings like this—a universal revival of common counsel. That is what investigations by Congress are for. I do not understand their primary object to be to get anybody in jail or, if it be to find out which men ought to be in jail and which ought not, it is with the confident expectation that it will be discovered that the vast majority ought not to be. But the majority are under suspicion until it is discovered who the minority are who ought to be in jail. No man could even get through a highly reputable company like this without investigation and put his finger on the innocent men. Not until everything about you is known is it possible to separate the sheep from the goats; but I have a confident expectation that the majority of sheep would be enormous and it would not be necessary to shear them.

You remember it was told of a certain United States Senator that he was so cautious in his statements that he was the despair of every newspaper reporter who sought to interview him. On one occasion he was on a train which was passing through a grazing country and saw a flock of sheep in the field. It was rather late in the season. One of his companions remarked, "That is very singular, those sheep are not sheared yet." The Senator answered, "So it would appear, looking at them from this side."

Now, the shearing time has not come in the great matter we speak of, and I do not think it will come; but the time has come to determine who are responsible for the things that ought not to be done, who are to be set free to do as they please, for that is the problem of honest business and right politics. The problem of politics is, who should be restrained and who should not; and the problem of business is, who should be restrained and who should not. The whole analysis of modern conditions is a discussion of control. Do not get impatient, therefore, gentlemen, with those who go about preaching, "We must return to the rule of the people." All they mean, if they mean anything rational, is that we must consent to let a majority into the game. We must not permit any system to go uncorrected which is based upon private understandings and expert testimony; we must not allow the few to determine what the policy of the country is to be. It is a question of access to our own Government. There are very few men within the sound of my voice who have any real access to the Government of the United States. It is a matter of common counsel; it is a matter of united counsel; it is a matter of mutual comprehension; it is a matter of mutual understanding.

I wish these matters could be more discussed, but it is very difficult to discuss them nowadays; there is too much noise in the air. I feel nowadays, not in gatherings like this, but in gatherings of the ordinary sort, very much as I felt at a certain county fair. The grand stand by the race track was set back from the track, I suppose 50 feet, and a speaker's stand had been erected just in front of it, opposite the little pagoda where the judges of races stood; and I was put up to address the grand stand. Just back of the grand stand there was a most obstreperous hurdy-gurdy accompanying the giddy motions of a merry-go-round, and while I was trying with my voice to compete with that they started a horse race behind my back. Not having the attention of the grand stand, I did what any normal man would have done; I stopped and watched the horse race. That is an allegory with regard to our present situation. It is very difficult to address the grand stand, and I am glad I got you off in a corner.

But what is at stake? That is what makes a man's thought infinitely sober, and sometimes touches it with a certain degree of sadness. What is at stake in this business? Why, nothing less than the content, the hope, and the life of the people of this country. Say what you please, the real basis of disturbance in the field of business just now is the suspicion of the great body of people in the United States concerning the methods and combinations of business; and business can not breathe an atmosphere of suspicion and live. You must, at any risk, remove that suspicion, or else there can be no normal business in the United States.

What is that suspicion based upon? It is not a contest between the men now in control of business and the men now in control of the Government of the United States. It is a contest between those men and the normal life of the country, and there is everything involved. How would it suit the prosperity of the United States, how would it suit the success of business, to have a people that went every day sadly or sullenly to their work? How would the future look to you if you felt that the aspiration had gone out of most men, the confidence of success, the hope that they might change their condition, if there was everywhere the feeling that there was somewhere covert dictation, private arrangement, as to who should be in the inner circle of privilege and who should not, a more or less systematic and conscious attempt to dictate and dominate the economic life of the country? Do you not see that just so soon as the old self-confidences of America, just so soon as her old boasted advantages of individual liberty and opportunity are taken away, all the energy of her people begin to subside, to slacken, to grow loose and pulpy, without fiber, and men simply cast around to see that the day does not end disastrously with them.

For 18 months now I have been on the inside of some things, and I owe it to a very elastic temperament that I have not become cynical. When I know that certain men actually do not possess political liberty because other men hold their notes, then I know that normal conditions do not exist in the United States; and that I do know, for I have had it from the mouths of the men who suffered thralldom. When I know that men very prominent in business dare not tell me what they think of some of the circumstances of the organization of modern business except privately and under pledge of confidence, then I know that something sinister has happened in America that has disturbed our intellectual manhood and our political liberty. I have made it my business to talk with men who understand the economic conditions of the country vastly better than I do, because they were concerned in large business transactions, and I have almost invariably found them disposed to ask me not to say where I got my information.

In God's name, gentlemen, where does that point! Is it possible that there is some financial tyranny obtaining in America? It is not necessary that the men who exercise it should entertain tyrannous purposes; they may be unconscious of it; they may feel the same impulse of patriotism that you and I feel. Is it possible that we have allowed the system to grow up which they use and that you and the other men are afraid of them? That's what we have to face, and our stake is the reputation and happiness of a great nation. Alas, that we should have to ask the question! Alas, that men who ask it should be supposed to be desirous of upsetting the institutions of the country! Some of the institutions of this country have been upset already, not by political agitators, but by those who have exercised an illegitimate control over the Government, over the legislatures of the States of the Union. There, again, I am on ground absolutely firm under my feet, for it is the ground of knowledge. I can furnish you a list of the partners, and I say that when that is true, if it can be true, then our duty is so plain, so luminous, so attractive that I do not see how any man can turn away from it. It is nothing less than to rehabilitate our own self-respect and our own liberty; it is nothing less than the opportunity, the glorious opportunity, to recover the institutions of the United States, to set them up again in their purity and integrity, and see to it that no man dare breathe a single breath of suspicion against them, to see that they are not tarnished by the defiling touch of any man with unclean hands.

We have come to an age when constructive statesmanship is imperative, and I thank God for it. Who will be the volunteers? Who will volunteer for immortality? Ah, how men deprive themselves of honor! How men live upon husks and throw away the thing that nourishes! How men lose the happiness of life by not seeing wherein it consists! How men selfishly decline to serve and so find out the infinite reward of unselfishness! How blind, how self-denying, how stupid we are!

There are some words about which we are very careful. There is not much discriminating use of individual words in America, but there is one word about which we are very careful. We use the word "great" to describe anybody who has been talked about. It does not require character to be great; it only requires size of achievement. You may throttle everybody else and get everything they own and be "great." You may be great and be feared; but there is one word which we bestow with great discrimination, and that is the word "noble." You can not be noble without character; you can not be noble and not be loved; you can not be noble and not serve somebody; you can not be noble and spend every energy you have on yourself.

Who are candidates for this open peerage of America? Who desires the patent of nobility amongst us? Only those who will enter upon this great enterprise of recovering the ancient purity and simplicity of our politics. We can do it by mere candor; we can do it by merely discussing the facts and meeting them; we can do it without disturbing one of the legitimate transactions of business.

I am always afraid that business men who are uneasy have something to be uneasy about, or that, if there is nothing in itself that justifies their uneasiness, perhaps they do not comprehend what their real situation is. You can find it out in this way. Take the experience in Wisconsin. The men who were in control of the public-service corporations of Wisconsin fought the plans of that State for the regulation of such corporations as they would have fought the prospect of ruin; and what happened? Regulation of the most thoroughgoing sort was undertaken, and the result was that the securities of those companies were virtually guaranteed to purchasers. Instead of being speculative in value, they were known to be absolutely secure investments, because a disinterested agency, a commission representing the community, looked into the conditions of this business, guaranteed that there was not water enough in it to drown in, guaranteed that there was business enough and plant enough to justify the charges and to secure a return of legitimate profit; and every thoughtful man connected with such enterprises in Wisconsin now takes off his hat to the men who originated the measures once so much decried. The chief benefit was not regulation but frank disclosure and the absolutely open and frank relationship between business and government. That's the advantage. The regulation may in some particulars have been unwise and hasty, but the relationship was absolutely normal and wholesome. That is the way, no doubt, in which a satisfactory relationship is going to be restored between the business of the country and the Government of the United States—by frank disclosure and well-considered readjustment.

Of course, there must be first a flood of released water. I have sometimes wondered whether that great, obstructing, "stand-pat" dam was not erected to restrain the release of watered stock. You must let it out sooner or later; and the sooner the better, because if we do it soon we will do it in good temper, and if late there is danger it may be done in ill-temper.

What is the alternative, gentlemen? You have heard the rising tide of socialism referred to here to-night. Socialism is not growing in influence in this country as a program. It is merely that the ranks of protestants are being recruited. Socialism is not a program, but a protest against the present state of affairs in the United States. If it becomes a program, then we shall have to be very careful how we purpose a competing program. I do not believe in the program of socialism. If any man can say he knows anything from the past, perhaps he can say that the program of socialism would not work; but there is no use saying what will not work unless you can say what will work.

A splendid sermon was once preached by Dr. Chalmers on "The expulsive power of a new affection."[5] If you want to oust socialism you have got to propose something better. It is a case, if you will allow me to fall into the language of the vulgar, of "put up or shut up." You can not oppose hopeful programs by negations. Every statesman who ever won anything great in any self-governing country was a man whose program would stand criticism and had the energy behind it to move forward against opposition. It is by constructive purpose that you are going to govern and serve the United States, and therefore a man ought to welcome the high privilege of addressing an audience like this. You can analyze, you can form purposes. Many of you do know what is going on. You know what part is wrong and what is right, if you have not lost your moral perspective, and you know how the wrong can be stopped.

Very well, then, let us get together and form a constructive program, and then let us be happy in the prospect that in some distant day men shall look back to our time and say that the chief glory of America was not that she was successfully set up in a simple age when mankind came to begin a new life in a new land, but that, after the age had ceased to be simple, when the forces of society had come into hot contact, when there was bred more heat than light, there were men of serene enough intelligence, of steady enough self-command, of indomitable enough power of will and purpose to stand up once again and say: "Fellow citizens, we have come into a great heritage of liberty; our heritage is not wealth; our distinction is not that we are rich in power; our boast is, rather, that we can transmute gold into the lifeblood of a free people." Then it will be recorded of us that we found out again what seemed the lost secret of mankind— how to translate power into freedom, how to make men glad that they were rich, how to take the envy out of men's hearts that others were rich and they for a little while poor, by opening the gates of opportunity to every man and letting a flood of gracious guiding light illuminate the path of every man that is born into the world.[6]

Printed in the *Cong. Record*, 62nd Cong., 2nd sess., Vol. 48, Appendix, pp. 392-96.

[5] For information about this famous sermon, see n. 5 to the after-dinner speech printed at Dec. 22, 1900, Vol. 12.

[6] There is a WWhw outline of this address, dated May 23, 1911 [1912], in WP, DLC.

Edward E. Grosscup to John James Gifford[1]

My dear Mr. Gifford: [Trenton, N. J.] May 23, 1912.

I understand that the same false statements are being made in Vermont about Governor Wilson's attitude towards party organization that have been made in other parts of the country. I am sure that you yourself know how false these statements are, but I dare say it will assist you in your contradiction of them to be able to say, on my authority as Chairman of the State Committee, that the charge is merely malicious and is entirely without foundation.

A mere casual glance at the appointments Governor Wilson has actually made will answer the charge in itself. A list of these appointments has been prepared for this very purpose, and I shall ask the men at the headquarters in New York to send you a copy at once. It will show that at least eighty per cent. of the appointments have been regular organization appointments.

This false report is due entirely to Senator James Smith, Jr., whose personal control of the Democratic party Governor Wilson has fought. Governor Wilson believes that party action can be effectively carried out only by party organization, and that so long as the organization honestly serves the party as a whole, it ought to be sustained by every form of legitimate recognition.

Very sincerely yours,
[Edward E. Grosscup]
Chairman, Democratic State Committee.

CCL (Governors' Files, Nj).
[1] Retired businessman of Newark, president of the Woodrow Wilson League of Essex County. At this time he was traveling through New England and the Middle West on behalf of Wilson's candidacy.

To the Democrats of New Jersey

[[May 24, 1912]]

Fellow Citizens:

Under the new legislation of the session of 1911, known as the "Geran Act," you are to have the opportunity, at the primaries to be held on the twenty-eighth of this month, to express your free preference as to who shall be nominated for the office of President of the United States. I am a candidate for nomination to that great office by the Democratic party. I was unwilling to canvass the State for your vote. I have spoken frequently in the past few months in other States, because my friends thought that I ought to make myself personally known there, but that could not be urged as a reason in New Jersey. You know me. For eighteen months I have sought to serve you as Governor of the State, with a full sense of the responsibilities you have imposed upon me, and my record all the State knows. Nothing that I could say upon the public platform could alter it, either for better or for worse. It would be unbecoming in me to commend it to you or to seek to give it color by my own exposition of it.

But I consider it my privilege and my duty, as your servant and representative, to speak of certain matters that enter very vitally into this contest.

Throughout many dark and disheartening years prior to the autumn of 1900 [1910], the masters of our State government were, on the Republican side, the notorious "Board of Guardians," made up now of this group of politicians and again of that, but with one or two charter and permanent members, like the treasurer of the State[1], and on the Democratic side, Mr. James Smith Jr., once a Senator of the United States.

While their control of the Legislature of the State was maintained, there was small chance of getting anything put on the statute books that they deemed hurtful to their own political interests, and they deemed anything hurtful to that interest that was not desired by the great corporations and moneyed interests which supplied them with campaign funds. But one measure, long ardently pressed for by the Democrats and the liberal Republicans of the State, did at last, in the session of 1907, slip through the Legislature, when the Democrats had a majority of one in the Assembly. That was the statute which gave the voters of this State the right to express their preference at the polls as to who should be selected as Senators of the United States from this State.

Just before my election as Governor, the Democratic voters of the State expressed their preference for Mr. James E. Martine. The first question presented to me as Governor was whether that preference should be respected or not. Mr. Smith insisted that it should be disregarded and that he should be sent to the Senate. He had known before my nomination that I would not support his candidacy and had declared that he would not be a candidate. My election as Governor made me the responsible spokesman and leader of my party. It would have been disgraced and discredited had it failed to redeem its pledges and sustain the great principle of popular choice which it had fought so hard to establish. I strove by every honorable means in my power to

[1] Daniel S. Voorhees of Morristown, for many years the Republican boss of Morris County.

bring about the election of Mr. Martine, as every Democrat was in honor bound to do. I won. Mr. Smith was overwhelmingly beaten; and everybody breathed more freely, to find that laws and party obligations meant something. It was a death blow to both machines. The most noticeable champions of Mr. Smith's candidacy had been the newspapers owned by Mr. David Baird, of Camden, one of the Republican guardians.

What followed was easy. The power, in both parties, that had held the legislature back from doing what the opinion of the State demanded was broken, and the Legislature moved forward with zest. Elections were freed from machine control by the Geran act, and from corrupt manipulation by the corrupt practices act. Power to control the great public service corporations, which had controlled Mr. Smith and the Board of Guardians, was conferred upon the Public Utilities Commission and law put above private interest. The Walsh act was passed which gave the urban municipalities of the State the right to put their government in the hands of responsible commissions, when they chose, and so do away with the hide-and-seek of their present complicated town and city governments, by which political machines and favored contractors had so much profited. Such measures had been often promised, but as often defeated, by the managers between elections.

The employers' liability and workingmen's compensation act was passed and the act obliging the railroads to pay their employees twice a month instead of only once, so that justice might be secured for those who did not contribute to campaign funds and had only the law to depend upon for their defense. No disinterested person doubted the justice of these acts, but disinterested persons had not often been allowed to determine what the legislation of the State should be. An act[2] empowering justices of the Supreme Court to empanel special grand juries and call upon the Attorney General of the State to undertake prosecutions whenever the sheriff of a county had brought himself under suspicion of illegal practices was another measure in the series intended to bring about a political emancipation.

I will not prolong the list. It is familiar to you. These acts passed the Legislature with surprising, with refreshing ease, though one house was Democratic and the other Republican. The power of both machines was broken with the downfall of one of the partners. But it was a great shock to those who had been accustomed to dictate what should and what should not be done at Trenton.

2 *Laws of New Jersey, 1911*, Chap. 184.

The president of the Public Service Corporation[3] is said to have shown angry surprise when he found that legislative action had escaped from his dictation, and to have scolded an independent Republican Senator[4] very roundly for so far forgetting the many obligations of his party guardians to that great corporation as to vote for a measure which placed public authority in a position to restrain private interest in behalf of an equitable and adequate service.

This is the whole ground of my offending. I insisted that the party should keep faith with the people, in the matter of the Senatorship as in all others. Senator Smith wanted its obligations ignored in order that he might be returned to the Senate. He seeks revenge, as do the guardians and all others who have been deprived of their private control. Their purpose is to regain their power and rule again as they please. I stand in their way, because I kept my own promises, every one, public and private, and insisted that the promises of the party should be kept as well.

What, therefore, is the present situation? What is happening now? What is happening within the Republican party is obvious to the whole country, and a very unedifying spectacle it is. But what is happening in this State within the Democratic party is not so obvious. It is, indeed, being done very quietly and very secretly, because it is being done by Mr. James Smith, Jr., who knows no other way of acting in politics and who has no suggestion to make to the voters of the State which he can quite venture to make in public. He does not, I understand, avow himself as in favor of any particular candidate for the Democratic nomination; he is only opposed to me; and the men he has induced to offer themselves as candidates to represent New Jersey in the national Democratic convention wish to be sent "without instructions."

It is interesting to note how large a proportion of them are men who were candidates for appointment to office, and whom I did not appoint. There are one or two very conspicuous instances and a great many minor ones of petty spite and disappointment. But that is not the important side of the matter; that is cause for contempt rather than for concern. What concerns us and makes the matter very much larger and more serious than the mere incidental question of whether I am to be nominated at Baltimore or not, is the fact that this is Mr. Smith's attempt to re-establish his control over the Democratic party and put himself once more in a position to make the Democratic machine

3 Thomas N. McCarter, Jr.
4 William James Lee Bradley of Camden County.

an adjunct and partner of the old Republican machine in serving the special interests in New Jersey. It is the last desperate attempt of the discredited old regime to destroy and supplant the new.

Shall the Democrats of New Jersey send delegates to Baltimore who are free men, or are the special interests again to name men to represent them? The representatives of special interests will be in a helpless, intriguing minority at Baltimore. Is the progressive Democracy of New Jersey to contribute to that minority?

We are speaking of very practical matters now and ought not to mince words. The question is, Do you wish to sustain the new regime; do you wish to support government conducted by public opinion, rather than by private understanding and management, or do you wish to slip back into the slough of the old despair and disgrace? This is a question to be asked on both sides of the house —by the men who are going into the Republican primaries as well as by those who are going into the Democratic primaries. It involves the reputation and the freedom of the State we love. On the Democratic side it affects my personal fortunes, but only because I happen to have been given the opportunity by the people of the State to represent the great ideas and principles which every honest man ought to represent. My heart is in them; the heart of every patriotic man in New Jersey is in them; and they are involved in this contest.

We are now to decide whether the State shall go forward or return to the things which besmirched and debased her. The voting on the twenty-eighth of this month will settle a great deal more than a mere personal preference. It will settle a fundamental preference. It will determine your choice between a government that is your own, to be conducted according to your own judgment and interests, and a government made to conform to private interest and the ambition of a small group of men who, by whatever party name they be called, are in the play for nobody but themselves. They care not a whit for principle. They love profit and power.

The choice in such a matter is so plain and obvious to every man who cares for principle and honor and free government that you will be apt to take it for granted that the result at the polls next Tuesday is a matter of course. But it cannot be. You dare not run the risk. The forces of the other side are marshaled and will be got to the voting places to the last man of them. If you stay away from the polls they will beat and laugh at you. You can win only by voting, and by voting your full strength. Every man who stays away from the polls on Tuesday deliberately deserts a great cause and hands his State over to be plundered of even her good name.

Woodrow Wilson, Governor.

Printed in the Trenton *True American*, May 25, 1912; with corrections from the text in the *Newark Evening News*, May 24, 1912.

A Campaign Address in Jersey City, New Jersey[1]

[May 25, 1912]

Mr. Chairman[2] and Fellow Citizens:

I think there is a touch of selfishness on my part in withholding from you the privilege of hearing the distinguished gentlemen who have so honored us by coming here to speak.[3] I feel particularly honored that they should have come here to speak in my behalf, for I know the great part they play in questions concerning the nation. I know how much they are sacrificing in order to do me this great service. I feel there is a touch of selfishness on my part in speaking now also because it is a matter of self-indulgence to speak to my own people. I feel that it is not necessary to establish any connections between you and myself. I feel like a man speaking at home and I feel particularly at home in Hudson County. There is so much militant democracy in Hudson County.

Just because we are speaking at home and to one another in the family we must speak very plainly indeed.

You know what the trouble is, you know exactly what is happening, but I want to put it in plain terms for you so you cannot in any way mistake it, and I want to point out to you at the outset that what we are engaged in discussing now is not of temporary significance but of permanent significance. It is of permanent significance to New Jersey as to who controls either of the great parties that contest for supremacy among the voters of the State, and it is perfectly plain to any man who has his eyes open who at present control the Republican Party in New Jersey. It may be that after next Tuesday the scene will change, but I am not interested in that. I am not particularly interested in who runs the Republican Party and for that reason I am not very interested, I must say, in the debate which is now proceeding between the two most distinguished Republicans in the country, that I understand them to be debating this question: which of them has been

---

[1] Delivered in the auditorium of the Jersey City High School.
[2] James A. Hamill.
[3] Congressmen Hamill and Robert L. Henry were to speak.

the more to blame in the things which have discredited the Republican Party. That is a family question about which it will be indelicate for me to express an opinion.

I was addressing a meeting in Springfield, Massachusetts, the other day which was very much in the nature of your case. The day before they had heard Mr. Roosevelt and the day before that they had heard Mr. Taft and I was moved to say to them: "After what you people have been through the last two days, perhaps you would like to know what the public questions of the day are." Because those questions and those questions only are of significance.

I feel sometimes in trying to attract the attention of audiences to the serious issues of the day, in view of the present performance, very much as I felt at a county fair not long ago, where they put me up to address the grandstand by the race track. The grandstand stood some forty or fifty feet back from the immediate edge of the running track and they erected a little platform just opposite the judge's stand and put me up to address the grandstand. Right back of the grandstand there was a most obstreperous hurdy-gurdy accompanying a merry-go-round, which it was very difficult to compete with, and finally after I had gotten launched and flattered myself that I was going to have the attention of the audience, they started a horse race behind my back, and I, like any other normal American, stopped and watched the horse race. Now, how can a man speak about the public questions of the day when there is a prize fight going on?

But this performance has invaded New Jersey for only a few days. We are going to be here when it goes away, and we have things to settle with which that performance has nothing to do.

We have to settle who are going to run the State of New Jersey. Are the people of the State of New Jersey going to run it or are those people to be delivered back into the hands of men who have discredited and debauched the State? That is the question.

Now, I am interested, in spite of what I said a few minutes ago! am interested, by way of illustration, in the question of who is running the Republican Party in this State. I was told by a very influential citizen of Essex County the other day that he could not get a single thing even proposed in the Legislature of last winter without first going to consult Mr. Dalrymple.[4] Did you ever hear of him? Mr. Dalrymple is the manager of the Republican Party in Essex County and has never been employed for that purpose by the people of Essex County.

4 Alfred N. Dalrymple, lawyer of Newark, chairman of the Essex County Republican Committee.

He has been employed by the managing politicians who mean to see to it that nothing is done by the Republican representatives inconsistent with their welfare and the Republican portion of the Legislature was last winter in the hands of organizations of that sort.

Very well, when I look back a few years I find the Democratic delegations from the County of Essex were sometimes under their similar control and that that control was for a long time excluded, at any rate, from the County of Hudson, but it has long tentacles, and with its long hands it stretches out in secret. Those hands are sometimes lined with gold and it is stretching over to take possession of the County of Hudson.[5]

What is the opposition and what are they opposed to? Who constitute the opposition in the County of Hudson? Who are the leaders? What are their records in court and out of court? Who induced them to take part in this contest, and if they succeed what will they do?

Ah, gentlemen, when you come to vote next Tuesday you will find a lot of delegates on the ticket with nothing opposite their names and you will be told that they wish the privilege of being sent to Baltimore uninstructed. If you vote for them do you suppose they will go uninstructed? The meaning of that blank space is that you shall not instruct them and that it's none of your business who does instruct them! They are to be privately owned, privately voting as it pleases those who own them.

Uninstructed, indeed! The only free men in a great domain are the men who are instructed by you people, for then they speak with the majesty of the people themselves; and the men who are in slavery, the men who are in thraldom, the men who are not their own masters, are the men who are privately instructed and so you are not to be misled for a moment, as intelligent voters, by the pretense that those gentlemen are to go to Baltimore to exercise their own discretion. They will exercise no discretion whatever, except to fulfill the understandings of those who trade in votes and who manipulate the results of conventions.

I said that I did not come here to mince words. I have come here to strip the facts naked and let you look at them, and these are the facts:

[5] He referred to the battle for control of the Hudson County Democratic organization then being waged between Mayor H. Otto Wittpenn and his erstwhile political lieutenant, Frank Hague. With James Smith Jr.'s support, Hague was using the fight against Wilson's endorsement in the presidential primary as a means of consolidating his personal power over the county organization. Hague had already persuaded several assemblymen to come out against Wilson.

Look all over the State of New Jersey and find out the process by which men were persuaded, after infinite difficulty, to allow their names to be put upon these ballots as uninstructed delegates and then run over them and find who they are and what their motives are. I am happy to say—for I don't like to have any picture look too dark in a State which I love—I am happy to say that there are men among those who from whatever motive they are acting, are honorable men and I would say nothing against them, but I also know so familiarly the names of many of them for they haunted my office for appointments and I have reason to know them. Some of them were worthy of appointment, I dare say, but when there are fifty applicants for one place one man has to be appointed and forty-nine have to go unappointed, and if the men who are not preferred in the choice thereupon turn about and try to break up the whole scheme upon which the Democratic party in New Jersey is working, what will you say of them? I cannot understand them. It would not make any difference to me how angry I was, I would be ashamed to stand up and admit it. I would be ashamed to have men say, "He is doing this out of disappointed ambition." The real sport, the man that I will grasp hands with every time, is the man who stays in the game when he's losing.

Don't you remember when we were boys how we used to despise those who would not play if they could not have the principal parts in the plot. Don't you know what we called them? Don't you know that you would have predicted their future careers? These childish, petulant, disappointed men, who, for the most part, will go uninstructed and do anything else to wreak revenge for their disappointment. A handsome picture indeed, and a picture that is deeply mortifying to anyone who understands the serious issues with which we are concerned.

Ladies and gentlemen, I wish you could spend a week with me in my office at Trenton, if there were room. I have day after day counted the amount of time I was permitted to spend in considering the serious interests of New Jersey and I have found it was just about one tenth; that the other nine tenths were consumed in listening to applications and sometimes to the most tearful petitions to be appointed to office; while the business of the State of New Jersey is waiting to be transacted men are filling that office for the purpose of getting jobs. Now, there is nothing disgraceful in seeking employment; I don't mean to imply that, and I don't mean to say that the Governor can sit as a sort of omnipotent being, but I do say that I want you to understand that there is altogether a disproportionate share of the energy of the

State devoted to the mere question of who shall fill offices, and
when it comes to a campaign like this and you find that question, and not questions concerning the fundamental interests
of the state, thrown forward as the determining question, then
it is time you knew how your public servants were employed.
The only time I have to consider, to read documents, to read the
more serious letters I receive, to consider the matters argued
before me in hearings, is when I crawl back to Princeton at night,
tired out with the work of the day, and in that little country town
have an hour or two to myself before I fall absolutely asleep
with the fatigue which has come upon me.

That is not fair to New Jersey. That is the travesty of government. Of course, the Governor makes a lot of mistakes about
appointments and everything else. He knows that a great deal
better than you, but if the men who want to criticise me would
only come down and sit quietly with me I could give them points.
But I take it that is not the way you look at your Governor, I
take it you know he has all sorts of limitations, but that you want,
above all things else, to have fair play; that you want, above all
things else, to take a man's average—to take his batting average
and see just how he plays—see when he lines out a hit clean and
when he makes a sacrifice and lets someone else come in.

Now, if these gentlemen are sent privately instructed to Baltimore, what will their instructions be? Their instructions will be,
though they come from New Jersey, "Anybody but Wilson!" Now,
I have some degree of sympathy with them. I sometimes wish
myself that it might be anybody but Wilson, but that is not the
case. I know the tremendous responsibility and the serious tasks
that await the next President of the United States. A man in my
judgment would be a misguided fool who was sure that he was
fit for the job. That isn't the point. The point is that whatever
accident has thrown a particular man forward, by whatever series of circumstances he has been enabled to render a service, it
is his business to go forward with that service no matter what
happens to him, no matter whether he is elected to office or rejected for office, no matter whether a few stand by him or if
everybody stands by him. If he has got any conscience under his
jacket he is enlisted for life, and I have again and again said
to my fellow citizens in New Jersey that as for me I am enlisted
for life. And if our notorious fellow citizen in Essex should get
rid of me from office, I'll know just about as much about him
then as I did before. I will have just as free a tongue then as I
have now. I will take the same liberty of addressing my fellow
citizens in New Jersey that I take now, and the game will be

just as lively as it has been. It's too late to call the game off. It's impossible now to stop it! And God help the man who is in the wrong.

Ah, how the man who works constantly in the dark makes it more and more evident that he is afraid of the light! How the man who intrigues makes it obvious that he dare not debate! How the man who lays trails of gold in order to lure men to do the wrong makes it evident that he is buying their souls, because he cannot convince them! . . .[6] So I want to serve notice that if this should be only a skirmish, the battle is to come, because I want you to realize what the stake is. I would if I could make you forget that I am concerned in any way. Suppose that it were a man of another name? Suppose a man of different character? Suppose somebody of whom I know nothing? What would be involved, no matter who the man was? The man is not of vital importance, the man is a mere incident. Life is a short thing at best, ladies and gentlemen, but the life of a community is endless and the issues are the issues of life and death, of moral and political life and death, and men are ciphers, mere pawns in the game, but the game goes on, played by the invisible, immortal hand which cannot be stayed from the victory, and so I want you to know that the issues of this campaign are permanent, not temporary. They are not the question of the rise or fall of individuals, they are the question of the permanency of institutions and of the purity of methods of your politics. They are the questions which go to the very life you are living and to the very life of the children whom you have begotten and for which you are now casting anxious thoughts forward into the future.

I read last night in the New York "Evening Post" or was it this morning's—it doesn't make any difference, I read it—a letter from a gentleman who heard me make an address last Thursday evening in New York[7]—an address to businessmen—and he confirmed the suspicion which I admitted I entertained when I began the speech. The presiding officer introduced me to this body of influential businessmen in such terms as these: "You already know the next speaker," and I said I wondered if they did. I said it depends upon which newspaper you read, and I am led to believe from some of the estimates formed of me that you have not read my speeches as some of the things attributed to me I have never entertained. Now, this gentleman, confirming the

<hr/>

[6] The Editors deleted a garbled sentence here.

[7] Drummond Fife to the Editor, May 24, 1912, printed in the New York *Evening Post*, May 25, 1912. Wilson summarizes it in the following text.

suspicion that he had never heard me make any speech or read any other speech that I made, said the businessmen of the country could trust Mr. Wilson if they believed his heart was really with the toiling millions who were concerned directly in the prosperity of the business of the country, because he pointed out what every man must see, that if business languishes or is thrown into despair, more men than ever would be thrown out of employment, and I read the article with pity and amusement. Here I have spent eighteen months trying to say what was the particular I was interested in—that I was not interested in the man at the top so much as the men in the ranks, and that every national question presented to its citizens is a question which affected them, affected the great body of citizens of this country, in all the purity of their interests, in all the purity of their lives, in all those things which make men talk quietly when they go to meet with those who are nearest and dearest to them, by which they will make their wages eke out to pay the bills. Why, there is not a man in public life worthy of the name whose heart is not heavy with that view of the situation.

Now, that is the reason I am interested in the contest next Tuesday, for I know this: that the men who are trying to take New Jersey away from the present control exercised by the Democratic administration are men who never in their lives have served the rank and file, but always have served the special interests, and the most conspicuous arch conspirator amongst them is the man who prevented the passage of the only systematic tariff that has been attempted in our time for the relief of the people of the United States.[8] The tariff question lies at the heart of every thing. The reason your money does not buy what it used to buy is because every attempt to serve you has been prevented by the expert lobbyists that have controlled the judgment of committees of Congress, until in the providence of God at the last general election at least one half of that Congress was released from their control and the men whom you are now to choose between, the men whose effort to recover control of the Democratic party you are to judge next Tuesday, are the men who have prevented every piece of legislation they could prevent that relaxed the hold of special interests upon the policy of the United States. They [have] done it in the State as well as in the Union. I did not come here tonight to talk to you on the affairs of the Union so much as the affairs of our beloved state. I did not know, although I thought I did, until I became Governor, just what a stranglehold these people had upon the legis-

8 A reference to Senator Smith and the Wilson-Gorman tariff debacle of 1894.

lation of New Jersey. The Legislature of New Jersey was not free until the session of 1911 set it free. I would like to claim as much credit as I can get for the outcome of the session of 1911, but I would not be frank with you if I did not tell you that most of the outcome was due to those men who acted according to their conscience[s] and not due to any astuteness nor power of persuasion on my part; so that for the first time in a generation you had a representative assembly who did not dare listen to any suggestions except the suggestions of public opinion in their own county.

There were some very amusing things said in connection with it. One very frank member of the Legislature came to me and said, "Governor, I don't agree with you but I would not dare go home if I do not vote with you," and he added with a sly wink, "they never get me if I see them first." Now, in his rough way he was describing the situation. He was listening to the counsel that came out of public utterances in his own county.

I am not one of those who believes that every judgment of public opinion is a true judgment, because the general public are apt to be mistaken upon occasions, but I do know this: that if they are mistaken it is in the judgment of their own interests. The judgment is made for the maintenance and protection of their interests and not of mine or anybody else's, and therefore I would a great deal rather accept an erroneous general judgment than an interested private judgment.

What we want is government by public opinion and not government by private arrangement—and that's what you have to determine on Tuesday.

I did not come up here because I was afraid of what you would do. There is only one thing I am afraid you won't do. This whole thing is so obvious, and the opposition is so outrageous, that I am afraid you will think everybody else thinks so and it is not necessary to vote. Well, now, don't deceive yourselves. Everybody on the other side is going to vote. Somebody is going to see to it that he does and if you don't vote you may wake up the next morning and find yourselves deeply humiliated and have simply delivered yourselves into their hands by not taking the trouble to go to the polls. Mind you, the polls are open until nine o'clock at night and any man can find time to vote between one o'clock in the afternoon and nine in the evening. And if you don't go what have you proved? You have proved that you do not admit that you are a trustee for New Jersey. Every voter in this commonwealth is a trustee for the general good, and if he does not vote he is recreant to his trust. He is not worthy of the name of citizen if he will not at least take the trouble to say what he thinks about public affairs, for the only disappointment, the only keen disappointment, I have experienced in some of the recent primaries in different parts of this country has not been that some of them went against me, but that the vote was so pitifully small that the people of this country did not seem to be interested in expressing a judgment as to who they thought should be President of the United States. This is the first year we have had presidential primaries for the expression of that choice, but it was amazing to me that only some eighteen per cent of the voters of our Party bestirred themselves to express any judgment at all. Don't they care? Do you suppose they are really indifferent? No! The truth of the matter is that the whole thing is too good to be true. They have taken part in so many primaries and have gotten dished by the managing politicians so often, they have been deprived of the results of their victories so repeatedly, that they are not going to believe it until it happens. I believe in my heart that the people of this country have in many places said to themselves, "What's the use, they are going to manage it so that we won't get it, so there is no use going to the polls because we are not our own masters, we are not permitted to be our own masters."

Ah, gentlemen, the only reason you are not your own masters is that you will not believe it.

You remember that story, which is such an admirable illustration of it, of some great elephant, not symbolical but real, which had spent year after year of his life in a certain paddock in a great zoological garden, chained by the legs, a very dangerous elephant, whom they had not dared to let loose, and when there was occasion to move him from one paddock to another after he had been chained for some ten years, they took the chains off his feet but he did not move. They put food just beyond his reach and he would reach for it, and when he could not get it trumpet in his distress. He did not know he was free, did not believe it, and they had to cruelly prod him in order to induce him to lift those massive legs and get out of the old tracks and find something of the breath of the old forest come upon him—a whiff of freedom in the air.

Sometimes I think people who have been chained by the machinery of politics so long do not know that the chains are struck off, but they are! You are your own masters! You need not do any master's bidding any longer than you please!

These men whom I have spoken of tonight wish to be your

masters. I, if you will permit me to say so, wish to be your servant, and I am not wholly unselfish in the wish. I flatter myself
that I know more than they do. It's a bigger thing to embody the
will of a people than to go cunningly about to deceive them. It
is a bigger job, because if a man is not big himself he can be
made big by the job with which he is entrusted. As he receives
into his limited lungs something of the afflatus that comes from
the general life of the people themselves, as he forgets himself
and loses his identity in theirs, there steals upon him something
of that dignity that lies upon the face of all great history, where
men are seen moving as if directed by the fingers of Providence,
connecting the parts, which seems to put into them the spirit
of the age.

There is a spirit of the age. It is change. It is not what it was
five years ago; it is not what it was one year ago; year by year
in the United States this spirit more and more displays itself.
Only those who can comprehend it can take any share in
the future. Those who have governed our affairs in this intriguing
way have not seen the signs of the times, and those conventions
that are going to meet in Chicago and in Baltimore, they are
going to have this critical choice to make: Will they recognize
the spirit of the age or will they not? If they do not they will discredit, dishonor and destroy their party. If they do they will have
taken title deeds to immortality. There is a spirit that rules us.
If I did not believe in Providence I would feel like a man going
blindfolded through a haphazard world. I do believe in Providence. I believe that God presided over the inception of this
nation; I believe that God planted in us the visions of liberty;
I believe that men are emancipated in proportion as they lift
themselves to the conception of Providence and of divine destiny, and therefore I cannot be deprived of the hope that is in
me—in the hope not only that concerns myself, but the confident
hope that concerns the nation—that we are chosen and prominently chosen to show the way to the nations of the world how
they shall walk in the paths of liberty.

How great a destiny it is and how small those who intrigue
against Providence. How God must laugh! I do not know his
ways; I do not know by what method he will work the great plot
out; but I do know that there is a power whose approaching
breath we can feel, that is going to purify the whole air of American politics, chasten every selfish man, drive out every corrupt
purpose, bring on the morning with its light, and as the day
broadens men shall look about them and say, "Behold the heavens

are clear again! God's sun is in the heavens and all shall be right."[9]

T transcript (Nj) with corrections from the partial text in the Jersey City
Jersey Journal, May 27, 1912.
    [9] There is a WWhw outline of this speech, dated May 25, 1912, in WP, DLC.

From Charles Sumner Moore

Personal

My dear Governor: Atlantic City, New Jersey May 25th, 1912.

Your letter[1] is excellent and I am confident it will help greatly. We had a splendid meeting here last Wednesday evening. The place was packed to the doors with an intelligent and enthusiastic audience of twelve hundred people. The speaking of Congressmen Hardy[2] and Palmer and Col. Bacon was of an exceedingly high order, and met with a hearty response from the audience.

Judge Cole and I have just talked the situation over and our impression is that the opposition is melting away. The trouble here as everywhere is the fact that the independent Republicans can't vote for us in our Democratic primaries.

La Follette's meeting was scarcely advertised at all yet he drew an audience of over three thousand people. It far outclassed Roosevelt's in every respect except size, noise, and "brag."

Sincerely yours   C. S. Moore

ALS (Governors' Files, Nj).
    [1] That is, Wilson's letter to the Democrats of New Jersey printed at May 24, 1912.
    [2] Rufus Hardy of Texas.

To Mary Allen Hulbert Peck

Dearest Friend,   Princeton, New Jersey 26 May, 1912

Many, many *happy* returns of the day! You are on the sea and I cannot send you a birthday message by wire, as I had intended to do. I *believe* that from this time on each year will find you happier,—as your life settles about you, becomes calculable, is spent altogether with those you love, and you are freed from intolerable uncertainty and conjecture. You are on the "home stretch" now, in the truest and deepest sense of the word,—and the skies will brighten about you as you realize it more and more, God bless you!

Alas! that it should be to-morrow that you are to reach New

York and that you are to be there only a day! It is the time of all others when I *cannot* get away. On Tuesday the vote comes which is to decide the action of New Jersey about my candidacy,—whether I am to have the support of my own State or not,—and *all* my friends and lieutenants will require of me that I "stay on the job" and be where they can resort to me and get in touch with me at any moment and on the shortest notice. I cannot stir. I will call you up on the telephone some time to-morrow and find out whether your plans are so fixed that you *cannot* linger longer in New York or not. It would be *so* delightful to turn aside from all this anxious hurly-burly of politics and have a good, old-fashioned talk with you all,—as if I were visiting you in Bermuda and all America had sunk out of my ken! What is to be your address at the shore? I find I have not the least idea and would not know how to get a letter to you there. You will seem *very* far away then, for I have never seen the place and will not be able to visualize your surroundings, as I was able to do after I had been at "Shoreby," at "Glencove," before your occupancy of it, and at Pittsfield. Please take photographs *galore* of it, from many sides, and both inside and out, so as to eke out my imagination!

I am well, and so glad that you are presently to be in America again, where your friends can get at you and you will no longer seem inaccessable, a sight of you past praying for. All join me in affectionate messages. My love to Mrs. Allen and Allen.

Your devoted friend   Woodrow Wilson

ALS (WP, DLC).

To Edith Gittings Reid

My dear, dear Friend,   Princeton, New Jersey 26 May, 1912

You must have *known* that I needed a letter[1] from you and that an expression of your generous confidence in me was just the tonic that would put me in form again! Everybody over here seems to agree that there has never been a campaign in which there was such a systematic and malevolent attempt to destroy a man's reputation for character and intellectual integrity as has been made by my opponents all over the country, including the representatives of the other candidates for the Democratic nomination, and in such circumstances one *needs* to hear the voice of true and loyal friends to keep him in heart.

Not that I actually lose heart. I find I am of too firm a fibre, and of too firm a faith, for that; but the world grows sometimes

to seem so brutal, so naked of beauty, so devoid of chivalrous
sentiment and all sense of fair play, that one's own spirit hardens
and is in danger of losing its fineness. I fight on, in the spirit of
Kipling's "If," but that is oftentimes a very arid air; and one's
heart softens and glows again and the colour comes back into
the world when a dear friend speaks and calls one's heart back
from its anxious quest amongst strangers. Your letter did me a
world of good. You are always *there*, to think about and depend
on; but when you speak the comfort and reassurance come in a
flood!

The political field is hopelessly confused: no one can confidently predict *any*thing,—not even the nomination of Roosevelt,
though that seems daily more probable. On the Democratic side
is [it] now looks as if the choice of the convention might lie between Bryan and me. I need not tell you how I feel about it,—
I am so sure you can divine. I dread the possibility and yet feel
that I must offer myself and not shirk. Your judgment of Roosevelt is mine own. God save us of another four years of him *now*,
in his present insane distemper of egotism!

Ellen and the girls join me in messages of deep affection. It
delighted us so to hear from you. I hope that you have got both
health and pleasure amidst your old haunts and friends.

Your devoted friend,   Woodrow Wilson

Alas! The Governor of N. J. (till 1914) cannot leave his bailiwick
to travel across seas!

ALS (WC, NjP).
    [1] Edith G. Reid to WW, May 11, 1912, ALS (WP, DLC), from Cambridge,
England.

To Thomas Bell Love

My dear Mr. Love: [Trenton, N. J.] May 27, 1912.

My heart goes out to you in genuine sympathy for the loss of
your Mother.[1] I understand fully how you feel and that detained
you from the Convention in Texas. You will be missed missed
[sic] there but nobody would expect you to go in the circumstances.

It was kind of you to write while under the weight of a great
loss,[2] and I sincerely appreciate your letter.

Cordially yours,   Woodrow Wilson

TLS (photostat in the T. B. Love Papers, Dallas Hist. Soc.).
    [1] Sarah Jane Rodgers (Mrs. Thomas Calvin) Love, who died in Mt. Pleasant,
Tex., on May 20, 1912.
    [2] Love's letter is missing.

From Willard Saulsbury

Dear Governor: [Dover, Del.] May 27th, 1912.

While you are awaiting the returns from New Jersey, you will probably not be displeased at the action taken by our little delegation here to-day, which is in accordance with program. I called a meeting of the delegation for this morning, when an order was unanimously passed instructing our Chairman[1] to vote for you until the delegation should otherwise direct, and you can readily understand that there will be no further direction unless we all become hopeless of the possibility of your nomination.

I have just taken a trip by automobile between three and four hundred miles through this state and Maryland, and it will doubtless please you to know that your friends are enthusiastic for your nomination and thoroughly convinced that no other man mentioned would so well satisfy the people of the country as yourself.

My own feeling has been that you have been forging ahead somewhat in the last two weeks and this is doubtless caused by my talks with strong and leading Democrats, so[me] of whom have a national reputation and are well known to you, and because I have been receiving letters from some of them who are now requesting interviews and meetings to talk things over where for two or three weeks before that I had been rather in the way of soliciting them myself. My feeling is that the people who have been furnishing the opposition in the Democratic Party with the sinews of war to defeat your nomination have become frightened at the measure of success their efforts have attained and because of their fear that Roosevelt will be nominated, those who have been opposing you are veering around to the point where they may advocate your nomination because of their willingness to accept your candidacy and what I regard as the certainty of your election if nominated rather than to take the chance of having Roosevelt elected.

While the undignified and disgraceful contest between President Taft and Roosevelt has to some extent obscured Democratic Booms, I think it has been for some weeks an affirmative benefit to you and my feeling is that we are in much better shape now than when I saw you personally in Princeton, when I feared that we were simply being trampled upon. I do not know exactly why I feel as I do but I have a sort of a sense that makes me believe the sober second thought of the Democrats is now asserting itself and that the abuse and villification which you have been subjected to by some of the friends of the other candidates

has disgusted the right-thinking Democrats of the country and
that there is a decided revulsion of sentiment. I sincerely hope
that the result in New Jersey to-morrow will be a great victory for
you and I believe it will put the final quietus upon the Taft candidacy.

As you know, I have not been very sanguine about the result
in this state at the next election, but going around as I have in
the last few days, I have gathered a great deal of information
from all people with whom I have talked which leads me to
believe that the nomination of Roosevelt would almost certainly
give you the electoral vote of this state, if you shall be nominated.
Some of the strongest Republicans I know are declaring without
any qualification that they will never under any circumstances
vote for Roosevelt and many of them say they would be glad
to vote for you. It is my belief that if an election were held in
this state to-day, you and Roosevelt being the candidates, you
would sweep the state. Of course the feelings of those who are
opposed to Roosevelt are running high now but this sentiment
will be greatly modified and people will come back into their
party alignments, but their contest has been so bitter and feelings
have risen so high that your election in my opinion if nominated
is almost certain.

With best wishes for New Jersey and in fact for the Democracy of the United States, believe me,

Yours very truly,   Willard Saulsbury

TLS (Saulsbury Letterpress Books, DeU).
[1] That is, Saulsbury.

A News Report

[May 28, 1912]

WILSON TO PRINCETON STUDENTS ON CAMPAIGN

PRINCETON, May 28.—In a final pre-primary appeal, flaying
privileged business and urging straight thinking and conscientious voting, Governor Wilson last night addressed parading
undergraduates from the steps of his home in Cleveland lane.
He remarked that the "two very militant gentlemen"[1] had made
things interesting in the campaign, but that the issue is not a
mere party matter.

The address followed that of Colonel Roosevelt by an hour.[2]
The lack of fair play in the system of "big business" and the failure of the Sherman law were emphasized by the Governor. In

spite of all that Presidents had so far done, he said, monopolies are steadily increasing in power.

"Business says, 'Let us alone,'" he said, "'and the country will take care of itself.' You cannot let business alone when you do not have fair play. There is no fair play for the laborer—I mean the men who receive wages. The men who are employed are at a disadvantage.

"The Sherman act was to have been expressed in terms unmistakable, but Senator Sherman did not have his way. It was changed so that it would be difficult for the courts to interpret it. We break up combinations, but not the things that are the root of the evil."

Because of the hostilities of the "militant gentlemen," the Governor said it had been difficult for the people to centre the[ir] mind on the serious problems of the campaign.

"There never was a time in this country when more brains were more necessary," the Governor declared in concluding.

Printed in the *Newark Evening News*, May 28, 1912.
1 Roosevelt and Taft.
2 He spoke from the balcony of Nassau Inn.

A Statement on the Results of the New Jersey Presidential Primary

[[May 29, 1912]]

I never doubted the result,[1] but I am none the less delighted and grateful that the Democrats of the State should have stood by me so generously and with so unmistakable a verdict.

Their approval makes me very happy, because it is their judgment of the new regime in our politics in New Jersey, and means that the new order is to be sustained with steadfastness and enthusiasm. New Jersey is permanently enrolled among the progressive States.

Printed in the Trenton *True American*, May 30, 1912.
1 Wilson lost Essex County on account of the opposition of the Smith-Nugent machine but won all the other counties by a landslide vote.

To John Wesley Wescott

My dear Judge Wescott,   Princeton, New Jersey 29 May, 1912

Now that there is no doubt about the willingess of New Jersey to support me, I am writing to ask if you will do me the honour of placing my name in nomination before the Baltimore Convention. I know of no one who could do it more impressively or convincingly, and it would give me great personal gratification to have you do so.

Affectionately Yours,   Woodrow Wilson

ALS (photostat in RSB Coll., DLC).

To Willard Saulsbury

My dear Mr. Saulsbury: [Trenton, N. J.] May 29, 1912.

Your letter of the twenty-seventh did me a lot of good. I read it with pleasure and gratitude. I am happy to read this morning that the results in New Jersey fulfill our highest hopes. They ought to do a great deal to strengthen our lines everywhere.

Gratefully yours,   Woodrow Wilson

TLS (W. Saulsbury Papers, DeU).

To Francis Griffith Newlands

My dear Senator: [Trenton, N. J.] May 29, 1912.

For fear you should feel some hesitancy about accepting a place as a delegate-at-large from Nevada, I am going to take the liberty of telling you that I should think it a real service to myself and to the cause of the party if you would go to the Convention in that capacity. Wise counselors and leaders will be needed.[1]

Pardon the suggestion, if it is a presumption.

Cordially yours,   Woodrow Wilson

TLS (F. G. Newlands Papers, CtY).
[1] See F. G. Newlands to WW, June 6 and July 1, 1912.

From William Gibbs McAdoo

PERSONAL.

Dear Governor: [New York] May 29, 1912.

My friends on the "World" tell me that something interesting will appear Thursday morning, the 30th, and that it ought to be pleasing to us.[1] Will you please look out for this edition?

Sorry I cannot sign this letter, as I am rushing for a train.

Very sincerely yours,   W G McAdoo

TL (LPC, W. G. McAdoo Papers, DLC).
[1] The New York World, heretofore one of Wilson's severest critics in the East,

published on May 30 a long editorial, "For President—Woodrow Wilson!," advocating his nomination on the ground that he alone among the Democratic candidates could defeat Theodore Roosevelt, the "most cunning and adroit demagogue that modern civilization has produced since Napoleon III." Stating that Wilson would be "a progressive constitutional President whom the American people could trust," the *World* appealed to Bryan and all delegates to the Baltimore convention to rally behind the New Jersey Governor.

Two Telegrams to Edward Mandell House

Princeton N. J. May 30th 1912

Would it be agreeable and convenient for me to call tomorrow Friday evening at your hotel?

Woodrow Wilson.

T telegram (E. M. House Papers, CtY).

✧

Trenton N. J. May 31/12

Thank you sincerely will join you at dinner to-night at eight.

Woodrow Wilson

Hw telegram (E. M. House Papers, CtY).

To Mary Allen Hulbert Peck

Dearest Friend, Princeton, New Jersey 2 June, 1912

It was a cruel disappointment not to see you when you were so near; but of course I understood why you could not wait on the convenience (or rather the chance liberty) of a poor, badgered politician, tied by the leg and obliged to carry his chains with him wherever he moves. I hope you were disappointed, too (so unselfish am I and willing to share *anything* with my friends), —so disappointed that you will soon come to this neighbourhood and try me again! Not that I see any greater freedom ahead for me, but I would not have to have much to break away in such circumstances. When shall we ever have a chance to sit down together for a real talk, and catch up? Only when the present battle is over, and (Beau)champ Clark or some other good Democratic [candidate] of the popular stamp is nominated? Politics and friendship seem mutually exclusive. That sounds like a very cynical remark; but it is not. It is only a very sad one. Moral: eschew politics and brighten your life with friendship.

Meanwhile (that is, while I fret and repine after this fashion) you are, I hope with all my heart, already enjoying Nantucket and *your own house.* I can imagine the caravan arriving,—the boxes, the trunks, the household belongings, and the dear tired people, and all the heat and labour, and the cantankerousness of New England helpers of the vicinage,—the masterful, capable lady in charge, using every o[u]nce of her vitality and diligently getting ready to collapse when it was all over,—but not *until* then, —the whole scene and the characters in the play! How I hope it is all over. How I hope you like,—even love,—the new home, and are satisfied with the alterations to which you gave so much thought. At last you are literally and truly *at home*. Does not the peace of it begin to steal over you at last and take the kinks out of your tired heart strings, wrung again and again and again until you feared that it was no longer possible to play any strain of happy music on them? Do you not hear the major chords come out, true and sweet, and the minor chords die away? God bless you, with every gift of peace!

I am well, singularly, persistently, *stubbornly* well, and quite philosophical about the possibilities of the month. All join me in affectionate messages to you all, and I am, as always,

Your devoted friend   Woodrow Wilson

Is it "Sandanmede"?

ALS (WP, DLC).

To John Wesley Wescott

Dear Judge: [Trenton, N. J.] June 3, 1912.

I want you to know how proud I am of the friends who exerted themselves in the recent campaign and at the recent primaries. My chief pride in the whole thing is that I was supported by thoughtful and disinterested men who represent the real interests of the State. This is an altogether inadequate message of sincere personal appreciation.

Cordially and sincerely yours,   Woodrow Wilson

TLS (J. W. Wescott Coll., NjP).

A News Report

[June 4, 1912]

WILSON ACTIVE IN GRAFT QUIZ

Governor Confers with Atlantic City Reformers,
and Elisor Jury May Be Drawn.

ATLANTIC CITY, June 4.—Having in mind the councilmanic scandal[1] here disclosed by Burns detectives[2] and dictagraphs,

Mayor [Harry] Bacharach said after a meeting of City Council last night, that "no one knows what is going to happen from hour to hour."

This statement epitomizes the situation here and more so since the arrival of Governor Wilson. The Governor was in conference until late last night with some of the men who have so effectively gone about the work of cleaning up the city.

"I shall do whatever is necessary to aid the work," stated the Governor after his arrival.

Whether the Governor will be compelled to take a hand depends upon the action that the Atlantic County Grand Jury, now in session, may take when the evidence obtained by the Burns detectives in the grafting cases is submitted to them.

If the grand jury does not act, then the Governor may direct Attorney-General Wilson to apply to Supreme Court Justice Kalisch for a grand jury drawn by elisors. . . .

Harvey Thomas, head of the municipal cleansers, met the Governor and Secretary Tumulty at the railroad station on their arrival and arranged for the night conference. Mr. Thomas later was one of the men at the conference held in the Marlborough-Blenheim, where the Governor stayed, and showed copies of some of the more important features of the Burns testimony to the Governor. The Governor, on his arrival, was met also by a party of newspaper men, who requested a statement from him.

"It has been wholesome work," the Governor stated. "I have come down here tonight to get into touch with those men who are behind the movement to clean the city, municipally and politically. I shall meet these gentlemen, or some of them, tonight and talk over the situation.

"I shall do whatever is necessary for me to do. The attorney-general may be called in by Justice Kalisch. In that case it would be up to the attorney-general to decide on the course to be pursued."

Printed in the *Newark Evening News*, June 4, 1912; one editorial heading omitted.
  1 Several councilmen stood accused of graft in connection with public works, city contracts, and liquor licenses. Four councilmen had already confessed.
  2 Detectives of the agency run by William John Burns.

To Alexander Mitchell Palmer

My dear Mr. Palmer: [Trenton, N. J.] June 4, 1912.

Since writing you this morning,[1] I received your letter[2] making the very acceptable and important suggestion that I hold a conference with you and the entire Pennsylvania delegation. The suggestion is a splendid one and I shall be very glad indeed to fall in with it.

Mr. Roland S. Morris of Philadelphia, has kindly offered to entertain the whole delegation at lunch at Princeton, if that would suit your ideas and convenience. Unfortunately, the accommodations at Princeton are monopolized until Tuesday night next, because of the Commencement season, and the crowds of visitors, but I am sure that the visit could be arranged for on Wednesday of next week. Do you think that a delay until that time would be putting the conference off too late? I should like very much to know what you think of this plan.

In the meantime let me thank you most warmly for your letter and for its thoughtful suggestion.

Cordially and faithfully yours,   Woodrow Wilson

TLS (WP, DLC).
    1 This letter is missing.
    2 It is also missing.

To Dan Fellows Platt

Dear Mr. Platt: [Trenton, N. J.] June 4, 1912.

I want you to know how proud I am of the friends who exerted themselves in the recent campaign and at the recent primaries. My chief pride in the whole thing is that I was supported by thoughtful and disinterested men who represent the real interests of the State. This is an altogether inadequate message of sincere personal appreciation.

Cordially and sincerely yours,   Woodrow Wilson

TLS (photostat in RSB Coll., DLC).

An Address of Welcome to the American Medical Association in Atlantic City, New Jersey

[[June 4, 1912]]

Mr. President[1] and members of the American Medical Association, ladies and gentlemen, I feel it a privilege, as representing the State of New Jersey, to welcome this great society to its session this year in Atlantic City.

A great many people come to Atlantic City on all sorts of errands, most of them not serious. The problems that Atlantic City is confronted by is that it is the refuge of the idle, and those

1 Dr. Abraham Jacobi of New York, the father of American pediatrics.

who are idle are apt to adjourn the ordinary standards of their lives. But you are doubly welcome here, because you have not come as idlers but as those who study the more serious problems of our lives, both individually and nationally.

Atlantic City is used now to investigation. You have come as investigators, not to investigate Atlantic City, except for your intimate knowledge of the make-up, the physical make-up of all citizens of the community, and I feel in facing a great association like this that I am facing a body of men and women who have a particularly intimate connection with the life of the country, because you are very much more than physicians individually. You are very much more than the advisers of individuals with regard to the problems of health. You are the guardians of communities. You are the guardians of communities not only with regard to those general sanitary problems which are summed up under the head of sanitation and general hygiene, for example, but of a great many moral problems also. In our day the old story that the physical welfare of man is very closely knit with the moral is very true, and as a man thinks so is he, a thing which comes very much nearer being a physical fact than is usually realized, because there is undoubtedly an air of morale in most of the problems that you have to deal with. At any rate, by way of preliminary determination and as counselors or individuals, you are the arbiters, to some degree, of the life of communities.

I have sometimes wished there might be some way of establishing an official connection between doctors and the State that has been found in the case of lawyers. Lawyers are officers of the court, and are subject to discipline as such. They hold in their hands the honor of obeying and carrying out the laws of the Commonwealth, and they are held amenable on that basis. It is on that basis that men are dealt with for contempt of court and lawyers are held to a code which has nothing to do with their knowledge of the law. Similarly, it seems to me, the doctor, by reason of the license he holds, is reputed to represent morality as well as the knowledge of the community. And the most interesting part of the profession is this, that knowledge is not vital unless it goes hand in hand with honesty and sympathy. I believe you will agree with me that one of the things to be regretted in modern times is that we have been obliged to specialize our professions to so great a degree, because in proportion as the medical profession is specialized, for example, the old family physician disappears.

I remember going over in my memory a single year of my

family life with my children when they were small and finding
that I had called in consultation 13 different specialists. There
was no ill luck in the 13, because it all came out very happily.
But where I had summoned 13 specialists my father would have
summoned 1 family physician. My father would not have got as
good advice as I got, and yet I lived through it. But every time
he sent for his doctor he was sending for a personal friend. He
was sending for a man who had his confidence in a peculiar degree. He was sending for a man who walked along the paths of
life with him as a comrade and confidant. There was something
very vital, there was something very useful in that relationship,
and although we have certainly yielded only to necessity, it is
unfortunate that we should have been obliged to specialize so
much as we have, and therefore it is necessary, it seems to me,
if you will permit me to suggest it, that we regeneralize our sympathies. I remember saying once, when I was following out a
certain occupation, that I understood the chief business of a
university was to make young men as unlike their fathers as
possible. I will hasten to explain that, as I did on that occasion.
I did not then, nor do I say that now, in disrespect to the fathers,
but merely this: By the time a man was old enough to have a
son in the university he became so immersed in a special occupation and narrowed to the point of a single calling, it was advisable that his son should be taken out on some place of vantage
where he could see the world, instead of seeing a single individual, a single community, a single profession. I understood
that to be the business of the university—to regeneralize each
generation of youngsters, show them the Nation, show them the
great infinite variety of human interests, show them the map
of the world, so that they would never forget, at any rate, their
general geographic relations to the races of mankind. So, it seems
to me, every profession, particularly a profession so absorbed as
yours is, and bent upon investigations, must find it necessary to
refresh its general sympathies by reconnecting itself with the
wider questions of our modern life.

As an American I feel that the task of a statesman in our day
is analogous to the task of the surgeon. There is a great deal that
is necessary to be cut out of modern life, and yet we must be
very careful not to injure any of the sound tissue in cutting it
out, and the various processes of politics are not unlike the processes with which you are familiar. The preliminary agitations
of a political campaign are a sort of prognosis and the platforms
are a sort of diagnosis, and then follows the critical part. Then
you have to study your materia medica; then you have to propose

a particular operation and determine exactly what you are going to do in following up your diagnosis to remove the disease, or, at any rate, to apply some tonic which will enable nature to assist herself.

The moral of that sort of thing is that the surgeon should know what he is about, and that rough and ready methods, methods of passion, methods of prejudice, are of all things the most dangerous. They are the methods of the quack; they are the methods of the uneducated, the uninstructed, the unlicensed practitioner, and therefore I have a sort of sympathy with you. It is very much easier for you to get at the difficulty and the particular phenomenon with which you have to deal than it is for the men who are wandering abroad amidst the general phenomena of society; and yet, it seems to me, that you can be infinitely instrumental in assisting the statesman, because there are a great many evidences and symptoms at this time of hysteria, and if you will only hurry home from this convention and calm your communities down we may be able to transact business.

I am very glad to have you all at once in New Jersey, but you can not calm New Jersey down by merely sitting here in Atlantic City. It will be necessary for you to disperse to your homes and get to work on the people you know. I know a great many people whom I would like to get to work on if I only knew the proper cure for hysteria, but never having, happily, felt the symptoms myself, I am unsympathetic about it. And yet, seriously, ladies and gentlemen, speaking of the problems of our life, they are all one. The thing I am particularly impatient with, ladies and gentlemen, is dividing our lives and our interests into sections and supposing you know nothing about anything, except one thing. The whole problem of modern society is infinitely complicated, just because it is variously specialized, and it should be our object to avoid the separation of interests; it should be our object to effect a union of purpose, to unite ourselves with one another, not as a body of competing interests, but a body of unified interests, moving forward to the common goal of general service. That, it seems to me, is the problem of all intelligent men in the United States and in the world at large. I can not do better, therefore, than to ask you in your modern occupation to harmonize the various parts of our whole life to one another, so that heat, hostility, and friction may be taken out and all the sweet and wholesome processes of life may be restored.[2]

Printed in the *Cong. Record*, 62nd Cong., 2nd sess., Vol. 48, Appendix, pp. 493-4.
[2] There is a WWhw outline of this talk, dated June 4, 1912, in WP, DLC.

A News Report and a Statement

[June 5, 1912]

PRESENT JURY TO SIFT GRAFT

Governor, Talking of Atlantic City, Says Politics Won't Figure in Probe.

ATLANTIC CITY, June 5.—That for the present there will be no special elisor-drawn grand jury to consider the municipal graft cases here was made known by Governor Wilson in a statement he made before leaving for Trenton. The Governor praised the character of the present grand jury.

With Secretary Tumulty, the Governor looked up the law before coming here and they made it plain to the local workers for good government that before elisors could be named it would have to be shown that the sheriff labored under some disability or was interested in some case under consideration.

This is not charged to Sheriff Ingersoll,[1] a former District Court judge. The Governor, moreover, does not wish to give any air of partizanship to the investigation and if the sheriff and grand jury show good faith they will receive only assistance. Mr. Tumulty remained here until today for further conferences on the graft cases. . . .

The statement of the Governor was as follows:

"There can be no suspicion or intimation that partizan politics has any part in the undertaking. From a knowledge of the project that goes back to its very beginning, I can declare that there has been no basis for any such suspicion, but henceforth any such intimation will be deliberately false.

"It is a system that has been under attack in Atlantic City; a system of politics and government whose practitioners have been bad men. They have been professional practitioners, which may be taken as accounting for their success.

"It is satisfying to see these fellows so beautifully caught when they try to play the old game. It is getting harder to play all the time; harder for the old fellows to guess what is going to happen. They sit back and decide the cat will jump this way only to find that it jumps that. It is far from pleasant for them, but if they are not becoming accustomed to it I fear they never will.

"Here they believed that the cat jumped during the days of the Macksey Commission,[2] to find that it had only been getting ready to jump.

---

[1] Robert H. Ingersoll, a state district court judge until 1911, when he was elected sheriff on the ticket supported by Louis Kuehnle, Republican boss of Atlantic County.

[2] A state legislative committee appointed to investigate frauds in the elections

"I should like, more than all else, to have my administration remembered as one during which the influences for good in the State became freed. All that the changes in the past few years mean is that these influences are being freed, and that under this freedom we are getting back to self-government. Men normally prefer to be governed by their better natures; even bad men had rather enjoy their self-respect.

"As Governor I took an oath to enforce the laws of the State, as every other Governor must take oath. This was not utterly idle, for no desire of mine, however ardent, could bring about fulfilment. There was nothing with which I might set about my task.

"If a sheriff belonged to a gang, the grand jury he drew was depended upon not to go too far.

"The prosecutor, if he belongs to the gang, will be discreet. The judge may be complaisant.

"Originally the attorney-general was the prosecutor for the whole people. As his work increased county prosecuting attorneys were appointed, intended to be deputies of the attorney-general. The attorney-general might intervene in any case.

"For reasons that should be manifest as we look back, power was withdrawn from the attorney-general and conferred upon the prosecutor. Finally no power of any value remained to the attorney-general, and by the same consequence the Governor's obligation to compel obedience to law became an empty thing.

"Justice Kalisch, now assigned to the circuit including this county, soon after he took office, came across a long-forgotten law empowering justices of the Supreme Court to appoint elisors to act when a sheriff should be under any disability.

"Disability meant prejudice or implication in some case under inquisition, which might mean that a jury he drew would fail or decline to take the action it should. Effective use of this ancient statute, which belongs to the common law, was made last year in this county,[3] as it has been made use of in Hudson County.

"This freed us in New Jersey from possible abuse of power by a sheriff set against the doing of justice. Then came the passage of a law empowering a Supreme Court justice to call in the attorney-general as special prosecutor in emergencies. This has freed us from possible abuse of power by a prosecutor. There remains, then, only the menace of a complaisant judge, which has at all times been the most remote of our dangers.

---

in Atlantic City in November 1911. The committee discovered that the rolls were padded with the names of 4,000 phantom voters and that the Kuehnle machine openly purchased votes.

[3] About this matter, see n. 1 to the platform printed at Oct. 3, 1911, Vol. 23.

"All this means that in our effort toward self-government we have gone backward. It is an instance where going backward means progress, and I believe that we might go still further. We have, as a matter of fact, gone but half-way back to the original provision for safeguarding our rights.

"Still it has been a long step and I believe we shall profit by it more than we have already.

"There are some admirable things about the judicial system of New Jersey, despite amusement sometimes affected regarding it. The Court of Chancery originally meant the king's conscience. To it were submit[t]ed matters deserving of adjustment for which there was no remedy specified by law. In our Courts of Chancery the minority stockholder is assured that he will be guaranteed his rights, and nowhere else in the United States is this true. At the point to which we have gone back in the other respects that I have spoken of, may I not say that the minority stockholder in the government will find his rights guaranteed to him?

"The situation in Atlantic City is, as I said, evidence that it is not safe to try to play the old game. It is evidence that years of safety do not mean perpetual safety. It is evidence that the influence[s] for good that have been freed are at work.

"The State will take a part in further investigation of the charges, only that nothing may interfere with relentless examination of them.

"There will be no recourse to an elisor-drawn grand jury, for in the case of the sheriff of Atlantic County, there is no disability. Nor is there any reason to feel anything but satisfaction over the character of the grand jury now in existence. Under all these circumstances the cases will be carried through with all possible speed. No one should yield for a moment to any fear that there may be partizan politics in this and that when the ends of politics have been served, there may come indifference to anything more.

"Some of the men who have given their support to this particular movement in Atlantic City have been working in the cause of good and clean government for years. One of them, I know, has been working toward that end for fifteen years. If they worked so tirelessly when all was dark, can anyone suppose that they will cease when the light has come?

"And if they should, authority in the matter has passed now from their hands. The State will see this through."[4]

Printed in the *Newark Evening News*, June 5, 1912; one editorial heading omitted.
[4] The grand jury completed its work on September 27, 1912, handing down nineteen indictments charging several councilmen and other individuals with conspiracy, embezzlement, and gambling.

To Alexander Mitchell Palmer

My dear Mr. Palmer: [Trenton, N. J.] June 5, 1912.

At last things are settled in New Jersey and I am at liberty to give myself the pleasure of turning for conference to my friends elsewhere. I wonder when it would be convenient for you to see me. Do you come home for the week-ends? If so, perhaps you could come over to Trenton for a conference, which I feel I stand very much in need of.

Cordially and sincerely yours,   Woodrow Wilson

TLS (WP, DLC).

To Josephus Daniels

Trenton, N. J. June 5th, [19]12.

Your telegram greatly appreciated[1] the support of Wake county[2] and your fight for me delights me. I am confident you will win tomorrow.   Woodrow Wilson.

T telegram (J. Daniels Papers, DLC).
  [1] It is missing.
  [2] The county seat of which is Raleigh.

To Roland Sletor Morris

Personal.

My dear Mr. Morris: [Trenton, N. J.] June 5, 1912.

Mr. Vick has communicated to me the interesting suggestion made by you and Mr. Wallenstein[1] to him about my meeting the entire Pennsylvania delegation. That would be more than agreeable to me. I should value the opportunity and I particularly appreciate your generous offer to have them lunch with you at the Princeton Inn. The difficulty just now is that until Wednesday of next week, everything is apt to be so congested here by reason of the commencement guests. Do you think that it would be too late after commencement? I have just written to Mr. Mitchell Palmer asking for a conference with him and if we could all get into communication with each other, I am sure we could arrange a conference which would be very useful.

With warmest appreciation,

Cordially and faithfully yours,   Woodrow Wilson

TLS (R. S. Morris Papers, DLC).
  [1] David Wallenstein, lawyer of Philadelphia and alternate delegate at large to the Baltimore convention.

To William Jennings Bryan

My dear Mr. Bryan: [Trenton, N. J.] June 6, 1912.

Your position about the temporary chairmanship[1] is altogether fair and is indicative of the wise position you are taking with regard to the whole arrangement for the Convention.

I agree with you that the temporary chairman should be acceptable to the leading candidates, and I shall certainly lend myself to any arrangement which can bring about a thoroughly satisfactory solution of the question. My own opinion is that the temporary chairman should come from one of the uninstructed delegations. My own thought had been centering upon Senator O'Gorman of New York, a man of admirable poise and capable of making a speech that would be absolutely fair to all concerned, and at the same time ring true and clear with regard to progressive policies.

Please present Mrs. Wilson's warm regard, as well as my own, to Mrs. Bryan[2] and say to her that it was a genuine disappointment to Mrs. Wilson not to be able to go to Washington to the Dolly Madison breakfast. Only a very painful accident prevented her being there.

Cordially and sincerely yours,   Woodrow Wilson

TLS (W. J. Bryan Papers, DLC).
    [1] Bryan's letter, to which this was a reply, is missing. "I wrote to Governor Wilson," Bryan reminisced, "and suggested to him that we should have a progressive chairman and that as neither [Clark nor Wilson] had a majority the choice would naturally fall to the candidate [i.e., Clark] having the largest number of votes. I called his attention to the fact that Ollie James, the candidate of the Clark delegates, was a progressive and a fair-minded man and suggested that he accept James in case it should prove impossible to elect the man of his own choice." William J. Bryan and Mary Baird Bryan, *The Memoirs of William Jennings Bryan* (Chicago, Philadelphia, and Toronto, 1925), p. 161.
    [2] Mary Elizabeth Baird Bryan.

To John Wesley Wescott

My dear Judge: [Trenton, N. J.] June 6, 1912.

You may be sure that your acceptance makes me very happy, and, too, the manner of your acceptance was quite like yourself.

Faithfully yours,   Woodrow Wilson

TLS (J. W. Wescott Coll., NjP).

To Edwin Anderson Alderman

My dear Dr. Alderman: [Trenton, N. J.] June 6, 1912.

I wonder if I may impose upon your generosity with a request of an unusual kind? I understand that Mr. J. W. Fishborn of

Charlottesville[1] is probably going to sit as a delegate from the Seventh Virginia District and that whereas he was one of the original "Wilson" men, he did not stand by us at Norfolk,[2] he needs a little tonic. Would you think that I was asking too much of you, if I asked that you take occasion to have a little talk with him? It would be a great service to me, for we find it necessary now to stiffen our lines at every point.

With warmest regard, and the greatest pleasure in thinking that I have so strong a friend in you,

Cordially and faithfully yours,   Woodrow Wilson

TLS (E. A. Alderman Papers, ViU).
  [1] John Wood Fishburne, a lawyer, who went to Baltimore as an alternate.
  [2] That is, at the Democratic state convention.

From Frank Irving Cobb

My dear Governor,   New York, June 6, 1912.

It will gratify you, I think, to know that no other editorial printed in The World in many years met with such public response as the one advocating your nomination for President. The letters of commendation are still pouring into the office. Unquestionably the thoughtful, intelligent, disinterested element of the party in the East is largely on your side, and the volume of independent Republican support that you can command is not the least interesting element.

Whether we win or lose at Baltimore we can at least make a real fight for a real principle.

Let me thank you for your letter.

With sincerest regards,

Faithfully yours,   Frank I. Cobb.

ALS (WP, DLC).

From Francis Griffith Newlands

My dear Governor Wilson: [Washington] June 6, 1912.

Prior to the receipt of your letter I had taken such a position regarding my going to the Baltimore Convention as to make it impossible for me to change my decision.

With best wishes, believe me,

Most sincerely yours,   [Francis G. Newlands]

CCL (F. G. Newlands Papers, CtY).

From William Gibbs McAdoo

PERSONAL.

Dear Governor: [New York] June 6, 1912.

I have reviewed with Mr. McCombs today the suggestion I made to you about inviting a representative man or men from the delegations in each of the states to call on you at Princeton, and have become convinced that it is inadvisable to proceed with this plan, because of the jealousies that may be aroused. I, therefore, think that this idea had better be abandoned.

I have your letter about Mr. Jones.[1] I am trying to get in touch with that situation and will advise you later. I continue to feel very much encouraged about your outlook.

Always, with warm regards,

Sincerely yours,   W G McAdoo

TLS (LPC, W. G. McAdoo Papers, DLC).
[1] A mysterious reference.

To James Sprunt

Trenton N J June 7 [1912]

Warmest congratulations and deepest appreciation[1]

Woodrow Wilson

T telegram (received from J. Sprunt, Jr.).
[1] The North Carolina state Democratic convention, meeting in Raleigh on June 6 and 7, elected an overwhelmingly pro-Wilson delegation to the Baltimore convention, but the opposition of the Underwood men was so determined that the Wilson managers abandoned their efforts to adopt a resolution instructing the delegates. The Wilson leaders settled for an endorsement of Wilson.

From Edward Mandell House

Dear Governor Wilson: Beverly, Mass. June 7th, 1912.

I have a letter from Mr. Love this morning telling me that he has suggested some things to you which I hope you will not consider.

If you should invite a number of delegates without inviting them all it would be sure to cause offense and if you should invite them all I think it would create a bad impression.

It might be well for Mr. McCombs to write to the *secretary* of each delegation that is instructed to vote for you, and tell them that in the event it was convenient and pleasant you would be glad to have them call at Princeton on their way to Baltimore.

In my opinion, everything is being done that should be towards influencing the delegates in your behalf. Plans for organizing them into an efficient and effective force at Baltimore are already under way and will be much more potent than anything Mr. Love has suggested.

If I see the situation rightly, there has never been a time when your nomination seemed so probable as now and if I were you I would move cautiously and do nothing further for the present.

I do not doubt but that a large part of your time has been taken up, as indeed has Mr. McCombs' and mine, by people giving advice which if acted upon would defeat our ends.

Do you recall what I told you concerning the conversation I had with Mrs. B[ryan]? I have a letter this morning from her containing this most significant sentence:

"I found Mr. B. well and quite in accord with the talk we had."

It encourages me to believe that Mr. Clark will never receive that influence and that you will. It also means that he will not want the nomination unless two republican tickets are in the field.

If your engagements will permit I hope that we may have the pleasure of seeing you here before the 25th.

Faithfully yours,   [E. M. House]

CCL (E. M. House Papers, CtY).

From Henry St. George Tucker

My dear Governor: Lexington, Va., June 8, 1912.

I got back home this morning and found your letter awaiting me of which you spoke to me yesterday. In thinking the matter over about your presentation to the convention, I take the liberty of suggesting to you that your nomination by New Jersey and Pennsylvania while eminently appropriate as to locality, would be too circumscribed for a national candidate (and not a favorite son) unless reinforced from the west and south. Your position is fortunate in this, and while the south makes large claims upon you I feel it would be manifestly impolitic for you to be put forward on the idea of being a southern man, but I feel with equal emphasis that the west and south should second your nomination, preferably Wisconsin or Oregon in the West.

I would be glad to hear from you when you have come to a decision about the matter. I am enclosing editorial from the Petersburg Index Appeal, an ardent Wilson paper. My mail brings me today much more hopeful news of the Virginia situation. Mayor Cameron, of Petersburg,[1] heretofore against you, is out in an interview stating that you are the man to be nominated, and I find on every hand a much more hopeful sentiment among your friends.

With best wishes for your success and that of the democracy I am   Very sincerely,   H S G Tucker

TLS (WP, DLC).
¹ George Cameron, Jr.

To Mary Allen Hulbert Peck

Dearest Friend,   Princeton, New Jersey 9 June, 1912

I was so glad to get your little note from Sandanwede. It had in it just what I wanted,—a love for the place you have at last found a haven in, and a sense of home. It had what I feared, too, a sense of the kind of labour and confusion of tasks which I have learned to dread in your case. But I feel confident, somehow, that the first will swallow the second up very promptly, and that, even when the physical reaction comes, it will be quickly offset and healed by the influences that will now more and more delight and soothe you. For there is a genuine note of enjoyment, and even of enthusiasm, in this note of yours, though it sounds only for a moment, in a line or two. Your love of wild nature and your womanly sense of pride and responsibility and possession in your new and beautiful home will pull you through everything. You have more natural resources within yourself than any one else I ever knew. There is a whole world within your own consciousness, on which you can live and be happy if the world *outside* of you will but give you half a chance! It is wonderful to catch even a glimpse of it,—and inspir[i]ting.

We go to the shore, to Seagirt, on Friday, the 14th,—at least the family goes. I never know from hour to hour where sudden calls, for political conferences and the like, will take me on any given date. It is of great service to me just now to be able to look on at the political game as if I had no part in it, at the same time that I am actively enlisted, and my own personal career involved. And it gives me, I think, a clearer vision and a steadier hand. Just between you and me, I have not the least idea of being nominated, because the make of the convention is such, the balance and confusion of forces, that the outcome is in the hands of the professional, case-hardened politicians who serve only their own interests and who know that I will not serve them except as I might serve the party in general. I am well and in the best of spirits. I have no deep stakes involved in this game.

I think Crane resigned[1] because he sees that the country at large, including his own State of Mass., has had enough of men who *manage* and do not *serve*. He is discreet; and H.C.L.[2] will some day have to follow his example.

All join me in affectionate messages to you all.

Your devoted friend   Woodrow Wilson

ALS (WP, DLC).
   [1] Winthrop Murray Crane had announced that he would not be a candidate for re-election to the United States Senate in 1912.
   [2] Henry Cabot Lodge.

To Edward Mandell House

My dear Mr. House: [Trenton, N. J.] June 9, 1912.

Thank you sincerely for your letter of June seventh. I am almost ashamed to say that I stood in need of the advice it gave, for I had at first thought that Mr. Love's suggestion ought to be acted on. But I am quite convinced to the contrart [contrary] and shall be very careful not to act independently in any matter of which I am not perfectly confident.

It was very gracious of you to wish me to visit you at Beverly, and I shall not give up the hope until it is plainly impossible.

Cordially and faithfully yours,   Woodrow Wilson

TLS (E. M. House Papers, CtY).

From Thomas Jones Pence

My dear Governor Wilson: Washington, D. C. June 10, 1912.

No doubt Mr. McCombs acquainted you with the ideas of Senator Gore and other friends here, with reference to having those Senators and Congressmen favorable to your nomination, who are delegates to the Baltimore convention, call at Trenton. Senator Gore, Senator Gardner, and Representatives J. Mitchell Palmer, Albert S. Burleson, and possibly Representative R. L. Henry, plan to call on you one day this week. No one knows of this contemplated visit except these gentlemen. It is the opinion of Mr. McCombs and your friends here that you should extend invitations to the other Senators and Congressmen friendly to your candidacy, who are delegates or alternates to the Baltimore convention, to visit Trenton. This list would include Senator Charles A. Culberson, of Texas; Senator E. D. Smith, of South Carolina; Representative McGillicuddy, of Maine, and Representative J[ohn]. J[efferson]. Whitacre, of Ohio. You know the attitude of Senator O'Gorman, of New York, whose hands are more or less tied. Mr. McCombs can best advise you about writing him.

I think you should also write to Senator Benjamin R. Tillman, of South Carolina; Senator Luke Lea, of Tennessee, and Senator-elect Robert Broussard, of Louisiana. All of these Senators are delegates-at-large. Senator Tillman is exceedingly friendly to your candidacy, though he has not declared himself. I am sure he is for you and will vote for you until the last ditch. Senator Luke Lea is your friend, though he will vote for Mr. Underwood on the first ballot. This arrangement was necessary in the interest of your candidacy. It is my suggestion that you should write Senator Lea a very friendly letter. He has a peculiar gift for political convention work, and his services at Baltimore will be of exceedingly great value.

Senator-elect Broussard has never declared for you, though he has been your friend and has done some quiet but effective work. All of us think that it is highly important that you invite him to come to Trenton. He is a delegate-at-large from Louisiana. I think you should also extend an invitation to Col. Robert Ewing, the Editor of the [New Orleans] Daily States, and the Democratic National Committeeman from Louisiana. He did magnificent work in your behalf in the Louisiana campaign, and is a delegate-at-large.

I would suggest that you do not write to any of these gentlemen until Senator Gore and your other friends determine what day they can go to Trenton. It is barely possible that one or more of the other gentlemen may go with them, and in that event it would not be necessary for you to write to them.

Of course, you have other strong friends in Congress who will be delegates-at-large to Baltimore, but unfortunately they are bound by instructions, and it would doubtless be unwise to invite them to go to Trenton. For instance, there is Senator John Sharp Williams, of Mississippi, who is insructed [instructed] to vote for Mr. Underwood. You have no stauncher friend in the world than Senator Williams. He will be on the floor of the convention voting for Mr. Underwood, but he will be for you every minute, and when the opportune time arrives, will be voting for your nomination. Senator Myers, of Montana, is also a delegate-at-large, and while he will have to vote for Mr. Clark under instructions, he does not hesitate to say that he favors your nomination.

This is true of other friends of yours here who were unable to control the actions of their State conventions.

With very best wishes,   Sincerely,   Thos. J. Pence

P.S.—I did not include the New Jersey Congressmen, who are alive to the situation. You can best decide as to the advisability of writing them.

TLS (WP, DLC).

From Henry St. George Tucker

My dear Governor,   Lexington Va June 10, 1912.

I am glad to be able to write you that all fear of the imposition of the Unit Rule against us in the Virginia Delegation is past, and that not only will you have *your nine*, but the evidence is quite convincing that you will exceed your original estimate, & invade the domain of the enemy.

I write hastily.   Very Sincerely   H S G Tucker

ALS (WP, DLC).

From Willard Saulsbury

Dear Governor: [Wilmington, Del.] June 10th, 1912.

My information bureau is working overtime and I think that you will like to know exactly how the various delegations stand that I satisfy myself about. I have been investigating carefully the Virginia situation. Virginia as you know has 24 votes in the convention provided that the unit rule should be applied to the delegation on the demand of 2/3 of the delegation. It is a very close question whether this can or will be done to your detriment. Our friends there claim 3 delegates at large with half a vote each or a vote and a half. Also from 6 to 8 of the district delegates, which makes from 7½ to 9½ out of the 24 votes. Our friends say that the opposition is not strong enough to apply the unit rule even should they want to and I have a great deal of confidence in this statement, although it is a fact that those who are opposed to your nomination in Virginia say that you only have 5½ votes, which would give us only 4 of the district delegates. This is the situation from both sides having as intimate knowledge of the local conditions as it is possible to obtain and I send it to you for your information.

Yours very truly,   Willard Saulsbury

TLS (Saulsbury Letterpress Books, DeU).

A Plank for the Democratic Platform[1]

[June 11, 1912]

TRUSTS—Under the stimulation of the opportunity afforded by the tariff, trusts have come into existence in this country with extraordinary rapidity and in extraordinary numbers during the last two decades, despite express provisions of law intended to prevent their successful formation and operation. Within that brief period they have managed to bring together under their control almost all of the more important business enterprises of the country. The general terms of the present Federal anti-trust law forbidding "combinations in restraint of trade" have proved utterly ineffectual against them. They have grown and flourished in spite of it, as if without let or hindrance. That law must, therefore, be strengthened and supplemented. The specific processes of monopoly, now many of them clearly disclosed, must one by one be dealt with by laws whose phraseology, whose purpose and whose method cannot be mistaken or explained away. Laws both civil and criminal must give vigor and definiteness to the policy of the government; must check and punish every arrangement and practice that has trammeled the freedom of enterprise or fixed prices or stifled competition, and must fix criminal responsibility definitely upon the persons who, whether individually or collectively, engage in them, so that those who defy the law may be punished while legitimate cooperation in large enterprises is left free of interferance. Where suitable and adequate judicial processes, civil and criminal, cannot now be found by which to disclose these practices and follow them to final verdict and judgment, they must be devised and supplied, and our procedure altered and adapted to that purpose.

We pledge ourselves to more than that. The law will not only have to deal with individual trusts and the processes by which they control prices and create monopoly. It will have to deal also with vast confederacies of banks, railways, common carriers, commercial and industrial corporations, and business companies of every kind, bound together by the fact that the ownership of their stocks and the membership of their boards of directors are controlled and determined by comparatively small and closely interrelated groups of persons who, by their confederacy, may control when they will both credit and enterprise. We pledge ourselves to undertake such legislation as will effectually break up these leagues and prevent any sort of monopoly of either credit or opportunity,—without destroying or hampering any sound or legitimate business enterprise.

CC T MS (WP, DLC).
¹ Wilson drafted this in response to a request from John Sharp Williams. See J. S. Williams to WW, June 13, 1912.

To Willard Saulsbury

Personal.

My dear Mr. Saulsbury: [Trenton, N. J.] June 11, 1912.

Thank you sincerely for your attention about Virginia. It tallies so near with what I hear from one source and another that I have no doubt it is right. I believe that the nine and a half is nearer than the five and a half to the actual hard pan.¹

It was very thoughtful of you to send me this information.

Cordially and faithfully yours,   Woodrow Wilson

TLS (W. Saulsbury Papers, DeU).
¹ Wilson was right. Virginia cast 9½ votes for him on the first ballot.

To Josephus Daniels

My dear friend: Trenton, N. J. June 11, 1912.

I am not sure that this will find you in Raleigh, but I am not certain just where to send it.

I appreciate your letter of the eighth¹ very much, and the editorial enclosed² was certainly most effective. I do not wonder that it may [made] Bankhead feel like folding his tent and stealing away.

The interviews I have read from you in the newspapers of the last day or two were fine and warm my heart. You are certainly a friend worth having.

The result in North Carolina has given me the deepest gratification and increase[s] my feeling of gratitude to my friends there.

Cordially and faithfully yours,   Woodrow Wilson

TLS (J. Daniels Papers, DLC).
¹ It is missing.
² "Do We Need Senator Bankhead, Underwood's Manager, At Our Convention?" Raleigh *News and Observer*, June 6, 1912. It declared that the Democrats of North Carolina would not welcome the appearance of Underwood's manager at the state convention (he was then in Raleigh) and warned him against attempting to influence the selection of delegates to the national convention.

From Josephus Daniels

Dear Governor: Hotel Belvedere Baltimore, June 11 1912

It has not been possible for me to send you a line since our Convention. We had a very warm fight. Toward the close the opposition was so well organized and so resourceful that we feared they would do more than they did on the final show-down. Considering all the circumstances, we did well, though I had hoped we would be solid.

One of the big things we must do is to have a platform that rings. I know you are burdened beyond your strength, and yet if you could give some attention to the platform I would be glad if you would write some of the more [important] planks, with an opening that would catch the attention and win the approval of the average man who has grown tired of "we view with alarm" and "we point with pride," and the lack of courageous and uplifting sentiments that this day demands. If you are not willing to write a platform, please draft some planks. If you send [them] to me at this hotel I will see that they go before the Committee either from you or not as you may prefer.

Sincerely Josephus Daniels

ALS (WP, DLC).

From George Foster Peabody

Saratoga Springs [N. Y.]

My Dear Governor Wilson, June 12th 1912

The enclosed letter is from the hopeful Democratic Candidate for U. S. Senator in New Hampshire[1]—a very nice fellow whom Mr Shepard[2] and I knew and thought well of. He is as you will see close to Mr Bryan in his own mind at any rate. I got the impression when I spoke with Mr Bryan that he well knew that you quite outclassed Mr Clark, but also that he knew the kind of people to whom Mr Clark appealed and therefore was not going to run crisscross with them. I think Mr Bryan's fundamental desire is the welfare of the people as he conceives it and therefore his first anxiety is to defeat the candidates of the Money Power whom he deems to be and correctly Gov'r Harmon and Chairman Underwood. I count therefore on Mr Bryan's not antagonizing your running ahead unless the T.F.R[3] people conclude to take him into camp in order to beat you and make him believe they will only accept him—W.J.B. If I get to Baltimore I shall hope to be of some service in that connection. Mr McCombs and Mr McAdoo each write me they think I should be there and I am now trying to arrange it. The time is particularly awkward for me because I am to lose then the Secretary of this Commission[4] and I must be in Washington on July first. As to this latter also I hope for a chance to talk with you beforehand. I have been summoned by Senator Clapp as Chm of Sub Comm of Privileges & Elections[5] respecting the funds for the 1904 campaign, when I was Treas'r of the [Democratic] Nat'l Comm

May I ask therefore if it will be convenient for you to see me on the 21st 22d or 23d if I go to Princeton? I should like a fairly full conference if not asking too much. I want to post you a bit on some political inside history.

I think I wrote to Mr McAdoo to get in touch with Mr Hollis. Will you kindly return his letter.

                    I am Sincerely Yours   George Foster Peabody

ALS (WP, DLC).
    [1] Henry French Hollis, lawyer of Concord; unsuccessful Democratic candidate for governor, 1902 and 1904; senator from New Hampshire, 1913-19.
    [2] Edward Morse Shepard, long-time reform Democratic leader of New York.
    [3] Thomas Fortune Ryan.
    [4] The State Reservation Commission of New York.
    [5] This subcommittee, headed by Moses E. Clapp of Minnesota, was investigating the funding of the preconvention and presidential campaigns of 1904, 1908, and 1912, and of the congressional campaigns during the same years and 1906 and 1910.

From Edwin Litchfield Turnbull[1]

My dear Gov. Wilson   [Baltimore, Md.] June 12 [1912]

I called on Cardinal Gibbons today and he said that if you would let me know, what day *after* convention you could be in Baltimore, that he would arrange to come in from his country home and meet you. I am sure you would have great pleasure in meeting the Cardinal and I think he is much interested in your career. If you would permit me to offer a suggestion, I think that if you were to send him one of your books now, with your autograph, that he would appreciate it very much. Simply Address

        James Cardinal Gibbons
            Baltimore

The Cardinal has met Mr Underwood and thinks very highly of him. The Cardinal told me today that he had accepted the invitation of the National Committee, to open the Convention with prayer.

If you could arrange to come to my office 12 E. Lexington St. we could walk to the Cardinal's residence which is nearby. His customary hours are 10-12. Or I could meet you at the Station or anywhere you suggest. I appreciate that you wish the meeting to be very informal and free from Newspaper men[.] We could "shake" everyone at my office and get to the Cardinals house by a quiet route[.] I have told the Cardinal that there is a rapidly growing sentiment among the Democrats that the wise thing would be for the party to unite in naming you. He commented on the great progress you had made since last I spoke with him.

Hoping to have the pleasure of seeing you soon and with very kind remembrances for Mrs Wilson and your daughters

Believe me

Yours very sincerely   Edwin L. Turnbull

ALS (WP, DLC).

[1] A.B., Johns Hopkins, 1893; in the real estate business in Baltimore; prominent in the musical life of that city.

To George Foster Peabody

My dear Mr. Peabody,   Princeton, New Jersey 13 June, 1912

Your letter of yesterday interests me very much. I am delighted that you are planning to go to Baltimore: it will be of real value to sane counsels.

So far as I now know, I shall be in Sea Girt June 21-23. It will be of great service to me to see you. Pray telegraph or telephone just before coming, to make sure I have not been called away unexpectedly.

In haste, with warm regard and appreciation.

Cordially Yours,   Woodrow Wilson

ALS (G. F. Peabody Papers, DLC).

From John Sharp Williams

My dear Governor Wilson: Washington, D. C. June 13th, 1912.

Yours of the 11th, together with the enclosed anti-trust plank, at hand. The last clause of it, which goes beyond the mere question of industrial trusts, is fine. What precedes it, however, is too general and indefinite; not specific enough. We ought to attack the evil *right at its root*, and the root is found in the charters granted by states, giving undue power, or neglecting to limit properly the powers granted. I want you to read over what I sent you again. Think about it carefully. My idea was to strike the evil specifically and to use the interstate commerce power of the United States in order to *persuade* the states to reform their charter grants.

I dictate this very hurriedly. Just got back from the University of Virginia, where I went to join the Phi Beta Kappa, and am rushing through my mail in order to get to the Senate.

I am, with every expression of regard,

Very truly yours,   John Sharp Williams

TLS (WP, DLC).

From Thomas Jones Pence

My dear Governor Wilson: Washington, D. C. June 14, 1912.

Upon receipt of your letter yesterday, I had the Elizabeth Times article[1] planographed, and mailed a copy to each delegate to the Baltimore convention. You will observe from the enclosed copy that I also incorporated an editorial from the New York World, which appealed to me as a strong argument to accompany the Evening Times article.

I am also enclosing herewith editorial expressions from the leading independent newspapers, located in every section of the country, backing up the position taken by the New York World in favor of your nomination at Baltimore. I am sending a lot of matter of this character to the delegates. I expect to conclude this work tomorrow and will go over to Baltimore Sunday, where I will remain until the convention is over. If you desire to address me after Sunday, I can be reached at the Emerson Hotel, Baltimore.

All of your friends are well satisfied with the situation, but impressed with the fact that they must go to Baltimore and work with unsparing effort towards the consummation of our great purpose.

With very best wishes,   Sincerely,   Thos J Pence

TLS (Governors' Files, Nj).
[1] No copies of the *Elizabeth Evening Times* for this period are extant, and all enclosures mentioned in this letter are missing.

A Statement on the Perth Amboy, New Jersey, Strike

[June 15, 1912]

I have just been in conference with General Sadler, over the wire, and believe that the situation in Perth Amboy[1] is beginning to improve. General Sadler went down at my request on Thursday evening and has been in conference with the local authorities and with the owners of the property threatened by the strikers, as well as with every one else who might throw any light on the situation. I have been in almost hourly communication with him by telephone since he went down and have kept in touch with each development.

Under the law, I am not at liberty to intervene in any way except as an adviser, until it has become evident that the local authorities can no longer maintain order and protect property.

The trouble came so suddenly that at first the local authorities did not have force to cope with it, but as the situation has developed they have got together a considerable force of apparently competent and steady men, and so far as I can tell at this hour, have the situation in hand.

I have tried again and again to find out some responsible representative or representatives of the strikers in order to form a judgment as to the basis and justice of their claims, and in order to get them directly into communication with the mill owners, who, General Sadler advises me, are willing to negotiate and consider any proposition that it is possible for them to meet.

So far as I have learned, the strikers are as yet without responsible leaders who could be dealt with or who could speak for them. I hope since[re]ly that some arrangement may presently be reached. It will be so soon as the parties can be brought together.

Printed in the *Newark Evening News*, June 15, 1912.
    1 Some five thousand workers of the Standard Underground Cable Co., the American Smelting and Refining Co., the Barbour Asphalt Co., the Atlantic Terra Cotta Co., and the Lehigh Valley Co. went on strike in Perth Amboy for substantial wage increases on June 11, 1912. During the first three days, the strikers rioted, damaged property, and beat up factory officials. Municipal police and factory guards shot and killed two strikers and injured ten others. The crisis passed as quickly as it had exploded, and negotiations between management and worker representatives were under way by June 17. By June 27 the strikers had accepted compromise pay increases and returned to work.

To Josephus Daniels

My dear friend: [Trenton, N. J.] June 15, 1912.

Thank you warmly for your letter of June eleventh and for all the fine things you have been saying outloud about me. It seems to me the fight in North Carolina was very handsomely won indeed, and that there is nothing to regret about it.

I am going to try to comply with your suggestion about the platform and am going to work on something to-morrow and hope sincerely that it will seem to you to have things in it worth noting.

In haste,
            Cordially and faithfully yours,   Woodrow Wilson

TLS (J. Daniels Papers, DLC).

An Outline of a Democratic Platform

                                    [c. June 16, 1912]

Planks
I.   Tariff
II. Monopoly "combination in restraint of trade" (confederacies)

III. Banking & Currency
IV. Labour conditions (Emp. liability)
V. Foreign trade (merchant marine)
VI. Conservation

Analysis.

Monopoly: Its tariff advantages destroyed[,] *its processes* met by the prohibitions and processes of law.

    Its confederacies broken up and credit & enterprise opened upon equal terms to all.

The qus. involved:

    Tariff, Trusts, Currency—
    Conservation, Development, Assistance
    Foreign policy of justice, vs. exploitation.

What Dems intend w. regard to each of these

    Standardize by "the power that tills the fields and builds the cities" "Democracy of the farms & cities."

Possible only w. emancipation fr. control—

    "the black magic of campaign funds"

How far the emancipation has gone (editorial)[1]

Organized and enthusiastic force standing ready,

    To which young men and all who desire free opportunity and a government that thinks of the average man, are flocking.

WWhw and WWsh MS (WP, DLC).
[1] A mysterious reference.

Planks for a Democratic Platform

[c. June 16, 1912]

Planks, 1912.

TRUSTS—The trusts, which have come into existence in this country with such extraordinary rapidity and in such extraordinary numbers during the last two decades and which have within that brief period managed to bring together under their control so large a proportion of the entire business of the country, have undoubtedly been bred and nurtured and made secure by the tariff, and a proper revision of the tariff, in the interest of free business and industry of every kind, will do a great deal towards weakening and ultimately destroying their power. But it will not be enough to alter the soil in which they have grown and flourished. It is necessary, besides, that the law should deal with them directly. The general terms of the present federal anti-trust law, forbidding "combinations in restraint of trade," have proved ineffectual. Trusts have grown under its shadow without let or hindrance. It has roared against them like any sucking dove. The processes by which they have established monopoly have not been so much as checked or seriously embarrassed. But those processes have now become known. We pledge ourselves to pass such laws both civil and criminal, as will effectually punish and prevent them, and to add such other laws as may be necessary to provide suitable and adequate judicial process, whether civil or criminal, by which to disclose them and to follow them to final verdict and judgment. They must be specifically and directly met by law as they develop.

We pledge ourselves to more than that. The law will not only have to deal with individual trusts and the processes by which they control prices and create monopoly. It will have to deal also with vast confederacies of banks, railways, manufacturing corporations, mining corporations, packing companies, power and development companies, and the like, bound together by the fact that the ownership of their stocks and the membership of their boards of directors are controlled and determined by comparatively small and closely inter-related groups of persons who, by their confederacy, may control when they will both credit and enterprise. We pledge ourselves to undertake such legislation as will effectually break up these leagues and prevent any sort of monopoly of either credit or opportunity,—without destroying or hampering any sound or legitimate business enterprise.

TARIFF—We declare our earnest opposition to the present protective tariff, and denounce the Payne-Aldrich Act as the most conspicuous example ever afforded the country of the special favours and monopolistic advantages which the Republican party has always shown itself willing to extend by legislation to those to whom it looked for financial support. We once more avow our conviction that the only legitimate object of such taxes, as of every other form of taxation, is to raise revenue for the support of the government. Tariff duties, as employed by the Republican party, are not a means of equitable "protection" but a method of fostering special privilege. They have made it easy to establish monopoly in our domestic markets. Trusts have owed their origin and their secure power to them. Our economic freedom, our prosperity in trade, and our free energy in manufacture depend upon their radical revision and immediate and systematic reduction.

We do not ignore the fact that the business of a country like ours is exceedingly sensitive to changes in the tariff schedules.

It has been built upon them and its foundations must not be too radically or suddenly disturbed. We shall act with due prudence and caution. It is obvious that changes should be made only at such a rate and in such a way as will least interfere with the normal and healthful course of commerce and manufacture. But we shall not act on that account with timidity, for we are certain of our ground and of our object.

Revision should begin with the schedules which have been most obviously used to kill all competition and to raise prices in the United States arbitrarily and without regard to the prices obtaining elsewhere in the markets of the world; and it should, before it is finished or intermitted, be extended to every item in every schedule which affords any opportunity for monopoly, for special advantage to limited groups of beneficiaries, or for subsidized control of any kind in the markets or the enterprises of the country; until special favours of every sort shall have been absolutely withdrawn and every part of our laws of taxation shall have been transformed from a system of patronage and special privilege into a system of just and reasonable charges which shall fall equally upon all.

We heartily approve and applaud the intelligent and statesmanlike course of the present Democratic majority in Congress with regard to the tariff and deplore the veto of the measures which it framed for the relief of the people.

CURRENCY—We recognize the fact that our present banking system and our present system of currency are entirely inadequate to serve the great commercial and industrial operations of the country, either promptly or when most needed, and that their inadequacy subjects the country not only to constant serious inconvenience but also to a constant risk of disastrous financial disturbance and to recurrent panics. We favor, therefore, changes in the regulation and credit basis of our currency which will connect it with commercial credits as well as investment securities and give it ready elasticity, and also changes in our banking laws which will govern the action of our banks in this matter in a common system of law and furnish the machinery by which the volume of currency may be adjusted with the greatest possible readiness to the varying demands for cash. This machinery, however, must not be subject to control by individual banks or groups of bankers. It must be under the control of the government itself or of some public instrumentality which the banks cannot manipulate or dominate.

Plank Sketches

POLITICAL ORGANIZATION is absolutely indispensable to the successful action of parties, and should not only not be broken up, but should be fostered so long as it constitutes the means of carrying out the principles of a party and of serving the public interest. It becomes hurtful and illegitimate only when it is perverted and degenerates into a mere "machine" for the advancement of the personal fortunes (either economic or politic) of one man or of small groups of men.

THE DIRECT ELECTION OF UNITED STATES SENATORS is a reform which now only awaits the formal action of the people. New Jersey has shown her devotion to the principle by her obedience to the choice of the direct primary in the selection of a Senator, and her Democrats are entirely committed to the principle.

THE PHYSICAL VALUATION OF RAILROAD PROPERTIES should undoubtedly underlie all efforts to fix a standard of just rates and of reasonable returns upon investment. There can be no reasonable return upon any investment which is not a real investment.

DIRECT PRIMARIES are an indispensable means of putting into the hands of the people the selection as well as the election of their public officers. Whenever the people choose to make use of them, they absolutely prevent the private manipulation of elections in the interest of particular groups and of the control of special coteries of men, working altogether in their own interest.

THE UNIT RULE can have no legitimate place where delegates are elected by direct primary. It violates every principle of popular rule in such circumstances as to prevent their voting as their constituents instructed them to vote.

COMMISSION GOVERNMENT FOR CITIES has not furnished a complete remedy for the evils of city government, but it has rendered the immense service of concentrating responsibility without vesting it in such a way that it can be privately exercised or used in behalf of special interests. Commission Government has constituted a great advance in the reform of city government.

INITIATIVE, REFERENDUM AND RECALL do not fall within the field of National questions. They are not inconsistent with the spirit of our institutions. The Referendum, on the contrary, has been at the center of our constitutional arrangements from the first. The object of the initiative and referendum is to control legislative action where the legislature of the state fails to respond to the stronger movements of public opinion, and the recall is a means of administering the control on the part of the people which is entirely consistent with all the most revered documents in which we have set forth popular rights.

IMMIGRATION[.] One of the most difficult of our national questions and yet one which must be faced with frankness and courage. Reasonable restriction safeguarding the health, the morals and the political integrity of the country, no one can object to, but regulation should not go to such an extent as to shut the doors of America against men and women looking for new opportunity and for genuine political freedom.

LABOR. The whole problem of modern legislation is how to do justice to each class of the community without setting class against class. So-called labor organization ought to be devoted at every point to securing justice to the laborer in respect to his employment, his environment while working, his health, and his opportunities for advancement. Workingmen's compensation and employers' liability acts illustrate what is necessary in order to secure justice. Factory legislation, legislation regulating the hours of labor and the sanitary conditions illustrate the regulation of environment and the safeguarding of health, and laws of this character are, all of them, in the interests not of a single class but of the welfare and wholesome life of the whole community.

T MSS and CC MSS (WP, DLC). These manuscripts, along with the outline printed above and a WWsh undated draft of the planks on trusts, the tariff, and currency, were found together in the Wilson Papers. It seems likely that they were copies of the planks and plank sketches that Wilson sent to Josephus Daniels about June 16.

From Thomas Joseph Scully

Washington D C June 16 1912
Shall be pleased to join you at Philadelphia Monday evening
Thos J Scully

Hw telegram (WP, DLC).

To Mary Allen Hulbert Peck

Governor's Cottage
Dearest Friend,   Sea Girt, New Jersey 17 June, 1912
Here we are at Sea Girt. We came down yesterday: the house was ready for us; it did not take long to unpack the trunks; and so we already feel very much at home again. The day is gray and

drizzly; the sea makes a dismal voice across the bleak camp ground in front of us; we have had to light a fire in the huge fire place to keep our spirits (and our temperature) up; but here we are a home group with that within us that can defy the depressing influences of the weather. What we now look forward to with not a little dread are the possibilities of the next fortnight in politics. I was saying at breakfast this morning, "Two weeks from to-day we shall either have this sweet Sunday calm again or an army of reporters camped on the lawn and an all-day reception." "Which would you rather have?" Nellie asked. "Need you ask?" I exclaimed; and that is the way I feel. Now that the *possibility* is immediately at hand (it is no more than a possibility, as things stand) I find myself dreading it and wishing most devoutly that I may escape. Not that I dread what would be really big and essential and worth while in the whole thing, but all that would go with—all that is *non*-essential, *not* of the *business*, merely distracting and exhausting and hateful without counting,—the excessive *personal* tax of a campaign. May the Lord have mercy on me! My heart is not faint, but my taste and my preference for what is genuine and at the opposite pole from mere personal notoriety revolts at the thought of what I may be in for!

Moral: turn away from it, to what is wholly delightful,— thought of faithful and loving friends by the quiet sea at Nantucket, and of all the things that the public cannot invade and make their own; the things they cannot spoil, that keep life sweet and supply it with motives and with enjoyments that make one better and happier and fitter for the things that are hard and bitter and disappointing! I am well (I do not count a teasing sick headache!) and underneath, deep down, my soul is quiet.

All join me in affectionate messages to you all, and I am, as always,   Your devoted friend   Woodrow Wilson

ALS (WP, DLC).

From Leon Rutherford Smith[1]

Dear Sir: Shreveport, La. June 17, 1912.

Answering your letter of June 6th, I will say that the Clerk of the Senate and House of Representatives was remiss in not forwarding you the resolution inviting you to address the State Legislature. It is past now, however, and the delegation has been selected and will go uninstructed. The Clark people claim that the same is 12 to 8, but, as a matter of fact, the delegation is

10 and 10. Governor L[uther]. E[gbert]. Hall had only been inaugurated one month and he took an active interest in attempting to shape the delegation for Speaker Clark. With all of his patronage being held back he was able to get for Speaker Clark a larger representation than would ordinarily have been the case.

The State of Louisiana is for you and if a resolution to force the unit rule had been attempted to be put through the Convention, the Convention would have sent an instructed delegation for you. We had a stormy Convention as it was and adjourned leaving the delegation uninstructed and not bound by the unit rule. If the pressure exercised by the Governor had not been used there is no doubt but that the Louisiana delegation would have honored you on the first ballot with its vote. Ex-Governor Blanchard[2] and National Committeeman Robert Ewing are both your strong friends. They are Delegates at Large.

I am proud of the fact that we made an earnest fight, and while we could not send a solid Wilson delegation we did the next best thing and sent a divided delegation which I feel sure will show a majority for you. In any event you will have half of such number.

Assuring you of my personal regards, I am,

Yours very truly,   Leon R. Smith

TLS (WP, DLC).
[1] Lawyer of Shreveport and member of the state House of Representatives from Caddo Parish.
[2] Newton Crain Blanchard of Shreveport, United States senator, 1894-97, governor, 1904-1908. Smith and Blanchard were partners in the Shreveport law firm of Blanchard, Barret & Smith.

From Patrick Henry O'Brien[1]

My dear Governor: Houghton, Michigan June 17th, 1912.

Your very kind favor of the 13th inst., came to hand yesterday. Permit me to state that in supporting you I have felt that I was not only doing my duty as a democrat and as a citizen, but also was doing what I could to give effective expression to the will of the masses of the Democratic party of Michigan. There is no doubt whatever that the sentiment of the Democratic party of this state has been but partially expressed in the personnel of the delegation to Baltimore.[2] However, I am sincerely hoping that the logic of the situation, which is every day making your nomination more necessary, will finally prevail.

I am not of the number of those who believe that any Democratic candidate can win this year. I cannot confess to such undiluted optimism. In my opinion a progressive candidate with a record for constructive public service, and with a background of sane conservatism, can win this year, and as I believe that you meet all of those requirements, I have given you, and will expect to give you as long as there is a chance for your nomination, my undivided and unqualified support. That being so, you can depend upon it that I will see every one of the Wilson delegates from Michigan, and any others that I may be able to influence, before the caucus is held. I expect to go to Baltimore on the special train, on which most of the Michigan delegation will travel, and in that way I believe I shall have an opportunity to see all of them.

If there is anything else that I can do to further your candidacy, you can count on me.

As far as Edmund C. Shields and Mr. Hemans[3] are concerned, I shall endeavor to sound them as soon as possible, and as soon as I learn of anything of interest I shall either write you personally, or see Mr. McCombs. As I understand it, Mr. Hemans is quite favorably inclined to yourself as his second choice, and as Mr. Shields is committed somewhat to Governor Marshall of Indiana, I should imagine that he would be susceptible to argument as soon as he sees, what I believe to be the fact, that Governor Marshall has absolutely no show.

With the best wishes for your success, and which will also mean the success of the party and the welfare of the nation, I remain,   Yours very sincerely,   P. H. O'Brien

TLS (WP, DLC).

[1] Judge for the twelfth judicial circuit of Michigan; he seconded Wilson's nomination at Baltimore.

[2] On the first ballot at Baltimore, Wilson received ten Michigan votes, Clark, twelve, Harmon, seven, and Marshall, one.

[3] Edmund Claude Shields, lawyer of Howell, Mich., chairman of the Democratic State Central Committee, and Lawton Thomas Hemans, lawyer of Mason, Mich. They were both delegates to the national convention.

From John L. F. Talton[1]

Governor Wilson: Kansas City, Mo., June 17th., 1912.

It has been some time since I wrote you and I take this method of informing you as to the progress of the "Negro Democratic Governor Woodrow Wilson for President Club." To date, the club has 131, one hundred and thirty-one members with bright prospects for as many more[.] The convention will soon convene in Baltimore, and I believe that you will undoubtedly be the choice of the convention.

Governor, I have been with you in my feeble way, supporting

you as best I could, ere you left the presidency of Princeton. I
must stay with you to the end. For that reason, I am going to
ask you to help me out in a very important matter. Governor,
after you have been nominated at Baltimore, please use your
influence with the National Committee to have me sent out as
one of the speakers in the campaign. I am very anxious to take
the stump in your interest. It is said by my friends that I make
an excellent and a rousing speech. I am principal of one of the
negro schools here in Kansas City and will be at leisure through
the months of June, July, and August. In September and October
I will be able to work every Friday night, Saturday and Saturday
nights. Governor, I would freely go on my own expense if I were
able. Not being able, I ask to be sent by the National Committee.
Hoping that you will consider my request, and permit me to
enjoy the extreme pleasure that it will give me to go on with you
to the end in your campaign for the presidency of the United
States, and again hoping that the rank and file of Democracy
will see the wisdom in putting you forward at Baltimore as the
logical standard bearer of the great Democratic party, I am, with
best wishes for you, most respectfully,

John L. F. Talton.

TLS (WP, DLC).
  1 Principal of the Blue Valley School in Kansas City, Mo., 1909-12, and of the
Wheatley School in the same city, 1913-19.

From Benjamin Ryan Tillman

My dear Governor Wilson: Washington, D. C. June 18, 1912.

I have your note of June 17th. Although some people think
differently, I have never considered myself as an expert in politics at all, and things are so muddled in the National Field just
now, that I am unable to offer you any advice. Presuming you
will be at Baltimore, it seems to me, if the opportunity should
come, you ought to be prepared to make such a speech as will
enthuse your friends and disarm, as far as possible, your enemies
among the democrats. The Presidency is such a prize that the
glamour is apt to blind people to the responsibilities and duties
of the office.

I do not think it would be wise for us to do away with the
two-thirds rule, and certainly not until after the nomination is
made. What a blessing such a rule would be to the Republican
party right now; for if the old adage be true, "whom the Gods
would destroy, they first make mad," it seems to me that the
G.O.P. is doomed.

I trust the democratic convention will attract support for the party, and emphasize the difference between real democracy,— a Government "of the people, by the people, and for the people," and a Government by money, for the trusts, and through politicians.

As you already know, the South Carolina delegation goes to Baltimore uninstructed, but our state convention endorsed you by a very large majority, and you have a strong following in South Carolina.

Allow me to express the hope that the choice of our people will be the choice of the Convention and that the choice of the Convention will be the next President of the United States.

Very sincerely etc.,   B. R. Tillman

TLS (WP, DLC).

From Richard Evelyn Byrd

My dear Governor,   Richmond June 18, 1912

Just a word of cheer on the eve of the engagement. I was not able to do what I hoped for you in Virginia but the odds were very great and we had neither money or machinery. The whole of the organized political forces of the State were put in action against us. Nevertheless I know that your generous heart will feel that I did what I could. We can I feel quite confident count on nine, strong Wilson delegates, affirmative and enthusiastic. My information now is that there will not be an attempt to strangle us with the unit rule which would require 2/3 of the delegation to enforce & then only after the first ballot. There are I think probably three Clark men on the delegation tho' they are keeping quiet. As against Bryan you would get the solid Virginia delegation. Underwood is the only formidable opponent you have with our delegation and this is due to the fact that he is personally very close to our members of Congress. As against Clark you would get all but four counting Thos F. Ryan as irreconcilable tho' even he would support you against Bryan. It is apparent to even the casual observer that in the last three weeks you have gained enormously & should the ratio of gain continue for a week longer your nomination is assured. I had a letter from a member of the staff of the Baltimore Sun who says the indications now all point to your nomination. Am enclosing an interview[1] in the [Richmond] Times-Dispatch which recently came out for you. I will leave for Baltimore Sunday noon. My dear Governor, I am praying for you[r] success heart & soul and will leave nothing undone which is in my power to do.

Your friend   R. E. Byrd

ALS (WP, DLC).
    [1] This enclosure is missing.

From Edward Amos Purdy[1]

My dear Governor: Minneapolis, Minn. June 18th, 1912.

Your thoughtfulness in finding time to write me a personal note under date of June Ninth, is deeply appreciated.

Such little courtesies as this certainly belie the insinuations and aspersions cast upon you by some of your critics and reassure us in the ranks that our leader has a heart as big as his intellect.

What little work I did in your behalf, Governor, was done because I sincerely believe in you and in the principles you stand for. You, and you alone, are the choice of my colleagues from this District and myself, and you can depend upon the Minnesota delegation to stand by you staunchly.[2]

My next communication to you, I confidently believe, will be one of congratulation upon your selection as the standard bearer of the Democratic Party in the coming election, but whether or not, you may depend upon it that you have, in this Campaign, won friends for yourself who are ever ready to follow when you may call.   Faithfully yours   Edward A. Purdy.

TLS (WP, DLC).
    [1] Managing editor of the *Western Architect,* delegate to the Baltimore convention.
    [2] The state convention had elected a full slate of Wilson delegates to Baltimore on June 6. They stood by Wilson through thick and thin.

A Letter and a Telegram from
Robert Foligny Broussard

My dear Governor Wilson: Washington, D. C. June 19th 1912.

It was only the other day that I returned to my office after a couple of weeks' absence; and I avail myself of this opportunity to write and express to you my many thanks for your appreciative letter of the 11th instant, congratulating me upon my election to the Senate.

With assurances of my high regard and esteem, I am,
                Very sincerely yours,   R. F. Broussard

TLS (WP, DLC).

Washington D. C., June 19, '12

Your letter inviting me to consultation at Sea Girt received. I shall be very glad to avail myself of this kindness and will proceed to Sea Girt just as soon as you wire me your convenience in matter   daily expecting Louisiana delegates to come to Washington on their way to convention at Baltimore   suggest therefore if you will permit that honor [the sooner] you arrange for this consultation the more satisfactory it will be to me.

R. F. Broussard.

T telegram (WP, DLC).

To Robert Foligny Broussard

[Sea Girt, N. J. June 19, 1912]

Am expecting to be continuously here 'til Saturday evening. Pray come at your convenience.   Woodrow Wilson.

Hw telegram (WP, DLC).

From Robert Bird Kirkland[1]

My Dear Governor: Jefferson, Wis. June 19, 1912

I am in receipt of your valued favor of June 17. In what little service I rendered in the Wisconsin campaign I simply did my duty, as I understood it, nothing more, nothing less. I have always believed in the words of the great Cardinal Richelieu, "In the bright lexicon of youth, there is no such word as fail." We are battling for the right, and cannot fail. At Baltimore your friends will be steadfast with the slogan, Never Surrender, emblazoned on their banner. I expect to see you nominated and hope the privilege of taking a hand in the battle, but not such a battle as is at present being so disgracefully waged by our Republican friends in the City of Chicago. The nominee of the Democratic party will be elected, and it goes without saying that I sincerely hope that the nominee will be none other than yourself.   Yours very sincerely,   R B Kirkland

TLS (WP, DLC).
    [1] Lawyer of Jefferson, Wisc., delegate to the Baltimore convention.

From Henry Marston Smith, Jr.

My dear Governor: Richmond, Va. June 19, 1912.

I have your favor of June 18th. The Virginia delegation will be quartered at the Rennert hotel, where my own room will be. Mr. Tucker has invited your friends to meet him at lunch at the Willard Hotel on Monday at one o'clock, of which arrangement I presume you are well aware.

Your friends on the delegation are enthusiastic, and we think our arguments are unanswerable.

I shall be pleased to have you communicate with me at the Rennert if you think it advisable, and you may count on my unswerving loyalty.   Very sincerely,   H M Smith Jr.

TLS (WP, DLC).

From John Sharp Williams

My dear Governor: Washington, D. C. June 20th, 1912.

I am just reading your letter of June 17th. I rather like your proposed anti-trust plank. Of course, I am somewhat partial to my own in preference, but I don't know but what you are right. Maybe mine goes too much into detail and might cause a discussion, whereas there is nothing in yours that would interfere with the remedy which I propose.

I am, with every expression of regard,
                    Very truly yours,   John Sharp Williams

TLS (WP, DLC).

From Edward Mandell House

Dear Governor Wilson: Beverly, Mass. June 20th, 1912.

I am sorry beyond measure that it is my fate not to be able to be at the Baltimore convention. Both my inclination and my deep interest in your success calls me there but I am physically unequal to the effort.

However, I have done everything that I could do up to now to advise and to anticipate every contingency. I have had interviews with many delegates and some of my warm personal friends on the Texas Delegation will be here tomorrow in order to have a final word.

Colonel Ball, who is perhaps the most forceful man on the Texas Delegation and the one best equipped for floor tactics, has wired me that he will be in Baltimore today.

I have told Mr. McCombs of those upon whose advice and loyalty he can lean upon most heavily and now I feel that I can do nothing further excepting to send my good wishes.

If Mr. Clark's strength crumbles on the second and third ballot, which I hope may be the case, then I believe that you will be nominated forthwith, but if on the other hand, his vote clings to him and he begins to get the uninstructed vote, he may be nominated.

We are sailing for England on the Cunard S.S. Laconia on the 25th at six o'clock but Mr. McCombs has promised to tell me of the result by wireless and if you are nominated I shall return almost immediately.

I shall at least have the benefit of the trip over and back and that is one of the reasons I am going on the 25th rather than waiting until after I know the result.

In the event of your nomination I would suggest Senator O'Gorman, Mr. Burleson and Mr. McCombs as being among those of your friends best fitted to conduct a successful campaign.

And if you will permit me to act as your friend in an advisory capacity, it will give me pleasure to use my every effort in your behalf.

With kind regards and best wishes, I am,

Faithfully yours,   [E. M. House]

P.S. My mail address while away will be, care, Brown, Shipley & Co., 123 Pall Mall, London, and my cable address will be, Emhouse, care Shiprah, London.

CCL (E. M. House Papers, CtY).

From Daniel John McGillicuddy

My dear Governor: Washington, D. C. June 20, 1912.

I am in receipt of your kind favor of the 17th instant, and beg to assure you that if I knew anything that was being omitted that would assist your candidacy, I would suggest it. I think your candidacy is being handled admirably, and I believe that it is making a deep impression on the rank and file of the voters of the entire country.

I would be very glad, indeed, to call to see you if I thought it would do any possible good, but I feel that you must be overwhelmed with visitors, and there is nothing I could suggest that in any way would assist. If there is anything later on that I can do, do not fail to call on me.

Very truly yours,   D J McGillicuddy

TLS (WP, DLC).

To George Foster Peabody

[Sea Girt, N. J.] 6/21 [1912]

Delighted to see you either tomorrow or Sunday.

Woodrow Wilson

T telegram (WP, DLC).

From John Haslup Adams[1]

Baltimore, Md. June 21st, 1912.

The evening Sun would like to have your views on the selection of Parker for temporary chairman. If you feel if you can at this time outline your position will you please prepare a statement and give it to Mr. Denneberg, a staff representative of the evening Sun[2] who will arrive in Sea Girt about noon today and who will call upon you immediately. Our position is outlined in the following editorial published in the Sun, this morning. Let the dead past bury itself, why not two men fresh from the people to preside over the democratic convention. Why stir the smoldering embers of the past? why invite a fight on the floor of the convention? why not ignore factions instead of reorganizing them without going into details about 1904 and 1908. The Sun strongly urges the National committee to keep off the grass on the both sides of the fence. Let them put up the kind of men that would have been chosen by the people—men who fill in hopes with the present hopes aspirations and principles of the democratic party. Gentlemen of the Committee don't start us off with an ugly gift [rift] that might wipe out the advantage that the republican split has given the democracy.

J. H. Adams, Editor.

T telegram (WP, DLC).
  [1] Editor of the Baltimore *Evening Sun.*
  [2] The Editors have been unable further to identify him.

To John Haslup Adams

[Sea Girt, N. J., June 21, 1912]

My friends in Baltimore, who are on the ground, will know how to act in the interest of the people's cause in everything that affects the organization of the convention. They are certain not to forget their standards as they have already shown. It is not necessary that I should remind them of those standards from Sea Girt; and I have neither the right nor the desire to direct the organization of a convention of which I am not even a member

Woodrow Wilson[1]

WWhw MS (WP, DLC).
  1 This was published in the Baltimore *Evening Sun*, June 21, 1912.

William Jennings Bryan to Woodrow Wilson and Others[1]

[Chicago, June 21, 1912]

In the interest of harmony, I suggested to the sub-committee of the Democratic National Committee the advisability of recommending as Temporary Chairman some progressive acceptable to the leading progressive candidates for the Presidential nomination. I took it for granted that no committeeman interested in Democratic success would desire to offend the members of a convention overwhelmingly progressive by naming a reactionary to sound the keynote of the campaign.

Eight members of the sub-committee, however, have, over the protest of the remaining eight, agreed upon not only a reactionary[2] but upon the one Democrat who, among those not candidates for the Presidential nomination, is, in the eyes of the public most conspicuously identified with the reactionary element of the party. I shall be pleased to join you and your friends in opposing his selection by the full committee or by the convention. Kindly answer here.   [William J. Bryan]

Printed in the New York *World*, June 22, 1912.
  1 Sent to Wilson, Clark, and several favorite son candidates.
  2 Alton B. Parker.

A Proposed Reply to William Jennings Bryan by William Frank McCombs

Baltimore June 21/1912

I quite agree with you that the temporary chairman of the convention should voice the sentiments of the Democracy of the nation which I am convinced is distinctly progressive, however before receiving your telegram I had given the following statement for publication in the Baltimore Evening Sun—My friends in Baltimore who are on the peoples cause in everything that effects the organization of the convention   they are certain not to forget their standards as they have already shown   it is not necessary that I should remind them of these standards from New Jersey and I have neither the right nor the desire to direct the organization of a convention of which I am not even a member
                                    McCombs[1]

Hw telegram (WP, DLC).
  1 About the discussion over this proposed reply, see the news report printed at July 3, 1912.

From Alfred Anthony Stein[1]

My dear Governor: Elizabeth, N. J. June 21, 1912.

Yours of the 15th instant received. Several of the Democratic Clubs appointed committees to arrange for a delegation to go to Baltimore on the 24th instant, and I was appointed general chairman at a meeting of the several committees and have been busy since then endeavoring to procure as many of our friends in Elizabeth, who can find the time to go to Baltimore in a body on Monday. We will wear badges reading "Win with Wilson," and we will endeavor to bring about your nomination for President of the United States for we believe we can "Win with Wilson" and with him only. We will be in Baltimore before the Convention opens and personally I shall remain until a nomination is made.

Outside of the pleasure your elevation in the services of the people would afford me, I hope that for the good of the party and its success in November, the delegates will see the wisdom of placing you in nomination.

Sincerely yours,   A. A. Stein

TLS (WP, DLC).
[1] Mayor of Elizabeth, N.J., 1910-1913.

To William Jennings Bryan

[Sea Girt, N. J., June 22, 1912]

You are quite right. Before hearing of your message I clearly stated my position in answer to a question from the Baltimore Evening Sun. The Baltimore convention is to be a convention of progressives,—of men who are progressive in principle and by conviction. It must, if it is not to be put in a wrong light before the country, express its convictions in its organization and in its choice of the men who are to speak for it. You are to be a member of the convention and are entirely within your rights in doing everything within your power to bring that result about. No one will doubt where my sympathies lie and you will, I am sure, find my friends in the convention acting upon clear conviction and always in the interest of the people's cause. I am happy in the confidence that they need no suggestion from me.[1]

[Woodrow Wilson]

T telegram (WP, DLC).
[1] There is a WWhw draft of this telegram in WP, DLC.

From Edwin Doak Mead[1]

My dear Mr. Wilson:　　　　　　　　Boston June 22, 1912.

I am writing you before news of the final action at Chicago has come, although men like myself are deeply gratified by the smashing of Roosevelt and his scheme for a third term, the success of which would in my judgment have been a serious blow to all our best democratic traditions. I am, as you know, an Independent in politics, bred in the Republican party, but having voted for Mr. Bryan in 1900 and 1908, largely because of his courageous and outspoken stand against our pestiferous new imperialism and militarism. I have been an earnest and grateful supporter of Mr. Taft during the last two years on account of his splendid services for unlimited arbitration. His election to the presidency this year seems to me impossible, if the Democrats realize the character of the contest and, avoiding follies of the kind which they have so often committed, nominate a ticket like yourself and Mr. Underwood. The only chance which the Republicans had for success seemed to me, as I have telegraphed during the week to my influential friends in the Chicago Convention, [lay] in the nomination of Judge [Charles Evans] Hughes and some advanced progressive like [Herbert S.] Hadley or [Albert B.] Cummins; but that seems now impossible. The action of thousands of men with whom a brave and broad international policy is the paramount issue, and who have been profoundly stirred by what Mr. Taft has done for this cause, will depend upon whether the Democratic platform at Baltimore makes such an advanced and courageous declaration upon the whole military evil as shall command signal attention and enthusiasm, and identify the party with this great movement in the highest measure. No perfunctory or compromised statement will satisfy this immense body of earnest men. They have been peculiarly moved by the resolute action of the Naval Committee of the House about naval increase; and they wait to see whether the Baltimore Convention will make a comprehensive declaration along that strong and salutary line. I take the liberty of sending to you, as the Democratic leader who commands my fullest confidence, the draft of such a plank for the Baltimore platform[2] as would satisfy the great American peace party, asking that, if it meets your approval, you will use your influence to secure its adoption. I am informed that Mr. Bryan himself has prepared or is preparing a statement condem[n]ing imperialism and supporting the Democratic declaration in Congress in behalf of Philippine independence. This anti-militarism statement of mine might well follow and supplement that declaration. As an illustration of the extent and arrogance now reached by militarism in this country, I submit to you the editorial statements of the *Army and Navy Journal*, upon which I comment in the enclosed recent editorial in the Boston *Herald.* I believe that the American people are heartily tired and sick of this whole un-American tendency, which Colonel Roosevelt has done more than any other among us to foster; and the political leader or party that makes courageous conflict with it a paramount feature of its endeavor and its program, will serve not only the country, but the world.

I am, with high regard,

Yours truly,   Edwin D. Mead.

I am taking the liberty of sending a copy of the enclosed statement to Mr. Edward A. Filene, of Boston, whose devotion to good citizenship and all good causes is, I think, known to you, who goes to Baltimore for the Convention.

TLS (WP, DLC).
1 Director of the World Peace Foundation of Boston.
2 This and other enclosures mentioned below are missing.

To Mary Allen Hulbert Peck

Dearest Friend,   Sea Girt, New Jersey 23 June, 1912

The Republicans have met,—and done their worst; and now the Democrats are to meet and—? But that is not what interests me just at this writing, because I am afraid that you are ill. I have not heard from you since your hard work of getting settled at Nantucket was finished (if it *is* finished!) and I know only too well how you spend all the strength that is in you, and more till Nature cries out against it and lays you low; and I do not know how many of these bankruptcies your store of vitality can stand. You are a very wonderful person, physically as well as every other way. Mind and body, you are one of the most wonderfully *vital* persons I have ever known. But there are limits even to the marvelous and some day you may presume upon your endowment of vigor and recuperative power once too often, —and I dread this constant experimenting with the lasting quality of the finest thing in the world, a life that makes other people happy! *Don't* do it any more! *Must* trunks and boxes be unpacked *at once? Must* all parts of a house be furnished and set in order within the week, whether anybody is left in condition to enjoy living in it or not? These are not questions patiently listened to by any housewife I ever knew; but maybe one's friends who *need* one, in order that they may be sustained for all the finest efforts of their lives may be forgiven for once and again insisting on raising and debating them. At any rate this one means to! He knows what friendships he lives by—and he means to fight for their continuance as he would for means of subsistence! He is himself too much involved. *He* is very well—so well as almost to argue lack of deep sensibility—and is to-day especially wide-awake and vigourous, because, after having been talked to by excited political friends night after night till one or two o'clock, he last night had twelve hours sleep and did not stop until he had consciously had enough!

If you read the papers you know all that I know of political happenings (except the details). We need not fill our letters with that, but with something more permanent.

All join me in affectionate messages to you all.

Your devoted friend   Woodrow Wilson

ALS (WP, DLC).

From Francis Fisher Kane

Philadelphia
My dear Governor Wilson: Sunday [June 23, 1912].

I am delighted over your telegram to Bryan. It was just right. It puts you just where you ought to be and with the right people back of you. And more than this,—it speaks the truth.

The people are not going to turn to the Democratic Party just because it is the Democratic Party—Governor Baldwin notwithstanding. They are interested in other things, and we owe it to them to say plainly whether we are progressives or reactionaries.

We also owe it to them to speak out plainly on the tariff. I am worried about that for I hear indirectly that Bryan is not going to force the issue with the members of Congress in the Convention. I hope that does not mean that there will be the usual cowardly equivocation in our platform instead of an out-and-out declaration for a tariff for revenue only as the goal to which we should strive.

I was in Baltimore on Friday night, but had to return here yesterday. I go back by the first train tomorrow.

All seemed right when I left so far as I could see. Your telegram to Bryan and the events of yesterday in Chicago seem to me to ensure your nomination.

Yours sincerely,   F. F. Kane.

ALS (WP, DLC).

From George Foster Peabody

My Dear Governor Wilson   [Baltimore, Md.] June 23d 1912

I must thank you for the honor of your so gracious hospitality to me and the confidence I appreciated.

I must also thank you for the word of masterful apprehension which your telegram to Mr Bryan gave forth as a true prelude to the leadership which he will I feel resign to your abler handling. I must congratulate the country on all it means to have one who can see and knowing has the courage to do and dare.

I found a fine state of enthusiasm and courage aroused by it here altho Senator Gore was evidently not so ready to put away the idea of harmony expressed by having both sides speak their discordant words—he is loyal however. I feel that the lines will now be drawn clearly and you alone could have done that. It is an accomplishment worth while. I cannot but think you will in consequence be nominated and thus be the Leader but surely the Country will now take your measure and call for your service

Sincerely Yours   George Foster Peabody

ALS (WP, DLC).

From Garrett Droppers[1]

Dear Governor Wilson: New York. Sunday June 23, 1912

I am simply delighted with your frank reply to Mr. Bryan. It was the only conspicuously straight-from-the-shoulder response to his request. I hoped, before I read your telegram, that you would answer it as you did, and I was not disappointed. It was good sense, good morals and I believe good politics. Thank you.

If there is the least taint of Murphy-ism in the Democratic Convention Roosevelt will sweep the country. I telegraphed Norman Mack yesterday to this effect and urged him to make the Democratic Party a haven of refuge for all progressives and insu[r]-gents.

The Clark leaders have in my opinion overshot the mark. They have made a deal with Murphy, or some thing like it[2]—and it will react against them—at least I trust so.

I am off for Baltimore by the next train. My district, as you doubtless know, gave you a majority in the Primary. I am grateful for that. Needless to add that you will have my whole-hearted support.

With best wishes

Yours very truly   Garrett Droppers

ALS (WP, DLC).

[1] Professor of Economics, Williams College, delegate to the Baltimore convention.

[2] He was right. Clark's managers concluded a bargain with Charles F. Murphy, leader of Tammany Hall, by which the Clark delegates would support Parker for the temporary chairmanship and New York's ninety votes would go to Clark at a crucial time in the balloting.

To Edward Mandell House

My dear Mr. House:　　　　　[Trenton, N. J.] June 24, 1912.

Your two letters have reached me and gave me additional proof of your thoughtful and admirable friendship. I am going to send them both on to headquarters in Baltimore so as to be sure that they will receive attention there.

I hope that you will have a most refreshing voyage. It leaves an empty feeling in my heart to have you away because it is good to know merely that you are within reach, but it would be selfish to ask you to stay.

Please give my warmest regards to Mrs. House,[1] and believe me,　　　　　Always affectionately,　Woodrow Wilson

TLS (E. M. House Papers, CtY).
[1] Loulie Hunter House.

From Josiah Strong, with Enclosure

Dear Governor Wilson:　　　　　New York June 24, 1912.

A few weeks ago I had a talk on the political situation with our mutual friend Mr. George M. La Monte, and expressed some ideas which he asked me to embody in a letter to him or to you. I have just dictated a letter to him which I hope may have some little possible influence in the Baltimore Convention, and herewith enclose a copy to yourself.

Wishing you the greatest success at Baltimore, I am,

　　　　　Yours faithfully,　Josiah Strong.

E N C L O S U R E

Josiah Strong to George Mason La Monte

My dear Mr. La Monte:　　　　　New York June 24, 1912

I have delayed my proposed letter to you because I have waited for the Republican situation to develop itself.

I do not imagine that I have anything to say that you have not already thought of, but I desire to say it as a lifelong Republican.

You are aware, as the elections of the last half-century have shown, that in the presidential years a majority of the voters of the United States are Republicans, and that if a democratic candidate is elevated to the presidency, he must be elected by republican votes. If, therefore, the convention now in session in Baltimore desires to nominate the next President of the United States, they must nominate a man who will be acceptable to a large number of Republican voters.

It is obvious that the voters whom you will aim to attract are not the dyed-in-the-wool stand-patters, but the independent Republicans, and it will be impossible to secure the support of such men for a pronounced conservative. If you are to gain a majority of the next electoral college, you must not only poll substantially the full democratic vote, but also a considerable independent republican vote. This of course points to the selection of a "safe and sane" progressive. Moreover, the organization of a third party with the present prospect of a democratic committee to secure democratic support for Colonel Roosevelt confirms the judgment that the nomination of a conservative at Baltimore would be suicidal. The "safe and sane" progressive will apparently be necessary in order to hold the progressive democratic vote, and certainly necessary in order to win the independent republican vote which is in no small measure disgusted with the existing situation in the Republican party.

In my judgment the index finger of the situation points unmistakably to Governor Woodrow Wilson as the man. I have talked with quite a number of Republicans in different parts of the country, and almost without exception they have expressed a desire to vote for Woodrow Wilson, and not one of them has expressed a preference for any other democratic candidate. Last week a gentleman whose position brings him in contact with people of all sections told me that he must have talked with at least fifty Republicans every one of whom expressed a desire to vote for Governor Wilson.

The situation in the Republican party to-day is not unlike that in the Democratic party in 1860, which gave the presidency to the Republican party and Abraham Lincoln to the world. The Baltimore Convention has now an opportunity to nominate another distinguished Kentuckian for the most exalted office in the land.

Permit me to add that for fifty years my choice for the presidency has been elected without a single exception.

With great esteem, I am,

                           Faithfully yours,   Josiah Strong.

P.S. I am sending a copy of this letter to Governor Wilson.

TCLS (WP, DLC).

From William S. Andrews[1]

Dear Governor Wilson,   Baltimore, June 24, '12

One of your best friends here has told me that some New York men, close to Mr. Murphy, have objected to you because of your alleged ingratitude toward those who have given you political support; which is the charge made by Senator Smith.

It may be that has been repeated to you.

I am authorized to assure you that has never been said by Mr. Murphy, or by anyone else having any right to speak for him.

On the contrary, any statements or insinuations made against you personally in opposition to your nomination are absolutely disapproved by Mr. Murphy.

In my several conversations with him, during the past year or more, relative to your candidacy, he has never expressed any thought or feeling unfavorable to you.

Be kind enough not to answer this. It is merely for your information and does not call for any reply.

                    Very sincerely yours   William S. Andrews

ALS (WP, DLC).
    [1] Commissioner of the Hall of Records of New York City.

From Frank E. Loughran[1]

My dear Governor,   Baltimore, Md. June 26th, 1912

The selection of Mr Parker was at first a disappointment to those who desired the Convention to be as progressive as Caezar's wife was virtuous but upon analysis it is not so bad for the vote did not furnish a test on this point, as the Clark vote that went to Parker did so for two reasons (1) to find favor with the N Y City organization (2) to eliminate the candidacy of Mr Bryan which they greatly fear. The N Y City organization cares little for Parker and the second reason has failed of its purpose as Bryan is far from eliminated.

It did however have the effect of showing Bryan upon whom

he could depend for progressive support and in this regard has helped the Wilson position decidedly.

It has been everybody's day at the Convention, everybody who had a speech, spoke it, the big ones from the platform, others to their own delegation on the floor, and the crowd had its say too and shouted itself hoarse. It was play-day at the Convention. Nobody is making serious predictions of the outcome. Another session of the Convention this evening, and a big parade of Wilson supporters scheduled under the leadership of Saml. Iredell of Bridgeton.   Very Truly   Frank E Loughran

ALS (WP, DLC).
    [1] Lawyer and notary of New York, who was working in McCombs' headquarters in the Emerson Hotel.

To Ralph Pulitzer

[Sea Girt, N. J.] June 27-[19]12

The work the World is doing fills every genuine progressive with admiration and some of us with deepest gratitude
                                                    Woodrow Wilson

T telegram (WP, DLC).

A News Report

[June 27, 1912]

WILSON QUITS GOLF TO HEAR RETURNS
GLAD UNIT RULE IS BROKEN

SEA GIRT, N. J., June 27.—Gov. Wilson gave up practice on the golf links this afternoon, ten minutes after the battling on the South Dakota contests began in Baltimore.[1] The Governor came off the links declaring that things were getting so interesting he couldn't keep away from the telegraph wire.

His direct wire to the convention hall brought him constant information throughout the afternoon. At 6 o'clock the Governor was smiling more broadly than he had throughout the day.

"The indications are," he said, "that the Progressives are in control and that is gratifying."

"Do you consider," a visitor asked, "that the balloting is demonstrating that your personal chances are improving?" The Governor indicated with a quick wave of the hand that the question was distasteful to him.

"That is not the way I care to think of it," he said. "I am confident that the nominee will be a Progressive, and that the platform will be Progressive."

The Governor plainly was elated at the action of the convention last night in abrogating the unit rule.[2]

"I have always maintained," he said, "that where delegates are instructed by districts in a primary election, they should vote accordingly, and not be bound by the unit rule. For instance, here in New Jersey we have twenty-four of the twenty-eight delegates—an overwhelming majority—yet we have never dreamed of enforcing the unit rule."

A question was asked about the South Dakota contest. Gov. Wilson said he did not know the details of the situation there enough to be able to estimate the exact meaning of the vote in the convention.

"I regard it as very fortunate," he said, "that the fight was started at the outset of the convention to make a straight lineup as between Progressives and non-progressives. When the first victory for Judge Parker was announced the people at home had a chance to let their delegates hear from them and the result seems to have been wholesome. I consider that the Progressives have been in command from the start. I have been unable to analyze the Parker vote fully."

A chill wind blowing in from the sea caused Mrs. Wilson to abandon an auto trip in the evening and have log fires lit in the large fireplaces of the Governor's residence. With Mrs. Wilson, the Governor sat through the evening in front of the fire.

Ex-Gov. Fort drove up to the Governor's residence at 9 o'clock and spent some time. When he left he said that his call was merely social. "I came over," he said, "because I realized that this would be an anxious night for the Governor, and as my home in Spring Lake was within motoring distance I thought I would keep the Governor company for half an hour and incidentally learn the late news from the convention.

"I did not mention the recent convention at Chicago in any way and did not say a word about the new party which Col. Roosevelt is forming."

After ex-Gov. Fort had gone, bulletins came to Gov. Wilson giving him the contents of Bryan's resolution declaring that it was the sense of the convention that agents of Wall Street should not be recognized as having any proper place within it.[3]

"Evidently," said Gov. Wilson, as he stirred the fire in the big fireplace, "Mr. Bryan is having a showdown on this matter. I could sleep through almost anything," continued the Governor, as he prepared to retire. "I may be able to sleep through the night, but I shall keep in touch with the telegraphic bulletins, and, of course, if they should begin to ballot I should not stay in bed."

Printed in the *New York Times*, June 28, 1912; two editorial headings omitted.
[1] About this contest, see Link, *Road to the White House*, pp. 440-441.
[2] See *ibid.*, pp. 438-440.
[3] See *ibid.*, pp. 441-45.

From Elgin Ralston Lovell Gould[1]

My dear Wilson:　　　　　　　Baltimore, Md. June 27, 1912.

I have been here working since the opening of the convention, and things have changed greatly in your favor.

1) The Clark people cannot hold their forces together after the first or second ballots. Too many are hearing from their constituents. I saw some of these telegrams yesterday.

2) Underwood's vote will largely go to you after the first two or three ballots. I have been working especially with this contingent.

3) The breaking of the unit rule helps you tremendously. Bryan has another good thing in reserve for to-day.

4) I have seen some near the seat of "the interests" whom I know well. Their attitude of confidence is changed, but their determination still is to beat you. But if Bryan holds firm and refuses the nomination under any circumstances, you can't be beaten. I feel sure you will win.

I shall be in New York Monday and ready for your further service.

　　　　　　　　Faithfully Yours,　　E. R. L. Gould

ALS (WP, DLC).
[1] Wilson's old friend, a pioneer in the development of low cost housing in the New York area. He was not a delegate.

From Alexander Crombie Humphreys[1]

Personal

My dear Governor Wilson:　　　　New York June 27, 1912.

After our talk over the 'phone this afternoon I reported to President Butler and to President Schurman what had passed between us. Previous to calling you on the 'phone we three had been over the file containing the correspondence had between you and President Pritchett in regard to the pension matter.[2] After our talk over the 'phone we continued the discussion at length and especially had under consideration the question whether it would be wise to issue any statement in regard to this pension matter. We finally decided not to make a statement because we feared that we might embarrass you rather than help you by any statement that might be made at this particular time. I want you, however, to understand that we three were more than anxious to make any fair statement which would show that nothing but the most friendly feeling had existed in the minds of the members of our committee towards you in connection with the pension application. It is to be borne in mind particularly that there has been only one meeting of the committee since the article in the *Sun*,[3] and this is the first meeting which has been held since the Miller letter in the *New York Times*, dated, I think, June 24. It is also to be borne in mind that we have been embarrassed in this matter through the long-continued absence of President Pritchett. As you know, we have been very careful in the committee to leave it to Pritchett to make statements for the public, and no doubt he has been somewhat handicapped in this matter by his absence from the headquarters.

I have felt from the first that the information that went to the public in regard to the application for a pension could not have been given out by any member of the committee. Our conference in the committee to-day more than confirms me in this opinion. As I said to you over the 'phone, President Butler informed us that he had been applied to a number of times to give information, but in every case he replied either orally or in writing that such matters were entirely confidential and no information was ever given out from the committee except through the president, namely, Pritchett.

I am only sorry that I was unable to see my way clear to do something that would clear up the situation in your interest, and in this feeling I am very sure that President Butler and President Schurman agreed with me.

With kindest regards, I am

Most sincerely yours,   Alex. C. Humphreys

P.S.—Since dictating the above I have read an editorial from the *Brooklyn Times* of yesterday which winds up to the effect that this is not the public's business and the Governor of New Jersey has wisely decided to say nothing about it, but evidently not all the Governor's friends have sense enough to understand that when a question of this kind is closed, it should be kept closed. Apparently, then, our decision of to-day is in accord with this editorial writing.

TLS (WP, DLC).

1 President of Stevens Institute of Technology, member of the executive committee of the board of trustees of the Carnegie Foundation for the Advancement of Teaching.

2 The controversy over Wilson's application for a Carnegie pension (about which, see WW to H. S. Pritchett, Nov. 11, 1910, n. 1, Vol. 22) had recently broken out anew. Dickinson Sergeant Miller, Professor of Philosophy at Columbia, in a letter and statement published in the New York Times, June 17 and 25, 1912, had accused Henry S. Pritchett, president of the foundation, of misleading Wilson and had come close to accusing Pritchett of leaking news of Wilson's application to the press.

3 Divulging Wilson's application. It is printed at Dec. 5, 1911, Vol. 23.

A News Report

[June 28, 1912]

WILSON IS SERENE AS VOTING GOES ON

Jokes with His Family, Reads Morley's
"Life of Gladstone," and Takes an Auto Ride.

TELLS A TALE WITH A MORAL

Which is, That He's Glad He Is Holding His Own—
Says Progressive Spirit Controls.

SEA GIRT, N. J., June 28.—While the delegates to the Democratic National Convention at Baltimore jostled his personal fortunes about through their long series of balloting, Gov. Woodrow Wilson spent his time here to-day in apparent freedom from the least concern as to the outcome. The Governor played with his daughters on the lawn, joked with Mrs. Wilson because her watch was slow, and offered to lend her his watch if she would be sure to return from an automobile ride in time to have him join her for a longer one.

He strolled about for ninety minutes while the second, third, and fourth ballots were being taken, and upon his return to the "Little White House" accepted with a smile the very meager reports from Baltimore which his secretary handed to him.

"The Progressive spirit continues in control," was his only comment as he looked over the bulletins and noted the steady increase in his total, with a corresponding failure of the Champ Clark column to take on headway.

All around the Governor's house the scene seemed exactly made to order to fit his own spirit of aloofness. No one came to see the Governor, and so far as could be learned no one called him up on the telephone or sent him any rush of personal messages. In front of his home the vast lawns of the Sea Girt rifle range stretched toward the sea without a single living thing to suggest that the "Little White House" stands close to living persons and crowded communities, and that the man who joked with his wife and children was waiting under tension for the outcome of events which the world was impatiently watching.

Sometimes from far down the rifle range the pop of rifles could be heard, but the firing squad was out of sight behind a group of buildings.

Gov. Wilson read for a time John Morley's "Life of Gladstone."

"It's a great book," he commented to a Times reporter. "I am quite absorbed in it."

"What is the latest word you have from the front?" asked the reporter.

"Now, really," said the Governor, "I guess my friends are so busy trying to nominate me that they have no time to bother sending me messages. Really, I have no word at all, and the best message I can give out is that if any of my good friends haven't read 'Molly Make-Believe'[1] they have missed a charming book. I like it even better than this fascinating life of Gladstone."

Some one asked Gov. Wilson what he thought of the situation.

"From what I know at present," he said, "the situation reminds me of a story they used to tell about a friend of mine. This friend was riding in a buggy one day and asked a man by the roadside how far it was to the next town. The man replied that it was twenty miles. He drove on a long way and asked a second man. This man also replied that it was twenty miles. In another half hour's driving a third passer-by was encountered, and he also said the distance was twenty miles. Whereupon my friend remarked to a companion in the buggy: 'Well, John, I'm mighty glad we are holding our own.' "

"May we print that?" chorused some reporters.

"You may," said the Governor, "but by morning it may seem sadly inappropriate."

Once only during the day was the persistent calm of the Wilson home invaded by a scene suggesting a political headquarters. As Gov. Wilson came out on the lawn to join his wife in an auto ride a moving picture man sprang suddenly in his pathway and began to operate his machine. As if by magic a dozen photographers appeared and for twenty minutes they clicked their machines.

A persistent rumor was to the effect that Mr. Bryan had telegraphed Gov. Wilson, urging him to come to Baltimore to address the delegates. Gov. Wilson said he had no communication with Bryan and was not expecting to leave his home. When he learned of the evening adjournment until 9:30 he ejaculated:

"My, what unheard-of hours they adjourn to. I wonder what makes them choose the hours they do?"

As the beginning of the ninth ballot in the convention was announced Melvin A. Rice,[2] who had remained among the group of reporters on Gov. Wilson's lawn, remarked that Princeton was famous for its rallies in the ninth and that this was the inning of the great Princeton victories.

"But it won't be in this case," said Gov. Wilson. "This is to be a ten-inning game, and I fear several more than that. I wish some candidate would come forward and make a sacrifice hit."

When the result of the ninth was read to the Governor at midnight he ordered a glass of buttermilk, remarking that things were too interesting for him to retire.

At midnight Gov. Wilson bade good night to the newspaper men, with whom he had been chatting around the telegraphers' tent on his lawn and retired. Mrs. Wilson and the Governor's three daughters were among those who had watched the bulletins from Baltimore all evening, analyzing the votes.

Printed in the *New York Times*, June 29, 1912.
[1] Eleanor Hallowell (Mrs. Fordyce Coburn) Abbott, *Molly Make-Believe* (New York, 1910).
[2] President of the linen importing firm of Donald W. McLeod and Co. of New York, member of the New Jersey State Board of Education.

From William Joel Stone

Balto Md [June] 29 [1912]

A majority of the national convention has voted for the candidacy of Champ Clark.[1] No one questions his fitness and loyalty to democracy and for seventy years the practice has been established of giving the nomination to the candidate who receives a majority we ask you in the interests of the party and in vindication of the democratic principle of majority rule to assist in making his nomination unanimous by the withdrawal of your candidacy.[2]

> William J. Stone,
> Chairman and rest of Missouri delegation in
> natl convention.

T telegram (WP, DLC).
[1] Murphy switched New York's votes from Harmon to Clark on the tenth ballot, giving the Speaker 556 votes, nine more than a majority. Wilson received 350½ votes, Underwood, 117½. The following evaluation of Clark by that wise student of American affairs, James Bryce, seems too good to remain buried in a governmental archive:
"At the beginning of 1912 the main thought in everyone's mind in both parties

was to the candidates whom they should choose at the nominating conventions to be held in the summer. On the Democratic side four persons were uppermost in men's minds. There was Mr. Champ Clark, the Speaker of the House, who had the advantage (though it is not always an advantage) through his position of being known to all politicians and tolerably well known to the general public. He had but recently emerged from obscurity when on the departure from the House for the Senate of Mr. John Sharp Williams, previously leader of the Democrats, Mr. Clark succeeded to the post, although he possessed no eminent gift beyond that of a genial western manner cultivated with extreme care, the gift of more or less humorous and sometimes shrewd speech, and the reputation of being a genuine 'son of the soil.'

"He had obtained the speakership in the dearth of stronger candidates by going round beforehand among his democratic friends, and asking them whether they would give him their votes if the Democratic party obtained a majority in the Congress elected in 1910; as it did obtain a majority and no other candidate appeared Mr. Clark was elected without difficulty. It might have been expected that his conspicuous deficiency in mental grip and force of character as well as in knowledge of the procedure of the House would have soon exposed his weakness in a post so trying as the Speakership. But that office had been shorn of two-thirds of its power by the revolt of the insurgents against Mr. Cannon at the last Congress, and thus Mr. Clark succeeded to an office whose duties almost any man of ordinary sense, and by the aid of a skilled adviser constantly at his elbow, could discharge without exposing himself to ridicule. Accordingly, he has made a tolerable Speaker, and as he used the powers which the post gives him of making friends and obliging people he had gathered a considerable support, and was in the beginning of 1912 the leading Democratic aspirant for the presidential candidacy, deemed even then more likely to be chosen than were the other three aspirants, although they were all known by those who saw them at close quarters to be greatly his superiors in ability and in character." James Bryce, *United States, Annual Report, 1912*, printed document (FO 371/1859, No. 10256, PRO).

2 Wilson sent a message to McCombs authorizing him to withdraw his name. About this message and the controversy over the decision to ignore it, see n. 3 to the news report printed at July 2, 1912.

Two Telephonic Messages to William Jennings Bryan

[Sea Girt, N. J., June 29, 1912]

It has become evident that the present deadlock is being maintained for the purpose of enabling New York, a delegation controlled by a single group of men, to control the nomination and thus bind the candidate to itself. In these circumstances it is the imperative duty of each candidate for the nomination to see to it that his own independence is beyond question. I can see no other way to do this than to declare that he will not accept a nomination if it cannot be secured without the aid of that delegation. For myself, I have no hesitation in making that declaration. The freedom of the party and its candidate and the security of the government against private control constitute the supreme consideration.[1]

T MS (WP, DLC).
1 There is a WWsh draft of this message in WP, DLC.

The only reason the Gov does not cause the publication of this statement is because his vote in the convention having stood still, he (the Gov) would regard it as a reflection on himself, because his position of independence is so well known.[1]

Hw MS (M. F. Lyons Papers, DLC) with heading: "Telephone message to Mr Bryan from Gov Wilson"

[1] Tumulty later told Colonel House that Bryan called Wilson by telephone (between the tenth and thirteenth ballots) and said that Wilson was beaten but had one chance left—to come out strongly with a statement declaring that he would not accept the nomination if it was achieved with New York's help. Wilson and Tumulty concluded that the situation was so desperate that Wilson had nothing to lose by following Bryan's advice. The Diary of Edward M. House, T MS (E. M. House Papers, CtY), entry for Dec. 29, 1912. The first statement printed above was telephoned to Maurice F. Lyons, McCombs' secretary and assistant, while the thirteenth ballot was in progress.

The second message was undoubtedly added at Mrs. Wilson's urging. Tumulty recalled that "her idea was that Mr. Bryan was not playing fair, and that it would place the Governor at a disadvantage and make his nomination impossible." In any event, Wilson never published the statement and (again, according to Tumulty) left it to McCombs to decide whether to deliver the statement to Bryan.

The only point in issue is whether the statement was in fact delivered. Lyons, *William F. McCombs, the President Maker* (Cincinnati, Ohio, 1922), pp. 89-92, claims that it was, and that it was instrumental in Bryan's decision to change his vote from Clark to Wilson on the fourteenth ballot. McCombs, *Making Woodrow Wilson President* (New York, 1921), p. 146, says that he decided, without consulting Wilson, not to deliver the statement.

A News Report

[*June 29, 1912*]

WILSON RESISTS APPEALS TO GO ON TO BALTIMORE.

Senator Stone's Telegram Asking Him to Withdraw in Favor of Clark Ignored—Calm Amid Excitement, He Watches the Balloting.

SEA GIRT, N. J., June 29.—It was a day of hopes and fears in "Camp Wilson," which is the official as well as the present political designation of the Jersey summer capital. Militiamen at target practice now constitute the mass of Sea Girt's population. Soldiers and the Governor's few neighbors kept inquiring anxiously at the army tent beside the "Little White House," where all day and nearly all night the telegraph clicked tantalizingly and uni[n]for[m]ingly most of the time.

Gov. Wilson, at all times the calmest person about the camp, was up at 7 to receive the latest news of Friday night's long session. He spent the morning on the shaded breakfast porch with his family or at the executive offices, dividing his time between routine business of the State and communications from his managers in Baltimore. By noon the Governor was being urged to consent to a plan to have him invited to Baltimore to address the convention, the proposal attributed yesterday to Bryan. Samuel Bigelow, jr., of Jersey City offered to supply a specia[l] train to take the candidate to the convention city, and other friends, fearful that the tide was turning against the Governor, urged him to go and take personal command.

But at no time did the Governor consider acceding to these requests, although the pressure was so strong that the Jersey Central Railroad prepared to have a train at the Governor's disposal at ten minutes' notice.

On the telegram of Senator Stone, requesting him to withdraw in favor of Champ Clark, the Governor gave his decision straight out from the shoulder. The newspaper correspondents had a bulletin of the Stone telegram from Baltimore before the message reached Gov. Wilson.

"What's the answer?" the Governor was asked.

"There will be none," was his prompt and laconic reply.

The Governor was sitting on the big front piazza at the head of the large journalistic class in political science when the Stone message was received. On top of it arrived the bulletin of Bryan's shift to the Wilson standard.[1] A pleased smile, but no comment.

Just then an enthusiastic Wilsonite, arriving from Baltimore with the latest personal intelligence, joined the circle and the sixteenth photographer trained his guns on the candidate. The Wilson worker, Frank E. Loughran, a New York attorney, accounted for Bryan's shift by the statement that Mr. Bryan had discovered that Clark has been from the first the choice of Alton B. Parker, Morgan J. O'Brien and other Wall street attorneys in the New York caucuses. Others attempted to analyze the Bryan move and its effect on the Wilson chances, but not one word from the Governor indicated that he had any feeling on the subject.

"It looks as though the Wall street crowd wanted Underwood, and failing to get him they wished to pick some man whom Taft could beat," said Mr. Loughran.

"A pretty difficult thing, I should say," interjected the Governor and the laugh was general at Mr. Taft's expense.

A wild bulletin came during the disorder accompanying the seventeenth ballot. "A general break all along the line for Wilson"—there the telegraph was interrupted. Everybody got excited except the Governor.

"Wonders will never cease," he remarked, with a grin. "Awkward, though, to be interrupted just at this time."

When the result of the ballot showed the break had not yet

arrived neither surprise nor disappointment marred the candidate's placid smile. As the Wilson vote climbed higher the candidate evidenced pleasure, but never elation.

Golf and motoring were both dropped from the day's schedule; otherwise the routine was no different from the preceding days. There were a few neighborly calls to ask "the latest news from the front." Mrs. Wilson and her daughters followed eagerly each development, manifested their interest in their unassuming, quiet way and kept well out of the photographer's sight.

Printed in the New York *World*, June 30, 1912.

[1] On the fourteenth ballot, when he announced that he would withhold his vote from Clark so long as New York supported him.

From Simon Faber[1]

My Dear Governor: Atlantic City, N. J., June 29, 1912.

In writing this to you I am reminded of the following sentence, contained in a message sent by the great Hungarian patriot, Louis Kosuth, to the Hungarian Nation many years ago, from Italy, his exile, when against his wishes he was elected to Congress!

From the heart to the head, from the head to the arm, from the arm to the hand, from the hand to paper, words are losing in weight and force. So it is with me in this instant. It is impossible for me to describe to you how deeply I was moved by all that occurred at the Baltimore Convention.

Returned at 6:30 a.m. tired in body and so hoarse that I cannot speak above a whisper, yet in fine spirit. I am returning, tonight, to Baltimore with a number of friends so as to be present at your nomination, and to assist in raising the roof off the Convention Hall, and then finish the job by painting Atlantic City red all over. The demonstration,[2] in your favor, began at 2 a.m. Thursday morning and lasted until 3:25 a.m., which had to be suppressed by police authority, was the greatest I ever witnessed. This demonstration in which thousands upon thousands of people coming from all parts of the country, participated in, shouting at such an unusual hour too, "We want Wilson," must have had an effect on the Delegates. It certainly must have put the representatives of the special interest to thinking.

Governor such a demonstration means something. It means a great deal. It means not only that the people want Wilson, but that at last our people are commencing to take the proper interest in the affairs of our institutions.

Judge Wescott's speech was great. It came from his very heart and met a responsive cord. The masses showing their appreciation at every opportunity.

Bryan himself never appeared to me as great as he did when he faced the enemy. He looked like an aroused lion. I shall never forget that moment.

The Princeton boys, who seemed to be all over the house, certainly did justice to their schoolmaster.

Whatever the outcome may be of this great meeting at Baltimore, one fact will remain undisputed, that Woodrow Wilson stands idealised by millions of our people who believe in him and trust in him.

Wishing you health and happiness, I am

                          Very sincerely yours,   Simon Faber

N.B. Have you received my telegram sent to you from Baltimore to Sea Girt.[3]

TLS (WP, DLC).
[1] Real estate broker and general contractor and builder of Atlantic City, leader in local reform movements.
[2] The demonstration in the early morning of Friday, June 28, which preceded Wescott's nominating speech.
[3] It is missing.

A News Report

[*June 30, 1912*]

GOV. WILSON SAYS: "THERE CAN BE NO TRADING DONE AT THE CONVENTION IN MY NAME"

SEA GIRT, N. J., June 30.—Gov. Wilson made very clear to-day to the assembled newspaper correspondents:

1. That there can be no trading or promise-making for the presidential nomination done in his name. There will be no deal for delegates with his knowledge or authorization.

2. He will not go to Baltimore, and he considers his uninvited appearance before the convention would be an act of impertinence to say the least.

3. He does not regard the loyalty of his followers as a testimonial to himself, but as a stand for principle.

"Of course I do not know in detail what my friends and supporters are doing," said the Governor when The World correspondent called his attention to remarks attributed to Murphy in response to alleged overtures for the New York delegation's support.[1]

"But I am morally certain," continued the Governor with great emphasis, "that they (his convention managers) are not making arrangements or attempting to come to an agreement with anybody. I am certain they are doing nothing that could not be done in the view of the whole country, and that their only means of getting support is argument. There cannot by any possibility be any trading done in my name; not a single vote can or will be obtained by means of any promise." . . .

In fact it can be stated that the Wilson managers in Baltimore have not consulted their chief on such a question, for they have well known what would be his answer. Consequently there has been for such circumstances an unprecedented lack of communication between the candidate and his headquarters in Baltimore.

Gov. Wilson has been for hours at a time uninformed of the progress of events on the line of battle excepting as it came through the corps of correspondents or by news bulletins received through the temporary telegraph office stationed on the Governor's lawn.

"It would be only on questions of principle, not details, that my managers would consult me," explained Gov. Wilson the other day in accounting for the infrequency of his communications direct with the convention leaders. There is a direct telephone from the Wilson headquarters in the Hotel Emerson to the Governor's cottage, but its use is surprisingly meagre. . . .

Correspondents have learned how useless it is to ask the Governor to talk about himself or his prospects. During the suspense of the balloting he must have been asked a hundred times what he thought of his chances of being nominated. Each time he patiently gave the same reply, usually with a joke to take the edge off the hopeful reporters disappointment.

What may have been the candidate's feelings as the political wind shifted from point to point in his favor, no look or word has yet betrayed. It was the same to-day when he was asked for judgment on the effect adjournment might have on the outcome. Testing every possible point for an opening, the newspaper men finally found one when they got around again to principles. What did the candidate think of the stand of the Wilson delegates? Gov. Wilson replied:

"My predominating feeling about the whole situation is one of pride that the men who are supporting me are doing so because of an evident conviction that they are standing for a principle. I should feel abashed if I thought it was mere loyalty to me as an individual, deeply as that would gratify any man. I feel it is a privilege to be supported as they are supporting me and to see the support grow as if in response to conviction and public sentiment." . . .

Telegrams continued to pour in upon the Governor from all parts of the country from personal friends assuring him of victory and congratulating him on prospective success. There were more frequent consultations to-day over the long distance telephone with Baltimore, but in spite of the demands for advice the candidate took the afternoon off for a motor ride with his family.

Up to 10 this morning the Governor slept, repairing the strain of the last few days. At 11 the Governor, Mrs. Wilson and their three daughters went by auto to the next village, Spring Lake, to the Presbyterian services. The Rev. Dr. Ludlow of East Orange[2] occupied the pulpit, and in the usual prayer for the Governor of the State besought success for him and all others who are struggling to uplift government. The remainder of the day and evening was spent indoors, answering telephone and receiving neighborly calls.

Printed in the New York *World*, July 1, 1912; one editorial heading omitted.
    [1] According to Louis Seibold in the New York *World*, June 30, 1912, Wilson's managers had urged Murphy to swing New York's ninety votes into line for the New Jersey Governor. Murphy replied: "Can't now. Bryan has disfranchised us. We'll have to stay by Clark. Bryan wants it himself. He will never get the vote of New York."
    [2] The Rev. James Meeker Ludlow, D.D., Princeton 1861, pastor of the East Orange Presbyterian Church.

From Allan Dudley Jones[1]

Balto Md June 30 [1912]

Your cordial wire recd   every Wilson delegate from Virginia will stand like Stonewall Jackson at Manassas

Allan D Jones

Hw telegram (WP, DLC).
    [1] Lawyer of Newport News, Va.; founder and publisher of the Newport News *Daily Record*, 1914-20.

From Royal Meeker

My dear Governor Wilson: Princeton, N. J., June 30, 1912

Mrs. C. B. Alexander and I came home after the adjournment last night. I fully expected that you would be the nominee of the Democratic Party before this. I am more confident than ever, that you will be named next Monday and only regret that I could not stay to witness the breaking of the delegations, which are pledged to Underwood, to your support. Then will come the land slide. I don't suppose my influence had any effect on any of the delegates with whom I talked, although I am sure I corrected some erroneous notions in the minds of some of them. Never before did I realize fully what you are up against. I am more a radical than ever, after the exhibition of cold blooded and hot blooded selfishness, chichanery, jobbery and corruption displayed by "the interests" bent on defeating you by any methods, short of open murder.

I wish, Mr. Wilson, you could have witnessed the superb devotion and fine fighting spirit of your followers, especially, those fellows from Texas and Pennsylvania. To be frank, I left the Convention Hall Saturday morning at 4 or 5 o'clock, very much discouraged. I felt that we,—that is you,—were licked. I went to the headquarters of the Texas and Penna. delegations. Those fellows declared they had not yet begun to fight! I never saw such splendid devotion.

Mrs. Alexander and I had the distinguished honor of sitting just behind the four rows of seats reserved for the use of the Honorable Norman E. Mack. We had ample opportunity to study at close hand the methods employed by the Murphy-Ryan-Hearst syndicate in packing Conventions, manufacturing "public opinion," and "taking care of the boys." I was subjected to such annoyance from some of these "boys," (i.e. door-keepers) that when I was obliged to leave the Hall to arrange for our transportation and sleeper tickets, I deemed it wise to remove my Woodrow Wilson badges. Otherwise I should, quite probably, have been prevented from returning to the Hall.

I hope you will not think me presumtuous in thus attempting to give you some side-lights of the Convention, from the standpoint of a mere onlooker. I have slept spasmodically perhaps 12 hours this week and I have totally forgotten the taste of civilized food. But I am a perfect Sybarite, compared to those men who are on the firing line fighting like lions for Woodrow Wilson and clean politics.

I have not had a bath or a shave for two days so I will now turn my attention from political cleanliness to personal cleanliness.   Sincerely and respectfully yours,   Royal Meeker

ALS (WP, DLC).

A News Report

[*July 1, 1912*]

GOV. WILSON WARNED TO BEWARE OF BRYAN

SEA GIRT, N. J., July 1.— . . . As the critical moment came when the forces of Champ Clark were overhauled and passed in the slow upward movement of the Wilson column at Baltimore to-day,[1] Gov. Woodrow Wilson was busily engaged in reciting limerick verses to Mrs. Wilson and her daughters on the veranda of the Governor's Summer home.

"There was a young lady from Niger," the Governor was reciting as an excited reporter burst upon him with a bulletin from the tented telegraph station on the lawn.

"Oh, you've passed him, you've passed him!" the reporter shouted with a flou[r]ish of the yellow bit of telegraphic paper in his hand.

"That's the stuff," was the Governor's only comment, and then, in a slightly more buoyant spirit, he continued with his limerick:

There was a young lady from Niger,
Who smiled as she rode on a tiger.
They came back from the ride with the lady
    inside,
And the smile on the face of the tiger.

The reporter waited anxiously for further comment. When he saw that none was to be offered he asked if the limerick was suggested by any present thought of Tammany.

"Of that," said the Governor, "you can guess as well as I can," and then he continued to recite more limericks.

It was too much for the reporter and his twenty-odd stampeded companions, who came up yelling and applauding the convention's action. "Oh, now, Governor," he persisted, "won't you please let us see you excited just for one minute. We have written about the quiet pastoral scene down here till we simply can't do it any longer. We've got to see how you behave when you're really stirred up. Now, please get a little excited."

Gov. Wilson smiled very broadly. "You might put it in the paper," he commented, "that Gov. Wilson received the news that Champ Clark had dropped to second place in a riot of silence."

The reporters retired to the telegraph station on the lawn. Another ballot was reported, in which it was shown that the Clark forces were losing, but not in any large numbers. This time Gov.

[1] On the thirtieth ballot, when Wilson received 460 votes, Clark, 455, and Underwood, 121½.

Wilson strolled over to the reporters to hear the result just as it was clicked off the telegraph wire. He heard the figures, and this was his exclamation:

"My, they're running like cold molasses!"

Gov. Wilson, for the first time since the convention opened, had work enough before him to occupy all of his time throughout the morning, to the exclusion of his usual pleasurable activities. The Governor's work was in connection with the hundreds of telegrams and letters which poured in upon him over Sunday. He dictated to his stenographer most of the morning, and then sent his colored butler, Sam Gordon, to the Post Office with a bundle of letters. Gordon passed a group of reporters on the way.

"I done suspect," he said, "that if you all throwed me down and took these here letters all away you would get some pretty fine sayings and such for the papers. My whiskers is gray and my haid is bald, but I'se a pretty good fighter yet, so I don't expect you all is a-goin' to see what's in here."

Then the aged butler passed along to the Post Office. He wore a Wilson button as large as his coat lapel could accommodate, and he was anxious to bet the Governor "would get there foh shore."

Judge Nelson T. Dungan of Somerset County was the Governor's only visitor before nightfall.

"Your column is climbing at a mightly slow rate," suggested Judge Dungan. "It has picked up only seventy-one votes all day. I'd like to see it forge ahead faster."

"But that's pretty fair," smiled Gov. Wilson. "You know it climbed all last week, and the whole week's work brought us only eighty-three. This isn't bad, considering."

It was clear that Gov. Wilson was very much satisfied with the slow, hammering progress of his supporters.

"Have you talked with your managers to-day?" a reporter asked when the Governor invited those present to visit him at 6 o'clock.

"No, I have not," he answered. "I have not talked with any one in Baltimore and have not had any important telegrams. I guess my supporters are kind of busy down there. The only message I have sent was one to the New Jersey delegation, congratulating them upon the spirit they are showing. I send them a telegram each day."

The Governor was asked about reports that his managers had offered to let the present convention adjourn as a deadlocked convention, provided the present managers for other candidates would agree upon a Nation-wide Presidential primary to be held between now and September.

Gov. Wilson shook his head and a slight frown overcast his features. "There is not a candidate in the country," he said, "who could stand the expense and the strain of such a plan. I should say that would be a futile thought. I don't think it is being considered."

For a time during the afternoon Gov. Wilson watched, and then umpired, a game of baseball between members of the colony of reporters established at his home.

"I never saw such uniform incompetents," he said, after three home runs had come in succession on three bad errors in the field. "You are worse than the worst reactionaries."

A stout player made a long slide to third and was put out, while ripples of laughter came from Mrs. Wilson and her daughters on the porch.

"That reminds me," smiled the umpiring Governor, "of a little phrase somebody got off about Col. Roosevelt. The phrase ran, in good baseball lingo, that in coming out for the nomination this year, Col. Roosevelt was 'trying to steal third.' "

The phrase disrupted the baseball game and there was an effort to have Gov. Wilson place himself on record as to the third term and the third party movement.

The Governor refused to follow up his base stealing comment and continued to upbraid his team for their poor playing until some one turned to a page in a biography[2] in which it was reported that Woodrow Wilson in college was a fine baseman and fielder, but was too lazy to run bases and shone only in making speeches of congratulation as he presented medals to the stars.

Gov. Wilson laughingly admitted that the book recorded the truth, and added that, for all his criticisms of the others, he would not dare to try his own pitching arm after its many years of disuse.

The cheerful comment that the reporters certainly had gone back to "primitive beginnings and forms of sport" irrevocably broke up the game. The team was disbanded.

Gov. Wilson, with an evening paper in his hand describing Bryan's attacks on Clark, left the baseball field. His final comment was that he had observed that Bryan had never attacked Hearst, but had confined his assaults to Clark's actions and the conduct of his supporters.

It was the universal view of those who watched Gov. Wilson's entire freedom from concern through what must have been the most trying day of his life, that there is no possibility of any

2 William Bayard Hale's.

crisis arriving within the next four years for which he will not have a limerick as handy as Lincoln kept his stock of anecdotes. The Governor himself insisted that he was too much used to living in his recent state of suspense to mind it any longer.

His secretary,[3] while he has smiled his way through it, has nearly collapsed under the strain.

Printed in the *New York Times*, July 2, 1912; one editorial heading omitted.
  [3] Tumulty.

To Royal Meeker

My dear Mr. Meeker:　　　　　[Sea Girt, N. J.] July 1, 1912.

Your letter of yesterday with its very striking sidelights on the Convention interests me deeply. I cannot tell you with what genuine pride my heart swells when I think of the splendid way in which selfsacrificing friends are fighting for me in the Baltimore Convention. Your letter only adds to the vivid impression and makes me search my heart to see whether I am worthy of representing the cause for which these men fight with so much forgetfullness of themselves.

Your letter written from the Convention Hall[1] was as moving to me as it was delightful.

With the warmest regard and esteem,

　　In haste,　　　　　Cordially yours,　　Woodrow Wilson

TLS (WP, DLC).
  [1] R. Meeker to WW, June 28, 1912, ALS (WP, DLC).

From Charles Henry Grasty

Confidential

My dear Governor:　　　　　Baltimore, Md. July 1, 1912

Before I go up to the convention hall I want to send you a line of greeting. The prospects seem bright this morning.

The Sun has tried to be wary as well as loyal and to avoid anything that might produce reaction. We sent the paper to all delegates for four weeks before they came to Baltimore and when they came they kept on reading it. We gave all candidates a fair show and this kept the minds of delegates open to our "poison." Our support has warmed up crescendo fashion, our editorial this morning[1] striking the top key up to date.

I write you all this because, whatever happens, I want you to know about it.

It does not matter a great deal, for the big compelling fact is that the great heart of the country is with you.

Sincerely yours   Charles H Grasty

I spent most of the Sunday afternoon with Bryan & had him at my house for supper. I pointed out as strongly as I could that you were the one man that New York could not taint.

ALS (WP, DLC).
[1] "Name The Strongest Candidate!" Baltimore *Sun*, July 1, 1912.

From Francis Griffith Newlands

My dear Governor: Baltimore, Md., July 1, 1912.

My last note to you[1] was written in a great hurry, just as I was about to start west with the remains of poor Senator Nixon.[2]

I am satisfied that I acted wisely in not accepting the position of delegate under instructions for Clark. The instructions bound the delegates to support Clark as long as he was a candidate and, I think, would have been very embarrassing to a man of honor. I think I have been able to serve the interests of your candidacy better than I would have been had I been a member of the delegation. The proxy of the National Committeeman was given me, and this enabled me to take an active stand in support of Bryan's position on the National Committee, and I have been able to bring the Nevada delegation to the support of the Bryan forces on all collateral propositions. Mr. Belford,[3] one of the delegation, who was chosen as one of the Committee on Platform, asked the Committee to accept me in his place; so I was appointed a member of the subcommittee on platform and collaborated with Bryan and O'Gorman in its preparation.

The Nevada delegation has gradually become convinced of the desirability of selecting you as standard-bearer, and has been very restive under its pledge. Compelled to vote for Clark, they have been free in their expressions of opinion and have helped to swell the western movement in your favor.

I have sent telegrams west which I hope will result in a movement of the delegates to the late State Convention to free the delegates from their pledges; but the distance and the scattered communities make this a difficult subject to deal with, and it is possible that they will have to go down with the Clark ship. But I wish you to understand that everything consistent with honor has been done to do away with the effect of the original blunder. Hearst's paper, the *Examiner*, has an enormous circulation in

Nevada, and I found on my trip there that it had poisoned the minds of the people against you. I have no doubt it is making such publications now as will tend to prevent a reversal of the pledges exacted.

The members of the Nevada delegation are convinced that the deadlock is so serious as to prevent the nomination of either Clark or yourself, and they have been desirous of starting a movement amongst the Western delegations for my nomination; but I have told them that in my judgment this whole movement would lack its proper climax unless you are nominated, and have insisted that nothing should be done in this direction so long as there is a possibility of your gaining the necessary two-thirds. They answer me with the statement that they can easily get absolved from their pledge in order to support me, and they insist that the solidification of the Intermountain and Pacific Coast vote in my interest would weaken Clark more than it would you. I wish you to understand, however, that nothing will be done in this direction with my consent which in any way tends to avert the climax to which I have referred and which I regard as essential to create the enthusiasm that will carry our ticket to victory.

I have found a very fruitful field of effort here in disarming the conservative forces, with which I happen to have some degree of influence, of their distrust of your candidacy. Throughout I have endeavored to impress them with the view that inasmuch as they cannot hope to get a reactionary, they should welcome the success of a Progressive who, whilst determined upon a radical cure, will apply all the palliative remedies necessary to save the life of the patient. I had an opportunity of urging this view today with great force upon a man[4] who stands in a position of exceptional strength with the Illinois delegation, and he promised me that he would take immediate steps to bring that delegation into line.

Wishing you every success, I am

Very sincerely yours,   [Francis G. Newlands]

P.S. July 2d. I have just been reading over my dictation, and am delighted to learn at this moment that you have got beyond the six hundred mark.[5]

CCL (F. G. Newlands Papers, CtY).

[1] F. G. Newlands to WW, June 6, 1912.

[2] George Stuart Nixon, Republican senator from Nevada, died on June 5, 1912, and was interred in Reno.

[3] Samuel W. Belford of Ely, Nev.

[4] Probably Roger C. Sullivan.

[5] On the forty-third ballot, when Virginia, West Virginia, and Illinois swung over, giving Wilson a total of 602 votes.

A News Report

[*July 2, 1912*]

GOV. WILSON NOT ELATED BY VICTORY

Feels the Tremendous Responsibility Even More
Than Honor of the Nomination.

SEA GIRT, N. J., July 2.—Gov. Woodrow Wilson received word of his impending nomination over the telephone from Baltimore at 2:48 o'clock, went upstairs to notify Mrs. Wilson, and, on coming down again, made this statement:

"The honor is as great as can come to any man by the nomination of a party, especially in the circumstances, and I hope I appreciate it at its true value; but just as [at] this moment I feel the tremendous responsibility it involves even more than I feel the honor. I hope with all my heart that the party will never have reason to regret it."

The word that the nomination had been made brought to an end an even week of tense feeling and suspense that wrecked nerves indiscriminately in Sea Girt, leaving to all appearances only the Governor unmoved and undisturbed.

The news was received in a spirit of solemnity. There were no cheers, no exclamations, no shouts. Even the soldiers on the rifle range near by ceased firing, and it was more than an hour later before the first demonstration commenced. The telegraph lines were clogged within ten minutes after the nomination was announced with more than a thousand personal messages to Gov. Wilson. Four extra telegraphers were sent for, and these, in addition to those already here, hoped to be able to handle the flood of work.

Mrs. Wilson's only sorrow as the break to her husband came was that Georgia, her native State, had not come to her husband's cause earlier in the battle.[1] Gov. Wilson's final smile before he became the candidate was inspired by the switch of Virginia, the State of his birth.

"That is fine," he said, "to feel my own native State coming over for me."

Informal receptions during the afternoon and the reading of personal messages of congratulation occupied the Governor's time until he retired. He found an opportunity, however, to summon to Sea Girt Edward I. Edwards, State Controller, who with the Governor comprises New Jersey's State House Commission.

---

[1] On the forty-sixth (and last) ballot, Senator Bankhead withdrew Underwood's name, and Georgia, along with the other Underwood delegations, went to Wilson, pushing him past the two-thirds mark.

Edwards was in conference with the Governor for thirty minutes. He emerged with eyes bulging, to declare in startled phrases that the Governor had remembered it was the scheduled day for the State House Commission to meet and that the meeting had been held in all its routine details.

"He never once mentioned the Presidency," said the puzzled State Controller.

In the Wilson home when the nomination was announced were seven persons—Gov. Wilson himself, his wife, his three daughters, Miss Hester Hesford, author of a biography of Gov. Wilson,[2] and Miss Mary Hoyt of Baltimore, a cousin of Mrs. Wilson.

Gov. Wilson received the news over the telephone from some one whose identity he did not learn. As he came from his library into the main reception room of his home his face was lighted by a characteristic expression of suppressed solemnity and strain under perfect control. He glanced about for the members of his family. They were nowhere in sight. Under sheer strain of the final minutes they had gone, one at a time, to their rooms upstairs.

Gov. Wilson walked slowly up the stairs, and in a minute came down again with Mrs. Wilson on his arm. There was a suspicious moisture in the Governor's eyes, but Mrs. Wilson, the strain broken, was smiling at the group of reporters, who had planned to do a serpentine dance to the home, but actually came hats in hands and in sober silence. Mrs. Wilson broke the strain for all.

"Isn't it fine?" she said. "I didn't think the hard, pounding battle could win. It is a hopeful thing, a beautiful thing, to see what the people can do when they take the case in their own hands. It renews hope for the people in me. Now I'm going to quit worrying. I never had a moment's fear about the outcome if Woodrow could only get the nomination, but I did fear he'd be defeated in the convention."

Mrs. Wilson was in a confidential mood, and she confided things that the colony of reporters stationed here through all the period of stress had not guessed. She confided that her husband had abandoned hope last Friday, and had begun to plan with her for a Summer trip to Europe.

"It was when the Clark column passed the point of a majority," said Mrs. Wilson. "Then we gave up. The Governor, as soon as he heard the news, sat down and wrote to Col. W. F. McCombs, releasing all his delegates. He told Col. McCombs that the dele-

[2] Hester Eloise Hosford, *Woodrow Wilson and New Jersey Made Over* (New York, 1912).

gates, especially the Jersey delegates, need not have the least
compunction about changing their votes; that they had done all
any man could expect for him.[3]

"It was a noble response the men made. Not one would accept
the release offered. They rallied to the Governor stronger than
ever, and that fine hammering for results was begun.

"Before Clark's lead was overcome the Governor told me to prepare for a trip to mount Rydal in Westmoreland, England. You
know we always loved Mount Rydal. It was Wordsworth's home.
Five years ago we[4] were over there and spent four months in one
of the Wordsworth cottages. See, here is a painting of it," and
Mrs. Wilson led the way to an oil painting near the large colonial
fireplace in the reception hall. "The painting," said Mrs. Wilson,
"was done for us by a friend[5] who lived in another cottage.

"And now isn't it strange, when I heard Gov. Wilson coming
up the stairs and I just knew it was all over I was thinking of
that dear little cottage at Mount Rydal.

"And what do you think the Governor said to me? He said,
'Well, dear, I guess we won't go to Mount Rydal this Summer
after all.' And I said, 'I don't care a bit, for I know lots of other
places just as good.'

"That is how I got the news from Baltimore."

For Mrs. Wilson to talk to reporters, knowing that they were
taking notes, was an entirely new experience. Throughout the
week they had coaxed for an interview in vain. Only an hour
before the nomination was made Gov. Wilson had been implored
to ask the members of his family to come out and be photo-
graphed.

"Gentlemen," he had answered, "my jurisdiction extends all
over the State of New Jersey, but when it reaches the front door
of the Little White House, there it stops. You will have to make
your appeals yourself."

The little party in Gov. Wilson's home, made up of those who
had been his intimates for a week, was quickly broken up by
arrivals from the outside. In an automobile Mayor R[eginald]. S.

[3] She referred to a message of June 28, which Wilson sent to McCombs on his
own initiative. Meanwhile, McCombs had lost hope and, early in the morning
of June 29, telephoned Wilson to say that the situation was hopeless and ask for
specific authorization to release the Wilson delegations, which the Governor
gave. Upon learning about this development, McAdoo urged Wilson to stand fast,
and Wilson countermanded the authorization. Link, *Road to the White House*,
p. 451; William G. McAdoo, *Crowded Years: The Reminiscences of William G.
McAdoo* (Boston and New York, 1931), pp. 153-54; Joseph P. Tumulty, *Woodrow
Wilson As I Know Him* (Garden City, N. Y., 1921), pp. 121-22. McCombs'
account in *Making Woodrow Wilson President*, pp. 143-45, is not reliable.

[4] Actually, it was in 1906.

[5] Frederic Yates.

Bennett of Asbury Park rushed up at top speed, and the Mayor ran up the front steps to be the first man from the outside to grasp the Governor's hand and greet him with the new salutation of "President." Judge W. S. Cobell[6] of Passaic arrived from Baltimore. He had come to bring good news of "breaks all along the line for Wilson," but arrived just in time to receive the news that had flashed ahead of him and invalidated the merit of his own.

As he turned from Mrs. Wilson to his visitors Gov. Wilson retained the same calm manner that has been his from the first. His secretary, on the other hand, had a serious fit of hysterics. With each of his visitors Gov. Wilson passed remarks on every subject but that of the Presidency.

"How did you get the news?" demanded Mayor Otto Wittpen of Jersey City, who had broken all speed laws and his automobile's running record in rushing to Sea Girt.

"To tell you the truth," said Gov. Wilson, "I don't know. I went to the 'phone, I could not make out who was talking. The connection was very bad. I gathered that some one had withdrawn Underwood and that some one else had moved to make it unanimous for Wilson, and then the 'phone was hung up."

Gov. Wilson's last day as a candidate for the nomination opened in a series of sensational flashes from Baltimore, which distracted every one but the Governor himself. While taking his morning bath word was carried to him that he had passed the six hundred mark. The reporter who galloped to the Wilson home with the bulletin read it wrong, and announced it as 700 instead of 600. There was a moment of elation all around, followed by a calm voice from upstairs saying: "I think there must be a mistake. That can hardly be."

The reporter looked again at the bulletin. Sure enough, he had read it wrong. But that was only the commencement.

"You're within 12 of enough," ran a bulletin received at noon. The cold, stern figures received a moment later belied the bulletin. But the atmosphere of impending victory was spreading everywhere and could not be suppressed.

Gov. Wilson came across the lawn to the press tent.

"I have something I want to say to you men, all of you," he remarked as he drew near.

The high seriousness of his manner impressed each reporter. This time there were to be no limericks, no anecdotes, no jokes.

"You must sometimes have wondered," the Governor went on,

6 W. Carrington Cabell.

"why I did not show more emotion as the news came from the convention, and I have been afraid that you might get the impression that I was so self-confident of the result that I took the steady increase in the vote for me at Baltimore as a matter of course.

"The fact is, the emotion has been too deep to come to the surface as the vote has grown, and as it has seemed more and more likely that I might be nominated I have grown more and more solemn.

"I have not felt any of this as if it were a thing that centred on myself as a person. The fine men who have been fighting for me at Baltimore I have not regarded as my representatives. It has been the other way around. I have felt all the while that they were honoring me by regarding me as their representative, and that they were fighting for me because they thought I could stand for and fight for the things that they believed in and desired for the country.

"I do not see how any man could feel elation as such responsibilities loomed nearer and nearer to him, or how he could feel any shallow personal pride."

Reporters asked Gov. Wilson to have his secretary write out his comment. Gov. Wilson said he would do so. While he was still standing near the telegraph tent this message was received from the leader of a far Western State's delegation:

"The switch of the Progressive leadership from Bryan to Wilson means that the Progressive movement is passing from emotionalism to rationalism. Bryanism is dead, a new Democracy is being born."[7]

"I think my Western friend phrases it about right, and he does it quite aptly," was Gov. Wilson's comment.

He retired to his library to dictate the statement he had given to the reporters. It was still in the typewriter when the message came that the nomination had been made. Gov. Wilson then added to it the words quoted at the beginning of this dispatch.

To reporters who rushed to the Governor's house as the first news reached them over the telegraph his secretary stated that the news they brought was old and that the Governor was already aware of the outcome and had completed the statement he had been dictating when the news arrived.

"It's remarkable, remarkable," added Gov. Wilson as the typewritten sheets were passed about. "I didn't think it would come so soon, but I saw they were ready for business as soon as they

[7] This telegram is missing.

went into session. When I heard of the Underwood break I didn't know how much of his vote would come to me, as it was regarded as highly conservative.["]

It was fully two hours after the news from Baltimore came that the first cheers echoed across the Sea Girt fields. A spell had held every one for that length of time, and it was not broken until a brass band, which had marched all the way from Manasquan, arrived in front of the Governor's home, the tired musicians blowing the notes of "Old Nassau" at the top of their lung power.

A flag had been run to the top of the pole in front of the Governor's home. Buggies and autos, all aflutter with flags, had lined up a mile deep at the side of the beach road. Behind the band was all of Manasquan's population. As the strains of Princeton's hymn died away cheers rose from a thousand throats and the long, tense silence was over for those who had watched from the first. They seized partners and danced on the lawn, and yelled themselves hoarse.

Calls for Wilson brought the Governor, minus his family, out on the veranda. He was in no mood for speech making. He stepped down among his neighbors, bared his head, and said softly:

"I cannot express the heartfelt emotions that I feel."

Some one in the crowd called out:

"We want Wilson and Evolution! It's all that will save us from Revolution!"

A tiny girl with a blue ribbon in her hair took Gov. Wilson's hand. He lifted her up in his arms. "I like to hold these tiny little hands," he said. A young woman in a blazer coat from a Summer hotel grasped the Governor's hand, and every one present fell in line for a handshake.

Henry Morgenthau arrived in an automobile and Gov. Wilson greeted him among the others. A telephone call took the Governor back into the house, and the crowd followed the band back home. The first demonstration for Democracy's candidate commenced at 4:30 o'clock. It ended at 5:10. . . .

Gov. Wilson had gone to bed before the nomination of Gov. Marshall for the Vice Presidency.[8] Earlier in the night, however, a premature report of Marshall's nomination had reached Sea Girt. At that time Gov. Wilson, referring to the Indiana Governor, said:

---

[8] Wilson's first choice, Underwood, would not accept the nomination. Without Wilson's knowledge, McCombs had traded the nomination of Marshall in return for Indiana's votes.

"An excellent man, one who is entirely satisfactory as far as I am concerned. I know Gov. Marshall and have been his guest on one occasion for thirty-six hours, and I am sure that his selection is another progressive triumph. It couldn't be anything else."

Printed in the *New York Times*, July 3, 1912; four editorial headings omitted.

From Champ Clark

[Baltimore, Md., July 2, 1912]

Just leaving for Washington. I congratulate you on your hard-earned victory and will do all I can to elect you.

Champ Clark

Printed in the Baltimore *Sun*, July 3, 1912.

A News Report

[*July 3, 1912*]

WILSON WON'T RESIGN AT ONCE

SEA GIRT, N. J., July 3.—This has been a field day for friends, neighbors, and hand-shaking enthusiasts, who have swarmed around Gov. Woodrow Wilson. . . .

For dinner to-night Gov. Wilson had as his guests Dean Harry Fine of Princeton University, and Mrs. Fine,[1] and Editor Gonzales of The Columbia State of Columbia, S. C. Gov. Wilson said that Editor Gonzales published "one of the most able papers" that he received in his mail, and that for that reason he was mighty glad to have him at his home. It was at a private school taught by a sister of Dean Fine[2] that Gov. Wilson's three daughters received their preparatory school education.

"I will lose Dean Fine's vote," said the Governor, "but, fortunately, it is a Jersey vote, and so I will be able to spare it. Dean Fine is departing to-morrow for Europe, to be gone a year. That is why I invited him here just at this time."

Following his dinner party Gov. Wilson received the members of his class in "Progressive Democracy," as he refers to the encamped reporters who have been here a week.

"Do you know," he smiled when asked about the platform, "they have kept me so busy to-day that I have had no chance whatever to read the platform. I have no idea what is in it."

Gov. Wilson was informed that the platform limited him to one term.

"So," he said, with an appearance of surprise. "I did not know it did that."

Friends of Gov. Wilson had urged him not to resign as Governor, because his administration would then pass into the hands of President John D. Prince of the State Senate, a regular Republican, who is Professor of Oriental Languages at Columbia University, and said to be a close friend of President Nicholas Murray Butler. Gov. Wilson was asked how he regarded this advice of his friends.

"As to my resignation," he replied, "I have not yet reached a conclusion. I shall not resign at once, but shall carefully consider the whole matter before I decide."

"The Governor would rather wait until a Democrat is elected President of the Senate," said one of his friends to-day, "and then turn the office over to him rather than a Republican, although he has a very high personal regard for Mr. Prince. We believe that the Governor is not required by law to resign. If this be true, he will probably continue in office until Jan. 1 next. His term expires on the third Monday in January, 1914."

Among the Governor's accomplishments is a mastery of shorthand. He displayed his knowledge of this to-day by making notes for dictation. As he wrote, leaning his pad upon the arm of his easy chair, the camera squad snapped him again and again, and a moving picture man recorded his movements.

"Shorthand?" asked the Governor, looking up in answer to a query, "why, yes, I write shorthand. I have written it for forty years. I taught myself how when I was 15 years old." . . .

With the coming of Walter Measday, who had charge of the Wilson Headquarters in Baltimore, and Dudley Field Malone, son-in-law of Senator O'Gorman, who was an active Wilson worker, the Governor was enabled to learn many details of the long-fought Baltimore battle. It came out that, in handling Bryan's telegram concerning the attitude to be taken toward Judge Parker for Temporary Chairman, Gov. Wilson had to meet again a problem similar to that he had to face in considering an offer of Ryan money from Col. Henry Watterson. In the Watterson case Gov. Wilson's managers were considered by Col. Watterson to be favorable to his plan, but Gov. Wilson said "Dirty money." In this case Gov. Wilson received from his friends in Baltimore a telegram urging him not to reply to Bryan until he should hear from them.

Gov. Wilson did hear from his friends. They inclosed to him a message to Bryan already written out ready for him to sign. It was a straddling message somewhat similar to that which cost Champ Clark so dearly before the convention.

"I cannot sign this," was Gov. Wilson's first comment on reading the message sent to him. He took up a pad of paper, sat on the edge of his bed, the prepared message having been handed to him while he was dressing, and began the substitute message of his own to Bryan with the words, "You are right."

The Wilson workers who joined in drafting the first undecisive message were so delighted with the outcome of Gov. Wilson's firm stand on the Temporary Chairmanship that they gladly told to-day of their own blunder in preparing the original draft. . . .

Printed in the *New York Times*, July 4, 1912.
  [1] Philena Fobes Fine.
  [2] May Margaret Fine.

To Oscar Wilder Underwood

Seagirt, N. J., July 3, 12

Your message of congratulations has given me deep pleasure.[1] It cheers me as much as it strengthens me to have the support of a man whose character and leadership in Congress all the country admires. Please accept my assurances of warm personal regard.   Woodrow Wilson.

T telegram (O. W. Underwood Papers, A-Ar).
  [1] It is missing.

From Walter Hines Page

My dear Wilson: Garden City, New York July 3, 1912

It's wrong perhaps to add to your present burden of letters. But I can't resist an expression of my joy.

To see a sincere effort made to work out democratic ideas in government and to have the democratic philosophy of society worthily formulated once more and with authority and fitted to present conditions—these are exciting prospects and most cheering. Sound economics, right social ideals, even an impulse towards sincerity and human sympathy in literature—all these will have a new impetus under your leadership. This will give a new impulse to work, a new zest to life. Surely it will give me a new impulse and all other men whose work is to try to think clearly, to keep the old democratic ideal always in view, and to tell the people the whole truth as we see it.

Your Administration, whatever statutes & decisions it may

bring forth or fail to bring, will clear up and strengthen the great people's vision of right human relationships.

After the failure of Cleveland to lead and of Bryan to see, I had almost despaired of seeing these things wrought out in our working-day; and now it is to come true! Your leading gives new hope & a profound joy to all men like me—all who have ever seen the fair vision of a real democracy and having once seen it could never escape from its radiance.

And the way it came is as fit as its coming; & the people will understand & respond.

Always heartily yours   Walter H. Page

ALS (WC, NjP).

From Robert Underwood Johnson

Dear Governor Wilson: New York July 3, 1912.

After telegraphing my Indiana brother,[1] Mr. Alton B. Parker and Mr. John Sharp Williams I went down to the Convention and took a hand in a humble way, telling our Southern friends that they must get their political eyes open or lose their chance for twenty years. Some time I'll tell you what I said to Bryan.

Well, the news is too good to be true and I am very happy over the situation.

Think of it!

I. The unspeakable Hearst is foiled.

II. The redoubtable Murphy rolled in the dust of his party's contempt.

III. Ryan and his "dirty money" scorned.

IV. Roosevelt and the third-term madness well-nigh put out of business.

V. Bryan's aspirations for the nomination—which would have been disastrous—squelched.

Sound the loud timbrel!

Of course Bryan created a favorable situation, but I feel sure he was hoping to profit by it himself.

I saw Underwood Tuesday morning. *There* is a high class man one can tie to with confidence.

I was greatly impressed by Mitchell Palmer and McCombs.

Faithfully yours,   R. U. Johnson

P.S. Here is the cartoon I spoke of.

ALS (WP, DLC).
[1] Henry Underwood Johnson of Richmond, Ind.; member of Congress, 1891-99.

From Samuel Untermyer

On Board R. M. S. "Caronia,"
Eastward Bound, New York to London,
My dear Governor: Wednesday, July 3rd, 1912.

On the receipt this morning at sea of a Marconigram announcing the glad tidings of your nomination I took the liberty of sending you the following Marconigram:

"I congratulate our country on its great opportunity to destroy Wall Street government and accomplish lasting economic reforms. Consider me unreservedly enlisted provided all Wall Street assistance is refused. Will gladly return if needed."
which I now beg to confirm.

The result is a splendid triumph in popular government over what seemed at one time to be almost insurmountable obstacles on the part of the great financial interests that have steadfastly and bitterly opposed your nomination.

I was compelled to leave my Delegation on Friday to reach my Steamer sailing the next day, but the caucus of our Delegation that had already been held showed the strong sentiment in your favor in spite of the animosities of a certain section of the Delegation.

It is only fair to say in this connection—and I think you should know the fact—that from the beginning Mr. Murphy maintained a surprisingly impartial attitude. He refused to vote or express his views in the caucus or to accept discretionary power that was offered him and encouraged independence of action in the Delegation. It was quite unlike anything I had known in my experience as a Delegate in any of the three preceding National Conventions.

The purpose of burdening you with this letter is not however to rehearse past history nor to assure you of my anxiety to assist in every possible way in your election but more particularly to call your attention to certain valuable information—available as campaign material—that will be found in the minutes of testimony of the so-called "Money Trust Inquiry."

The Investigation has as you know barely begun. We are awaiting the passage of a Bill to amend the Banking Law that is now pending in the Senate before the main branch of the Inquiry can be entered upon. Meantime the Committee held only five sessions, which were devoted to collateral subjects affecting the concentration of the Money Power, connected with the Clearing Houses and Stock Exchanges.

The investigation into the main phases of the subject will involve the examination of accounts and is likely to occupy months of time.

It is to the last day's proceedings of the Committee that I desire at this time to call your particular attention. It appears from the testimony of Mr. [George Bruce] Cortelyou—the then Secretary of the Treasury—and from figures put in evidence from the Treasury Department and from the books of J. P. Morgan & Co. that at the time of the Panic in 1907 the Government deposited approximately $39,000,000 within three or four days in the National Banks of New York. These deposits were manifestly made under the direction of Morgans, and mainly in Banks controlled by them.

Of this sum $18,000,000 was used to relieve the stringency in the Stock Exchange on October 24th, 1907. The amount that each Bank was to loan on the Stock Exchange was designated by Morgans, who apparently controlled the entire disposition of the Government funds.

The Clearing House Committee apparently had nothing to do with it.

All of this $39,000,000 was deposited without interest and a large part of it was left in Morgan Banks where it was loaned at substantial rates of interest. $10,000,000 of the amount was, according to Mr. Cortelyou's own statement, intended for the relief of the "Trust Company situation"—by which was meant the then precarious situation of the Trust Company of America. It was widely advertised at the time that Messrs. Morgan had come to the relief of the Trust Company and of the Stock Exchange—presumably with their own money; but it appears from this testimony that they never contributed a penny and that their Banks made substantial profits out of the Government moneys that they received without interest and loaned at interest.

All this time the National Banks were holding on to the balances of the out-of-town Banks that were on deposit in New York and the merchants of the country, who were in great distress for money, were unable to get it because the Government's resources were being used to relieve stock gamblers and to assist the Morgan Banks.

There are other features of the Inquiry connected with the uncontrolled and irresponsible power of the New York Clearing House which have been developed in the few hearings that have been had that might be of aid to you but I desire to commend to your consideration the relations between the Government and Wall Street during the Panic of 1907.

The Record shows a scandalous condition. On January 25th, 1908 when the Panic was over, the Record shows, as I claim, that the Clearing House deliberately wrecked three entirely solvent Banks, of which for some reason they wanted to rid themselves. All these Banks paid their depositors in full and even in liquidation showed excess assets for their stockholders of from $200 to $50 or more per share of stock.

If you care for this data and will have someone communicate with my son, Mr. Alvin Untermyer,[1] 37 Wall Street, New York City, he will send you the minutes of the testimony, or will have them analyzed for you if you prefer that course.

In the interest of the country I wish you every success and will be more than pleased to do whatever may be asked of me to contribute to that result. If it is believed that my presence in America before the date of my intended return (September 13th) will be of aid to the cause I will willingly return at the conclusion of my cure at Baden-Baden (August 15th).

Very respectfully yours   Saml. Untermyer

TLS (WP, DLC).
[1] Lawyer in his father's firm of Guggenheimer & Untermyer.

From Samuel Huston Thompson[1]

My Dear Governor,   Pittsburgh, Pa. July 3. 1912.

You will be overwhelmed, and whether your eye lights on this or not, the hearts back of it are just about as happy as it is ever given for those of mortals to be.

After the 6th Ballot and I saw the trend, and noted reply telegrams, I felt that nothing but a tragedy could stop you, hence my telegram *"The Thompson family congratulate their next President in advance—God bless him."* That telegram will hold good next Nov.

But as "faith without works is dead," we have been all at it, and altho' 70, I have only had the first fair sleep in a week. We swung the four old Pa 'hacks' into line, & the way we did so was too comical. You must know all about it someday.

We expect Marshall (AM.T) this morning, and learn that he is about as much dead as alive. He worked, as did all of us, from the standpoint of Republicans, and it has proved a good lever.

Glad Marshall is with you. Splendid man. Now I wish that the old fossilised Democrats would take a back seat. You are the great leader of a practically new party. The Republican's & Dem's.

have sold their birthright, but there will be no place for Teddy unless he turns in with you, or leads a small minority of his followers.

I am asking brethren in many States to keep you in constant remembrance before The Throne.

Hope the great lesson will not be lost on Prin. Univ. reactionaries. We have the pictures this mor'g of yourself & family. Be careful of your movements, cranks are always around at such times.   S. H. Thompson Senr.

ALS (Governors' Files, Nj).
    [1] Father of Wilson's students and friends, Alexander Marshall Thompson and Samuel Huston Thompson, Jr. He was a retired Presbyterian minister who had served in Pennsylvania, New York, Iowa, Maryland, Minnesota, and New Jersey and was at this time financial secretary of the Pittsburgh Association for the Improvement of the Poor.

From George Howe III

Dear Uncle Woodrow,   Chapel Hill, N. C. July 3, 1912
    Not all the telegrams & letters in the world can tell you how happy I am in the great victory! And such a unique victory! You can bet your bottom dollar we have been celebrating. The little town has yelled itself hoarse, built bonfires, & had a mass meeting. The joy is not for you alone but for the whole broad country of ours. We *know* that your election will follow and that it will mean a turning point in the history of our nation. We are going on now away from greed & selfishness to better things—hurray! Our faith is pinned to you, & our joy knows no limits!

    I wish I could be there to congratulate you & to join in with the family in its happiness. You will, of course, have no time to answer this—but I am going to try to get a handshake at least on my way to Europe. I shall be passing through in a couple of weeks.

    Love to all the family. Hurray! And a thousand more hurrays!
                        Affectionately,   George Howe

ALS (WP, DLC).

From Richard Theodore Ely

                                        Madison [Wisc.]
Dear Governor Wilson: July third, Nineteen hundred twelve.
    Cordial congratulations on your nomination! I feel proud of you as a former student of mine, and I trust that you will allow me just a little bit of reflected glory.

For the first time I expect to vote for a Democrat for president. All here are enthusiastic, and I think you will have a pretty nearly unanimous vote from our faculty.

Mrs. Ely[1] also is delighted that your name is to be added to the list of Virginia presidents. She joins me in all good wishes to you and Mrs. Wilson.

Ever faithfully yours,   Richard T. Ely

TLS (WP, DLC).
[1] Anna Morris Anderson Ely, who had come from Richmond, Va.

From Francis L. Corrao[1]

Honored Sir,   Brooklyn, N. Y. June [July] 3rd 1912.

I write you as an Italian-American to sincerely congratulate you on your nomination.

I beg to assure you that the intelligent portion of my fellow co[u]ntrymen and citizens have with a becoming sense of propriety declined to pay any attention to the things which some political enemies of yours have in bad faith endeavoured to ascribe to your pen as derogatory of the people of my race.

Long before you wrote the letter of February, 7, 1912, to "L'Araldo Italiano" relative to the matter I as well as every sensible Italian-American believed that you were one of those who "y[i]elded to no one in your ardent admiration for the great people of Italy and that no one who loves the history of liberty should fail to accord to Italians a great place in the history of political freedom."

I shall therefore be very glad to support you with all my power and assure you that every honest Italian-American will do the same.   Respectfully yours,   Francis L. Corrao.

TLS (WP, DLC).
[1] Lawyer and Democratic politician of Brooklyn, who had organized the Italian Columbus Society.

From Frank William Taussig

Vereerter Mynheer Dr. Professor
forkonftiger Präsident Wilson!   Amsterdam, July 3 1912

De nieuw in het dagblad von de sehere candidatuur von Dir is de beste nieuw dat eder ein Fremder het gehebt in ein Fremd Land von sein leiwes Vaderland. Oh Gott im Himmel, is dat eine Freude![1] In fact, as you see, it is quite beyond the range of ordinary language. I have followed the course of events in Baltimore with a lively interest mostly enhanced by the necessity of working out the meaning of the blessed pigeon-german-english of this free country and now I find it impossible to express my satisfaction except in a hodpodge of my own. But Gott im Himmel, it *is* a Freude! To think that in November I shall be able to cast a self-respecting vote for a candidate whom I can unhesitatingly support! So feel I, and hundreds of thousands of independent-minded voters. I can not forbear saying this much to you, even at the risk of adding to your mountain of letters. I am confident you will be the next president, & in that office won't disappoint even the high expectation of your friends & admirers, among whom I am proud to place myself.

Truly & sincerely yours   F. W. Taussig.

Gott im Himmel, don't acknowledge this,—you couldn't anyhow, for I am on the road, not due in U.S. until late July.

ALS (Governors' Files, Nj).
[1] Taussig's mixed Dutch and German reads something like the following in English:
"Honored Mr. Dr. Professor future President Wilson: The news in the newspapers of your nomination is the best news that a foreigner has ever received in a foreign land from his beloved homeland. Good heavens, is not that a joy!"

From William Jennings Bryan

Chicago Ills July 4th 1912

Beg to suggest expresident Roosevelt's attitude makes it necessary for you to select campaign committee composed of most prominent progressives in Contested states   do not desire any more prominence than you think helpful to you but will serve on such committee if you wish.   W. J. Bryan.

T telegram (WP, DLC).

From Francis Fisher Kane

My dear Governor Wilson: Philadelphia. July 4, 1912.

I have waited purposely until today to write to you, but must now give myself that satisfaction. Sure it will be my particular celebration of the day—that glorious Fourth of July, 1912, when we are all saying our Thanksgiving.

Those were brave and honest men who fought for you at Baltimore, and I must admit that I had a feeling of intense gratification as I watched Palmer and our people work for you. For once I had not been in error in my judgment of men. But it was you, Sir, and what you stood for that carried them to victory. That is the moral of it all. They could not have won, had they been fighting for a lesser man, a lesser cause.

Perhaps it is the old mugwump spirit in me, but I like the Evening Post's résumé.[1] I cut it out, and although you probably saw it, I'll enclose it. You have what the Evening Post had, and of course a great deal more—your appeal is to the people. Still, you were the only man before the Convention who had, and who has, the mind and ability to guide as well as give. And therefore (am I the less a Democrat?) I am a Wilson man.

We in Pennsylvania are in a state of ecstasy. I cannot yet work at things quietly and soberly. Am I dreaming or do I really see things as they are? Pennsylvania carried for the Democratic candidate for President? Yes—so it will be, let Teddy do his worst. The enthusiasm for you will be so great that, third party or no third party, you will sweep the State. Berry[2] must be kept from making a fool of himself, but the man's heart is sound if he is a bit irresponsible at times. And his popularity is great.

Wonderful, that with those tariff-for-revenue-only sayings in our platform we should carry Pennsylvania! The explanation of it all is Woodrow Wilson.

Please do not trouble yourself to acknowledge this letter.

Your faithful servant,   Francis Fisher Kane.

ALS (WP, DLC).
[1] He referred to an editorial, "Wilson's Nomination," in the New York *Evening Post*, July 3, 1912. It described Wilson's gifts of political leadership and called his nomination a "popular uprising" which had left the political bosses discredited and defeated.
[2] William H. Berry, former Pennsylvania state treasurer, who had run unsuccessfully for governor in 1910 on a third-party ticket, the Keystone party, supported by progressive Republicans and Democrats.

From William Joseph Martin[1]

My dear Mr. Wilson: Davidson, N. C. 7/4/12

For the college as well as for myself I congratulate you cordially on your recent nomination to the Presidency of our Nation. Still more do I congratulate our party on its selection of its standard bearer and our country on our next President.

I thank God that such a man as yourself can be nominated by one of our great political parties & will be, as I trust, elected in November to our highest office.

Pardon me if I say that I see more in this than your elevation in office & the winning of a Democratic victory. I believe it means that the bed rock of Christian principle & religious freedom is still & will continue to be the real foundation of our Nation.

With hearty goodwill from the old college which is honored in her slight touch with your early life, & with cordial regards for yourself and your family, I am,

Sincerely yours,   Wm. J. Martin

ALS (WP, DLC).
1 President of Davidson College.

To Francis Griffith Newlands

My dear Senator Newlands: [Sea Girt, N. J.] July 5, 1912.

Thank you sincerely for your frank and interesting letter of July first. Though I am reading it after the nomination and after the struggle was all over, I am nonetheless impressed by its candor and insight, and I want to tell you how warmly I appreciate the actions and motives on your part which it so graciously discloses. I am looking forward with the most confident hope to cooperating with you in the future in the interest of real progressive action.

Cordially and faithfully yours,   Woodrow Wilson

TLS (F. G. Newlands Papers, CtY).

From Elisha Benjamin Andrews

My dear Governor Wilson: Lincoln, Nebraska July 5, 1912

I hope it is not too late to offer you my congratulations upon your nomination. I believe you will be elected, in which case the Democratic Party will have before it the most brilliant prospects it has enjoyed since the days of Jackson. Tho myself a New Englander, I rejoice in you as a Virginian and a Southerner, the kith and kin of Washington, Jefferson, Marshall, Madison, Monroe and Robert Lee. It will be given you to restore and cement the Union as has not yet been done.

I glory in your nomination as a recognition of academic worth, training, and attainments. In this aspect your elevation will be gloriously unique. In scholarly and theoretical preparation for the Presidency, you are the peer if not the superior of the finest Chief Executives the Nation has had. I shall expect you to succeed so well that scholarship and politics will be more commonly and more successfully joined in our public life than they have ever been. This will mean for our prosperity more good than words can describe.

I believe that you will be enabled really and justly to reform our damnable tariff, a work worth living and dying for. Poor Cleveland did his best at this, but he lacked both information on the subject and the gift of leadership, in both which particulars natural and acquired gifts render you in my judgment pre-eminent.

As surely as I am able, I shall take the stump for you in October. If I cannot stump, I shall be able to write. I stumped for Cleveland in two campaigns and should speak with much greater cheerfulness and certainty for you.

I take occasion again to thank you for your great kindness in calling upon me at the Sanitarium a year ago.[1] You will of course not think of replying to this.

Yours with the highest esteem and admiration,

E. Benjamin Andrews.

HwLS (WP, DLC).
[1] See the news reported printed at May 27, 1911, Vol. 23.

From Oscar Wilder Underwood

My dear Governor Wilson: Washington, D. C., July 5, 1912.

I am in receipt of your kind telegram this morning and wish to thank you for the kindly words you say in reference to myself.

I feel sure you will be elected President next November and am glad to render any aid in my power to accomplish the desired result. As floor leader of the party in the House of Representatives, I wish to say to you that our action between now and the time of adjournment may affect the campaign and I hope you will not hesitate to advise with me freely as to any matters transpiring in Washington which you may consider essential for the good of the cause.

With kindest regards, I am,

Yours very truly,   O W Underwood

TLS (WP, DLC).

From Hardwicke Drummond Rawnsley

Dear Mr Woodrow Wilson   Keswick [England]. July 5, 1912

I cannot express to you my delight in the result of your nomination as President, and for the sake of probity in politics and high ideal as well as for the sake of literature, I feel I must just

shake hands with you across the Atlantic and send you greeting
from the Lakeland which you love

Yours truly   H D Rawnsley

How glad Wordsworth would have been to know of this success.

ALS (Governors' Files, NjP).

To Mary Allen Hulbert Peck

Dearest Friend,   Sea Girt, New Jersey 6 July, 1912

How often—not to say how constantly—I have thought of you
throughout these two (to me) momentous weeks! It was hard,
very hard, to know, last week, that you were in New York and
not only not come to see you but not even send you a message,
and it will be hard for you to believe that it was literally impossible to do either. You cannot (at least I hope, for your own
comfort, that you cannot) *imagine* such days as I have spent
since I last wrote to you. While the convention was in session
there was hardly a minute between breakfast and midnight
when some one of our little corps was not at the telephone,—on
some business or inquiry connected with the convention. All day
and all evening reporters were in and around the house, without
excuse or ceremony—not a minute of privacy—the transactions
of the convention pervading the whole premises by one wire or
another (for the Western Union had established itself in a tent
on the lawn) and I, your humble servant, expected to be within
touch always—even when all well conducted persons had long
ago gone to bed;—and *this* week, *since* the nomination, an invasion by the people of the United States! I had read of the like,
and *dreaded* it, but of course had never *realized* what it was to
the principal victim. Now I know—and this is actually the first
breathing space, if I was to sleep at all, in which I have been
able to turn to the dear friend to whom my thought has turned
hour after hour, wondering what *she* was thinking about and
doing and feeling. My nomination was a sort of political miracle.
"There is nothing in our political history with which it may be
compared. No man heretofore ever obtained a presidential nomination with such circumstances of distinction, honour, and freedom." (I am quoting from the letter[1] of a student of our history).
I am wondering how all this happened to come to *me*, and
whether, when test is over, I shall have been found to be in any
sense worthy. It is awesome to be so believed in and trusted. It

makes me feel a sort of loneliness, because I cannot speak of it without seeming to be thinking of myself—and reporters haunt me the livelong day. I want my friends to talk to,—and I want them to talk to me! I wonder if a letter from you has been lost to me in the bushels of mail now pouring in upon us, to be opened by clerks? I need one very much. Are you well? I think of you with a great solicitude. Please write. It will so refresh and reassure me! All send most affectionate greetings. When am I to be within reach of seeing you again?

Your devoted friend,   Woodrow Wilson

ALS (WP, DLC).
  ¹ It is missing.

To William Jennings Bryan

[Sea Girt, N. J., July 6, 1912]

Thank you sincerely for your telegram. Your judgment in the matter is absolutely sound and you may be sure that it is also mine. On all sides I hear the finest things said about your part in the convention.   Woodrow Wilson.

T telegram (WP, DLC).

To George Howe III

My dear George: [Sea Girt, N. J.] July 6, 1912.

Thank you with all my heart for your letter of July third. I knew how you would feel, but it is very delightful to have you say it.

For myself, I feel very solemn about the whole thing. It is a very deep responsibility just because I have been so trusted and the nomination has been won in such a way as to leave me absolutely free of private obligations.

All join me in the warmest love to you, and we shall count on seeing you on your way to the steamer.

Affectionately yours,   Woodrow Wilson

TLS (photostat in RSB Coll., DLC).

To Oscar Wilder Underwood

My dear Mr. Underwood,   Sea Girt, New Jersey 7 July, 1912

May I not send you this additional line, to bear my most cordial greetings and to express the hope that, so soon as your duties in

Washington will permit, I may have the pleasure of seeing you here. I would greatly enjoy, and should greatly profit by a talk with you on the policy best for the party.

Cordially and Sincerely yours,   Woodrow Wilson

ALS (O. W. Underwood Papers, A-Ar).

To Walter Hines Page

My dear Page,   Sea Girt, New Jersey 7 July, 1912

I have wanted to write you a line of grateful appreciation ever since I received that delightful little note of hope from you written on June 19, but it has been impossible until this moment. Even now I can write only a line; but it is full of warm feeling. Your friendship and your generous faith in me are a source of cheer and of strength to me all the time.

Sincerely Your Friend,   Woodrow Wilson

ALS (W. H. Page Papers, MH).

From Richard Evelyn Byrd

My dear Governor,   Sea Girt, New Jersey Sunday [July 7, 1912]

I did not drop in yesterday because I know the immense strain you must be undergoing in seeing so many people. I thoroughly enjoyed seeing you & meeting your family and am grateful for your kindness and consideration. I am going back to Virginia to see to it that you get a great & memorable majority.

Do husband your strength my dear Governor. Don't see any more people than you can help. Take all the rest you can.

Faithfully yours,   Richard Evelyn Byrd

P.S. I promised to mention the fact that Mr. William Rozell of Richmond has a patent method, of dealing with trusts which he will communicate to you. Please consider it mentioned.

REB

ALS (Governors' Files, Nj).

To William Jennings Bryan

My dear Mr. Bryan: Sea Girt, N. J. July 8, 1912.

I have not seen the full text of it as I hope I shall, but your "valedictory," spoken in the last hours of the Convention at Baltimore, seems to me a peculiarly noble thing and constituting a fitting close to a Convention in which you played a part which the whole country now recognizes and assesses at its true significance.

Will you not let me send you this additional cordial message of regard with the hope that as soon as convenient to you, when you come East again, I may have the pleasure and profit of a talk with you.   Cordially yours,   Woodrow Wilson

TLS (W. J. Bryan Papers, DLC).

From Sydney Brooks

Dear Governor Wilson,   Kensington, W. July 10/12.

It seems almost absurd to "congratulate" anyone on assuming so vast & sobering a responsibility as has been laid upon you; & I flatter myself that even though we have only met once, we understand one another well enough to dispense with such formalities. But I should like to say this—that your nomination fills me with a new hope for American politics.

You will win of course; & though it is foolish to prophesy about any politics, & almost immoral to do so about American politics, I predict it will be by a majority such as has never yet been registered in the Electoral College. Allow me to say that I regard that prospect with some mingled feelings on your own account but with the profoundest satisfaction from the standpoint of your country's welfare & the sanity of its development. I look forward especially to your doing two things. One is making the Democrats—if anything can make them—a Party. The other is making the Presidency, what it has never been in my time, a centre of intellectual statesmanship. And I promise myself the pleasure of coming over to America & observing your performance of these tasks at close range.

I think I do more writing on American affairs in the English papers & reviews than any other man; & I venture in that capacity to ask if you will be so good as to give my name & address to the Manager of your Campaign Press Bureau, with instructions to forward to me all the "literature"—some of it, I fancy, will wring your soul—that is published on your behalf. I should particularly like your own speeches & addresses during the past two years.

Will you also kindly recall me to your two daughters whom I had the pleasure of meeting & believe me, with hearty good wishes,   Yours very sincerely   Sydney Brooks.

ALS (Governors' Files, Nj).

From Oscar Wilder Underwood

My dear Governor Wilson: Washington, D. C., July 10, 1912.

I am in receipt this morning of your kind note of the seventh instant and shall be pleased to come to Sea Girt to call on you at an early date. On account of several matters of importance now pending in the House, I will be prevented from leaving here this week but I will be glad to come down to see you not later than the early part of next week.

The party is in entire harmony in the House and I feel assured of your election in November from the good news I am hearing from over the country.

Sincerely yours, O W Underwood

TLS (WP, DLC).

To Cyrus Hall McCormick

Personal.

My dear Cyrus: [Sea Girt, N. J.] July 11, 1912.

Your friendship is always so generous and your confidence in me so delightful that I hardly know how sufficiently to thank you for your notes of the eighth.[1] I feel that I have a very high standard to live up to just because I am so trusted and believed in, and it touches me very deeply that you should feel as you do. Our life-long friendship has given you a real chance to test me and you must realize how particularly grateful it is to me to be assured that the test has not lessened your affection for me. I know that I may trust you in every way.

Affectionately yours, Woodrow Wilson

TLS (WP, DLC).
[1] C. H. McCormick to WW, July 8, 1912 (two letters), ALS (WP, DLC).

From Luke Lea

My dear Governor: Washington, D. C. July 13th, 1912.

I had hoped all week that the Lorimer case might be finished so I could go to Seagirt and present to you certain questions as they appear to your friends here. As soon as the vote was taken Saturday I telephoned your secretary for an en[g]agement with you Sunday, but found you would be out of the city until Monday, and as I must be in Nashville Tuesday it rendered a personal visit at this time impossible and made it necessary for me to present by letter the matter I had in mind.

Yesterday I had a long talk with Senator La Follette about you and your candidacy and it was at his urgent request that I determined finally to make certain suggestions to you in regard to your campaign. He wanted his position made clear that under no circumstances does he now expect to give you active support. On the other hand he does not want any condition to arise that will cause him to attack you or your candidacy. He called attention to the active support that is being given to you by the President of the University of Wisconsin[1]—a close personal friend of his—and The Journal, the most influential paper in Milwaukee which is edited by a devoted friend of his.[2] He said he believed you would carry Wisconsin if your presidential campaign impressed the country as quite as progressive as your pre-convention campaign. La Follettee expressed the belief that the real fight would be between you and Roosevelt in November and that Taft would not win the electoral vote of more than six states— a view very generally shared by the shrewdest of the Washington correspondents and by many well-informed members of Congress.

La Follettee then wanted me to advise you that it would be a great mistake for you to appoint or have Mr. McCombs selected as your campaign manager or chairman of the National Committee and gave the following story as partial evidence of the weakness of such a selection:

According to La Follette George L. Record, formerly his and your warm supporter, but now a devoted Roosevelt adherent, and the sponsor for New Jersey of Roosevelt's Progressive party, told him (La Follette) that after your speech upon the money trust you had an interview with him (Record) and explained that at McCombs' suggestion you were going to stop making such progressive speeches for a time; that the Progressive Democrats were for you and it was the part of discretion[,] according to McCombs, for you not to alienate entirely the conservative element of the party; that while you did not agree with McCombs nevertheless you had agreed to such a policy for the time being. La Follette believes you had such a conversation with Record and that for this reason, if for no other, you should not select McCombs as your manager, as it will place a weapon in the hands of your keenest competitor that it is unnecessary for him to have. La-Follette is confident that Record has communicated to Roosevelt this alleged interview with you. He stated further that he was most anxious for you to make no mistakes that would result in Roosevelt's election.

Irrespective of whether you had this conversation with Record or not it would seem that your selection of McCombs would be unfortunate for many reasons:

First—Roosevelt would attempt to make much of the Record interview, and McCombs' opposition to Progressive ideas if McCombs was your selection.

Second—McCombs' selection would not be regarded by a great many Democrats as a Progressive appointment, as he is believed to be reactionery in his beliefs and desires and entirely out of sympathy with progressibe [progressive] policies except for campaign purposes.

This estimate of McCombs is doubtless due in part to severe criticism he made of Bryan during the pre-convention campaign. He went so far on one occasion as to criticise Bryan most severely in the presence of Senator Briggs of New Jersey and Louis Brownlow, a newspaper man of this city, when the criticisms were absolutely unjust. He also dissaproved openly and loudly of every move made by Bryan at Baltimore, although they subsequently resulted at least in defeat of Clark. It is reported that this was especially true of his attitude toward Bryan's opposition to Judge Parker, the Ryan-Belmont resolution and the manner in which Nebraska's vote was changed from Clark to Wilson.

Third—McCombs' selection would tend to separate rather than to cement the personal and political relations between Mr. Bryan and yourself, for this relationship to be most intimate is regarded by your true friends as of the utmost importance. Rumors to the contrary Bryan does not desire to dominate or dictate any feature of your campaign or administration, and I do not believe he would accept a cabinet position in your administration, as has been so often suggested in the press, even if all of the cabinet positions were welded into one and that one offered him. Mr. Bryan, however, must be recognized as a tremendous force for good in the party and in the nation and nothing could be more unfortunate than for the new and old leader of progress in the party to be separated in the hour of victory when the opportunity for service is dawning.

Fourth—Your nomination was not the result of organization or management, but of the spontaneous demand of the country for your nomination on account of the enemies you have made as well as the principles your candidacy embodied. Hence there was not opportunity for any exhibition of managerial ability and the general verdict at Baltimore among the delegates and visitors—, only a small number of whom even knew any one was your manager,—was that you won in spite of having neither effective management or organization. Therefore, McCombs' ability, not

being regarded as sufficiently extraordinary to justify his appointment, his appointment would be believed to have been
made on account of these things that are so objectionable to one
element of the party.

Fifth—An Eastern man, from a state adjoining yours, should
not be selected. If he is the proper man at all, his appointment
should not strengthen you with the powers that be in New York
and since the Baltimore convention New York Democracy has
not been very popular with that of the rest of the country.

Summing up, McCombs' selection would be a mistake on account of his location, because it would ultimately alienate from
you a large part of the rank and file of the Bryan following; because it would drive away, instead of drawing to you, the bulk
of the Progressive Republican vote; and because it would be regarded as the resuscitation of those elements that were crushed
in the death struggle at Baltimore. . . .

If this letter contains any suggestion that may be of service
to you, I shall be recompensed for overcoming my hesitancy and
reluctance to write you thus. If on the other hand it is worthy
only of the waste basket I will nevertheless feel that I have convinced you of one fact at least—my great interest in all that pertains to you and your successful leadership of our party.

Very faithfully yours,   Luke Lea.

P.S.—It is unnecessary for me to state the reasons that I beg
that this letter be treated as absolutely confidential.

TLS (WP, DLC).
[1] Charles R. Van Hise.
[2] Lucius W. Nieman.

From Akos Weltnar and Cornelius Csongrávi[1]

Dear Mr. Governor: New York, July 13, 1912

In a certain literary work of yours you talk disparagingly of
our fellow Hungarian-Americans. We are sure you are wrong in
this respect. But inasmuch as many of our readers are Democrats, that is to say, are believers in the principles the American
Democratic Party stands for, and are looking to us for advice
how to vote in this campaign, our board of directors appointed a
committee to ask an audience with you to ascertain your present
views as to the American citizens of Hungarian birth.

Now we ask your Excellency most respectfully are you willing
to receive this committee? And should you be willing to grant

an audience to them, please be kind enough to notify us of the day and place where and when should they ask to see you.

Yours most respectfully,

Akos Weltnar,

Cornelius Csongrávi.

ALS (WP, DLC).

¹ Weltnar was the president and Csongrávi the editor and secretary of the Concord Publishing Co. of New York, publishers of *Egyetértés* (*Concord*), a Hungarian-language daily newspaper.

From David Benton Jones

Personal suggestions

My dear Governor: Chicago July 13, 1912.

I want to make an attempt to reduce to a very few sentences the general conclusion of numerous conversations which have taken place at our luncheon table when only Mr. Wilson,¹ my brother and myself have been present. As you know, Mr. Wilson is in the throes of making an attempt to reorganize the International Harvester Company in conformity with the Sherman Law and the suggestions of the Government; and as my brother is a member of the Board, consideration of the subject has not been academic in character.

We are all agreed, first, that supervision or regulation of trusts by commission is not practicable or possible.

Second, that the Government must establish and maintain *competitive conditions* in the industrial field. It cannot compel competition, but it can prevent a corporation from monopolizing the raw materials of production and it can and must prevent agreements and practices which limit or restrain trade in the distribution of its products. If it does this it is certain that in time competition or the danger of competition will be a powerful regulator of prices.

Third, that the decrees of Court in the interpretation or enforcement of the law are certain to become more and more drastic as the earlier decrees are found to be ineffectual or defective in accomplishing the purposes for which the law was enacted. If, therefore, people can possess themselves in patience the Courts, in the interpretation of the anti-trust law, are certain to see to it that the purposes of its enactment will find effective interpretation in the decrees of Court.

The treatment of the trust problem is the great puzzle of the present time. You are, as I see it, not compelled to enter upon a detailed exposition of your views on this subject. No one is far-seeing enough to make that a safe venture at the present time. What gives Mr. Roosevelt his great power and advantage before the country is the fact that he merely asserts his determination to establish righteousness even if he has to destroy representative government and violate the great majority of the ten command-ments in doing it. If he were compelled to define exactly what he meant by establishing righteousness he would make himself ridiculous. He is that as it is in the eyes of sane people.

It is almost cruel to send you a letter of any kind when your mail is so burdensome, but on this one subject of the trusts I am confident you cannot get from outside wiser or more disin-terested and experienced judgment than Mr. Wilson's. Naturally his conclusions should not be quoted as his. In the peculiar posi-tion that he occupies it would be misunderstood.

Very sincerely yours,   David B. Jones.

TLS (WP, DLC).
  [1] John P. Wilson, senior partner of the legal firm of Wilson, Moore and Mc-Ilvaine. He represented many leading corporations.

To Mary Allen Hulbert[1]

Dearest Friend,   [Atlantic Highlands, N. J.] 14 July, 1912

What *does* this pathetic little note from The Manhattan mean? *What* has the world taken away from you? Let me tell you some-thing. Not until yesterday did I see your sweet letter of the fifth.[2] It had been engulfed in the flood of letters (five thousand of them) that poured in on me after the nomination,—and is still running strong—and, notwithstanding my best search for it—for I was wondering all the while what could have become of it, since I never doubted for a moment that you had written, unless you were ill—had waited for the slow and stupid sorting which green and dull clerks had been attempting. When I got hold of it I devoured it with delight. It was like one of your old letters. A little peace had crept into it,—a quiet enjoyment of the quaint people you were working with, and that deep joy in the splendid nature that was about you that is so characteristic of you. You belong in every fibre to the world of natural, beautiful, exquisite, free, and untainted things that God has made and man has not spoiled. By the sea or in the woods or on the open heath, or in the old, romantic lanes of a place like Bermuda, where the very work of man seems the work of nature—in the sawn-out walls

and the cottages built out of the very ground they stand upon,—
you are yourself, and happiness wells up in you, despite every
adverse circumstance of your life; and those who know you and
are close to you feel the thrill of one of the sweetest, freest, no-
blest natures God ever put in a beautiful and noble form. But in
New York, in a hot hotel, just back from I know not what
trying experiences at Pittsfield, no wonder a cry of pain comes
from you. I understand and I sympathize till it cuts to the quick
and hurts. But what have you lost? Do you mean the chance to
see those who understand and who are your devoted friends?
That is only for a little while. The life I am leading now *can't*
keep up. It is inconceivable that it should. I wish I could describe
it to you, but I fear it is as indescribable as it is inconceivable.
Not a moment am I left free to do what I would. I thought last
night that I should go crazy with the strain and confusion of
it,—and so I ran away! I am not at Sea Girt. I am just outside the
little village of Atlantic Highlands by Sandy Hook. A good friend
here, Mr. Melvin Rice, has a big place ("Drynock Farms") where
he lives in lonely state with his wife (no children). He saw my
distress, beset and helpless at the Governor's Cottage and took
pity on me. He insisted that I take asylum with him whenever
the hunt harassed me beyond endurance. Last evening, therefore, after an intolerable day, in desperation, I telephoned him
I was coming. At six I got in a motor, at seven thirty was here;
had a delightful dinner and a quiet chat (ah, what a luxury!)
on the lawn under the trees, and at half after nine turned in. I
slept till noon to-day, like a tired boy, and now (how much better than a chat on the lawn!) am opening all my mind to my
dear friend who is never again going to distress me with a note
like that. If *I* ever change it will never be at the heart! The morning (I awoke long enough to see) was overcast. Just after I got
down, at 1.15 a violent thunderstorm broke, and now we are
shut in by a steady, cool, friendly rain which makes our chat
doubly secure.

And now tell me what has happened. You sign that pitiful little
note "M. A. Hulbert." If I wanted to tease you, I would conjecture
that what you had lost was indicated by the signature! Is it indeed over? Have you been set free? I hope with all my heart
that the dreaded trial is entirely over, and that there was less
hateful talk and publicity than you feared there would be. I am
very, very anxious to hear all about it. Remember that I have
plenty of time to listen to what I want to hear and to think of
those of whom I want to think. These flocking people monopo-
lize my time, but not my thoughts. They cannot crowd in there,

or take possession of my soul. Indeed, the more these things crowd upon me the more I seem to be dependent for peace and joy upon those I love. The more public my life becomes the more I seem driven in upon my own inner life and all its intimate companionships. Letters have come to me from persons of the first consequence and the most valued judgment, for example, which have bestowed upon me praise and encouragement which ought, I suppose, to have made me very proud and very happy. But they have not weighed with me at all as compared with the unselfish joy of a letter like yours from "Sandanwede," with its affectionate confidence in me and its message (it seemed a message from beginning to end, as all your letters do) of deep, abiding friendship. I bless you for it! These things keep me alive and fresh and ready for the trial, the long, unbroken trial, of what I must now go through. Nothing has been lost,—or, if it has, it is only for a little while and will presently be recovered, fresher and finer than ever!

All would join me in affectionate messages if they were here. Ellen begged me to thank you most warmly for your letter to her.

Your devoted friend   Woodrow Wilson

If you will mark your letters "Personal and Private" they will not go through the mill, but will come direct to my hands.

W. W.

ALS (WP, DLC).
[1] She changed her name to Hulbert on receiving her divorce on July 9.
[2] It is missing, as are most of her letters for this period.

To Nicholas L. Piotrowski

My Dear Mr. Piotrowski: Sea Girt, N. J. July 15, 1912.

I am sure that you will understand the way in which my days have been absorbed by things important and unimportant since the nomination and that you will have already made generous allowance for my delay in replying to your generous letter of July fifth.[1] I have received no letter which I value more highly. Your kindness is very great and I am sure that the assistance you will give will be absolutely invaluable. I am going to take the liberty of turning to you a little later just as soon as we have effected our campaign organization. In the meantime will you not accept my warmest assurances of personal regard and of the high value which I hold your kind friendship?

Cordially yours,   Woodrow Wilson

TCL (RSB Coll., DLC).
[1] It is missing.

From Thomas Jones Pence

Chicago Ills July 15/12

McCombs elected chairman [Joseph E.] Davies secy and resolutions for appointment committe[e] of nine went through unanimously   meeting harmonious and enthusiastic and splendid good spirit prevails   every member confident of your election and ready for success of ticket   Thos J Pence

T telegram (WP, DLC).

To William Jennings Bryan

My dear Mr. Bryan: [Sea Girt, N. J.] July 16, 1912.

Thank you for your note[1] about Mr. Osborn[2] and Senator O'Gorman. I am very much pleased indeed that your judgment is what it is of Senator O'Gorman, and I shall greatly rely upon his judgment in matters concerning New York.

I wish you could hear what I hear on every hand with regard to your action in the Convention. By your stand there you have made yourself what would have seemed impossible—a bigger man than ever in the estimation of the people of the country.

I warmly appreciate your generous notes.

Cordially and sincerely yours,   Woodrow Wilson

TLS (W. J. Bryan Papers, DLC).
[1] W. J. Bryan to WW, July 12, 1912, ALS (WP, DLC).
[2] Thomas Mott Osborne.

From John H. G. Davis[1]

Dear Sir   [Chicago, Ill.] July 16 1912

We have just concluded a Straw Ballott of about 3000 which showed among my people that 1500 were for Teddie 400 for Taft 1100 for you which I consider an exceptionally good showing for you. I joined the Democrat party in 1910 and have been a fierce & fearless agitator every since. I only think it necessary to put some good men in the field to convince the Negro that you & your party will be our friends & goodly number of the colored voters will support the party this fall. hoping you every success I am at your services & remain   J. H. G. Davis

ALS (WP, DLC).
[1] A porter for the Chicago, Milwaukee & St. Paul Railway in Chicago.

From Charles Richard Van Hise, with Enclosure

Manhattan Beach, N. Y.

My dear Governor Wilson,   July 16, 1912

When I returned to New York from Sea Girt, I had a message from Col. Roosevelt saying he wished to see me. The subject with which we conferred was his platform. In this connection, without any suggestion from me, he said he was going to wire Dr. McCarthy[1] to come on to help him. This put me in a very embarrassing position. Considering what I had said to you, I hardly knew what to do, but finally decided to wire Mr. Crane[2] at Chicago the facts.

This morning I have a telegram from Dr. McCarthy which I enclose for your information.

With high regard, I remain

Very sincerely yours,   Charles R Van Hise

ALS (WP, DLC).

[1] Charles McCarthy, Ph.D., Wisconsin, 1901, of Madison, Wisc., expert on state government and legislation, organizer and director of the first state legislative reference library and bill-drafting bureau in the United States, author of *The Wisconsin Idea* (New York, 1912). Roosevelt did send a telegram to McCarthy on July 14, requesting his assistance with a draft platform and speeches. McCarthy conferred with Roosevelt on July 20. Edward A. Fitzpatrick, *McCarthy of Wisconsin* (New York, 1944), p. 157.

[2] Charles Richard Crane, Chicago manufacturer of plumbing equipment. He was the largest single contributor to Senator La Follette's campaign for the Republican presidential nomination, giving $26,684.40 of the Senator's reported $67,815.56 in contributions. He gave $10,000 to Wilson's preconvention campaign in two installments on March 28 and April 30, 1912, while still making frequent sizable contributions to La Follette. His objective, he said later, was to secure the nomination of a progressive by one or both of the major parties. See *Campaign Contributions: Testimony before a Subcommittee of the Committee on Privileges and Elections*, United States Senate, Sixty-Second Cong., 3rd sess. (2 vols., Washington, 1913), I, 570-571, 573-77. Crane was soon to become vice-chairman of the finance committee for Wilson's campaign and the largest single contributor ($40,000).

E N C L O S U R E

Charles McCarthy to Charles Richard Van Hise

Madison Wis July 16 [1912]

Am going east in a couple of days   If W. wants to see me I shall go if he wires[1]   Chas McCarthy.

Hw telegram (WP, DLC).

[1] Wilson did telegraph McCarthy on July 17, requesting a "talk" with him when he came east. He came to Sea Girt about July 20 but was not permitted to see Wilson due to some confusion among the staff. See C. McCarthy to WW, Aug. 17, 1912, TLS (WP, DLC), and Fitzpatrick, *McCarthy of Wisconsin*, pp. 157-58.

A News Report

[July 17, 1912]

WILSON SOON TO STATE POSITION

Will Tell Whether or Not He Will Remain in Gubernatorial Chair.

PLEASED WITH UNDERWOOD

SEA GIRT, July 17.—In the next few days Governor Wilson is going to have something positive to say publicly about the question of his retaining the Gubernatorial chair. . . .

Governor Wilson returned to his cottage here last night in high good humor. It had been an extremely satisfying day for him. His talk with Representative Oscar W. Underwood at the Mercer County Country Club, near Trenton, was both instructive and productive of much happiness.

Mr. Underwood made a hit with the Governor and the Governor was pictured in glowing terms by Underwood. The two men got along famously during the afternoon; in fact, one could not help contrasting the attitude of Mr. Underwood with the demeanor of Champ Clark when he came to Sea Girt last Saturday afternoon.

Mr. Underwood emphasized the difference between himself and Mr. Clark when he declared that "when he pulled down the banner there were no sore spots left."

The Governor had this to say concerning Mr. Underwood:

"I don't know of any man that I have met in a long time that I have taken such a fancy to. I found him entirely charming. He has a singular frankness and openness and charm about him. We had a fine talk, going over the situation in the debatable States in a way that was most satisfactory. We talked like two men who had known each other for a long time." . . .

Governor Wilson smiled when told that Mr. Underwood had referred all inquirers to him for information, and remarked that there was really no reason why he should have taken that stand, as there was nothing at all of a private nature in their talk.

"We discussed the whole political situation as two friends equally interested in the success of our party," was the way the Governor summed up what had taken place at the meeting. "We discussed it up and down in all its aspects, interspersed with just enough stories to prevent its becoming monotonous."

The Governor and Mr. Underwood returned to the State house shortly after 3 o'clock in the afternoon.

The Governor at once resumed the task of receiving callers, who by that time had congregated in some numbers in the big reception-room. . . .

Governor Wilson's last callers before he left Trenton were a delegation of colored men, who were brought here by A. B. Cosey, of Newark.[1] The visitors were Rev. J. Milton Waldron, of Washington, organizer for the National Independent Political League; William Monroe Trotter of Boston, editor of The Guardian, which is the official organ of the league; Robert N. Wood, of New York,[2] and William C. Harris, of Washington.[3] They had a long conference with the Governor, at the close of which the Governor returned to Sea Girt by automobile.

Printed in the *Newark Evening News*, July 17, 1917.
  [1] Alfred B. Cosey, lawyer of Newark.
  [2] Robert N. Wood, inspector in the New York City Bureau of Highways, member of the Democratic State Committee, active for many years in Tammany Hall.
  [3] William C. Harris, a mechanic at the Washington Navy Yard.

To Edward Mandell House

My dear Friend: Sea Girt, N. J. July 17, 1912.

I value most highly your letter of July ninth.[1] It read like familiar matter because when you outlined your plan of campaign to me, orally, it made such an impression on me that I have carried it in my head ever since with great distinctness. But there are additional details, as you now outline it, and I am extremely obliged to you for letting me have this memorandum.

I need not tell you how warmly I appreciated your message of congratulation[2] or how eagerly I shall wait your return. It is selfish to wish for you and I hope that you will not risk anything in regard to your health by coming too soon, but it will be delightful and reassuring to see you.

With warmest regard,
                          Gratefully yours   Woodrow Wilson

TLS (E. M. House Papers, CtY).
  [1] It is missing in WP, DLC, and in the House Papers.
  [2] It is missing.

To Ralph Pulitzer

Personal.

My dear Mr. Pulitzer: Sea Girt, N. J. July 17, 1912.

I am sure you have attributed my delay in replying to your kind message of July third[1] to the real cause, the necessity for meeting the many distracting calls upon my time which have been made and inevitably made, since the nomination. I am sure also that I need not assure you of the pleasure that your message gave. The generous support of the World had already made me aware of your own feeling about the nomination, and I am sure that it had the greatest influence upon the result. I am honored to be so supported.

Cordially and sincerely yours,   Woodrow Wilson

TLS (WP, DLC).
¹ R. Pulitzer to WW, July 3, 1912, Hw telegram (WP, DLC).

To Walter Hines Page

My dear Page: [Sea Girt, N. J.] July 17, 1912.

Never do it again! Never go by without invading my office if I am not otherwise accessible. I must plunge now into the preparation of my speech of acceptance. I am given so little time to do anything that I am fearful I shall not be able to do it as well as it ought to be done. But just so soon as that is off my hands, I shall be a trifle freer. Let me know by telephone or telegraph when you are coming this way again and we *must* hit it off.

Cordially and sincerely yours,   Woodrow Wilson

TLS (W. H. Page Papers, MH).

To Charles Williston McAlpin

My dear McAlpin: [Sea Girt, N. J.] July 18, 1912.

Your telegram and your letter of July tenth¹ made me very happy. I have several times tried to tell you what your friendship has meant to me but have always failed to do it adequately, and now it seems to me that it has a particular value and the pleasure it gives has added poignancy. Those were dark days, some of them, in Princeton and your constant confidence in me and our frank conferences together meant a vast deal to me. You won then and shall always have my genuine affection.

Pray, come down to Sea Girt any time you choose except next week when I shall be much of the time away. It would be delightful to see you.

Mrs. Wilson joins me in warm regards to Mrs. McAlpin² and I am,   Always your sincere friend,   Woodrow Wilson

TLS (photostat in RSB Coll., DLC).
¹ Both are missing.
² Sara Carter Pyle McAlpin.

From William Monroe Trotter

Dear Sir: Boston, Mass July 18, 1912

I write to thank you for the considerate hearing you gave us on Tuesday. In my eagerness not to waste time in getting to the main point I forgot to present the letter of introduction from Governor Foss which I now enclose[1] because he wrote it and that you may know of my sincerity in trying to do away with color prejudice and its horrible effects in color segregation, disfranchisement and lynching.

I also enclose the editorial leader of the leading Republican Colored paper[2] to show that an occasion has been already created for your making now a public statement on your attitude when elected toward Colored Americans.

I am saying that you told us that you were not in sympathy with race and color prejudice, or with discrimination, disfranchisement or lynching because of race or color, that you respect the constitution in its entirety including the amendments and will carry out the law not only according to its letter and spirit, but in the spirit of the Christian religion, endeavoring to be a Christian gentleman to all, according even-handed justice and equal rights to all regardless of race, color or nativity.[3]

I find many Colored men ready to vote for you if assured by you that in so doing they would not be voting for a President who would disregard the fourteenth and fifteenth amendments as part of the supreme law of the land. They sincerely desire to feel that you will be the democrat to begin the end of democratic aggression against their civil and political rights and that you will if elected exercise your personal influence with the Southern democracy in favor of fairer treatment of their Colored neighbors as men.

You could hardly realize the deep earnestness of this feeling. That is why we are glad you expressed yourself as willing to make a statement. No statement second-handed will satisfy the Colored people. To be credited it must come from you. When you say you accept the Amendments as the settlement of the issues arising out of the Civil war, thousands will flock to your standard to rebuke recreant Republicanism and begin the era of friendship with traditional foes.

Yours very sincerely,   Wm. Monroe Trotter.

TLS (WP, DLC).
[1] It is missing.
[2] The enclosure was the clipping of an editorial, "Wilson and the Negro," *New York Age*, July 11, 1912. The gist of its argument came in the first paragraph: "The NEW YORK AGE does not see how it will be possible for a single

self-respecting Negro in the United States to vote for Woodrow Wilson. He was born in Virginia and lived a good part of his life in Georgia and Alabama. Both by inheritance and absorption, he has most of the prejudices of the narrowest type of Southern white people against the Negro." The editorial continued with other statements to support this assertion. Princeton University, under Wilson, was "the one large institution in a Northern State" that closed its doors to Negroes. As governor, Wilson had "not by the turn of the finger recognized a single Negro in New Jersey," though he owed his election to black votes. Moreover, even if Wilson personally was favorably disposed to the recognition of Negroes, he was the nominee of a party which had refused to put "a single word" regarding Negroes in its platform, and he was beholden for his nomination to such southern demagogues as James K. Vardaman and Benjamin R. Tillman.

3 Trotter probably published a statement along these lines in his *Guardian*; however, no issues of this newspaper are extant for this period, and his statement was not reprinted.

From Charles Sumner Hamlin

Dear Gov. Wilson: Boston, Mass., July 18, 1912.

I enclose herewith an editorial from the Boston Herald of July 17, 1912.¹ This paper has several times made references to this subject and I am inclined to think that there is to be a general attack upon you all along the line as to this matter.

I wish very much that I could some time have a talk with some representative of yours with regard to this in order to be able to meet it decisively at the proper time. I think a decisive word at the outset may stop this annoying kind of attack. If you could have a very short statement made, it would give your supporters here an opportunity, I think, to end the matter decisively.   Very sincerely yours,   Charles S. Hamlin

TLS (WP, DLC).
1 The editorial, "The Wilson Mystery," raised the question of Wilson's conduct during the graduate college controversy at Princeton University. The writer apparently had access to inside information supplied by Wilson's opponents on the Board of Trustees. He referred in particular to Wilson's conduct at the meeting of January 13, 1910, especially his denial that he had read Andrew F. West's brochure, *The Proposed Graduate College of Princeton University*, at the time that he wrote its preface (see the Editorial Note, "Wilson at the Meeting of the Board of Trustees of January 13, 1910," Vol. 20). The writer of the editorial mentioned the Rev. Dr. John DeWitt as one trustee who could give the true story. While professing that the *Boston Herald* was not "disposed to speak unkindly" of Wilson, the writer added that the facts relating to these matters should be made public and the views of Wilson's opponents at Princeton should be sought out before the nation made its choice of the next President of the United States.

To William Joseph Martin

My dear President Martin: Sea Girt, N. J. July 19, 1912.

It was very delightful to get a greeting from my old college and I want to thank you very cordially for it and for the message

of your letter of July fourth. It is messages of this kind that make
public life worth while.

Cordially and sincerely yours,   Woodrow Wilson

TLS (W. J. Martin Papers, NcDaD).

To Oscar Wilder Underwood

Personal.

My dear Mr. Underwood: Sea Girt, N. J. July 19, 1912.

I have just had a talk with my friend, Representative Jones of
Virginia, about the Philippine bill.[1] He tells me that he learns
from Ex-Governor Curry[2] that Mr. Roosevelt has certain purposes
about the treatment of the Philippine question in his platform[3]
which led me to believe that it might be wise to reconsider our
judgment of the other day about the immediate passage of Mr.
Jones' bill.[4]

The net result of my conversation with Mr. Jones is this: So
far as I myself am concerned and so far as the tactics of the
campaign are concerned, I think it a matter so debatable, whether
it would give us embarrassment or give us an advantage, that I
am perfectly willing to leave the whole matter to the judgment
of the leaders of the House. I shall be perfectly willing to have
the bill brought up at any time that it seems best to them. I do
not think that it would embarrass the campaign in any way and
that perhaps there is a slight preponderance of argument in
favor of the immediate passage of the bill.

I am very much obliged to you for having paid me the compliment of consulting me in this matter.

With the pleasantest recollections of our meeting the other
day, I am,

Cordially and sincerely yours,   Woodrow Wilson

TLS (O. W. Underwood Papers, A-Ar).
   [1] On March 20, 1912, William A. Jones of Virginia introduced H.R. 22143,
largely drafted by Manuel L. Quezon, which reorganized the government of
the Philippines and set a definite date for the independence of the islands. It
provided for elected lower and upper houses of the Philippine legislature, independence eight years thereafter, and the stationing of American troops in the
islands for twenty additional years to protect the new government against foreign interference. The bill was reported out of committee on April 2, 1912.
See Peter W. Stanley, *A Nation in the Making: The Philippines and the United
States, 1899-1921* (Cambridge, Mass., 1974), pp. 172-73.
   [2] George Curry, congressman from New Mexico, 1912-13; governor of New
Mexico Territory, 1907-11; various posts in the Philippines, 1899-1907.
   [3] As it turned out, the Progressive platform did not mention the Philippines.
   [4] When he was in Washington on April 4, Wilson told Representative Jones
that the Democratic party had better campaign issues than the Philippine question and ought not to divert attention from them by raising the question of
independence. Stanley, *A Nation in the Making*, pp. 173-74, 300n56.

To Mary Allen Hulbert

My dearest Friend,   [Atlantic Highlands, N. J.] 21 July, 1912

All week I have turned the hundreds of letters over that came in by each post in the vain hope of finding a letter from you! I hope, I *hope* you are not ill, that you are not blue,—that nothing but what affects neither your health nor your happiness has prevented your writing; but I cannot help being anxious. My thoughts turn constantly to Nantucket, searching for my dear friend,—seeking some glimpse of what she is doing or thinking. I am not writing from Sea Girt,—the caption of this paper to the contrary notwithstanding,—but am again in asylum at my good friend Rice's quiet place,—where I may spend the greater part of the week so as to be free to write my speech of acceptance. I do not *like* to be away from home,—the fact is I get very homesick,—but it is literally impossible to have an uninterrupted hour, even on Sundays, at that little house standing there accessible to everybody on the open camp ground. The idle and curious crowds, collected from one end of the long coast to the other, surge at our very door as the sea surges at yours, and without stirring in us the emotions that the sea stirs in you. I like to think of you out there upon Nantucket island! You do not belong in New England: you never did belong there; but you are not caged now. You are free. You are like a splendid flower, native of rich woods or the breezy mountain side, transplanted to those sands, to dominate them with a new note of life and colour. Or, rather,—for you are not like anything inanimate and rooted to the spot,—you are like some free creature, some child of beauty and free force, who might have been born in Greece or in Scandinavia, or in the free West, where there are no *types* but untrammeled people,—almost anywhere except among a Latin people or in New England (You are essentially Greek or Anglo-Saxon or Scandinavian) now set down to surprise a neighborhood caught in a mould, stiff, narrow, inelastic, and yet which is itself neighbour to the sea and the boundless, lawless sand, to which you are from all time kin. You could not endure those stiff folk, however much they may interest and amuse you, if you could not turn to your cousin elements. Please turn to them very often! Turn to them for me. You are no longer in a cage. You can turn back to where you left off when you were thrust in the cage, and can recover all the unspoiled elements that have been suppressed in you, or have asserted themselves only now and again because irrepressible or in rebellion. While *I* have reversed your story. *I* am now in a cage,—of a very different sort and yet a cage, and

made of triple steel and brass,—a man without individual freedom or privacy. You must read nature to me. You must remind
me, from your free shore and your free choice of occupation and
of thought, what the lessons of freedom are. For the dear people
of my little household are also caught and imprisoned within
these singular impalpable walls of publicity and constant, necessary preoccupation with affairs not their own. I try to discipline
my spirit to it, but often I find myself beating my very head
against the walls in a sort of despair. I love my freedom. It is
the breath of life to me. Now that I have lost it and you have
found it, do you not see that I must depend upon you to supply
me with air for my lungs? You must not let me suffer the sort
of blindness and atrophy public men so often suffer. You must
keep me supplied with an atmosphere,—must tell me what normal
people are thinking who are not flattered and fussed with and
banged about by other persons' interests and views and designs.
You must let me feel through you the fresh, untainted breath of
the sea, which is shut off from me by the crowds on the lawn. I
must see through your eyes the free beauty of the curving shore,
for I am not allowed to see it myself. Am I talking nonsense or
poetry or—what? I am trying to release what is in my mind about
you—and cannot find the words. I am trying to let you see what
you really embody to my thoughts—a noble, sweet, free, unspoiled, inspiriting womanhood, for which nature found a fit
form and a fit instrument of utterance.

I am dead tired today. All the spunk has gone out of me. I
am the worse for wear. *I* am not the chap to cheer and hearten
my friend, for my digestion is not working, my vocabulary is
mislaid, I am disgusted and discouraged. But, dear me, that does
not matter! Have I not the most generous loving friends a man
ever had—and the most delightful and interesting and every way
engaging? I am happy even when I am miserable, and can always recover my spirits by thinking of them.

With love to all,

Your devoted friend   Woodrow Wilson

ALS (WP, DLC).

A News Report

[*July 22, 1912*]

WILSON IN HIDING TO WRITE SPEECH

SEA GIRT, N. J., July 22.—Gov. Woodrow Wilson held political
conferences today with the original Wilson man of the House
of Representatives and two ardent Clark men from Missouri.

When his visitors left at 3:30 P.M., he came out on his lawn attired in a natty gray coat of an Atlantic City boardwalk design. An automobile was waiting for him at the end of the walk.

At his left and right on the walk as he sped along were scores of Jerseymen employed in their usual afternoon diversion of waiting for their daily handshake with their candidate. They exacted their toll of handshakes before they would let him pass and poured upon his patient shoulders their usual gallons of advice.

The reason for his going was simple. The Governor's good neighbors had seized possession of his home. He had to work on his speech of acceptance. If his good neighbors would persist in seizing his home, then—well, he could surrender so completely that it would amount to an evacuation of the premises.

"Where are you going, Governor?" asked a persistent Jerseyman, as Gov. Wilson was permitting the forty-seventh handshake.

"Oh, away from here," he replied.

"And are you going to rest up? You need it."

"No. I am going away to work."

By that time Gov. Wilson had tunneled an opening to his waiting automobile.

"Now for the speech of acceptance," he called out, and told the chauffeur to turn on the speed lever.

Before leaving the Little White House, Gov. Wilson had a long talk with Gezea Kende, editor of the Amerikar-Magyar Nepszava,[1] a Hungarian paper published in New York. Mr. Kende came to ask him to answer W. R. Hearst's exploitation of the phrase "Men of the meaner sort from the South of Europe," taken from his historical writings.

Mr. Kende told him thousands of Hungarians considered him their enemy and were withholding their support until they could learn more about his view of them as immigrants.

Gov. Wilson received the editor and chatted with him for some time. Afterward on a railroad train headed away from Sea Girt a friend of the editor received and made public the substance of the interview and a signed statement furnished by Gov. Wilson for publication in Mr. Kende's paper.

The Hungarian editor came here, he said, to sound the Governor on immigration matters largely because he wished to come out for him and did not dare to do so in the face of the opposition to the Governor among his constituents.

Gov. Wilson assured him that he would be indeed an ignorant person if he were not well aware of the vast service done by the

Hungarians in Europe for the cause of European freedom. He said he had stepped from a scholastic life into politics in a very natural manner and found his new environment not at all strange, since he had taught politics to his students for many years. The editor asked Gov. Wilson if he did not think the question of immigration was the most important one before the people at this time.

Gov. Wilson said he thought it was one of the greatest questions, and said he was in sympathy with "sound" immigration, and that he was in favor of "only such regulations and restrictions of immigration as would help the health and moral conditions of the United States."

In response to a question as to the exact scope of the word "sound" Gov. Wilson dictated this statement for publication, signing it after his stenographer had written it out.

> I believe in the responsible restrictions of immigration, but not in any restrictions which will exclude from the country honest, industrious men who are seeking what America has always offered—an asylum for those who seek a free field. The whole question is a very difficult one, but, I think, can be solved with justice and generosity. Any one who has the least knowledge of Hungarian history must feel that stock to have proved itself for liberty and opportunity.

Gov. Wilson promised Mr. Kende that he would take up very fully the question of immigration either in his speech accepting the nomination or in a speech to be delivered later. . . .

Only the Governor's most intimate friends know where he went. He carried with him two large books for shorthand notes. The speech that he will read to the Democratic Committee on Notification on Aug. 7 he will write out entirely in shorthand, and afterward he will dictate his shorthand draft to a stenographer.

The Governor's secretaries were left at Sea Girt and were told they could take a two-day vacation. Enough is known of the Governor's favorite campaign ideas to make it certain that he wishes to have his speech reach a high-water mark that no other campaign effort will need to approach.

Printed in the *New York Times*, July 23, 1912.

[1] Geza Kende, assistant editor of *Amerikai Magyar Népszava (American-Hungarian People's Voice)*, the largest Hungarian-language newspaper in the United States.

From William Jennings Bryan

My Dear Gov: Lincoln, Neb., [c. July 22, 1912].

Your kind letter at hand. I enclose a copy of my "valedictory." It was called out by a speech from Dist of Col, putting me in nomination for V. P. I was opposed to Marshall, first, because he took the Parker side, which I think will lessen his popularity in Ind &, second, because he went out of his way to attack the in[it]iative & referendum for which you stand. They are not in the campaign but they indicate a fundamental bias toward aristocracy or toward Democracy. But, in favoring Burke & Chamberlain[1] I was looking to our chance of carrying the N.W. States. Burke is a Catholic but such an excellent man that his nomination could not be criticized on religious grounds. We need to do something to bring back the Catholics who voted for Taft in 1908 & who will vote for him this year. *That is the one weak point* in our fight this year. I see, already, evidence of activity along this line. I am sending a Catholic friend to you Mr Michael F. Doyle of Philadelphia.[2] He was my secetary at Baltimore. He is high up in Catholic circles & I think he can be of service to you. I commend him to your confidence. I enclose a check for $1000 which [I hope you will][3] turn over to to [sic] the treasurer as soon as one is appointed. Feel free to call on me on any subject and feel just as free to reject my advice. You are the one to decide all questions pertaining to the canvas and I would not interfere with that freedom. I welcomed advice from all sources & then followed my own judgment & conscience[.] I commend the rule to you—am inclined to think that is your rule already[.] My brother C. W. who called upon you is also at your service.
Sincer[ely yours,   W. J. Bryan]

Do not count on carrying N. Y. The reactionary (Wall Street) influences are too strong & the Catholic vote will be largely against you there. As I see it your fight must be won in progressive states[.] You will carry the West & NW.

ALS (WP, DLC).
[1] John E. Burke and Senator George Earle Chamberlain of Oregon.
[2] Michael Francis Doyle, lawyer of Philadelphia active in Democratic politics.
[3] Words obliterated.

From Oscar Wilder Underwood

My dear Governor Wilson: Washington, D. C., July 22, 1912.

On my return to Washington I found your letter of the 19th instant awaiting me here.

I note what you say in reference to your consultation with Representatives Jones of Virginia about the Philippine Bill, and as I judge from your letter you do not think the consideration of the bill at this time would be embarrassing to your campaign, I shall advise the Rules Committee to report a rule giving Mr. Jones an opportunity for the consideration of the bill before Congress adjourns.[1]

Assuring you of my appreciation of your kindness and courtesy during my recent visit to Trenton, I am,

Sincerely yours,   O W Underwood

TLS (WP, DLC).
[1] Actually, the House never debated or voted upon H.R. 22143.

From Alexander Jeffrey McKelway

Dear Governor Wilson: Atlanta, Georgia. July 23rd, 1912.

Perhaps you remember that when I met you at lunch in Philadelphia, a little over a year ago, I told you of a general agreement among several representative men of the National Conference of Charities and Correction, which had just met in Boston, to support you for the Presidency as against President Taft. The President had showed absolutely no sympathy, so far as any activity of his was concerned, with the aims and purposes of the "human welfare" folks.

I was talking to-day with Mr. J[oseph]. C. Logan, Secretary of the Associated Charities of Atlanta, who has done more for the enlightenment and redemption of Atlanta during the last seven years than any man in it. He is a Virginian, has never voted anything but the Democratic ticket but he was seriously considering enrolling himself with the Roosevelt party in this State. In fact he had then an appointment with one of the Colonel's organizers here. I told him some of the views you entertained about social betterment; that you felt, for example, that the emphasis should be laid upon "States' Functions" rather than upon "States' Rights", what you had done for child labor reform, and so forth; and he told me after his interview with the other man that I had persuaded him to abide in the Democratic ship.

I feel sure that the whole multitude of social workers throughout the country would come to the same conclusion, or would take passage on that ship for the first time, if they knew your opinions as well as I do.

I know in advance what the Roosevelt platform is going to be on these very questions, which come very near to the life and work of many good people who ought to be permanently with the Progressive Democracy.

I am taking the liberty of suggesting that in your speech of acceptance, especially, as that will precede the adoption of the Third Party Platform, you give a few words to the discussion of these problems. You can say that the Federal Government can set the example to all municipal corporations and in some respects to the states by making a model city of the National Capital, in its laws and institutions. Again it can furnish standardized information concerning these human welfare problems, by collecting and publishing the facts ascertained through Federal Bureaus and Commissions, a task that the Federal Government is alone competent to do. As for example through the Children's Bureau, which was passed by the Democratic House, Speaker Clark and Mr. Underwood both favoring it, after it had been turned down by Speaker Cannon in the preceding Congress. Then you can say that the Progressive Democracy of the States, through State legislation, should adopt the most advanced principles of Prison Reform, of the care and protection of the dependent, the delinquent, the afflicted children; of child labor reform; while in the cities they should work out the solution of the housing problem, of the prevention of tuberculosis, etc., as is being done in Cleveland under that splendid young Democrat, Mayor Baker.

I take the liberty of enclosing the platform of social standards of industry,[1] presented to the National Conference recently in session at Cleveland. I think if you have time to read the platform itself, printed in the large type, it will give you some suggestion as to what the "Humanists" are setting forth as their ideal. It will also occur to you that the Federal Government can do little here, but the States much. President Roosevelt had the confidence of these people because he gave them his sympathy and co-operation. I believe you can spike one of his main guns by some declaration of your own, in your own inimitable way, of such sympathy.

There was nobody in the United States outside of your own family happier to hear of your nomination than I was. I think your election is as sure as your calling. But for the future of the party I believe that we should pay some attention to these matters.   Cordially yours,   A. J. McKelway.

P.S. Could you not also adopt another plank of the New Party's platform, with a slight change in spelling and punctuation, thus: "Thou shalt not, Steel."[2]   A.J.McK.

TLS (WP, DLC).

[1] This enclosure is missing. The platform is printed in *Proceedings of the National Conference of Charities and Correction* . . . (Fort Wayne, Ind., 1912), pp. 388-94.

[2] An allusion to Roosevelt's close relations with the House of Morgan and the United States Steel Corp., then being divulged by the Stanley Committee.

To William Frank McCombs

[Sea Girt, N. J.] July 24, 1912

Would be very much obliged if you would notify McAdoo at once that he is to act as Vice Chairman of the National Committee. This is of the first consequence.   WW

Hw telegram (WP, DLC).

From Newton Diehl Baker, with Enclosure

My dear Mr. Wilson: Cleveland July 24th, 1912.

The enclosed letter from Harry Tucker is self explanatory, but proposes a puzzle for which I do not know the answer. It is entirely likely that you know conditions in Virginia very much better than I. As I understand them from my intimate friends there Senator Martin, backed by the railroad interests, has for a number of years dominated the politics of the State. This is extremely distasteful to the old element of which John Randolph Tucker, Harry Tucker's father, was in many senses the leader. Now that "Old Ran" is dead Harry Tucker and the younger element have been very restless under the Martin domination, and, of course, have been anxious to rescue the State to its better traditions. I saw Harry Tucker at the Baltimore Convention and he was undoubtedly the main inspiration of so much of the Virginia delegation as steadfastly adhered to our side from the beginning. Richard E. Byrd, to whom Mr. Tucker refers in his letter, is much more of a politician than Mr. Tucker, and is a very adroit, capable fellow, not so high a type as Mr. Tucker or those with whom the latter is working, and I can well understand how a story if started would gain credence among the Virginians who have watched Mr. Byrd's career, to the effect that his activities were intended ultimately to reconcile the old state machine to the new conditions which you are to bring in. I hope you will not infer from this that I undervalue the efficiency, zeal, or intelligence of Mr. Byrd's services, but I do know that those with whom Mr. Tucker is associated have a larger hold on the old Virginia traditions which you and I both know[1] than is likely to be found anywhere else in the state outside of their circle.

If you will be good enough to have your Secretary return Mr. Tucker's letter to me for my files, and will yourself not take the trouble to make any acknowledgement of this matter which is transmitted to you only for your private information, I will be most grateful.   Cordially yours,   Newton D. Baker

¹ He grew up in Martinsburg, West Va., and attended Washington and Lee University Law School.

E N C L O S U R E

Henry St. George Tucker to Newton Diehl Baker

My dear Newt: Lexington, Virginia July 22, 1912

Thank you for your letter just received. You will find the paper I sent you of interest in view of the present condition of things.

I may want your help in a matter in reference to Virginia affairs here. Your relations to Mr. Wilson and to his campaign committee are such that I want to invoke your aid in the interest of the old State. The great enthusiasm of our people which was stifled at Norfolk, in sending the delegation to Baltimore, is largely due to the fact that Wilson had the nerve and pluck to take hold of the bosses in New Jersey and throw them to the ground. We have the same state of things in Virginia and while nobody doubts Mr. Wilson's sincerity on these lines there is a condition that causes us some trouble. Richard Evelyn Byrd, who belongs to the machine in the state, for political reasons was appointed to manage his campaign in the state. He is supposed to have the ear of Wilson and the committee. There would be no kick from our people were Byrd's efforts for Wilson to be rewarded by giving him an office commensurate with his claims, but our people wil not stand for his being the representative of Mr. Wilson in Virginia, for the idea has gotten abroad that he is to be the go-between with Wilson and the machine in order to save the latter in the state. This wont do and would ruin Wilson in Virginia. Wilson's campaign and victory has been that of the People over the Bosses, and there should be no failure in this direction in Virginia, his own native state.

I write you this confidentially, but feeling sure that I can count on your help.

I was greatly delighted at meeting you and was ready to vote for you for Vice-President had you allowed your name to be used.
                    Yours very truly,   H S G Tucker

TLS (WP, DLC).

From William Gibbs McAdoo

Dear Governor: New York June [July] 25, 1912

Mr. McCombs told me late yesterday afternoon that you had requested that I be named Vice Chairman of the National Committee.

I greatly appreciate this exhibition of your confidence and the honor it implies. You are the only man living for whom I would accept this post. I do not say this to impress an obligation. I am sure that you know me too well to think that. I only mean that it is an exceedingly difficult situation and that I realize my limitations any way, and more particularly under the circumstances. But I am so interested in you and the cause you represent, that I will accept and put my soul into the work. If I do less well than you expect, only remember that I am not in command and that that necessarily restricts opportunity. I do not offer this as an excuse but as a possible explanation.

As soon as definite announcement is made, as it will be, doubtless, on Monday next when the Committee is to meet, I shall take hold vigorously and do all I can to get something started. There is much to be done and we have lost some valuable time.

My great hope is for your success and that I may so acquit myself as to justify your confidence.

                    Sincerely Your Friend   W G McAdoo

ALS (WP, DLC).

From Alexander Mitchell Palmer

My dear Governor Wilson: Washington, D. C., July 25, 1912.

Honorable Ollie James talked with me yesterday about the advisability of submitting to you in advance a copy of his notification speech. I told him I thought it would be very wise for him to read or show his speech to you so that if any part of it called for any particular attention on your part, you would know in advance how to handle it. I trust you will approve of this suggestion, and in pursuance of it Senator James will probably call on you next week for the purpose of going over his speech with you.

There is a matter pending in the Committee on Appropriations about which the Democratic members of the Committee desire me to get your views before any action is taken. It is a proposition to appropriate $250,000. for the celebration of the anniversary of the Emancipation Proclamation by the colored people of the country. The various negro associations everywhere are putting up a pretty strong fight to get this money.

I may say for your information that the association in Philadelphia, which has corresponded with me about it, has a number of honorary officers, white men, every one of whom I recognize as a strong Penrose machine Republican.

Of course, the House is attempting to keep its record for economy straight, but in matters of this kind we recognize that in the middle of a political campaign we must consider the political effect. I would be glad to have your views in relation to it.*

Yours truly,   A Mitchell Palmer

*Of course, whatever you may think about this will be communicated to Chairman Fitzgerald as *my* views, not yours. He understands,—and you will have said nothing.[1]

TLS (WP, DLC).

[1] The House Appropriations Committee referred Senate Bill 180, providing funds for the celebration of the fiftieth anniversary of the Emancipation Proclamation, to the Committee on Industrial Arts and Expositions with the recommendation that it investigate the costs of the proposed celebration. Wilson's reply to Palmer is missing. However, as late as January 5, 1913, Wilson was urging approval of the appropriation. See WW to A. S. Burleson, Jan. 5, 1913, Vol. 27. The committee never reported the bill.

From William Jennings Bryan

My Dear Gov   McPherson, Kansas, [July] 26 1912

I enclose copy of speeches made at Baltimore. You only asked for valedictory but I send salutatory & intermediate speeches. Also send editorial on Roosevelts criticism of our platform. Have asked my brother to send you my speeches on Tariff, Trusts & Imperialism.

In trust question you will notice that stress is laid on opposition to the principle of private monopoly.

Am very much pleased with your campaign com. You will need some one in charge at Chicago or at least as an adviser. Hon J. G. Johnson of Peabody, Kas[1] is the best man I know for the place. He was at headquarters in all three of my campaigns & also in Parker's campaign. Hudspeth & Gore will tell you about him.

I shall be ready for campaign work about Sept 10.

Yours truly   W J Bryan

ALS (WP, DLC).

[1] John Gilmore Johnson, lawyer of Peabody, Kan., member of the Democratic National Committee, 1896-1904. He became secretary of the "national advisory committee" for the campaign of 1912.

To Mary Allen Hulbert

Dearest Friend,   On Board Corona 28 July, 1912

I ran away from home about a week ago. Cleveland Dodge, my class-mate, said I might have his yacht as long as I wanted her; I not only needed rest and refreshment, I also needed five or six days in which to prepare my speech of acceptance and so (nobody knowing whither we were bound—for I am even now supposed to be "in retreat" with a friend near Atlantic Highlands) Ellen and Margaret and I—with Dudley Malone, a young *fidus Achates* of mine,—bundled into an automobile, went down to the dock at Atlantic Highlands, which is just by Sandy Hook, and came aboard *The Corona*; since when we have been cruising in the Sound. My first thought on going aboard was that we could run to Nantucket and see a dear friend of ours; but no such luck. We got no further than New London; and to-morrow we are to be towed through Hell Gate and down East River again on our way back to duty. The *Corona* is a very smart boat, a beautiful 129 ton schooner; but the airs hereabout were light, the Captain is afraid of the waters about Nantucket and I could get nothing that I wanted! I had to content myself with finishing the speech. It is ready, poor thing, such as it is,—and we have had a truly delightful and refreshing little cruise, away from everybody, safer in our seclusion than if we had been at sea,— for sailing yachts have no wireless. If *thinking* of you could have transported me to Nantucket, I would have been there every day. How *do* you get there? What is the quickest and best way from New York, if a fellow ever *could* get away for a Sunday (say), and what is the briefest time in which it could be done, allowing at least a bit of a day at Nantucket? I am deeply anxious to see you, in a nest of your very own. Having been a week away I have not seen a line from you since I wrote last Sunday. I am eagerly hoping that I shall find a letter, a good long letter, telling me all about everything, when I get back. We are all well. Our days are not our own any more and are very laborious, but we keep heart and would be all right if we could only see our real friends.   Your devoted friend   Woodrow Wilson

All send love.

ALS (WP, DLC).

Ellen Axson Wilson's Description of Her Husband

[July 28, 1912]

PERSONAL.

VOTER.—We find this interesting description of the Baltimore nominee for President: Gov. Wilson is 5 feet 10½ inches in height, chest measurement 39, collar 16, size of hat 7⅜, weight 170 pounds. His weight has been practically the same for 10 or 15 years. He has good shoulders, the neck round, strong and very young-looking. He has no accumulation of flesh about the waist. He has an excellent constitution—very elastic—steel rather than iron. He is a splendid sleeper—can go to sleep at any moment that he makes up his mind to do so. He decides beforehand just when he will wake up, and always does it to the moment, with his mind perfectly clear. He is in much better physical condition than when he was a young man. Then, owing to bad food at colleges, etc., he suffered from chronic indigestion, but, living since under more wholesome conditions, he has entirely outgrown all tendency to trouble of that sort. He had once an attack of writer's cramp (in his author days), which makes his friends a little anxious as to the handshaking ordeals. He has dark brown hair, now turning iron-gray, a rather dark and somewhat ruddy complexion and very large, dark gray eyes, with dark eyebrows and very long, dark lashes. People are apt to say after meeting him that, strange as his face is, they were even more impressed with the sympathy and kindliness of expression of his eyes and his smile.[1]

Printed in the *St. Louis Post-Dispatch*, July 28, 1912.

[1] Accompanying this clipping in WP, DLC, is a handwritten note from "Ed Answers and Queries" of the *St. Louis Post-Dispatch*, July 28, 1912, which reads as follows: "Mrs. Wilson: Many thanks for your kindness and good sense. No person here, myself excepted, knows anything whatever of the request I made. See checked clipping inclosed."

To Cleveland Hoadley Dodge

Dear Cleve., On Board Corona 29 July, 1912

You have given us six of the happiest days I remember and my heart is full of gratitude to you. You are an ideal friend: you do everything in the best and most generous way. The speech is written, and I am at the same time refreshed and reinvigorated.

All join me in affectionate and grateful messages.

Your devoted friend, Woodrow Wilson

Malone will send you the "Log."

ALS (WC, NjP).

From Roy Dee Keehn[1]

My dear Governor Wilson: Chicago July 29th 1912.

I have yours of the 19th acknowledging mine of the 3rd.[2] I assure you that I fully appreciate that any seeming delay in answering letters has been unavoidable. I note that you state you hope that a little thinking space will come in which you may have a talk with me. I will be glad to hold myself in readiness to come at your command, and will do anything I can to help the particular situation in mind, which I feel is somewhat critical. The ticket deserves the heartiest support of the Hearst papers and should get it. I believe I can offer some helpful suggestions, and it is for this reason only that I have written so freely. I know you understand that it is in the interest of the ticket only that I have made these suggestions.

Sincerely yours,   Roy D. Keehn

TLS (WP, DLC).
   [1] Lawyer of Chicago, general counsel for the *Chicago Examiner* and *Chicago American*, Hearst newspapers.
   [2] R. D. Keehn to WW, July 3, 1912, TLS (WP, DLC), congratulating Wilson upon his nomination and offering his aid in obtaining Hearst's support for the ticket. Wilson's letter to Keehn is missing.

A News Item

[July 31, 1912]

SYMPATHY FOR NEGROES.

A delegation from the United Negro Democracy of New Jersey called on the Governor and told him that men of their race wanted to support a candidate in sympathy with their aims and ambitions in life. "I was born and raised in the South," the Governor told them. "There is no place where it is easier to cement friendship between the two races than there. They understand each other better than elsewhere. You may feel assured of my entire comprehension of the ambitions of the negro race and my willingness and desire to deal with that race fairly and justly."

Printed in the *Trenton Evening Times*, July 31, 1912.

To Charles Wayland Bryan

My dear Mr. Bryan: Sea Girt, N. J. July 31, 1912.

Thank you very warmly for your interesting and important letter of July twenty-second,[1] enclosing the letter from your brother. I have noted with genuine gratification your approval of the campaign appointments, so far as made. After our long talk here at Sea Girt, I was particularly interested to learn your judgment about them.

It is very gratifying, indeed, to know that you have started the appeal for a campaign fund again. I have no doubt that it will have as rich results as it had last time.

The suggestions in your letter seem to me of real importance and I am going to take the liberty of sending them on to Mr. Davies, the Secretary of the Committee, by whom, I am sure, they will be brought to the proper people in the campaign committee when the organization is finally effected, which now lags a bit because of our effort to choose the very best people everywhere.

With warm appreciation,

Cordially and sincerely yours,   [Woodrow Wilson]

TCL (WP, DLC).
1 It is missing.

To Francis L. Corrao

My dear Mr. Corrao,   Sea Girt, N. J. July 31st, 1912.

I am very much chagrined that so many important letters that have reached me have had to wait so long for a reply. But I am sure my friends will be generous enough to understand that it has not been through any neglect on my part but only because of the absolute impossibility of keeping up with my correspondence in the midst of the days when every other sort of demand was made upon me. Pray, pardon my delay in replying to your letter of July third.

Your letter gave me genuine gratification. I took it for granted that intelligent and well-informed men everywhere understood how grossly my views had been misrepresented, but it is nonetheless deeply gratifying to have such assurances of your generous feeling. It would distress me very much to have any of my Italian fellow-citizens think that I was so ignorant and so unjust as not to appreciate the great Italian people at their full worth and distinction.

Cordially and sincerely yours,   Woodrow Wilson.

CCL (WP, DLC).

To Franklin Potts Glass

My dear Glass: Sea Girt, N. J. July 31, 1912

It is a source of real distress to me that I am obliged to delay replying to the letters even of old friends. But I know you will not expect me to apologize. You will be generous and understand.

Your letter of July sixth[1] gave me the deepest kind of pleasure. It was characteristic of you and it gave me just the sort of assurances of your interest which went straightest to my heart. I knew all along, of course, where you were in the Convention and I am sure I have no criticism to offer of anything that the Alabama delegation did. As you point out, they were extremely serviceable in resisting the break that might have been made when it looked as if things were going against us.

Mrs. Wilson and my daughters join in cordial messages. I hope sincerely that it will be possible for me to meet Mr. Hanson,[2] and I beg that you will convey to him my cordial regards.

Always faithfully yours,   Woodrow Wilson

TCL (RSB Coll., DLC).
[1] F. P. Glass to WW, July 6, 1912, TLS (WP, DLC).
[2] Victor Henry Hanson, publisher of the *Birmingham News*.

From Edward Mandell House

Dear Governor Wilson: London. July 31st, 1912.

Thank you so much for your letter of July 18th. It is a joy to work for such an appreciative friend.

We are sailing for Boston, August 6th, on the Laconia, and we should arrive on the morning of the 14th. From then until November every hour of my time will be devoted to your cause.

There are many things I would like to say which had better not be written, and I shall be unhappy until I can come in closer touch with you. I wish you would steal away for a day or two and be with me when I first reach Beverly. It would give you rest and a better chance to think out the problems which confront you. Please do it if you can.

At present your election seems as certain as anything political ever is, but it can be lost, and I think I see ways by which it may.

Blaine was elected as surely as you are, but five days before the people could confirm it at the ballot box he made his famous "Rum, Romanism and Rebellion" speech and Cleveland won by the narrow margin of eleven hundred votes.

Your election means so much to our country that I shall have no peace of mind until I can address you as "Mr. President."

Your very faithful,   E. M. House

TLS (WC, NjP).

From Samuel Untermyer

My dear Governor: Baden-Baden, Germany, July 31st, 1912.

I thank you for your very kind and cordial letter of the 16th inst. which has been forwarded me here. My son writes me that he is making an analysis of the testimony thus far taken in the Money Trust Inquiry, which he has probably forwarded you by this time. In writing you I assumed that the Committee had completed the analysis which it was undertaking and that this might be placed at your service.

Accompanying you will please find a brief summary I have dictated from memory and which may serve your purpose if you conclude to take up the subject for discussion. You understand of course that we are barely on the threshold of this Inquiry and have not touched upon the vital subject of the dangerous and rapidly increasing concentration of the Money Power. That will not be possible until the pending legislation amending the National Banking Law which has passed the House and is now pending in the Senate has been secured,[1] after which we shall require months of painstaking investigation of the books and transactions of certain of the New York National Banks in order to secure the necessary data for the examination of witnesses.

I accepted the retainer of the Committee on the express condition that this legislation would be enacted and upon the understanding that the main branch of the Inquiry would be postponed until after election so as to secure for the Investigation the confidence of the public as a judicial, non-partisan undertaking.

I am expecting to reach New York on September 1st and would gladly come sooner if any of your advisers are of the opinion that my earlier return would be of the slightest aid to your cause, in the success of which I am intensely concerned as a citizen interested in decent and progressive government. Your election would mark the greatest triumph that has been scored in that direction in my day.

Please do not bother to acknowledge this letter.
Again thanking you for your letter believe me
Sincerely yours   Saml. Untermyer

TLS (WP, DLC). Enc.: T memorandum.
[1] On May 4, 1912, Representative Arsène Paulin Pujo of Louisiana introduced H.R. 24153 to amend and re-enact a section of the law of 1864 regulating
national banks. The purpose of Pujo's bill was to make explicit the right of
Congress to investigate national banks, thus putting an end to a question
which had been raised as to whether or not the Pujo Committee to investigate
the "Money Trust" had the power to extend its inquiries to national banks.
The House approved the bill on May 18. However, the Senate Finance Committee on July 29 issued a report recommending against passage. Despite repeated statements by Pujo and others that failure to enact this measure was
hampering the work of the committee, the Senate took no action on the bill.

To Richard Heath Dabney

My dear Heath: Sea Girt, N. J. August 1, 1912.

I was stupid enough not to notice the address you gave me
and, feeling that my letters would wander around Europe seeking for you, I have not acknowledged sooner the letters from
you[1] which have given me so much delight. I have a sort of feeling
that after your troubles and after the political disappointment
in Virginia, this result at Baltimore is a sort of message of cheer
to you yourself. Certainly, I know that nobody has been more
generously interested in it than you have been. My letters have
piled in on me so that I cannot write more than a few lines, but
these are lines of sincerest affection. Please take care of yourself
and be sure to come back well and in restored spirits.
Affectionately yours,   Woodrow Wilson

TLS (Wilson-Dabney Corr., ViU).
[1] They are missing.

To James Sprunt

My dear Mr. Sprunt: Sea Girt, N. J. August 1, 1912.

I am very much chagrined that so many important letters that
have reached me have had to wait so long for a reply. But I am
sure my friends will be generous enough to understand that it
has not been through any neglect on my part but only because
of the absolute impossibility of keeping up with my correspondence in the midst of the days when every other sort of demand
was made upon me. Pray, pardon my delay in replying to your
letter of July sixteenth.[1]

I am deeply obliged to you for all your generous support.

Somehow, it particularly strengthens me to have the people who have known me since I was a lad come to my support with such entire generosity and enthusiasm. I wish that my dear father could have lived and see these days of fighting for the things that we believe in and I am sure that he believed in as we do.

Cordially and sincerely yours, Woodrow Wilson

TLS (received from J. Sprunt, Jr.).
1 J. Sprunt to WW, July 16, 1912, ALS (WP, DLC).

To Samuel Huston Thompson

My dear Mr. Thompson: Sea Girt, N. J. August 1, 1912.

I am very much chagrined that so many important letters that have reached me have had to wait so long for a reply. But I am sure my friends will be generous enough to understand that it has not been through any neglect on my part but only because of the absolute impossibility of keeping up with my correspondence in the midst of the days when every other sort of demand was made upon me. Pray pardon my delay in replying to your letter of July third.

I do not know any friends whose support has given me greater happiness than the remarkable members of the Thompson family. Your sons have told me so much about you that I feel as if I knew you much better than I do, and I want to tell you how entirely I have admired the splendid chaps you sent to Princeton who have honored me with their friendship since graduation. May I not return to the Thompson family, in response to their generous telegram and your equally generous letter, my sincerest messages of friendship and regard.

Cordially yours, Woodrow Wilson

TLS (photostat in RSB Coll., DLC).

From William Cox Redfield

My Dear Governor Wilson: New York, August 1st, 1912.

I confirm my telephone message of this morning to your Secretary disavowing the "Times" interview printed today. Despite this, I should doubt my acquital of conduct unbecoming a gentleman or at least of blazing indiscretion were it not for the "Sun" and the "World" reports of the same interview today. These have restored my self respect and I trust will prevent my losing your confidence in my judgment and courtesy.

The "Brooklyn Eagle" of tonight may, both in its columns and editorially, readjust matters and I have told the "Times" plainly what I think of their statements.

As a matter of record between us, however, I wish you to know that I declined to say to the reporters anything of what you had said to me. For this I referred them to you. Nor did I say to them or to any one that your speech of acceptance had, either in whole or part, been read, heard or seen by me. I did not refer to it. The "Times" head-line scheme of 5 per cent annually for four years[1] was new to me when I saw it in the "Times" today. No one ever spoke of it to me nor has the idea ever been my own. I do not approve it. The mass of the interview printed in the "Times" has chiefly to do with explanations of my personal views which had and have no relation whatever to my talk with you and in which I did not assume you were or are interested. Your courtesy of yesterday was appreciated highly; it must have seemed to you to have met with a very poor return, which I much regret. I think you will not disapprove the "Sun" interview, by which I stand and I should add that the three reporters were together when I spoke to them.

Yours very truly,   William C. Redfield

TLS (WP, DLC).
  [1] That is, Wilson favored tariff reduction in this fashion.

From Louis Dembitz Brandeis

My dear Governor Wilson: Boston, Mass. August 1, 1912.

This morning's news that you will suggest dealing with the tariff by reducing the duties gradually at the rate of five per cent. a year is further evidence that the Country may expect from you a wisely progressive administration.

No other method of securing relief from tariff burdens is consistent with the demands of business; and there is probably no business in the Country which cannot adjust itself to such a gradual reduction.

The simple plan which you suggest is true statesmanship; and the real tariff reformers should rally to your support.

With best wishes,

Very truly yours,   Louis D Brandeis

TLS (WP, DLC).

From Robert Lee Henry

My dear Governor: Washington, D. C. August 1, 1912.

I am sending you a letter[1] of importance and value in my judgment. Untermyer is right. From my experience and information, I don't doubt it. We have secured the reporting of minority views to the Senate and will get to fight the matter out on the floor.

But the thing that I really desire to get before you is the last half of the enclosed letter. It has so impressed me that I feel it my duty to enclose it to you for your perusal and consideration. When you have finished with it, please return it to me.

With cordial regards, I am,

Sincerely yours,   R. L. Henry.

TLS (WP, DLC).
[1] It is missing.

From Charles Sumner Hamlin

My dear Gov. Wilson: Boston, Mass., August 1, 1912.

I trust you will pardon me for taking up your valuable time but I feel that I ought to say to you that there is a strong feeling in the community here that in your coming letter of acceptance you will radically attack the existing banking and financial conditions and this idea is being so assiduously cultivated that it is causing some uneasiness for fear lest you will rest content upon attacking the existing system without constructive suggestions as to needed reforms.

A great many business men in the community here rather regret the attack on the so-called Aldrich Financial Bill in the National Democratic Platform.[1]

I have given very careful study to this Bill and while I believe that under its provisions many existing evils would be corrected and that the theory upon which it rests is sound, yet I am not quite certain that under its operation the various reserve associations could not be controlled by the centralized financial capital of the country.

I presume that you have read the book published by Dr. Laughlin called "Banking Reform"[2] which has been issued by the National Citizens League of Chicago[3] and which is devoted largely to an explanation of the Bill of the National Monetary Commission, otherwise called the Aldrich Bill, as to which, as I have said, I am not quite yet convinced that the proposed reserve

associations could not be controlled. I decidedly believe, however, that many existing defects in our banking system pointed
out in this book are real evils which could be met constructively
without endorsing the plan of the Monetary Commission. For
example, if National Banks could be given the power to accept
strictly commercial bills of exchange, it would create a discount
market in the United States similar to that now existing in London, Paris and Berlin and would tend to regulate and lower the
rates our merchants have to pay for their strictly commercial
transactions.

It is certainly an anomaly that at the time of our greatest
prosperity, when enormous crops are being moved, that is the
time when our business interests, under existing methods, are
most apprehensive.

It is certainly a further anomaly that the rates which the business people of the United States have to pay for their strictly
business transactions should depend upon call loan rates on
stock exchange transactions in the New York market.

If the power were given to National Banks to accept commercial bills, or if some relation were fixed by law between the
amount of commercial bills accepted and other paper, in proportion to the ratio between commercial and savings deposits,
adding to the latter the capital and surplus funds, I believe we
should see a commercial revolution in this country in the way
of distinct advantage to our commercial interests.

If it were pointed out, as Dr. Laughlin admits, that the proposed National Reserve Association is not absolutely necessary
to correct these admitted evils and a suggestion were made for
correcting them without the use of the machinery provided by
the so-called Aldrich Bill, I believe it would be most helpful and
would go far to assuring the people that the Party has its mind
upon constructive financial legislation.

Among other remedies suggested by the above book are the
prohibition of corporations owning national bank stock and the
prohibition of national banks from direct or indirect control of
the stock of other banks, this latter recommendation having been
already made by President Taft; also the prohibition of holding
companies in connection with national banks.

As I have said above, the power of accepting bills of exchange
under proper limitations would create a discount market in the
United States for commercial bills, resulting in a comparatively
stable rate and going far to divorce strictly commercial transactions from speculative transactions of the New York stock exchange. It would also tend to bring the capital of Europe to the

United States because it could safely invest in bills accepted by the banks of the United States, whereas now it could not purchase the notes of individuals with any safety and such foreign capital is not much attracted by the violent fluctuations in the call loan rates of the country.

Furthermore, it would enable the people of the United States to finance for themselves the payment of the vast and increasing mass of imports coming into the United States the profit on which now is practically absorbed by foreign banking houses.

I am sure you will excuse my writing to you in this way but I feel that you ought to know exactly what the various communities of the country are thinking about and in view of the splendid possibilities for Democratic success in this State, I venture to send you these suggestions for what they are worth.

With again my best wishes for your success, I am,

Very sincerely yours, Charles S. Hamlin

TLS (WP, DLC).

[1] The platform declared: "We oppose the so-called Aldrich bill for the establishment of a central bank; and we believe our country will be largely freed from panics, and consequent unemployment and business depression by such a systematic revision of our banking laws as will render temporary relief in localities where such relief is needed, with protection from control or domination by what is known as the money trust."

[2] James Laurence Laughlin (ed.), *Banking Reform* (Chicago: National Citizens' League, 1912).

[3] An organization devoted to winning public support for banking and currency legislation.

A News Report

[*Aug. 2, 1912*]

WILSON TO STAY AS GOVERNOR OF NEW JERSEY

Sea Girt, August 2.—Governor Wilson this morning announced definitely his intention to remain in the chair as the Governor of New Jersey. It has been a matter of open question with him ever since the Democratic national convention at Baltimore, and the arguments of his friends and fellow-Democrats have prevailed. Although he has been urged continually not to drop the reigns of the State government, the incumbent was undecided until this morning.

It is said that his determination to remain in the office now until he leaves for the White House, or until the end of his term, as the election may decide, is due to a great extent to his wishes to see the results of the working out of problems now before commissions which are investigating the tax conditions in the State and matters pertaining to the State efficiency.

Edward E. Grosscup, chairman of the Democratic State committee, who was here this morning, heard the announcement of the Governor's intention with genuine satisfaction. He said that it was an announcement which would bring the Democrats of the State closer to their leader, and one that would entirely satisfy his following in New Jersey, excepting, perhaps, a few Democrats who had wanted him to resign. . . .

Governor Wilson is still facing the same old strain of letter writing and signing. He has discarded the rubber stamp, which bore his signature, and which he used to use in signing the thousands of letters which he is sending in reply to messages from people in all parts of the country. He said this morning that he was gaining and losing at the same time. Every day that he is undisturbed he spends several hours in signing his name to letters which are written by his force of typewriters. On days when he has a host of callers, like yesterday, he loses ground and the letters pile up. Last night, after he had closed his conference with Mr. [Joseph E.] Davies, he sat for an hour signing his name to hundreds of letters. His messenger stood beside him and blotted the letters as they were signed. . . .

"I remind myself of the frog that was trying to jump out of the well," said Governor Wilson as he turned away from a desk piled high with letters awaiting his signature. "My correspondence work is getting heavier and heavier, and, like the frog, I find that for every foot I jump up I fall back two." . . .

In describing his recent yachting trip to Mr. Davies today Mr. Wilson quoted the following limerick:

"I wish that my room had a floor;
    I don't so much care for a door,
But this waiting around without touching the ground
    Is getting to be such a bore."

Printed in the Trenton *True American*, Aug. 3, 1912.

To Edward Graham Elliott

My dear Edward: Sea Girt, N. J. August 2, 1912.

Extraordinary things have happened to the letters that came to us just after the nomination. Our little office staff was entirely unprepared for the deluge and it is actually a fact that your letter of July third[1] got buried in the avalanche. I did not see it until today, when I came upon it in my steady digging toward the bottom of the pile. Pray, forgive me for not having written.

I am sure I need not tell you how genuinely I enjoyed reading it or how welcome and refreshing the message was. We think of you all very often. You seem very far away[2] but a letter now and then brings us close again. Pray, take care of yourselves to the limit.

I am overwhelmed with all sorts of interviews and business that is not business and feel very gravely the responsibility that has been put upon me, but the old thoughts are the permanent thoughts.

With the warmest love from us all to you both.

Affectionately yours,   Woodrow Wilson

TLS (WC, NjP).
[1] E. G. Elliott to WW, July 3, 1912, ALS (Governors' Files, Nj).
[2] He and his wife, Margaret Randolph Axson Elliott, were vacationing on a ranch at Buffalo, Wyo.

To Charles Sumner Hamlin

My dear Mr. Hamlin: Sea Girt, N. J. August 3, 1912.

Circumstances over which I seemed to have no control have prevented my replying sooner to your valued favor of July eighteenth, enclosing the abominable editorial from the Boston Herald of July seventeenth.

I don't know whether you saw the comment upon that editorial in the New York Evening Globe;[1] it seemed to me to give it its proper assessment. It undoubtedly refers to some of the slanders uttered against me at Princeton, where I excited the animosity of men who were interested in things I could not possibly support. For the rest, I do not know anything that it can possibly refer to, of course. If the paper ever dares to become specific, we can handle it without gloves.

Cordially and sincerely yours,   Woodrow Wilson

TLS (C. S. Hamlin Papers, DLC).
[1] "The Wilson Mystery," New York Globe and Commercial Advertiser, July 20, 1912. This editorial defended Wilson's conduct during the graduate college controversy, reproached the Boston Herald for attacking Wilson with innuendos, and challenged it to print the facts, concluding: "If it has not such facts it is small and contemptible to emit hints and to indulge in winks and knowing looks."

A News Report

[Aug. 4, 1912]

WILSON HERE; DINES AT A LUNCH COUNTER

Unnoticed and unrecognized by the throngs among whom he passed, Gov. Woodrow Wilson came into New York last evening, ate his dinner perched on a stool in the lunch room of the Pennsylvania Railroad Station, and then went to the University Club for a long, possibly an all night conference with Chairman William F. McCombs, of his newly organized Campaign Committee.

It had previously been announced that Col. McCombs was going to Sea Girt to see his chief, and why the candidate should come to New York was a problem which puzzled many of the Governor's friends and for which none of them could get an answer. . . .

In every way Gov. Wilson's trip to New York last night from Sea Girt was the flight of a person who felt that he wished to be alone without interruption.

At the little railroad station in Sea Girt, where every trainman knows the Governor, he stood waiting for his train with his face buried deep in a magazine. Beside him on the platform was a small handbag of leather which he had carried with him on foot from the Little White House. None of those who recognized Gov. Wilson approached him as he seemed to be so intent upon his magazine reading, and the trainmen merely looked at him from a respectful distance.

The Pullman porter who took his handbag as he stepped aboard a train bound for the Pennsylvania Station at Thirty-third Street and Seventh Avenue, did not recognize him. Inside the car there was no other passenger except the newspaper reporters who have been encamped for several weeks on the Governor's lawn. The Governor sat alone and read throughout the journey.

At the Pennsylvania Station the negro porter was too slow in picking up Gov. Wilson's handbag to have an opportunity to carry it from the car. Gov. Wilson gathered it up himself and stepped down into a typically surging New York crowd. They were all in a hurry, and they jostled him, crowded past him, shouldered him aside, but they did not recognize him.

Gov. Wilson caught the infection of the hurrying multitudes and walked through the wide waiting room so rapidly that the reporters accompanying him had to run to keep him in sight. As he gained the west end of the long arcade, leading from Seventh Avenue, the reporters watched, expecting the Governor to hurry forward to the taxicab stands and drive away towards the club, where he had his appointment to meet Col. McCombs.

Instead they saw Democracy's candidate glance for an instant into the well-appointed dining room to his right and then into the lunch counter with its scores of stools all in a row to his left. He turned abruptly and disappeared into the throng of those who were eating hurried lunches.

"He's surely missed his way," remarked a dozen of those who were following him. "He must think the taxicab stands are in that direction."

But the candidate had not lost his way. He was headed direct for a stool before a large stack of assorted fruits on the counter and in less than a minute he was spreading an abbreviated lunch counter napkin out on his knee and was ordering a simple dinner. It consisted of a glass of buttermilk and a sandwich. It was then 7:25 o'clock and Gov. Wilson had been on the train since 5:10 o'clock, his usual dinner hour at Sea Girt having passed by 90 minutes before a negro waiter brought him his meal. After he had eaten he took a taxicab to the University Club.

At midnight Gov. Wilson and Chairman McCombs left the University Club, the Governor to go to his over-Sunday retreat, and Mr. McCombs to return to his hotel. To reporters who were waiting Gov. Wilson handed this statement, which he had written out before leaving the clubhouse:

"I came to New York for the purpose of having a quiet conference with Mr. McCombs on general plans, where we would be most likely to be uninterrupted. It was the first opportunity I have had to talk over with him the choice of a Treasurer, of a Chairman of the Finance Committe, and a head for the headquarters, which are to be established at Chicago.

"We have agreed on the Treasurer,[1] but have not yet had an opportunity to communicate with him. Mr. Henry Morgenthau, of New York, will take the Chairmanship of the Finance Committee, and Mr. Joseph E. Davies, of Wisconsin, will take charge of the Chicago headquarters.

"We also discussed the committees other than the Campaign Committee, which are to be formed and which will be made as representative as possible. That is a bigger task, which we did not finish. The Campaign Committee is making very satisfactory progress toward organization and expects to be in full action by the time the notification exercises take place." . . .

There was much anxiety at Sea Girt as to whether Gov. Wilson's unexpected visit to New York implied any interruption of the harmonies of the Wilson campaign committee.

"Are you going to iron out any ruffles while you are in New York?" the Governor was asked.

"Absolutely none," he replied. "We have differences of opinion, of course, but not disputes. We are just going to have a round-up of all the matters connected with the campaign. I have not seen

---

[1] Rolla Wells, prominent businessman of St. Louis, mayor, 1901-1909.

Col. McCombs for two weeks, and as he and I are equally responsible we must get together on plans already suggested."

An effort was made to have Gov. Wilson name an hour when newspaper reporters might see him. He said he planned to talk to Col. McCombs for a long time.

"You know," he remarked, "that every time I see McCombs I find his head so filled with good suggestions that I have to listen a very long time to get them all out of him. After we are through I plan to sleep as late as I possibly can on Sunday morning. And after that I shall rest. I shall see nobody until Monday on any political business."

The Governor finally consented that the reporters could telephone to him at 11 P.M., by which time, he said, "he would know how his time was shaping up."

Before leaving Sea Girt Gov. Wilson definitely authorized an announcement that, regardless of what the other candidates might do, his plan of campaign would not include any stump speaking from the rear end of Pullman cars, or any extended tours of the country.

"I intend to discuss causes and principles and not personalities," he said, "and I will make speeches only in response to invitations from sections of the country I find it practicable to visit."

"But surely," suggested a friend with whom Gov. Wilson was discussing his speaking plans, "you will hold yourself at the disposal of your Campaign Committee, and will make such speeches as the committee deems desirable?"

"Yes," the Governor replied, "if I agree with 'em."

The intermountain tier of States was mentioned by a Far Westerner, who suggested that the people out that way would like to see Gov. Wilson, and become better acquainted with him.

"But going to that country," said the Governor, "would involve a stumping tour, and I shall not make any such a tour as that."

"But Bryan will speak for you?" some one asked.

"Yes," replied Gov. Wilson, "I hope so."

The news from New York that Chairman McCombs had announced the appointment of William G. McAdoo as Vice Chairman pleased Gov. Wilson very much.

"McAdoo was my original choice," he said, "and I am particularly glad to have him associated with me in the campaign. It is fine of him to give up his time to the work."

Gov. Wilson said it was probable that other Vice Chairmen would be named to take charge of the Chicago headquarters and of the Far Western headquarters, which, it is expected, will be opened within a few weeks.

"The campaign," he said, "will open about three weeks after the speech of acceptance is made, so far as the speaking is concerned. Of course, there will be steady work from the day of the acceptance, but it will consist of organization efforts and the preparation of campaign literature. The delivering of speeches should be under way about Sept. 1. That is the usual time for such work to begin, I believe."

Printed in the *New York Times*, Aug. 4, 1912.

INDEX

NOTE ON THE INDEX

THE alphabetically arranged analytical table of contents at the front of the volume eliminates duplication, in both contents and index, of references to certain documents, such as letters. Letters are listed in the contents alphabetically by name, and chronologically within each name by page. The subject matter of all letters is, of course, indexed. The Editorial Notes and Wilson's writings are listed in the contents chronologically by page. In addition, the subject matter of both categories is indexed. The index covers all references to books and articles mentioned in text or notes. Footnotes are indexed. Page references to footnotes which place a comma between the page number and "n" cite both text and footnote, thus: "624,n3." On the other hand, absence of the comma indicates reference to the footnote only, thus: "55n2"—the page number denoting where the footnote appears.

We have ceased the practice of indicating first and fullest identification of persons and subjects in earlier volumes by index references accompanied by asterisks. Volume 13, the cumulative index-contents volume is already in print. Volume 26, which will cover Volumes 14-25, will appear soon after the publication of Volume 25.

The index supplies the fullest known form of names and, for the Wilson and Axson families, relationships as far down as cousins. Persons referred to by nicknames or shortened forms of names can be identified by reference to entries for these forms of the names.

Beginning with this index, all entries consisting of page numbers only and which refer to concepts, issues, and opinions (such as democracy, the tariff, the money trust, leadership, and labor problems), are references to Wilson speeches and writings. Page references that follow the symbol Δ in such entries refer to the opinions and comments of others who are identified.

INDEX